Politics
USA

Politics USA

Robert McKeever

John Zvesper

Richard Maidment

PRENTICE HALL

LONDON ■ NEW YORK ■ TORONTO ■ SYDNEY ■ TOKYO ■ SINGAPORE

MADRID ■ MEXICO CITY ■ MUNICH ■ PARIS

First published 1999 by
Prentice Hall
An imprint of
Pearson Education Limited
Edinburgh Gate
Harlow
Essex, CM20 2JE
England

Typeset in 9.75/12pt Sabon
by Mathematical Composition Setters Ltd, Salisbury

Printed and bound in Great Britain by Redwood Books, Trowbridge, Wiltshire.

Library of Congress Cataloging-in-Publication Data

Available from the publisher

British Library Cataloguing in Publication Data

A catalogue record for this book is available from
the British Library

ISBN 0-13-354151-7

1 2 3 4 5   03 02 01 00 99

The authors dedicate this book to Jack, Elise and Anthony McKeever; to Thomas, Jonathan and Louis Zvesper; to Alice, Adam and Eleanor Maidment and to Eva and Katja Tausig.

Contents

Preface

The principal objective in writing *Politics USA* is to provide students with an understanding of the politics and government of the United States. The American political system is extremely complex. It is a political system which requires a careful and precisely-structured account if students are going to come to terms with this the most complex of political processes. We hope that *Politics USA* has achieved this goal.

Non-American students bring many assumptions to studying the United States, notably that the United States is not a foreign nation. The mass consumption of American music, cinema and television programmes has created a sense of comfort and ease with American society. These cultural products have generated an intimacy and familiarity which has eroded the foreignness of the American experience. However this sense of familiarity is to some extent illusory. The United States is a very distinctive society with a political system that is strikingly different to any other liberal democratic polity. Consequently, the American political process can only be understood within the context of its distinctive historical experience as well as a unique constitutional framework.

Politics USA offers a comprehensive account of the American political system and how it functions. It examines the institutions of government as well as the processes through which public policy is made. It locates these accounts within a broad historical sweep as well as within the American constitutional framework.

The distinctive quality of American political life is strikingly illustrated by the events of the last twelve months. At the point of writing this preface, the United States has just about worked its way through the gravest constitutional and political crisis for at least a generation. However, the impeachment of President Clinton and the subsequent trial, which culminated in his acquittal by the United States Senate will not fade easily from the collective political consciousness, but will continue to reverberate through the political system for many years, if not decades. Interestingly, it was a crisis that most foreign observers found almost entirely inexplicable. They could not quite understand how a sex scandal could be transformed into a constitutional problem of such gravity that it placed the presidency in jeopardy. Their lack of understanding is a testament to the unique characteristics of the American constitutional and political system.

However, while foreign observers were perplexed by the drama unfolding in Washington, there were many domestic commentators who were profoundly concerned about the impeachment of President Clinton. On December 19, 1998 the House of Representatives impeached the President. The House passed two articles of impeachment, alleging that the President committed perjury and obstructed justice. In many respects, this was a surprising turn of events. The impeachment occurred against a backdrop where the view of the American people has been explicit and clear about this matter. From the start of the scandal concerning the President and Ms Lewinsky, opinion polls consistently reported a substantial majority against impeachment. Whatever the constituency polled – the entire electorate, registered voters or likely voters – there was a majority, between 63 per cent and 75 per cent, who opposed impeachment. Even the sample least sympathetic constituency to President Clinton, those who voted in the recent 1998 congressional elections, which was disproportionately Republican and approximately 38 per cent of the electorate, overwhelmingly rejected impeachment, according to all the exit polls that were conducted. The American public, failing any new revelations, had made up its mind on the issue of impeaching the President on account of his relationship with Ms. Lewinsky or on his attempts to conceal it. They did not want it. Indeed, after the House took the decision to impeach the President, opinion polls recorded an increase in his approval ratings by up to 10 per cent. So why did American politicians who usually are so responsive to public opinion disregarded it on this particular occasion?

Over the coming years there will be many attempts to answer this question, but certainly one point is clear even at this stage, no institution or individual comes out of the impeachment saga with an enhanced reputation. The President's behaviour has been described as deplorable and unacceptable even by his own lawyers and political allies. He may not have committed perjury, but his testimony was designed to mislead. In addition he lied to the American people over his relationship with Ms Lewinsky. It is one of the striking and, to a large extent, unexplained characteristics of this episode that President Clinton's approval ratings significantly improved as the scandal unfolded. Nevertheless, at the very minimum, President Clinton has not enhanced his reputation and will be recalled as the first elected President to have been impeached in American history. But if the President's behaviour was less than commendable, then virtually all the other participants have fared equally poorly.

The Congress, particularly the Republican majority, appeared to be determined, from the outset, to impeach the President. The behaviour of the Judiciary Committee of the House of Representatives, which dealt with the issue of impeachment initially, suggested that the Republican members wanted to engineer an impeachment rather than establish bipartisan and broadly accepted impartial procedures for dealing with this issue. As a result, the Judiciary Committee divided on strict party lines. The full House of Representatives also divided on a partisan basis with only a handful of members crossing the aisle. To some extent the Senate avoided the intense and bitter partisan divisions of the House, but no Democrat in the Senate voted to find the President guilty and only a handful of Republicans broke ranks with their colleagues. The result of this bitter party conflict was an impeachment and trial that was viewed by too many voters as partial and tainted with only one central objective, that of removing the President without any regard to fairness and to their wishes.

If the reputation of the Presidency and the Congress has suffered, so has that of the Office of the Independent Counsel. This Office was created to provide an effective and important check on any abuse or illegal behaviour by the Presidency. However it is widely believed that the investigation conducted by the Independent Counsel, Kenneth Starr was deeply flawed. His investigation was viewed without any enthusiasm by the electorate and opinion polls have recorded some of the highest disapproval ratings of any public figure. He needed to convince both parties in the Congress and the wider public that his investigation was scrupulous, unbiased and above all fair. In this respect Kenneth Starr failed. The report was seen as tainted and partial. As a result one of the most important and effective institutional safeguards, the Office of the Independent Counsel, against the abuse of power by the Presidency has been damaged perhaps fatally so.

There have been other institutions of American government which have also suffered a degree of damage to their reputation. The United States Supreme Court did itself no favours by permitting a sitting President to be sued in a civil case. The Court's view that the case brought by Paula Jones alleging sexual harassment by Bill Clinton, was unlikely to absorb too much of the President's time appears, especially in retrospect, quite extraordinary.

The scandal and the impeachment process has been a deeply dispiriting episode. It has raised many concerns about the US political system and the manner in which it functions. However this saga makes it all the more important that this extra-ordinarily complex political system is understood. We hope that *Politics USA* makes a contribution to this process.

Robert McKeever
John Zvesper
Richard Maidment

March 1999

Acknowledgements

Having been a rather longer project than originally planned, the completion of this book is due in no small measure to the enthusiasm and patience of the three editors at Prentice Hall who have worked on it. Clare Grist initiated the project and put it on a substantial basis. When Tony Johnston took up the reins, he drove it forward with impressive energy. And finally Tim Pitts pulled it altogether, ably assisted by Lyn Roberts and Susannah Gee. To each of these the authors are indebted for their friendship and support as well as their endurance.

We are also grateful to all those colleagues and friends who have contributed short pieces to this book. It is surely a sign of the healthy state of the study of American politics in Britain that we could call on so many experts for help.

1

The view from the nineties

Introduction

Henry Luce, the founder of the news magazine *Time*, believed that the twentieth century was the American century. This was the century, Luce felt, in which the United States was going to leave an indelible mark on the rest of the world. The USA was going to be the dominant power in the globe, not only militarily but politically and culturally as well. To a striking extent Luce's prophecy has been fulfilled. The United States did emerge as the most powerful nation in the world during the course of the twentieth century. Certainly by 1945 its pre-eminence was clearly established. In the years immediately after the end of the Second World War, the United States was the key player in the globe. The American economy generated almost 50 per cent of the world's gross national product (GNP), its technology was supreme, and there was no doubt about which nation was militarily the most powerful. Moreover, US cultural products, films, music and subsequently television, appeared to have captured the popular imagination of the rest of the world. The Americanisation of the globe was proceeding apace. The fifteen years after the end of the war were, for the United States, a period characterised by enormous self confidence and assurance. No problems or difficulties, foreign or domestic, were insoluble. There was peace as well as prosperity. These were exceptionally good years for Americans, and they believed that their nation had, in a telling phrase, a 'rendezvous with destiny'.

To some extent, however, these years were the height of American power. The view from the end of the twentieth century is rather different. To some extent the self assurance has substantially diminished. The mood has soured. At home and abroad there is a degree of uncertainty. The country is very unsure about its role in the world. The source of the uncertainty is clear. It lies with the war in Vietnam. The US involvement occurred during the 1960s and 1970s and it was a very unhappy experience. These memories have not been laid to rest, but continue to loom over American foreign policy. Every major foreign policy decision is affected, to some degree, by the failure of that military adventure. Even the success of the Gulf War in the 1990s did not allow Vietnam to settle. It emerged, once again, in the debate over the commitment of US troops in Bosnia. The key aim for many Americans is to make sure that the Vietnam experience will never be repeated. This is an interesting and rather curious obsession because the central objective of post Second World War American foreign policy has been achieved. The United States won the cold war, despite Vietnam. The demise of the Soviet Union and the communist regimes of eastern Europe produced a world where the United States was once again the militarily dominant power. The United States is currently the only superpower in the world: but this has not restored a sense of direction and purpose to foreign policy. There continues to be this uncertainty over how the United States should conduct itself in this post cold war globe. There are powerful voices arguing for a neo-isolationism, a partial withdrawal from what they see as dangerous foreign entanglements. Even those who wish to see the United States fully engaged in the international community are cautious over the degree and extent of the involvement, and are very aware of an electorate that is sceptical, if not hostile, to foreign involvement and appears to be increasingly absorbed by domestic problems.

The uncertainty and absence of confidence over foreign policy is also visible over domestic issues. The belief that most problems could be solved has also diminished. The country appears to be confronted by a long list of very difficult problems. Until the first Clinton administration in 1993, the economy would have appeared on the list of these problems. Certainly for the preceding quarter of a century, the US economy did not perform as well as many other economies in recent decades. In the view of many observers, the American economy was in a state of relative decline. It had grown but not as fast as others. Put bluntly, other nations reduced the gap and in some respects surpassed the United States. The United States now produces approximately 20 per cent of the world's GNP. The economies of Europe, particularly in the 1950s and 1960s, and notably those of the nations of the Asia Pacific had grown faster than the American economy and in certain sectors, notably manufacturing, have overtaken their American counterparts. The sense of American economic pre-eminence and invincibility has been dented. The endemic trade gap with Japan, and now China, reflects the fact that, in some sectors, American products are second best. Frequently the products are uncompetitive and perhaps not as well designed. The quality control in several sectors of American manufacturing industry is inferior to that of their competitors in the Asia Pacific. These were unpalatable facts for the American electorate, but to some extent they have been modified by the performance of the economy for most of the 1990s. The US economy has responded flexibly to global competition, and has grown consistently throughout the decade, with low inflation and unemployment at historically low levels. Moreover, the nations of the Asia Pacific have been enveloped in a financial crisis that suggests the economic miracle of the region is stalled if not over. Without diminishing the resurgence of the 1990s, the economy continues to pose certain problems. Despite the overall growth, certain sectors do not function well. There is increasing income inequality, and the standard of living for the bottom 50 per cent has barely grown over the past two decades. This is a particularly difficult for a nation which has been in a constant process of creating and recreating itself for the past two hundred years. Change and reconstruction have been the American hallmarks, but the end of the twentieth century appears to be a singularly difficult time.

There are other ailments, and one of them is the state of American education and training. Far too many pupils are graduating from high school barely literate and numerate. International comparative tests suggest that American children are up to a couple of years behind children in several nations of the Asia Pacific region, in both mathematics and verbal comprehension. Moreover, this gap is not being closed. Schools appear to be increasingly unable to provide their pupils with the appropriate and necessary skills. Consequently, the United States now possesses a workforce which is comparatively underskilled in relation to its European as well as its Asia Pacific competitors, at a time when the skill of the workforce is central to economic success.

The schools which fail their pupils are disproportionately concentrated in the inner cities. These urban areas offer a dismal panorama of economic, social and cultural deprivation. They are ridden with crime, family breakdown, and are being destroyed by the widespread use and trafficking of drugs. Simply, these areas are a source of despair both to the inhabitants and to those who attempt to deal with the problems. There is an absence of potential solutions and, perhaps of even greater concern, a growing sense that a majority of the electorate and their representatives no longer care. They do not wish to deal with the inner cities as long as the consequences are kept at a distance.

The problems of the inner cities are, of course, linked to the perennial issue of race. The integration of African Americans into the mainstream of American life has been the dominant domestic problem of the United States. It has also been the most striking failure of the political system since the creation of the republic. While slavery and legal segregation have been abolished, the full integration of African Americans remains the most difficult issue on the political agenda. The presence of a large black underclass in the inner cities, the continuing existence of widespread racial discrimination and increasing doubts over some of the remedies that were put into place to deal with this discrimination show that the condition and treatment of African Americans remains the most profound unresolved domestic issue.

The list of problems can be easily extended. The welfare system is in urgent need of reform. The changes that were made in 1996 are already coming under strain. The basis of the 1996 legislation – that the transition from welfare to work could be made without dislocation and hardship – is not being borne out in quite the way that its sponsors argued. The United States spends more on health care than any other nation, but even so, 40 million Americans have no health cover. Violent crime is socially disabling. There is little point in continuing. The point is made. The agenda of problems is extensive. In some respects, of course, other nations have to confront a similar if not identical list of difficulties. However, the position in the United States is that the agenda is allied to a sense that little can be done about it, in a nation which has historically possessed a belief in its ability to mould the future. Perhaps this is the central problem: Americans have lost a considerable degree of their faith in their collective ability to deal with these concerns. They have lost faith in their politics, politicians and in their political process. The political system does not really have the confidence of a clear majority of Americans because it no longer appears to function satisfactorily. Opinion polls from the 1970s onwards have consistently recorded a substantial level of disenchantment with all the institutions of American government, as well as parties and politicians. Opinion polls have registered an improvement in public confidence in some of these institutions during the late 1990s, but this is most likely a reflection of a strong economy rather than a change in fundamental attitudes towards politics. Even more persuasive indicators of the view of voters have been the decline in electoral participation rates, the sharp reduction in identification with the Democratic and Republican parties, the quite striking volatility in the behaviour of the American electorate, and broadly a loss of trust in the entire political process. The loss of faith and confidence is of profound importance.

The politics of the 1990s

The principal complaint, that is frequently voiced, is that the political process in the United States simply does not work. The most striking characteristic of policy-making during the 1980s and 1990s has been the apparent inability of the political process to address some of the most pressing problems confronting the United States: a phenomenon known as gridlock. The institutions, for instance, had grappled with the question of the budget deficit of the federal government for well over a decade before any resolution was in sight. Health policy, similarly, has also exercised the electorate for several years. There is all but universal dissatisfaction with the current system of health care. No significant element of opinion and no major interest endorses the health system that has evolved. It has no support and yet significant reform appears unlikely because any possible reform alienates one or more of the significant participants within the industry. There is a further and equally fundamental concern about the political system. It is not a democracy. Its democratic credentials are increasingly suspect. Despite universal suffrage, which interestingly in the case of the United States was only achieved during the 1960s with the passage of the Civil Rights Act and the Voting Rights Act, the political process has ceased to be representative; or rather it represents 'special interests' rather than the wider electorate. Too frequently, access is reserved for the powerful and the wealthy; the average voter has to some extent lost the franchise because neither politicians nor government respond to their desires and worries. So what kind of political system has emerged in America at the end of the twentieth century? To a degree any answer has to be located in the historical experience of the country. The concern over democracy and effective government is not new. It resonates throughout the eighteenth and nineteenth centuries. It is part of a continuing and, to some extent unfinished, debate in the United States.

The politics of the 1780s

The government of the United States, unlike the government of virtually every other western liberal democracy, operates within a constitutional structure that was created at the end of the eighteenth century and which remains essentially intact. The objectives and the concerns of those who framed the Constitution at the federal convention of 1787 were not those of democrats. They were strongly influenced by the writings of John Locke, David Hume and Montesquieu, which were imbued with the doctrine of liberalism but not with notions of democracy. They endorsed the principles of consent, liberty, political and property rights but not the other key ideas and practices that are central to modern democratic beliefs. The American colonists used the language of liberalism to make their case against the manner in which successive British governments had behaved towards the colonies. Thomas Jefferson in 1776 documented these grievances against Britain and George III in the Declaration of Independence. He and his fellow colonists attributed these problems to the corruption of British political institutions that allowed both the Crown and politicians at Westminster to behave in a tyrannical and autocratic manner. However, the solutions that the colonists sought to prevent a recurrence of such behaviour in a newly independent America were not democratic solutions but in essence liberal ones. There was little demand for even universal white male suffrage and no sense that the new constitutional and political arrangements should enshrine majority rule. Indeed, the tenor and thrust of the debate in the federal convention was directed towards the creation of a set of governmental institutions and a political process that controlled and limited the influence and power of the simple majority. The primary concern of the delegates was to protect the individual rights of speech, press, religion as well as property and to protect them against the will of the majority.

The strategy deployed to control the majority faction revolves around three elements. The first element is that certain crucial matters are removed from the arena of everyday politics. A good example is the first ten amendments to the Constitution, also known as the Bill of Rights, where particularly important civil liberties are guaranteed. These constitutional guarantees can only be modified or rescinded by a process of constitutional amendment, and cannot be tampered with by either the president or by legislation of a traditional kind. Furthermore, the process of constitutional amendment is long and elaborate and has been used successfully on only seventeen occasions since 1787, bar the Bill of Rights. The second element was the adoption of a federal structure which created two principal levels of government, one at state level, the other nationally. Moreover, the national or federal government was given very specific and limited responsibilities and powers. The third and final element of the strategy established that the powers designated to the federal government were allocated in such a manner that the institutions of the federal government would be profoundly suspicious of each other and consequently would find it extremely difficult to act in concert if they were not clearly acting in the public interest.

The delegates very deliberately established each of the three branches of the federal government with a degree of constitutional independence from each other. The presidency, Congress and the federal judiciary were endowed with designated and limited powers which could not be modified by the other branches. Nevertheless, the Constitution also built in a degree of interdependence, which was intended to heighten the friction between the institutions. The presidency was not designed solely as an executive institution, it was also given a legislative role through the power of veto over legislation passed by the Congress. Similarly, the Congress was authorised to intervene in matters traditionally within the domain of the executive. Moreover, all of the political institutions of the government had different constituencies with differing methods of election, which the Convention assumed would result in members of the House of Representatives, the Senate as well as the occupant of the White House having very different perspectives and agendas. The clear intention behind this very elaborate and complex governmental structure was to produce a political process that did not act easily and smoothly. Indeed, the overriding desire was to create a system that functioned only when an overwhelming majority of Americans were in agreement. In the absence of such agreement the conflict designed and built into the political process would prevent any faction, but particularly the faction of a majority of 50 per cent plus one, from controlling the government and making policy which would put in jeopardy the liberty and property of their fellow citizens. There was one further element of this structure which was also the final safeguard in the event that Congress and the president did manage to co-operate in infringing constitutionally guaranteed rights – the Federal judiciary. There is a scholarly debate over the precise intentions of the delegates regarding the role and powers of the federal judiciary, nevertheless the powers of the judiciary to be the guardians of the Constitution were soon established. Federal judges possess the authority to declare unconstitutional actions of the president as well as federal and state legislation. If the political institutions either fail to protect civil liberties or property rights or themselves are the source of threat, then the courts have the power to intervene. Moreover, federal judges are appointed, not elected, and can only be removed by the process of impeachment, a difficult and rarely used procedure. Thus the protectors, in the last resort, of the Constitution were and continue to be unelected judges, which is the most telling indicator of the American constitutional system's profound suspicion of politics, politicians and the dangerous instincts and tendencies of majority opinion.

By the third decade of the nineteenth century, however, the fear of majorities, and mass opinion had receded sharply. The political culture was imbued with a populist impulse. The period identified with the presidency of Andrew Jackson (1829–37) was a watershed in American political history. At about this point, the political process was irrevocably transformed into a mass political system. Even property qualifications, which were still in place in several states, were no longer a significant barrier to a broad spectrum of participation. Almost 80 per cent of white males exercised their right to vote in presidential elections and the political system, by no stretch of the imagination, could any longer be described as elite, even if it could not be described as democratic. Increasingly, American political culture was in the sway of a majoritarian impulse. The expansion of the electorate resulted in a striking change in political discourse. Concerns about majorities were no longer electorally productive. This majority was now required to provide an election victory. The electoral connection between the rulers and the ruled ensured that politicians sought to identify, rather than distance themselves from the views and aspirations of their constituents and sought to represent their values and beliefs in the full range of political institutions. The language of American politics now paid homage to mass opinion.

This transformation reflected the substantial changes that were occurring in American society. Waves of immigration, westward expansion, and the growing industrialisation of the economy were altering the social structure. The elites that dominated colonial society were primarily based in agriculture and the traditional professions, and now found their position challenged. The rapid expansion of commerce and industry provided new sources of economic power and they required and demanded political representation. The map of political influence in the United States was being redrawn. It was difficult, if not impossible, to resist the claims and demands of the newly arrived and the newly propertied to participate, at the very least, in the political process.

How were these new voters, with their demands and desires, to be accommodated within the American constitutional system. The answer was with a considerable degree of difficulty. The accommodation never fully occurred. There was an uneasy fit between the populist impulse and a constitution which had no enthusiasm for majorities. The result was tension; a tension which has endured. The tension between a constitutional process profoundly suspicious of majorities and a culture of populism has remained one of the central features of the American political system. It emerged during the nineteenth century and has not disappeared. It has never been decisively resolved in favour of the majoritarian impulse. The United States, at the end of the twentieth century retains a Constitution devised and designed in the late eighteenth century which operates in an assertively populist culture, and the consequences are apparent.

The politics of frustration

It is no exaggeration that there has been a collapse in trust in the political system. Opinion polls regularly record the electorate's distaste for the institutions of government, politicians of all parties, and the very activity of politics. There is an extraordinary cynicism about politics which manifests itself in the volatility of the electorate, the decline in voter identification with either of the major parties and a level of voter participation that is the lowest amongst liberal democracies. In the presidential election of 1992, approximately 55 per cent of the electorate voted, but in 1996 the figure was closer to 50 per cent. The voters who do go to the polls appear to change their minds with a bewildering frequency. At the time of writing only one president since 1961, Ronald Reagan, has served two full terms in office. Virtually every other administration, regardless of party, has ended with the smell of failure. The presidencies of Lyndon B. Johnson, Gerald Ford, Jimmy Carter, George Bush and, above all, Richard Nixon culminated in defeat or resignation. In 1992, the victory of Democrat Bill Clinton was owing in large part to a sense that it was time for a change, only for the electorate to establish Republican majorities in both houses of Congress in 1994. Clinton's second term has been dominated by a series of scandals that, at a minimum, has absorbed the energies of the Clinton White House and diverted its attention from the serious affairs of state. The incessant scandals have reinforced the instincts of an electorate that has little sympathy with politics and politicians to represent their values, beliefs or aspirations. They have lost their trust in the key and central mechanism of a democratic political process. The reasons for this lie in the perception that the American political system has not dealt effectively with many of the nation's most pressing problems and that the political system no longer reflects the opinion of the nation at large but the views of organised and powerful interests, which are now in control of policy making in Washington DC.

Why is the political system apparently unable to provide coherent policy responses to the most important issues and concerns that confront the electorate? The fundamental reasons for this, as we have seen, are historical and systemic. The division of power between the three branches of government, the different systems of election and representation that each is founded on, the significant devolution of power to the states all help ensure that decision making is protracted, minority voices can be heard and agreement is difficult. This was the way that the American government was supposed to function. However, there have been some new developments over the past three decades that have exacerbated the problem of governance in the United States and made gridlock all the more severe and dissatisfaction with democratic politics more widespread. Blaming the recent malfunctioning of the political system on the Constitution overlooks the importance of these developments. These developments include party fragmentation, the hyperpluralisation of the policy process, a shift in power from mass opinion to organised interests, and the enduring exclusion in policy making and electoral contests of the interests of the poor.

The first of these is the continuing decline of the Democratic and Republican parties. Parties have provided a degree of cement in this divided and fragmented political system, even though by the standards of most other liberal democracies, American parties have never possessed similar levels of organisational and programmatic cohesion. They have always been large coalitions of diverse interests and beliefs. During the early decades of this century, the parties were able to act in concert on a sufficient number of occasions, notably during the New Deal in the 1930s for a substantial legislative programme to be passed. However, since the end of the Second World War there has been a decline in the ability of parties to put together a legislative programme and enact it.

Parties have lost control over the nomination process. The widespread use of primary elections has transferred control over the process from party organisations to the electorate. The key players are no longer party officials but candidates and those who are expert at winning elections, the political, financial and media consultants as well as opinion pollsters. Individual candidates construct their own organisations and raise their own finance in order to contest both primary and general election campaigns. Parties in a meaningful sense have been replaced by individual campaign organisations. Politics, in this respect, has been privatised. The consequences of this development for governance are profound. Candidates, if elected, owe few if any debts or obligations to their parties. Their success is due to their own efforts. Party discipline in the Congress has diminished and is lower than in the legislatures of other western democracies. More importantly there has been a sharp decline in a shared political identity, of a common purpose and set of objectives. The combination has resulted in a Congress that finds it difficult to pass a substantive legislative programme. The election of a Republican Congress in 1994, campaigning on the basis of a shared programme, Contract with America, appeared to suggest the possibility of a resurgence in party cohesion. The performance of that Congress as well as the Republican-controlled Congress elected in 1996 indicates that both parties continue to have profound internal divisions.

Secondly, the decline of party has been mirrored by an explosion of interest-group activity over the past few decades. The American political system is now characterised by hyperpluralism, and the range of interests, their demands and their ability to influence government appears to overload or deadlock the political process. To some extent this has occurred because the parties are no longer able to develop and implement coherent legislative programmes. The two major parties as corporate national organisations are not the prime focus for attention. They are no longer that important. Groups now feel that it is necessary for them to operate extensively in Washington at all levels of government to protect their interests, and it is the case that the divided system of government does allow them both far greater access and influence than any other western democracy. Over thirty thousand interests are registered in Washington with a significant number who are important 'players' in the governmental process. In addition, the American legislative process has more built-in hurdles which have to be successfully negotiated than in any comparable system, with a far larger number of opportunities to obstruct and hinder the development and passage of legislation. Health care illustrates this. Most voters have wanted to put in place a health care system that has universal coverage but where costs are controlled and are roughly in line with other western countries. It has not been possible to achieve these objectives because of the vast range of interests involved and because of their individual and collective power to prevent the passage of legislation. Politicians have been unable to impose a settlement. In 1993–95, a Democratic president with a democratically controlled Congress was unable to do so.

It is striking that the power of interests is primarily exercised in a negative manner. They are more able to prevent reforms than to sponsor and put into place new and innovative legislation. The balance of power, by and large, favours those interests that are established and have been players in Washington for some considerable time. Thus while hyperpluralism does mean that the process is open, accessible and that there are a host of players capable of influencing policy outcomes, it does not mean that the playing field is level. Interests which are well organised, well funded with long-established networks and a record to defend are better placed. These include producer groups, professional associations, those who are focused on a single interest (of which abortion is a good example), labour unions, plus a host of associational groups, such as the National Rifle Association (NRA) on the right or the National Educational Association (NEA) on the left. They work through the Democratic and Republican parties both in Washington and in the electoral districts. Consequently, politicians of both parties are very reluctant, for instance, to oppose the NRA. The NRA has a large, active and a strongly motivated membership. It is well funded and organised, and able to mobilise supporters. Moreover, it makes substantial financial contributions during elections. The laws regulating the funding of elections in the United States vary, but in all elections money is a critical factor for success. A generous supporter is assiduously cultivated and, accordingly, no politician alienates the NRA, or comparable interests with equanimity.

Gun control provides another example where the opinion of the electorate has been clear and consistent. A considerable majority of Americans over a substantial period of time has been in favour of a degree of regulation over the possession of firearms. Yet no substantial regulatory legislation has been passed, owing to the influence of the NRA. Majority opinion is not channelled to have the greatest impact. Nor is it well funded or organised. It is simply politically ineffective. The NRA has been able to frustrate and obstruct proposals for gun control.

By contrast, those who are on the periphery of economic life are not as effective in participating in the political system as those at the centre, which heightens their sense of alienation from politics. That part of the population which depends on income from welfare – the urban dispossessed, which comprises a disproportionate percentage of African Americans and Hispanics – constitutes a substantial element of the total population, approximately 25 per cent, but it is marginalised politically. These adults vote less frequently and they are not organised, with the inevitable result that the political process does not respond proportionately to their concerns. It is no coincidence the agenda of American politics in the late 1990s includes welfare reform, a sharp reduction in governmental social expenditure, the ending of affirmative action programmes and so on. All of these issues are ones that work to the disadvantage of the poor and some ethnic minorities. The entry cost to be an effective participant in the political process is high, and a significant percentage of the electorate and their representatives are unable to cross this barrier, which is a serious problem for a political system that views itself as the epitome of the democratic tradition.

Conclusion

The view from the 1990s does appear rather bleak. Perhaps the sense of pessimism can be overdone; the position may not be quite so grim. The American economy may have its problems, but it is still the largest in the world by a very considerable margin and it appears to be performing better than some of its competitors. There are sectors of the economy that clearly lead the rest of the world for innovation, such as information technology. Even manufacturing industry has made a modest comeback. Race relations continue to be difficult but they are in a much better state than they were in 1950. Legal segregation has ended. There are many more African Americans in managerial and professional positions. The percentage of African Americans in higher education has grown remarkably over the past five decades. Even the levels and frequency of crime have shown signs of being brought under control. Interestingly and regardless of all its problems, the United States is viewed as the destination of choice of so many who leave their country of origin. Immigrants from all parts of the world want to live in the United States more than in any other nation. America clearly retains its attractions whatever its problems.

Even while noting the resilience and strengths of the United States and not underestimating them, it is difficult to escape the fact that the closing years of the twentieth century have been difficult. The principal source of that difficulty has been the political process. It has few defenders. Everybody is a critic and the criticisms are endless. The institutions are insufficiently representative and they do not operate efficiently. Politicians are corrupt and they only consider the interests of the wealthy. It continues in this vein. The consequences, as noted above, have been the rapid growth of cynicism, distrust and frustration which has bred a disillusionment with politics and politicians, and a disillusionment that has had a corrosive effect on American society. There is no indication that the general atmosphere is changing. Indeed the conduct of politics has become, if anything, even more mean spirited and bitter during the first six years of the Clinton presidency. Nor is there a sign that reforms, particularly constitutional reform, which may address some of the problems are likely. It is far more likely that the current state of affairs will continue, which does not offer a very positive prognosis for the American polity in the new millennium.

The constitutional dimension of American politics

In no country has politics been influenced by written constitutions as much as in the United States. Therefore it is neither romantic antiquarianism nor dry legalism that makes it common for the study of American politics to begin by analysing the Constitution of 1787 and the way that this Constitution has developed over the years, shaping and being shaped by political debates and events.

During the last quarter of the twentieth century, two further good reasons for paying close attention to the formation and development of the Constitution have appeared. Many of those who complain that American government is malfunctioning argue that the troubles afflicting the polity are rooted in the Constitution. At the same time, the American Constitution has been held up as a model for those responsible for assembling governments in the new liberal democracies.

The first part of this book surveys the constitutional context of politics in the United States. Chapter 2 examines the Constitution as it was constructed in 1787. In order to do this, consideration is first given to the American Revolution and the political ideas and practices developed in America during the period of the founding, a period of which the Constitution was but one moment. Then Chapter 3 examines the way that the political and legal interpretation of the Constitution proceeded when confronted by the changing social and economic circumstances of the nineteenth and twentieth centuries, and by the shift of the political agenda in the 1950s towards questions of civil rights and civil liberties. Finally, Chapter 4 focuses on federalism, a pervasive feature and perennial issue of American politics and one of the United States' particular contributions to governance.

Contents

2

The making of the Constitution

The American Constitution of 1787 was a product of the political, revolution- and constitution-making experience of the British North American colonists in the seventeenth and eighteenth centuries, and of the citizens of the newly independent states in the 1770s and 1780s. Many of the abiding concerns of American politics had their origins in this experience. Contributions to the theory and practice of American politics made both by those who favoured the ratification of the Constitution (the Federalists) and by those who opposed it (the Antifederalists) are still highly relevant today.

The federal government of the United States is based on the Constitution that was written by a convention that met in Philadelphia in the summer of 1787. This Constitution replaced the Articles of Confederation that had previously served as the written basis of the federal government. The work of the Philadelphia convention, and the ensuing deliberations among the people and in the conventions that ratified this Constitution in each of the thirteen states have inspired much admiration. In *Democracy in America*, a classic early nineteenth-century study of the American polity, Alexis de Tocqueville praised the work of the Constitutional convention in glowing terms, comparing the making of the Constitution very favourably to the achievement of American independence:

> The spectacle of a nation struggling energetically to obtain its independence is one which every century has seen. Moreover, the efforts made by the Americans to throw off the English yoke have been much exaggerated. With twenty-eight hundred miles of ocean between them and their enemies, aided by a powerful ally, the United States owed their victory much more to their position than to the valor of their armies or the patriotism of their citizens. ... But that which is new in the history of societies is to see a great people, warned by its lawgivers that the wheels of government are stopping, turn its attention on itself without haste or fear, sound the depth of the ill, and then

wait for two years to find the remedy at leisure, and then finally, when the remedy has been indicated, submit to it voluntarily without its costing humanity a single drop of blood.

(Tocqueville, 1835; 1969, p. 113)

Even without sharing Tocqueville's belittling of the American Revolution, we have to agree with him that there is clearly something quite awe-inspiring about that spectacle of

---

Box 2.1

Chronology: the founding of the USA

1763 End of Seven Years' War
1764 Parliament introduces taxes that provoke non-importation agreements in Boston
1765 Protests against Stamp Act culminate in intercolonial Stamp Act Congress
1766 Repeal of Stamp Act
1767 Townshend Acts establish new customs board to enforce collection of new taxes
1768 British troops arrive in Boston to protect customs board
1770 Repeal of Townshend taxes, except on tea
1773 Boston Tea Party: colonists dump tea into Boston harbour
1774 Coercive Acts close Boston port and curtail Massachusetts government
      First continental congress meets and agrees Continental Association for uniform policy on non-importation
1775 Battles of Lexington and Concord; martial law in Massachusetts and Virginia
      Second continental congress establishes Continental Army
1776 Colonies start adopting new constitutions
      Declaration of Independence
1777 Second continental congress proposes Articles of Confederation
1778 Treaty between United States and France confirms military cooperation
1781 Articles of Confederation ratified by last state
      British forces surrender at Yorktown
1782 Provisional peace treaty signed, recognising independence
1783 Treaty of Paris confirms provisional peace treaty
1786 Annapolis conference ends with call for constitutional convention
      Debtors in various states close courts and attack tax collectors
      Congress defaults on loan payments to Europeans
1787 Constitutional convention at Philadelphia, 25 May to 17 September
1788 Ninth state ratifies Constitution
1789 First Congress under the Constitution proposes Bill of Rights
      George Washington elected President
      Judiciary Act completes constitution of federal courts
1790 Last state ratifies Constitution
1791 Amendments 1–10 (Bill of Rights) ratified

a country rationally and peacefully adopting a new constitution to remedy the ills of the old one. Shortly after the Philadelphia convention had completed its work, Alexander Hamilton, in the first issue of *The Federalist* (the famous essays arguing in favour of the ratification of the Constitution), drew attention to the frequently noted fact that 'it seems to have been reserved to the people of this country, by their conduct and example, to decide the important question, whether societies of men are really capable or not of establishing good government from reflection and choice, or whether they are forever destined to depend for their political constitutions on accident and force.'

Of course, as both Hamilton and Tocqueville were aware, the making of the Constitution did not begin in 1787. Tocqueville took pains to point out that the political principles on which the Constitution was based had been developed and had become familiar to what he called the 'Anglo-Americans' long before 1787 (see Box 2.1 for a chronology of the founding of the USA). For one thing, the original thirteen states had already individually gone through the process of making constitutions in the years from 1775 to 1780. The state governments, and their component town and county governments, came first in the political loyalties of most citizens – certainly this remained true when Tocqueville was writing in the 1830s, and arguably it remains true today even though the political and constitutional developments of the twentieth century have made the federal government more central to Americans' lives. However that may be (this question is pursued in Chapter 4), the state constitutions came first in time, and heavily influenced the content of the federal constitution. As Tocqueville explained: 'The federal government was the last to take shape in the United States; the political principles on which it was based were spread throughout society before its time, existed independently of it, and only had to be modified to form the republic' (Tocqueville, 1835; 1969, p. 61). Therefore, to understand the making of the Constitution, we have first to take into account the early political and constitutional experience of the states.

Moreover, since the drafting and adoption of constitutions by the individual states were part of the process of becoming politically independent from Britain, we have first of all to appreciate something of the causes and results of the American Revolution. It could well be maintained that it is the Revolution rather than the Constitution that has been the more formative experience, closer to the heart of American political life. The Constitution has been and still is greatly venerated, but at critical moments in American political history, successful political leaders have appealed to the patriotism and purity of ideals expressed in the Revolution, more than to the cool compromises of the Constitution. Even if that were not true, it is difficult to understand the Constitution of 1787 except as one moment in the creation of the American republic, a creation that began with the Revolution.

The American Revolution

For some decades before the American Revolution there had been predictions that the British colonies on the North American continent would eventually seek and gain independence from Britain. These predictions were based on the observation of certain demographic, economic and political facts.

Demography

When the first of these colonies had been established in the early seventeenth century, it seemed that the choicest spots for European colonisation had already been taken by other Europeans, and that English colonisers had been relegated to the economically less promising regions. These colonies in their first decades had indeed to struggle for their very survival. However, starting in the middle of the seventeenth century, population growth and economic growth in general showed very impressive and sustained gains. The population of the colonies increased from about 50,000 in 1650 to 250,000 in 1700, to over 2 million by 1770. Roughly half a million of these were slaves, but in none of these continental colonies was there a large majority of slaves, as there was in Britain's island colonies of Jamaica and Barbados, where continued British rule was seen by the slaveholding class to be necessary to protect them from the huge slave population. It is also worth noting that many of the 'Anglo-Americans' were not of English ancestry. Especially outside the New England colonies, there were many communities with non-English majorities – largely Irish, Scots, Welsh and Germans. The elements and the balance of this ethnic composition, as well as the rapid growth in population, distinguished these 'English' colonies from Britain. The diversity of the religious backgrounds of the colonists, who had loyalties (of varying strengths) to a wide variety of Christian denominations, was another important difference from Britain, although this was a fact that constituted important differences among the colonies as well.

Economic growth

An expansive economy accompanied the expanding population. Economic growth in the colonies from the beginning to the middle of the eighteenth century took the future United States from an economy less than 5 per cent as large as Britain's in 1700 to one not far short of 40 per cent of Britain's by 1775 (Perkins, 1991, p. 53). Projections of such trends easily showed that the American economy would overtake Britain's in the not-too-distant future. Given these economic realities, continued political dependence of the colonies on the 'mother country' seemed to make less and less sense.

Intercolonial communication and common wartime experience

At the same time, and as part of the same economic and social development, communications among the colonies gave the people of each colony a slight but increasing sense of solidarity with each other. Partly in order to avoid the risk of diseases brought back to the colonies by graduates of Oxford and Cambridge, wealthy colonial families began sending their sons to American universities instead, creating a basis for a continental-minded political class. Nearly one-sixth of the delegates to the constitutional convention of 1787 (including James Madison) were to be graduates of the College of New Jersey at Princeton. It is difficult to see much real American nationalism being expressed until independence from Britain was being seriously considered. However, plans to unite the colonies had been explored since the late seventeenth century, and effective intercolonial co-operation can be traced at least as far back as the wars of Britain (and British Americans) against the French and the 'Indians' in the 1750s. This common wartime experience also helped to educate a class of American military professionals – such as George Washington – who would later make it possible for the Americans to secure their independence.

Political maturity

The 'Anglo-Americans' joined an increasing level of political competence to their increasing level of economic prosperity:

1. **Representative institutions of government were ubiquitous and increasingly important,** both at the local (town and county) level and at the colonial level. At the colonial level, government typically consisted of a governor appointed by the king; and a legislative assembly, with an upper house called the council, nominated by the governor and formally appointed by the king's privy council, and an elected lower house, variously named. The political importance of the lower houses of colonial assemblies *vis-à-vis* the governors and councils tended to increase after the Whig understanding of the Glorious Revolution of 1688 had emphasised the crucial role of representative bodies in preserving rights against tyrannically inclined executives, whether it be, as in England, a king and his ministers, or, as in the colonial case, the governor and his chosen council. The lower houses became more jealous and assertive, especially in matters concerning taxation. By the beginning of the eighteenth century these lower houses had become the dominant bodies in colonial politics, in spite of British imperial administrators' hopes to make the governors the dominant force. These lower houses were parts of the structure of British imperial government, and were by no means centres of disloyalty to Britain, but they did provide the colonists with political experience that made them more formidable when the issue of independence arose, and they gave the newly independent states a wealth of experience to draw upon in their independent conduct of politics.

2. Elections to the colonial assemblies were based on a relatively **broad franchise** (much broader than in England, or anywhere else, in the eighteenth century). The effect of property qualifications varied from place to place, but in most cases they left a large majority of white male adults eligible to vote. Elections at town and county level were generally even less exclusive than at colonial level.

3. There was generally an **open political climate**, with a free and active press.

4. In these circumstances, an **experienced and confident political class** emerged in the colonies, enjoying the deference of the electorate and providing confidence and stability to colonial politics.

The new imperial policy

If all these conditions signifying socio-economic distinctiveness and dynamism and political maturity made eventual American independence seem very likely, what actually precipitated it was the British government's determined policy to tighten up the administration of the Empire at the end of the Seven Years' War in 1763. In fact, already by the 1750s British policy-makers, witnessing the growing economic and political strength of the American colonists, had concluded not that the colonies were bound to become more independent and therefore should be more liberally administered, with a policy of 'salutary neglect' that had in effect been the policy up to that point, but that they should be more tightly controlled, to ward off the perceived danger that these now prosperous people might either become objects of interest to imperial rivals, or become interested in going their independent way. Since the colonists were equally determined to resist being more strictly ruled, the British government's anxiety about the loss of the American colonies proved to be self fulfilling. The Seven Years' War interrupted the implementation of the new, tighter imperial policy, but also produced a plausible reason for this intended rationalisation of colonial administration to be pursued, because the war greatly enlarged the Empire. Victorious Britain gained Quebec, Florida and French-claimed territories east of the Mississippi River, as well as India and much of the West Indies.

It took little more than a decade for the contradiction between this new imperial desire to govern and to tax the American colonies more, and the colonists' undiminishing desire to be governed if anything somewhat less – and certainly not to be taxed without their representatives' consent – to result in armed conflict, soon followed by the colonists' decision to try to establish their political independence. The independence that they declared in 1776 was made good by the victory of their armed forces (eventually and crucially aided by the French) in the war with Britain that had begun in earnest during 1775 and that formally ended with the Treaty of Paris in 1783.

The Declaration of Independence

The political life of the United States legally began not with the Constitution of 1787, but with the Declaration of Independence in 1776. This Declaration is the first constitutional law of the United States (see Box 2.2 below and Appendix A to this book). Its statement of the justification for 'dissolving the political bands' between Britain and America tells us much about the thinking that was to enter into the federal Constitution. Historians sometimes treat the Declaration and the Revolutionary period as more enthusiastically democratic phenomena than the more sober Constitution and Federalist period, and there are important differences between the two, but there are also important continuities.

Although, as Tocqueville noticed (above, pages 15–16), successful wars for independence had frequently occurred before 1776, the American Revolution was in many ways a first. Most importantly, it was the first in a series of modern revolutions inspired by and inspiring the idea of political progress built on the spread of enlightenment about universal human rights. It is the first time in human history that a country was explicitly founded on a universal truth about human nature. Thomas Jefferson, the principal author of the Declaration, looking back on it fifty years later, expressed the hope and expectation that the Declaration might prove to be a signal arousing human beings everywhere 'to burst the chains under which monkish ignorance and superstition

Box 2.2

The Declaration of Independence

When in the Course of human Events, it becomes necessary for one People to dissolve the Political Bands which have connected them with another, and to assume among the Powers of the Earth, the separate and equal Station to which the Laws of Nature and of Nature's God entitle them, a decent Respect to the Opinions of Mankind requires that they should declare the causes which impel them to the Separation. WE hold these Truths to be self-evident, that all Men are created equal, that they are endowed by their Creator with certain unalienable Rights, that among these are Life, Liberty and the Pursuit of Happiness – That to secure these Rights, Governments are instituted among Men, deriving their just Powers from the Consent of the Governed, that whenever any Form of Government becomes destructive of these Ends, it is the Right of the People to alter or to abolish it, and to institute new Government, laying its Foundation on such Principles, and organizing its Powers in such Form, as to them shall seem most likely to effect their Safety and Happiness. Prudence, indeed, will dictate that Governments long established should not be changed for light and transient Causes; and accordingly all Experience hath shewn, that Mankind are more disposed to suffer, while Evils are sufferable, than to right themselves by abolishing the Forms to which they are accustomed. But when a long Train of Abuses and Usurpations, pursuing invariably the same Object, evinces a Design to reduce them under absolute Despotism, it is their Right, it is their Duty, to throw off such Government, and to provide new Guards for their future Security. Such has been the patient Sufferance of these Colonies; and such is now the Necessity which constrains them to alter their former Systems of Government. The History of the present King of Great Britain is a History of repeated Injuries and Usurpations, all having in direct Object the Establishment of an absolute Tyranny over these States. To prove this, let Facts be submitted to a candid World.

(for the full text of the declaration, see appendix A)

had persuaded them to bind themselves, and to assume the blessings and security of self-government' (letter to Roger C. Weightman, 24 June 1826, in Peterson, 1975, p. 585). In this view, agreement on universal but *natural, secular* political principles furnishes the means of overcoming the profound political conflicts and consequent human misery that had been caused by the belief in universal *otherworldly, religious* political principles. In the case of the USA, acknowledgement of these natural universal secular political principles provided, and continues to provide, the major (not to say always perfectly successful) means of defining a common citizenship for a 'people' composed of a great and growing diversity of ethnic and religious loyalties.

The Declaration rests the case for the American choice of independence on certain truths about members of the human species: that they possess by nature 'unalienable rights', among them 'life, liberty and the pursuit of happiness'. These are called 'self-evident truths', which means that their truth is contained in the definition of what it is to be human. Jefferson was following (among other precedents) the seventeenth-century English philosopher John Locke's formulations in his *Second Treatise* (sections 4 and 5), where Locke points out that the equality of humans by nature is 'evident in itself, and beyond all question, ... there being nothing more evident' than that human beings, as members of the same species, are equal to one another: there is no natural 'subordination or subjection' of one human being to another. Human beings can be seen as natural rulers of members of other species, and rule them without their consent, but for one human being to treat another in this way is unjust by nature. As Jefferson was to put this thought fifty years later, 'the mass of mankind has not been born with saddles on their backs, nor a favored few booted and spurred, ready to ride them legitimately, by the grace of God' (letter to Roger C. Weightman, 24 June 1826, in Peterson, 1975, p. 585). Similar sarcastic language had been used in the colonists' Declaration of the Causes and Necessity of Taking Up Arms (6 July 1775):

> If it was possible for men who exercise their reason to believe that the divine Author of our existence intended a part of the human race to hold an absolute property in, and an unbounded power over others, marked out by his infinite goodness and wisdom, as the objects of a legal domination never rightfully resistible, however severe and oppressive, the inhabitants of these colonies might at least require from the parliament of Great Britain some evidence that this dreadful authority over them has been granted to that body.

The most obviously unjust political practice in violation of this natural human equality is slavery. (The restriction of the public world of politics to men, and the exclusion of women from voting, were practices that did not appear unjust to many observers at this time; see Box 2.3 below and also Chapter 7 for a discussion of developments on these issues.) Many of the American founders were slaveholders. Since the middle of the nineteenth century, many people have concluded from this fact that the founders did not mean what they said when they talked about human equality, that they must have consciously or unconsciously excluded Africans from their assertion that 'all men are created equal'. However, this easy dismissal of the seriousness of their assertion is mistaken, both *logically* and *historically*. Students of American politics need to be wary of these common mistakes.

From the logical standpoint, it follows from the observation of natural human equality that slavery is always an evil, but – unfortunately – it does not follow that it is never a necessary evil. That slavery had for a time to be tolerated as a necessary evil is the judgement that was made by many Americans between the Revolution and the Civil War. This judgement was based on the view that freeing the slaves, even if it were done by schemes of compensated emancipation so that slaveholders suffered little financial harm, would leave the former slaveholders subject to (understandable and justifiable) physical assaults by former slaves. Jefferson – a Virginia slaveholder – remarked that emancipation of the slaves without their expatriation was not practicable, because of the widespread belief that peaceful coexistence of large numbers of former slaves and former masters was impossible: 'we have the wolf by the ears, and we can neither hold him, nor safely let him go. Justice is in one scale, and self-preservation in the other' (letter to John Holmes, 22 April 1820, in Peterson, 1975, p. 568). By the logic of equal natural human rights, slaves had the right (but not often

Did the Declaration of Independence include women?

Gordon Wood, a leading historian of the American founding, writes: 'we know [that the Declaration of Independence] did not mean that blacks and women were created equal to white men.' This is today's conventional wisdom. Yet it it not true.

In 1764, in a pamphlet formally endorsed by the Massachusetts Assembly, James Otis wrote: 'Are not women born as free as men? Would it not be infamous to assert that the ladies are all slaves by nature?'

For the American Founders, the idea of equal natural liberty meant that no one, male or female, has the right to rule another without that other's consent. There are no natural masters or natural slaves. That includes women.

In his *Notes on Virginia*, Thomas Jefferson, the author of the Declaration, reproaches the Indians for failing to acknowledge this equality: 'The [Indian] women are submitted to unjust drudgery. This I believe is the case with every barbarous people. With such, force is law … It is civilization alone which replaces women in the enjoyment of their natural equality.' Jefferson says 'replaces' ('puts back') because barbarism deprives women of the equal natural rights that they are born with.

Many today think women's liberty and well-being are better secured when the law guarantees their voting rights, the right to practice the sexuality of one's choice, and identical legal rights and responsibilities for both sexes.

Jefferson disagreed. He thought the main protection for women's rights was the civilized family, with its traditional division of labor. The husband was to take on the most physically demanding work, so as to acknowledge 'the rights of beauty and feminine weakness' (to quote James Wilson, another leading Founder).

This does not mean that the Founders absolutely rejected voting rights for women.

James MacGregor Burn's textbook *Government by the People* typically but mistakenly claims that 'All states [in 1787] barred women from voting.' The U.S. Constitution deals with the right to vote by turning the matter over to the states. Not one word of the Constitution had to be changed for women to obtain the vote.

In fact, New Jersey women had the right to vote during the late 1790s and early 1800s. They voted in large numbers. The reason: Americans believed in equality. This belief by itself was not enough to bring about female voting all at once. But it made it thinkable as an option. New Jersey exercised that option then, as the whole United States does today.

Based on West, T.G., *Vindicating the Founders: Race, Sex, Class, and Justice in the Origins of America*, Washington: Rowman & Littlefield, 1997.

Contributed by Dr Thomas G. West of the University of Dallas

the power) to escape or to rebel, and to kill their masters if necessary. They had no duty to respect the laws that held them without their consent. They were not common citizens with their masters, but remained in a state of nature with them. In such a state, everyone has the right to judge for themselves what is necessary for their self preservation. However, by the same harsh state-of-nature logic, slaveholders (before the Civil War Amendments to the Constitution, which not only freed the slaves but also made them citizens) had the right to maintain their slaveholding system until it could be abolished without (in their judgement) endangering their self preservation.

From the historical standpoint, while Americans of the founding generation can surely be faulted for not doing enough to change the conditions necessitating the continuance of slavery, the efforts that they did make in this direction show that the universal applicability of the doctrine of human equality was well understood by them, and that Africans were not excluded from it. Before independence, slavery was legal throughout the colonies. (Jefferson's draft of the Declaration had included a condemnation of the king's frustration of colonial efforts to prohibit the 'execrable commerce' of the slave trade.) In 1787, in the Northwest Ordinance, which set down the rules for the pre-statehood governance of the territories between the Ohio River and the Great Lakes, Congress outlawed slavery in those territories. The Constitution of 1787 avoided the use of the term 'slavery', even while incorporating compromises that countenanced its existence. Several northern states legislated against slavery and the slave trade in the Revolutionary decades. With effect from 1 January 1808 – during Jefferson's presidency, and at the first moment allowed by the Constitution – Congress outlawed the importation of African slaves into the United States and its territories. These Acts fell well short of dooming slavery in the southern states, where it was most economically entrenched; this task had to be taken up by a later generation. However, these Acts do reveal a consciousness of the injustice of slavery, a consciousness based on acknowledgement of human equality, that is, of the equality of all humans everywhere. Even today that consciousness is not universal in the United States (nor anywhere else), and it diminished in many parts of the country in the years leading up to the Civil War. Nevertheless, it was a real and animating force in the country's founding, as well as in the refounding of the republic in critical moments such as the conflicts that led to the Civil War.

Four kinds of political conclusion logically follow from the natural equality of human beings (that is, from their natural freedom) that is asserted in the Declaration:

1. **The natural ends of government.** Government is naturally necessary, and government has certain naturally just purposes. Natural freedom understood as a condition without government is not an attractive condition for any length of time, and one of the first things that revolutionaries have to do is to establish 'new government'. (Moreover, one of the worst things that government itself – or a part of a government, such as the king and his agents, the colonial governors – can do is to interfere with properly constituted government actions, such as those of the colonial legislatures.) However, not just any government will do; by nature, governments have certain purposes, and it is right to establish governments with those purposes in mind. Therefore written constitutions are useful, to specify in so far as is possible what those purposes are, and to organise political institutions in a way

that makes it likely that those purposes will be served. In the words of the Declaration, governments are instituted 'to secure' the natural rights of the people concerned, and 'to effect their safety and happiness'.

From the Declaration, as well as from numerous other documents of the American Revolution, we learn that one of the signs of unjust, tyrannical government is taxation without consent. In part, this is because any government without consent is unjust (see item 2 below). However, in part, this is also because securing the right to property is one of the natural purposes of government. This is a principle that Americans had learned especially from John Locke's teachings, conveyed to them by successors and popularisers of Locke as well as by Locke's writings themselves. In English law, the principle had been affirmed several times since it had first been asserted in the Magna Carta in 1215.

Especially when the importance of securing property is emphasised as a purpose of government, government designed to secure rights can be understood as a radically liberal or libertarian government, designed only to secure the 'negative liberty' of the comfort and security of private life. Louis Hartz, in an influential interpretation of American political thought published in 1955, characterised that thought as thoroughly liberal and Lockean (Hartz, 1955). More recently, historians have argued that at least in the Revolutionary period, it is more accurate to categorise American political thinking as *republican* rather than as *liberal*. They admit that American republicanism has often been merely the expression of a kind of bad conscience that Americans have felt about the reality of their liberal, individualistic, competitive society; but they also show how it has had substantial meaning and impact on American political practices. Americans have paid more than lip service to republican ideals that emphasise communal, political responsibilities as well as individual, private rights. In the founding, this republicanism can be seen in the fact that the Declaration says it is a human duty (and not merely a human right) to participate in politics, and in the fact that the signatories to the Declaration pledge to each other, in the last words of the document, their 'sacred honor': the patriotic words and deeds of the American revolutionaries cannot be understood simply as cool calculations of 'liberal' maximisers of private utility. It can also be seen in the fact that the boundaries between state and society were not drawn with a doctrinaire, libertarian precision in the American founding. For example, while it was apparent that the separation of church and state was, at least at the national level, going to be established in America more strictly than anywhere before – if only because of the necessity of toleration in a country containing such a diversity of sects, with none in the majority – it was also widely understood that government would not and should not be indifferent to religion. Thus, in the laws set down for the territories the Northwest Ordinance, which had provided in its first article that, 'No person, demeaning himself in a peaceable and orderly manner, shall ever be molested on account of his mode of worship or religious sentiments,' added in the third article that, 'Religion, morality, and knowledge, being necessary to good government and the happiness of mankind, schools and the means of education shall forever be encouraged.'

When considering the difficulties of characterising and categorising the thinking of the founders that is expressed in such documents as the Declaration, it helps to recall Thomas Jefferson's later description of the Declaration: 'Neither aiming at originality of principle or sentiment, nor yet copied from any particular and previous writing, it was intended to be an expression of the American mind, and to give to that expression the proper tone and spirit called for by the occasion. All its authority rests then on the harmonizing sentiments of the day, whether expressed in conversation, in letters, printed essays, or in the elementary books of public right, as Aristotle, Cicero, Locke, Sidney, etc.' (letter to Henry Lee, 8 May 1825, in Koch and Peden, 1944, p. 719). Jefferson perceived a 'harmony' of the classical principles of such writers as Aristotle with modern principles such as those of Locke. Both these classical principles and these modern principles agreed that a naturally just political constitution must be directed at the good of the community and of the individuals within it, and not merely at the good of a ruling class. (This does not mean that a politically dominant class is *ipso facto* illegitimate, but it does mean that such a class must be expected to work for the good of the whole community.) Moreover, in the modern world, both classical and modern principles can be seen to agree that certain kinds of human activity – most clearly and primarily, religious beliefs – should be kept at a safe distance from politics (and vice versa). Politics had enough hard work to do just in securing the rights to 'life, liberty and the pursuit of happiness', and in legislating 'for the public good' in this world, without being troubled by taking on responsibility for the salvation of souls in the next world.

2. **Government by consent.** Government must be instituted and operated by 'consent of the governed', since no human being is the natural (or supernatural) ruler of any other human being. Of course (as we shall see in some detail in Part III of this book) what is required for 'consent of the governed' has been and remains today a controversial question in American politics. However, from before the Revolution there has been widespread agreement that active consent by means of elections and representative institutions is required for legitimate government. Most of the items in the Declaration's lengthy list of particulars that are cited to prove that imperial policy has tended to establish 'an absolute tyranny' concern the interference of the king and his colonial governors with the existence and the actions of representative colonial legislatures: refusing to assent to laws 'necessary for the public good' that were passed by these legislatures, dissolving these legislatures for opposing invasions of the people's rights, and on the other hand assenting to 'acts of pretended legislation' by Parliament, where there was no American representation.

    Note that there is a massive problem in reconciling the requirement for a government with just purposes (item 1) with this requirement for government by consent. As the example of slavery discussed above very clearly shows, consent must be enlightened before it can be depended upon to support naturally just policies. Government by consent means government, ultimately, by public opinion, and if powerful public opinion is prejudiced (as it often is), perfectly just policies may well not be practicable. Nevertheless, the principle of human equality demands both just policies and government by consent, and to deny one of these in favour of the other is to deny the principle of equality that underlies both. This problem within the idea of equality provides the greatest trials for liberal democratic political systems such as that of the United States.

3. **The right of revolution.** When a government 'becomes destructive' of its natural ends, 'it is the right of the people to alter or to abolish it, and to institute new government'. In other words, there is a natural right of revolution, or (as John Locke had put it) of resistance to tyranny, even though (as Locke also said) there may be prudent reasons not to change governments until a 'long train of abuses and usurpations' has clearly demonstrated a tyrannical design. As we have just noticed (in item 1 above), the Declaration adds that political resistance to tyranny is a 'duty' as well as a right: citizenship in a modern republic requires something of the public spiritedness urged by the classical republicanism of ancient Greece and Rome. In American politics, it has been one of the functions of civil associations and political parties not only to form channels of consent, but also to maintain this necessary level of attention by citizens to public affairs, to prevent the people from becoming apolitical, in order to prevent governments from becoming tyrannical and inviting revolutionary resistance.

4. **Natural constitutional right.** The fact of natural human equality means not only that it is naturally unjust for some human beings to be treated as less than human, and governed without their consent, but also that it is unwise to treat those who govern by consent as more than human, as either infallible or totally selfless and disinterested. That is another reason for representative government, so people can keep an eye on government actions. It is also another reason why taxation without consent is unjust: it gives governments too much scope for misbehaviour. Several other constitutional arrangements are logically connected to this recognition that the power of government, while necessary, must be constrained to ensure that it does not stray from its duty to serve its natural purposes: the independence of judges from absolute control by the executive or the legislature, subordination of the military to the civil power, trial by jury – these all fall under the heading of what some Americans had begun to call 'natural constitutional right'. Thus, in the Declaration the violation of these arrangements by the king is cited to prove that he is 'a tyrant … unfit to be the ruler of a free people'. These constitutional arrangements were thought of both as rights of Englishmen and as natural rights; the natural rights had been 'ingrafted into the British constitution' (Commager, 1973, vol. 1, pp. 65–6). Among these naturally just constitutional arrangements, one that was visible in 1776 but would be given much more attention and development in the making of the Constitution of 1787 was the separation of legislative, executive and judicial powers.

This logic of the Declaration – the logic of natural equality, liberty and constitutionalism – coupled with the evidence that the Declaration then proceeds to assemble about the unjust British policies towards the colonists, leads the representatives of the 'United States of America' (thus named for the first time), in the name of the people of the colonies, to declare their status as 'free and independent states'. Not all of the American colonists agreed with the decision to declare independence, but even among those (perhaps 20 per cent of the population) who remained loyal to Britain, the ideas expressed in the Declaration found much support. They were, after all, ideas about English liberties as well as about natural equality and liberty. However, it made a profound difference to American politics that the Declaration's arguments based on universal truths, arguments that were much less explicit in the Glorious Revolution of 1688, were made so explicit and publicly declared at the origins of American politics in the Revolution of 1776. John Locke and others had tried with little success to move English political culture towards a greater consciousness of the universal, natural foundations of their political liberties. Locke's abstract principles were much more widely accepted in America. This difference has continued to affect the differing styles of political discourse in Britain and America. For example, American political conservatism has been very different from British conservatism, by being much more open to abstract theories. Burkean conservative distrust of abstractions can be found in America, but it is nothing like as dominant as in British conservatism.

Constituting independence before 1787

One of the first tasks that the American revolutionaries had to undertake was to establish independent governments, both in each state and at the confederal, interstate level. By 1776, the British colonies on the North American continent had had a decade of intermittent experience in intercolonial political co-operation. (This dated from their successful protest against the Stamp Act in 1765, a protest which included a meeting of delegates from nine of the colonies – later known as the Stamp Act Congress – which sent to king, Lords and Commons petitions for the repeal of this revenue Act.) This co-operation had been mounted in order to resist British policies that violated traditional and natural liberties of the colonists, principally their right not to be taxed by legislative bodies (such as Parliament) in which they had no representatives, but also their right not to have a standing army quartered among them in peacetime. The continuous political co-operation of the colonies, later states, can be traced to the First Continental Congress, which assembled delegates from the colonies in Philadelphia in 1774, two years before the Declaration of Independence, to discuss and to co-ordinate measures of resistance, for example agreements not to import or to consume goods from Britain. In the spring of 1775, after the conflict between Britain and the colonists had begun to take on a military form with clashes between British troops and Massachusetts militia, the Second Continental Congress began to advise individual colonies on their efforts to write constitutions to establish governments for the purpose of carrying them through the continuing hostilities with Britain.

Many colonists who supported these political and constitutional initiatives from the 1760s up to 1776 did so without assuming that American political independence from Britain was either desirable or inevitable. They thought of these initiatives as efforts to bring British officials to their senses, and to maintain political order while those efforts proceeded. However, after a policy of independence was chosen and publicly declared, the Second Continental Congress – which became formally known as the United States in Congress Assembled, and which acted as the federal government until the end of the war – sought to formalise its authority with written Articles of Confederation. These were drafted by Congress itself in 1776 and 1777, and ratified by most of the state governments by 1778, but by the last of these only in 1781. Perceptions of the defects of these Articles as a constitution for the United States, perceptions that were widespread even before its final ratification, helped shape the Constitution that was to be drafted by the convention in Philadelphia in 1787 – a convention that in fact had been called for the purpose merely of proposing revisions to the Articles. This convention also had the benefit of learning from the experience in constitution-making that the individual states had acquired from 1775 to 1780.

The first state constitutions

In each of the colonies, just as was the case with the Continental Congress, governing bodies unconnected with and unrecognised by the British government sprang up to organise resistance and to conduct public business during the revolutionary crisis. First came 'committees of correspondence' and 'committees of safety' – revolutionary devices used by the colonists to exchange and to agree plans of resistance. (These devices were to be imitated by political party organisations when partisan opposition became part of the political system.) These committees also helped the process of creating more formally constituted independent governments to get under way. By the time the Second Continental Congress agreed to declare independence in July 1776, seven of the newly independent states had already taken formal steps to reconstitute their governments, by adopting written constitutions. By April 1777, all thirteen states had done this. Two of these states (South Carolina and Massachusetts) had a second go at writing their constitutions (in 1778 and 1780), so a total of fifteen constitutions were produced during this period (see Lutz, 1988; Wood, 1969).

Most of the first state constitutions contained declarations of rights substantially similar to, and in some cases preceding in time, Jefferson's 'harmonising' statement of natural rights in the Declaration of Independence. (These state declarations also anticipated much of the federal Bill of Rights, the first ten amendments to the Constitution of 1787.) The governments instituted to secure the declared rights were models that were to be both emulated and departed from by the federal Constitution. Four sets of issues confronted the state constitution makers:

1. **Constitutions as fundamental laws.** Americans working on these new state constitutions only gradually came to pursue the full implications of the distinctive legal characteristics of republican constitutions, as *basic laws* unalterable by ordinary acts of legislation, that needed to be based directly on *popular consent*, and that therefore ideally needed specially elected conventions to draft them, and popular referenda to approve them. In many cases, the state legislatures drafted and approved constitutions just as if they had been standard pieces of legislation, although this generally took place only after a legislative election in which it was made clear that the newly elected legislature would be taking on this responsibility. It was not until the eighth new state constitution that a specially elected legislature, rather than the sitting legislature, was used to draw up the document. Only with the last of these constitutions (Massachusetts' second, in 1780) was a constitutional convention used for drafting, and a referendum election used for ratification. (Interestingly, in this referendum the votes of two-thirds of all free

male adults were required for approval; the usual property qualifications were waived.)

2. **The expansion of electoral politics.** Many revolutionary leaders were aware that enlarging the electoral base of politics could help to enlarge the popular support for revolutionary action. The new state constitutions maintained or expanded the role of the lower houses of the colonial assemblies, and replaced with elected offices the elements of government that had consisted of the royally appointed governors and councils. In the two colonies – Connecticut and Rhode Island – where the governors had been popularly elected since the middle of the seventeenth century, less constitutional change seemed to be needed, but generally the pattern was for politics to become more completely based on elections, for a widening suffrage, and for election results that placed newer and younger faces alongside the established political leaders. (In a few states – New York, North Carolina and Pennsylvania – suffrage laws placed free black males on the same basis as white males.)

3. **Legislative–executive relations.** From the perspective of the last in this series of state constitutions (Massachusetts 1780), as from that of the federal Constitution of 1787, the outstanding feature of the first state constitutions was the weakness of the executive offices that they created. From that perspective, these constitutions imperfectly embodied the principle of the separation of powers. The first state executives were designed to be closely overseen by the legislatures, who were often responsible for electing the executive and were invariably in a position to dominate that office. In some cases, the executive was simply a committee of the legislature. The reason for this – apart from the speed with which many of these constitutions were made – was the assumption that the legislature, which was elected annually, was a true representation of the electorate, and therefore did not need to be balanced by the executive. (This was also one of the reasons why these legislatures were at first deemed to be fit bodies to write and to approve constitutions.) When the new state legislatures, now even more dominant than they had been in the colonial system, began to exhibit signs that the factional divisions within them did not always faithfully reflect the opinions of the electorate, questions began to be raised about their unchecked powers.

   New York's constitution, the thirteenth in the series, made some important moves towards strengthening the executive against the legislature, by making the governor part of a council that could veto legislative acts (subject to the veto being overridden by a two-thirds vote), and by giving the governor more say in executive appointments. The Massachusetts constitution of 1780 went much farther along this road, giving an annually elected governor, with 'an honorable stated salary', the (overrideable) veto power unconstrained by having to agree with a council when to use this power. In these ways, the New York and Massachusetts governors were steps towards the office of the presidency under the federal Constitution. The period from 1775 to 1787 can thus be seen as a period during which experience and reflection brought American constitution-makers to explore more profoundly how republican government can include an energetic executive.

4. **Representation and the new rationale for bicameralism.** A further prominent part of this learning process concerned the way that popular consent and representation

were conceived and structured. The Pennsylvania constitution of 1776, often seen as a relatively radical democratic experiment, was in some ways atypical, but it illustrates very clearly a problem facing American constitution-makers at both the state and the federal level. The problem was how to understand the purpose of bicameralism: in republican politics, with neither royalty nor nobility, what was the purpose of an 'upper' house in the legislature? There was much confusion about this in the 1770s and 1780s. Some argued that the senate was to bring wisdom and stability to the representative body by giving special attention to property rights, and several states required higher amounts of property to qualify as a candidate for the senate than for the lower house. However, others pointed out that the lower house was already designed to protect property rights, and accordingly enjoyed the right of initiating taxing and spending bills.

Pennsylvania's constitution (until it was revised in 1790) provided for a unicameral legislature, dispensing altogether with the upper house (senate) that formed part of all of the other state constitutions (except for Georgia, which also had a unicameral legislature until it changed its constitution in 1789). Taking the place of a senate's role in revising laws emanating from the lower house was the unusual provision that ('except on occasions of sudden necessity') no public bill should become a law until a second reading took place during the legislative session in the year subsequent to the bill's introduction and first reading. Since an annual election would have intervened between the two legislative sessions, laws were expected to be 'maturely considered, and the inconvenience of hasty determinations as much as possible prevented', by the general public's having an opportunity to read the bill. All bills were therefore to have their 'reasons and motives ... clearly expressed in the preambles'. Thus, all laws were in principle subject to a kind of popular referendum, in that legislators were expected to justify their votes to their constituents in order to be returned to the legislature.

In the end, this model failed to appeal widely, and it was soon abandoned in Pennsylvania itself, where critics pointed out that its effect was less to enhance the quality of legislative deliberations than to make second chambers out of the beer taverns where the proposed laws were posted and where the quality of debate was not high. However, in arguing against the Pennsylvania model, opponents of unicameralism were obliged to clarify the argument in favour of a senate in the new political circumstances of Revolutionary America. In a republican political system, they had to emphasise that a senate was simply a second 'representation of the people', rather than a chamber representing a distinct interest or class. A senate could be expected to impart wisdom and stability to the legislative process by acting as second agent of the people, monitoring the work of the first agent. The implication might well be that the senate should be distinguished from the lower house simply by being smaller (as was usual), by having a longer term of office (as was the case in five of the thirteen bicameral constitutions written between 1775 and 1780), and by having staggered elections, that is with only some seats being filled at any one time (as was the case in three of those constitutions). That, at least, was to be the lesson taken from this experience to the Philadelphia convention of 1787.

Congress and the Articles of Confederation ▬▬▬▬▬▬▬▬

The questions concerning representation and executive–legislative relations that had been put onto the agenda of the Philadelphia convention by the experience of the new states were complemented by related questions that arose out of the experience at the federal level during the period from independence to 1787.

The Articles of Confederation were proposed by the Second Continental Congress in wartime circumstances that made it difficult for a full discussion of political and constitutional issues to take place, and several issues remained unsettled in the minds of the delegates when the Articles were nevertheless finally drafted and submitted to the states in November 1777. Congress hoped that the quick and unanimous approval of the states would be forthcoming, in order to put the federal government in a better position to secure an advantageous alliance with France, so delegates agreed to answers to certain important questions more in the interests of speed than out of conviction that these answers were really at all satisfactory.

1. They agreed that one state, one vote should continue to be the rule by which Congress operated (many in the more populous states thought this was unfair).

2. They agreed that the expenses of the government should be met not by federal taxes but by requisitioning the states in proportion to the surveyed value of land and buildings in each state (thus side-stepping the question of whether, if this apportionment had been based on population instead of land, slaves would be counted, thus increasing the liability of the southern states).

3. Perhaps most controversially, they agreed that the western lands claimed by certain states would not be turned over to the United States to serve eventually as a resource to pay the debts being incurred to fight the war (as states without such lands had urged should happen).

In the event, because of the hasty and unsatisfactory deliberation of these issues, the ratification of the Articles was delayed for more than three years: strong objections of a few states to the failure of the Articles to nationalise the western territories prevented the Articles from coming into effect until March 1781, by which time the 'landed' states had begun to agree to cede these territories to the union.

The Articles left federal affairs in the hands of Congress, with two to seven members to be appointed annually (and recallable at any time) by each of the state legislatures, no person being permitted to serve more than three years out of any six. Members were thus very much delegates from the state governments, appointed and paid by them. They were not allowed to hold offices under the United States. That was the extent of the separation of powers provisions, however, since the executive body was to consist simply of a committee of one of the delegates from each state. (Administrative boards were appointed by Congress, but these were civil servants, not political officers.) This Committee of the States (or any nine of them) was empowered to act when Congress was in recess, but it was limited in its ability to act independently of the whole Congress because it was barred from acting on any of the important matters on which Congress itself was to act only with at least nine states agreeing. These matters included all of the major federal responsibilities: engaging in war, fixing the size and appointing commanders of the armed forces, making alliances or treaties, determining the amounts of expenditures, and borrowing or coining money.

This list of responsibilities that the Articles gave to Congress was accompanied by a set of prohibitions on the states. States were not allowed to have diplomatic relations or treaties with foreign powers, nor to make treaties between themselves unless approved by Congress; nor were they allowed to tax foreign commerce in any way that might interfere with the treaty powers of Congress. Here is the contradiction at the heart of federal politics in this period. On the one hand, Congress was expected to exercise a fair amount of power to accomplish important tasks, and the states were expected not to interfere. On the other hand, not only could a minority of any five states constitutionally prevent it from deciding to use this power, but also, and more importantly, since Congress was not given the power to tax (that probably would have prevented ratification), apart from just printing money and borrowing from abroad it had to rely on the states to supply the men and money that Congress decided were needed. It had no way of coercing the states into supplying these needs – which were not always forthcoming, especially when the war was winding down or ended. In 1781, Congress proposed an amendment to the Articles, to permit it to collect taxes on imports, but this proposal ran aground on the same contradiction: under the Articles every state had to agree to any amendment; in this case, one small state prevented the amendment from being adopted.

Congress under the Articles repeatedly tried to reform itself to put its political and financial house in order, but was always hampered by these constitutional impediments to making and executing decisions. Therefore the end of the war effort that had inspired and sustained the actions of and loyalty to Congress threatened to lower expectations of the federal government. For example, some nationalist-minded politicians in the early 1780s hoped that the creditors of the states could be attached to the government of the union by a federal takeover of the states' war debts. Not only were they soon frustrated in this hope but they also had to watch these creditors being attached more firmly to the states, some of whom actually started paying the federal debts rather than the other way around. By 1786, Congress had begun defaulting even on its foreign loans. Nor was Congress able to sustain a vigorous foreign policy after the war. Unable even to issue orders to individual citizens, and impotent to force states to compensate loyalists, as agreed by the peace treaty, Congress was not in a strong position to compel Britain to relinquish forts that it had agreed to relinquish in that treaty.

In addition to these discouraging difficulties at the federal level, developments in politics and economics at the state level gave many Americans reason to fear for the future of their republican political systems. Many of these developments were related to the federal difficulties. For example, the financial weakness of the federal government put more pressure on state governments. The Articles did not forbid the states to print money, and the means chosen by the states to retire war debts was simply to inflate their currencies by printing more money, which caused grief to some sections of the community. When state policies were less inflationary, they caused grief in another section, and in some cases provoked armed rebellion against debt collections, as in Massachusetts in 1786–87. The hunger for imports from Britain after the war ended dashed idealistic hopes for republican austerity, and caused large trade imbalances in many states. With Congress having no power to regulate either foreign or interstate commerce, states competed against each other with commercial regulatory regimes that disadvantaged every state in the long run.

The Philadelphia convention and the Constitution of 1787

It was not inevitable that these problems of the 1780s should produce an attempt to replace the Articles with a new federal Constitution, but they presented an opportunity to those political leaders who feared that the union would not survive without such a refounding, and they made such an attempt seem reasonable to many Americans. Therefore, when an abortive interstate commercial convention at Annapolis in 1786 ended by issuing a call for a convention to propose constitutional revisions, twelve states responded and sent delegates to Philadelphia in May 1787. This convention worked on the Constitution for nearly four months. (See Appendix B to this book for the full text of the Constitution and amendments.)

The delegates chosen by the state legislatures to be sent to the Philadelphia convention were well educated men, relatively young (their average age was 40), but experienced in politics, law and business. George Washington, the heroic general of the Continental Army, soon to be the first president, presided over the convention. Most of the delegates had served in the war, in colonial or state legislatures, or in Congress; a few had been state governors. Some of them had helped draft constitutions for the states. Most of them were wealthy, and this fact has been used as evidence that the Constitution represented a conservative, property-protecting reaction (Beard, 1913). However, some of their personal economic interests were adversely affected by the Constitution, and many Americans with similar socio-economic backgrounds opposed their work, so concentrating on this point can mislead.

Besides, there were clearly great differences of opinion among the delegates. James Madison, a Virginia delegate who played an important part in the convention, also kept detailed notes on the proceedings (which were published only after his death in 1836: Farrand, 1937; see also Rossiter, 1966), from which we can appreciate the range and the dynamics of the discussions. The convention kept its proceedings secret while it met, and adopted other rules that helped make discussions frank and open within the convention hall, encouraging an atmosphere in which delegates felt free both to express their thoughts and to change their minds. These rules helped to maximise the advantages that Americans had discovered in using conventions to propose constitutions, rather than expecting regular legislatures to draft and even to enact them. The momentum was with the nationalist-minded, and substantive discussions opened with the presentation of a nationalist-oriented plan of government proposed by delegates from Virginia. However, few delegates, even among those who opposed strengthening the federal government as much as the Virginia plan proposed, were made to feel marginalised in the debates, and in fact no state's delegation was always on the losing side in the important decisions. In general, delegates were genuinely concerned to persuade rather than merely to outvote each other, in order to enhance the chances for acceptance of the convention's proposals.

Representation, the large republic and federalism

In the federal convention, the issue of representation, which had been an important part of the debates about the state constitutions, was tied up with the issue of federalism. The basic constitutional question facing the country was whether the federal government was to consist of anything more than an assembly of representatives of each of the states, each state having an equal legal voice in the decisions of the United States. In other words, was the federal government to be a real government, based on the consent of individual citizens and empowered by them to act directly on individual citizens, rather than being restricted to acting on (or rather, merely trying to persuade) the states? In fact, the expression 'federal government' was (and perhaps still is) something of a contradiction in terms, since a federation (as the Latin root of the word implies) rests on the faith of each of the parties, whereas a government implies a degree of decisive power and authoritative coercion agreed to be exercised by the governing authority.

The Articles of Confederation had begun by stating the principle that 'each state retains its sovereignty, freedom and independence', and then described the purposes of their 'firm league of friendship: their common defence, the security of their liberties, and their mutual and general welfare'. The *Virginia plan* was explicitly based on the reasoning that such a 'merely federal' union could not achieve these objects, and that what was needed was a 'national government ... consisting of a supreme Legislative, Executive and Judiciary', the officers of all three to be paid salaries from the national treasury. This plan (presented on 29 May by Edmund Randolph, but drafted by James Madison) envisaged a rather parliamentary system, and a more thoroughly national system than the Constitution finally incorporated. One legislative house would have popularly elected members from each state, subject to recall, and for a single term, the length later set at three years. A second house, with a term of office 'to ensure their independency' (later set at seven years), would consist of members nominated by state legislatures but elected by the first house. This bicameral national legislature would choose a national executive (for a single term, length unspecified, later set at seven years) and a national judiciary (for 'good behaviour'). While the states were by no means to be abolished, the national legislature was to have the power to veto any state laws that it judged to be contrary to the constitution of the union. Moreover, representation at the national level was not to be based on the principle of the equality of the states. The numbers of each state's representatives in both houses would be in proportion either to the state's quota of financial contributions to the national treasury or to its number of free inhabitants.

Discussion of the Virginia plan modified many of its details in significant ways, even while maintaining its overarching national character, basing representation on proportionality rather than on state equality. It was decided to base each state's representation on its population (which was assumed to be roughly equivalent to wealth, and potential taxes) – using a formula that had been proposed by Congress in 1783 for tax quotas, whereby the number of slaves ('all other persons' was the euphemism to be employed in the Constitution) were counted as three-fifths their actual numbers. With deference to the more state-minded delegates, it was decided to have the second house of the national legislature elected (not just nominated) by the state legislatures. On similar grounds, but also with a view to practicability, it was decided to drop the provision for using force against any state failing in its federal duties.

During these discussions, Madison was particularly effective in countering lingering doubts about the wisdom of the decision to proceed on the basis of the Virginia plan. He tellingly pointed out the necessity of avoiding the fatal contradiction inherent in the Articles, the contradiction of demanding much of the federal government without giving enough power to that government. It was also during these discussions that he argued, against the weight of tradition, that *republican* government could be more safely constructed in a *large* territory that encompassed a large *variety of interests*, than in a small, homogeneous community. After all, he remarked, the new republican governments of the individual states were hardly exhibiting signs of political health. To thrive for any length of time, republics needed to be large and heterogeneous. In small republics (as in certain states) it was too easy for majorities to get unjust laws passed by compliant legislatures. In a large republic, with a greater multiplicity of interests, it would be less easy for individual interests to get such oppressive measures passed, because they would be competing for political attention with many other interests, and because political representatives with long-term views of the public good would be elected more often in the larger electoral districts of such a republic. This was the novel argument that Madison was famously to repeat in *The Federalist* no. 10 (see Box 2.4). It is often interpreted as an antimajoritarian argument, and a proof that the framers of the Constitution were antidemocratic. However, apart from the fact that this novel argument was not unquestioningly accepted by Madison's contemporaries, or even by Madison himself, especially in later years, it was obviously intended as an argument not against majority rule, but against unwise (short-sighted) or unjust (tyrannical) majority rule. It was precisely because the framers saw that majorities would continue to rule in American politics that they sought to set up representative institutions that would favour wise and just majority decisions and discourage – if only by delaying – unwise and unjust majority decisions. Ultimately, of course, they recognised that no institutional structure can guarantee that majority rule will always be wise and just, but they thought that such structures could make an improving difference.

At this point (14 June) those delegates who had most doubts about the national scope of government being considered by the convention proposed what is known as the *New Jersey plan* (presented by William Paterson, a delegate from that state, but assembled by delegates from three or four other states as well). This plan offered a last opportunity for delegates to opt for a 'purely federal' system, in which the states would retain their equality of representation in Congress. The New Jersey plan reveals how far even the doubters had moved in the direction of strengthening the federal government. In this plan, Congress was to be granted the powers to raise revenues, not only by taxing imports but also by stamp and postage charges; and to regulate foreign and interstate commerce. Acts and treaties of the United States were declared to be 'the supreme law' of the states. A salaried executive council was to be elected by Congress, and empowered to use force to compel obedience to Congressional acts and treaties. (A similar coercive provision in the Virginia plan had been dropped, but with state equality of representation now being put forward, it looked like it might be more necessary.) A salaried federal judiciary was also part of

Box 2.4

James Madison's argument for a large republic

The two great points of difference between a ['pure'] democracy ['a society consisting of a small number of citizens, who assemble and administer the government in person'] and a republic ['a government in which the scheme of representation takes place'] are: first, the delegation of the government, in the latter, to a small number of citizens elected by the rest; secondly the greater number of citizens and greater sphere of country over which the latter may be extended.

The effect of the first difference is, on the one hand, to refine and enlarge the public views by passing them through the medium of a chosen body of citizens, whose wisdom may best discern the true interest of their country and whose patriotism and love of justice will be least likely to sacrifice it to temporary or partial consideration. Under such a regulation it may well happen that the public voice, pronounced by the representatives of the people, will be more consonant to the public good than if pronounced by the people themselves, convened for the purpose … .

The other point of difference is the greater number of citizens and extent of territory which may be brought within the compass of republican than of democratic government; and it is this circumstance principally which renders factious combinations less to be dreaded in the former than in the latter. The smaller the society, the fewer probably will be the distinct parties and interests composing it; the fewer the distinct parties and interests, the more frequently will a majority be found of the same party; and the smaller the number of individuals composing a majority, and the smaller the compass within which they are placed, the more easily will they convert and execute their plans of oppression. Extend the sphere and you take in a greater variety of parties and interests; you make it less probable that a majority of the whole will have a common motive to invade the rights of other citizens; or if such a common motive exists, it will be more difficult for all who feel it to discover their own strength and to act in unison with each other. Besides other impediments, it may be remarked that, where there is a consciousness of unjust or dishonorable purposes, communication is always checked by distrust in proportion to the number whose concurrence is necessary.

Hence, it clearly appears that the same advantage which a republic has over a ['pure'] democracy in controlling the effects of faction is enjoyed by a large over a small republic – is enjoyed by the Union over the States composing it.

From *The Federalist*, no.10.

the New Jersey plan. Many of the provisions and formulations of this plan were to appear in the final draft of the Constitution. What was not to appear was the basis of the plan, the retention of the simple equality of states in Congressional representation. The New Jersey plan was rejected, over the objections of three states, within five days of being presented.

However, the most that the deliberations had so far established was that at least one house of a new federal legislature would be elected in proportion to population. What about the other house? Many delegates, not least those who had favoured the New Jersey plan, remained unhappy with the comprehensive nationalism involved in having the number of each state's representatives in both houses determined by population. Many delegates, especially those from less populous states, felt their state's interest required some institutional protection for the interests of the states as such. Therefore, debates on the subject of representation continued, often becoming acrimonious. The *Connecticut compromise* (based on suggestions from delegates from Connecticut) was eventually the agreed solution. The second house – the Senate – would retain the equality of the states, by having the same number of representatives from each state; at the same time, it was agreed that revenue bills would originate in the first house, the House of Representatives. Oliver Ellsworth of Connecticut described the resulting system as 'partly national, partly federal' (30 June). This 'middle ground' was accepted only by a narrow vote, and many (including James Madison) remained unhappy with this concession to pure federalism. Nevertheless, this decision, along with the decision to drop the national legislature's veto on state legislation, ended most of the anti-nationalist grumbling at the convention, and produced the only unamendable part of the Constitution of 1787: each state's equal suffrage in the Senate. Each state would have two senators, and each senator one vote. Thus was brought forth to the world a hitherto unknown species of government, partly national and partly federal – to the edification or confusion, the frustration or delight of observers from 1787 onwards.

Box 2.5 sets out the legislature designed at the Philadelphia convention.

Enumerated and implied powers

Once the great issue of representation was settled, the convention was able to focus on the powers that the new government was to have. Of great significance here was the general fact that the new government, without depending on the states as its agents, would be able to enforce its laws, acting directly upon individual citizens. This is the aspect in which the Constitution's mixture of federal and national elements is most simply national: in 'the operation of the government on the people in their individual capacities, in its ordinary and most essential proceedings' (*The Federalist*, no. 39).

Specific enumerations of powers included the main items that had been missed by Congress under the Articles of Confederation. The war and treaty powers that Congress exercised during the war and then formally held under the Articles were to be enhanced by a grant of powers 'to raise and support armies' and 'to provide and maintain a navy'. These powers made the US government far less dependent on military contributions and co-operation by the states. 'To pay the debts and provide for the common defense and general welfare of the United States', Congress was granted the power 'to lay and collect taxes, duties, imposts and excises'. A further important departure from the Articles was the grant of power 'to regulate commerce with foreign nations, and among the several states'. (This power was complemented by powers to coin money, to punish counterfeiting, to grant patents, to establish post offices and roads, and to establish uniform laws of bankruptcy.)

Box 2.5

Congress: The legislature designed at the Philadelphia convention, 1787

House of Representatives
Number of Representatives from each state in relation to population
Popularly elected
Not subject to recall
Suffrage same as for the state legislature's lower house
Two-year terms of office; no limit on number of terms
Twenty-five years minimum age; no property qualification

Senate
Two Senators from each state
Elected by state legislatures
(Changed to direct popular election by Seventeenth Amendment, 1913)
Not subject to recall
Staggered elections, so one third of Senate is elected every two years
Six-year terms of office; no limit on number of terms
Thirty years minimum age; no property qualification

To become law, bills must pass both houses and be approved by the President, or be passed by two-thirds of each house over the President's veto. Revenue bills must originate in the House of Representatives.

As under the Articles, the state governments were prohibited from engaging in war, having diplomatic relations and making treaties. In addition, they were forbidden to tax imports or exports, to coin or to print money, and to make any law impairing the obligation of contracts.

Finally, whereas under the Articles each state had retained every power not 'expressly delegated' to Congress, the Constitution finished its enumeration of powers granted to Congress by noting powers implied in that enumeration: 'To make all laws which shall be necessary and proper for carrying into execution the foregoing powers, and all other powers vested by this Constitution in the government of the United States.'

North and south: commerce and slavery

Several issues settled at the convention were compromises between the economic interests of northern and southern states. The north was less economically dependent on slavery and agricultural exports, and more dependent on shipping. The 'three-fifths' rule (mentioned above) for counting slaves for purposes of taxation and representation was one of three constitutional clauses explicitly dealing with slavery (while always keeping the word itself out of the document, to avoid, as Madison said, admitting the expression of 'the idea that there could be property in men'). The federal government was prohibited from taxing exports, which would have burdened the south (it was recognised that the south would already be paying more heavily than the north for taxes on manufactured imports); and, at the insistence of those southern states most in need of importing more slaves, congressional power to outlaw the importation of slaves from abroad was delayed for twenty years. In return for these concessions to the south, the power of Congress to regulate commerce by favouring American (largely New England) shipping was left intact, instead of being subjected (as some southern delegates had proposed) to a requirement of a two-thirds majority in each house. (Southerners did, however, succeed in their demand that treaties be subject to a two-thirds vote in the Senate.) The third reference to slavery was the clause stating that a 'person held to service or labor in one state' who escapes to another must be 'delivered up on claim of the party to whom such service or labor may be due'.

Executive power

In addition to the enlargement of the powers of the federal government and the nationalising of its representative basis and operational method, the third great innovation of the Philadelphia convention was the creation of the presidency as a relatively strong and independent executive office. Discussion of the constitution of this office was rendered difficult by the absence of any models (although recall the steps that New York and Massachusetts had made towards energetic executive offices at the state level); by the anti-executive bias of much of the republican thinking (and action) of the Revolution; and by the somewhat awkward fact that George Washington, the presumptive first president, was presiding over the convention's discussions of that office. Nevertheless, early on in the convention's discussion of the Virginia plan, the executive office was clearly seen in an expansive light, when it was decided to give the executive a veto over national legislation (overrideable by two-thirds of each house), unencumbered by the council that the Virginia plan had proposed for the executive to consult when deciding when to exercise this veto. This emphasis on the singularity of the executive persisted in later discussions, and heads of executive departments emerged not as members of an executive council, but as clearly subordinate to the president. There remained questions that had to be settled about the term of office and the method of election of the executive. There were also questions, and perhaps some unspoken assumptions, about the powers of the president. Some pregnant ambiguities remained here, which (as we shall see in Chapter 13) have been interpreted and exploited in various ways by various presidents.

The presidential term was eventually set at four years, with no limit on the number of terms. A determined minority of delegates persuaded the majority to agree to a method of election as independent as possible from the legislature: again, a significant departure from the Virginia plan. After considering many variations, it was agreed that presidential electors would be appointed as each state legislature directs (this was expected to be by popular election), and that these electors should vote for two candidates, one of them not an inhabitant of their state, thus encouraging the search for a nationally recognised candidate. Each state has the same number of electors as it has members of the House of Representatives and Senate; this emphasises the federal aspect of presidential elections, which, even without this extra weighting for small states, require the search for a geographically distributed majority. As a fallback position, if no candidate receives a majority of electors' votes, the House of Representatives – each state delegation having one vote – chooses the president from the five candidates with the greatest number of electoral votes.

The 'executive power' vested in the president in Article II of the Constitution was not qualified by the phrase 'herein granted' (as had been used with 'legislative powers' in Article I), and it was soon to be argued that this meant that the president had been assigned a broad 'executive power', not confined to the specific powers then mentioned. Even the specific powers mentioned in Article II as belonging to the president came out of the final drafting stages at the convention looking quite formidable: commander-in-chief of the armed forces, chief executive, chief diplomat, chief appointer of members of both the federal executive and judicial branches (with the Senate's 'advice and consent'); even chief legislator, armed not only with a veto power (overrideable by two-thirds of both houses), but also with a constitutional duty to recommend legislation to Congress. Significantly, whereas representatives, senators, and other federal officers and judges are required to agree 'to support this Constitution', the oath of office prescribed for the president requires this officer to 'preserve, protect and defend the Constitution', suggesting somewhat supraconstitutional duties for this constitutional office.

The federal judiciary

The judiciary occupied less of the convention's time than the legislature and executive, but it was recognised at Philadelphia that the new federal judiciary would play a vital, if somewhat unpredictable, role in the new government. For one thing, the federal legislature's power to veto state legislation, a power proposed in the Virginia plan, had been dropped in favour of the 'supremacy clause' that had its origins in the New Jersey plan. This made both state and federal judges recognise the Constitution, laws and treaties of the United States as the supreme law of the land, taking precedence over the constitutions and laws of any state.

The Constitution vested 'judicial power' in 'one Supreme Court, and in such inferior courts as the Congress may from time to time ordain and establish'. Federal judges, appointed by the president (with the Senate's confirmation), hold their offices for 'good behavior'. Many of the details of the structure and jurisdiction of the judicial establishment were left to be set by Congress. There was also some ambiguity in the extent of 'judicial power'. Federal courts were clearly expected to resolve legal conflicts between federal and state governments, and to do this by treating the federal Constitution and laws as supreme. However, it was not explicitly stated in the Constitution that federal courts would have the power of 'judicial review', that is, the authority to declare unconstitutional acts of Congress, President, and state government. This possible implication of the Constitution was left to be drawn by subsequent commentaries and decisions (which are discussed in Chapter 17).

The characteristics of American constitutional politics

We have seen in this chapter that three basic characteristics pervade American constitutional politics: representation, federalism and separation of powers.

Representation in the large republic bases government on consent, but, following the Federalist theory, tries to filter this consent, to frustrate unreasonable majority impulses while enabling reasonable majority views to find expression in policy-making.

Federalism divides consent into two pathways, legitimising two governments each with a direct relationship to individual citizens, and treating neither state government nor federal government as the creature of the other.

We shall be analysing the representative process in Part III, and having a closer look at federalism in Chapter 4. All three characteristics will appear as necessary explanatory devices at other places in the rest of this book. At this point, it will be helpful to reflect on the way that the *separation of powers* was treated in the constitutional deliberations that we have been examining.

The limited extent and constructive purpose of separating powers

Two points are worth emphasising because they are important but frequently misunderstood. The first is the *limited extent of the separation of powers*, that is to say, the separation is not absolute.

Americans quickly learned that separation of legislative, executive and judicial functions and offices would not work unless each office were assigned a share in the two functions primarily assigned to the other offices. This feature of the separation of powers, which had been recognised by political science in the early eighteenth century, was often lost sight of in the midst of the American Revolutionary resentment of executive action against colonial legislatures. Thus, the early state constitutions, even when proclaiming the separation of powers doctrine, often ended up in practice promoting domination by the legislature. For example, Jefferson criticised the Virginia constitution of 1776 for failing to make executive and judicial offices independent of the legislature for their subsistence or continuance in office, with the result that all the powers, even the judicial power, ended up being exercised by the legislature, who in the natural way of such things were bound sooner or later to make interested use of such an accumulation of power (*Notes on the State of Virginia*, 1787, Query 13, in Peterson, 1975, p. 165). Madison emphasised, both at the Philadelphia convention and in *The Federalist*, that merely to proclaim that the powers were to be kept separate was insufficient; one had to give constitutional powers to each branch so each would have a 'partial agency' in the acts of the others (*The Federalist*, no. 47). This is necessary for the different branches to be able to communicate effectively with each other. It is also a means of avoiding the inherent weakness of the executive and judicial branches against the legislative branch of republican governments. In republics, the legislature is generally where power tends to accumulate, because legislators can claim to be the most immediate representatives of the people, so fortifying the executive and judiciary with a partial agency in legislation is a constitutional priority.

The second point worth noting is the *constructive purpose of separating powers*. The separation of powers in the American Constitution is intended not only to provide a checking, controlling, restraining influence on government (especially on the legislature), but also, more subtly but perhaps more importantly, to provide a means of invigorating or empowering government. Commentaries on American politics generally appreciate that the separation of powers is designed to help preserve liberty, by helping to prevent tyrannical actions by government. What is less widely appreciated but at least as important for serious students of American politics to see, is that the separation of powers in the Constitution of 1787 was intended to help establish good, competent government. The Constitution does this by trying to attract fit characters to public office, by setting up offices with scope for them to display their fitness.

The thought here is not that elected and appointed officials will be totally selfless in their dedication to the public good, but that the ambitions of politically oriented persons can be fulfilled in a regime that gives them the means to initiate and to achieve public projects, and that rewards them with recognition by their colleagues and with public honour. The regime thus aims to exploit and to channel the talents of the ambitious to advance the public good. It does this partly by enabling them to protect the position of their respective offices, 'giving to those who administer each department the necessary constitutional means and personal motives to resist encroachments of the others' (*The Federalist*, no. 51); but, more completely, simply by enabling them to do their jobs well. Two-year (rather than annual) terms for representatives and six-year terms for senators, and the small size of both houses give these legislators the opportunity to learn to do their job of deliberating with a view to the public good as well as to the interests of their constituents. The Senate's staggered elections and longer terms add stability to the legislative process. The president's unity (rather than the plurality involved in an executive committee or council), and consequent capacity for secrecy and speed, along with the chance to be re-elected, add to the 'energy' and 'firmness' of this office, and therefore to the probability of its being filled by 'characters preeminent for ability and virtue' (*The Federalist*, nos 68–72). The life tenure of federal judges makes them sufficiently independent to follow the Constitution and the laws in their rulings. The opportunities that federal offices give their holders for fulfilling the responsibilities of governing well are expected to attract able and ambitious characters to those offices.

So the United States was *not* intended to have a government of 'separated institutions sharing power', as is so often claimed. Rather, each branch is 'vested' with a specific *kind* of power, a specific function, with which it is expected to make specific contributions to governance. We have seen in this chapter that, from the point of view of the framers of the Constitution, this framework of government was intended not to weaken but to invigorate the federal government. From this viewpoint, the separation of powers is a division of labour, designed to get the job of governing done more efficiently and capably. In this light, the partial agency of each branch in the others is not just a way of each branch balancing and checking the others, it is also a means of doing its own specific part of the job well, and of contributing to the work of the whole government. For example, a presidential veto (or the possibility of it) can improve the quality of a piece of legislation; or a Senate confirmation (or the possibility of non-confirmation) can improve the quality of presidential appointments, and so on. Thus the separation of powers is not designed to make the government feeble or inactive, or regularly deadlocked or gridlocked.

In measuring the success of the Constitution and its adequacy today, one must bear in mind this ambitious and constructive purpose of the separation of powers. Both liberal critics and conservative admirers of the Constitution often miss this crucial point, and criticise or admire the Constitution with the false assumption that the separation of powers was intended to weaken American government (Zvesper, 1999).

The Antifederalist critique

According to its final clause, the Constitution had to be ratified by conventions in only nine of the thirteen states in order to come into effect 'between the states so ratifying'. This violated the Articles of Confederation, which required the consent of every state to any amendments. However, the proponents of the Constitution had been determined from the beginning to avoid this crucial problem inherent in the Articles, the problem of desirable changes being stopped by one or two states. In *The Federalist* (no. 40) Madison cited the right to revolution described in the Declaration of Independence to justify this irregularity, and pointed out that the Constitution was, after all, being put to the people themselves in each state to decide whether or not to adopt it.

The proponents of the Constitution being called and calling themselves Federalists, it was their opponents' fate to become known as Antifederalists. Although defeated in 1788, many of their views survived, and some of their criticisms of the Constitution have modified the way that the Constitution has been interpreted and has worked in practice. Some Antifederalists disagreed with Federalists about the urgency of the crisis of American politics; but even those who agreed that constitutional change was needed, disagreed with Federalists in their views on the three basic characteristics of American constitutional politics (Eliot, 1891; Storing, 1981):

1. **Representation.** Antifederalists favoured a much more literally 'representative' system, in which elected office-holders more closely mirrored the major parts of American society. They proposed a more numerous representation – in other words, smaller electoral districts. They charged that the Federalists were setting up a system in which the 'middling class', mainly the yeomanry, who could still find a voice at the state level, would have little chance of being elected to federal offices, so that even without titles of nobility the new government would be dominated by an aristocracy. They also feared that the elitist politics would support monopolistic economic practices, favouring the privileged few rather than releasing the commercial energies of the many. Federalists argued in favour of 'refining' popular views in order to improve deliberation in government; Antifederalists feared that this would mean excluding the views of some classes of respectable citizens whose views deserved to be carried to the federal government, and looked for deliberation to take place among the people rather than in the government. They made a case for keeping government on a tighter leash, by making public opinion more directly influential in policy making. Federalists thought about elected officials' 'responsibility' (a noun that was coined by Madison in *The Federalist*) as responsibility *for*

certain duties; Antifederalists talked more about ensuring that elected officials remained responsible in the sense of *accountable to* the people. They called for shorter terms of office, limits on the number of terms that could be served, and the right of the people to instruct and to recall representatives.

This basic disagreement between Federalists and Antifederalists soon took on a new life, in the partisan divisions that began to shape American politics after the new government started up in 1789. A partisan opposition to the policies of the Federalist administration appeared (led in the House of Representatives by none other than James Madison, 'the Father of the Constitution'), and soon came to be known as the Republican party. This party, which many who had been Antifederalists supported or led, and which dominated American electoral politics for three decades, voiced Antifederalist ideas, stressing both the importance of social unity rather than the diversity of the large republic, and the usefulness of public opinion having a direct impact on government. These more purely democratic ideals of representation (as we shall see in Part III) have continued to be central to American politics, legitimising at the national level extraconstitutional practices such as opinion polling and the transformation of the presidency into a more plebiscitary office, as well as constitutional devices at the state level such as recall, ballot initiatives and referenda.

2. **Federalism.** Antifederalists often simply denied that sovereignty could be divided between two governments in the way that Federalists seemed to suppose was possible. They continued to insist that the union was a union of states rather than of individual citizens. They also questioned the amount of power that was being given to the federal government – especially the unlimited power to tax and to raise armies – and proposed that the powers granted to Congress be limited (as in the Articles of Confederation) to those 'expressly delegated'. Without such limits, they feared that the new system, even if it started out 'partly national and partly federal', would function in such a way that it would inevitably move towards a 'consolidation' of government power into the national centre. The advantages of local diversity and locally based public-spiritedness would be lost.

These questions have also reverberated through the development of American politics, starting with the conflict between the Federalists' liberal construction, versus the Republican party's 'strict construction', of the federal government's powers, and continuing right down to current debates about the limits on federal power, the significance of the role of the states in such policy areas as welfare provision, and the role of local communities and associations in maintaining public-spiritedness.

3. **Separation of powers.** Antifederalists criticised the Constitution for its inadequate separation of legislative, executive and judicial powers. Especially in the Senate, with its share of executive and judicial appointment powers added to its legislative role, they saw the danger of too many kinds of powers being held by the same people. They warned that the federal judiciary would use its power of judicial review against the will of Congress. They also opposed the re-eligibility of the president, and suggested an executive council to assist the president with information and advice, thus questioning the unity of the office defended by the Federalists.

More than the Federalists, they retained a traditional British Whig and American Revolutionary suspicion of executive power.

The Antifederalist critique thus again anticipated the partisan divisions that have animated American politics from the 1790s down to today. Madison's and Jefferson's Republican party (the precursors of today's Democratic party), even while supporting victorious candidates for president from 1800 onwards, championed the more directly republican legislative branch both against the 'monarchising' tendency of the presidency as it had been interpreted by Alexander Hamilton, and against the high-profile federal judiciary led by John Marshall. Today, as throughout American history, the Constitution still invites partisans to see one branch of government as the most legitimate or most defensible branch.

The dialogue between Federalists and Antifederalists thus continues in our time. 'There had always been something artificial in the means and temporary in the resources which maintained the Federalists' (Tocqueville, 1835; 1969, p. 176). Federalists (narrowly) won the ratification battle of 1787–88, but they did not so decisively win the war to determine the way that Americans have thought about their Constitution.

The Bill of Rights

One of the most common and effective objections of the Antifederalists was that the Constitution lacked a bill of rights, such as had been included with most state constitutions. Several delegates to the convention suggested adding a bill of rights, but this was judged unnecessary by the majority, at the end of the long discussions in Philadelphia. This judgement proved to be too hasty, and it was only with the promise of the subsequent addition of a bill of rights that the Constitution was approved by conventions in enough states to ensure its adoption. The first ten amendments, proposed by the first Congress, were ratified in 1791.

In fact, as Alexander Hamilton had pointed out in *The Federalist* (no. 84), the Constitution did already contain several items that might well logically appear in a bill of rights, for example a guarantee of trial by jury in criminal cases, and prohibitions against bills of attainder, *ex post facto* laws, titles of nobility, and suspension of habeas corpus. The first ten amendments (see Appendix B to this book) add guarantees of religious freedom, freedom of speech and of the press, the right of the people peaceably to assemble and to petition the government, the right of the people to bear arms (for the purpose of maintaining 'a well regulated militia'), the right to trial by jury in some civil cases, and various rights of the accused in criminal proceedings. As we shall see in subsequent chapters, the application and interpretation of this part of the Constitution have at times supplied lively controversies to the American legal and political scene.

The Bill of Rights is not opposed to the main body of the Constitution; nevertheless, while the emphasis of the Federalists' Constitution is on the establishment of competent government, the emphasis of the Bill of Rights is on the limits of government power. It can thus be seen as one of the most important achievements of Antifederalism, even though it did not make any of the structural changes to the Constitution that Antifederalists favoured. As we shall see in the following chapter, it was an achievement that was to be central in the future development of constitutional law.

Summary

The American Revolution and the constitution making of the 1770s and 1780s set out an enduring and demanding set of political principles, and based American constitutionalism, in contrast to European constitutionalist traditions from which it arose, more explicitly on natural-rights thinking. The system of separating legislative, executive and judicial powers into three governmental bodies was developed in the early state constitutions, and this experience was built upon by the framers of the federal Constitution of 1787. Studying Federalist thinking about the structure and purposes of the Constitution makes more intelligible the workings of American government today. Antifederalists contributed a more traditionally democratic way of thinking to the development and current functioning of American politics.

Topics for discussion

1. What was the most significant influence of the colonial and revolutionary experience on the future of American politics?
2. Were the founders of the American republic self contradictory in basing their politics on natural human equality but condoning the continuation of slavery?
3. What do the principles proclaimed in the Declaration of Independence imply about the proper constitution of legitimate government?
4. What are the constructive purposes of the separation of powers?
5. What were the most telling points made by the Antifederalist critique of the Constitution?

Further reading

The *Blackwell Encyclopedia of the American Revolution* (Oxford: Blackwell, 1991, eds Jack P. Greene and J.R. Pole) is a useful starting point for further reading on the Constitution as well as on the Revolution. *The Federalist* is essential reading for students of American politics. It is widely available in print, and can be downloaded from the Library of Congress Internet site (http://thomas.loc.gov) – which is a gateway to a wide variety of sources on American national, state and local government. David F. Epstein offers a good interpretation of *The Political Theory of* 'The Federalist' (Chicago: University of Chicago Press, 1984). Colleen A. Sheehan and Garcy L. McDowell (eds) Present allies of *The Federalist* in *Friends of the Constitution: Writings of the 'Other' Federalists 1787–1788* (Indianapolis: Liberty Fund, 1988) Herbert Storing edited *The Complete Anti-Federalist* (7 vols, Chicago: University of Chicago Press, 1981); W.B. Allen and Gordon Lloyd (eds) provide *The Essential Antifederalist* (Lanham, MD: University Press of America, 1985). Thomas G. West, in *Vindicating the Founders: Race, sex, class, and justice in the origins of America* (Washington DC: Rowman & Littlefield, 1997), explains and defends the American founders' views on these perennially controversial subjects. On the problem of characterising the political thinking of the founders, see also West's 'The classical spirit of the founding' and Charles R. Kesler, 'The founders and the classics', both in J. Jackson Barlow, Leonard W. Levy and Ken Masugi (eds), *The American Founding: Essays on the formation of the Constitution* (New York: Greenwood Press, 1988); John Zvesper, 'The American founders and classical political thought', *History of Political Thought*, vol. 10, no. 4 (1989), pp. 701–18; and Paul A. Rahe, *Inventions of Prudence: Constituting the American regime*, volume 3 of Rahe's study *Republics Ancient and Modern* (3 vols, Chapel Hill: University of North Carolina Press, 1994).

References

Beard, Charles A., 1913, *An Economic Interpretation of the Constitution of the United States* (New York: Macmillan)

Commager, Henry Steele, ed., 1973, *Documents of American History* (9th edn, 2 vols, Englewood Cliffs: Prentice Hall)

Eliot, Jonathan, ed., 1891, *The Debates of the State Conventions on the Adoption of the Federal Constitution* (3rd edn, Philadelphia: Lippincott)

Farrand, Max, ed., 1937, *The Records of the Federal Convention of 1787* (rev. edn, 4 vols, New Haven: Yale University Press; reprinted 1987 with vol. 5 *Supplement*, ed. J.H. Hutson)

Hartz, Louis, 1955, *The Liberal Tradition in America* (New York: Harcourt Brace Jovanovich)

Koch, Adrienne and Peden, William, eds, 1944, *The Life and Selected Writings of Thomas Jefferson* (New York: Modern Library)

Lutz, Donald S., 1988, *The Origins of American Constitutionalism* (Baton Rouge: Louisiana State University Press)

Perkins, Edwin J., 1991 'Socio-economic development of the colonies', pp. 53–63 in *The Blackwell Encyclopedia of the American Revolution* eds Jack P. Greene and J.R. Pole (Oxford: Blackwell)

Peterson, Merrill D., ed., 1975, *The Portable Thomas Jefferson* (New York: Viking)

Rossiter, Clinton, 1966, *1787: The Grand Convention* (New York: Macmillan)

Storing, Herbert J., ed. and intro., 1981, *The Complete Anti-Federalist* (7 vols, Chicago: University of Chicago Press)

Tocqueville, Alexis de, 1835, *Democracy in America*. Reprinted 1969, ed. J.P. Mayer, trans. G. Lawrence (Garden City, New York: Doubleday)

West, Thomas G. 1997, *Vindicating the Founders: Race, sex, class, and justice in the origins of America* (Washington DC: Rowman & Littlefield)

Wood, Gordon S., 1969, *The Creation of the American Republic, 1776–1787* (Chapel Hill: University of North Carolina Press)

Zvesper, John, 1999, 'The separations of powers in American Politics: why we fail to accentuate the positive', *Government and Opposition*, vol. 34.

3

A constitution to endure

The Constitution of 1787 has endured only because it has been adapted to changing economic, social and political circumstances. Both formal and informal constitutional changes have taken place ever since government officials first took up their offices under the Constitution in 1789. Some constitutional issues remain unresolved; this state of affairs ensures the continuing importance of constitutional issues in American politics.

On the campaign trail in 1912, in a successful bid for the presidency, Woodrow Wilson (an academic political scientist) expressed an opinion that he had reached in his study of American politics, an opinion that has been shared by progressive, reform-minded commentators on American politics throughout the twentieth century:

> The makers of our Federal Constitution ... constructed a government as they would have constructed an orrery – to display the laws of Nature. Politics in their thought was a variety of mechanics. The Constitution was founded on the law of gravitation. The government was to exist and move by virtue of the efficacy of 'checks and balances.' The trouble with the theory is that government is not a machine, but a living thing. It falls, not under the theory of the universe, but under the theory of organic life. It is accountable to Darwin, not to Newton. It is modified by its environment, necessitated by its tasks, shaped to its functions by the sheer pressure of life. ... Society is living organism and must obey the laws of life, not of mechanics; it must develop. All that progressives ask or desire is permission ... to interpret the constitution according to Darwinian principle; all they ask is recognition of the fact that a nation is a living thing and not a machine.
>
> (Wilson, 1916, pp. 40–1)

In this progressive or (what is now called) liberal view, the Constitution as it was originally conceived is not suitable to the tasks of governance in the modern world, and must be substantially changed – if only by major reinterpretation – in order to

Box 3.1

Pragmatism and American politics

American politics is both admired and criticised elsewhere in the world for its apparent escape from the ideological battles usually associated with the European categories of 'left' and 'right' originating in the French Revolution. It is difficult to overlay a simple template of 'radical' and 'conservative' on particular controversies and issues in American politics.

Nonetheless, American politics was not 'born free' of ideology in quite the way that some commentators admiring the apparently fresh start of the Constitution would like to claim. There are powerful eighteenth-century liberal commitments built into all of the founding documents of the republic. Equally, the religious basis of many of the communities present at the creation has powerfully influenced the way in which the states in particular have conducted their affairs.

However, the strongest link that can be claimed between the practice of American politics and the history of academic philosophy concerns neither liberalism nor religious doctrine but the emergence in the twentieth century of *pragmatism*.

The development of pragmatism as a philosophical doctrine was the work of three very different men.

The philosopher *Charles Sanders Peirce* (1839–1914) first proposed the pragmatic maxim in a series of papers given at Harvard in the 1870s. His technical formulation was as follows:

> Consider what effects, that might conceivably have practical bearings, we conceive the object of our conception to have. Then our conception of these effects is the whole of the conception of the object.

In ordinary language, this says that an idea's meaning rests in the possible consequences of acting upon it.

Peirce was appalled by the highly effective way in which his friend and personal benefactor *William James* (1842–1910) took over the concept. James, brother of the novelist Henry James, as well as having been one of the founders of modern psychology, is arguably America's most popular philosopher. In his hands pragmatism became a call to action, cast in quasi-religious terms, as in his essay *The Will to Believe*.

It was, however, in the hands of *John Dewey* (1859–1952) that pragmatism entered the mainstream of political thinking, stripped of its metaphysical and religious overtones which were replaced by an overwhelming confidence in the capacity of modern science. Dewey inspired a generation of social scientists and policy analysts to adopt a version of the pragmatic test, allied with confidence in progress, which therefore he called 'experimentalism' or 'instrumentalism'. For him, science and democracy were harnessed together in a mission which should free democracy from the other-worldly errors of the nineteenth century. As he wrote in *Liberalism and Social Action* (1935):

> Liberalism is committed to an end that is at once enduring and flexible; the liberation of individuals so that the realization of their capacities may be the law of their

life. It is committed to the use of freed intelligence as the method of directing change ...

Several historians, including David Hollinger (*In the American Province*, Bloomington: Indiana University Press, 1985) and Alan Ryan (*John Dewey and the High Tide of American Liberalism*, New York: Norton, 1995), have noted how between the late 1930s and the 1970s Dewey's ideas directly influenced American managers and bureaucrats.

More recently there have been some interesting attempts to revive the original religious and moral themes in pragmatism, as in the work of *Cornel West*, the most celebrated black social theorist working within the academy. In a number of public political pronouncements West has attempted to establish an activist 'prophetic pragmatism' with special resonance for black intellectuals (see his *Keeping Faith: Philosophy and race in America*, London: Routledge, 1993).

Contributed by Professor David Watson, University of Brighton

carry out those tasks. In particular, it must be changed to avoid the policy-making and administrative difficulties entailed by the separation of powers, since (in Wilson's words) 'no living thing can have its organs offset against each other as checks, and live'. One of the main worries from this point of view – a worry that came to be expressed very forcefully as a reaction against the rapid economic growth and large-scale, confident, and often unscrupulous economic enterprise that took place in the decades after the Civil War – has been that American government is incapable of rising to the challenge of the tyranny that comes in the shape of powerful concentrations of economic power and their subversion of democratic forms. Liberals have also been concerned, most conspicuously in the second half of the twentieth century, that American politics is incapable of dealing with just demands for the legal protection of the civil liberties and the rights of individuals and groups.

Assessing the accuracy of this critique of the adaptability of the Constitution would require a review and analysis of the whole course of American political history. In this chapter we can only begin such an assessment. We here examine how adaptable the Constitution has been in these two important areas (economic policy, and civil rights and liberties), by focusing on the most salient and persistent conflicts of constitutional interpretation the changing resolution of which has reflected and influenced political developments in these areas.

While liberals tend to complain that the Constitution has been incapable of evolving to address modern economic and political problems, conservatives tend to complain that it has evolved all too much and metamorphosed into a new and inferior form of government. In fact, the Constitution has been neither as unadaptable as that liberal complaint assumes nor as malleable as that conservative complaint assumes.

It is important to note that in the twentieth century there appeared deep philosophical as well as political differences between liberal (or progressive) views of the Constitution and conservative views. The philosophical *pragmatism* that has inspired many liberal reformers and technocrats is profoundly opposed to the enlightenment liberalism of eighteenth- and early nineteenth-century America. Pragmatism takes an instrumental approach to political principles, and rests on a rather postmodern disillusionment with the belief in the universal human standards that form the basis of earlier American revolutionary and constitutional thinking (see Box 3.1).

An adaptable constitution

In an important Supreme Court decision in 1819 (*McCulloch v. Maryland*), Chief Justice John Marshall, writing the opinion of the Court, emphasised the necessity of interpreting the powers given to Congress by the Constitution in a way that would make sense of the fact that the Constitution was a basic framework of government '*intended to endure for ages to come, and, consequently, to be adapted to the various crises of human affairs*' (emphasis added). This intention, said Marshall, meant that Congress had to be allowed to exercise much discretion in choosing the means to carry into execution the powers conferred on it by the Constitution. His view of the latitude that the Constitution allows Congress in this choice was very sweeping:

> Let the end be legitimate, let it be within the scope of the Constitution, and all means which are appropriate, which are plainly adapted to that end, which are not prohibited, but consist with the letter and spirit of the Constitution, are constitutional.

If this discretion had not been intended, then the Constitution, Marshall argued, would have been much more restrictive and detailed – in fact, it would have had to be so prolix that it 'could scarcely be embraced by the human mind':

> To have prescribed the means by which government should, in all future time, execute its powers, would have been to change, entirely, the character of the instrument, and give it the properties of a legal code. It would have been an unwise attempt to provide, by immutable rules, for exigencies which, if foreseen at all, must have been seen dimly, and which can be best provided for as they occur.

Marshall's opinion in this case has been widely cited and relied upon, and his argument is very persuasive. However, it should be remembered that this opinion was controversial. His liberal interpretation of the 'necessary and proper' clause in the Constitution, arguing that 'necessary' did not here mean 'absolutely or indispensably necessary,' has not been shared by all Supreme Court justices, nor by all Congresses and presidents. When, some years after Marshall's opinion in the McCulloch case, the same question arose – namely, whether chartering a national bank was a 'necessary and proper' exercise of Congressional fiscal power – President Andrew Jackson successfully vetoed a bill to recharter such a bank. Jackson's veto message – which became a rallying point for his party in the election of 1832 – stated his opinion that the proposed charter for the Bank of the United States would have conferred or continued quite unnecessary powers and privileges on the Bank, and on the 'many ... rich men' who stood to gain economically from the bank's recharter, men who 'have not been content with equal protection and equal benefits, but have besought us to make them richer by act of Congress' (Commager, 1973, vol. 1, pp. 272–4). Jackson's view was not without political precedent. After all, Marshall was one of the many Federalists who had been appointed to the federal judiciary just before the Jeffersonian

Republican party opposition to the Federalists took over the presidency in 1801, and his liberal constitutional interpretation, although shared by most Federalists, was not shared by everyone at that time. In 1791, Jefferson (as secretary of state) and Hamilton (as secretary of the Treasury) had written for President Washington opposing opinions on the constitutionality of the first national bank. Hamilton had anticipated Marshall's argument in the McCulloch case, but Jefferson had urged Washington to veto the bill, insisting that if the word 'necessary' were read as meaning 'merely convenient', Congressional powers would in effect be constitutionally unlimited. Washington signed the bank bill, but Jefferson's 'strict construction' of the Constitution became a dogma of his party: a party which, with Jackson's party as its successor, dominated American national politics from the beginning to the middle of the nineteenth century.

Marshall's and Hamilton's liberal or 'loose' construction of the Constitution has long since become the ruling paradigm, and there was perhaps always an element of mere rhetoric in the appeal to strict constructionism. However, this conflict between Marshall and Hamilton on the one hand, and Jackson and Jefferson on the other, illustrates four important and still relevant points about the 'adaptation' of the Constitution 'to the various crises of human affairs' that American politics has encountered during the past two centuries:

1. On many important and controversial policy issues, it is possible to produce plausible constitutional positions that conflict with each other.

2. The American Constitution sets up no final arbiter in such conflicts, unless it be the popular and nationally distributed majorities that are necessary to pass formal amendments to the Constitution. (Notice that, even here, minds can change, as happened on the question of the legality of alcoholic drinks, prohibited by the Eighteenth Amendment in 1919, and re-legalised by the Twenty-first Amendment in 1933.) There is a continuous constitutional dialogue among the various parts of the polity.

3. Connected with the battles over constitutional interpretation (just as there had been over the ratification of the Constitution) are often sharp differences of judgement about whether a particular measure contributes to the common good, or confers too many particular and private benefits. While it is usually too crude to see constitutional positions as mere rationalisations of economic interests, the combination of a constitutional position with a coalition of economic interests is a powerful and recurring event in American politics.

4. There is a strong tendency in American politics for substantive policy issues to be discussed and fought over in terms of constitutional interpretation. This constitutionalisation of politics baffles and annoys many observers, but it is clearly a major feature of the American political landscape.

It should not be concluded from these considerations that interpretations of the Constitution are always controlled by politics. The relationship between constitutional interpretation and politics is a two-way street, with influences going in both directions. If that were not the case, it would be pointless to study the basic characteristics of the Constitution and the way these have been adapted in changing circumstances. The

Constitution is adaptable, but it is not so malleable that it can be rendered meaningless or ignored. There are really very few words or phrases in the Constitution that have occasioned persistent controversy. If the Constitution had been completely inflexible, it would not have endured; but if it had been infinitely flexible, it might well have become a thin façade behind which the really efficient forces of politics worked.

Changing the Constitution

The Constitution of 1787 endures today, then, partly because the meanings and therefore the political effects of this Constitution change – not in every respect and all the time, but to some extent, from time to time. This is not to deny that in one sense (and this was the main point in Marshall's *McCulloch* opinion), Congress interprets the Constitution almost every day, every time it acts in a way that specifies how it will put its powers into execution, and it can and does change these specifications. Larger and longer-term changes in the Constitution come from at least six sources, most of which we shall be returning to in our analysis of the workings of American politics in the remainder of this book:

1. **Formal amendments.** In addition to the first ten amendments (the Bill of Rights), there have been seventeen further formal amendments (see Box 3.2 below, while Appendix B to this book includes the full text of these amendments). Article V of the Constitution sets out two methods of proposing amendments, and two methods of ratifying them. The usual combination of methods has been for two-thirds of each house of Congress to propose, and the legislatures in three-quarters of the states to ratify. The one exception was the Twenty-first Amendment – the repeal of prohibition – ratified by conventions in three-quarters of the states; Congress judged that too many state legislatures would oppose ratification. The alternative method of proposing – a national convention called at the request of two-thirds of the state legislatures – has never been used (although in the 1990s, the call for a convention to pass an amendment requiring a balanced budget has come from thirty-two states, only two short of the required two-thirds). The ratification process can be frustratingly long, although it has taken as little as three months, and only six amendments proposed by Congress have failed to be ratified. Congress usually includes a time limit on the ratification process, but the newest amendment (the twenty-seventh, ratified in 1992, prohibiting raising the salaries of the current Congress) was actually one of the twelve amendments proposed by Congress as a Bill of Rights in 1789. Formal amendments can be used (as was originally anticipated) as corrections of technical flaws or corruptions of original provisions of the Constitution (for example, Amendments 12 and 25). They can also be used (for example, Amendments 13 to 18) for more directly policy-related purposes.

2. **Congressional legislation completing the constitutional framework of government.** As we saw in Chapter 2, the Constitution leaves some things for Congress to decide in completing the framework of government, most obviously in the case of the judicial branch. Congress has decided these matters differently from time to time: for example, changing the number and size of executive departments, the number of

Box 3.2

Amendments to the Constitution, 1795–1992

Amendment	Year ratified	Substance
11	1795	Guarantees states immunity from suits started in federal courts by individual citizens
12	1804	Adjusts rules for presidential elections
13	1865	Prohibits slavery
14	1868	Guarantees persons subject to US jurisdiction rights of citizenship and of due process and equal protection of the law
15	1870	Guarantees against denial of right to vote 'on account of race, color, or previous condition of servitude'
16	1913	Grants Congress power to tax incomes
17	1913	Guarantees direct popular election of US senators
18	1919	Prohibits manufacture of and commerce in 'intoxicating liquors'
19	1920	Prohibits denial of right to vote 'on account of sex'
20	1933	Changes dates of congressional and presidential terms of office
21	1933	Repeals Amendment 18
22	1951	Limits presidents to two terms of office
23	1961	Adds District of Columbia to presidential electoral college system
24	1964	Prohibits denial of right to vote 'by reason of failure to pay any poll tax or other tax'
25	1967	Rules for determining presidential disability and succession, and filling vice-presidential vacancy
26	1971	Prohibits denial of right to vote 'on account of age' to citizens who are eighteen years or older
27	1992	Prohibits congressional pay rises from taking place until after the subsequent congressional election

lower federal courts, and (more infrequently) the size and the jurisdiction of the Supreme Court. Congress also determines the number and responsibilities of departments in the executive branch. The first Congress established the important principle that the presidential power to remove appointed officials is not subject to Senate approval.

3. **Executive actions that become accepted practice.** As we shall see in greater detail in later chapters, the constitutional position of the president has changed as a result of the initiatives taken with respect to federal management of the economy, and the

growing importance of foreign policy in American politics during the twentieth century. The expansion of the size and of the amount of responsibility of the executive branch has not always gone unchallenged. Moreover, it has been argued that the more plebiscitary modern presidency is actually constitutionally less energetic than was originally intended, since it is so immediately dependent on public opinion. However, the point is that customary expectations of the office of the president have clearly changed.

4. **Judicial interpretation.** Congressional completion of the judicial branch of the government was supplemented by the Supreme Court's development of its claim to judicial review. This claim having been established, the centrality of the Constitution (and its amendments) in American politics ensures the importance of shifts in judicial interpretation of the Constitution. Courts often simply follow precedents rather than creating them, and, as we shall see in Part VI, creative judicial interpretations are not always quickly accepted and implemented. Nevertheless, the judicial branch have greatly influenced the adaptation and endurance of the Constitution, sometimes by co-operating with the other branches and sometimes by standing in their way.

5. **Extraconstitutional institutional developments.** A large federal *bureaucracy* has grown up in recent decades. *Political parties*, not anticipated by the Constitution, have altered the way that the constitutional organs are selected and the way that they act and interact with each other. A dense jungle of *interest groups* and sophisticated networks of professional *lobbyists* have entwined themselves around these other extraconstitutional bodies as well as the constitutional offices themselves. The growth in the political centrality of the *mass media* has added yet another informal branch to American government, and another necessary chapter in books about American politics.

6. **Public opinion, responding to changing perceptions of the economic and political world.** Related to many of these other sources of informal constitutional change, and behind the formal amendments, are changes in public opinion, often following from economic crises and wars. For example, the expansion of the federal government's responsibility for the economy required not only different judicial interpretations of what the constitution permits the federal government to do, but also decisive shifts in public judgements about the rights and wrongs of federal government activity in this field. Without the shifts of public opinion, the shifts of judicial interpretation might not have happened, or might not have been accepted. In American constitutional politics, ultimately, as Abraham Lincoln argued, 'he who moulds public sentiment, goes deeper than he who enacts statutes or pronounces decisions. He makes statutes and decisions possible or impossible to be executed' (Angle, 1991, p. 128).

Crises and adaptations: economic policy

In spite of their frequent republican nostalgia for agrarian simplicity, and occasional socialist doubts about capitalism, Americans since colonial times have been pretty massively committed to an enterprising, capitalist economy. However, this generally agreed commitment has left room for deep disagreement on the proper relations between government and economy. The understanding of the framers of the Constitution was that government must have the power to regulate economic activities – primarily *not* in order to oppose public and private interests, but in order to harmonise them, to make the private creation of wealth (which is in the public interest) harmonise with the other purposes of civil society. This understanding rules out the view that economic policy should be based on the assumption that the public interest is deeply opposed to private economic interests. In other words, it rules out the socialist view that successful capitalists are enemies of the people. However, it leaves many questions to be determined by political deliberation. Should government engage in indicative planning, subsidy, close regulation, or even occasional outright ownership and operation of economic enterprises? Or should government take a less directive role, simply maintaining peace and leaving the economic players free to get on with the game? If the latter, then what are the exceptions to such a position? For example, what should government do about the growth of business monopolies and labour unions? Furthermore, what, if anything, is the government's responsibility for the provision of welfare assistance to those who, for whatever reason, are less benefited than others by the workings of the modern capitalist economy? (This last question, of great current interest outside as well as inside the United States, is discussed in Chapter 20.)

Disagreements about such economic policies have been connected with changing constitutional interpretations ever since the first years of the operation of the Constitution. As we saw in Chapter 2, establishing a common internal market, unfettered by individual states' regulatory barriers, had been one of the main purposes of the nationalist movement that resulted in the adoption of the Constitution. In the 1790s, Federalists, especially those who agreed with the programme of legislation advanced by Alexander Hamilton, went further down this road, by favouring a form of what today would be called 'development economics'. In this Hamiltonian plan, the early republic's financial, commercial and manufacturing interests (all relatively small compared with the overwhelming dominance of agricultural interests) would be supported and encouraged, by Congress' exercise of its powers to borrow money, to regulate commerce, to tax imports, and to pay the debts of the United States; and those business interests would, in turn, support the new federal government. Jeffersonian and later Jacksonian policies in the early decades of the nineteenth century rejected much of this Hamiltonian vision. Jeffersonian and Jacksonian rhetoric often harked back to a simpler, agrarian and allegedly more moral society and policy. However, less nostalgically and more effectively what the Jeffersonians and Jacksonians did (as is indicated by Jackson's veto message, quoted above) was not to try to turn back the tide of commercialisation and industrialisation, but to challenge the exclusivity and elitism of their partisan opponents in their use of the federal government (as opposed to the state governments) to structure and to stabilise American economic development. (Constitutional and policy debates about the federal government's economic involvement thus often turned on questions about the proper division of responsibilities between federal and state governments. We shall be studying this development of federalism in Chapter 4.)

Because many Federalists retreated from elective offices to the judiciary after the Jeffersonian 'revolution of 1800', the constitutional basis for wide-ranging regulation of the economy by the federal government was developed and articulated by the judicial branch before it became the normally acknowledged basis of action by president and Congress. Supreme Court Chief Justice John Marshall was the leading developer and articulator. In 1824, in the case of *Gibbons v. Ogden*, he set out a generous interpretation of the Constitution's grant of power to Congress 'to regulate commerce ... among the several states'. This *interstate commerce clause* has been one of the most controversial parts of the Constitution. It continues today to provide fuel for political and legal disputes. Three questions have arisen. What is 'commerce': just buying and selling, or other activities more or less directly connected with that? For what purposes may Congress legally 'regulate' commerce: merely for economic efficiency, or for broader social ends? Finally, can states also regulate interstate commerce, or must their powers in this area all yield to the federal government's authority?

Gibbons v. Ogden involved a challenge to a long-established but rather unpopular monopoly that a steamboat company (with Aaron Ogden as its current licensee) had persuaded the New York legislature to grant to it, to operate steamboats in New York waters, excluding all competitors. The challenger, Thomas Gibbons, licensed by the federal government to engage in coasting trade, began running services between New York and New Jersey, in defiance of the New York monopoly. Having been enjoined by New York courts from running this service, Gibbons appealed to the United States Supreme Court, which reversed the New York decision. Marshall's opinion for the Court (in contrast to Justice Johnson's concurring opinion) avoided making any final pronouncement on the question of whether the federal government's power to regulate interstate commerce completely extinguishes the states' powers in this area, as Gibbons claimed. A nationalistic pronouncement on this question would have been highly controversial, and was not necessary to the Court's decision. The Court's opinion rests rather on the more modest ground that Congress' coasting legislation, as part of the 'supreme law of the land', must take precedence over any state law conflicting with it, as did the New York law granting the monopoly. Less modestly, on the way to deciding against the monopoly (generally a popular decision), Marshall's opinion laid down three very definite and very broad ideas about what interstate commerce is and what the federal government can legally do in regulating it:

1. Commerce is not (as Ogden had claimed) simply 'buying and selling, or the interchange of commodities'; it comprehends not only (as in this case) navigation, but also all other parts of 'the commercial intercourse between nations, and parts of nations, in all its branches'. The power to regulate commerce may entail the power to regulate all economic activities that form part of that commerce: the breadth of the power is very great (even if it does not extend as far as federal judges since 1937 have generally suggested: an issue we return to below). Moreover, it is a power that can easily expand to cover new forms of commercial transactions introduced by economic and technological innovations such as rail and air traffic, interstate stock market quotations, telecommunications, and radio and television broadcasting. Understood with this breadth and elasticity, the commerce power is the federal government's most important peacetime power.

2. The phrase 'among the states' means concerning more states than one, but it does not restrict congressional regulation to the borders between states. On the contrary, argued Marshall, 'among' means 'intermingled with', so this phrase extends federal power over commerce to any location within a state where a commercial activity affects other states. On a liberal interpretation of Marshall's already liberal opinion, any economic transaction in the United States that is, 'in any manner, connected with' foreign or interstate commerce is subject to congressional regulation. Of course, as Marshall knew, with the development of the economy and its increasing division of labour, fewer and fewer activities in America could be regarded as 'completely internal commerce of a state', and therefore reserved from congressional power; his definition of interstate commerce was a recipe for the growth of the federal government's power.

3. The power 'to regulate' commerce is the power 'to prescribe the rule by which commerce is to be governed. This power, like all others vested in Congress, is complete in itself, may be exercised to its utmost extent, and acknowledges no limitations other than are prescribed in the Constitution.' This reading of the commerce clause permits Congress to regulate commerce for any constitutional purpose, including non-commercial, social policy purposes (for example, attacking racial discrimination).

Congress did not use its commerce power for non-commercial purposes during Marshall's day, and in fact during the first century of American politics it used this power very sparingly even for commercial purposes. Especially in the last half of the nineteenth century, business interests, now thriving quite nicely without needing to rely on 'development economics' and a broad, Hamiltonian view of the economic power of the federal government, adopted a strict-construction, states' rights position that had previously been associated with Jeffersonian views of America. They believed that this position would help them in their efforts to prevent state and federal governments from being pushed by popular movements to control the excesses of capitalism. These same business interests were inconsistently but understandably happy for government to intervene in the economy to assist their enterprises, with protective tariffs, infrastructure improvements (road and harbour construction, telegraph lines, finance for canals, land surveys, land grants for schools and universities), and subsidies (steamships, fishing fleets); and they were grateful when the government opposed the organisation of trade unions. Nonetheless, laissez-faire was the major theme of the constitutional interpretation that these interests favoured.

Thus, the Hamiltonian and Marshallian vision of the scope of the federal government's economic regulatory power came into its own only when the political response to industrialisation in the late nineteenth and early twentieth centuries finally prompted Congress to use its commercial power somewhat more vigorously – both for strictly commercial and for broader social purposes, in this way combining Hamiltonian means (energetic federal government) with Jeffersonian ends (protection of the interests of the many). The Interstate Commerce Act of 1887 began an intermittent series of federal Acts designed to promote economic efficiency and fairness (in this case, by attempting to enforce standard and 'reasonable and just' charges for rail services). Many state legislatures also began enacting regulatory legislation at this time, often under the impulse of progressive reformers' desires to adjust American politics and economics to the emergence of large-scale industrial and corporate capitalism. However, by this time, the federal and state courts had developed constitutional doctrines that made them much more wary than Marshall's opinions had been of such legislative vigour. Therefore, for several decades political battles over economic policy were often conducted in the context of conflicting interpretations of the Constitution, with the courts ruling against economic legislation in many cases. This was the 'Lochner era', named after the 1905 Supreme Court decision that struck down a New York statute that had restricted bakery workers to a ten-hour day, the Court deeming this an unreasonable interference with the liberty of the individual to enter into labour contracts (*Lochner v. New York*). Only in 1937, when the Supreme Court began approving most New Deal economic and social legislation, did this narrowly conservative contribution of the courts to the constitutional arguments in economic policy significantly diminish. This long history of judicial constitutional interpretations that often opposed even the most reasonable economic and social legislation lent credence to the progressive critique of the Constitution as an outdated, eighteenth-century, 'Newtonian' system that could not easily adapt to meet the administrative, economic and social needs of the modern world – although, as we have seen, the framers of the Constitution actually did not hold the strict laissez-faire views that the conservative judges of this era read into the Constitution.

The contraction of the scope of the interstate commerce clause introduced by this judicial conservatism can be seen very clearly in the Sugar Trust case (*United States v. E.C. Knight Company*). In 1890, Congress passed the Sherman Anti-Trust Act, outlawing contracts, combinations or conspiracies 'in restraint of trade or commerce among the several states, or with foreign nations', in particular, any 'attempt to monopolize any part of' this commerce (Commager, 1973, vol. 1, p. 586). This Act, along with the Federal Trade Commission and the Clayton Anti-Trust Acts of 1914, are still today important tools in the federal government's antimonopolistic activities. However, the Sherman Act soon suffered a constitutional weakening, in the Sugar Trust decision. In this case, the federal government charged the defendant company with violating this Act, following its purchase of several competing sugar refining companies in Philadelphia, a purchase which had given the company control of over 95 per cent of the country's sugar refining business. The Supreme Court decided that the company was not guilty, on the ground that the Act must be interpreted – as the commerce clause must also be interpreted – as applying only to *interstate trade*, and not to the *intrastate manufacturing* of the products traded: 'the contracts and acts of the defendants related exclusively to the acquisition of the Philadelphia refineries and the business of sugar refining in Pennsylvania, and bore no direct relation to commerce between the states or with foreign nations.' The Court admitted that a monopoly on manufacturing within one state 'might unquestionably tend to restrain external as well as domestic trade, but the constraint would be an indirect result, however inevitable and whatever its extent … '.

Related constitutional considerations led the Court to strike down the Federal Child Labor Act of 1916. This Act, in order to discourage the employment of children in mining and manufacturing, prohibited the interstate trade of goods which had been produced in places where children under fourteen were employed, or where children under sixteen were permitted to work either for more than eight hours, or at night (after 7pm or before 6am), or more than six days per week. In *Hammer v. Dagenhart* (247 US 251 [1918]), the Court (albeit with four dissenting justices) decided that Congress could not use such an act to prevent Dagenhart from continuing to employ his young sons in his cotton mill, because, although the goods produced entered interstate commerce, 'before transportation begins, the labor of their production is over, and the mere fact that they were intended for interstate commerce transportation does not make their production subject to federal control under the commerce power'. The opinion of the Court acknowledged that the Court had in the past approved federal laws that prohibited interstate traffic in some things (lottery tickets, impure food and drugs, prostitutes), but in these cases, the interstate traffic itself had 'harmful results', whereas, in the case before the Court, the harm had already taken place: 'The goods shipped are of themselves harmless.' In other words, the Court was here saying not only (as in the Sugar Trust case) that the definition of commerce in Article I needs to be construed narrowly, but also that the fullness of the power 'to regulate' must be qualified in a way that had not hitherto been evident. Congress' attempt to respond to this decision by using its tax power to discourage the use of child labour was also found unconstitutional by the Court (*Bailey v. Drexel Furniture Company*).

The Court's sharp distinctions in these cases between *manufacture and commerce*, and between *direct and indirect effects* of economic activity – distinctions which John Marshall might have found implausible – were difficult distinctions to maintain and to apply. There were many cases in which the Court kept a lower profile, and much important economic and social legislation was passed, especially by state and local governments, which was allowed by the courts to stand. Reviewing the history of the Supreme Court in this period, one can even conclude that 'the dominant tendency had been to moderate the regulatory movement without attempting to destroy it, to nudge and advise democracy rather than to frustrate it' (McCloskey, 1960, p. 168). Nevertheless, these sharp distinctions were used by the Court to frustrate several congressional Acts, right down to the mid-1930s, even after the onset of the Great Depression. The Court (with bitter dissenting opinions) accepted the constitutionality of some of the New Deal legislation enacted in response to the Depression (for example, the ending of the gold standard, and the social security system), but in 1935 and 1936 the Court used its heavy distinctions between production and commerce, and between direct and indirect economic effects, to rule out New Deal legislation designed to assist economic recovery in manufacturing, mining and agriculture. The Court also ruled some of this legislation unconstitutional because it *delegated legislative power to administrative agencies*, thus violating the principle of separation of powers.

Judicial hesitations and refusals in the field of economic policy dramatically declined in 1937, when, under the threat of President Franklin D. Roosevelt's Court-packing plan (a confrontation that will be described in Chapter 18), the Court began leaving economic policy to the elected branches of the federal and state governments. The Court abandoned its absolute distinctions between production and commerce, and between direct and indirect effects, which had made the commerce clause more constraining than empowering. It began approving congressional regulation of any commercial activity that has *substantial effects* on interstate commerce. Significantly, one of the first cases in which it did this was when it affirmed the constitutionality of the National Labor Relations Act of 1935 (the 'Wagner Act'), a law that protected the rights of labour unions to organise and to bargain collectively, on the grounds that the exercise of these rights helped prevent industrial conflicts that seriously disrupted interstate commerce (*National Labor Relations Board v. Jones & Laughlin Steel Corporation*). This was significant because it showed that the New Deal was giving greater political recognition to the economic role of manual workers. (At the same time, it did not elevate them into a ruling class; in fact, recognition of unions – in the plural – was also a means of keeping labour divided, complementing business plural-ism with labour pluralism.) In the Fair Labor Standards Act of 1938, Congress pro-hibited interstate commerce in, and the production for that commerce of, goods made by employees whose wages and hours do not meet standards prescribed by Congress. This Act was upheld by the Court in a unanimous decision (*United States v. Darby Lumber Company*, overruling *Hammer v. Dagenhart*).

The commerce clause was not the only part of the Constitution that was given a more liberal treatment by legislatures and courts in the aftermath of the Depression. In a 1934 case (*Home Building and Loan Association v. Blaisdell*), the Supreme Court ruled that a Minnesota law authorising temporary emergency delays in mort-gage payments was 'consistent with the spirit and purpose' of the Constitution's contract clause ('No state shall ... pass any ... law impairing the obligation of con-tracts'). After 1936, the Court began to approve the federal government's use of its tax powers for non-revenue purposes (for example, to support farm prices, disal-lowed in 1936 (*United States v. Butler*) but allowed in 1939 (*Mulford v. Smith*); or to discourage gambling (*United States v. Kahriger*). It also began to allow Congress to delegate broadly drafted powers to administrative agencies, thus facilitating its economic regulation (Corwin, 1973, pp. 7–8).

When Roosevelt first took office as president in 1933, in his inaugural address he had confidently stated:

> Our Constitution is so simple and practical that it is possible always to meet extraordinary needs by changes in emphasis and arrangement without loss of essential form. That is why our constitutional system has proved itself the most superbly enduring political mechanism the modern world has produced.
>
> (Commager, 1973, vol. 2, p. 242)

Although this confidence did not invariably prove to be warranted in the years that fol-lowed, at least after 1936 few constitutional challenges were involved in setbacks to Roosevelt's economic policies. The New Deal's emphasis on the federal government's responsibility for the economy – specifically, for economic recovery, for reform and supervision of the financial sector, and for certain kinds of relief – was soon accepted in principle by the moderates who began to dominate the Republican party, and became the ground of a constitutional and political consensus for several decades. This consensus was reinforced by the experience of the Second World War, during which the federal government directly and successfully managed the economic planning needed for the war effort, and after which America's enlarged international role included commitments involving the federal government's superintendence of the national economy as well as continued direct participation in that economy by way of military and other purchases. (We look more closely at the origins of this historical consensus, and its decline, in Chapter 5.)

In the 1960s and 1970s, growing public interest and concern with consumer and environmental protection added new kinds of federal economic policy (and new policy-making agencies) to the set established in the 1930s and 1940s. Today, Congressional legislation and federal administrative regulations decide all kinds of economic questions, reaching deeply into the country's business activities and the lives of individual citizens.

The interpretations of the Constitution that have ruled since 1937 onwards permitted rather than required this enlargement of the federal government's economic policy responsibility, so they have also allowed a retreat from that enlargement in the era of greater public scepticism towards the federal government that has unfolded since the 1960s. Federal government action in economic policy has remained a politically contentious subject throughout the twentieth century, even during the post New Deal period of consensus. The point is that constitutional barriers to this action have been greatly reduced, so economic policy conflicts have occurred mainly in the crowded and chaotic political arena rather than in the constitutional arena.

It is possible that the constitutional dimension of economic policy will one day again loom large in American politics. For example, liberal interpretations of the commerce clause that have ruled since 1937 have recently been brought into question. Since the 1930s, Congress has used its interstate commerce power – for both commercial and non-commercial purposes – to regulate a great variety of intrastate economic activities that 'substantially affect' interstate commerce. For instance, the Supreme Court unanimously approved the application of limits on the amount of land on which wheat is grown to a small Ohio farmer who exceeded his allotted acreage in order to grow extra wheat destined solely for consumption on his own farm (on the grounds that if many farmers did this it would greatly affect wheat prices: *Wickard v. Filburn*), and it unanimously upheld the application of prohibitions on racial discrimination to a family-owned restaurant, with a largely local customer base (on the grounds that some of the food served had travelled in interstate commerce: *Katzenbach v. McClung*). However, in 1995, in *United States v. Lopez*, the Supreme Court (by a five to four majority, affirming a lower court of appeals decision) ruled against the constitutionality of the Gun-Free School Zones Act of 1990, by which Congress had made it a federal crime (as it was already a crime in more than forty states) to possess a gun in or near a school. The ruling held that this could not be regarded as a proper exercise of the interstate commerce power, because it was 'a criminal statute that by its terms has nothing to do with "commerce" or any sort of economic enterprise, however broadly one might define those terms.' To the government's argument that guns in schools might well have substantial interstate economic effects (higher insurance premiums, discouragement to live in and to travel to violent areas, less productive citizens), the Court replied that accepting this argument as a basis for congressional legislation made it 'difficult to perceive any limitation on federal power, even in areas such as criminal law enforcement or education where states historically have been sovereign.' If the government's argument were accepted, the Court would be 'hard-pressed to posit any activity by an individual that Congress is without power to regulate.' The further expansion of the commerce power involved in this Act of Congress would 'convert congressional authority under the commerce clause to a general police power of the sort retained by the states.' In support of its decision, the Court quoted Marshall's opinion in *Gibbons v. Ogden*, for even Marshall had emphasised that in the commerce clause, 'the enumeration of the particular classes of commerce to which the power was to be extended would not have been made had the intention been to extend the power to every description. The enumeration presupposes something not enumerated ... .' In a concurring opinion, Justice Thomas pointed out that, while the case before the Court turned on the fact that the activity being regulated was not commerce, the 'substantial effects' test itself has the defect of being too elastic – that is, of excluding in principle no commercial activity. In other words, he pointed out that the 'something' that Marshall had pointed out was presupposed by 'the enumeration' in the commerce clause is something *commercial*. Justice Thomas suggested that the Court might therefore modify its commerce clause jurisprudence accordingly in an appropriate case in the future. The constitutional dimension of economic policy may be dormant but it is not dead.

Crises and adaptations: civil liberties and civil rights

After the constitutional revolution of 1937, interesting constitutional conflicts shifted away from economic policy towards social issues, civil rights and civil liberties. For three decades, no federal law based on the commerce clause was invalidated by the Supreme Court. In that same period, the Court's protection of constitutional liberties felled dozens of federal laws and many more state laws. There were several reasons for this shift:

1. **Bigger government.** This shift of constitutional concerns followed in part as a reaction against the newly enlarged size and activities of the federal government stemming from the Great Depression and the Second World War: a more prominent government inspired more solicitude for the protection of liberty against that government. Conservatives, who might have appealed to the freedom that had traditionally been accorded to the business classes before those classes had been perceived as having failed the nation by failing to prevent the depression, found that they could still respectably appeal against big government and its threats to individual liberty. Many libertarians continue to cultivate this suspicion of big government today.

2. **New Deal coalition.** However, the rise to prominence of civil liberty issues also followed from the changes in the coalition of interests that normally enjoyed majority status in the federal government. The New Deal Democratic party, with its economic policies, has looked after the interests of the soldiers of industry (particularly the unionised ones) – not altogether neglecting the captains of industry, but not treating them with the degree of deference and respect that pre New Deal governments gave them. Some Americans who favoured New Deal economic policies directed towards the interests of the less privileged saw these policies as an enlargement of civil liberty. For example, in 1938 the American Civil Liberties Union characterised the Supreme Court's upholding of the Wagner Act and of the activities of the National Labor Relations Board as 'the most important single step toward the attainment of meaningful freedom of speech which has taken place in modern

times' (Murphy, 1972, p. 172). However, New Deal Democrats have also looked after the interests of liberal politicians, professionals and intellectuals, religious groups and leaders, publishing and media businesses, and others who have been concerned with furthering the freedoms of religion, speech, press, assembly and privacy. In addition, increasingly in the decades after the Second World War, the Democrats have looked after the interests in civil rights of ethnic and 'racial' minorities and women. These groups of citizens have perceived the possibility of the federal government acting as a direct and positive promoter of, rather than as a threat to, civil liberties and civil rights.

3. **Totalitarianism.** A third reason for the more frequent appearance of civil liberties on the agenda of constitutional politics was the growing threat to liberal democracies from totalitarian states in the 1930s. Looking at attacks on civil liberties in fascist and communist tyrannies – in their persecution of ethnic and 'racial' minorities, their intolerance of critical political speech, and their dismissiveness of fair procedures in criminal trials – made many Americans more sensitive to these issues at home.

4. **Violent domestic and international conflicts.** At the same time, the recurring involvement of the United States in wars through much of the twentieth century, and the intensive and often violent domestic conflicts between labour and capital, increased the threats to domestic civil liberties that generally accompany such conflicts. The American Civil Liberties Union was originally set up during the First World War to defend domestic critics of the war.

5. **Greater cultural diversity.** Successive waves of immigration, and home-grown alternative lifestyles, have increased the number and variety of cultures in the United States, providing difficult tests for the ideal of toleration that the freedoms of religion and speech embody.

The constitutional conflicts and changes associated with the new emphasis on civil liberties and civil rights have involved a new focus on and new interpretations of several amendments to the Constitution: the First Amendment, which deals with the freedoms of religion and speech; Amendments 4 to 6, establishing fair legal procedures, especially in criminal cases; and the first section of the Fourteenth Amendment, especially its command that no state 'deny to any person within its jurisdiction the equal protection of the laws'.

That section of the Fourteenth Amendment has been doubly important, because it has been used to 'incorporate' many of the freedoms in the Bill of Rights – which applies directly only to the federal government – so that these freedoms apply to the state governments as well. This process has been carried out by the changing interpretation of the Fourteenth Amendment's provision that no state 'deprive any person of life, liberty, or property, without due process of law'. During the late nineteenth and early twentieth centuries, the judiciary's use of this 'due process' clause had complemented their constraining use of the interstate commerce clause (discussed above). It was used to protect property rights and to deny state governments the capacity to enact economic regulations that the courts 'found to be arbitrary, oppressive, and unjust' (concurring opinion of Justice Bradley in *Davidson v. New Orleans*) – for example, minimum wage laws for women and children, struck down in *Adkins v. Children's Hospital*. In the 1930s, just as the interstate commerce clause was being liberally reinterpreted, this conservative 'substantive due process' line of argument was repudiated (for example, *Nebbia v. New York*, upholding milk price controls, and *West Coast Hotel Company v. Parrish*, upholding the state of Washington's statute prescribing minimum wages for women, which had been passed in 1913 and continually enforced in spite of the *Adkins* decision). It was gradually replaced with a liberal 'substantive due process' line of argument, which was developed and applied by the courts in civil liberty and criminal procedure cases, thus 'incorporating' (or 'absorbing' or 'embracing') Bill of Rights freedoms into the Fourteenth Amendment's 'due process' limitations on state governments.

This transfer of judicial scrutiny of federal and state legislation from economic liberties to civil liberties was joined to the development of a controversial new judicial philosophy. Not all judges have shared this philosophy, and it is still widely contested in the United States today, but it offers a plausible rationale for the political, especially the judicial, emphasis of the libertarian aspects of the Constitution. It sees the courts as having two distinct but greatly intertwined functions. They are:

1. The natural champions of *rights*, especially of the rights of individual citizens and groups who are otherwise excluded from the political process.

2. The natural protectors of the safe and proper operation of that *democratic process*, by being the protectors of the fundamental freedoms presupposed by that process.

Under this philosophy, even if the 'incorporation' of the Bill of Rights into the Fourteenth Amendment is left out of the picture, the courts have a particular duty to focus on violations of a free and open political process, in the interests of maintaining fundamental rights that are 'of the very essence of a scheme of ordered liberty' (*Palko v. Connecticut*). In a famous footnote to a Supreme Court opinion (*United States v. Carolene Products Company*), Justice Harlan Stone explained the implications of the Court's connected concerns with the political process and with certain minorities' rights: legislation restricting access to or participation in the political process (for example, laws establishing electoral practices that fall short of fair representation) may 'be subjected to *more exacting judicial scrutiny*' than other legislation (emphasis added). Moreover, 'similar considerations [may] enter into the review of statutes directed at particular religious, ... or national, ... or racial minorities', since '*discrete and insular minorities*' may not enjoy the protection normally offered by the operation of the majoritarian political process (emphasis added).

Underlying this philosophy is a belief that judicial protection of the processes of government and of the rights of individuals in excluded groups is more likely than judicial determinations of the intrinsic justice of legislative policies to lead to desirable results. This belief is grounded both on a conservative, sceptical assessment of the policy-making capacity of judges and on a liberal optimism that the flourishing of free speech and other civil liberties will lead to a healthy competition of interests and ideas from which the public good will reliably emerge.

This role that the courts have found for themselves in modern America after their retreat from the economic policy arena may seem natural and defensible, and when Americans now think of their Constitution they tend to think first of the Bill of Rights.

However, this libertarian constitutional focus is not uncontroversial, partly because in pursuing it the courts have tended to heighten some of the intrinsic conflicts between the needs of governance on the one hand and intense concern for procedural correctness and individual freedom on the other. Of course, these may be vital rather than morbid conflicts in liberal democratic politics.

The emergence and the persistence of such conflicts can be seen by briefly reviewing constitutional developments in the four most important areas of civil liberty, and seeing the extent to which crucial constitutional issues in these areas remain unsettled:

1. Freedom of speech
2. Religion
3. Rights of criminal suspects
4. Rights of victims of unfair discrimination

These liberties can conflict with each other. For example, the freedom of speech ('and of the press') may render a fair trial by an impartial jury very difficult, or may incite racial violence. Nevertheless, especially when the courts began occupying this territory in the 1930s and 1940s, 'these categories of rights were logically hard to separate', and 'alertness to one tended to stimulate alertness to all, so that they mutually animated one another' (McCloskey, 1960, p. 182). Minorities subjected to racial discrimination were very often also victims of violations of free speech or of improper criminal justice procedures.

First Amendment freedoms: speech

The freedoms of speech, press and peaceful assembly are clearly fundamental to liberal democracy. In Justice Louis Brandeis' words, 'freedom to think as you will and to speak as you think are means indispensable to the discovery of political truth; … without free speech and assembly, discussion would be futile; … with them, discussion affords ordinarily adequate protection against the dissemination of noxious doctrine …' (concurring opinion in *Whitney v. California*). However, does this mean that the freedom of speech must be absolute? Or even if not absolute, should it occupy a 'preferred position' in constitutional law? Are there circumstances in which discussion will not be 'adequate protection against the dissemination of noxious doctrine'? Must political speech that rejects freedom be protected from legislative restriction? And what protection, if any, must be given to non-political speech?

Although some Americans (including at least one Supreme Court justice, Hugo Black) have argued that the First Amendment forbids all legislative interference with speech, American constitutional law has permitted exceptions to this absolute freedom of speech. However, there remains uncertainty about why and where to draw the line. The attempt to formulate a general test to help draw the line in individual cases has not been successful. In the first half of the twentieth century, the Supreme Court developed, and for a time regularly applied, the *clear and present danger* test, which assumed that legislation could rightly restrict speech in attempting to prevent evils, but required that the government prove in each case that the defendant's 'words are used is such circumstances and are of such a nature as to create a clear and present danger that they will bring about' those evils (*Schenck v. United States*). This test, which gave freedom of speech a 'preferred position', was announced in a case brought under the Espionage Act of 1917 against the general secretary of the Socialist party, Charles Schenck, who had violated the Act by posting 15,000 leaflets urging potential military draftees to resist the draft. This Act was a wartime measure, and Schenck's conviction for obstructing military recruitment was upheld by a unanimous Court, noting that 'when a nation is at war many things that might be said in time of peace are such a hindrance to its effort that their utterance will not be endured so long as men fight and that no court could regard them as protected by any constitutional right.' It is difficult for a libertarian-oriented constitutional law to formulate and to uphold a standard of free speech that can be maintained in wartime.

During the period in which the 'clear and present danger' test was regularly used by the Court (1937 to 1950), convictions under statutes limiting free speech were rarely upheld. This was true even during the Second World War, when a prosecution similar to that by which Schenck had been convicted in 1917 failed the test (*Hartzel v. United States*). (This was America's most popular war, so political leaders were largely successful in their efforts to avoid the free speech problems encountered in previous wars [Murphy, 1972, pp. 225–47].) This lengthy run of speech limitations failing the test made the test seem too demanding to some, and the next wartime experience – the Korean War and the cold war – soon proved too much for this libertarian test. When the Court upheld the conviction of several Communist party leaders for violating the Smith Act, an Act of Congress that made it a crime to advocate the overthrow of the government by force or violence, it had to reduce the 'clear and present danger' test to a clear and 'probable' danger test, since it recognised that the danger in this case was not present, that is imminent (*Dennis v. United States*). This radically modified the test, and in the judgement of one commentator 'came close to abandoning altogether the concept of judicial limitation' on legislative restrictions of political speech (McCloskey, 1960, pp. 196–7).

It is true that the Court has since then tended to adopt a less formulaic approach to free speech issues. However, its more ad hoc, *balancing* approach has included special weighting for free speech. It has by no means lost its attachment to free speech as one of its special objects of care, even while it balances competing private and public interests against each other on a case-by-case basis rather than applying a libertarian formula. For example, in cases involving national security, the Court soon reintroduced a more libertarian note than could be detected in the *Dennis* opinion, first by limiting the reach of such laws as the Smith Act to apply only to advocacy of actual revolutionary action, as opposed to advocating the doctrine that revolutionary action is desirable (*Yates v. United States*), then by adding that the lawless action thus advocated must be 'likely to incite or produce such action' (*Brandenburg v. Ohio*); it also began restricting various government loyalty programmes and congressional investigations into subversive activities.

Nor has libertarianism disappeared from other political speech issues. The libertarian proposition that truth results from competition in the marketplace of ideas has been one of the elements in recent judicial decisions that have struck down legislated limits on *electoral campaign spending*. Very provocative 'symbolic speech' acts (for example, burning the American flag, and Nazi displays of swastikas and marches through Jewish districts) have recently found constitutional support from the Court, with angry reactions from Congress and state legislatures.

In the non-political speech field, although laws against obscenity can still be constitutional, defining obscenity and distinguishing it from art has proved to be difficult. Nude dancing (among other things) has been deemed to be at least 'marginally' within the First Amendment's protection. Courts have permitted cities to use planning laws ('zoning') to confine commerce in pornography to certain areas. Laws restricting the advertising of harmful products or activities (for example, tobacco, alcohol and gambling) are usually upheld, but restrictions on professional advertising (for example, by lawyers and accountants) are not, since they are judged to serve no clear public interest. Laws against such abuses of speech as false advertising and libel are constitutionally permissible; however, defence against libel actions is easier in the United States than in many other countries: a statement will not be held libelous or slanderous if it can be shown to be true, and for public figures the statement must be shown to be not only false but also maliciously intended.

The 'balancing' approach to freedom of speech has clearly not always produced uncontroversially balanced constitutional law. However, at least it has produced less erratic constitutional law than previous attempts to apply a general rule in this inherently controversial area of politics and law.

First Amendment freedoms: religion

In the liberal political tradition the freedom of speech is intimately connected with religious freedom. Genuine religious discussions, beliefs and worship – 'the rights of conscience' – are seen as needing protection from political dictation, and political practice is seen as needing protection from religious dictation. In this tradition, the separation of church and state is compatible with mutual recognition and some interchange between religion and politics, and in a multi-religious society like America, government can be supportive of religion in general (for example, by granting tax exemptions to religious organisations) as long as it does not favour one religion over another.

During the twentieth century, this traditional understanding has been challenged and legally largely displaced by a more libertarian view. In the 1980s and 1990s the traditional view has been reasserted in both the legislative and the judicial branches of the federal government. The basic constitutional rules remain libertarian, but these rules are more frequently and more tellingly challenged. There is currently a policy debate between, on the one hand, those who fear the marginalisation of religion and the loss of religious contributions to democratic politics (they cite, for example, the role of the churches in the civil rights movement; see, for example, Neuhaus, 1984; Carter, 1993), and, on the other hand, those who support libertarian arguments against reducing the separation of church and state (for example, Kramnick and Moore, 1996). This debate is part of the current division between cultural conservatives and cultural liberals in American politics.

With religious freedom, as with freedom of speech, the new libertarian focus of constitutional law led to attempts to find general formulas to apply the principle to the various cases that arise. There has been an attempt to erect a libertarian 'wall of separation' between church and state, to make government completely indifferent towards religion, that is, neutral to religion in general (versus irreligion) as well as to all particular religions. At the same time, there has been an attempt to compel governmental accommodation of minority religious practices. These contradictory efforts have taken place in the context of the growth of government activity (thus greater potential for conflicts between that activity and religious activity), and the proliferation of religious denominations and cults inviting legal accommodation. The result has been an extraordinary degree of perplexity in this area of constitutional law.

The First Amendment forbids laws 'respecting an establishment of religion, or prohibiting the free exercise thereof'. The libertarian interpretation usually given by post Second World War courts to both the 'establishment' and the 'free exercise' clauses has made these clauses inconsistent with each other, the former demanding no government favouring of religion, and the latter demanding governmental accommodation of certain religions.

The *establishment clause* has been interpreted to mean that 'neither a state nor the federal government ... can pass laws which aid one religion, *aid all religions*, or prefer one religion over another' (*Everson v. Board of Education*, emphasis added). On this understanding, it is difficult to justify even such general political encouragement of religion as tax exempt status, although the Supreme Court has in fact upheld this practice, noting that it has for more than two centuries been 'deeply embedded in the fabric of our national life' (*Walz v. Tax Commission*). State requirements for prayers in public schools, even for non-denominational prayers, or even simply setting aside one minute each day for silent meditation or prayer on a voluntary basis, have been invalidated (with noisy political objections), as have requirements that 'creationism' be taught alongside evolutionism. State financial aid to private religious educational establishments has been sharply restricted, virtually extinguished at the school level (apart from such things as bus transportation, normal emergency services, and lunch subsidies, which have indisputably secular purposes), although allowed for significant secular elements (for example, buildings) in higher education, where religious indoctrination is not a primary purpose of the establishment. (In contrast to sectarian schools, it is judged that secular and religious education are not inextricable in most higher education establishments.) The Court has allowed a local government to erect a Christmas nativity scene in a public park in a shopping district, not, however, because it is permissible for government to encourage religions, but only because such a display is a common practice of Christmas holiday celebrations, with primarily a clearly secular purpose (*Lynch v. Donnelly*). The Court has found that a state law giving employees an unqualified right to refuse to work on their sabbath day violates the establishment clause (*Thornton v. Caldor*). In the 1980s and 1990s, some decisions by a very divided Supreme Court have recognised somewhat greater rights of state financial support for religious groups, for example, subsidies for religous student groups' publications where secular student groups' publications are being subsidised (*Rosenberger v. Rector and Visitors of University of Virginia*). However, establishment clause reasoning remains fundamentally antagonistic to state support for religions.

The interpretation of the *free exercise clause* has, at least until the 1990s, gone in the opposite direction, mandating not less but *greater* government attention to religious sensibilities. Up to the 1960s, the Supreme Court demanded little concession to religious beliefs that clashed with legitimate governmental ends. Religious scruples could not (and still cannot) exempt you from compulsory smallpox vaccination, or blood transfusion required for your child, or laws against polygamy. In a 1961 case, the Court added a requirement that the legitimate governmental end be one that could not be advanced by a less restrictive means. In that case (*McGowan v. Maryland*), the Court upheld a Sunday closing law (which burdens those whose sabbath day is not Sunday), but two years later it used this new rule to decide against a state unemployment compensation law that denied benefits to a claimant who, on religious grounds, refused to accept jobs that required work on Saturday, the claimant's sabbath (*Sherbert v. Verner*). Congress, in its civil rights legislation since 1964, has also heightened the legal accommodation of minority religious practices. This extension of the free exercise clause has meant in one sense that government has to be *more* involved with religion, simply to determine what counts as religion and whether individuals' claims to religious motivation are sincere.

This extension thus increased the inconsistency between the free exercise clause and the Court's current interpretation of the establishment clause. As Justice Stewart pointed out in his concurring opinion in *Sherbert*, in the Court's ('historically unsound and constitutionally wrong') libertarian construction of the establishment clause, a refusal to work on Saturdays based on religious reasons logically has to be treated in the same way as a refusal based on secular reasons ('on indolence, or on a compulsive desire to watch the Saturday television programs'). A less 'insensitive and sterile' construction of the establishment clause, requiring government 'to create an atmosphere of hospitality and accommodation to individual belief or disbelief', would allow decisions such as the one reached in this case without making the demands of the two religion clauses inconsistent with each other. On this construction of the establishment clause, and others (such as that recently voiced by Justice Rehnquist) that would abandon the 'wall of separation' ideal of government neutrality to religion versus irreligion, government aid to religious education and non-sectarian arrangements for prayers in school would also become less constitutionally infirm. Government could pursue 'legitimate secular ends through nondiscriminatory sectarian means' (Rehnquist's dissenting opinion in *Wallace v. Jaffree*).

In fact, in the 1990s, Supreme Court opinions have tended towards reducing the contradiction between establishment clause and free exercise clause decisions; however, they have done this by modifying the interpretation of the free exercise clause rather than of the establishment clause. In 1990, the Court (by five to four) decided *not* to apply the *Sherbert* rule that would have required finding a 'compelling state interest' in order to override a religious group's claim to exemptions from a generally applicable law (a group had sought an exemption from drug laws, in order to use peyote in religious rituals: *Employment Division v. Smith*). This decision inspired Congress to pass the Religious Freedom Restoration Act of 1993, which aimed to restore the 'compelling interest' test. However, this Act was in turn declared by the Court to be an unconstitutional exercise of power by Congress, in an opinion that clearly was not the Court's final word on the subject (*Boerne v. Flores*). A dissenting opinion in this case noted several unsatisfactory results of the 1990 (*Employment Division v. Smith*) decision, which could well be challenged again, either legislatively or judicially.

The very divided opinions on the proper constitutional form of the freedom of religion both on the Court itself and elsewhere in the polity in recent years suggest that the evolution of the Constitution in this area has not reached a steady state.

Criminal procedure

More than half of the rights named in the Bill of Rights are rights specifically connected with crime and punishment, in the Fourth, Fifth, Sixth and Eighth amendments. The ambiguity in some of the wording of these amendments has left room for interpretative expansion. Even when there is little such ambiguity, judges have felt it necessary to update the meanings of these liberties, to keep the Bill of Rights in touch with what Chief Justice Earl Warren called the 'evolving standards of decency that mark the progress of a maturing society' (*Trop v. Dulles*). The controversy thereby roused by judicial decisions in this area has been increased by the fact that the application (by 'incorporation') of these parts of the Bill of Rights to the states, in a series of decisions during the quarter-century starting in 1948, has been a lengthy but thorough process, requiring radical changes in local and state police and judicial behaviour. (There was much room for improving the standards of this behaviour, which were often lamentably low.) In some cases some states have led the way in the liberalisation of criminal procedural rights, but it has been easy to caricature the federal courts' decisions as being responsible for having tipped the balance far too decisively against police, prosecutors and victims. Public controversy about the judicial reform of criminal procedure has also been magnified by the adoption of the 'exclusionary rule' (used in federal cases since 1914, and imposed on state trials since 1961) to bar from trials evidence obtained by faulty criminal investigations, instead of (as in many other legal systems) using the tainted but relevant evidence and prosecuting the offending police work as well, as a deterrence to errors in criminal proceedings.

In spite of all the controversy, the courts have been able to claim a certain authority in this area, which seems part of their natural domain and their area of expertise, and – with the co-operation of Congress in its crime legislation (for example, laws defining what constitutes a 'speedy' trial, guaranteed by the Sixth Amendment) – they have established several major changes in the understanding of constitutional rights. For example, the understanding of the right of counsel (in the Sixth Amendment) has been broadened by unanimous Supreme Court decisions to mean that in all state and federal felony trials the court must appoint an attorney to act if a defendant cannot afford to do so (*Gideon v. Wainwright*), and that 'absent a knowing and intelligent waiver, no person may be imprisoned for any offense, whether classified as petty, misdemeanor, or felony, unless he was represented by counsel at his trial' (*Argersinger v. Hamlin*). This right to counsel has been expanded to include the right to psychiatric expertise (*Ake v. Oklahoma*), and extended chronologically from the trial backwards to in-custody interrogation and forwards to appeals and parole proceedings. In *Miranda v. Arizona*, in order to free courts from having to decide what constitutes an 'uncoerced' confession, standard procedures for police interrogations were established (under the threat of the exclusionary rule if not followed): before interrogation, accused persons must be warned of their right to remain silent, that anything they say can and will be used against them in court, that they have the right to consult with a lawyer and to have a lawyer present during interrogation, and that a lawyer will be appointed for them if they cannot afford one.

Since the 1970s, a few minor exceptions to the exclusionary rule used to enforce these procedures have been formulated by the Court (for example, when the requirement of public safety allows a police officer to ask someone where they have discarded a gun following a felonious assault, before giving them their *Miranda* warnings: *New York v. Quarles*), but the procedures remain well established in constitutional law. Controversy about these reforms continues but is more subdued; it seems more widely appreciated that law and order can be better served where fair and humane procedures are the recognised national standards, even if these standards are not always followed in practice.

Fourteenth Amendment: 'equal protection' and discrimination

The Fourteenth Amendment became part of the Constitution in 1868, as a result of the victory of the Union in the Civil War. This most important formal amendment to the Constitution (passed and ratified before the rebellious southern states had regained their political footing) could be said to illustrate the capacity of the Constitution to change well ahead of corresponding economic, social and political changes.

Before the Civil War, the possibility of American citizenship for people of African descent had been subjected to extreme doubt (although many free Africans had in fact been citizens in some states). At that time, most of the citizens and politicians who favoured containing and eventually extinguishing slavery in the United States did not envisage the co-citizenship of African Americans with other Americans. Many (such as Abraham Lincoln) were pessimists on the question of the possibility of racial harmony, and thought the best policy would be a gradual, compensated emancipation coupled with provision for the emigration of freed slaves to Africa. In the infamous case of *Dred Scott v. Sanford* the Supreme Court (inaccurately, as we have seen in Chapter 2, page 24) interpreted both the Declaration of Independence and the Constitution as denials of the natural and constitutional rights of persons of African descent, and concluded from this that such persons could not be American citizens.

The first section of the Fourteenth Amendment (repeating much of the language of the Civil Rights Act of 1866; see Commager, 1973, vol. 1, p. 464) reverses the *Dred Scott* decision by ensuring United States citizenship for African Americans, including former slaves (and anyone else 'born or naturalized in the United States, and subject to the jurisdiction thereof'). It also provides that 'no state shall make or enforce any law which shall abridge the *privileges or immunities* of citizens of the United States; nor shall any state deprive any person of life, liberty or property, without *due process* of law; nor deny to any person within its jurisdiction the *equal protection* of the laws' (emphasis added).

The intention of this amendment was to base the security of the civil rights of African Americans as of other American citizens on congressional specification and protection of 'the privileges or immunities of citizens', that is, of their fundamental rights as citizens of a free country – their rights to 'life, liberty and the pursuit of happiness'. However, this *privileges or immunities* clause was rendered quite insubstantial by interpreting it (as the Supreme Court has since 1873) as referring only to a narrowly defined range of rights of *United States* citizenship (for example, the rights to engage in interstate and foreign commerce, and to sue in federal courts), and not the full range of fundamental economic and civil rights that was and remained under the protection of the *states*. In the decisive interpreting cases, the five-man majority of the Court simply could not accept that this clause was 'intended to bring within the power of Congress the entire domain of civil rights heretofore belonging exclusively to the states' – although the four dissenting justices saw that this was precisely what had been intended, and that the majority's emasculating interpretation transformed the clause into 'a vain and idle enactment, which accomplished nothing, and most unnecessarily excited Congress and the people on its passage' (*Slaughterhouse Cases*).

While the Fourteenth Amendment's privileges and immunities clause thus has not borne the weight that was intended, the due process clause and the equal protection clause have borne much more than intended. Originally thought of as protecting procedural rights, they have both been used to protect substantive rights. We have seen above (pages 66–7) how the due process clause has been transformed and used in this substantive way, first to support conservative economic policy, then in a liberal vein with the application of the Bill of Rights against the states. The equal protection clause has been similarly transformed, and has helped make the Court that interprets it what the majority in 1873 feared: 'a perpetual censor upon all legislation of the states, on the civil rights of their own citizens.'

However, this transformation, and the resulting promotion of the Fourteenth Amendment to the vanguard in the protection of the civil rights of African Americans (and others), arrived painfully slowly. In 1875, Congress passed 'an Act to protect all citizens in their civil and legal rights', which made racial segregation in public accommodation unlawful, declaring that 'all persons within the jurisdiction of the United States shall be entitled to the full and equal enjoyment of the accommodations, advantages, facilities, and privileges of inns, public conveyances on land or water, theaters, and other places of public amusement' (Commager, 1973, vol. 1, p. 536). This Act would not have been passed by the less egalitarian-minded Congresses that followed, and these Congresses did not react when the Act was found unconstitutional by the Supreme Court. The Court interpreted the Fourteenth Amendment to apply only against 'state laws, or state actions', narrowly defined, not against action by such private persons as innkeepers, theatre owners, or railway operators (*Civil Rights Cases*). Justice Harlan's dissent pointed out that the activities of such persons were not wholly unconnected with state governments, which licensed them and charged them with certain public duties. This point was to be picked up by much later Court majorities, which have, for example, invalidated political party primary elections restricted to whites, on the ground that the party was acting as 'an agency of the state' (*Smith v. Allwright*); and barred court (i.e. state) enforcement of contracts in which property owners agreed not to sell to non-whites (*Shelley v. Kraemer*).

In 1896 the restriction of the Fourteenth Amendment to state action was further confined when the Court decided that a state law requiring 'equal but separate' railway accommodation 'for the white and colored races' did not violate the Amendment: 'the enforced separation of the two races' (for the sake of 'the preservation of the public peace and good order') does not stamp 'the colored race with a badge of inferiority' (*Plessy v. Ferguson*). The view that facilities separated by state law had to be 'equal' left a ground for legitimate constitutional complaint, but it was not until the 1930s and 1940s that the fraudulent claim that the separate provisions for white and coloured Americans were actually equal was successfully challenged in the courts, most often in cases concerning higher professional education (for example, law schools), where the inequality of provision was most undeniable, and where the decisions in favour of African Americans affected relatively few other Americans. Finally, in 1954, in the famous case of *Brown v. Board of Education of Topeka*, the Court unanimously concluded 'that in the field of public education the doctrine of "separate but equal" has no place. Separate educational facilities are inherently unequal.'

Significantly, the Court in this case did not adopt Justice Harlan's famous dissenting opinion in *Plessy*, in which he asserted that 'our Constitution is color-blind ... and takes no account ... of color when ... civil rights as guaranteed by the supreme law of the land are involved.' Rather, it emphasised that public education had, by the middle of the twentieth century, become much more important in state and local government and in most citizens' lives, and that segregation (contrary to the finding, but not the reasoning, in *Plessy*), *does* generate in African American schoolchildren 'a feeling of inferiority as to their status in the community that may affect their hearts and minds in a way unlikely ever to be undone.' The reasoning of Justice Harlan's *Plessy* dissent could have enforced Linda Brown's right to attend her local public school (the equivalent of the British state school) in Topeka because no state law, 'proceeding alone on the grounds of race', could prevent her attendance without thereby infringing her objective 'personal liberty', and denying her 'equal protection of the laws'. Such infringements of liberty and denials of equal civil rights can be perceived without reference to the subjective feelings of the victims. In contrast, the reasoning of the Court's opinion in *Brown* (which, admittedly, probably would not have been a unanimous decision if Harlan's logic had been adopted) actually accepted the *Plessy* majority's reasoning, and enforced her right because of her (putative) subjective 'feeling of inferiority', in the absence of which there would have been little constitutional barrier to continued segregation.

After the *Brown* case, other decisions in the 1950s and 1960s extended the equal protection against racial discrimination and segregation to many other public facilities and accommodations. The Civil Rights Act of 1964 (based on Congress' commerce power, which, as we have seen, was by then far-reaching) codified this extension – and gave the US attorney-general power to enforce it. In public education, it remained to be settled what counted as unconstitutional segregation: do residential patterns resulting in racially unmixed schools – '*de facto* segregation' – call for (publicly controversial) legal remedies (for example, re-zoning and cross-town busing)? In the 1970s, judicial decisions often side-stepped this question by finding significant *de jure* (that is, state action) elements (for example, school board policies that perpetuated racial segregation patterns) in many (though not all) cases of *de facto* segregation. However, the Supreme Court has also held that once a segregated school system has been integrated, and the racial balance of schools within that system then changes solely because of demographic changes, there is no case for further desegregation orders (*Pasadena City Board of Education v. Spangler*). More recently, demographic change causing resegregation has been used to justify ending a busing scheme that had not yet reached the goal of an integrated system (*Freeman v. Pitts*).

In spite of these quarrels concerning its implementation, the principle that public acts of discrimination against African Americans are unconstitutional is less problematic than principles in the other contested areas of civil freedom that we have examined. Constitutional protection of freedoms of speech and religion, and rights of suspects, has always to be balanced against legitimate constitutional protection of public order and security. The only thing that protection from legal discrimination against 'racial' minorities has to be balanced against – apart from the need to respect federalism – is the majority's prejudiced but powerful resistance to that protection. As was pointed out in Chapter 2, to ignore powerful public opinion is undemocratic as well as foolish, but the direction in which prejudiced opinion should be led if one can lead it is clear. In this way, the establishment of equal civil rights – though long delayed – has enjoyed a certain clarity and simplicity.

In contrast, the substantive dimensions of the equal protection standard, and the difficulties of constitutional judgement in applying it, have been magnified by its extension in the 1960s and 1970s to cases where legislative classifications and public discriminations have been challenged not on behalf of African Americans or other 'racial' minorities, but by those who object to discrimination based on gender, age, poverty, illegitimacy, and alienage; and by those who object to 'reverse discrimination' in 'affirmative action' programmes set up to benefit victims of more traditionally recognised forms of discrimination. Although the Fourteenth Amendment was incontestably written with African Americans in mind, it is also true that 'its language is general, embracing all citizens' (Justice Bradley's dissenting opinion in the *Slaughterhouse Cases*) – indeed, it embraces all 'persons' – so the equal protection clause is clearly logically open to this extension. However, this extension has been politically and constitutionally unsettling. Justice Stone's famous footnote (quoted above, page 66) suggesting the modern constitutional need for 'more exacting judicial scrutiny' of some kinds of legislative classification has been most prophetic in this extension of the equal protection clause. Which classifications are 'suspect,' and what level of 'judicial scrutiny' is required with each suspect classification, are questions that continue to bedevil American constitutional thinking.

Rather confusingly, the Supreme Court has decided that state laws cannot forbid aliens (non-citizens) to practise law, but can forbid them to be police officers or public school teachers. It has refused to treat as suspect (and therefore subject to strict, – usually unapproving – scrutiny) legislative classifications bearing against older people (for example, requiring certain public servants to retire at 50 or 60) and poorer people (for example, a public school system in which schools' financing varies in relation to the wealth of the district). Gender classifications, both those favouring men and those favouring women, have met mixed fates; they have – eventually – been subjected to an 'intermediate' level of judicial scrutiny, which offers the advantage of allowing flexibility in deciding cases as they arise, but also seems to admit that a clear and predictable equal protection standard is unsuitable in this area. Here, at any rate, constitutional deliberation has left much for politics to decide. The Court's refusal constitutionally to *require* strict non-discrimination on the grounds of age, poverty and gender does not prevent Congress or state and local governments from acting against discrimination on these grounds, nor from writing their laws in a strictly non-discriminatory way if they choose to do so. For example, in 1986 Congress enacted a law phasing in a ban on states' compelling their employees to retire at age 70.

The subjective and psychological reasoning of the *Brown* opinion has played a large part in equal protection arguments against those claiming to be the victims of unconstitutional discrimination in schemes of 'affirmative action'. Defenders of such schemes often argue that these 'victims' cannot claim the protection of the Fourteenth Amendment because they do not suffer the 'sense of inferiority' or 'stigma' felt by victims of more traditional forms of racial classification. In this view, not racial classifications as such, but psychologically damaging racial classifications, are unconstitutional. Critics of 'affirmative action' argue that this kind of reasoning is too subjective and standardless, and emphasise that the Fourteenth Amendment protects the rights of individuals without reference to their group affiliation or to their subjective feelings. This constitutional debate continues today, and forms part of the contemporary politics of race and ethnicity, discussed in Chapters 8 and 20.

Summary

The Constitution has endured by changing – not completely, but in several politically significant ways. It would be wrong to conclude that the Constitution of 1787 is no longer relevant; both conservative fears and liberal hopes to that effect seem misplaced. Nevertheless, both in economic policy and in civil rights and liberties, the changing interpretation of the Constitution (and of its amendments) has adjusted the original constitutional design to changing economic, social and cultural circumstances. In recent decades, Supreme Court justices, although not altogether abandoning their attempt to shape economic policy with constitutional arguments, have more visibly laboured in the field of civil rights and civil liberties, trying to define these in ways that meet conflicting political demands while maintaining genuinely constitutional standards.

Topics for discussion

1. What is the most significant way in which constitutional changes come about?
2. Which parts of the Constitution have changed most since 1787?
3. How did judicial conservatism on economic policy in the nineteenth and early twentieth centuries depart from John Marshall's views?
4. In which area of civil liberties and civil rights has the Supreme Court been most, and in which area least, successful in balancing individual liberty against the needs of governance?
5. Is the Constitution too unadaptable to meet the needs of the twenty-first century?

Further reading

Students of American constitutional law need to remember to read the Constitution (see Appendix B at the end of this book), as well as judicial and other pronouncements on its meaning. Robert G.

McCloskey's *The American Supreme Court*, which describes and analyses the development of judicial interpretation of the Constitution, has been updated in a second edition co-authored by Sanford Levinson (Chicago: University of Chicago Press, 1994). Summaries and extracts of important Supreme Court opinions can be found in Louis Fisher, *American Constitutional Law* (2 vols, 2nd edn, New York: McGraw-Hill, 1994), Joel B. Grossman and Richard S. Wells, *Constitutional Law and Judicial Policy Making* (3rd edn, London: Longman, 1988), and Ralph A. Rossum and G. Alan Tarr, *American Constitutional Law: Cases and interpretation* (4th edn, New York: St Martin's Press, 1995). One of the best Internet sites through which to find both old and recent court opinions is maintained by the Legal Information Institute (http://www.law.cornell.edu).

References

Angle, Paul M., ed., 1991, *The Complete Lincoln–Douglas Debates of 1858* (Chicago: University of Chicago Press)

Carter, Stephen L., 1993, *The Culture of Disbelief: How American law and politics trivialize religious devotion* (New York: Anchor)

Commager, Henry Steele, ed., 1973, *Documents of American History* (9th edn, 2 vols, Englewood Cliffs: Prentice Hall)

Corwin, Edward S., 1973, *The Constitution and What It Means Today* (13th edn, revised by Harold W. Chase and Craig R. Ducat, Princeton: Princeton University Press)

Kramnick, Isaac, and Moore, R. Laurence, 1996, *The Godless Constitution: The case against religious correctness* (New York: Norton)

McCloskey, Robert G., 1960, *The American Supreme Court* (Chicago: University of Chicago Press)

Murphy, Paul L., 1972, *The Constitution in Crisis Times* (New York: Harper & Row)

Neuhaus, Richard John, 1984, *The Naked Public Square: Religion and democracy in America* (Grand Rapids: Eerdmans)

Wilson, Woodrow, 1916, *The New Freedom* (London: Dent)

4

The federal dimension

The federal aspect of the political system adds a teasing complication to politics. It is often difficult but almost always important to understand both the constitutional (or legal) and the political side of American federalism. American federalism is in essence ambiguous, but one thing that is clear about it is the interdependence of constitutional questions and political issues. This was seen at the beginning of American politics, and it remains true today.

In Chapter 2 we saw that the most striking novelty of the Constitution of 1787 was its combination of purely federal (or confederal) elements with purely national (or unitary) elements, producing a hitherto unknown species of government: a 'compound republic', partly federal, partly national (*The Federalist*, nos 51 and 39). Today, the term 'federal' is used to describe the governmental systems of the United States and various other polities (for example Australia, Canada, Germany) that follow the American example and combine unitary and confederal features. Federalism refers to the division of sovereignty in such a system between governments at two different levels: one at the level of each territory (state), and one at the centre. Federalism can also refer to the advocacy of such a divided political system – an advocacy which generally involves inventing or strengthening the government at the centre. 'Federal government' is also used in those two senses: as a synonym for such a federal system of governments, or (more frequently) to refer to the central government in these combined systems (for example, the government based in Washington DC).

In Chapter 3 it became clear that, in the United States, differing views on the constitutional rights and duties of the federal government, in relation to the rights and duties of the state governments, have been deeply implicated in the development of policies in economics, civil liberties and civil rights. One of the reasons that American political debates in these and many other areas are so often conducted in constitutional language is that arguments about policies are conceived and conducted in terms of arguments about which level of government – federal or state (if either) – is constitutionally empowered to set the policy.

Federalism, alongside representation and the separation of powers, is traditionally identified as a basic characteristic of American constitutional politics. However, in recent decades doubts have been raised about its significance. It can sometimes seem (although, as we shall see, it is not the case) that the nationalisation and centralisation of American politics, starting with the Civil War and intensifying during various crises during the twentieth century, have made federalism merely a superficial phenomenon, a vestigial reminder of the past glory of the states. Although the Constitution was a product of centralising pressures and of a recognition of the incapacity of the states to perform certain desired governmental tasks, the states clearly retained a significant political role. The purpose of the Constitution (as stated in its preamble) was 'to create a more perfect union' – not a wholly perfect union, not a complete consolidation that would entirely abolish the sovereignty of the states. The Constitution delegated certain enumerated powers to the federal government; the states retained their 'police power', a general power to legislate to protect their citizens' safety, health, welfare and morals. In theory, at least, this remains the case. States still have governments, and many of the paraphernalia of sovereignty: constitutions, flags, even official state songs, birds, flowers and so on. They, and the local governments which are legally their creatures, remain active in such important areas as education, health, transportation, criminal justice and planning (land use). However, the two centuries of political development and constitutional adaptation that we surveyed in Chapter 3 might seem to have reversed the original situation, elevated the federal government to the role of general protector, and degraded the states to serving merely as instruments of the federal government's policies.

To assess the extent to which this is true, and to appreciate the contemporary political importance and constitutional status of federalism, we need first to review and to analyse the changing meanings of federalism in American political history.

'The compound republic': a composition of federal and national

The pre-1787 understanding

Before 1787, a government partly national, partly federal was, as James Madison claimed, a 'non-descript' – a hitherto unclassified species. In the pre-1787 understanding, federalism and confederalism were synonymous terms, as were federation, confederation and confederacy (Diamond, 1974). A federal system was (as in today's parlance, a confederation still is) distinguished from a national or unitary government in several ways in this understanding:

1. **Whose consent legitimates the central government?** The consent of the governments of the member states (and not, as in a unitary state, of the individual citizens) is understood to be the origin and the legitimating force of the federation (or confederation).

2. **Which level of government is the creature of the other?** In a unitary state, local

government organisations are creatures of the central government. They live or die at the central government's will. A confederacy, on the other hand, is the creature of its member states, and cannot exist without them, while they can survive its dissolution.

3. **What is the basis of representation in the central government?** Each member state, no matter how large or populous or wealthy, is understood to be equal in the representation and deliberations of a confederacy. In a unitary state, subordinate governmental bodies have no such claim to equality, although they might be treated equally by the state.

4. **Are acts of the central government addressed to member governments (who might decline to consent to them) or to individual citizens?** The central representative body of a federation is understood to act not (as in a unitary state) on individual citizens, but on member states, and generally with the consent of those member states rather than by coercing them. (Recall that the Articles of Confederation required the agreement of the delegations of nine of the thirteen states on any important decision.) The lack of a lawful power of coercion means that a federation is not truly a government: in the older sense of the word 'federal', federal government is an oxymoron. In any case, the purposes of a confederacy typically call for action (often military) that primarily affects third parties rather than member states.

5. **How limited are the purposes of the central government?** The purposes of a confederacy are understood to be strictly limited (although possibly very important – confederacies have usually been constructed for military co-operation).

The post-1787 understanding

The United States has a federal system in the post-1787 understanding, which means that it combines some of the elements of this older federalism with some of the elements of national governance. This newer federalism differs decisively from the older on each of the five points just mentioned, without veering totally into a purely unitary system:

1. **Whose consent legitimates the central government?** Both the state and the central (now somewhat confusingly called federal) governments are understood to rest on the consent of individual citizens, who are at once citizens of a particular state and of the United States. The citizens of the United States act together only by acting also as citizens of one of the states (or – since the Twenty-third Amendment – of the District of Columbia). Constitutionally, they never act as a mere national aggregate. Even in ratifying the Constitution, Madison remarked, 'the people of the United States' were acting 'not as individuals composing one entire nation, but as composing the distinct and independent states to which they respectively belong'. Likewise, the ratification of amendments is 'neither wholly national' – a simple national majority is not sufficient: three-quarters of the states must agree – 'nor wholly federal' – not every state must agree (*The Federalist*, no. 39).

2. **Which level of government is the creature of the other?** It follows from the first point that neither state nor federal government is the creature of the other.

Constitutionally, the United States is an 'indestructible union, composed of indestructible states' (*Texas v. White*).

The states are not in the same relationship to the federal government as local government units (towns, cities, counties and so on) are to the states, liable to be rearranged or abolished at will: Article IV of the Constitution forbids changes in state boundaries without the consent of the affected states, and Article V forbids even constitutional amendments to deprive any state of its equal suffrage in the Senate, without its consent. Furthermore (as elaborated in point 3 below), the states play a significant role in electing and removing federal officers, while the opposite is not the case.

Nor does the existence and continuance of the federal government depend on the will of the states. At times – especially before the Civil War – claims have been made that the states created the union and can therefore 'nullify' acts of the federal government, 'interpose' themselves between that government and their citizens, and even lawfully and peacefully secede from the union if they choose. This theory, discredited by the outcome of the Civil War but still voiced from time to time, was developed notably by John C. Calhoun, a senator from South Carolina. Calhoun inspired South Carolina's Ordinance of Nullification of 1832, which declared the high protective tariff Acts passed by Congress in 1828 and 1832 'null, void, and not law binding upon this State, its officers or citizens', and threatened to secede if the federal government tried to force its compliance with these laws (Commager, 1973, vol. 1, pp. 261–2). As President Andrew Jackson said in his spirited reply to South Carolina, this theory is a 'strange position', quite inconsistent with the letter and the spirit of the Constitution (*ibid.*, pp. 264–5). The nullifiers of 1832 claimed the support of James Madison, who in 1798, in partisan opposition to Federalist policies, had drafted the Virginia Resolutions, calling on other states to join Virginia's declaration of the unconstitutionality of the Alien and Sedition Acts of 1798. Unfortunately for the nullifiers, Madison was still alive and thinking, and able to demonstrate that Calhoun's theory (unlike Madison's own superficially similar expressions in the Virginia Resolutions) mistook the *natural, revolutionary* right of a state (or any number of individuals) to resist tyranny (an undeniable right, but one that entailed a return to a state of nature, and quite possibly involved making war) with a *legal, constitutional* right of a state to nullify undesirable laws, and to be allowed peacefully to secede if and when it chooses (Jaffa, 1974).

Calhoun is reported to have remarked that sovereignty is like chastity: you cannot surrender it in part. American federalism depends on the possibility of sovereignty being more divisible than that, so that both the federal government and the state governments are sovereign in certain respects.

3. **What is the basis of representation in the central government?** Federal and national elements are thoroughly mixed in political representation at the national level. Members of the House of Representatives (each with one vote in the ordinary proceedings of that chamber) are chosen in proportion to population. However, there are federal elements even in this more national chamber: each state has at least one representative, and they are elected by the people within states – since 1842 (by an Act of Congress under Article I, Section 4), from dis-

tricts within states, the boundaries of these districts being determined by each state's legislature. Each state has two senators – originally chosen by state legislatures, now (since the Seventeenth Amendment in 1913) always by state-wide popular elections. The Senate (thus the more purely federal chamber) advises and consents on appointments to the judiciary made by the president (the most nationally representative office). The president and vice-president are chosen by electoral votes won in each state separately, and there is more federal weighting in this process in that even the smallest states have three electoral votes (one per representative plus one per senator). Federal executive and judicial officers are removable by impeachment, in which process the House impeaches and the Senate sits in judgement.

4. **Are acts of the central government addressed to member governments (who might decline to consent to them) or to individual citizens?** The acts of the federal government can command directly both individuals and states. For example, as pointed out in *The Federalist* (no. 39), states can be parties in cases before federal courts, and subject to the decisions of those courts. However, for the most part the federal government uses its ability (newly granted by the Constitution) to address its commands to individual citizens. The advantage of this method of action is that it avoids the natural tendency of state and local governments to display 'an impatience of control' by the federal government and 'to judge the propriety' of federal actions 'in a spirit of interested and suspicious scrutiny', even though they do not have a constitutional right to withhold their consent (*The Federalist*, no. 15).

5. **How limited are the purposes of the central government?** As we have seen in Chapter 2, the Constitution delegates a large number of powers to the federal government, for purposes both domestic and foreign, and vests in Congress the power 'to make all laws which shall be necessary and proper for carrying into execution' those powers (Article I, Section 8). At the same time, it does not give the federal government that 'indefinite supremacy over all persons and things, so far as they are objects of lawful government' that is given to purely 'national' governments. In America, the states retain 'a residuary and inviolable sovereignty over' the lawful objects of government that are not delegated to the federal government (*The Federalist*, no. 39).

This fifth point contains the seeds of the current doubts about the continuing significance of federalism. The Constitution does allow for – and, as we have seen in Chapter 3, American political history has precipitated – an expansion in the means chosen by the federal government in order to pursue its delegated purposes. So students of American politics have to consider whether that process of federal government expansion has gone so far that it has reduced to insignificance the objects and powers of government reserved to the states. Even if we decide that it has, there remain the elements of state sovereignty mentioned in the first four points, so America's Constitution still remains 'in strictness, neither a national nor a federal Constitution, but a composition of both' (*The Federalist*, no. 39). As recent Supreme Court decisions have shown (we look at these below), those elements are not empty: respecting the structural dual sovereignty that they impose can still require limits on federal government actions.

The dynamics of federalism

A composite of federal and national is a complicated constitutional arrangement. The combination of purely federal and purely national can be a very unstable compound, when political partisans are tempted to try to reduce it to its simply federal elements or to its simply national elements. Such temptations, and resistance to them, characterise the history of American federalism. The Civil War was the product of, among other things, one such confrontation of temptation and resistance: a clash between supporters and opponents of the theory of absolute state sovereignty that had been championed by Calhoun. Less violent and more nuanced examples have been – fortunately – more common.

The complications and ambiguities intrinsic to federalism (in the post-1787 sense of the word) make it a dynamic form of politics. Presiding over these dynamics has been the Supreme Court, to which the Constitution left the job of deciding 'controversies relating to the boundary between' the objects of federal and state governments (*The Federalist*, no. 39). However, many decisions affecting federalism are made in Acts of Congress that are not contested in the courts.

The dynamics of federalism work in two different dimensions: changes in the size and content of state and federal spheres of activity, and changes in the degree of overlap in state and federal jurisdictions.

Changing size and content of state and federal spheres of activity

The growth of one level of government need not always require the shrinkage of the other (nor vice versa): in the twentieth century, especially since the 1930s, both federal and state governments have grown. However, there is always the potential and often the reality of a shift of responsibility (and, it is hoped, corresponding power) between federal and state governments. The New Deal entailed a shift to the federal government of some responsibility for the reform of banking and finance and for the relief of economic hardship. The civil rights movement of the 1950s and 1960s, 'Great Society' antipoverty, education, health and welfare programmes in the 1960s, and consumer and environmental movements in the 1960s and 1970s augmented this shift towards national responsibilities. Since the 1970s, efforts have been made to reverse some of these shifts, with some degree of success (as we see below).

Constitutionally, all of these shifts must be compatible with the powers delegated to the federal government and those reserved to the states, but we have seen in Chapter 3 that the Constitution is adaptable – not to say infinitely flexible – on the question of the boundary between federal and state powers. The frontier is movable, because, as Chief Justice John Marshall remarked in *McCulloch v. Maryland*, 'The question respecting the extent of the powers actually granted [to Congress], is perpetually arising, and will probably continue to arise, as long as our system shall exist', and different answers can be given to that question in changing circumstances. (On this question as on others, the Supreme Court is not infallible, but, as Marshall said in another case, 'Questions may occur which we would gladly avoid; but we cannot avoid them.

All we can do is, to exercise our best judgement, and conscientiously to perform our duty' (*Cohens v. Virginia*). The frontier is also movable because formal constitutional amendments can greatly affect it. The enlargement of the federal government's authority to protect civil rights (by the Civil War Amendments, 13 to 15) eventually (when they finally came to be enforced) sharply constricted state governments' sovereignty in this field.

Changes in the degree of overlap of jurisdictions: duality versus co-operation and conflict

Even when the respective jurisdictions of state and nation are more or less settled, the extent to which they overlap can vary.

Especially at those times when less is expected of federal government, it can plausibly be maintained that the two levels of government can operate for the most part in separate, self-contained spheres, not often touching and therefore not often conflicting with each other. This was the view embodied in *dual federalism* thinking in the nineteenth and early twentieth centuries. With separate and well defined responsibilities, it was thought that the federal government could avoid both conflict and co-operation with state and local governments. In fact, there was some intergovernmental collaboration even in this period when strict dual federalism was the official constitutional view. The federal government with its wealth of revenue and land actively assisted state and local governments in developing transport, communication and educational projects; and federal and state governments co-operated in law enforcement and in the establishment of military bases (Elazar, 1962). However, dual federalist doctrines, articulated by a federal judiciary that was determined to counteract the nationalising tenor of the Marshall Court (Chief Justice Marshall was replaced by Roger Taney in 1835), did prevent or delay the federal government's addressing some grave national problems. For example, the Supreme Court (with some strong dissenting opinions) decided that Congress lacked the power (which it had exercised since 1789) to exclude slavery from prospective new states (*Dred Scott v. Sandford*), the power to ban monopolies in manufacturing within a state, no matter how much interstate commerce was affected (*United States v. E.C. Knight Company*), and the power to restrict child labour in the production of goods destined for interstate commerce (*Hammer v. Dagenhart*). These and other such decisions in the period up to 1937 were based on the view that the federal government's use of its own powers must never invade the sphere of activities that belongs to the states, and that both state and federal governments must exercise their powers in such a way that neither interferes with the other. Dual federalism thus buttressed the barriers to federal economic policies that had been read into the interstate commerce clause and other parts of the constitution in that period (see again Chapter 3, pages 59–61.)

In one of these decisions (*Hammer v. Dagenhart*), the Court notoriously misquoted the Tenth Amendment, inserting the word 'expressly' before the word 'delegated' in that amendment's reservation to the states of 'powers not delegated to the United

States'. In fact (as the Marshall Court had pointed out in *McCulloch v. Maryland*), the Tenth Amendment had been formulated intentionally leaving out that word (which, by contrast, had appeared in the corresponding phrase in the Articles of Confederation). Moreover, James Madison, in 1791, during Congress' consideration of the bill to establish a national bank, had noted the irrelevance of the Tenth Amendment to such considerations: 'Interference with the powers of the states' is not a constitutional objection to the exercise of 'the power of Congress'. The federal Constitution and laws are the supreme law of the land; if Congress has been given a power, it can exercise it, even if that exercise 'should interfere with the laws, or even the Constitution of the states' (quoted in Corwin, 1973, p. 369). The only proper constitutional question is whether Congress has been delegated a power, not whether using that power might invade the sphere of state legislation. Conflicts were inevitable, and when they occur, state laws and actions must yield to Congress' use of its delegated powers.

After the New Deal, when more came generally to be expected of the federal government, the official dual federalism view was displaced by *co-operative federalism*, the view that the spheres of federal and state (and local) governments naturally overlap in many important domestic policy areas, and that some governmental functions cannot be designated clearly as belonging to one sphere or the other. Political scientists began to use the metaphor of a marble cake, in contrast to a layer cake, to describe this intermingling of federal, state and local functions, whereby, for example, a local health official, meeting national standards of qualification, is paid by a combination of federal, state and local funds, and enforces regulations issued by all three levels of government (Grodzins, 1966). The Tenth Amendment was now more accurately interpreted as nothing more than a declaration 'of the relationship between the national and state governments as it had been established by the Constitution before the amendment' (*United States v. Darby Lumber Company*), rather than (as dual federalism had seen it) a new limitation on federal powers by the erection of a wall of separation between federal politics and state politics. The partnership rather than the rivalry of the two levels of government was emphasised. 'Intergovernmental relations' replaced 'federalism' as the vogue expression.

Of course, the overlapping of federal and state spheres can lead to conflicts as well as to co-operation, and the co-operation remains legally voluntary, so states can still choose to go their own ways. Since the 1970s this has been more remarked upon, and some observers have begun to talk of the conflicting, competitive or coercive rather than the co-operative character of American federalism. In this view, while co-operative and interdependent efforts still characterise federal–state relations, many state governments are now finding more onerous the closer association between the federal government and state and local governments that has developed since the 1930s. Without returning to the earlier assumptions of dual federalism, doubts have grown about the unprincipled and overnationalising tendencies of co-operative federalism. Co-operative federalism was a view that developed as a reaction against the extreme antifederal government view of dual federalism – which in turn had been a reaction against Marshallian nationalism. It is not surprising therefore to find that co-operative federalism is itself now being seen as veering too much towards the antistate government extreme.

Controlling and empowering purposes of federalism

The federal division of power functions, and is intended to function, as an empowering rather than a merely controlling device. Like the separation of legislative, executive and judicial powers (recall the discussion at the end of Chapter 2, pages 42–4), the federal allocation of power to different levels of government has both a restraining and an invigorating purpose. As with the separation of powers, the restraining purpose is more obvious: 'The different governments will control each other… ' (*The Federalist*, no. 51). However, the energising purpose was evident from the outset, as well. This purpose affects both government and citizenship.

Energising government

With the two different levels of government monitoring each other, Americans could more confidently vest enough power in these two levels of the 'compound republic' to enable it to accomplish the desirable ends that neither states nor union had succeeded in accomplishing under the Articles of Confederation. The Constitution increased the power of the federal government more than it diminished the power of the state governments. At the same time, the state and local governments, being closer to the people, continued to enjoy the strength that came from popular 'affection, esteem and reverence' (*The Federalist*, no. 17).

A certain amount of constitutional ambiguity can be a useful way of retaining the loyalty of citizens with different constitutional views. This very old political truth (noticed by Aristotle in his *Politics* [IV, 1294b14–40] is given a new twist by American federalism. Citizens who want to see the country as mainly national can do so; while those who want to see it as mainly federal can also do so. The opposing views can clash, and do from time to time, but they can also peacefully co-exist for long periods. Federalism can thus increase the popular support for government.

At several points in American history, the existence of two levels of government has served not to prevent or to delay policy making but to make it more possible for sound policies to be initiated or retained. This can be seen to have happened in at least three different ways:

1. As with the separation of powers, the federal division of power can bring about a synergistic collaboration by different governmental bodies. There have always been elements of co-operative federalism in American politics.

2. Even when the federal government has pursued policies against the wishes of some states, it has been able to do so only because the people of other states (as well as minorities within the resisting states) have supported those policies. In other words, the enlarged republic, which was made possible only by the device of federalism, has to be given credit for the success of such policies. For example, critics of federalism who emphasise its retarding and restraining effects rightly point out that American federalism long sheltered such evils as racially discriminatory state laws and customs. However, if federalism is to be blamed in this way, it must also be praised when the policy changes. Defenders of federalism –

understood not as states' rights but as a mixture of federal and national governance – can thus claim some credit for the fact that the federal government (which had itself been guilty of racial segregation and discrimination) led the way in civil rights policies in the middle of the twentieth century, against many states' indifference or resistance.

3. Nor is it always the national element (the federal government) that is in the forefront of liberal or progressive policies; in fact, such policies almost always have initial successes somewhere at the state or local level. Liberals as well as conservatives have found reason to be grateful for the partial sovereignty of the states. Many state and local governments were well in advance of the national government in their efforts to regulate the economy in the late nineteenth and early twentieth centuries, and to protect the environment in the 1970s. In the 1980s, many state governments countered decreases in federal government welfare provision and consumer protection with compensating increases. In the 1990s, state governments initiated health care reforms, while the federal government remained unable to agree to a national health care plan. (Some of the states' initiatives provided ideas for President Clinton's unsuccessful effort to get agreement to such a national plan in 1993.) The states have also been much more effective than the federal government in campaign finance reforms. State courts sometimes reach more liberal conclusions than federal ones; for example, in 1989 the Texas Supreme Court, following leads by courts in California and Connecticut, decided that the state's school financing system greatly favouring schools in wealthy districts – which had been held by the United States Supreme Court not to violate the Fourteenth Amendment's equal protection clause – violated the Texas constitution (Zimmerman, 1992, p. 179). It has long been noted as one of the advantages of federalism that the states can serve as 'laboratories of democracy', experimenting with policies that, if successful, can later be taken up by other states or by the federal government. One of the arguments that persuaded the Supreme Court to invalidate the Gun-Free School Zones Act of 1990 (in *United States v. Lopez*, discussed in Chapter 3, page 63) was that the Act 'forecloses the states from experimenting and exercising their own judgement in an area to which states lay claim by right of history and expertise' (concurring opinion of Justices Kennedy and O'Connor). In the 1990s, several states developed policies (for example, welfare reforms and abolition of telecommunications monopolies) later imposed on the remaining states by Acts of Congress.

Federalism furnishes the opportunity for a gradualistic method of reform, which some participants and observers find more satisfactory than reform initiated from the top. For example, the gradual reform of abortion laws that was occurring in the states might have led to be a more consensual and durable set of laws than was imposed on the states by a sweeping Supreme Court decision, *Roe v. Wade*, in 1973.

Proponents of federalism also claim as one of its advantages the fact that uniform regulations in some areas simply do not make sense. American states and cities have very different standards in such important areas as educational policies, crime and punishment, restrictions on pornography, taxation and incorporation laws. A unitary system that uses decentralised administration can also operate with due attention to differences in local needs, but federalism ensures that decentralisation is constitutionally guaranteed.

Energising citizenship

The retention of healthy state and local governments with a constitutionally guaranteed existence multiplies the access points to political power. Groups that feel frustrated at one level of government can approach another. It also makes possible more citizen participation in politics, necessary (although not sufficient) for the survival of civic-mindedness. There are currently more than 80,000 units of government in the United States (see Box 4.1), with over 500,000 elected officials: 537 federal, plus about 8,000 state and 494,000 local (US Bureau of the Census, 1996, pp. 282–3). Some twenty states now impose limits on the number of terms that state legislators can serve, thus further enlarging the scope for citizen participation. This energising of civil society can work against the energising of government, by clogging up the smooth operation of government, but in the longer run it can make government more efficient, by making it more responsive and better informed. This Antifederalist view of the advantages of federalism (noticed in Chapter 2, page 44–6) is quite compatible with the way that American federalism has actually developed.

Box 4.1

Eighty-five thousand American governments

Type	Number of government units	
Federal government		1
State government		50
Local government:		
County	3,043	
Municipal (city)	19,279	
Township and town	16,656	
School district	14,422	
Other special district (e.g. airport authority, water supply, sewage treatment)	31,555	
Total local government		84,955
Total		85,006

Source: US Bureau of the Census, 1996, p. 295

Intergovernmental relations and federalism at the end of the twentieth century

Current doubts about the continuing importance of federalism arise from two kinds of concern: practical and constitutional. Practically, although the co-operation of state and local governments with federal policies is in theory voluntary, the federal government is often in a position to make this co-operation seem financially irresistible; furthermore, the institutional capacity of state and local governments has often come into question. Constitutionally, it has appeared more and more difficult for the judiciary to discern (and therefore to maintain against Congress and the president) any limits on powers delegated to the federal government, and therefore any content in the 'residual and inviolable sovereignty' of the states. However, on both the practical and the constitutional fronts there are signs that American federalism is surviving and even reviving.

Fiscal dependence and institutional inferiority

State and local governments share with the federal government the power to tax. However, the federal government's tax base has generally given it a fiscal potential overmatching that of the subnational governments.

In the nineteenth and early twentieth centuries, protective tariffs usually produced more revenue than the federal government needed. The constitutionality of a federal income tax (first used briefly during the Civil War) was confirmed by the Sixteenth Amendment in 1913. This tax has helped to secure the relative fiscal strength of the more active post-1930 federal government. In the 1920s, state and local governments spent twice as much as the federal government; by 1940, federal spending equalled state and local spending, and since then it has exceeded it (Kincaid, 1994, p. 207). The federal government's fiscal advantage over the states is increased by the fact that it can more easily than they spend more than it taxes.

These fiscal advantages have allowed the federal government to initiate and to subsidise many programmes that are administered by state and local governments. In 1927, less than 2 per cent of state and local spending came from the federal government. From the 1930s this financial dependence rose steadily – and in the 1960s quite sharply – to a high of 27 per cent during the 1970s. It dropped back to the 1970 level (19 per cent) during the 1980s, and has again risen slightly (to 22 per cent) in the 1990s (see Box 4.2). The federal money flowing to the states has usually come with many strings attached, including the requirement that it be supplemented (if only by a small percentage) by state revenues.

There have been two main incentives for the growth of federal aid to state and local governments. First, in the 1930s, the federal government often took up its new responsibility for overseeing the national economy by collaborating with state governments. Several New Deal social programmes (for example, welfare and unemployment insurance) were co-operative efforts by federal and state governments. State and local politicians were naturally pleased to be able to claim some of the credit for benefits brought to their constituents without the need to raise all of the money to pay for those benefits

Box 4.2

Federal grants-in-aid, selected years 1970–96

Fiscal year ending	Total (billions of 1987 dollars)	As percentage of:		
		State and local outlays	Federal outlays	GDP
1970	73.6	19	12.3	2.4
1975	105.4	23.5	15.0	3.3
1980	127.5	26.3	15.5	3.5
1985	112.9	21.3	11.2	2.7
1990	119.5	18.7	10.8	2.5
1991	130.9	19.5	11.7	2.7
1992	146.7	20.8	12.9	3.0
1993	155.5	21.2	13.7	3.1
1994	165.9	21.8	14.4	3.2
1995	172.7	22.2	14.8	3.2
1996 est.	177.3	n/a	15.1	3.2

Source: US Bureau of the Census, 1996, p. 300

by state and local taxation. Secondly, the sharper increase of federal aid occurred in the 1960s, and much of that increase was motivated less by the thought that the federal government, able to regulate the whole national economy, was the only political unit that could reasonably be expected to finance and to co-ordinate certain things, than by the perception that the states were performing badly some of the jobs of governance that were still deemed to be their responsibility, such as education, civil rights, crime-fighting, urban renewal and environmental protection. Federal programmes and aid in these areas were therefore developed to encourage improvements in the performance of state and local governments. Aid often went directly to local governments, bypassing the states. The 1960s has been called a period of 'creative' federalism, since the federal government was trying to alter the way that states and cities did their jobs, going beyond the collaborative framework of 'co-operative' federalism.

Resurgence of the states

If that were the end of the story, then the idea that the history of federalism has been an inevitable advance of centralisation, and therefore has produced an inevitable decline in the substance of federalism (divided sovereignty), might be validated. However, since the 1960s there has been a 'resurgence of the states' (Bowman and Kearney, 1986), assisted by several acts of the federal government, which has helped to swing the pendulum of federalism in the opposite direction. Especially since the

1980s, a push for devolution of responsibility to the states has been part of the conservative drive to reduce government and taxation at all levels, but liberals have also registered a renewed interest in federalism.

In the 'creative' 1960s, much more federal aid was given to the states than before, but the conditions attached to federal grants became more demanding. States' complaints about this situation soon received a federal response. Since the late 1960s, presidents (especially Republican ones) and Congresses (especially after the Republicans took control of both chambers in 1995) have been more attentive to states' demands that more discretion be given to them in spending money granted to them. A 'general revenue sharing' scheme gave a small proportion of federal grants to states and localities with no conditions attached, between its launch in 1972 (as part of Richard Nixon's New Federalism initiative) and its demise in 1986 (when it fell victim to budget cuts). Since 1966, 'categorical' grants, with fairly precise restrictions on the use of the funds, have been replaced to some extent with 'block grants', which consolidate categorical funds and direct them at specific problems (such as urban development) but allow more local decisions on how to spend them. One of the most revolutionary domestic policies in recent years was the decision, in 1996, to transform a significant part of the federal government's welfare programme (Aid to Families with Dependent Children) into a block grant (Temporary Assistance to Needy Families), with much greater state control over eligibility and benefits – although also with strict work requirements and limits on the period of individual recipients' eligibility. See Chapter 19 for further discussion of this innovation.

State governments, many of them justly condemned as amateurish and irresponsible in the 1950s and 1960s, have been reformed since then, improving the capacities of governors and legislatures. In many states, gubernatorial terms were lengthened, governors were made eligible for re-election, and they were given somewhat greater appointment and removal powers. Legislative districts were reapportioned (the Supreme Court decided that even state senates had to be elected on the 'one person, one vote' ideal), and legislatures began meeting for longer sessions. Both governors and legislatures acquired more professional staff. Although public confidence in all levels of government has declined in recent decades, confidence in state and local government has declined far less than confidence in the federal government. Concerns are now often voiced about the institutional capacity of the federal government rather than that of state governments. A recent opinion poll asking whether the interviewee trusted the federal government or the state government to do a better job of running things, found more than twice as many Americans picking their state governments (Weissert and Schram, 1996, pp. 2–3). Fears that federal government programmes have become too diverse and unmanageable are expressed not only by popular opinion but also by respected liberal elites (Rivlin, 1992).

The resurgence of the states has been fiscal as well as institutional. In fact, state and local governments did not reduce their spending when the federal government began spending more in the 1930s. Since that period, states and localities have raised and spent impressive amounts of money. In spite of the growth in federal government spending during the New Deal and the Second World War, it was not until the late 1950s that federal government spending on domestic programmes first exceeded spending by subnational governments from their own resources (that is, leaving federal grants out of the picture) (Rivlin, 1992, p. 86). Since the 1970s those governments have broadened their own revenue bases, by adding income taxes and user fees to their traditional arsenal of sales and property taxes, and by finding other sources of income (for example lotteries). Moreover, since the 1980s, cuts in federal income tax rates, and the adjustment of tax brackets for inflation, have reduced the tendency for federal revenues from this source to grow faster than the economy, thus lowering the fiscal advantage of the federal government. In the 1980s, subnational revenues grew faster than federal revenues, and federal domestic spending is now regularly exceeded by state and local spending.

Some states are still much less institutionally and fiscally fit than others, and some local governments remain inefficient and corrupt. Moreover, the federal government, with its more flexible tax base and less regressive taxation, continues to enjoy at least a potential fiscal superiority (Wallin, 1996). Nevertheless, the recent experience of stronger state and local governments has very effectively made the point that fiscal dynamics and institutional capacity do not always favour the federal government.

Continuation of federal constraints

This is not to say that the pendulum has swung completely to the opposite point. State and local governments still feel constrained by federal dictates, which take four main forms:

1. **Federal pre-emption.** The use of the constitutional power (under the supremacy clause) of federal pre-emption, or supercession of state legislation, in various fields has greatly increased since 1965. Using this power, the federal government can stop state and local governments from legislating in areas that it chooses to start legislating in (assuming that it has the constitutional power to legislate in that area). It can also allow states and localities to continue or to resume legislating in such areas if they conform to federal standards. Courts have become less willing to infer pre-emptive intent when Congress does not state it in an Act, but Congress has become more inclined to make its pre-emptive intentions explicit. The effectiveness of the federal government's policies to deregulate some commercial activities (for example air and bus transportation) and to establish uniform national rules in cases where it judged that states' regulations had been either too lax (for example air and water pollution standards) or too strict (regulation of mutual funds and agricultural chemicals) has required it to prohibit or at least to strictly limit state regulation in those areas.

   However, it should be noted that policy-making involving federal pre-emption is not always a one-way street; states contribute to the process. When a federal pre-emption draws strong objections from several states, Congress sometimes enacts pre-emption relief laws that adjust the pre-emption to meet the objections. Moreover, federal pre-emption laws often contain provisions for returning 'regulatory primacy' to any state once its own regulatory regime meets minimum federal standards (Zimmerman, 1992, chapter 4 and pp. 197–203).

2. **Judicial orders.** Federal courts, especially in interpreting the Fourteenth Amendment,

still order many state and local government actions, some of them (such as those affecting schools and prisons) requiring significant expenditures by states and localities, with no federal subsidy.

3. **Funding.** Subnational governments are still significantly dependent on federal funds, and categorical grants still far outnumber the less conditional block grants, which account for only about 10 per cent of total federal aid (Kincaid, 1994, p. 211). (The more diffuse coalitions of interests that favour the more general block grants are usually less effective in lobbying Congress than the more specific interests favouring categorical grants.) The costs of some co-operative programmes with large state financial involvement have greatly increased (for example, Medicaid, the health programme for the poor).

4. **Unfunded mandates.** Federal orders now often arrive without any funding incentive, but with threats to cut funding in other areas or to prosecute officials if the orders are not followed. These strings without money require state and local efforts and expenditures to meet prescribed standards for such things as pollution control, antidiscrimination policies, minimum wages, disabled persons' access to buildings and transportation, AIDS testing, and (as noted above) transforming welfare beneficiaries into employed workers. An Unfunded Mandate Reform Act (supported by President Clinton, the new Republican majority in Congress, and the new Republican majority of state governors) was passed in 1995, but it allowed many exceptions and in any case sought only to require that Congress deliberate somewhat more carefully before enacting such mandates. The Act raises awareness of the problems that unfunded mandates can pose, but does not dispose of those problems.

Constitutional uncertainty

Since 1969, more conservative presidents have appointed more conservative federal judges, who have been trying to develop a solid constitutional basis for a federalism that gives due acknowledgement to the importance of the states without returning to the simplistic assumptions of a doctrinaire dual federalism.

In 1976, the Supreme Court for the first time in forty years declared unconstitutional an Act of Congress based on the interstate commerce clause. It did this in order to protect federalism. The Court decided (by a five-to-four majority) that Congress' application of minimum wage and maximum hours legislation to employees of state and local governments was an unreasonable interference with the way that the states carried out their constitutional responsibilities: it threatened to 'displace the states' freedom to structure integral operations in areas of traditional governmental functions' (*National League of Cities v. Usery*).

However, this particular attempt to limit congressional authority over subnational governments did not last long. The decision was overruled (in another five-to-four decision, one justice having changed his mind) in 1985, when the Court rejected the idea that it had a duty to protect federalism by discerning constitutional 'limitations on the objects of federal authority'. It was enough, said this Court, to rely on the way that 'the structure of the federal system' gave the states important roles 'in the workings of the national government itself' (*Garcia v. San Antonio Metropolitan Transit Authority*). Congress' adjustment of federal wages and hours legislation to accommodate some state and local concerns soon after this decision seemed to prove that reliance on this federal structure, and on the ability of governors and mayors to lobby Congress, was not wholly misplaced. However, the leading dissenting opinion (by Justice Powell, joined by Chief Justice Burger and by Justices O'Connor and Rehnquist) accurately noted that political and constitutional developments in the twentieth century, such as 'adoption of the Seventeenth Amendment [providing for direct election of senators], the weakening of political parties on the local level, and the rise of national media, among other things, have made Congress increasingly less representative of state and local interests, and more likely to be responsive to the demands of various national constituencies.' The dissenters emphasised the duty of the Court to continue to exercise judicial review in federalism cases, to weigh 'state autonomy as a factor in the balance when interpreting the means by which Congress can exercise its authority on states as states', and not to decide such cases as if a state were merely a private party.

In fact, the Court has not been shirking its duty. It continues to engage in the battle. The *National League of Cities* and *Garcia* cases have turned out to be only the first skirmish in the late twentieth century struggle to determine what the constitutional maintenance of American federalism requires. Chief Justice Rehnquist (one of the dissenters in *Garcia*) is now joined by three or four other justices in giving more substantial support to states' interests in federalism cases. Although this group favouring a less centralising federalism has enjoyed some success, it has yet to establish a firm direction for the whole Court, which remains sharply divided on federalism issues.

In 1992 Justice O'Connor wrote an opinion for the Court in a decision that struck down part of the Low Level Radioactive Waste Policy Amendments Act of 1985, on the grounds that it violated the Tenth Amendment's reservation of powers to the states. The Act offered three kinds of incentive to states to establish by specified deadlines sites for the disposal of radioactive waste: financial subsidies, the right to deny access to their sites to waste generated in states that fail to meet the deadlines, and the obligation to take legal title to (and responsibility for) such waste in their state if they did not meet the deadlines themselves. The Court decided that this third incentive was unconstitutionally coercive, offering states a false 'choice' between taking possession of the waste or regulating as Congress had prescribed, in effect compelling 'states to enact or administer a federal regulatory program' (*New York v. United States*).

Similar reasoning was used successfully to attack the provision in the 'Brady Act' (a federal law passed in 1993) that required local law enforcement agents to do background checks on handgun purchasers during a five-day waiting period, as an interim measure until a national system of instantly checking prospective purchasers was put into operation. This part of the Act was challenged by law enforcement officers from some counties in Montana and Arizona, who objected to being compelled by an Act of Congress to administer, even on a temporary basis, this federal regulatory programme. A five-person majority of the Supreme Court decided these officers were right, and that the federal government 'may neither issue directives requiring the states to address particular problems, nor command the states' officers, or those of their political subdivisions, to administer or enforce a federal regulatory program', because such commands would 'compromise the structural framework of dual sovereignty' (*Printz v. United States*). Justice O'Connor's concurring opinion underlined the distinction between 'purely ministerial reporting requirements' that some federal laws impose on the states (for example, they report to the federal government such things as missing children, traffic fatalities and potentially environmentally hazardous storage facilities), and the offending requirements of the Brady Act, 'which directly compel state officials to administer a federal regulatory program', and therefore 'utterly fail to adhere to the design and structure of our constitutional scheme'.

The Court's invalidation of the Gun-Free School Zones Act in the *Lopez* decision in 1995 (mentioned above, page 88, and discussed in Chapter 3, page 63) has inspired several challenges to other federal criminal statutes (for example, those directed against arson, carjacking, selling drugs near schools, violence against women, and failure to pay child support). So far, most of these challenges have failed, but some have yet to be decided by the Supreme Court.

In another 1995 decision, *US Term Limits v. Thornton*), the Court (by five to four) refused to approve a state's imposition (by state constitutional amendment) of term limits for that state's members of Congress. The Court agreed with the Arkansas Supreme Court that such a limitation violates the United States Constitution by adding qualifications to those already enumerated in Article I, Section 2 (minimum age, minimum period of US citizenship and state residency). A vigorous dissent argued that a state's option to impose term limits on its members of Congress – a reasonable attempt to balance the well known advantages of incumbency in modern congressional elections – could not logically or historically be read out of the powers that the Tenth Amendment reserved to the states.

The following year, the dissenters in this case were joined by one of the majority to form a five-justice majority in a ruling against Congress' Indian Gaming Regulatory Act of 1988. The Act (passed pursuant to the power of Congress 'to regulate commerce ... with the Indian tribes') set up a statutory basis for regulating gambling operations by Indian tribes, allowing them to engage in such commercial ventures only after agreeing to a set of rules with the state in which the operation is located. The Act provided that a tribe may sue a state in federal court in order to compel it to negotiate such an agreement. The Supreme Court ruled that this provision violated the Eleventh Amendment's restrictions on federal court jurisdiction in suits against state governments (*Seminole Tribe of Florida v. Florida*). Determined dissenters again disputed the logic and the history of the majority's opinion.

Thus many recent decisions have moved towards insisting that 'state autonomy is a relevant factor in assessing the means by which Congress exercises its powers' (Justice O'Connor's dissenting opinion in the *Garcia* case).

Federalism is currently a more salient issue in constitutional law than it has been for many decades. Many of the current federalism cases are complex and dry, but politicians and interest groups realise that much is at stake in them. Therefore, even if constitutional law clearly and firmly shifts in a direction that complements the fiscal and institutional resurgence of the states, constitutional quarrels about the demands of federalism can be expected to continue.

Summary

The United States has a 'compound' governmental system, 'partly national, partly federal'. This American form of federalism has served both as a control on and as an enhancement of government activity. Changes in expectations of government in the twentieth century have enlarged the sphere of activity of the federal government, but the states have remained very significant, and since the 1960s they have become more vigorous. Recent Supreme Court opinions on federalism questions have reflected this fact. However, it remains clear that politics and public opinion contribute at least as much as constitutional doctrine to the determination of such questions. As both Madison and Hamilton emphasised, 'the federal and state governments are in fact but different agents and trustees of the people' (*The Federalist*, no. 46), so their competition for popular support ultimately determines the relative strength of each level of government more than any fixed legal statements of their proper ends can or should do. As long as the 'compound republic' continues, the interaction of politics and constitutional doctrines that characterises the federal dimension of this republic will also continue, adding both ambiguity and enrichment to American politics.

 Topics for discussion

1. How did the federal system invented in 1787 differ from previous federal systems?
2. What causes changes in the activities of the states on the one hand and the federal government on the other?
3. How strong is the 'resurgence of the states'?
4. What are the empowering purposes of federalism? How well are these purposes served today?

 Further reading

The character and problems of federalism are discussed in *The Federalist*, especially nos 14–17, 27, 31, 39, 45 and 46. Both historical and recent Supreme Court opinions on federalism can be read on the Internet, starting at the Library of Congress site (http://thomas.loc.gov) and following the links to the judiciary (or through the site listed under Further Reading in Chapter 2). The 'Thomas' site also leads to a wealth of information on state and local government activities. Up-to-date scholarly articles on American federalism are published in the quarterly journal *Publius*.

 References

Bowman, Ann O'M. and Kearney, Richard C., 1986, *The Resurgence of the States* (Englewood Cliffs: Prentice Hall)

Commager, Henry Steele, ed., 1973 *Documents of American History* (9th edn, 2 vols, Englewood Cliffs: Prentice Hall)

Corwin, Edward S., 1973 *The Constitution and What It Means Today* (13th edn, revised by Harold W. Chase and Craig R. Ducat, Princeton: Princeton University Press)

Diamond, Martin, 1974, 'What the framers meant by federalism', pp. 25–42 in *A Nation of States: Essays on the American federal system*, ed. Robert A. Goldwin (2nd edn, Chicago: Rand McNally)

Elazar, Daniel J., 1962, *The American Partnership: Intergovernmental cooperation in the nineteenth-century United States* (Chicago: University of Chicago Press)

Grodzins, Morton, 1966, *The American System: A new view of government in the United States* (Chicago: Rand McNally)

Jaffa, Harry V., 1974, 'Partly federal, partly national', pp. 109–37 in *A Nation of States: Essays on the American federal system*, ed. Robert A. Goldwin (2nd edn, Chicago: Rand McNally)

Kincaid, John, 1994, 'Governing the American states', pp. 200–17 in *Developments in American Politics*, eds Gillian Peele *et al.* (2nd edn, London: Macmillan)

Rivlin, Alice M., 1992, *Reviving the American Dream: The economy, the states and the federal government* (Washington DC: The Brookings Institute)

US Bureau of the Census, 1996, *Statistical Abstract of the United States* (116th edn, Washington DC)

Wallin, Bruce A., 1996, 'Federal cutbacks and the fiscal condition of the states', 1996, *Publius*, vol. 26, no. 3, pp. 141–55

Weissert, Carol S. and Schram, Sanford F., 1996, 'The state of American federalism, 1995–1996', *Publius*, vol. 26, no. 3, pp. 1–26

Zimmerman, Joseph F., 1992, *Contemporary American Federalism: The growth of national power* (Leicester: Leicester University Press)

part II

The socio-economic contexts

We saw in Part I that American government and politics operates within the framework provided by the Constitution. Equally important, however, are the social and economic frameworks. In the first place, social and economic realities give life and substance to the constitutional system, as institutions and individuals seek to put into practice the abstract framework bequeathed to them by the Founding Fathers. Moreover, the very agenda of American politics is determined largely by the social and economic problems and opportunities which present themselves in any particular historical era. In this Part, therefore, we examine in detail some of the key socio-economic contexts of American politics in the second half of the twentieth century. In Chapter 5, we analyse the economic and social roots of the political consensus which characterised American politics from the end of the Second World War until the mid-1960s. For many, this is now viewed as a 'golden age' when American pre-eminence in prosperity and power made the political process relatively straightforward. In that sense, it established a model of how the political system could and should operate. It did not last, however, largely because its economic and social bases were severely dislocated by domestic and international change. In Chapter 6, then, we examine how the American economy began to decline relative to its principal competitor nations until, by the 1980s, it was considered to be in deep crisis. In Chapter 7, we analyse the rise to prominence of a major contemporary social issue, that of gender relations. Socially, as well as economically, the United States is a markedly different country from that which existed during the postwar consensus. Among the many challenges to traditional social arrangements, feminism and the campaign for greater gender equality stands out as the most fundamental: and it is precisely for this reason that it has generated some of the fiercest debates in contemporary American politics. In Chapter 8, we look at some new aspects of an old issue in American history: immigration and the ethnic and racial composition of American society. The diversity of its people is one of the country's greatest strengths, yet it also creates tensions and problems that at times seem insoluble. The four chapters which make up Part II by no means paint a complete social and economic portrait of the contemporary United States. They do, however, make clear that, as the United States enters the twenty-first century, its political process is under considerable pressure from social and economic problems and constraints that seem often to be beyond its control.

Contents

5

The rise and fall of consensus since 1945

This chapter examines the political consensus which underpinned both domestic and foreign policy in the decades following the Second World War. From the perspective of the 1990s, many Americans regard this as a great period in their history: one when social and ideological cohesion promoted affluence and stability at home and American power abroad.

In 1945, the United States was indisputably the world's greatest economic and military power. Indeed, it had no serious rival in either sphere of activity. Its economy had recovered from the Great Depression of the 1930s, thanks mainly to war contracts; yet unlike the other belligerents, its cities, factories and farms had suffered no devastation during the Second World War. Thus, despite four years at war in Europe and Asia, the American economy was not merely intact, but was ready to expand around the world. Its military machine possessed the same capability. Its troops and weapons had been the decisive factor in defeating both Germany and Japan and, most important of all, the United States alone possessed the awesome power of the atomic bomb.

Such economic and military prowess, however, was by no means an unproblematic source of joy to Americans and their political leaders. On the economic front, the spectre of recession or even depression loomed. After all, if war contracts had ended the Great Depression, it was by no means unreasonable to suppose that the disappearing stimulus of war would throw the economy into reverse. Most immediately there was also the problem of how to reintegrate some 15 million service men and women, all clamouring for rapid demobilisation, back into the civilian economy.

It must be remembered that the prewar years had witnessed considerable political strife over fundamental socio-economic issues. The Democratic party had largely united behind President Franklin D. Roosevelt's New Deal, of which the central feature was the acceptance of responsibility by the federal government for the general health of the economy and the welfare of the people. This in turn had entailed much experimentation in both governmental process and policy. There had been, for example, a shift in political power from the states to the federal government, and to the presidency in particular; government intervention in the economy on an unprecedented scale; government promotion of worker power through pro-union legislation; and the creation of a fledgling welfare state.

These departures from traditional laissez-faire, pro-business American practice had incurred the wrath of most Republicans and, increasingly, of conservative Democrats. Thus, while the electorate continued to send Roosevelt to the White House and a Democratic majority to the Congress, New Deal innovation had all but come to a halt by 1938. It was by no means clear, therefore, whether the New Deal philosophy would be sustained in postwar America.

On the foreign policy front, the debate had been equally fierce during the interwar years. A bitter struggle over American participation in the League of Nations after the First World War had been followed by retrenchment and a strong tendency towards isolationism. This persisted right up until Pearl Harbour, even though by then President Roosevelt and other political leaders had become convinced of the need for the United States to enter the Second World War, (see Chapter 22). Most Americans therefore entered the global conflict reluctantly and, with the war over in 1945, assumed their country would once again turn inwards.

On the other hand, both economic and national security factors counselled against any such 'neo-isolationism'. The health of the American economy depended in part upon access to overseas markets and raw materials. Yet by the end of the war, there were very few countries with the wealth to import the goods that the United States had to offer. Furthermore, the policy of American neo-isolationists to terminate the loans which had been extended to European allies to fight the war would only make this situation worse.

As for access to raw materials, this depended upon ensuring global stability in general, and the freedom of the high seas in particular. With respect to the latter, the United States had always been able to count upon the protection afforded by the British navy. The old imperial order, however, had been put under terrible strain by the costs of defeating Germany and the capacity of Britain to continue playing the role of 'world policeman' was in doubt. In addition, should Britain prove unable to resume its prewar role, who but the United States was in a position to take up the mantle on behalf of western capitalism and democracy?

On the evidence of prewar political conflicts in the United States, these dilemmas over postwar domestic and foreign policy might easily have plunged the country into turmoil after 1945. Instead, a combination of unprecedented economic prosperity and the threat posed by the Soviet Union produced a platform for consensus on both domestic and foreign policy.

Postwar prosperity

Rather than lapsing into recession, the postwar American economy boomed. As a result of wartime prosperity, American gross national product (GNP, the value of all goods and services produced in the country) stood at a healthy $212 billion in 1945. Yet by 1960, that figure had more than doubled and by 1971 had reached over $1 trillion. This wealth was, as Carl Degler put it, 'the first big fact of the postwar economy' (Degler, 1975, p. 165).

The failure of the anticipated recession to materialise was owing in part to pent-up consumer demand. Americans had relatively few opportunities to buy consumer goods during the wartime austerity and had therefore saved considerable sums which they were now eager to spend. However, the key factor in sustaining the postwar boom was government expenditure: on defence, highways, education and housing, in particular. By the mid-1950s, purchases by government were more than one-fifth of total national purchases (Degler, 1975, p. 167). Government commitment to high defence and other expenditures encouraged American industry to invest in research and the development of new techniques and products. In consequence, manufacturing became increasingly automated and computerised, and ever more efficient at producing goods either for the government or for consumers.

Despite periodic recessions, consumer purchasing power increased enormously in the postwar decades. The proportion of Americans with an annual income of (in real terms) $10,000 or more rose from 9 per cent in 1947 to 33 per cent in 1968; during the same period, the proportion of those with an income of less than $3,000 fell from 34 per cent to 19 per cent. Thus, 'the distribution of income gave the American social structure the shape less of a pyramid than of a diamond, with a vastly expanded middle class' (Leuchtenburg, 1983, p. 48).

As well as being newly affluent, this burgeoning middle class had more leisure time, as hours of work were reduced and paid vacations increased. On top of this came a credit boom, with short-term consumer credit rising from $8.4 billion in 1946 to almost $45 billion in 1958. To facilitate this further, Diners Card introduced the first credit card in 1950, soon to be followed by American Express and others (Leuchtenburg, 1983, p. 43).

The result of all this was a mass consumer society. The first steps towards this had been taken in the 1920s, but those gains had been wiped out by the Depression. Now, in the postwar years, the great majority of Americans could purchase cars, televisions, refrigerators, washing machines and so on (see Box 5.1). They also consumed increasing quantities of convenience foods and patronised 'fast food' restaurants: in 1954, the first McDonalds was opened in San Bernadino, California. In 1956, in Minneapolis, came the first of another great symbol of modern American consumerism, the enclosed shopping mall.

Along with the consumer and leisure boom came the baby boom, the housing boom and the rapid expansion of suburbia. The birth-rate in the postwar years was remarkable, owing perhaps to a combination of rising prosperity, optimism and improvements in medical care. Whatever the reason, there were one-third more Americans in 1960 than there had been in 1940 (Dubofsky and Theoharis, 1983, p. 105). The population growth was especially pronounced in western states: by 1963, California had overtaken New York as the most populous state.

Wherever the population increased, however, it lived increasingly in suburbia. In the immediate postwar years, the federal government guaranteed the mortgages of millions of first-time home buyers. Many of these found the affordable homes they sought

Box 5.1

Distribution of durable consumer goods in American families, 1946–56

Percentage of families owning

Year	Car	TV	Fridge	Freezer	Vacuum cleaner	Washing machine	Air conditioner
1946	na	–	69.1	–	48.8	50.5	0.2
1947	na	–	71.2	–	49.5	63.0	0.2
1948	54	2.9	76.6	4.3	51.7	67.4	0.3
1949	56	10.1	79.2	5.2	52.8	68.6	0.4
1950	60	26.4	86.4	7.2	56.5	71.9	0.6
1951	65	38.5	86.7	9.3	57.7	73.5	0.8
1952	65	50.2	89.2	11.5	59.4	76.2	1.4
1953	65	63.5	90.4	13.4	60.5	78.5	2.6
1954	70	74.1	92.5	15.1	62.2	81.3	4.0
1955	71	76.1	94.1	16.8	64.3	84.1	5.6
1956	73	81.0	96.0	18.0	66.7	86.8	7.6

Source: Diggins, 1988, p. 186

in the new, prefabricated suburban developments, such as those built by William Levitt in Pennsylvania and New York. These 'Levittowns', although later derided as 'little boxes on a hillside', had enormous appeal for those seeking a stable, family life away from the noisy, dirty cities. Highway construction and automobiles made commuting relatively easy.

For many Americans, then, postwar affluence meant a better material life, with work, family and home at the heart of a consumer-oriented society. It also meant that Americans were becoming more like each other in their lifestyles, with mass culture diminishing regional, ethnic and class differences. Regrettably, 'commentators found the United States not only homogenous but homogenized. The typical American, social analysts complained, had become both conformist and bland. Each morning Mr Jones put on a standard uniform of button-down shirt, sincere tie, and charcoal-grey flannel suit, and adjusted his perpetual smile' (Leuchtenburg, 1983, p. 70). The rest of the Jones family seemed equally uninspiring. While Mr Jones set his sights upon climbing the corporate ladder, Mrs Jones was apparently content to aim for perfection as a homemaker. As for their children, even the college students were conformist and apolitical.

Of course, millions of Americans – black and white, young and old – did not share in the postwar economic boom or the lifestyle that went with it: and not everyone who did was willing to conform, as the 'Beats' and bikers of the 1950s attest. Yet even the

Beats were disengaged rather than challenging, while other sections of America's youth were 'rebels without a cause'. The prevailing cultural mood of the postwar years, then, was one of contentment; and inevitably, this was reflected in the politics of the day.

Political consensus

The New Deal had lost much of its impetus by 1938. Moreover, when Roosevelt died in April 1945, he was succeeded by a man whom few believed capable of reviving the liberal legacy of the 1930s. Harry Truman was a relatively unknown Missouri senator, who had been chosen as his running-mate by Roosevelt in 1944 because of his solid, if unspectacular record. Many leading Democrats did not think him worthy of Roosevelt's mantle and the Republicans were confident that he could not beat them in a presidential election. These assessments seemed borne out by the 1946 mid-term elections, when the Republicans won a crushing victory, capturing both the House and the Senate for the first time since 1928.

Yet, in 1948, Harry Truman caused the greatest upset in American electrical history by winning the presidency in his own right. To be sure, this was in part owing to his growing reputation as a tough, decisive and plain-speaking leader. The underlying reason for his victory, however, was the fact that he grasped better than his rival what a majority of Americans desired and feared: 'Truman appealed to both lower-class Americans eager for housing and welfare legislation and to an emergent middle class still too insecure of its own status to turn against the New Deal' (Diggins, 1988, p. 109). In other words, Truman's campaign promise to protect and extend the New Deal legacy touched a political consensus that had its roots in the 'affluence and anxiety' of the postwar years (Degler, 1975).

At the heart of this continuing adherence to New Deal liberalism was the belief that the federal government must be active in helping to produce a healthy economy and in protecting the people from the worst depredations of recession. This was the political lesson that a majority of Americans had learned from the experience of the Great Depression. In concrete policy terms, this meant maintaining high levels of federal expenditure, the minimum wage, agricultural subsidies and the safety-net of the welfare state. As long as the Republican party threatened the economic security of a majority of Americans by attacking these basic elements of the New Deal, the Democrats seemed assured of political dominance.

So it proved until the New Deal consensus began to crumble in the late 1960s. Between 1932 and 1964, the Republicans won just two presidential elections out of nine. Moreover, their two victories, in 1952 and 1956, were gained at the cost of explicit acceptance of some key elements of New Deal liberalism. Thus, during the 1952 campaign, the Democrats reminded the electorate time and again of the disastrous, ineffectual record of the last Republican president, Herbert Hoover, during the Depression. The response of Dwight D. Eisenhower, the Republican candidate, was to pledge repeatedly that he would use the resources of the federal government to combat recession, should it arise. In the 1956 campaign, Eisenhower implicitly disowned his party's past by referring to his own philosophy as 'Modern Republicanism'. This he defined as 'the political philosophy that recognises clearly the responsibility of the

Federal Government to take the lead in making certain that the productivity of our great economic machine is distributed so that no one will suffer disaster, privation, through no fault of his own' (Alexander, 1975, p. 191).

The Eisenhower equilibrium

Eisenhower's philosophy of modern and moderate Republicanism was an astute blend of the most popular aspects of the New Deal and traditional conservative American values. Combined with his considerable personal popularity, this enabled him to construct what historians have termed 'the Eisenhower Equilibrium'. On the one hand, Eisenhower not only promised to use the resources of the federal government during recession, but he acquiesced in an extension of social security coverage and an increase in the minimum wage. On the other hand, he insisted that private enterprise should be free from government controls, that the budget should be balanced and that Americans should not expect their education or housing to be directly subsidised by the federal government. In short, he advocated traditional individualism, backed by a federal government guarantee of support if times became hard.

For a while in the mid-1950s, it seemed that the Eisenhower Equilibrium had taken America beyond the political divisions and strife generated by the Great Depression. Americans at this time 'appeared generally satisfied with their economic system, their political system, and themselves. They seemed scarcely interested in ideological controversy, in searching analyses of social ills, or in seeking alternatives to the status quo' (Alexander, 1975, pp. 147–8).

This complacency would be challenged on both the domestic and international fronts before the decade was out. There was, however, more to the apolitical mood of the 1950s than affluence and self satisfaction, for owing largely to the perceived threat of communism both at home and abroad, political criticism and dissent became difficult, and even downright dangerous to express. This suppression of radical politics has its origins in the cold war consensus in foreign policy.

Foreign policy consensus

There had been considerable disagreement over foreign policy in the interwar period, and even during the war 'there had been only a fitful semblance of bipartisanship in foreign policy' (Barnet, 1990, p. 272). Yet, between 1945 and 1950 not only did a bipartisan foreign policy emerge, but it was one based on a radical departure from certain fundamental precepts that had held good since 1789.

We shall examine the traditions of American foreign policy in greater detail in Chapter 22. Suffice it to say at this point that the foreign policy of the United States had always been based upon the desire to avoid involvement in European conflicts. Americans generally considered European interstate politics to be corrupt and corrupting. Above all, therefore, the United States should steer clear of 'entangling alliances', as Thomas Jefferson put it, for these would surely drag America down to the level of the Old World. When the United States defied this tradition and belatedly entered the First World War, the experience proved so bitter that it served only to intensify distaste for involvement in Europe.

It is truly remarkable, then, that by 1950, the United States had entered into a series of military alliances with western European states and more generally accepted the political, economic and military burden of 'leader of the free world'. It is even more remarkable that this should have come about by a broad and deep bipartisan consensus.

It has been suggested that there were three main aspects to the foreign policy consensus that emerged in the United States after 1945: cultural cohesion, policy itself and procedural aspects (Melanson, 1991, p. 3). Cultural cohesion is important to foreign policy because it strengthens the sense of national identity. This in turn embraces values which may be considered not only worth defending, but also exporting for the 'benefit' of other peoples. American culture had always been based on both these estimates of its own worth, and the postwar economic boom served only to enhance them. While some considered American life to be 'homogenized', most ordinary Americans fervently subscribed to 'normal' and 'respectable' values such as stable nuclear families, community, religion, home ownership and the pursuit of prosperity (Melanson, 1991, pp. 8–9). While Americanism and its antithesis, un-Americanism, elude precise definition, most Americans in the postwar years thought of their national culture in these terms. It was these values which inspired a fierce patriotism, and even more so when they were threatened by 'atheistic communism'.

Policy itself is concerned with the grand design, strategies and tactics by which the nation should defend itself and its interests. In the postwar years, consensus on these was achieved on the basis of certain widely accepted propositions (see Box 5.2).

While there were specific areas of foreign policy on which there was sharp disagreement, there was little dissent from these fundamental foreign policy precepts,

Box 5.2

The postwar foreign policy consensus: some fundamental precepts

■ The United States was uniquely positioned materially and morally to create a just and stable international order

■ The interests of the United States were global

■ Soviet-Communist aggression was the main threat to world peace

■ Containment was the best means of preventing this aggression

■ Nuclear weapons were essential to deterring Soviet expansion

■ A stable, open world economy required American leadership

■ The United States must assume leadership of international organisations, such as the United Nations

Source: Melanson, 1991, pp. 4–7

either among the general population or the foreign policy elites. Together they impelled the United States towards a central and global role in the postwar international system.

The procedural aspects of foreign policy concern the process by which policy is formulated and implemented. Here again, there was a marked change after 1945, but one which received bipartisan approval. The central feature of this procedural consensus was the primacy of the presidency in foreign policy making. Both the Constitution and traditional practice had always promoted presidential leadership in the making of foreign policy. Now, however, Congress tacitly yielded to the president even its most fundamental constitutional powers, such as authority over war-making. Not one of the wars, conflicts or interventions in which the United States has been involved since 1945 has been accompanied by a formal declaration of war by Congress.

The reasons for this accrual of foreign policy making powers to the executive branch are numerous (see Chapter 22), but none was more important than the common perception that, at a time of permanent crisis and threat, the presidency was better equipped to discern and protect the national interest than Congress. The presidential branch included the expertise of the foreign policy making bureaucracy, the intelligence services and the armed forces. Moreover, as a unitary branch of government, it was better equipped to maintain secrecy and to take decisive action, particularly in a crisis. Underpinning these presidential advantages over Congress, were the other two aspects of the foreign policy consensus. Because fundamental cultural values and policy precepts were shared by most Americans, Congress was unusually willing to entrust the safety of the nation to the president.

It should not be assumed, however, that the postwar foreign policy consensus came about effortlessly. Indeed, there was considerable political calculation behind it by those who believed that US foreign policy must be actively internationalist. The most famous instance concerns President Truman's request for aid to anti-communist forces in Greece and Turkey in 1947. Meeting with a bipartisan congressional leadership delegation, Truman and his Secretary of State Dean Acheson asked how Congress could be persuaded to vote the funds. The Republican chairman of the Senate Foreign Relations Committee, Arthur H. Vandenberg, told him that the only way to produce the necessary consensus was to exaggerate the communist threat and 'scare the hell out of the country'.

Others emphasise the political deal between Democrats and Republicans that supported the consensus, with each side hoping to reap electoral gains from the show of unity (see Box 5.3). And yet another slant on the consensus draws attention to the advantages that bipartisanship offers to the president, in a system of 'separate institutions sharing powers' and where the opposition party may control the Congress. Secretary of State Acheson himself expressed this bluntly:

> Bipartisanship in foreign policy is ideal for the Executive because you cannot run this damned country any other way except by fixing the whole organization so it doesn't work the way it's supposed to work. Now the only way to do that is to say politics stops at the seaboard – and anyone who denies that postulate is a son-of-a-bitch or a crook and not a true patriot. Now, if people will swallow that then you're off to the races'.
>
> (Rourke, 1983, p. 81).

For all the cynical exploitation of bipartisanship, however, there was real substance to the new foreign policy consensus: a shared fear of communism, the perception of a

---

Box 5.3

Politics and the postwar foreign policy consensus

'The myth of the postwar bipartisan consensus is that the same lightning struck Democratic and Republican statesmen at the same time, causing them to put aside partisan quarrels in the face of an overwhelming external threat. What actually happened is less miraculous but more interesting. In return for a share of the credit key Republican leaders offered qualified support for the critical provisions of the foreign policy consensus taking shape within the Truman administration. In turn the rhetoric of the new foreign policy was carefully crafted to please not only Republican politicians whose votes were needed on foreign aid, loans and military appropriations, but also to win over their constituents to the Democratic Party in the 1948 election.'

Source: Barnet, 1990, p. 272

---

global threat and the determination to contain Soviet expansion. Indeed, where significant disagreements over foreign policy occurred, they were usually provoked by charges that measures against communism were too mild, lenient or limited. Even here, however, consensus often eventually triumphed. Thus, when out of office in the early 1950s, some Republicans, like the future secretary of state John Foster Dulles, wanted the country to go beyond containment and to 'roll back' communism from the gains it had already made in Europe and Asia. Once in office under Eisenhower, however, the Republicans practised containment: thus, they made no attempt to roll back communism in North Korea, nor would they come to the aid of Hungary in 1956 when the Soviet army crushed a popular uprising.

A consensus developed behind containment because roll-back was simply unfeasible in the nuclear age. Containment, therefore, met a felt need to combat communism vigorously without embarking upon a 'hot war' with the Soviet Union. In short, there was no credible alternative to containment, for if roll-back was too dangerous, both isolationism and appeasement of the Soviet Union seemed incapable of defending America's interests.

There was, however, still one further element that promoted and sustained the postwar foreign policy consensus: the crude suppression of dissenting voices and views.

McCarthyism

The infamous postwar 'witch-hunt' against alleged communist subversion in the United States is often given the blanket label of McCarthyism. The eponymous junior senator from Wisconsin rampaged through American politics from 1950 to 1954, making reckless and unsubstantiated accusations of disloyalty. While he ruined the lives and careers of thousands of innocent Americans, not once did he uncover any real spies or examples of espionage. At his peak, Joe McCarthy held the nation in thrall with his spectacular displays of macho interrogation of 'witnesses'; he also intimidated his fellow politicians to the point where few were openly willing to challenge either his methods or his mendacity. Even presidential candidate Eisenhower was anxious not to offend McCarthy. He dropped approving references to his great military friend and statesman General George C. Marshall from his 1952 campaign speeches after McCarthy had questioned Marshall's patriotism.

For all his notoriety and power, however, McCarthy was not the instigator of the anticommunist hysteria of the 1940s and 1950s. He merely exploited to great personal advantage a collective paranoia that others had already brought to the fore by the time he rose to prominence in 1950. For example, the House Un-American Activities Committee (HUAC) had begun its work as a temporary committee of the House of Representatives in 1938, and had been made a permanent standing committee in 1945.

HUAC achieved considerable publicity in the immediate postwar years by conducting investigations into the influence of communists and communist sympathisers – dubbed fellow travellers or pinkos – in a variety of professions. Most profitably, HUAC went to Hollywood to investigate communist influence in the movie industry: there were indeed some communists and former communist actors, directors and screenwriters but there was no evidence of any subversive activity. In fact, the main purpose of HUAC's trips to Hollywood was to gain valuable publicity for the committee's members, through the televised hearings featuring Hollywood stars as 'witnesses' and as they posed for the photographers with the idols of the silver screen.

There was actually little evidence of communist subversion generally in the United States at that time. Certainly it was revealed in 1950 that a British scientist, Klaus Fuchs, had passed atomic secrets to the Soviets when he had worked on the bomb project in Los Alamos during the war, and that he had been abetted by members of the American Communist party, including Julius and Ethel Rosenberg, who were later executed. Beyond that, however, there was little of substance. Ironically, this was demonstrated by the enormous publicity given to relatively insignificant cases. For example, Richard Nixon launched his national political career by using his seat on HUAC to pursue Alger Hiss, a former State Department official who had attended the Yalta conference. Hiss was accused by Whittaker Chambers, a former communist giving evidence to HUAC, of being a member of the Communist party in the 1930s and a spy. Hiss himself appeared before HUAC to deny the allegations, whereupon he was indicted for perjury. His first trial in 1949 ended in a hung jury; but after a second trial in 1950, he was convicted. The evidence against Hiss was, at best, flimsy and circumstantial, and he was never indicted, let alone convicted, for espionage. Nevertheless, a man hesitantly convicted for lying to a congressional committee became the object of a national drama and a debate which continues even to this day. Such was the power of the anticommunist paranoia in the United States in the postwar years to transform a non-event into headline news.

What, then, really lay behind 'the Great Fear'? (Caute, 1978). The Communist party had never been strong in the United States, even in the 1930s. No rational person could conceivably consider it a threat of such magnitude as to justify mass public hysteria. Historians have suggested a variety of explanations, some of which go deep into the psyche of a nation troubled by sudden changes in its domestic and international environment.

Earl Latham, however, suggests a more prosaic, political explanation. At heart, anti-communism was a weapon employed by conservatives to suppress liberal and radical thought. It was used by Republicans to attack Democrats, and by conservative Democrats to attack liberal elements of their own party coalition. If communist subversion was the rallying cry, the real target was the New Deal. Whether it was Alger Hiss, Dean Acheson or Harry Truman himself; whether it was labour unions, the State Department or the Office of Price Administration; whether it was schoolteachers, screenwriters or state employees, the aim and the effect was to put New Deal liberalism on the defensive and its more radical elements beyond the pale.

As we saw above, the concrete policies of the New Deal were too popular to be assailed directly. However, indirect attack through allegations of red or pink sympathies had the desired effect in two most important respects. First, in 1952 the Republicans recaptured both the White House and the Congress after twenty-two years of almost complete Democratic ascendancy. Secondly, the anticommunist witch-hunt reinforced both the domestic and foreign policy aspects of the postwar consensus. The mere suspicion of disloyalty, or even of harbouring un-American ideas, was often enough to lose people their job, their passport and their friends. Criticism from the left of governmental policy was grounds for suspicion, especially if it coincided with 'the communist line'. Thus, to argue on economic grounds for a reduction in the budget of the Voice of America (VOA) was enough to raise Senator McCarthy's suspicions, since the Kremlin would also like to see VOA broadcasts curtailed.

In the 1940s and 1950s, then, the United States experienced a domestic and foreign policy consensus that had both natural and contrived roots. Unprecedented and widespread prosperity bred both contentment and anxiety that it might all end, and naturally enough led to support for the status quo. Soviet expansion into eastern Europe after the war, combined with the weakness of western Europe, led to unsurprising agreement in many quarters on the need for 'containment'; and although no artificial reinforcement was needed, McCarthyism bolted these bases of the postwar consensus into place by eliminating the contemplation of alternatives.

The existence of such a consensus does not mean that there was no political debate in the United States in the postwar years, or that the two main parties did not compete vigorously, but politics was confined within a narrow and rigid framework. If the more liberal Democratic party strove to prove that it was not 'soft on communism', the Republicans had to demonstrate that they were not unsympathetic to the less fortunate in America. In that sense, there was a considerable degree of 'me-tooism' in both parties. This playing to the consensus continued into the 1960s. Around the middle of that decade, however, the fundamental weaknesses inherent in the domestic and foreign policy consensus forced their way to the surface of American politics with dramatic and enduring consequences.

The Kennedy/Johnson years

The administrations of John F. Kennedy and Lyndon B. Johnson (1961–69) witnessed both the apogee of the postwar consensus and the developments which led to its demise. This is true for both domestic and foreign policy.

In the first half of the 1960s, the consensus that the federal government could ensure economic growth and social justice was manifested in ambitious new policies. President Kennedy, for example, overcame the cautious economic orthodoxies of the business community, as he pioneered the 'new economics'. This involved, for example, the implementation of tax cuts and budget deficits to stimulate economic growth, even when there was no recession to justify what were previously considered emergency measures (Morgan, 1994, pp. 35–40). More generally, the 'new economics' symbolised the belief that the government now had the knowledge and power to iron out the traditional ups and downs of the business cycle, and ensure steady, continuous expansion and prosperity.

Moreover, the Johnson administration in particular had ambitions to produce not just a wealthier America, but a Great Society (see Box 5.4). This was a vision of an America in which there was no poverty, squalor, ignorance, fear or hatred, and where the quality of life opened the door for all Americans to fulfil their human potential. The rhetoric of the vision far outstripped the practical implementation. Nevertheless, an impressive array of legislation was enacted. In 1964, the self-styled 'War on Poverty' was launched through the passage of the Economic Opportunity Act: this involved a number of programmes designed to improve the education, training and job opportunities of the poor. Later measures included Medicare and Medicaid, designed to improve medical provision for the aged and the poor, respectively. Welfare programmes like Social Security and Aid to Families with Dependent Children (AFDC) were greatly expanded to provide the poor with a minimal standard of living, and there were measures to improve housing and the environment in the run-down inner cities.

The extent to which the War on Poverty and the Great Society achieved their goals, or even how seriously the Johnson administration took them in terms of financial provision, are matters which are still hotly disputed. Yet regardless of the successes or failures, it is important to recognise that there was a political consensus in the United States at this time that deemed such measures desirable and feasible. This was indicated by the landslide presidential election victory of Johnson over the arch-conservative Barry Goldwater in 1964. While it would be a mistake to interpret this victory as evidence of popular enthusiasm for the Great Society, it did at least demonstrate that Americans were far more comfortable with the idea of extending the philosophy of New Deal liberalism than they were with the prospect of its demise.

The domestic political consensus of the early 1960s also encompassed that historically most divisive of American issues, race relations. Outside of the south, there was a growing recognition among whites that full political and legal equality for black Americans was long overdue. In the 1950s, the civil rights movement had gathered great momentum, as it campaigned to end the racial segregation and discrimination that was endemic in the south and some border states. However, despite winning the moral argument, and having achieved a symbolic victory with the Supreme Court's 1954 decision declaring school segregation unconstitutional, there had been no legislation with the muscle to turn theoretical rights into practical realities. As Kennedy took office, most southern schools were still segregated, and so too were restaurants,

Box 5.4

Lyndon B. Johnson and the Great Society

'For a century we labored to settle and to subdue a continent. For half a century we called upon unbounded invention and untiring industry to create an order of plenty for all our people.

The challenge of the next half century is whether we have the wisdom to use that wealth to enrich and elevate our national life, and to advance the quality of our American civilization.

… For in your time we have the opportunity to move not only toward the rich society and the powerful society, but upward to the Great Society.

The Great Society rests on abundance and liberty for all. It demands an end to poverty and racial injustice, to which we are totally committed in our time. But that is just the beginning.

The Great Society is a place where every child can find knowledge to enrich his mind and to enlarge his talents. It is a place where leisure is a welcome chance to build and reflect, not a feared cause of boredom and restlessness. It is a place where the city of man serves not only the needs of the body and the demands of commerce but the desire for beauty and the hunger for community.

It is a place where man can renew contact with nature. It is a place which honours creation for its own sake and for what it adds to the understanding of the race. It is a place where men are more concerned with the quality of their goals than the quantity of their goods.

But most of all, the Great Society is not a safe harbor, a resting place, a final objective, a finished work. It is a challenge constantly renewed, beckoning us toward a destiny where the meaning of our lives matches the marvellous products of our labor.'

(President Lyndon B. Johnson, Remarks to the Graduating Class, the University of Michigan, 22 May 1964, often referred to as the Great Society Speech)

'We stand at the edge of the greatest era in the life of any nation. For the first time in world history, we have the abundance and the ability to free every man from hopeless want, and to free every person to find fulfilment in the works of his mind or the labor of his hands.

Even the greatest of all past civilizations existed on the exploitation of the misery of the many.

This nation, this people, this generation, has man's first chance to create a Great Society: a society of success without squalor, beauty without barrenness, works of genius without the wretchedness of poverty. We can open the doors of learning. We can open the doors of fruitful labor and rewarding leisure, of open opportunity and close community – not just to the privileged few, but to everyone.'

(President Lyndon B. Johnson, fundraising dinner, Detroit, 26 June 1964)

hotels, swimming pools, transportation and other public facilities. In addition, despite having been guaranteed the vote by the Fifteenth Amendment in 1870, most southern blacks were still unable to exercise this basic political right.

One of the main obstacles to effective federal legislation on civil rights had always been the power of the white south in presidential elections and in Congress. Even liberals such as Kennedy were fearful of offending the white south by pushing meaningful reform. In 1964, however, a combination of factors brought about a consensus on the need for action that overwhelmed southern resistance. The most important of these was the moral and political pressures brought to bear by the civil rights movement. This forced Kennedy to introduce a major civil rights bill into Congress in 1963. The bill was subjected to the usual blocking tactics by southern members, but the emotional aftermath of the assassination of President Kennedy in Dallas enabled President Johnson to obtain its passage.

The Civil Rights Act of 1964 demolished the legal edifice of racial discrimination and provided the basis for later remedial measures under the banner of 'affirmative action'. The following year, Congress passed the Voting Rights Act which obliged southern states to cease their discrimination against black voters.

It is clear, then, that the period from 1961 to 1965 saw a consensus behind the most ambitious programme of federal government responsibility and action in the history of the United States. While there were, of course, many Americans who deplored these developments, most were willing to give the federal government its head in attempting to solve the economic, social and political problems that remained. Behind the consensus, then, lay not only a basic contentment, but also optimism and confidence that things could get better still. In a very short time, however, both the mood and the consensus were to be shattered.

The end of the postwar consensus

The collapse of the postwar consensus is a complex phenomenon, but on both the domestic and foreign policy fronts, it involved a sharp and sometimes radical challenge to traditionalism. The roots of the collapse lie partly in the perceived policy failures of the 1960s and partly in fundamental socio-economic changes that have been transforming the United States from an industrial to a postindustrial society.

We examine some of these issues in other chapters. Thus, in Chapter 22, we analyse the role of the failure in Vietnam in ending the consensus behind containment and calling into question the efficacy and morality of American military power. In Chapter 20 we see how the consensus underpinning the civil rights movement collapsed amid ghetto riots and the introduction of affirmative action policies. And in Chapter 7, we examine the rise of feminism, its impact upon traditional gender relations and the consequent demand for new policies to further gender equality.

As we shall see in Chapter 6, however, these developments themselves owed much to the changing socio-economic structure of the United States. The transformation from an industrial to a postindustrial economy and society, and later the impact of globalisation upon the economy, brought about an era of reduced opportunity for many Americans. It also created a new division between those well educated Americans who could easily adapt and prosper in the new economic context, while lesser educated Americans tied to 'old' industries struggled to maintain their living standards. Unsurprisingly, this division was reflected in the realm of policy, both social and economic. The successful 'new class' of postindustrial society tended to favour policies which stressed the autonomy of individuals from governmental and societal control, while those who were losing out tended to look to the recent past as a moral and social compass.

Of course, this is an oversimplified picture. However, it serves to illustrate the deep-lying strains that have been present in American society since the 1960s. Just as stability, prosperity and consensus left their mark upon the political process of the immediate postwar decades, so too have fundamental change, economic difficulty and lack of consensus affected the conduct of politics in significant ways.

Postindustrial politics

The government and politics of the United States today are characterised by a lack of faith in government and an inability to produce a new consensus to replace the old one. One obvious manifestation of the latter is the tendency towards 'divided government' since 1968, where one party captures the White House but cannot gain control of Congress. There has been great speculation on the exact causes of divided government, but it seems that the inability of either party to unite the country around a political philosophy or programme encourages the electorate to ensure that neither of them exercises much control.

The most distinctive change of the postindustrial political era, however, is the loss of faith in government. Both liberals and conservatives became critical of many policies in the 1960s and 1970s, as the old centre-ground of politics became unacceptable to both. Precisely because government was accorded so much of the blame for policy failure, the capacity of government to solve problems is in doubt for most Americans. The tables in Box 5.5 indicate just how different this is from the days of the postwar consensus, when government was trusted and respected by the great majority of Americans.

The postwar consensus and the prosperity that underpinned it seem like a lost 'golden age' today. Such nostalgia probably involves a mistaken belief that things were 'simple' in the postwar halcyon years: whatever problems there were could be solved by government on the basis of compromise and consensus. At the end of the twentieth century, however, it is impossible for most Americans to believe either that problems have simple solutions or, therefore, that the federal government and the political process can be relied upon to devise satisfactory policies. In other words, one major casualty of the breakdown in the postwar consensus is faith in government and politics.

Box 5.5

Public attitudes towards government

Question: Is the federal government too powerful?

1941

	Yes	No	Don't know
Do you think there is too much power in the hands of the government in Washington?	32%	56%	12%

1960

	Yes	No	Don't know
Do the activities of the national government tend to improve conditions in this country?	78%	22%	–

1996

	Yes	No	Don't know
Is government trying to do too much in solving national problems?	62%	28%	10%

Question: How much of the time do you think you can trust the government to do what is right – just about always, most of the time, or only some of the time?

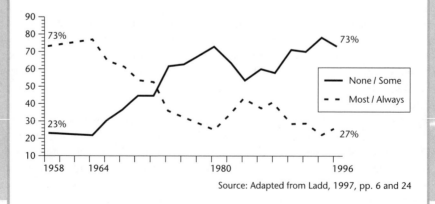

Source: Adapted from Ladd, 1997, pp. 6 and 24

Summary

The postwar consensus in the United States was based on a widely shared set of both fears and hopes. The major fears were of a return to economic depression and communist expansions. The optimism was based upon America's economic and military pre-eminence. Even when problems such as poverty and race discrimination came to the fore, there was a 'can do' attitude that suggested that solutions could be found. All this added up to a reasonably contented, if conformist, society that was willing to entrust unprecedented power to the federal government in peacetime. In turn, the political process worked satisfactorily, with bipartisan agreement on the fundamentals of both domestic and foreign policy. The consensus, however, lasted but a couple of decades, overtaken by structural change at both national and international level. In its wake emerged a political process far more fractured and less inclined to optimism and grand visions.

References

Alexander, C., 1975, *Holding the Line: The Eisenhower era, 1952–61* (Bloomington: Indiana University Press)

Barnet, R., 1990, *The Rockets' Red Glare: When America goes to war* (New York: Simon & Schuster)

Caute, D., 1978, *The Great Fear* (London: Secker & Warburg)

Degler, C., 1975, *Affluence and Anxiety: America since 1945*, (2nd edn, Glenview: Scott, Foresman)

Diggins, J., 1988, *The Proud Decades: America in war and peace, 1941–1960* (New York: Norton)

Dubofsky, M. and Theoharis, A., 1983, *Imperial Democracy: The United States since 1945* (Hemel Hempstead: Prentice Hall)

Ladd, E., 1997, '1996 vote: the "No Majority" realignment continues', *Political Science Quarterly*, vol. 112, pp. 1–28

Leuchtenburg, W., 1983, *A Troubled Feast: American society since 1945*, (rev. edn, Boston: Little, Brown)

Melanson, R., 1991, *Reconstructing Consensus: American foreign policy since the Vietnam War* (New York: St Martin's Press)

Morgan, I., 1994, *Beyond the Liberal Consensus: A political history of the United States since 1965* (London: Hurst)

Rourke, J., 1983, *Congress and the Presidency in US Foreign Policymaking: A study of interaction and influence, 1945–1982* (Boulder: Westview)

6

Economy and society

The American economy is a vital factor in American politics. Most obviously, the state of the economy goes a long way to defining the political agenda and the range of possible policy choices in relation to both problems and opportunities. Equally important, however, is that the 'American dream' is premised upon the ability of American capitalism to generate ever more wealth to satisfy the aspirations of an ambitious people. In this chapter, therefore, we examine the current state of the American economy and the anxieties that have arisen as a result of its perceived weaknesses.

The United States is probably the greatest economic success story in human history. Measured in terms of economic production and personal wealth, the United States transformed itself in the nineteenth century from an economic minnow into an agrarian and industrial superpower. Already in the 1920s, Americans could experience a level of material consumption undreamt of by earlier civilisations and generations, and for much of the twentieth century, the United States was the unchallenged leader of the world economy.

To be sure, this economic success was in part based upon appalling and ruthless practices such as slavery and harsh exploitation of wage labourers. Moreover, the United States has experienced some severe economic recessions and, of course, the Great Depression of the 1930s. Nevertheless, for the successive generations of immigrants who went to America to pursue 'life, liberty, and happiness', the economic system gave them the opportunity to rise far above the material station of their counterparts in Europe and elsewhere. Thus the American economy always seemed to offer the hope – and usually the reality – that each generation of Americans would be richer than the last. American capitalism appeared to be infinitely capable of expansion, of producing ever higher standards of living and of dominating the global economy.

This was never more true than in the years following the Second World War. With economic rivals like Germany, Japan and Great Britain exhausted, if not destroyed, by the war, the United States built upon superior technological and managerial methods developed before the war to become peerless in economic power. As a result, the United States was virtually able to write the rules of international economic trade: for only the United States had the capacity and the will to become the engine that would drive the world's economy, thereby bringing new life to the economies of war-torn Europe and Asia. The greatest symbol of American economic predominance was the almighty dollar, which the Bretton Woods agreement of 1944 made as good as gold for the purposes of international exchange.

At home, more and more Americans enjoyed a rapidly improving standard of living that was the envy of the rest of the world (see Chapter 5). While the United States certainly exported goods to the rest of the world, it was the vast, rich domestic market of consumers that was the focus of American economic output. The American economy used most of the world's raw materials and produced most of the world's goods – and the American population consumed most of those resources and goods.

The success of postwar American capitalism was the foundation stone of a political consensus that lasted for twenty-five years. Most Americans were content with their political system and their government and were prepared to accept the expenditure of vast sums of money on the nation's military capacity in order to defend capitalism and democracy. When problems were 'discovered' at home – race discrimination in the 1950s and poverty in the 1960s – the economy was sufficiently productive to allow the government to fund relatively ambitious attempts to solve them. As long as the majority could see themselves getting better off in their own and in their children's lifetime, Americans avoided serious internal dispute and gave the government a free hand within the limits of the consensus. In short, for most Americans, a successful economy made for a successful political system.

This picture of the American economy, still valid in the mid-1960s, no longer holds true. The final quarter of the twentieth century has seen the American economy succumb to a series of major problems that have long been familiar to other nations: high unemployment, low productivity growth, inflation and a loss of market share to rival nations. While the1990s witnessed a marked improvement in America's economic prospects, there remain some worrying signs and some stubborn weaknesses. As a result, Americans are having to come to terms with a loss of economic dominance and the need to adapt traditional economic principles and practices to a more competitive and global economy. This in turn has heightened political tensions and made political debate more fractious. For the first time since the Great Depression, many Americans have been learning to live with the reality of tight economic restraints and lowered expectations of the future.

Relative decline

In broad terms, the United States has been suffering what is called 'relative decline'. This means, for example, that although the American economy has continued to grow, it has been doing so at a slower rate than its main economic competitors, especially Japan and Germany.

The analogy of a long distance race helps to clarify the picture. In 1960, the United

States held a huge lead over the other competitors. Since then, however, the field has been closing in on the leader. At first unaware of what was going on behind, the United States continued to dawdle complacently. When Americans finally heard footsteps right behind them, it proved too difficult to accelerate and Japan and West Germany swept past. Worse still, other 'Asian Tiger' nations and members of the European Union (EU) were also bearing down on the country. Within a relatively short period, the United States had not only lost the lead, it was struggling to hold its own with competitors from the second and third ranks of nations. Once assured of the gold medal, the United States seemed in danger of being relegated to the also-rans.

Relative decline: the statistics

Economic performance can be measured in numerous ways and even experts often disagree about which statistics give the truest picture of the American economy. Nevertheless, the relative economic decline of the United States since 1960 is beyond serious dispute. The official government figures on perhaps the most important indicator, US economic productivity, are presented in Box 6.1. They show that the growth rate of US manufacturing productivity (output per hour) was already below that of its main competitors in the otherwise satisfactory period 1960–73. Following the huge oil price increase of 1973, however, US productivity growth dipped to a very poor annual rate of 1.7 per cent for the rest of the decade.

The situation deteriorated significantly in the 1980s, with an average annual figure of just 1.2 per cent. This only permits the US standard of living to double every 58 years, compared with every 21 years in the period 1947–67, when annual productivity growth averaged 3.3 per cent (Thurow, 1994, p. 165). Moreover, official government statistics suggest little improvement in productivity growth in the first half of the 1990s, with the annual rate around 1 per cent. However, there is considerable technical doubt about these statistics and they may not reflect very accurately the real

---

Box 6.1

US economic productivity in manufacturing in relation to selected other nations, 1960–80

Annual percentage change

	United States	Japan	France	Germany	UK
1960–80	2.7	9.4	5.6	5.4	3.6
1960–73	3.0	10.7	6.0	5.5	4.3
1973–80	1.7	6.8	4.9	4.8	1.9

Source: Thompson, 1994, p. 121

performance of the US economy (*The Economist*, 21 June 1997, p. 49). Certainly, as we shall see below, other economic indicators suggest the US economy recovered well in the 1990s.

Nevertheless, the broad picture over the past thirty years is clear enough: American productivity growth has fallen both in absolute terms and relative to many of its major competitors. This in its turn has sparked a political crisis, as radically different recovery plans have been proposed.

The role of government

If there is widespread recognition that US productivity has fallen to unacceptable levels compared with that of other nations, there is no agreement on either the causes or the solutions. Generally speaking, conservatives believe that the United States has lost its way because it has abandoned its traditional values and practices. On the economic front, they accuse the federal government of too much meddling in the free market. They believe that entrepreneurs have been saddled with regulations and obligations towards their workforce and the public that cause inefficiencies in their businesses.

They also reject the Keynesian economic policy of successive administrations from the 1930s to the 1970s, which involved the federal government in stimulating and managing consumer demand so as to produce constant economic growth and full employment. Instead, they advocate 'supply-side economics', which emphasises reducing the costs – including wages and taxation – of producing goods and services. At the risk of oversimplification, conservatives believe that the 'golden age' of American economic success was based on free market capitalism and minimal government involvement; a return to those practices should therefore involve a return to American economic pre-eminence.

On the liberal side of politics, advocates of old-style Keynesianism are few and far between. Rather, they have been replaced by those who believe that the German and Japanese models of close governmental co-operation with business is the key to future economic progress in the United States. After all, they reason, if Japan and Germany have produced their own economic miracles and overtaken the United States in many respects, then logic suggests they have something to teach Americans. Supporters of their view believe that government must be active in producing an economic infrastructure, a skilled and educated workforce and a socially just society.

These different tendencies lead to radically different policies, both domestic and foreign. For example, those who emphasise a return to free market economics want to apply pressure to foreign governments to reduce the support they give to their businesses and thus to compete with American businesses on a 'level playing-field'. At home, they also believe that free markets in employment, health care and education are likely to produce more effective results than government programmes and regulation.

Those on the liberal-left of politics also agree on the need for level playing-fields, particularly in the case of trade with Japan. However, they also believe that American business needs the active support of its government abroad if it is to survive even on a level playing-field. At home, they emphasise the need for an inclusive and fair society as a prerequisite for a thriving, well-motivated workforce and economy. Unlike conservatives who believe that government is part of the problem, liberals believe that government is part of the solution.

Research and development

As well as the role of government in the economy, there would seem to be other causes of American decline. One is the relatively low level of finance invested in research and development (R&D) in the United States, particularly when it comes to non-military goods and manufacturing processes. American investors tend to take a more short-term approach than their Japanese or German counterparts and demand quick rewards in profits and share dividends. They are less likely to invest large sums in long-term projects which for many years may yield only modest returns.

Moreover, it is argued that Americans have funded insufficient research into manu-facturing processes, as opposed to product development. This has meant that while the United States has continued to invent innovative and popular products, other nations have been able to produce these goods more cheaply and increase their share of the market at the expense of the United States.

Consumption and savings

It has also been pointed out that ordinary Americans also have a tendency towards short-term gratification, which means there is a far greater emphasis upon consuming goods and services than on saving money. These lower savings levels mean lower investment levels.

Unemployment

Whatever the causes of America's recent low productivity growth, the phenomenon has produced economic difficulty in a variety of forms. Box 6.2, for example, shows unemployment levels in recent decades.

Even those in work, however, are often worse off than they were, for while the American economy has continued to grow and create new jobs, the benefits have been made available only to a minority of employees. Thus between 1973 and 1990, the American economy grew by 28 per cent, yet the real hourly wage for non-supervisory workers (about two-thirds of all employees) actually fell by 12 per cent and real weekly wages fell by 18 per cent (Thurow, 1994, p. 53). This means, of course, that about one-third of Americans are far better off than they were in the 1970s, even as a majority of their compatriots have to cope with a fall in their living standards.

The reasons for this growing gap between the incomes of the well-off minority and the losing majority are mainly to be found in two major developments in the American economy: postindustrialism and globalisation.

Box 6.2

US unemployment levels in comparison with selected nations, 1975–96

Annual percentages

	United States	Japan	France	Germany	UK
1975	8.5	1.9	4.2	3.4	4.6
1980	7.1	2.0	6.5	2.8	7.0
1985	7.2	2.6	10.5	7.2	11.2
1990	5.6	2.1	9.1	5.0	7.0
1996	5.4	3.4	12.6	7.2	8.3

Source: US Bureau of Labor Statistics, July 1997

Postindustrialism

The United States has been transformed in recent decades into a postindustrial economy and society. Whereas an industrial economy relies mainly on the extraction and processing of raw materials, a postindustrial economic system centres upon the provision of services. For example, instead of the predominance of coal and steel production, or the manufacture of relatively simple goods, the emphasis is upon telecommunications, financial services or high value-added products such as pharmaceuticals or computers. By 1980, at least two-thirds of all American employees were working in the service sector of the economy, as opposed to the manufacturing sector (Thompson, 1994, p. 106).

A postindustrial economy requires a more educated workforce than an industrial economy. Unsurprisingly therefore, it is those Americans with the most education and skills who have fared well in the past twenty years, while those without college education have fared worst. Box 6.3 shows that the American workforce has become much better educated in recent years, with well over half now having had some college education. Moreover Box 6.4 shows not only that the likelihood of being unemployed is much greater the less education you have, but also the gap between the employability of the least and most educated Americans has grown in recent decades. This reflects the decrease in the number of unskilled jobs in the American economy.

Box 6.3

Composition of the workforce by educational attainment, 1970–95

Percentages

	Less than high school diploma	High school graduate	Some college	Graduate
1970	36.1	38.1	11.8	14.1
1980	20.6	39.8	17.6	22.0
1990	13.4	39.5	20.7	26.4
1995	10.8	33.1	27.8	28.3

Source: US Bureau of the Census, 1996, p. 395

Box 6.4

Percentage unemployment by educational attainment, 1970–95

	Less than high school diploma	High school graduate	Some college	Graduate
	%	%	%	%
1970	4.6	2.9	2.9	1.3
1980	8.4	5.1	4.3	1.9
1990	9.6	4.9	3.7	1.9
1995	10.0	5.2	4.5	2.5

Source: US Bureau of the Census, 1996, p. 415

Globalisation

Along with postindustrialism has come the globalisation of the American economy (see Box 6.5). In 1960, the United States had few serious rivals as a producer of goods that the rest of the world, or indeed Americans, wanted. Today, however, the United States must compete both at home and abroad with an ever increasing range of rivals. Included in these are low-wage economies which specialise in producing industrial

---

Box 6.5

The North American Free Trade Agreement 1993

The North American Free Trade Agreement (NAFTA) treaty was negotiated by President George Bush. It formed a free trading block of the United States, Canada and Mexico. It eliminated high tariffs on goods traded between the three nations and allowed each to have access to the others' energy sources at prices paid by home companies. For those who supported it – including President Clinton, most Republicans and most leaders of big business – it was a timely move in the process of globalising the economy and emulating the expansion of the European Union as a free trade bloc. American companies would benefit by being able to export more advanced and high value goods and services to Mexico and Canada. In due course, other nations in the western hemisphere might join NAFTA.

Opponents of the treaty feared it would entail the loss of blue-collar jobs to companies in Mexico. Companies operating there could produce some kinds of goods – textiles and steel, for example – much more cheaply than those operating in the United States, for not only were wages much lower, but companies were not required to meet American standards on matters such as workers' health and safety and environmental protection. Thus, billionaire businessman and independent presidential candidate H. Ross Perot predicted that NAFTA would cause 'a great sucking sound' as thousands of American jobs were drawn to Mexico. Unsurprisingly, many union leaders and their political allies in the Democratic party also opposed the treaty. When President Clinton asked for congressional approval of NAFTA, one of his leading opponents was the then House majority leader, and fellow Democrat, Dick Gephardt.

In many ways, the debate over NAFTA epitomised the divisions in the economy and in politics caused by postindustrialism and globalisation.

---

goods. This means that Americans still working in unskilled or semi-skilled jobs in the industrial sector find themselves in competition with Korean or Indian employees who are willing to work for much lower wages.

Globalisation is thus forcing a levelling down of American industrial wages and the wages of the underskilled in general. This transformation of the economy heralds the end of the American dream for many, since even an expanding economy no longer promises a higher standard of living. As one analyst put it:

In an isolated national economy, President Kennedy could talk in 1960 about how a rising economic tide would raise all boats. In an American economy floating in a world economy, his famous dictum no longer holds. The general economic tides [the per capita GNP] have been rising, but a majority of the boats [individual wages] have been sinking.

(Thurow, 1994, p. 53)

The twin deficits

Two of the greatest indicators of American economic decline are the trade and the budget deficits.

The balance of trade deficit

The balance of trade is the difference between the value of what a country exports and what it imports. As befits the world's leading economy, the United States had a balance of trade surplus every year from 1893 to 1971, when its first deficit of the twentieth century occurred. The surplus was then restored for a decade, but then virtually collapsed after 1983 (Thompson, 1994, p. 112). In the twelve months ending June 1997, the United States trade deficit had reached a staggering $197.9 billion. This contrasts, for example, with a Japanese trade surplus of $86.1 billion and a German surplus of $67.7 billion (OECD Economic Indicators, *The Economist*, 16 August 1997, p. 97).

Box 6.6

The budget deficit, selected years, 1950–96

$million

	Deficit/surplus
1950	−3,119
1960	+301
1970	−2,842
1975	−53,242
1980	−73,835
1982	−127,989
1985	−252,748
1990	−221,194
1991	−269,359
1992	−290,403
1993	−255,140
1994	−203,104
1995	−163,920
1996	−107,268
1997	−115,000 (est.)
2001	−36,141 (est.)
2002	+16,969 (est.)

Sources: US Bureau of the Census, 1996, p. 330; *Washington Post*, 6 February 1997

The budget deficit

There have been few more politically contentious issues in recent years than what to do about the budget deficit. As Box 6.6 shows, the United States is long used to such a deficit, but in the 1980s and again in the early 1990s it appeared to be spiralling out of control.

In one sense, the deficit was not as disastrous as many thought. For example, measured as a percentage of gross domestic product (GDP), the deficit in 1995 was actually somewhat lower (2.3 per cent) than that in 1975 (3.5 per cent). Indeed, for a while politicians were content to await a new spurt of economic growth and tax revenues to bring things back to manageable proportions.

The politics of the budget

The policies of the Reagan administration turned the deficit into a major political issue which deeply divided the two main parties. Generally speaking, Republicans wanted to increase spending on defence, cut taxation and compensate for these measures by reducing expenditure on social welfare and other domestic programmes. Democrats, on the other hand, refused to cut those domestic programmes significantly and, since they controlled the House of Representatives, they could not be ignored. Ultimately, both Democrats and Republicans got much of what they wanted, but the result was that the budget deficit went into orbit (see Box 6.7).

Equally important was the fact that for economic conservatives, a balanced budget became an article of political faith. The perceived need to spend no more than the government received in revenue transcended economics and became almost a moral crusade for some. It was for them yet another symbol of the nation's abandonment of what were believed to be sound, traditional economic principles.

Congress did pass the Balanced Budget and Emergency Deficit Control Act of 1985 (the Gramm–Rudman–Hollings Act), which empowered the Comptroller General to make necessary cuts in budget legislation where the politicians could not come to an agreement. This, however, was declared unconstitutional by the Supreme Court.

Virtually every year since then has witnessed a major political battle over the budget between a president and Congress controlled by different parties. In some years, such as 1995, no budget at all was passed in time to prevent a shutdown of government offices due to a lack of funding. Meanwhile, Republicans and some conservative Democrats turned to an effort to pass a balanced budget amendment to the Constitution. This came within a whisker of being passed in March 1997, when the Senate voted 66 to 34 in favour – just one vote short of the required two-thirds majority. The House of Representatives had voted overwhelmingly for the amendment in the previous Congress and would certainly have done so again.

This failure, however, may turn out to be of little significance. For in August 1997, President Clinton signed budget bills that promised to eliminate the deficit altogether by 2002. Clinton heralded the legislation as a milestone for the nation and a symbol of America's ability to restore its economic strength:

Box 6.7

The budget deficit controversy

The federal budget has been balanced only eight times since 1930, most recently in 1969. Since 1970 the US has operated its longest continuous sequence of unbalanced budgets, with deficits well in excess of $100 billion – a hitherto unprecedented level – the norm in the 1980s and 1990s. Many economists believe that mushrooming deficits: (1) undermined national saving; (2) led to artificially high interest rates which hurt US competitiveness in world trade; (3) raised the national debt/GNP ratio towards potentially harmful levels; and (4) made interest repayment on the national debt the second largest item in the federal budget, behind only social security, thereby taking funds away from other programmes, especially public infrastructure investment.

Democrats and Republicans have long agreed about the need to eliminate the deficit but not about the means. Determined to preserve the Reaganite agenda of low taxes and strong defence, Republicans favoured domestic spending retrenchment. True to the New Deal legacy, most Democrats preferred to raise taxes and cut defence. This disagreement has shaped political debate in the post-1980 era of divided party control of government. Deficit reduction plans occasioned controversy in 1990, 1993, and – most acrimoniously – in 1995, when failure to agree a budget on schedule resulted in temporary shutdown of some government offices. Negative public reaction to this episode, which was popularly blamed on House Speaker and right-wing Republican Newt Gingrich, led to more constructive debate between President Clinton and congressional Republican leaders in 1997. This produced a new agreement to eliminate the deficit by 2002 through a combination of spending cuts and tax measures.

This plan also depends on economic growth to deliver sufficient tax revenues to balance spending. If its estimates prove too optimistic, demand for a constitutional amendment to require balanced budgets will probably grow. Congress came close to approving such a proposal in 1982, 1995, 1996 and 1997. Its supporters, mainly Republicans and conservative Democrats, contend that politicians are too beholden to the selfish concerns of voters and interest groups to be trusted to balance the budget and safeguard future generations from a crippling public debt. Critics charge that the amendment is an expression of partisan ideology which does not belong in the Constitution, and its terms would either deprive the government of flexibility to respond to a crisis or contain so many loopholes to cover emergencies as to be an ineffective constraint on spending.

Source: Contributed by Professor Iwan Morgan, London Guildhall University

It wasn't very long ago that some people looked at our nation and saw a setting sun. ... The sun is rising on America again. For too long, it seemed as if America would not be ready for the new century, that we would be too divided, too wedded to old arrangements and ideas ... . After years in which too many people doubted whether our nation would ever come together again ... we set off on a new economic course.

It remains to be seen whether the United States really will eliminate its budget deficit by 2002: much depends upon its future economic performance and therefore its tax revenues. If it does, however, or even comes close to doing so, then it will remove one of the most significant and defining issues of recent decades from the American political agenda.

A debtor nation

One consequence of America's economic decline is that the United States has been transformed from being the world's banker to the world's greatest debtor. From 1915 until 1981, the United States was a net creditor – that is, American-owned assets abroad were greater than foreign-owned assets in the United States (Friedman, 1989, p. 227). By 1992, the United States was a debtor to the tune of $600 billion.

Recovery in the 1990s

Just as there is little doubt that the US economy endured a sustained crisis from 1973 until the early 1990s, so too it is clear that economic prospects improved significantly thereafter. Despite the lack of clarity on productivity, gross domestic output is up, and inflation, unemployment and interest rates are down to acceptable levels (see Box 6.8). The chairman of the Federal Reserve Bank, Alan Greenspan, was confident that the recovery would last at least until 1998. In July 1997, he told Congress that the economy was performing exceptionally well, with strong growth and low inflation. He also speculated cautiously that this improvement could reflect a permanent halt in the

---

Box 6.8

Recovery: the US economy in comparison with selected nations, 1997

Percentages

	GDP % growth	Inflation	Unemployment
United States	3.1	2.3	4.8
Japan	2.6	2.2	3.5
Germany	1.4	1.9	11.5
UK	3.4	3.3	5.5

Source: *The Economist*, 16 August 1997, p. 96

nation's decline:

> We do not know, nor do I suspect can anyone know, whether current developments are part of a once- or twice-in-a-century phenomenon that will carry productivity trends nationally and globally to a new higher track, or whether we are merely observing some unusual variations within the context of an otherwise generally conventional business cycle expansion.
>
> (*Washington Post*, 23 July 1997, p. A1)

The worst of America's economic crisis may well be over. Even if it is, however, the United States faces problems at home and abroad.

The first major fact for Americans today is that they can no longer dominate the world's economy as they once did (see Box 6.9). The European Union is now the biggest single market in the world, and although Germany has experienced economic problems following reunification, it is likely to regain its power in due course. It is the economic performance of Japan, however, which has shown up the American weaknesses in recent decades. The Japanese economy has not been without its own problems, including a recession in the early 1990s and the fall-out from the near-collapse of

---

Box 6.9

The economy and American world leadership

The dominant political and military position of the United States in the cold war era ultimately rested upon its dominant economic position. The question now is whether or to what extent the United States can exercise global political leadership without its economic ascendancy. The United States is unlikely to recapture its unquestioned leadership of the West given its relative economic decline and the end of the cold war. Indeed, it became clear as early as the Vietnam War in the 1960s that the US economy was struggling to pay for the demands of world leadership. Furthermore, the massive defence build-up under President Reagan in the 1980s proved economically incompatible with other goals, such as tax cuts and the maintenance of domestic programmes. It was even suggested that the American 'empire' might be destined to go the way of other great empires before it: into inevitable and continuous decline. Like Rome and Great Britain, the United States could become a victim of 'imperial overstretch', in which the nation's economy could not match its global responsibilities and ambitions (Kennedy, 1988). However, the United States will remain the world's leading nation if only for the simple fact that it has no rivals for this role. The European Union and Japan are powerful economic competitors, but neither is capable of providing political and, especially, military leadership for the world. At present, they lack both the means and the will. As the Gulf War and the Bosnian conflict made clear, world leadership is still nothing if not American leadership – and as was the case with the Gulf War, the United States is ready to demand that its rich allies pay the economic costs that it can no longer afford to bear.

some Asian Tiger economies later in the decade. Nevertheless, like Germany and the European Union, Japan will undoubtedly prove a fierce competitor for the United States in an increasingly global market.

It must be stressed that none of this means that the United States is a weak economy or doomed to continual decline. It does mean that the country will be obliged to lower its expectations. Several other nations are now in a position to oust the United States from foreign markets if it fails to compete in terms of products and costs – and without the discipline once imposed by the cold war, America's capitalist allies are free to compete as ruthlessly with the United States as they can.

The constraints of a new phase of fierce competition will continue to have an impact upon domestic policy options. As noted above, a globalised capitalist economy will tend to equalise wages across nations. For those Americans at or near the bottom of the economic ladder, often underskilled and undereducated, the future may continue to be one in which, rather than realise the American dream, they fall further behind.

The United States is thus haunted by the spectre of greater inequality. Far from being eliminated, as was hoped in the 1960s, poverty may become more entrenched than ever. Moreover, given that African Americans and Hispanic Americans are counted disproportionately among the poor, growing inequality may exacerbate racial tensions.

The United States already has significant problems which it lacks the financial means to solve: the welfare crisis, the health care crisis, the race crisis, the drugs crisis and the crisis of an ageing population. Money alone cannot provide an answer to these problems, but a lack of adequate public funds narrows available options.

On the other hand, it is clear that the prolonged economic decline of recent decades has discredited government 'tax and spend' solutions to social problems. The demise of effortless American economic superiority has also terminated its flirtation with generous welfare-statism. As the United States adapts to living within more restricted economic parameters, Americans seem increasingly to turn back to its traditional ideology of individual responsibility. The decline in economic power, then, entails a concomitant decline in government power in many issue areas.

 ## Summary

Since the early 1970s, the United States has been in relative economic decline. Other nations in Europe and Asia now rival or even surpass the performance of the American economy. The United States has consequently been engaged in a heated debate about what has gone wrong with its economy and how it can be restored to its former glory. Inevitably, this debate has taken centre-stage in American politics, as Americans have argued over taxes, welfare, defence expenditures and the very role of government itself in promoting economic strength. Although the economy now appears to be over the worst, the United States has not and cannot recapture its former economic pre-eminence. While still the most powerful single nation, many Americans are learning to live with lower expectations than previous generations. Moreover, in an era of relatively scarce government resources, the political fight over the distribution of those resources will continue to be fierce.

References

Friedman, B., 1989, *Days of Reckoning: The consequences of American economic policy under Reagan and after* (London: Pan)

Kennedy, P., 1988, *The Rise and Fall of the Great Powers* (London: Unwin Hyman)

Thompson, G., 1994, 'From the long-boom to recession and stagnation? The post-war American economy', in *The United States in the Twentieth Century: Markets*, ed. G. Thompson (London: Hodder & Stoughton)

Thurow, L., 1994, *Head to Head: The coming economic battle among Japan, Europe and America* (London: Nicholas Brealey)

US Bureau of the Census, 1996, *Statistical Abstract of the United States* (116th edn, Washington DC)

7

Gender and American politics

The struggle to achieve equality of the sexes goes back a long way in American history. Yet still today the political system reverberates with impassioned debate over what such equality demands of public policy. In this chapter we shall see that, despite great progress in the achievement of formal political and legal equality, women remain disadvantaged in important respects compared with men. We shall examine different views on why these inequalities persist and how they have dramatically expanded the political agenda in the contemporary United States.

Sex, gender and politics

What exactly do people mean when they talk about 'gender politics'? The key to understanding this issue is to appreciate the distinction between sex and gender. Sex is a biological given: men and women are physically different by nature. Gender, by contrast, refers not to these biological differences, but to the social construction of roles based upon them (Barnard, 1971, p. 16).

Thus, while no one disputes the fact that men are generally physically stronger than women, there are wide disagreements over the political and social consequences of that biological fact. Does it mean, for example, that men and women should be employed in different jobs and, furthermore, that 'men's jobs' should be better paid than 'women's jobs'?

While that particular aspect of gender politics is now less contentious than it once was, there remains a fundamental disagreement over the political, economic and social implications of the reproductive differences between men and women. For example, does the fact that women bear children mean that they should also assume primary responsibility for raising them? Moreover, if it is accepted that women should perform that role, does it further justify the segregation of women and men into 'separate spheres': men assuming responsibility for the public sphere of economics and politics, while women take responsibility for the private sphere of the home and especially the kitchen and the children?

The link between sex and gender, then, is the question of whether physical differences between men and women are accompanied by attitudinal and behavioural differences which are also determined by nature. Thus, it has traditionally been argued that men are, by nature, more aggressive and rational than women: characteristics that make them better suited to the world of work and politics. On the other hand, traditionalists say that women are less selfish and more nurturing than men and that these traits determine that they should be preoccupied with supporting and caring for other members of their household.

Patriarchy and feminism

Traditionalists believe that such differences as just described are natural and therefore unchangeable. Their opponents – often labelled feminists – argue that they are neither natural nor unchangeable. Rather, these attitudes and roles are ascribed to men and women by a culture which systematically privileges men to the disadvantage of women. This is the cultural system known as patriarchy.

Patriarchy, say feminists, is based on the belief that men are superior to women. It permeates all facets of society and always with the same result: the roles played by men are deemed superior and more important than those played by women. This is reflected in the fact that men are generally better paid than women and in the fact that 'men's characteristics' are accorded a higher status than 'women's characteristics'. Thus, patriarchal society has traditionally assumed a distinction between, say, 'male rationality' and 'female intuition' and placed a higher value on the former. Feminists believe that this assumption is simply false and that it can and should be changed.

Unsurprisingly, these debates have given rise to a raft of questions about the appropriate public policies to deal with them. Throughout American history, both traditionalists and feminists have fought for policies which reflect and support their view of gender. Because feminists have challenged the established social order, they have taken the political initiative. The history of American gender politics, therefore, can be profitably viewed through the successes and failures of the so-called women's movement.

The women's movement, 1789–1920

Women's rights in the early republic

For much of American history, the women's movement concentrated on the struggle to achieve formal legal and political equality with men. Although there was some discussion over the nature and extent of 'real differences' between men and women, the focus was upon whether men and women should have the same formal rights, regardless of any such differences. This is quite understandable, given the gross formal inequalities that existed well into the twentieth century.

Box 7.1

Marriage and patriarchal power

In 1855 Lucy Stone married her fellow abolitionist activist, Henry Blackwell. Both were feminists and objected to the marriage laws as they affected women's rights. Upon their marriage, therefore, they jointly published the following statement:

PROTEST

While acknowledging our mutual affection by publicly assuming the relationship of husband and wife, yet in justice to ourselves and a great principle, we deem it a duty to declare that this act on our part implies no sanction of, nor promise of voluntary obedience to such of the present laws of marriage, as refuse to recognise the wife as an independent, rational being, while they confer upon the husband an injurious and unnatural superiority, investing him with legal powers that no honourable man would exercise, and which no man should possess. We protest especially against the laws which give to the husband:

1. The custody of the wife's person.

2. The exclusive control and guardianship of their children.

3. The sole ownership of her personal property, and use of her real estate, unless previously settled upon her, or placed in the hands of trustees, as in the case of minors, lunatics, and idiots.

4. The absolute right to the product of her industry.

5. Also against laws which give to the widower so much larger and more permanent an interest in the property of his deceased wife, than they give to the widow in that of the deceased husband.

6. Finally, against the whole system by which 'the legal existence of the wife is suspended during marriage', so that in most States, she neither has a legal part in the choice of her residence, nor can she make a will, nor sue or be sued in her own name, nor inherit property.

We believe that personal independence and equal human rights can never be forfeited, except for crime; that marriage should be an equal and permanent partnership, and so recognised by law; that until it is so recognised, married partners should provide against the radical injustice of the present laws, by every means in their power.

We believe that where domestic difficulties arise, no appeal should be made to legal tribunals under existing laws, but that all difficulties should be submitted to the equitable adjustment of arbitrators mutually chosen.

Thus reverencing law, we enter our protest against rules and customs which are unworthy of the name, since they violate justice, the essence of law.

The law discriminated against women in many ways. Upon marriage, for example, all a woman's possessions became her husband's property. If the marriage ended in divorce, the husband retained this property and custody of any children. This was true, even where the husband was responsible for the breakdown of the marriage. Thus, as Barbara Deckard wrote, 'Married women did not exist as legal entities apart from their husbands' (Deckard, 1979, p. 259).

The notion of separate spheres determined that women should not generally seek employment outside the home, and hence they were excluded from educational opportunities and entrance to many professions and occupations.

Most important of all, women were denied the right to vote. When the new Constitution came into force in 1789, it allowed the individual states to determine for themselves the extent of the franchise. However, with the exception of New Jersey, no state deemed it appropriate for women to vote. In New Jersey, female suffrage had been granted in 1776 and thus New Jersey women became the first in western history to be placed on an equal voting basis with men. However, in 1807, New Jersey fell into line with the rest of the United States and deprived women of the franchise.

Feminist activism

While there is plenty of evidence to suggest that women did not happily acquiesce in this discrimination, it was some years before a determined political campaign was launched to challenge it. As was often to prove the case, feminist political activism was inspired by women's involvement in other reformist movements. The first such movement was that to emancipate America's slaves, a campaign that had achieved great political significance by the mid-eighteenth century.

Women played a major role in the abolitionist movement. There were up to one hundred women's antislavery societies in the 1830s and women provided over half the signatures on antislavery petitions to Congress (O'Neill, 1969, p. 20). Moreover, some of those who were to become leaders of the movement for women's rights were very active abolitionists – women such as Lucy Stone (see Box 7.1), Elizabeth Cady Stanton, Angelina and Sarah Grimké, Lucretia Mott and Susan B. Anthony.

The Seneca Falls Convention

Despite the fact that many male abolitionists sympathised with the cause of women's rights, there was a tension between the two movements. The antislavery campaign was highly controversial and most male activists did not wish to attract further hostility by being associated with the even more radical cause of women's rights. As a result, feminist abolitionists were advised to keep quiet about women's rights and were even denied platform seats at some antislavery meetings.

Women responded by deciding to hold their own convention, dedicated solely to the cause of gender equality. In 1848, they organised the Women's Rights Convention, at Seneca Falls, New York. The convention resulted in the first manifesto for women's rights in the United States, the Seneca Falls Declaration.

The declaration made five demands in particular:

First, equal educational opportunities
Second, entry into the professions
Third, equal property rights
Fourth, an end to double standards of morality
Fifth, the vote

(Banner, 1974, p. 4)

These demands were cleverly justified by appropriating Jefferson's Declaration of Independence for the purposes of women's rights. Thus, the Seneca Falls Declaration began, 'We hold these truths to be self-evident: that all men and women are created equal... '. It further paraphrased Jefferson when it substituted his protest at King George III's goal of tyranny over Americans, with that of men over women: 'The history of mankind is a history of repeated injuries and usurpations on the part of man toward woman, having in direct object the establishment of an absolute tyranny over her (O'Neill, 1969, pp. 108–11).

Women's suffrage

The fact that women could so easily justify their cause in terms of American political philosophy did not mean that government would act swiftly upon the Seneca Falls agenda. It would, in fact, be over seventy years before the most important demand – the vote – was achieved.

The principal obstacle for women was patriarchy, an even more deeply rooted ideology than Jefferson's vision of equal rights. Indeed, many women activists themselves were not wholly convinced that 'women's nature' was compatible with the vote. This was indicated by the fact of all the demands made at Seneca Falls, only the franchise was disputed by the delegates and failed to pass unanimously.

As a result, the campaign for the vote was often couched paradoxically in terms of fundamental differences in men's and women's natures and even the notion of separate spheres. In effect, many women claimed that their special capacity for nurturing, moral education and decency made it imperative that they should be able influence public policy through the ballot box.

Nevertheless, this argument worked against women rather than for them throughout the nineteenth century, both on the suffrage question and others. For example, in 1873, in the case of *Bradwell v. Illinois*, the Supreme Court upheld the right of the state to exclude Myra Bradwell from the legal profession simply because of her sex. While the Court's opinion turned on a technical issue, Justice Joseph Bradley wrote a concurring opinion which was based on very crude patriarchal thought (see Box 7.2).

Just two years later, in *Minor v. Happersett*, the Court applied similar logic in denying that women had a constitutional right to vote under the Fourteenth Amendment.

Having failed to obtain a constitutional ruling in their favour, women turned to a state-by-state campaign for the franchise. This produced meagre results, however. By 1910, only four states had responded positively – Colorado, Utah, Wyoming and

---

Box 7.2

The law and gender relations

The following is an extract from Justice Bradley's concurring opinion in the *Bradwell v. Illinois* (1873) case

> ...the civil law, as well as nature herself, has always recognised a wide difference in the respective spheres and destinies of man and woman. Man is, or should be, woman's protector and defender. The natural and proper timidity and delicacy which belongs to the female sex evidently unfits it for many of the occupations of civil life. The constitution of the family organization, which is founded in the divine ordinance, as well as in the nature of things, indicates the domestic sphere as that which properly belongs to the domain and functions of womanhood. The harmony, not to say identity, of interests and views which belong or should belong to the family institution, is repugnant to the idea of a woman adopting a distinct and independent career from that of her husband … .
>
> It is true that many women are unmarried and not affected by any of the duties, complications, and incapacities arising out of the marital state, but these are exceptions to the general rule. The paramount destiny and mission of woman are to fulfil the noble and benign offices of wife and mother. This is the law of the Creator.

Idaho. Part of the problem was that suffragist organisations found their efforts countered by other groups who adhered to the view that it was 'unnatural' for women to vote. Thus the National American Woman's Suffrage Association was opposed by the National Association Opposed to the Further Extension of Suffrage to Women. This group believed that the entry of women into the public sphere of politics would lead to the break-up of the home and undermine family values.

However, a variety of factors soon combined to secure the vote for women. First, the early twentieth century in the United States saw a widespread movement for reform, known as Progressivism. Women active in a variety of Progressive causes drew upon the opportunities provided by the reformist ferment to advance the suffragist cause.

Secondly, the entry of the United States into the First World War in 1917 entailed many women replacing men in the workforce. This experience not only enhanced women's own ambitions, but also helped to convince some doubters that women were the equals of men.

Thirdly, women exploited growing nativist fears in the country. The late nineteenth and early twentieth centuries saw a dramatic increase in the number of immigrants from southern and eastern Europe – Italy, Russia and the lands of the Austro-Hungarian Empire. Anglo-Saxon Americans feared that this influx threatened their cultural and political dominance and sought to introduce strict new immigration laws. Suffragists argued that the enfranchisement of American women would help to counter what was seen as the harmful political and cultural effects of the new immigration.

In 1919, Congress passed the Nineteenth Amendment and the following year it was ratified by the states. It read:

> The right of citizens of the United States to vote shall not be denied or abridged by the United States or by any State on account of sex.

Women had won their greatest political battle: yet it had been achieved with considerable help from an essentially patriarchal ideology. Although women and men were now politically equal, the notion of separate spheres still pervaded most facets of American culture and society. As a result, for all its potential for transforming the status of American women, the franchise in fact changed relatively little. Socially and economically, women were still greatly disadvantaged compared with men.

Gender politics today

The period from 1920 to 1960 promised much but achieved little of substance in the cause of gender equality. Having won the right to vote on the basis of the distinctive contribution women could make to politics, women behaved politically more or less like men.

Moreover, in the 1920s, many women, like men, lost interest in reformist politics. This decade was followed by the Great Depression of the 1930s, a period in which the sheer struggle for survival took political precedence over all.

The Equal Rights Amendment

There were some important feminist initiatives in the interwar years, however; none more so than the introduction into Congress of the Equal Rights Amendment (ERA) to the Constitution in 1923. In its original form it read:

> Men and women shall have equal rights throughout the United States and every place subject to its jurisdiction.

The ERA was the work of the radical Women's Party, founded by Alice Paul in 1916. Although it would be subject to judicial interpretation, it appeared to call for an end to all legal distinctions on the basis of sex. For this very reason, however, it was opposed not only by traditionalists, but also by other women activists who wanted to preserve so-called protective legislation for women.

Chief among these opponents were women's trade unions. They argued that whatever the desirability of the ERA in theory, the practical reality for most women in the workplace was that they were more vulnerable to exploitation by employers than were men. Without current legislation that fixed maximum hours and other conditions of work for women, though not men, the economic position of women workers would deteriorate.

The debate over the ERA illustrates one of the most difficult dilemmas for contemporary feminism. Should the movement seek absolute formal legal equality of the sexes, in which no legal distinctions are permitted, or should it acknowledge the real disadvantages women suffer and campaign for laws which discriminate *in their favour*? As we shall see later, any answer to this question must in part depend on the extent and origins of the socio-economic inequalities which have persisted until today.

The contemporary women's movement

The period 1920–1960 saw few substantial gains in the cause of gender equality. Indeed, there is some evidence to suggest that the cause suffered some reverses. For example, in 1920, male college students outnumbered females two to one, but by 1958 it was three to one; and in 1940 women held 45 per cent of jobs classed as professional but in 1967 only 37 per cent (Banner, 1974, p. 226).

Some progress had been made towards better pay for women, but women still lagged far behind men, even within the same professional categories. Thus, as Box 7.3 shows, among professional workers, women's earnings were 61 per cent of men's earnings in 1939 and just 64 per cent in 1960. Among clerical workers, women earned 68.5 per cent of men's wages in 1939 and 68.3 per cent in 1960.

Why had so little progress been made since the 1920s? This is puzzling, especially when we remember that during the Second World War, women entered the workforce in huge numbers in order to compensate for the mass mobilisation of men into the armed forces. Moreover, while many of these women were obliged to give up their jobs at the end of the war, a large number soon returned to the workforce. The reason was simple: the American economy was producing a vast array of consumer goods, but most families required more than one wage to afford them.

Thus, by 1960, some 38 per cent of women aged sixteen and over were employed outside the home. This compared with a figure of 25 per cent in 1940. Moreover, the kind of women in the workforce was also changing significantly. Before the war, the typical female worker was single and in her early twenties. After the war, she was married and more likely to be in her late forties (Gatlin, 1987, p. 25). In short, the long-standing tradition that women should work outside the home only until they married was disappearing.

Box 7.3

Women's wages as a percentage of men's

Category	1939	1960
Professional	60.8	64.0
Managerial	54.0	57.6
Clerical	68.5	68.3
Sales	51.3	42.2
Service	59.6	59.1

Source: Adapted from Gatlin, 1987, p. 41

The 'feminine mystique'

Despite this basic fact of life, the notion of separate spheres stubbornly persisted. While ideological change usually lags behind material change, it is also true that the postwar years witnessed an intense reaffirmation of patriarchy. Psychologists, sociologists, fashion designers and the media all placed renewed emphasis on traditional concepts of femininity, beauty and, above all, women's vocation as wife and mother. In 1963, Betty Friedan coined the term 'the feminine mystique' to describe what was, in effect, a neo-Victorian concept of women (Friedan, 1963).

Friedan vigorously challenged the idea that women should or could be satisfied by the model of domestic bliss conjured up by the feminine mystique. Rather, she argued, it alienated women in the most destructive fashion by denying the reality of their modern social and economic roles. Moreover, self-fulfilment for women lay not in some traditionalist fantasy of a woman's sphere, but in allowing them to share the male sphere of education, career and public life.

The 'new' feminism

By the early 1960s, economic changes in women's lives were clearly leading to new feminist perspectives on gender politics. Unlike previous feminist waves, the 'new' feminism of the 1960s demanded more than political, legal or even economic equality. It also urged a fundamental reassessment of gender relations that left virtually no aspect of American culture and practice untouched. As we shall see below, contemporary feminist thought is truly revolutionary in that it suggests that the whole of private and public life is gendered along patriarchal lines. Consequently, it is not merely the obvious forms of sex discrimination that have been challenged, but also 'apolitical' issues such as language, personal relations, sexuality and portrayals of women in the arts and media.

First, however, it is important to note how economic and philosophical change were translated in political action.

Feminist political organisation

As in previous eras, feminist political activism was boosted by a wider spirit of radical reform. The decade of the 1960s was one of the most turbulent in American history. The civil rights movement increasingly turned to direct, mass political action and the Black Power movement denounced American society as irredeemably racist. The anti-Vietnam War movement took to the streets in massive numbers and its more radical activists denounced American foreign policy as both racist and imperialist. Meanwhile, American youth was pioneering a new personal lifestyle that rejected the values of their parents: traditional dress codes were abandoned, a relaxed attitude to sex and drug use was prevalent and hippies advised young Americans to drop out of mainstream society and to experiment with alternative ways of living. In short, the cultural and political consensus that had long commanded respectful observance was torn apart.

Under these circumstances, it is hardly surprising that feminists should seek to add their own demands to the nation's political agenda. Moreover, just as feminists in the nineteenth century abolitionist movement had been urged to adopt a low profile in order not to damage 'more important' causes, contemporary feminists found 1960s reformers and radicals unwilling to address their issues. As a result, feminists broke away to establish their own organisations, dedicated to action on an agenda of gender politics.

Two distinct strands have been identified in the contemporary women's movement, corresponding to what can be called the reformist (or liberal) and radical tendencies.

Reformist groups are those whose goals are in essence to obtain for women equal status and opportunities within the present system. Their methods are those used by other mainstream interest groups – lobbying legislatures, litigating in the courts, working in elections, building up membership and publicising issues through group literature and the media.

The leading reformist group is undoubtedly the National Organization for Women (NOW). It was founded in 1966 by women attending a convention of state commissions on the status of women. When the convention refused to accept a resolution which equated sexism with racism, its proponents quit the meeting and decided to establish NOW.

NOW was soon followed by the establishment of other groups, dedicated to furthering some aspect of what was being dubbed 'women's liberation'. The Women's Equity Action League (WEAL) was formed to campaign on economic and educational issues. The National Women's Political Caucus (NWPC) was created to bring more women into politics (Gatlin, 1987, pp. 117–18). These and other groups have achieved many notable successes. Their victories, according to some, have been due in no small part to the very fact that they have worked within the system, both in methods and goals (Gelb and Palley, 1982, p. 7). Thus, they have been able to maximise support from non-feminist organisations through an appeal to familiar American values of egalitarianism and individual rights.

Radical feminists have attracted more hostility. Although far less organised than reformist groups, they have often been on the 'front line' of the contemporary women's movement. They have pioneered debate on certain issues and placed those issues on the political agenda, with the more moderate groups embracing them at a later stage. This was true, for example, of such issues as violence against women, especially rape, of pornography and lesbian rights.

Whereas liberal feminists tend to de-emphasise the differences between men and women, radicals highlight them and incorporate them into their strategies and policies. Thus, they have been separatist, excluding men from their groups and activities, as well as advocating social and living arrangements excluding men (Gatlin, 1987, pp. 130–7). Above all, perhaps, radical feminists have been famous for their attack upon the traditional family, which they see as fundamentally patriarchal and a prime source of the oppression of women.

In short, radical feminists call for the overthrow of what they see as a thoroughly patriarchal society, while liberal feminists seek to improve current society by eliminating its patriarchal aspects. Despite these differences of policy, strategy and rhetoric, however, it is worth emphasising that the two strands of the contemporary women's movement have a great deal in common. Radical feminists support equal rights for women and liberal feminists support lesbian rights and campaigns against sexual harassment and violence against women. Indeed, it is precisely because women of varied ideological persuasions have identified a common agenda of previously ignored issues, that feminism has become a powerful political force today.

The success of modern feminism

While contemporary feminism has its determined opponents, it has nevertheless achieved some notable successes since the 1960s. As measured by the acquisition of equal rights with men and the establishment of a political agenda that reflects feminist concerns, it can be argued that the women's movement has made a fundamental break-through (see Box 7.4). Exploiting the numerous points of access provided by the American political system, the movement has persuaded all the major institutions of the federal government to respond to its demands. As we now go on to examine some of those successes, however, it will be obvious that the victories are far from complete.

Equality in the workplace

By the late 1950s, it was becoming clear that the recent shift of women into the work-place in large numbers was a permanent phenomenon. As noted above, a booming economy based on mass consumerism required both more workers and more pur-chasers. Women formed a large pool of untapped labour and their wages provided additional consumer power.

The federal government recognised these new economic facts of life and President Kennedy set up the Presidential Commission on the Status of Women. When it reported in 1963, the Commission recommended action to eliminate discrimination in the workplace and the first concrete result was the Equal Pay Act of 1963. Although limited in the occupations covered, it was nevertheless a landmark because it was the first attempt by the federal government to promote greater economic equal-ity of the sexes. Furthermore, its coverage was extended in 1972 to cover executive,

---

Box 7.4

Landmarks in the campaign for equality of the sexes

1848 The Seneca Falls Declaration.
The first manifesto of the women's movement, demanding among other things, the right to vote

1873 Bradwell v. Illinois
The Supreme Court denies that women have a constitutional right to enter the legal profession

1875 Minor v. Happersett
The Supreme Court denies that women have a constitutional right to vote

1920 The Nineteenth Amendment ratified
Women acquire the constitutional right to vote

1963 Equal Pay Act
For the first time, the federal government requires women to be paid the same as men for doing the same job

1964 Civil Rights Act
Title VII of the Act outlaws sex discrimination in employment

1971 Reed v. Reed
For the first time, the Supreme Court rules that a state law favouring men over women violates the Equal Protection Clause of the Fourteenth Amendment

1972 Education Amendments Act
Title IX of the Act prohibits most sex discrimination in education establishments and programmes receiving federal government finance

1973 Roe v. Wade
The Supreme Court announces that a woman has a constitutional right to an abortion

1974 Equal Credit Opportunity Act
Women acquire the same right to obtain credit as men

1978 Pregnancy Discrimination Act
Congress reverses a Supreme Court decision and forbids discrimination against women employees on grounds of pregnancy-related absence from work

1981 Supreme Court justice
Sandra Day O'Connor becomes first female justice of the US Supreme Court

1984 Presidential elections
Geraldine Ferraro, Democratic vice-presidential candidate, becomes first woman to be nominated by a major party in a presidential election

1986 Meritor Savings Bank v. Vinson
The Supreme Court rules that sexual harassment in the workplace is a form of discrimination forbidden by Title VII of the Civil Rights Act of 1964

1987 Johnson v. Transportation Agency
For the first time, the Supreme Court upholds an affirmative action plan that discriminates in favour of women

administrative and professional workers, and again in 1974 to cover federal, state and municipal employees (Mezey, 1992, p. 92).

The Equal Pay Act did end the most obvious form of discrimination against working women, but, as Box 7.5 shows, it has not equalised the earnings of men and women. Why women still lag so far behind men in income is a complex and disputed question.

The Equal Pay Act applied only to women doing virtually the same jobs as men. It did not therefore address the fact that many occupations are, to a considerable extent, segregated by sex. Moreover, those occupations dominated by men tend to be much better paid than those dominated by women (see Box 7.6). In short, women earn less than men in large part because 'women's work' is deemed less valuable than 'men's work'.

Box 7.5

Women in the 1990s: basic statistics

Population, 1990

	Women	Men
	51.3%	48.7%

Electorate, 1992

	Women	Men
Voting-age population	52.3%	47.7%
Reporting registered	69.3%	66.9%
Reporting voted	62.3%	61.2%

Participation in workforce, 1992

	Women	Men
Single	66.4%	74.6%
Married	59.2%	77.6%
Other (widowed, separated, married but spouse not present)	47%	68%

Median weekly earnings $, 1992

	Women (% of men's earnings)	Men
Managerial, Professional	562 (72.3%)	777
Technical, sales, administrative	365 (70.3%)	519
Service	248 (75.2%)	330
Skilled workers	336 (66.8%)	503
Semi-skilled, unskilled	279 (70.1%)	393

Source: US Bureau of the Census, 1993

Box 7.6

Selected occupations by sex

Percentage women

	1983	1992
Education		
Pre-elementary	98.2	98.6
Elementary	83.3	85.4
Secondary	51.8	55.5
College/university	36.3	40.9
Engineers		
Civil	4.0	7.9
Electrical	6.1	8.4
Industrial	11.0	14.0
Mechanical	2.8	5.3
Managers		
Financial	38.6	46.3
Personnel	43.9	58.9
Purchasing	23.6	33.2
Marketing/advertising	21.8	33.6
Health		
Dentists	6.7	8.5
Doctors	15.8	20.4
Nurses	95.8	94.3
Pharmacists	26.7	37.8
Other professions		
Architects	12.7	15.3
Accountants/auditors	38.7	51.2
Maths/computer scientists	29.6	33.5
Lawyers	15.3	21.4
Service		
Private		
Child care	96.9	97.1
Cleaners	95.8	94.8
Public		
Waiters/waitresses	87.8	79.6
Child care	na	98.7
Manual		
Car mechanics	0.5	0.8
Construction	1.8	1.9
Textile	82.1	76.4
Truck drivers	3.1	4.6

Source: US Bureau of the Census, 1993

It can also be seen from Box 7.6 that many occupations still reveal the impact of traditional gender roles. Thus women predominate in jobs involving young children, nursing and personnel aspects of management. Feminists believe that this pattern stems from patriarchal conditioning: society permits and encourages women to aim for these careers and discourages them from seeking employment as, say, engineers or car mechanics. Antifeminists disagree, asserting that women choose these occupations because they involve the type of work that appeals to them. In other words, the debate turns yet again on the issue of whether men and women have fundamentally different natures, values and priorities.

One attempt to overcome the financial consequences of job segregation has been to advance the policy of 'comparable worth'. This is based on the premise that different jobs can be objectively rated according to the skills and responsibility they involve. Once measured, its proponents argue, jobs making comparable demands should be paid the same. In this way, it might be possible to argue that a nurse, say, is required to have qualities comparable to those of a skilled industrial worker and should therefore receive the same pay.

Opponents dismiss the comparable worth approach on a number of grounds: but most importantly, they argue that employee pay is in essence a market decision, based on the supply of and demand for the particular skills involved. Moreover, the 1985 Civil Rights Commission on unequal pay denied that it was the result of discrimination and instead pointed to three main characteristics of working women: lower job expectations, educational and job choices which accommodate child-rearing and interrupted participation in the workforce.

Feminists counter that these findings are not supported by statistical evidence measuring the relation between occupation and parental or marital status. So far, however, they have been unable to persuade either courts or legislatures that segregation and unequal pay result from discrimination (Mezey, 1992, p. 98). There is little sign, therefore, that government will endorse comparable worth in the near future.

Reproductive issues

The basic biological fact that women, not men, bear children looms large in gender politics. As we have seen, traditionalists believe that this makes women's nature, values and social roles different from those of men. Even leaving aside that debate, however, there are important political questions concerning the extent to which public policy should accommodate reproductive facts.

First, there is the controversial matter of the reproductive autonomy of women. To what extent should women be allowed to determine for themselves whether to bear children and, if so, how many and when?

Contraception

Great advances in contraceptive science in the second half of the twentieth century have dramatically improved women's reproductive autonomy. By the 1960s, most states had repealed their restrictive nineteenth-century laws banning artificial contraceptives, and in 1965, when the state of Connecticut persisted in restricting the availability of contraceptives, the Supreme Court declared its law unconstitutional in the case of *Griswold v. Connecticut*.

Abortion

However, as we shall see in Chapter 21, the issue of abortion rights has proved far more controversial. Feminists regard easily available abortion as a precondition not merely of reproductive autonomy but also of many other aspects of gender equality. For if women do not have ultimate control over their child-bearing, how can they compete with men in the workplace? Quite simply, a woman's educational or career goals may be delayed or sabotaged altogether by unwanted pregnancies.

Those opposed to abortion generally place what they see as the rights of the fetus above those of the mother. Suffice it to say at this point that, while it has been unable to ban abortions altogether, the anti-abortion movement has succeeded in making public policy hostile to abortion in important respects. Thus, for example, with few exceptions, the federal government does not permit public health funds to pay for abortions for poor women, even though they do pay for all other medical treatments, including childbirth costs. Furthermore, many states do not permit public hospitals or their staffs to perform abortions.

Pregnancy disability

A further major reproductive issue in contemporary American politics is that of the rights of pregnant employees. Until the 1970s, it was assumed that pregnancy was a private matter and that neither employers nor government had any responsibility for its impact upon women workers. As a result, women employees who became pregnant were not entitled to either paid or unpaid sick leave, could be dismissed merely for being pregnant, had no rights to return to their job following birth and, when they did return, found that they had lost benefits such as seniority rights. Underlying these practices were further assumptions that pregnant women and mothers of young children could not and probably should not be in the workforce.

However, the increasing participation of women of child-bearing age in the workforce (see Box 7.7), invited a change of policy.

The first major attempt came in 1972, when the Equal Employment Opportunity Commission (EEOC) issued guidelines with three main stipulations. First, employers should not refuse to hire women because they are or might become pregnant. Secondly, employers should treat pregnancy disability the same as other temporary health reasons for absence. Thirdly, employers should not single out pregnancy-related absences as a cause for dismissal (Mezey, 1992, p. 113).

However, the Supreme Court took a less sympathetic position on pregnancy disability. Two decisions were particularly worthy of note, *Gedulig v. Aiello* (1974) and *GEC v. Gilbert* (1976). In these cases, the Court determined that the exclusion of pregnancy disability from insurance programmes protecting employees against other temporary disabilities did not constitute sex discrimination. The Court's reasoning was somewhat bizarre, in that it said such programmes did not distinguish between women

Box 7.7

Percentage of married women in the workforce, 1960–92

Age	1960	1970	1980	1992
All	31.9	40.5	49.8	59.2
16–19 yr	27.2	37.8	49.3	49.0
20–24 yr	31.7	47.9	61.4	66.3
25–34 yr	28.8	38.8	58.8	70.9
35–44 yr	37.2	46.8	61.8	74.8
45–64 yr	36.0	44.0	46.9	58.6
Over 65 yr	6.7	7.3	7.3	7.9

Source: US Bureau of the Census, 1993

and men, but rather between 'pregnant women and non-pregnant persons'. In effect, the Court held that pregnancy-based discrimination was not sex-based discrimination (McKeever, 1995, p. 201).

These decisions prompted a coalition of more than fifty women's and other interest groups to launch the Campaign to End Discrimination Against Pregnant Workers. It achieved its main goal in 1978 when Congress passed the Pregnancy Discrimination (or Disability) Act. This explicitly included distinctions based on pregnancy within the meaning of sex discrimination in Title VII of the Civil Rights Act of 1964.

Many feminists do not believe, however, that it is sufficient to treat pregnancy disability as any other temporary disability. Rather, they argue that pregnancy has such a disadvantageous effect on women's careers that it requires *preferential treatment* compared with other disabilities. This is just one facet of a wider feminist view that a focus on equal treatment with men ignores the real disadvantages that women face even when formal equality is required. Thus both the short-term and long-term consequences of bearing children are far more significant than those resulting from other, truly temporary disabilities.

In the 1990s, legislative efforts on behalf of pregnancy rights focused upon the Family and Medical Leave Act, eventually passed in 1993. In its various forms, this bill sought to mandate employers to give unpaid leave to pregnant women and unpaid parental leave for men and women to care for their sick children. Although it first passed Congress in 1990, President George Bush vetoed the bill on the grounds that such leave, while desirable, should be a voluntary decision for employers.

The underlying reason for the president's veto was the fear of the business community that it would prove too costly in financial terms. According to government estimates, the Act would cost employers about $200 million a year. However, a change of administration in 1992 saw the last political barrier removed and President Clinton signed the bill into law in 1993.

Sexual harassment

Yet another issue to appear on the nation's political agenda because of feminist campaigning is that of sexual harassment in the workplace. The definition of sexual harassment can include a range of behaviour, running from unwanted physical advances to sexual comments. Typically, sexual harassment is practised by a senior employee upon a junior. Sometimes such harassment is accompanied by offers to advance the victim's career or threats to wreck it. Even in the absence of such inducements, sexual harassment can create a hostile working atmosphere that causes much personal distress and serious damage to an employee's efficiency.

Like many issues in the new 'sexual politics', sexual harassment is an age-old practice, yet until the 1970s, it drew little public or political attention. Many people believed that it was a more or less natural and inevitable aspect of human behaviour and therefore to be tolerated. Those who were its victims tended to keep quiet about it, or change job, fearing the embarrassment that would follow a public complaint. In essence, men had defined the workplace culture for so long that neither women nor the law challenged sexual harassment. As one writer observed, 'What men often experience as fun or flirtation, women often experience as degrading and demanding. And it is male experience that has shaped the law's traditional responses to sexual harassment' (Rhode, 1989, p. 233).

It was the combination of the increasing number of women in the workforce, their rising ambition and confidence and the perspectives offered by the new wave of feminism that identified sexual harassment as a major problem.

In 1976, the feminist magazine *Redbook* published a study of nine thousand working women: some nine out of ten reported being the object of sexual harassment of one kind or another (Gatlin, 1987, p. 229). Other studies followed, and while the incidence of reported harassment varied, the evidence pointed unmistakably to the fact that it was a widespread phenomenon. Thus, in the 1980s, the United States Merit Protection Board found that 42 per cent of women had been harassed in their present job: they further estimated that 85 per cent of women could expect sexual harassment at some point in their working lives. Of course, men are also sometimes the victim of sexual harassment, but far less so than women (Rhode, 1989, p. 232).

Although there was no law against sexual harassment itself, political efforts focused on the attempt to persuade courts that it came within the definition of sex discrimination contained in Title VII of the Civil Rights Act of 1964. Early cases were unsuccessful, but the federal government took a decisive step in 1980 when the Equal Employment Opportunity Commission issued new guidelines on the subject. The EEOC declared that sexual harassment was sex discrimination whether it was tied to other offers or threats or whether it simply created a hostile working environment (see Box 7.8).

Even more important was the 1986 decision of the Supreme Court in *Meritor Savings Bank v. Vinson*. Despite the fact that the justices were frequently in disagreement on gender issues, here the Court was unanimous in declaring that sexual harassment was a form of sex discrimination within the meaning of Title VII. Then, in 1993, in *Harris v. Forklift Systems, Inc*, the Court made it easier to sue for damages in alleged cases of sexual harassment. Whereas a lower court had ruled that a person

---

Box 7.8

Equal Employment Opportunity Commission guidelines on sexual harassment, 1980

Unwelcome sexual advances, requests for sexual favours, and other verbal or physical conduct of a sexual nature constitute sexual harassment when (1) submission to such conduct is made either explicitly or implicitly a term or condition of an individual's employment, (2) submission to or rejection of such conduct by an individual is used as a basis for employment decisions affecting such individual, or (3) such conduct has the purpose or effect of unreasonably interfering with an individual's work performance or creating an intimidating, hostile, or offensive working environment.

---

could only sue employers for sexual harassment when she had suffered severe psychological damage, the Supreme Court unanimously decided that a victim need only show that a 'reasonable person' would have found the workplace environment a hostile one.

Together, these Supreme Court decisions constitute a major legal victory. Moreover, they have spurred many employers to adopt sexual harassment policies and complaint procedures. Thus, a practice which had been the accepted norm less than twenty years earlier, has been stigmatised and outlawed by the political efforts of the contemporary feminist movement.

Equality in politics

Despite enfranchisement by the Nineteenth Amendment in 1920, the number of women holding high political office has been almost negligible for much of the twentieth century. This is particularly true at the federal level. Thus, there has never been a woman president or vice-president, nor even a female major party presidential nominee. The only such nominee for the vice-presidency was Geraldine Ferraro, nominated by the Democratic party in 1984.

Considering that Congress has 435 House seats and 100 Senate seats, the record there has been equally disappointing until quite recently. Before the 1992 elections, the Senate had never had more than two women members at the same time and the House had never had more than thirty.

As for the Supreme Court, the first woman justice was not appointed until 1981, when Sandra Day O'Connor took her seat. It was not until 1993 that the second was appointed, Ruth Bader Ginsburg.

Nevertheless, the recent wave of feminism has at least given rise to greater expectations of increased numbers of women holding high political office. This became clear when journalists, looking ahead to the forthcoming electoral cycle, dubbed 1992 'The Year of the Women'. This was not the first time that a breakthrough by women candidates had been anticipated. For example, in 1990, eight women had contested Senate seats, but only one – Nancy Kassebaum (R–Kansas) – was elected and she was an incumbent.

However, 1992 did produce evidence of a marked shift in favour of women candidates. Of 106 women candidates for the House, 47 were successful; and 5 of the 11 women candidates for the Senate were elected. In one election cycle, then, the number of women representatives rose from 28 to 47. With the victory of Kay Bailey Hutchison in the Texas seat vacated by new treasury secretary Lloyd Bentsen, the number of women senators rose to 7, compared with 2 in 1990.

This progress continued, and by 1998 there were a record 54 women in the House of Representatives and 9 in the Senate. Moreover, at the state level, there were in 1998 some 1615 women state legislators, that is 21.8 per cent of all state legislators (Center for the American Woman and Politics factsheet, 1998).

It would seem, therefore, that the American electorate is becoming increasingly comfortable with the idea of voting for women candidates. It would not be unduly optimistic to expect a snowball effect, in which the more that women are elected to office, the more that women will be encouraged to stand, and so on.

Antifeminism

Although the women's movement has not achieved all its aims, it has undeniably made significant progress. Even where concrete results have been disappointing, there have been important changes in public attitudes. For example, although there are still relatively few women holding high electoral office, it is no longer regarded as unnatural or undesirable that women should aspire to such positions.

Almost inevitably, the changes brought about by modern feminism have provoked opposition and resistance. Some criticism of feminism is simply reactionary in its desire to resist any change to the privileges afforded by the status quo. Others, however, while originally sympathetic to feminist goals, contend that the movement has either failed to produce the desired results or has been so successful that it is no longer relevant to contemporary society. This latter group is sometimes labelled postfeminist. In as much as it opposes the values and policies espoused by the contemporary women's movement, however, postfeminism may be regarded as one facet of a broader antifeminist backlash (Faludi, 1992).

Antifeminism is nothing new. Every historical phase of feminism has provoked a reaction from those, both men and women, who have viewed the new ideas as inimical to society. Its contemporary political strength is most obviously manifested in the movement known as the New Right. This first came to prominence in the 1970s and advocated a mixture of conservative values in economics, foreign policy and social issues.

With regard to social issues, the New Right, and especially the evangelical New Christian Right, celebrates what it sees as traditional family values. The New Right believes the traditional nuclear family to be the most important pillar of a moral and successful society. It explicitly endorses the notion of separate spheres, in the belief that men and women are biologically destined to play different, but complementary roles in society. Thus men should be the breadwinners, working outside the home to provide for the material needs of his family. Women, by contrast, are best suited to the role of wife and mother, catering especially to the moral, spiritual and emotional needs of her family.

George Gilder is a leading exponent of such traditional views. In the early 1980s, he argued that separate spheres was the natural and desirable consequence of biological differences. Moreover, any attempt to merge or abolish the two spheres entailed serious damage to both the economic and social fabric of the United States. Men are naturally more aggressive than women, says Gilder, and more suited to leadership roles: 'Because of the long evolutionary experience of the race in hunting societies, the provider role accords with the deepest instincts of men' (Gilder, 1981, p. 136). Feminism undermines this natural domination of women by men, leaving men without a socially productive focus for their aggressions. The result is social, familial and economic disruption.

The Equal Rights Amendment

The power of antifeminism was demonstrated in the battle for ratification of the Equal Rights Amendment (ERA) to the Constitution. The ERA had first been introduced into Congress in 1923. It was not until the contemporary wave of feminism arrived, however, that it looked set for success.

The modern version of the Amendment read: 'Equality of Rights under the law shall not be denied or abridged by the United States or by any State on account of sex'. The House of Representatives passed it in 1971 by a vote of 354 to 23. The following year, the Senate voted 84 to 8 in favour. It only remained for three-quarters of the state legislatures to pass it and women would have a constitutional right to equal treatment with men. This appeared little more than a formality, as by early 1973, thirty states had already voted for ratification.

From this highly unpromising situation, antifeminists organised a successful rearguard action. Their campaign against ratification of the ERA demonstrated both the disquiet about gender equality that a significant minority of Americans still felt and the difficulties involved in trying to amend the Constitution. The antifeminist coalition was led by Phyllis Schlafly and her organisation, STOP-ERA. Her strategy was to represent the ERA as a radical measure that went well beyond what most Americans would find acceptable. Thus, among the most frequent allegations were that the ERA would make unisex toilets compulsory; would force women to be drafted into combat roles in the armed services; and would force states to recognise homosexual marriages.

STOP-ERA was instrumental in persuading a sufficient number of states to reject ratification, thereby blocking the ERA. Requiring the approval of thirty-eight states by 1982 for passage, the amendment got stuck on thirty-five. According to many commentators, the failure of the ERA suggested that lurking beneath the surface of the widespread acceptance of gender equality lies a deep anxiety about any truly fundamental shift in gender roles. Thus, as one wrote:

> The campaign against the ERA succeeded because it shifted debate away from equal rights and focused it on the possibility that the ERA might bring substantive changes in women's

roles and behaviour. In this era, the American public, though changing its outlook, still objected to any major changes in traditional roles of men and women.

(Mansbridge, 1986, p. 20)

As the failure of the ERA suggests, the momentum behind contemporary feminism has slowed considerably since the 1970s. Partly this is because the early gains, involving decisive changes in the law, seem spectacular compared with the more piecemeal translation of those abstract rights into everyday reality. It is also due, however, to rising doubts about their movement from some erstwhile feminists. As Susan Faludi noted, 'By the mid-1980s, the voices of feminist recantation became a din' (Faludi, 1992, p. 352). No less a modern feminist pioneer than Betty Friedan alleged that the movement had been misguided in its attempts to achieve equality without regard to biological differences (Friedan, 1981).

What explains this antifeminist and postfeminist backlash is not possible to say with certainty. A combination of factors may be responsible: the greater social conservatism generally since the late 1970s; a measure of disillusionment within the feminist movement, as anticipated gains have not been fully achieved; continuing resistance from a political and social culture imbued with patriarchy; and a generational shift, involving young women less politically attuned than their mothers.

Nevertheless, none of this should be taken as signalling the end of gender politics as a major political, social and cultural issue. In the first place, there are now enough women in most occupations to ensure that continuing areas of inequality do not go unchallenged. Moreover, women's organisations are now deeply entrenched within the political process and are therefore well placed to defend the gains that have been made and to press for others. The 'gender revolution' is by no means complete, but the women's movement may increasingly be seen as part of the political status quo.

 ## Summary

The campaign for gender equality has deep roots in American history and its progress has at times been painfully slow. The main reason for this has been the fundamentally patriarchal nature of American society, which conditioned both men and women to think of themselves as so different as to justify widely disparate treatment by law. The contemporary women's movement has challenged patriarchy and has undermined much of its influence on public policy. This represents a profound change in American society and politics and has come about only after years of controversial political struggle. This political and cultural transformation has its origins in the changing economic role of women in the workforce, the broad breakdown in cultural consensus in the 1960s and in the efforts of women to organise themselves politically.

 ## References

Banner, L., 1974, *Women in Modern America: A brief history* (New York: Harcourt Brace Janovich)
Barnard, J., 1971, *Women and the Public Interest* (Chicago: Aldine Atherton)
Deckard, B., 1983, *The Women's Movement* (New York: Harper & Row)
Faludi, S., 1992, *Backlash: The undeclared war against women* (London: Chatto & Windus)

Friedan, B., 1963, *The Feminine Mystique* (London: Gollancz)

Friedan, B., 1981, *The Second Stage* (New York: Summit Books)

Gatlin, R., 1987, *American Women Since 1945* (Basingstoke: Macmillan)

Gelb, J. and Palley, M., 1982, *Women and Public Policies* (Princeton: Princeton University Press)

Gilder, G., 1981, *Wealth and Poverty* (New York: Basic Books)

Mansbridge, J., 1986, *Why We Lost the ERA* (Chicago: University of Chicago Press)

McKeever, R., 1995, *Raw Judicial Power? The Supreme Court and American society* (Manchester: Manchester University Press)

Mezey, S., 1992, *In Pursuit of Equality: Women, public policy, and the federal courts* (New York: St Martin's Press)

O'Neill, W., 1969, *The Woman Movement* (London: Allen & Unwin)

Rhode, D., 1989, *Justice and Gender* (Cambridge, Mass.: Harvard University Press)

US Bureau of the Census, 1993, *Statistical Abstract of the United States* (113th edn, Washington DC)

8

Immigration, ethnicity and race in American politics

In the United States, as in many other countries, division based on ethnicity is high on the list of social influences on politics. The American polity has attempted – never completely successfully – to subordinate ethnic consciousness to a common American civic culture, and, more recently, to remove the detrimental political effects of racial consciousness. In this chapter we focus on the current state of ethnic politics, examining it in the light of the development of immigration policy, which has often been affected by ethnic and racial considerations. (In Chapter 20 we return to the perennial and perplexing problem of race in American politics.)

The political importance of ethnicity and race

Scientifically, both ethnicity and race are very ambiguous if not totally nonsensical ideas. Yet they are important political facts in liberal democracies, where widely held political opinions, no matter how unscientific, are politically weighty. As long as citizens in these regimes base political preferences on ethnic and racial distinctions, these distinctions, no matter how prejudiced they may be, will be forces to be reckoned with. In the United States, perceptions of racial and ethnic differences have played a large if not always determining role in party alignments and in many areas of both domestic and foreign policy.

Ethnic diversity

One of the basic reasons for the importance of racial and ethnic categories in American politics, and one of the determinants of the manner of that importance, is the very diverse ethnic composition of the population. The first British colonists encountered 'Indians' (native Americans), who as tribes – when not exterminated (by European diseases as well as weapons) – were expropriated and pushed steadily into reservations, but who as individuals also intermingled with the European settlers (although there was far less interbreeding than in Central and South America, where the European newcomers were mainly men rather than, as in British America, colonies of men, women and children). Even if the American continent had not already been popu-lated by these aboriginal peoples, ethnic diversity was established well before the American Revolution. As noted in Chapter 2, the 'English' colonies contained within themselves several communities with majorities of non-English Europeans – mainly Irish, Scots, Welsh and Germans. Indeed, in 1790, the English were only 60 per cent of the white population (Mann, 1979, pp. 48–9). There were also large numbers of Africans: many slaves and a few free. As the United States expanded westwards and southwards, it incorporated some French- and many Spanish-speaking inhabitants and some Pacific Islanders. On top of this basic ethnic mixture in territories that were to be parts of the United States came several waves of non-English immigration in the nine-teenth and twentieth centuries, first mainly from Europe (but also from China), later from Japan, and more recently from elsewhere in Asia, and from Latin America and the Caribbean. Today the United States is the most ethnically diverse country in the world.

Racial diversity

The 'racial' composition of the American population is more difficult to describe, since racial categories are both more imprecise (if not totally meaningless) and generally more invidious than ethnic categories. It is this invidious use of racial distinctions that has made them politically salient even though they are scientific nonsense. Skin colour, one of the most common markers used by humans to discriminate 'races' (though not the only one – for example, height has also been used) – has been used in the United States as a basis to distinguish 'whites' from 'blacks' and other 'racial' groups, particu-larly American aboriginals and Asians. Mexican or more general Hispanic categories have also been thought of as racial classifications. The distinction between whites and blacks has been the most persistent and troubling racial distinction in American pol-itics, although conflicts between whites and other groups, as well as between non-white groups, have also been intense and violent at times. Surveys show that racial prejudice among both whites and blacks has declined in recent decades, and friendships between blacks and whites have multiplied. Nevertheless, the black/white divide is what Americans have in mind when they register gloom on the future of race relations. As President Clinton prepared a major speech on race relations in June 1997, a Gallup poll indicated that 55 per cent of Americans believe that relations between whites and blacks will 'always be a problem' (Holmes, 1997).

Counting racial and ethnic group membership

Both the scientific imprecision and the political salience of race and ethnicity have made the official recognition and counting of racial and ethnic categories controversial matters. The decennial census has from the very first (1790) counted whites and blacks (as well as tribal Indians) separately, since the Constitution required that slaves be counted in order to determine slave states' entitlements to representation in the House of Representatives and tax liabilities. More recently, in addition to counting whites and blacks, the Census Bureau has attempted also to determine the membership of diverse groups in two other broad 'racial' categories: Asian and Pacific Islander, and American Indian, Eskimo and Aleut. It also counts those 'of Hispanic origin' (who officially are allowed to be of any 'race' – for example, there are both black and white Puerto Ricans). The total population estimated by the Census Bureau for 1998 (270 million) includes:

223 million whites	(82.6 per cent)
35 million blacks	(13.0 per cent)
10 million Asians and Pacific Islanders	(3.7 per cent)
2 million Indians, Eskimos and Aleuts	(0.7 per cent)

Among these 'racial' groups are 30 million (11.1 per cent) of Hispanic origin (mostly counted as whites).

The Census Bureau is often pressured either to increase or to decrease the number of racial and ethnic categories and questions that it uses. For the 1980 census, it added a question on 'ancestry', out of deference to the new white ethnic consciousness expressed in the 1970s. Previously, census enumerators had simply asked if a person, or that person's parents, were foreign-born; and, if so, in what country. This meant that third-generation white immigrants were not differentiated from other white Americans. In response to the new ancestry question, many people have either declined to answer, or have reported difficult-to-classify mixtures of ethnicity. In the 1990s, there has been a debate about adding a 'multiracial' category to the census. This has been resisted by some in those groups (for example blacks and Hispanics) who fear their official numbers and therefore some of their political strength would diminish as a result. In October 1997 the Office of Management and Budget decided that the multiracial category will be used in preparations for the 2000 census, but this remains a controversial matter.

American reflections and policies on immigration, ethnicity and race

While ethnically (that is, in terms of the genetic and geographical origins of its population) the United States is the most diverse country in the world, linguistically and culturally it is strikingly homogeneous. It is much less multilingual than, for example, India, Belgium or Switzerland. The common 'American' culture is strong enough to provide a common bond of citizenship for individuals of all groups, and to seem threatening to many outside the United States, as well as to some groups within it (such as orthodox Jews or the Old Order Amish), who wish to resist its attractions.

This cultural homogeneity stems from the fact that at least since the Revolution, Americans have taught themselves that they are 'one people', bound together by their recognition of certain universal truths about the human species and the political implications of these truths, and by opposition to regimes that deny these truths. In the nineteenth and early twentieth centuries, 'Americanisation' programmes sometimes rather brutally assaulted immigrants with the imperative of accepting these ideas. In the softer approach of the later twentieth century, immigrants have been left a little freer to discover for themselves the superiority of American political ideas. In fact, liberal intellectuals in this century, affected by postmodern doubts about universal truths, have been much less sure that liberal political principles and American civic culture can really be based on 'self-evident' truths about all humans everywhere; in other words, they have been less confident than earlier liberals that American political ideas *are* superior. Nevertheless, the story of the transformation of immigrants into Americans remains one of the major themes of the political culture, and of the political reality experienced by millions of American citizens.

From the beginning of American history, observers, statesmen and citizens have reflected on the advantages and difficulties presented by the ethnic variety of the American regime. Should diverse ethnic origins be celebrated and perpetuated, or should they be played down or suppressed in the interests of a common political culture, political unity and patriotism? This question continues to occupy American citizens today, as immigration continues in impressive numbers and variety.

Assimilation and amalgamation

Extreme responses are sometimes given to the above question, and have sometimes been incorporated into laws and attitudes affecting immigrants (or potential immigrants) and ethnic groups. Some of those who have feared the foreign customs or loyalties of non-English immigrants have produced schemes designed to compel them to *assimilate* to a white Anglo-Saxon Protestant (WASP) cultural model. Since the 1980s a relatively mild form of this kind of thinking has appeared in the 'official English' movements that have pushed several states to enact laws making English their official language. There were more states that considered but declined to do so than did so; earlier versions of this assimilationist thinking had led to much harsher attitudes and practices towards some immigrant cultures and languages (Fuchs, 1990, p. 463; Hartmann, 1948, chapter 10.) Another, perhaps somewhat more liberal but also more utopian kind of thinking preoccupied with producing political unity out of ethnic diversity has been to imagine that the interaction and intermarriage of all the different ethnic groups (Anglos included) would produce a new race of ethnically undifferentiated Americans. Much of this *amalgamation* or 'melting' has occurred, and it continues to break down many ethnic differences, but their total obliteration is not yet in sight.

The opposite extreme: cultural pluralism

These extremes stressing the need for cultural or genetic homogeneity for the sake of political unity, whether by assimilation or by amalgamation, have been challenged by those who favour the opposite extreme, seeing no need for political unity to have such a basis and such a destructive effect on ethnic cultures. In the 1920s (when restrictive immigration laws were passed, partly out of fears for the nation's cultural integrity), 'cultural pluralism' became fashionable among some intellectuals, who opposed the spread of a unifying but superficial 'American' culture and upheld ethnic cultures, with their allegedly more satisfying warmth and depth. This rather romantic approach was echoed by some who supported the revival of ethnic consciousness among white ethnic groups in the late 1960s and early 1970s (for example Novak, 1971). More recently it has been adopted by some of the advocates of 'multiculturalism' who fail to see why ethnic cultures should be subordinated in any decisive way to a unifying national political culture. For example, some advocates of bilingual education (teaching students in their first language as well as in American English) have been more interested in the long-term maintenance of the first-language cultures than in easing recent immigrant children into the common national language and culture (Thernstrom, 1980; Porter, 1990). Reactions against this kind of cultural pluralism have recently appeared across the country in such forms as Proposition 209, the California legislative initiative approved by voters in 1998, which requires that schools in that state focus their efforts on teaching immigrants English.

Between the two extremes

American immigration policy has followed a course between extreme demands for unity and extreme demands for plurality. Although (as we shall see) this policy has had its illiberal moments, in general it has been remarkably liberal.

The first sense in which it has been liberal is in its openness to immigration from many places. The United States was the first country to adopt a policy of receiving immigrants (Mann, 1979, chapter 4). One of the complaints that the American revolutionaries made against King George III in their Declaration of Independence was that he had obstructed 'laws for the naturalisation of foreigners' and refused 'to pass others to encourage their migrations hither'.

The Constitution gave to Congress the power to establish a 'uniform rule of naturalization' (Article I, Section 8). Starting in 1790, it used this power to regulate immigration, assuming that few would immigrate without the prospect of citizenship. After the Fourteenth Amendment was interpreted to mean that resident non-citizens' children born in the United States are citizens, laws more directly affecting immigration were necessary in order to control it, since potential immigrants now had the incentive of citizenship for their American-born children.

In regulating naturalisation and immigration, politicians in the United States have developed a second and more important and controversial dimension of 'liberal' policy, by trying to ensure that the character of immigrants be such as will make for good republican citizens. For example, Thomas Jefferson, the main author of the Declaration of Independence, later (in his *Notes on the State of Virginia*, 1784) expressed fears that immigrants might bring antirepublican opinions and unrepublican habits to the United States. Jefferson continued to voice the first sense of liberality, by concluding that while 'extraordinary encouragements' should not be offered to immigrants, if they come on their own initiative 'they are entitled to all the rights of citizenship'. However, he also introduced a second sense of liberality, the desire that immigrants be as fit as possible for a republican life of 'temperate liberty'. He feared that immigrants from despotic European regimes might be either too careless of their rights, or, passing in reaction 'from one extreme to another', tempted to lead lives of 'unbounded licentiousness'. (Peterson, 1975, p. 125).

American immigration policy was to be liberal in this second sense as well, most clearly in expecting immigrants to learn and to be loyal to the liberal political principles that define the regime and that provide a means of binding the various ethnic groups or nationalities into one people. This requirement has led to difficult decisions about which countries are more likely to send immigrants whose cultural background makes it easy to make them into Americans.

One of the most powerful statements of the role of liberal ideas in the formation of United States citizenship was made by Abraham Lincoln in July 1858, in a speech reflecting on the function of the Declaration of Independence as a set of political principles that makes it possible for even the most recent immigrants to see that they have roots in the foundation of the republic that are equal to those of the Revolutionary generation:

> We are now a mighty nation, we are thirty – or about thirty millions of people, and we own and inhabit about one-fifteenth part of the dry land of the whole earth. We run our memory back over the pages of history for about eighty-two years and we discover that we were then a very small people in point of numbers, vastly inferior to what we are now, with a vastly less extent of country, – with vastly less of everything we deem desirable among men, – we look upon the change as exceedingly advantageous to us and to our posterity, and we fix upon something that happened away back, as in some way or other being connected with this rise of prosperity. We find a race of men living in that day whom we claim as our fathers and grandfathers; they were iron men, they fought for the principle that they were contending for; and we understand that by what they then did it has followed that the degree of prosperity that we now enjoy has come to us. We hold this annual celebration to remind ourselves of all the good done in this process of time, of how it was done and who did it, and how we are historically connected with it; and we go from these meetings in better humor with ourselves – we feel more attached the one to the other, and more firmly bound to the country we inhabit. In every way we are better men in the age, and race, and country in which we live for these celebrations. But after we have done all this we have not yet reached the whole. There is something else connected with it. We have besides these men – descended by blood from our ancestors – among us perhaps half our people who are not descendants at all of these men, they are men who have come from Europe – German, Irish, French and Scandinavian – men that have come from Europe themselves, or whose ancestors have come hither and settled here, finding themselves our equals in all things. If they look back through this history to trace their connection with those days by blood, they find they have none, they cannot carry themselves back into that glorious epoch and make themselves feel that they are part of us, but when they look through that old Declaration of Independence they find that those old men say that 'We hold these truths to be self-evident, that all men are created equal', and then they feel that that moral sentiment taught in that day evidences their relation to those men, that it is the father of all moral principle in them, and that they have a right to claim it as though they

were blood of the blood, and flesh of the flesh of the men who wrote that Declaration, and so they are. That is the electric cord in that Declaration that links the hearts of patriotic and liberty-loving men together, that will link those patriotic hearts as long as the love of freedom exists in the minds of men throughout the world.

(Basler, 1953–55, vol. 2, pp. 499ff)

In this understanding – more confident than the more disenchanted view that is typically taken by liberal intellectuals today – not ethnic patriarchs but ideological 'founding fathers' are the focus of American political loyalty, so ethnic background does not determine one's civil rights.

This view of the process of Americanisation does not require either assimilation to a pre-existing ethnic pattern, or ethnic amalgamation and the disappearance of separate ethnic groups. However, because (like Jefferson's earlier thoughts) it acknowledges that some humans may be by their experience and education better prepared than others for the opinions and habits needed to sustain healthy republican politics, it can be and has been understood at times to favour some groups of potential immigrants over others. Therefore it has been and remains today very difficult to disentangle legitimate concerns for ensuring that immigrants are good citizenship material from racial and ethnic prejudices.

Many ethnic groups in the United States – or, more precisely, many individuals within them – have been intolerant of other groups. Furthermore, many 'immigrants' have in fact been *sojourners*, intending or required to return to their own countries, and often doing so, either temporarily (for example, migrant workers from Mexico, both legal and illegal) or permanently – return migration has run as high as one-third of the total immigration (Mann, 1979, p. 84). Even with firmly settled groups, it has sometimes been difficult to judge when an ethnic group's natural concern for its country or people of origin becomes unacceptable distortion of American foreign policy. Thus sometimes there have been good liberal reasons for making exceptions to the basic liberality of American policy concerning immigrants.

Even in the absence of such reasons, many exceptions have been made on less legitimate grounds of ethnic or racial hostility, often combined with economic rivalries. These motives, as well as concern for the moral and political character and beliefs of immigrants as potential citizens, have led to the restriction or exclusion of certain categories of immigrants. These less noble motives have also led to the curtailment of the economic opportunities and civil liberties of some of these immigrants and their descendants, producing a substantial catalogue of exceptions to the liberality of immigration and ethnic policies. While immigration restrictions and some discrimination in favour of citizens over resident aliens can be defended in terms of liberal policy and the principle of government by consent, once individuals become citizens, ethnic and racial discrimination becomes illegitimate.

In the following sections of this chapter, we briefly examine the experience of some of the major immigrant groups. This will enable us to see how various ethnic groups have made their way and contributed to the formation of the 'one people' of the United States in spite of the hostility and opposition that they have often faced, and to see how the political system has been affected by the repeated experience of mass immigrations.

'Racial' exceptions to the liberality of immigration policy ▬▬▬▬▬▬

Blacks

The first category of legally excluded immigrants was free blacks. There were plenty of black slaves. From the beginning of the European colonisation of the Americas up to the nineteenth century, nearly 10 million African slaves were brought (against their will) to the western hemisphere. Only a small percentage of these went to what was or became the United States; yet the abundant reproduction of the slaves in United States territory meant that by 1800, slaves were nearly one fifth of the total population. However, naturalisation of free black immigrants was legally forbidden. Until 1870, only 'free white persons' were legally welcomed by being made eligible for naturalisation. Courts had difficulty defining what counted as a 'white' person, and many exceptions were made, but legally blacks were welcomed into the country only as slaves – and not even as slaves after their importation was outlawed in 1808.

There were, in addition to 5 million black slaves, nearly half a million free blacks ('free persons of colour') in the United States by the time of the final federal emancipation in 1865. However, this population – which, although very poor, enjoyed an adaptive head start over slaves freed in the 1860s – derived not from (voluntary) immigration but from earlier emancipations at the state or local level, or at the individual level. Many free blacks were mulattos, and more of them were women than men: the free black population included many children of white slave masters, and the mothers of these children. These blacks who were free before the Civil War and their descendants, as well as the blacks who have emigrated from the Caribbean in the twentieth century and their descendants, still form populations that can be distinguished by their social and economic standing from the larger population of blacks freed by the Civil War and their descendants (Olson, 1994, pp. 299–301; Sowell, 1981, chapter 8).

However, all American blacks were subject to legal violations of their civil rights under the state and federal discriminatory and segregatory regimes that flourished from the end of the nineteenth century to the middle of the twentieth. They also continued to be subject to physical assault; for example, lynching, a long-standing southern practice by whites, gradually came to be directed primarily at blacks rather than other whites.

It is difficult to judge how much the long history of discrimination and violence against black Americans has affected and continues today to affect their social and economic standings. Black leaders tend to be more pessimistic on this question than black Americans more generally (Fuchs, 1990, p. 444). National statistical comparisons can be misleading: a larger proportion of blacks than whites live in the south (where incomes are lower than average), and there is a larger proportion of blacks than whites in low-income age groups. In fact, in some categories (for example young two-earner married couples outside the south), black incomes have been higher than those of whites (Sowell, 1981, p. 222). The differences in life expectancy between blacks and whites (currently about six years) has been narrowing. Infant mortality rates have been falling for both blacks and whites – although much faster for whites. Since the 1960s, black Americans have greatly progressed in terms of political and cultural representation.

Some indicators of black/white social integration have gone up. The rates of intermarriage between blacks and others has increased dramatically since 1970 (Fuchs, 1990, p. 328), although it still remains low compared with intermarriage rates between different white ethnic groups, or even between whites, Asians and Hispanics. Mixed residential patterns have also become more common in this period.

Many of the overall improvements in black Americans' economic, social and political conditions have led to a sharper division between successful and unsuccessful blacks. One of the most worrying of recent statistics is the rate at which black males in their twenties are, on any given day, subject to imprisonment, probation or parole. The 1990s war on drugs in the inner cities has helped push this up to one in three: much higher than the rates for whites and others.

The standard portrait of blacks as a group failing to be accepted as equals and failing to reach the average level of economic achievement of other Americans thus ignores important distinctions among black Americans, and overaccentuates the negative, but it is not wholly lacking in substance. That portrait continues to sustain the view that how well blacks do is one good test of how well the American political system is working, and to support public and private affirmative action favouring blacks (which may or may not be a good remedy: see Chapter 20 for further consideration of this issue).

Chinese

Another category of people subjected to legal exclusion and deprivation of civil rights was the Chinese. In the nineteenth century many of the Chinese who came to the United States (not much more than 100,000, but geographically concentrated) were males, who came as sojourners, or as tentative immigrants, leaving families behind for the moment. Their experience in the United States often discouraged their desire to remain there, and a large proportion returned (although some who wanted to return could not afford to do so). The Chinese were not only non-white, they were also non-Christian, and they seemed to be very foreign. Physical harassment of Chinese soon became a well established tradition in the western states where most of them settled. Labour unions, who saw Chinese workers as rivals and strikebreakers, led the way towards the Chinese Exclusion Act of 1882, which curtailed further immigration. Other laws prevented Chinese from testifying against whites (thus reducing their legal recourse against assaults by whites) and made it impossible for them to become citizens.

The Exclusion Act of 1882, which was repealed only after sixty years had passed, had a great effect on the number of Chinese in America and on the quality of their lives. The number declined (an unusual event for an American immigrant group) by more than 50 per cent from 1890 to 1920; it then gradually rose again, not surpassing its earlier peak before 1950. The reason for this decline was the vast sexual imbalance of the Chinese in America (more than 27 men per woman in 1890). Many more men than women had come from China before the Act, and they were both socially and legally forbidden to marry white American women. In fact, many of these Chinese men had wives and children back in China, whom they were now unable to bring to the

United States, and whom they found it difficult to return to because of the cost of the return journey. This massive disruption of family life, coupled with continued physical and legal harassment, helped produce American 'Chinatowns', enclaves of stranded sojourners. These were centres for prostitution, opium and gambling, but they were also centres for self-help networks that made it possible for Chinese Americans to survive economic bad times with little reliance on public assistance, and to begin building up capital and business experience.

During and after the Second World War, labour shortages and educational and housing opportunities drew many Chinese Americans out of their traditional Chinatown occupations. By 1960, most Chinese Americans did not live in Chinatowns; they remained members of a self-contained ethnic community, infrequently marrying outside their group, but they had become well represented in business and the professions, and their average income had begun to exceed the American average. Initially, Chinese immigrants came overwhelmingly from one district of one province; in recent decades, Chinese immigration has included many Chinese with origins and dialects from different regions of China, often by way of Hong Kong or Southeast Asia, thus greatly diversifying the Chinese-American presence in the United States.

Japanese

In spite of the fact that the American way of life was extolled in Japan in the late nineteenth and early twentieth centuries, Japanese immigrants were also subject to discriminatory practices and legislation; for example California forbade aliens ineligible for citizenship to own land: a law directed mainly at first-generation Japanese immigrants, which was repealed only in 1956, after a successful challenge in the Supreme Court. However, because the Japanese government in the early twentieth century was effective in protecting the immigrants that it had carefully selected to send to America, growing hostility to Japanese immigrants took the form not (as with the Chinese) of a unilaterally imposed limitation, but of a 'gentlemen's agreement' in 1908, whereby Japan agreed to limit the number of its emigrants and the United States agreed to allow wives and other relatives to join the existing immigrants.

Soon after the Japanese surprise attack on the United States in December 1941, President Roosevelt issued an executive order authorising the army to evacuate from 'military areas' (defined to include the west coast) anyone they decided was a threat. More than 100,000 Japanese Americans were removed from the west coast, and many of them were interned behind barbed wire for many months in rugged, makeshift camps in inhospitable locations. The public support for this internment stretched across the political spectrum, 'from the Hearst newspapers and racist bigots like columnist Westbrook Pegler on the Right to outstanding liberals like Earl Warren and Walter Lippmann, to Leftists like Carey McWilliams, Vito Marcantonio, and the editors of the Communist *Daily Worker* and *People's World*' (Sowell, 1981, p. 172). The Supreme Court unanimously upheld the executive order when it was challenged.

This wartime hysteria did not last for long. In 1944 Roosevelt and other politicians were publicly defending the loyalty of Japanese Americans, many of whom had fought and died for their country in battles against German forces, or played a crucial role as interpreters in the war against Japan. However, the devastation of the evacuation and internment severely interrupted the economic progress that Japanese immigrants had been making. It is also argued by some (including some Japanese Americans) that this experience, along with the brave comportment of Japanese American soldiers in spite of the internment policy, in the long run actually improved their social and economic mobility and acceptance: today, Japanese Americans do well economically, and they frequently intermarry with 'whites'. Nevertheless, in the 1980s, Congress decided to pay more than $1 billion to compensate Japanese American losses caused by the evacuation.

Filipinos

The Philippine Islands became a United States territory as a result of the Spanish–American War in 1898, so Filipino immigration was not legally restricted until 1935, when the islands moved from territorial to commonwealth status and were therefore subject to the 1924 National Origins Act (see below). After the Philippines became an independent republic in 1946, further immigration was prohibited, but 200,000 immigrants had already come to the United States (or Hawaii). Their slow economic advancement, relative to other Asian groups, has been attributed to their internal heterogeneity (they came from different islands with different languages) and the consequent lack of the self-help networks that assisted the advancement of those other groups in spite of the discriminatory treatment that was meted out to them as well as to Filipinos.

Mexicans

Relatively few Mexican Americans trace their origins to people who lived in territories that became parts of the United States at the end of the war between Mexico and the United States in 1848. Most have come as immigrants, mainly in the twentieth century. For some decades, American policy on immigration from Mexico was influenced by two, sometimes conflicting, desires: the desire to have on tap a cheap labour supply, and the desire to treat Mexicans as an inferior race.

In the late nineteenth and early twentieth centuries, Mexican Americans were in many places subjected to legal segregation and disenfranchisement. The segregation of Mexican American communities was also based on the fact that many Mexicans were employed in railroad, mining or agricultural work that encouraged them to reside in Spanish-speaking enclaves; and on the fact that the large amount of back-and-forth migration between Mexico and the United States maintained the Mexican culture of Mexicans north of the border. This segregation was not as systematic or as durable as the system imposed on black Americans, and it had a less retarding effect on the economic progress of Mexican Americans (Fuchs, 1990, pp. 138–9), but it reflected the difficulty that many 'white' Americans have had in treating 'non-whites' as equals, and in recent years it has helped to justify the inclusion of Hispanic Americans as targets of affirmative action programmes.

Immigration across the 2000-mile border between Mexico and the United States has always been difficult to control, and the greater economic opportunity generally available on the American side has attracted large (although difficult to count) numbers of immigrants or sojourners. However, during the bad economic times of the 1930s, the number of Mexicans in the United States declined; many returned voluntarily to Mexico, and many (including US citizens) were illegally deported. During the labour shortage caused by the Second World War, immigration from Mexico, at least in the form of temporary contract workers, was again officially encouraged, but in the 1950s massive deportations once more took place – although with greater respect for the rights of US citizens this time. The third great wave of Mexican immigration started in the 1960s and continues today (see below).

'New immigrants' and the National Origins Act of 1924

In addition to these 'racial' exceptions to the liberality of ethnic and immigration policies, the openness of immigration policy was further reduced by the National Origins Act of 1924. This Act (as amended in 1929), which formed the basis of US immigration policy until 1965, restricted the total number of immigrants from the eastern hemisphere to 150,000 per year and allocated shares of that number to eligible countries (mostly European) in proportion to the number of people with origins in each of these countries who were already present in the United States in 1920.

One of the purposes of this policy was to counteract the shift of immigration away from northern Europe towards southern and eastern Europe. Rightly or wrongly, many Americans believed that this shift entailed a greater danger of morally and civically dubious characters becoming residents and citizens. The shift had taken place as industrialisation and the commercialisation of agriculture spread to these parts of Europe, and as improvements in transportation (for example the development of the steamship) made travel between these parts and America more feasible. More than half of the 22 million immigrants into the United States from 1890 to 1940 came from Italy (4.3 million), Austria–Hungary (3.9 million) and Russia (3 million) (Olson, 1994, p. 113; see also Box 8.1). These 'new immigrants' were mostly non-Protestants (Eastern Orthodox Christians, Catholics and Jews). Many of them were sojourners – though this was not true for the 2 million Jews among them, many of whom were families fleeing persecution in Russia and eastern Europe.

Throughout the nineteenth century, Catholic immigrants from Ireland, Germany and Canada had been subject to ethnic or racial abuse and assaults, and to local restrictions on some of their activities (for example the banning of German shooting clubs and mutual aid societies). Parochial (Catholic) schools were generally refused public financing, and by the 1880s the use of French or German as a language of instruction in parochial as well as state schools was outlawed by several states. The two major political parties in the early nineteenth century – the Whigs and the Democrats – differed on their attitude to and reception of immigrants (especially Irish Catholic immigrants). The Whigs depended on support from WASP and 'nativist'

Box 8.1

American immigration, 1890–1940

	1890s	1900s	1910s	1920s	1930s	Total
Austria–Hungary[1]	592,707	2,145,266	900,656	214,806	31,652	3,885,087
Denmark	50,231	65,285	41,983	32,430	2,559	192,488
Finland[2]			756	16,691	2,146	19,593
France	30,770	73,379	61,897	49,610	12,623	228,279
Germany	505,152	341,498	143,945	412,202	114,058	1,516,855
England	216,726	388,017	249,944	157,420	21,756	1,033,863
Scotland	44,188	120,469	78,357	159,781	6,887	409,682
Wales	10,557	17,464	13,107	13,012	735	54,875
Greece	15,979	167,519	184,201	51,084	9,119	427,902
Ireland	388,416	339,065	146,181	220,591	13,167	1,107,420
Italy	651,893	2,045,877	1,109,524	455,315	68,028	4,330,637
Netherlands	26,758	48,262	43,718	26,948	7,150	152,836
Norway	95,015	190,505	66,395	68,531	4,740	425,186
Poland[3]	96,720		4,813	227,734	17,026	346,293
Portugal	27,508	69,149	89,732	29,994	3,329	219,712
Rumania	12,750	53,008	13,311	67,646	3,871	1150,586
Spain	8,731	27,935	68,611	28,958	3,258	137,493
Sweden	226,266	249,534	95,074	97,249	3,960	672,083
Switzerland	31,179	34,922	23,091	29,676	5,512	124,380
Russia	505,290	1,597,306	921,201	61,742	1,356	3,086,895
China	14,799	20,605	21,278	29,907	4,928	91,517
Japan	25,942	129,797	83,837	33,462	1,948	275,166
Turkey	30,425	157,369	134,066	33,824	1,065	356,749
Canada	3,311	179,226	742,185	924,515	108,527	1,957,764
Mexico		49,642	219,004	459,287	22,319	750,257
Total	3,611,313	8,511,098	5,456,867	3,902,415	471,719	21,953,412

[1] Austria–Hungary includes Austrians, Hungarians, Galician Poles, Czechs, Slovaks, Rusins, Ukrainians, Slovenes, Croatians and Serbians

[2] Finland was part of Russia until after the First World War

[3] Poland was not really independent until after the First World War, and Polish-speaking people were scattered throughout Austria–Hungary, Russia and Germany

Source: Olson, 1994, p. 113. Copyright © 1994 by St Martin's Press, Inc. Reprinted with permission of St Martin's Press, Inc.

(anti-immigrant) voters, although they were never officially nativist (as was the 'American' or 'Know Nothing' party, an important minor party in this period). The Democrats depended on many recent immigrants' support, and their platforms denounced political crusades against Catholic and foreign-born Americans.

The 'nativist' reaction to the 'new immigration' from southern and eastern Europe in the late nineteenth and early twentieth centuries that helped to prompt the National Origins Act was a development of the earlier nativism. Although the new immigrants were 'white', their differences (real and imagined) from previous white immigrants inspired hostility to the continuation of their immigration in massive numbers, along with Americanisation programmes in schools, churches, patriotic societies, civil groups, and chambers of commerce. A national crusade was launched, designed to make the new immigrants 'forget Old World languages, shed Old World customs, abandon parochial schools, and discard Old World political loyalties' (Olson, 1994, p. 178). The new immigrants were often victimised by the criminal justice system, and convicted and executed (or lynched) in cases where there was very doubtful evidence against them (most notoriously, Nicolo Sacco and Bartolomeo Vanzetti, in a case that lasted from 1920 to 1927). It was not only white nativists who reacted against the new immigrants; for example, black American residents of certain neighbourhoods in New York and Detroit fled from these neighbourhoods when Polish and Italian immigrants moved in (Sowell, 1981, p. 277).

At the end of the twentieth century, the economic distinctions and the cultural differences between old and new Euro-Americans have greatly declined. Much intermarriage has taken place. For example, for Italian Americans under 25 years of age, the exogamy rate is more than 75 per cent (Wattenberg, 1991, p. 17). However, the new immigrants of the late nineteenth and early twentieth centuries did not simply assimilate or amalgamate. Some of them established cultural values that continue today to rival the dominant 'Protestant ethic' with its emphasis on individual economic success and social and geographical mobility: stable families, stable neighborhoods, religious loyalty, and hard work were the immigrant Catholic alternatives to the Protestant ethic in America (Olson, 1994, p. 138). Others – notably Jewish Americans, who were excluded by the dominant Protestants from many established routes to economic success – demonstrated that 'Protestant' middle class values and habits could carry them from the slums to the suburbs in spite of such discrimination.

Immigration and ethnic politics since 1965

The new immigration regime

Between 1945 and 1965, some exceptions were made to the 1924 immigration rules, in order to allow entry by war brides (and children) and by refugees from Europe, China and Cuba, but the 1924 regime remained in place until 1965. Then, partly because of pressure from ethnic groups whose further immigration had been restricted in 1924, and partly because American public opinion in the civil rights era of the 1950s and 1960s had become less content with basing immigration preferences on national origins, the Immigration and Nationality Act established a new system of immigration, which remains in place today. It set a yearly limit of 20,000 for every country in the eastern hemisphere, up to a total of 170,000. This Act also for the first time set a ceiling for immigration from the western hemisphere: 120,000 per year. At first no limit was set for each country in this hemisphere, but in 1976 the 20,000 limit was applied to western hemisphere countries as well, because of growing unease at the number of Mexican immigrants. (At the same time, Cuban refugees were exempted from the western hemisphere quota.) In 1978 the two hemisphere ceilings were combined to form a worldwide ceiling of 290,000. By 1996, the overall limit on legal immigration had been raised to about 775,000 (plus about 130,000 refugees – separately counted – and asylum-seekers).

As part of this new immigration system, preference is given to immediate relatives of US citizens and other US residents, and to those with professions and skills needed in the United States. In 1990 the annual quota for the latter was raised from 54,000 to 140,000, and, in what has been criticised as a 'give me your rich and well-to-do elites' programme, 10,000 annual places were established for those willing and able to invest at least \$1 million (or \$500,000 in certain high unemployment areas) in an American business employing at least ten people. So far, the take-up on this programme has been slight (936 in 1996, including immediate relatives of the investors).

The newest immigrants

Since 1965, several million immigrants have settled in the United States under this new immigration regime, and some millions have settled illegally. By 1996, the foreign-born population of the United States, according to the Census Bureau, was 24.5 million: about 9.3 per cent of the population, the highest proportion since the Second World War (though well short of the record 14.7 per cent recorded for 1910).

When the new system was initiated in 1965, it was expected that (as its sponsors intended) it would bring an increase in immigration from southern and eastern Europe, without much if any increase in immigration from other areas. However, what has actually happened is that the occupational preferences, coupled with the traditional family preferences, have helped to create a vast new wave of immigration by Asians (largely Koreans, Indians, Filipinos, Chinese and Indochinese) and Latinos during the past three decades. During this period, many immigrants have first entered the United States on non-immigrant visas (for example students or tourists), later (by marriage or employment) secured immigrant status for themselves, and then brought their immediate relatives in under the family preference rules. Another basis for immigration based on family preference rules has been armed service spouses from such countries as Korea, Japan, the Philippines and Vietnam. Refugee and asylee admissions have provided yet another basis, with large numbers entering as refugees from Cuba, Southeast Asia, Afghanistan, Ethiopia and elsewhere, then sponsoring entry by their family members after they had themselves been granted immigrant status. Illegal immigrants have also been able (through marriage, parenthood or employment) to gain immigrant status and therefore become the basis of a chain of immigration based on immediate relative status (Fuchs, 1990, pp. 279–83).

In the decade before the 1965 reforms, 50 per cent of immigrants were from Europe;

by the 1980s European immigration had fallen to 10 per cent. For the 1990s, the European percentage will no doubt have fallen further. If recent Census Bureau projections prove to be accurate, by 2050 these new immigration patterns, coupled with different age and birth patterns among different groups, will produce a US population that is 24.5 per cent Hispanic (up from 10.2 per cent today), 8.2 per cent Asian-Pacific (from 3.3 per cent), 13.6 per cent black (from 12 per cent), and 53 per cent non-Hispanic white (from 74 per cent). Of course, increasing intermarriage rates, among other things, might well make these projected classifications look absurd.

The large wave of Mexican immigration that started in the 1960s has taken place during a period of somewhat heightened sensitivity to civil rights and greater politicisation of Hispanic Americans. However, immigration from Mexico continues to pose particular policy problems for both federal and state governments, partly because it continues to involve numerous illegal as well as legal immigrants. A study sponsored jointly by the US and Mexican governments has concluded that the number of undocumented Mexican workers settling in the United States in the ten years up to 1996 is just over 1 million – far lower than some politicians have suggested, but still a substantial number – taking the estimate for the total Mexican-born US population to just over 7 million, with just over 2 million of these being unauthorised residents (Dillon, 1997).

Ethnic coalitions and conflicts

The traditional tendency for recent immigrants to identify with the Democratic party more than with the Republican party (the successor to the Whig party as the major party opposing the Democrats) grew – and black Americans began switching from Republican to Democratic identification – when the Great Depression and the New Deal increased the Democratic party's support in northern cities. This tendency was further strengthened when the Democratic party took up more energetically than the Republicans the cause of minority group members' civil rights during the 1960s. However, the post-1965 immigration has taken place while new, candidate-centred campaign techniques have made parties and party identification less important in electoral politics (as we shall see in Part III), and many of the new immigrant groups have learned that contributing money directly to candidates' campaigns is the most efficient way to gain political influence. In the 1980s and 1990s, many Asian American groups (including Taiwanese, Indians, Pakistanis, Filipinos, Vietnamese, Cambodians and Koreans) have been politically active in this way and have been targeted by fund-seeking politicians.

The various new ethnic minorities have not always shared the same interests or views, either with each other or with older ethnic minorities. Post-1965 immigrants have tended more than previous cohorts to reside in cities inhabited by large numbers of black Americans. Possibilities for both co-operation and conflict between blacks and these new immigrants have arisen out of this fact. Some Latino and Asian groups of recent immigrants share with black Americans lower than average levels of income and wealth. Some of them feel victims of discrimination by whites in the same way that some blacks do. In pursuing their political interests, they have been able to use some of the same political

strategies and tactics as blacks. For example, when the Voting Rights Act of 1965, originally designed to secure the rights of disenfranchised southern blacks, was renewed in
1975, it was extended to the south west, making it available for use by Latinos.

However, as in the past, the different ways that ethnic groups earn their livings, as
well as their different residential patterns and cultural backgrounds, divide them even
when gross economic characteristics might seem to unite them. Even on economic
issues, there are important differences between these various 'non-white' groups. For
example, Asian Americans who own and run shops in areas with many black and
Latino customers often reside elsewhere, in a white-majority area, and this can be a
recipe for mutual resentment more than for interracial harmony:

> The Asian shopkeepers are driven by economic necessity to do business in ghetto areas
> with relatively cheap family labor, since they are competing in a market sector in which
> the odds of failure are much higher than the odds of success. At the same time, this strat-
> egy limits employment opportunities for the neighboring residents and contributes to the
> chronic ghetto problem of circulating more money out of the neighborhood than back in.
>
> (Cain, 1994, p. 50)

Moreover, since politics concerns not only economic but also social and foreign
policy issues, it is important to note that many of the newest immigrants (particularly
Asians and Cuban Latinos) are more conservative than liberal on such issues as abortion, school prayer, school busing, affirmative action and homosexual rights, as well
as on foreign policy issues. This conservatism, along with the variety of ethnic or
national loyalties within their 'racial' group, distinguish them from the majority of
black Americans, who identify themselves as Democrats and as liberals or moderates,
and who have far fewer ethnic or nationality differences than are found among Asians
and Latinos. (There are notable exceptions to this generalisation: English-, Spanish-
and French-speaking black immigrants from the Caribbean and Latin America, as well
as black African immigrants, do not always identify with native-born black Americans
[Fuchs, 1990, p. 333].) In general, as the Democratic party was increasingly seen to be
embracing liberal social and foreign policy positions in the 1960s, 1970s and 1980s, it
had difficulty in obtaining votes among the newer ethnic groups as well as in maintaining its electoral strength among its traditionally supportive ethnic groups.

On top of economic and social policy differences between many Asians and Latinos
on the one hand and blacks on the other, any potential for a 'rainbow coalition' of all
non-white groups has declined as it has become more common for black political
leaders to question some of the standard liberal positions on immigration. Some of
these leaders fear that spending public educational funds on bilingual education programmes (favoured by many Latino leaders) reduces the amount of money available
for more general educational purposes, and that the continuation of large-scale immigration threatens the employment prospects of black citizens.

On immigration policy, there are also important divisions among different groups of
Latinos: Puerto Ricans, who are all US citizens by birth, and Cuban immigrants, many
of whom have refugee status, have not shared the concerns felt by Mexican Americans.
Mexican Americans themselves have not always stood united on the question, or on the
importance of the question, of Mexican immigration. During the first half of the twentieth century, it became usual for Mexican American *citizens* to distance themselves

from new Mexican *immigrants and sojourners*, and officially to oppose further massive immigration. They felt this immigration depressed their wages and detracted from their dignity in the eyes of other American citizens. In the 1960s and 1970s, the Chicano movement pushed Mexican American opinion away from this traditional tendency, towards regarding Anglo racism rather than Mexican immigration as the main enemy. The main concern of Mexican Americans during the 1980s' debates on how to control illegal immigration was that their rights and economic opportunities should not be jeopardised by the steps being taken to reduce illegal immigration. For example, they worried that employers punished for employing illegal residents would thereby be encouraged to discriminate against legal ones. Thus, as the Chicano movement had desired, immigration itself had become a less important issue for Mexican Americans, who were more concerned about education and welfare policy; but their distancing from recent or would-be immigrants from Mexico remained (de la Garza, 1992).

Since 1960, there has been a quickening pace of ethnic interaction in American society. Although some ethnic group members remain isolated, Americans of different ethnic backgrounds now more commonly encounter one another in neighbourhoods, churches, schools, workplaces and government bodies, and see each other in advertising and on television broadcasts. This has not removed all sources of ethnic hatred and conflict, but it has helped to create a greater amount of mutual recognition and respect. It has also increased the extent to which ethnic boundary lines have become blurred, allowing some Americans to claim the ethnic identification that they feel best suits their interests (Fuchs, 1990, chapters 16–17).

Political reactions against the newest immigration

The surge of immigration in the past thirty years, like previous episodes, has inspired some political opposition, but no Americanisation crusade or policy change as extreme as those of the 1920s (see Box 8.2).

One of the novelties of the new immigration is that, in spite of the fact that a greater variety of languages are spoken by these immigrants than by previous waves of immigrants, a majority (or a near-majority) of the new immigrants who speak a foreign language speak the same language (Spanish). As noted in the discussion of assimilation policy (above, page 162), the growth of Spanish-language areas in the United States inspired some laws – with relatively mild effects – establishing English as the official language in some states.

There have been discussions in Congress in the 1980s and 1990s about cutting the numbers of legal immigrants, but in both decades it was decided not to do so, but to try instead to deal with the more difficult problem of illegal immigration.

In 1986, the Immigration Control and Reform Act imposed penalties on employers who hire illegal immigrants, while at the same time offering many currently residing illegal immigrants the opportunity to legalise their status. Three million of them did so.

In 1994, California voters (through a ballot initiative, Proposition 187) decided to bar illegal immigrants from public education and from some health and social services. However, in 1995, in a case still working its way up to the Supreme Court, a federal district judge ruled that illegal immigrants could not be asked to reveal their status

Box 8.2

Patrick J. Buchanan, immigration and American identity

Patrick Buchanan, the conservative TV commentator and former speechwriter who sought the Republican party's presidential nomination in both 1992 and 1996, attempted to make immigration a central campaign issue. He called for a five-year ban or 'moratorium' on all legal admissions together with measures that would put a final halt to illegal immigration. These included the deployment of the National Guard and the fortification of America's southern border.

Buchanan's calls for immigration reform find an echo across established ideological and partisan boundaries. Some black leaders, long allied with liberalism, fear the impact of mass immigration on the unskilled labour market. A number of environmentalists argue that population growth intensifies the pressures on America's natural resources. In a number of states, strains on welfare provision, education and other public services are widely attributed to the presence of immigrants.

However, either indirectly or indirectly, Buchanan and some other conservatives introduce a further argument in support of restrictionist claims. They assert that the United States has a distinct national culture and an ethno-cultural character that evolved from a northern European core. Over the years, the original core was extended and remoulded by the 'frontier spirit', a sense of determination and individualism derived from the conquest of a continent.

Contemporary immigrants, it is argued, do not share the defining characteristics of this national culture. The emergence of Hispanic, Asian and east European enclaves, and the promulgation of 'multiculturalism', therefore threaten to weaken or even destroy America's identity as a nation-state. From this perspective, the United States faces the prospect of fracture and 'Balkanisation'.

However, restrictionist arguments have not gone unchallenged. Indeed, much of the opposition to Buchanan has come from within the conservative movement itself. The leading business newspaper, the *Wall Street Journal*, went so far as to propose a five-word constitutional amendment: 'There shall be open borders'. The paper's declaration stemmed from its commitment to the free movement of *both* labour and capital. Other conservatives observe that immigrants are largely of working age, and therefore, as a group, contribute rather more in taxes than they take in social benefits.

The proponents of immigration also confront the concept of a US national culture. They assert that the process of becoming an American, and the character of the United States as a nation, rest solely upon a faith in principles such as individualism, democracy, self reliance and economic enterprise. American identity has been, and will continue to be, structured around a plethora of cultural and ethnic forms.

These differences have led to an increasingly open rift within the conservative movement. Although Buchanan's successes in the Republican primaries gave his arguments a degree of credence, those who argue that conservatism can only prosper if it establishes a more positive relationship with minorities have also gained ground. As William Buckley Jr, the founder of *National Review*, the most widely circulated of America's conservative journals, noted: 'the two camps are now out in the open, moving towards one another with sabers drawn'.

Contributed by Dr E. G. C. Ashbee, Denstone College, Staffordshire

when applying for such services, since this would be an unconstitutional state usurpation of the federal government's power to regulate immigration.

Partly as a response to the support visible for measures like Proposition 187 during the congressional election campaigns of 1994, in 1995 a bipartisan congressional panel (and, for a time, President Clinton) supported a reduction in the number of legal immigrants, but pressures from a wide variety of sources – ranging from manufacturers to religious leaders to both liberal and conservative think tanks – helped persuade Congress to decline to adopt this proposal. Instead, in the spring of 1996, Congress passed laws designed to improve border controls, to streamline deportation procedures, and to make it more difficult for illegal immigrants to receive certain education and welfare benefits. In 1995 the Census Bureau had reported that 5.7 per cent of recent immigrants have received public welfare assistance, compared with 2.9 per cent of native-born Americans. (However, if refugees are excluded from these numbers, the immigrant and native-born percentages are much closer to each other.)

Just before the 1996 elections, Congress passed and President Clinton signed a welfare reform Act (discussed in Chapter 19). This Act included provisions that barred *legal* immigrants who are not citizens from certain welfare benefits (which led to a large increase in the numbers being naturalised). Clinton promised to try to get Congress to agree to remove those bars, and in 1997 and 1998 Congress did so. The anti-immigrant lobbies' bark evidently remains worse than their bite. However, some liberals as well as some conservatives continue to push for restrictions on the numbers of immigrants, pointing out that the United States takes half of the total of legal immigrants in the world, and that consideration of the quality as well as the quantity of immigrants is legitimate and desirable. A gradual cutback in the number of legal immigrants (to 550,000 per year by 2002) is one of the proposals made by a bipartisan Commission on Immigration Reform that reported in October 1997.

This Commission report also emphasised the continuing importance of Americanising new immigrants by teaching them the primacy of 'the rights of individuals over those of groups'. As we noted above, one of the weaknesses of the support for Americanisation in recent decades has been the decline in confidence (although often an increase in stridency) in those who make the case for emphasising the unifying elements of America's civic culture. Even American liberals who (like the liberal historian, Arthur Schlesinger) have recently rejected disunifying appeals for multiculturalism, have often done so not on the grounds that the rights of individual human beings are natural and self-evident for everyone everywhere, but merely on the grounds that these individualistic 'values' are historically 'our own', and that they 'work for us' (Schlesinger, 1992, p. 137).

Summary

In spite of a number of illiberal episodes, the American polity has been remarkably successful in accepting large numbers of immigrants with an enormous variety of ethnic backgrounds and turning them into Americans without requiring them altogether to dispense with their ethnic identifications and loyalties. Since the 1960s, the coercive aspects of the ethnic and racial pluralism of the American polity have declined. The caste-like character of ethnic and racial distinctions has diminished both legally and socially. Many individuals and groups still claim ethnic identifications, but this is now a more optional and voluntary choice than it was in the past.

This generally more liberal and democratic climate does not mean that ethnic or racial tensions have been steadily decreasing in politics, or that they can be expected to disappear from the American political scene. Even if, objectively, most indicators of equal opportunities for ethnic and racial groups are improving (and some are not), subjective judgements, which can vary from objective reality, can be more politically relevant. In a famous passage in *Democracy in America* that could be applied to economic class and gender politics as well as to ethnic and racial politics, Alexis de Tocqueville suggests one of the reasons why Americans sometimes seem greatly discontented and why their politics seem greatly embittered precisely when many relevant conditions are becoming less unequal:

> When inequality is the general rule in society, the greatest inequalities attract no attention. When everything is more or less level, the slightest variation is noticed. Hence the more equal men are, the more insatiable will be their longing for equality. ... That is the reason for the strange melancholy often haunting inhabitants of democracies in the midst of abundance, and of that disgust with life sometimes gripping them in calm and easy circumstances.
>
> (Tocqueville, 1835; 1969, II.ii.13, p. 538)

 References

Basler, Roy P., ed., 1953–55, *The Collected Works of Abraham Lincoln* (9 vols, New Brunswick: Rutgers University Press)

Cain, Bruce, 1994, 'Developments in racial and ethnic politics', in *Developments in American Politics*, eds Gillian Peele *et al.* (2nd edn, London: Macmillan)

Dillon, Sam, 1997, 'Study cuts into high estimates of illegal Mexicans in US', *International Herald Tribune*, 1 September, p. 5

Fuchs, Lawrence H., 1990, *The American Kaleidoscope: Race, ethnicity, and the civic culture* (Hanover, NH: Wesleyan University Press)

de la Garza, Rodolfo O., 1992, 'Immigration reforms: a Mexican-American perspective', in *Developments in American Politics*, eds Gillian Peele *et al.* (2nd edn, London: Macmillan)

Hartmann, Edward George, 1948, *The Movement to Americanize the Immigrant* (New York: Columbia University Press)

Holmes, Steven A., 1979, 'US poll gloomy on race relations', *International Herald Tribune*, 12 June, p. 3

Mann, Arthur, 1997 *The One and the Many: Reflections on the American identity* (Chicago: University of Chicago Press)

Novak, Michael, 1971, *The Rise of the Unmeltable Ethnics* (New York: Macmillan)

Olson, James Stuart, 1994, *The Ethnic Dimension in American History* (2nd edn, New York: St Martin's Press)

Peterson, Merrill D., ed., 1975, *The Portable Thomas Jefferson* (New York: Viking)

Porter, Rosalie Pedalino, 1990, *Forked Tongue: The politics of bilingual education* (New York: Basic Books)

Schlesinger, Arthur M., 1992, *The Disuniting of America* (New York: Norton)

Sowell, Thomas, 1981, *Ethnic America: A history* (New York: Basic Books)

Thernstrom, Abigail M., 1980, 'Language: issues and legislation,' pp. 619–29 in *Harvard Encyclopedia of American Ethnic Groups*, ed. Stephan Thernstrom (Cambridge, Mass.: Harvard University Press)

Tocqueville, Alexis de, 1835, *Democracy in America*. Reprinted 1969, ed. J. P. Mayer, trans. G. Lawrence (Garden City, New York: Doubleday)

Wattenberg, Ben J., 1991, *The First Universal Nation: Leading indicators and ideas about the surge of America in the 1990s* (New York: Free Press)

The representative process

The importance of political representation has been stressed throughout American history. The rallying cry of the American revolutionaries in 1776 was 'No taxation without representation'. When Abraham Lincoln sought to justify the bloodshed of the Civil War and the preservation of the Union in his Gettysburg Address of 1863, he spoke of preserving 'government of the people, by the people and for the people'. Even the most casual observer of American politics cannot fail to notice the pronounced populism of both political practice and rhetoric in the United States. In Part III we examine the detailed attention paid by the framers of the Constitution to notions of popular representation and the modes of election designed to give them effect. In analysing American elections today, we examine how voters respond at the polls and why. Particular attention is paid to the role of the media, especially television, and its power and influence over the conduct and outcome of elections. We also examine the spontaneous growth and development of other institutions of political representation, especially parties and interest groups. Throughout Part III, we will be addressing the major criticism aimed at American elections today: for all the rhetoric, do they actually deliver on the promise of representative democracy?

Contents

9

Elections and voting behaviour

This chapter begins with an examination of the complex arrangements made by the framers of the Constitution for the election of the president and members of Congress. We shall see how these arrangements have changed over time and how they translate into political practice in the modern day. We then turn to an analysis of how American voters respond to election campaigns.

The constitutional framework of elections

The Constitution of 1787 was founded upon the principle of popular sovereignty, the notion that government ultimately derives its authority from the consent of the people. This did not mean, however, that the framers were committed to democracy as we understand it today. Whilst they favoured a *republic*, they were opposed to creating a *democracy*, which many of them equated with mob rule. The constitutional framework for elections, therefore, attempted to blend the principle of popular sovereignty with a desire to restrict the power of the people to actually govern the country.

You are already familiar with the idea that the Constitution's 'separation of powers' and 'checks and balances' were intended as antimajoritarian devices. To further reinforce these restraints on democracy, the framers decided that separate institutions would be elected by separate constituencies, operating separate electoral procedures. In other words, the president, the Senate and the House of Representatives would be chosen in different ways, by different people and at different times. Rival institutions would thus check each other by representing the interests of rival constituencies.

The House of Representatives

The House was intended to be the popular, democratic institution of the federal government. Consequently, its members would be kept close to the people:

1. By being directly elected by the voters.
2. By frequent elections – every two years.
3. By representing relatively small, local constituencies, apportioned by population.

Originally, the Constitution envisaged the House containing one representative for every 30,000 people. The subsequent growth in population, however, has made this apportionment redundant: on the basis of the 1990 census population figure of over 248 million Americans, constituencies of 30,000 would create a House with 8,270 representatives. Congress has therefore fixed the number of representatives at 435 and growth in population simply means that the size of House constituencies, or *districts*, increases accordingly. Today, a House district contains on average approximately 570,000 persons.

Apportionment by population means that some states send many more members to the House of Representatives than others. Every state is entitled to at least one representative, and this is the case with Wyoming (population 454,000) and Vermont (population 563,000), for example. The largest states fare much better: California (population 29,760,000) has fifty-two representatives and Illinois (population 11,431,000) has twenty.

Members of the House, however, are not intended primarily to represent state interests, but rather the interests of their district – and these can vary considerably even within the same state. For example, the New York inner-city voters of Harlem have very different needs and concerns from rural constituents in upper New York state.

Members of the House, both individually and collectively, are obliged to keep in close touch with constituency opinion by the fact that they serve for only two years before facing re-election. With such a short period between elections, voters are unlikely to forgive or forget any representative who has seriously offended public opinion on a salient issue. As a result, representatives keep in constant touch with constituency opinion by, for example, making frequent trips back home from Washington and conducting polls in their district on major issues.

Some critics argue that two-year terms make representatives virtual 'slaves' to public opinion and have advocated replacing them with four-year terms. They also argue that it means that representatives spend too much of their time on electioneering in one form or another, and too little of their time on governmental duties. Whatever the merits of these criticisms, however, the present system does help fulfil the framers' aim of subjecting the House of Representatives to more popular influence than any other branch of the federal government.

The Senate

The representative functions of the Senate were intended to be significantly different from those of the House. First, instead of representing the voters *per se*, the Senate was to represent the states. As such, every state is entitled to two senators, regardless of population. Thus, while we saw above that Wyoming has one representative and California fifty-two, both these states have two senators. This system was a concession to the least populous states, who feared being swamped in the national legislature by the largest states. In line with this representative function, senators are elected by the voters of the whole state.

The second major representative difference is that whereas the House was designed to be the popular chamber, the Senate was designed to be a more 'aristocratic' chamber which checked the popular will. In fact, as many historians have pointed out, the framers thought of the Senate's relationship to the House as somewhat similar to that between the British House of Lords and House of Commons. In line with this aristocratic bent, senators were not originally to be elected directly by the voters. Instead, the legislatures of the states would each decide for themselves how to elect or appoint US senators. This system remained in operation until replaced by the Seventeenth Amendment, ratified in 1913, which instituted the direct election of senators by the voters.

The Constitution further distances senators from popular control by giving them a six-year term of office. This enables senators to take a more long-term and independent view of issues than representatives. If a senator goes against his or her constituents' views on an issue, the chances are that by the time the next elections come around the voters' memories will have faded and their political passions cooled.

Nevertheless, the framers established yet another device that protects the Senate as a whole from the popular political pressures of the moment: *staggered elections*. While all senators serve six-year terms, they are not all elected at the same time: one-third of senators come up for re-election every two years. This means that even if a ferocious political wind should blow in any election year, fully two-thirds of the senators will be electorally unaffected by it. While the House can change direction radically as a result of one year's election results, the Senate is much more resistant to sudden change – hence, its ability to act as a brake upon the House.

The presidency

The president and the vice-president are the only politicians in the United States who are elected by a national constituency. Logically enough, then, they were intended primarily to advocate and represent the national interest, as opposed to state interests (Senate) or local interests (House of Representatives).

Just as the presidency's representative function is different from those of the Senate and House, so too are its terms of office and its mode of election. The president serves a four-year term and, since the passage of the Twenty-second Amendment in 1951, is restricted by the Constitution to a maximum of two terms of office. In fact, however, the very first president, George Washington, had established the custom of not seeking a third term and the Constitution was only amended in the wake of Franklin D. Roosevelt's break with this precedent. The fear which lies behind the two-term limit is of a president who can combine executive power with personal electoral popularity and thereby gain unhealthy control over the rest of the political system.

Federal government election cycle, 1996–2000

1996	Presidency House – All 435 seats Senate – 1st one-third of seats
1998	House – All 435 seats Senate – 2nd one-third of seats
2000	Presidency House – All 435 seats Senate – 3rd one-third of seats

As a result of the different terms of office for president, Senate and House, it takes four years and three successive elections to complete a full electoral cycle for the federal government (see Box 9.1).

The electoral college

The method of electing the president is again different from anything else. The first thing to note is that Article II, Section 1(ii) of the Constitution established an indirect method of election, once again taking the direct choice of president out of the hands of the ordinary voters. The framers had several reasons for this. First, the least populous states feared that the most populous would always supply the president. Secondly, the framers did not believe that in such a large country, the ordinary people would have sufficient knowledge of the qualities of presidential candidates. Thirdly, the framers were wary of too much popular control over the choice of president, fearing that this would encourage demagoguery. They preferred a statesman rather than a tribune as president.

The president therefore would be chosen by an electoral college, in which each state had a number of delegates, called electors. It was left to the states themselves to decide how they would choose their electors. Originally, most state legislatures simply appointed them, but the practice quickly developed of holding some kind of popular vote on the question. By 1832, only South Carolina did not permit a popular vote. Even so, electors were not bound to vote for any particular candidate in the electoral college; rather, they were supposed to use their wisdom and experience to select the best potential president. Today, however, with exception of the odd maverick, electors cast their vote for the candidate who has won the popular election in their state.

Electoral college arithmetic

The number of electors for each state is fixed by adding the number of its representatives to the number of its senators. To calculate the number of electors from any state, then, is easy. For example, as we saw above, Illinois has two senators, like every other state, and twenty members in the House. Therefore the number of delegates in the electoral college from Illinois is twenty-two. Wyoming, one of the least populous states with just one representative, has three votes in the electoral college; and California, the most populous, has fifty-two representatives and therefore fifty-four electoral college votes.

The total number electors in the electoral college, then, is equal to the number of representatives and senators in the Congress, plus three from the federal District of Columbia: that is, 538 all together.

Any presidential candidate must win over half the electoral college votes and therefore the minimum number required for victory is 270.

Electoral strategy

In an important sense, the American presidential election is not just one single election, but rather 51 separate elections in the states and the District of Columbia. What determines victory is not the percentage of votes won in the national popular ballot, but the

---

Box 9.2

Minority presidents

Percentage of popular vote	President	Year of election
49.72	Kennedy	1960
49.54	Polk	1844
49.52	Truman	1948
49.24	Wilson	1916
48.50	Cleveland	1884
48.27	Garfield	1880
47.95	Hayes[a]	1876
47.82	Harrison[a]	1888
47.28	Taylor	1848
46.05	Cleveland	1892
45.28	Buchanan	1856
43.42	Nixon	1968
43.29	Clinton	1992
41.84	Wilson	1912
39.82	Lincoln	1860
30.92	Adams[a]	1824

[a] Fewer popular votes than opponent

Source: *National Journal*, 5 November, 1992, p. A40

number of electoral college votes obtained by winning the elections in the states. For example, a candidate who takes California by a single vote bags all its fifty-four electoral college votes. The same candidate then loses, say, Illinois (twenty-two electoral college votes) by 1,000,001 votes. Although he is now 1 million votes down on his opponent in the national popular vote, he is nevertheless ahead 54–22 in the vote that counts, the electoral college vote.

It is thus not necessary to win 50 per cent of the *popular* vote in order to win the presidency. In 1992, Bill Clinton became the fourteenth president in America to do exactly that. Indeed, on three occasions it has not even proved necessary to win more of the popular vote than one's chief opponent (see Box 9.2).

Moreover, even where a candidate wins both the popular vote and the electoral college vote, the margin of victory in the latter is often a gross distortion of the former. Thus, a candidate who appears to have won a landslide in the electoral college may only have won the popular vote by a relatively narrow margin, as Box 9.3 shows.

Thus, it can be seen that, in 1988, George Bush took just over half the popular votes, but because he won the contests in forty states he took nearly four-fifths of the electoral college vote. In 1992, Bill Clinton took only just over two-fifths of the popular vote, but more than two-thirds of the electoral college vote. It is important to bear this in mind when considering how much of a mandate a winning presidential candidate can claim.

Box 9.3

Distortion of winning popular vote margin by the electoral college system since 1960

Winner	Year	States won	Percentage of popular vote[a]	Electoral college votes	Percentage of electoral college
Kennedy	1960	27	50%	303	56%
Johnson	1964	44	61%	484	90%
Nixon	1968	32	43%	301	56%
Nixon	1972	37	61%	520	97%
Carter	1976	26	50%	297	55%
Reagan	1980	44	51%	489	91%
Reagan	1984	49	59%	525	98%
Bush	1988	40	53%	426	79%
Clinton	1992	32	43%	370	69%
Clinton	1996	31	50%	379	70%

[a] Figures are rounded

Sources: Adapted from *National Journal*, 5 November 1992, p. A40; Pomper *et al.*, 1997, p.176–8

Presidential candidates must therefore adopt the electoral strategy of winning states, rather than the national popular vote *per se* – and, of course, they must seek above all to win the states with the most electoral college votes. In theory, a candidate could win the presidency by carrying just the eleven largest states, including California, New York, Illinois, Texas and Florida. In practice, such a clean sweep of the big states is achieved only in the greatest of landslides. Bill Clinton, for example, had to carry the twentieth largest state before he secured victory in 1992. In 1996, however, he needed victory in only fourteen states to garner enough votes to win re-election.

Third party candidates

The electoral college, combined with the simple majority voting system (first past the post, winner takes all), not only exaggerates the mandate of the victorious candidate, it seriously disadvantages any third party candidate. In 1992, for example, Ross Perot took almost 19 per cent of the national popular vote, yet because he failed to come first in any state, he received no electoral college votes at all. Other third party candidates have fared little better, as Box 9.4 shows.

The difference between Ross Perot in 1992 and George Wallace in 1968 was that, although Perot had broader appeal nationally, Wallace had a strong base in the south which enabled him actually to win some states.

Strong third party candidates, however, pose a significant potential problem under the electoral college. If the contest between the Democratic and Republican candidates is close, then a third candidate with some electoral college votes could hold the balance

---

Box 9.4

Third party candidates in recent elections

Candidate	Year	Party	Percentage of popular vote	Electoral college	Percentage of electoral college
Ross Perot	1996	Reform	8.5	0	0
Ross Perot	1992	None	19	0	0
John Anderson	1980	National Unity	6	0	0
George Wallace	1968	American Independent	13	46	8

Sources: Adapted from *National Journal*, 5 November 1992, p. A40; Pomper et al., 1996, p. 178

of power. The framers of the Constitution did anticipate this and they provided that, where no candidate has a majority of electoral college votes, the election shall be decided in the House of Representatives. For this purpose only, however, each state delegation in the House, rather than each representative, is entitled to one vote. Although this mechanism has not been invoked for over a century, the mere possibility that a 'maverick' candidacy could throw the electoral process into confusion generates periodic calls for the reform of the electoral college system. Until a crisis actually materialises, however, nothing is likely to be done. Meanwhile, the United States continues with this arcane method of choosing its president.

Presidential nominations

The presidential election itself always takes place on the first Tuesday after the first Monday in November, but the campaign for the presidency begins long before that. The first task of anyone seeking the presidency is to secure the nomination of one of the major political parties. Both the Democratic and Republican parties hold a *nominating convention* in the summer prior to the November election. The delegates at these conventions choose who shall be the party's nominee for the November general election. For the candidates, then, the goal is to ensure that a majority of the convention delegates are committed to support them. This is achieved by winning votes in pre-convention elections.

The primary campaign

There are two methods prevalent today for selecting convention delegates: the *primary election* and the *caucus election*. The rules governing these elections vary somewhat between states and between the Democratic and Republican parties, but the broad outlines are as follows. In the period between February and June of election year, each state holds either a primary or a caucus election for each of the parties. Since 1968, more and more states have opted to hold primaries, mainly because these elections make it easier to meet the technical rules governing issues such as the gender and racial composition of state delegations to the convention. Whereas in 1968 there were just seventeen primaries, in 1996 there was just one Republican caucus, in Louisiana, and fifteen Democrat caucuses (Jackson and Crotty, 1996, pp. 221–2).

In a primary election, participants simply enter the polling booth and cast their vote for the delegate or presidential candidate of their choice. Caucuses are more time consuming. Voters physically gather in rooms and may spend several hours determining who they will support.

Both primaries and caucuses may be either 'closed' or 'open'. If 'closed', then only those voters officially registered as Democrats may vote in the Democratic primary or caucus, and the same for the Republicans. If the election is open, however, officially registered independents or even members of the other party may opt to vote in either the Democratic or Republican choice.

The number of convention delegates from each state is not purely a function of its population or even size of electorate. Rather it depends to a significant degree on the number of those who voted for the party in recent elections. As a result, the number of delegates from a state is different for the Democratic and Republican conventions. Nevertheless, it is still the most populous states which send the most delegates to the convention, so, as in the November election, candidates must try to win primaries and caucuses in the larger states.

Although candidates will not campaign hard in every state primary, serious contenders will try to collect a winning number of delegates to take to the convention. This means that the campaign must be planned well before the first primaries and caucuses take place. This has become even more true of recent elections, because of the tendency towards 'frontloading' the primaries and caucuses. Thus, in 1996, approximately three-quarters of convention delegates had been chosen after just six weeks of the primary season.

The impact of frontloading is debatable. Some believe it favours candidates who are already well known and those who can raise very large campaign funds in the pre-primary season. Others believe it enables a relatively unknown candidate to make a dramatic breakthrough and leave the frontrunner without sufficient time to recover. If anything, the 1996 Republican campaign for the nomination tends to support the former theory. Certainly the millionaire businessman Steve Forbes and the combative populist Pat Buchanan did steal an early march on Bob Dole, the frontrunner. Yet Dole's bedrock support among party stalwarts and the huge campaign chest he had been able to amass saw him overcome his initial setbacks and move decisively ahead by the beginning of March.

Whichever theory is correct, frontloading has one undeniable effect: it means that the unofficial campaign for the presidency must begin earlier than ever before.

Advantages and disadvantages of the primary system

Primaries were introduced in the early twentieth century as a means of democratising the selection of presidential nominees by removing the corrupt control of the process by party bosses. Today that democratisation can be criticised both as having gone too far and as having not gone far enough.

In regard to the former, critics argue that the elimination of party boss control has gone so far that the parties have lost almost any real say in who gets their nomination. In 1968, the Democratic party establishment was able to impose the nomination of Hubert Humphrey, the incumbent vice-president, even though he had not entered a single primary. The outcry against this led to the rule changes which encouraged more primaries and required any serious candidate for the nomination to enter at least some of them.

The results of these changes were, however, unsatisfactory to many Democrats. Candidates could now appeal directly to the voters in primaries, thus bypassing the need for support from the party establishment. This led to the nomination of candidates such as George McGovern (1972) and Jimmy Carter (1976), men who were in significant ways at odds with traditional Democratic policies. McGovern lost heavily to his Republican opponent, while although Carter won the presidential election, the lack of enthusiasm he generated among other Democrats, particularly in Congress, hampered his ability to govern and contributed to his defeat by Ronald Reagan in 1980.

The Democrats in particular, then, have fiddled with the rules governing primaries and nominating conventions continuously since 1968, in an attempt to produce a popular, winning nominee and a subsequently successful president. Changes introduced for the 1992 election, for example, included mandatory proportional representation and an increase in the number of convention 'superdelegates' appointed by the party establishment to 750 – about 20 per cent of all delegates (Cook, 1991). Over the years, however, the results of such changes have not been encouraging. In the eight presidential elections between 1968 and 1996, the Democrats have won only three times. In truth, the nominating system is just one factor in explaining the Republican ascendancy in this period, and probably a minor one at that.

Despite these rule changes, it can be argued that the nomination process is not very democratic in practice. Most obviously, voter turn-out in both primaries and caucuses is very low. In recent elections, the average turn-out in primaries has been 21 per cent, and in caucuses just 7 per cent (Wayne, 1996, p. 91). In 1988, in the key opening primary in New Hampshire, 34 per cent of the electorate voted; and in the very first test, the Iowa caucus, the turn-out was just 10 per cent (Cook, 1991).

Moreover, the relatively few people who do bother to vote tend to be the committed partisans of both parties and are not necessarily typical of the electorate at large. The risk is that the party will find itself with a relatively extreme nominee who has pleased the activists but who alienates the more typical voter at the general election in November. This was the case with George McGovern in 1972. Even where such a radical candidate fails to win the nomination, he may command enough delegates to force the party towards a more extreme platform (manifesto) than it would otherwise have chosen. This happened to the Republicans in 1992 (see Box 9.5).

Box 9.5

Buchanan hijacks the 1992 Republican convention

In the 1992 Republican primary elections, the right-wing populist Pat Buchanan secured enough support to make his presence felt at the nominating convention. Not wishing to alienate Buchanan and his supporters, the victorious Bush campaign agreed to give Buchanan a prime-time speech slot. As it turned out, Buchanan's intemperate speech left the Republican party – and the Bush candidacy – tainted with extremism.

> It began with a mistake – a deal making Pat Buchanan the *de facto* keynote speaker for a slash-and-burn appeal to the hard right. ... For four nights in Houston, it was as if the melancholy state of the union counted for little as against the scarlet sins of liberals, lesbians, gays, Democrats, feminists, Congress, Greens, trial lawyers, women who aborted babies. ... The die had been cast with the decision, after the primaries, that Buchanan had to be appeased, that he and his brigades could wreck the convention if they were not made part of it.
>
> (*Newsweek*, 16 November 1992, p. 35)

Perhaps the greatest disadvantage of the primary system, however, is the danger of self-inflicted damage upon the party's eventual nominee. In a long and fiercely fought nomination campaign, candidates will seek not only to enhance their own image and prospects, but also to undermine those of their competitors. This can sometimes erupt into bitter conflict between candidates from the same party, bordering on political fratricide. Even incumbent presidents seeking renomination do not always emerge from this phase of the campaign unscathed. Not only did Pat Buchanan launch damaging attacks upon President Bush in 1992, but Senator Edward Kennedy did likewise against President Carter in the Democratic nomination struggle in 1980. In both cases, the eventual nominee was already in a weakened state by the time the 'real' campaign began in September.

Presidential election campaigns

By custom, the general election campaign begins after the Labor Day holiday in September. The two-month campaign, however, rarely determines who shall become president, since 'for the vast majority of citizens in America, campaigns do not function so much to change minds as to reinforce previous convictions' (Polsby and Wildavsky, 1995, p. 162). Thus, candidates who trail their opponent in the opinion polls on Labor Day usually do the same in the real poll on election day. The last surprise result in this respect occurred in 1948, when Harry Truman defeated Thomas Dewey against all the pundits' expectations: but that was in the days when opinion polling was much less accurate than it is today. In more recent times, only Hubert Humphrey's late rally in 1968 threatened to reverse the September opinion polls, although many elections show something of a swing towards the governing party candidate as election day nears.

The fact is, then, that most people have already made up their minds by Labor Day. While the campaign is by no means irrelevant, it is rarely decisive. This is not surprising once we appreciate that Americans engage in what is sometimes called *retrospective voting*. This means simply that the election tends to be a referendum on the past four years. If the nation has experienced both peace and economic prosperity, the party currently in power is likely to be re-elected, especially if an incumbent president is standing again (Polsby and Wildavsky, 1995, p. 166). If, on the other hand, the country is in serious trouble at home or abroad, the rival party is likely to win.

Thus, in 1968 the Democratic administration of Lyndon B. Johnson was heavily criticised over its Vietnam policy and the Democratic candidate, Hubert Humphrey, lost the election. Similarly, President Carter had a range of foreign policy difficulties coming up to the 1980 election, in particular his failure to secure the release of the American embassy personnel held hostage in Iran.

However, even more important than foreign policy is the state of the economy. For all his foreign policy problems in 1980, the main cause of President Carter's defeat was dissatisfaction with the economy. The importance of the economic issue was again clearly illustrated in 1992 when, despite a wide perception of his foreign policy record as excellent, President Bush was defeated by an equally wide perception that the economy was stagnant and unlikely to improve under his guidance. His opponent Bill

Clinton had learned the lesson of past elections. In order to ensure that his campaign team never lost sight of the issue that could bring him victory, he had a sign prominently displayed at campaign headquarters which said simply, 'It's the economy, stupid!'

The Clinton victory in 1992 was all the more remarkable in that on other issues which have influenced previous presidential elections, such as foreign policy and personal character, he was noticeably weaker than President Bush. An opinion poll taken in March gave the president a 26 per cent lead over Clinton on the question of personal honesty. Clinton's personal integrity and trustworthiness had been severely challenged by, for example, alleged marital infidelity and allegations that he had sought to avoid military service during the Vietnam War. Although the Bush campaign hammered away at the character issue, it failed to overturn Clinton's lead on economic issues (see Box 9.6).

What was true of 1992 was doubly so in 1996. President Clinton was even more beset by financial and sexual scandals than he had been in 1992 and a majority of the electorate believed he was neither honest nor trustworthy. Yet some 55 per cent also believed that the economy was in good or excellent shape and only 20 per cent thought that they were worse off economically than they had been in 1992. It was largely on this basis, then, that 56 per cent of the electorate agreed that the president was doing a good job (Pomper et al., 1997, pp. 192–3).

Box 9.6

Voters and issues in the 1992 and 1996 presidential elections

1992 election

1. Which issues mattered most in deciding how you voted?

	Percentage Voting For		
	Clinton	Bush	Perot
Economy/jobs (43% mention this issue)	53	24	23
Budget deficit (21%)	37	26	37
Health care (20%)	67	19	14
Family values (15%)	24	65	11
Taxes (14%)	27	56	17
Abortion (13%)	38	54	8
Education (13%)	62	23	15
Environment (6%)	74	14	13

2. Is the condition of the economy:

	Clinton	Bush	Perot
Excellent (1%)	58	32	11
Good (18%)	9	82	9
Not so good (48%)	44	36	20
Poor (32%)	65	10	24

3. Which candidate qualities mattered most in deciding how you voted?

Will bring about needed change (38%)	59	19	22
Has the best plan for the country (25%)	52	26	21
Has the right experience (18%)	23	63	14
Would have good judgement in a crisis (15%)	26	63	11
Is honest and trustworthy (14%)	30	49	21
Has strong convictions (14%)	34	42	24
Cares about people like me (14%)	57	24	20
His choice of Vice-President (8%)	63	25	12
Is my party's candidate (5%)	47	40	12

1996 election

1. Which issues mattered most in deciding how you voted?

	Percentage Voting For		
	Clinton	Dole	Perot
Economy/jobs (21%)	61	27	10
Medicare, social security (15%)	67	26	6
Education (12%)	78	15	4
Budget deficit (12%)	28	52	19
Taxes (11%)	19	73	7
Crime, drugs (7%)	41	50	8
Foreign policy (4%)	35	55	8

2. Is the condition of the economy:

Excellent (4%)	78	18	3
Good (52%)	62	31	5
Not so good (36%)	34	52	12
Poor (7%)	23	50	21

3. Which candidate quality mattered most in deciding how you voted?[a]

Is honest and trustworthy (20%)	9	84	7
Shares my view of government (20%)	42	45	10
Has a vision for the future (16%)	77	13	9
Stands up for what he believes in (13%)	42	40	15
Cares about people like me (10%)	72	17	9
Is in touch with the 1990s (10%)	89	8	4

[a] Different wording from the question asked in 1992. The 1996 version allows only one quality to be selected

Sources: Data for 1992 adapted from *National Journal*, 7 November 1992, p. 2544, based on Voter Research and Surveys exit polls; data for 1996 adapted from *National Journal*, 9 November 1996, p. 2048, based on Voter News Service exit polls

If the economy provides the main issue context of presidential elections, that does not mean that other issues are irrelevant. Foreign policy has sometimes been very important to the outcome of elections, even if it seemed to have disappeared in 1996. In some respects, each presidential election is unique, and different issues may exert different degrees of influence at different times. Since 1968, for example, a cluster of issues, sometimes referred to simply as 'the social issue', has been of continuing, though variable influence. The social issue brings into electoral play attitudes on matters such as abortion, affirmative action for racial minorities and women, the death penalty, gay rights, and the place of religion in public life.

Before the cultural upheavals of the 1960s, there was a broad social consensus on these issues and, therefore, they did not figure prominently in elections. However, beginning with the election of 1968, a number of presidential candidates sought to profit from the divisions that emerged from these issues, most notably Ronald Reagan. As we shall see in Chapter 11, some political analysts believe that the social issue is one of the keys to explaining the dominance of the Republican party in presidential elections since 1968.

Beyond the policy issues that determine the outcome of presidential elections, there is also the matter of the personal characteristics of the candidates. We should not be surprised that personal character is important in presidential elections, since the voters are choosing an individual, rather than a party. The president, moreover, represents the nation as 'head of state', as well as being expected to provide able political leadership.

Precisely how much influence personal character has in elections is difficult to assess. Some presidential candidates, such as Ronald Reagan, are so well liked by a majority of voters that they are forgiven for unpopular policies. Reagan was dubbed 'the Teflon President', because the public seemed unwilling to attach blame to him for his administration's faults. George Bush, on the other hand, won in 1988 and lost in 1992 without his character being of major importance in either election, while although Bill Clinton was not particularly well liked in 1996, he was better liked than his opponent, Bob Dole (Pomper *et al.*, 1997, p. 193).

Box 9.7

Presidential election calendar 2000

Pre-nomination campaign	Nomination campaign	Party conventions July/Aug. 2000	Presidential election campaign
1999 – Feb. 2000	Feb. – June 2000		Sept – Nov. 2000
Candidates make appearances, visit key states, establish organisation, raise money	Primary and caucus elections, beginning with the Iowa caucus and the New Hampshire primary	Delegates gather to nominate party candidate, candidate selects vice-presidential running-mate	Presidential/ vice-presidential candidates campaign around the country, take part in TV debates

Box 9.6 shows what voters say influenced them in the 1992 and 1996 elections. We can see in the responses to questions 1 and 2, that voters thought economic issues to be the most important ones and that they preferred Bill Clinton to George Bush on these issues. Similarly, in response to question 3, voters believed change to be the highest priority and Bill Clinton the best equipped to bring that about. These factors outweighed the public's perception that George Bush had better experience, would have better judgement in a crisis and was more trustworthy and honest. The fact is, then, that in 1992, the social issue and the character issue counted for far less than the economic issue.

The presidential election calendar for the year 2000 is set out in Box 9.7.

Congressional elections

Divided government in modern America

When the framers of the Constitution opted for different procedures for electing the president, the House of Representatives and the Senate, they created the possibility of divided party control of the federal government. In other words, in today's terms, it is possible for the Republicans to control the presidency but for the Democrats to control the Congress, and vice versa. This clearly presents problems of governance, since the president is expected to provide policy *leadership*, but only the Congress can actually *pass* the legislation necessary to implement his policies.

Despite the obvious problems created by divided government, this situation has become the rule rather than the exception in contemporary America. Box 9.8 shows you the extent of this electoral phenomenon.

Two things stand out in the Box 9.8. First, out of the twenty-six elections involved, thirteen resulted in fully divided control of the presidency and the Congress. On a further three occasions under President Reagan, one chamber of the Congress was controlled by the non-presidential party. Divided government is thus very much a political reality in the United States.

Secondly, until 1994, the pattern of divided government was for a Republican president to be faced with a Democratic Congress. However, the 1994, 1996 and 1998 elections saw President Clinton become the first Democratic president to be faced with a Republican Congress since President Truman (1946–48).

The reasons for divided government will be explored more fully in Chapter 11. For the moment, it is enough to note that American voters clearly have different political criteria for choosing a president from those which determine their choice of senator or representative.

We have seen that economic, foreign policy and social issues, as well as character, can all influence the vote for the president. What then are the different factors which appear to operate in congressional elections?

Constituency service

Beyond anything else, voters in congressional elections value the local and personal

Box 9.8

Divided party control of the federal government, 1948–96

Election Year[a]	President	Senate majority	House majority
1948	**Truman (Dem.)**	**Dem.**	**Dem.**
1950		Dem.	Dem.
1952	**Eisenhower (Rep.)**	**Rep.**	**Rep.**
1954		Dem.	Dem.
1956	**Eisenhower (Rep.)**	**Dem.**	**Dem.**
1958		Dem.	Dem.
1960	**Kennedy (Dem.)**	**Dem.**	**Dem.**
1962		Dem.	Dem.
1964	**Johnson (Dem.)**	**Dem.**	**Dem.**
1966		Dem.	Dem.
1968	**Nixon (Rep.)**	**Dem.**	**Dem.**
1970		Dem.	Dem.
1972	**Nixon (Rep.)**	**Dem.**	**Dem.**
1974	Ford (Rep.)[b]	Dem.	Dem.
1976	**Carter (Dem.)**	**Dem.**	**Dem.**
1978		Dem.	Dem.
1980	**Reagan (Rep.)**	**Rep.**	**Dem.**
1982		Rep.	Dem.
1984	**Reagan (Rep.)**	**Rep.**	**Dem.**
1986		Dem.	Dem.
1988	**Bush (Rep.)**	**Dem.**	**Dem.**
1990		Dem.	Dem.
1992	**Clinton (Dem.)**	**Dem.**	**Dem.**
1994		Rep.	Rep.
1996	**Clinton (Dem.)**	**Rep.**	**Rep.**
1998		Rep.	Rep.

[a] Bold type indicates presidential election year, light type indicates mid-term elections

[b] President Nixon resigned in August 1974 over the Watergate scandal and was replaced by Vice-President Gerald Ford

services rendered by their representatives and senators. If a member of Congress is perceived as having served the constituency well, he or she will almost certainly be re-elected. The notion of constituency service includes, for example, ensuring that a slice of federal job or construction schemes, or grants for education and social services, are brought back home to the member's district or state. Representatives, in particular, may also act as a kind of ombudsman, intervening with government bureaucracy to help constituents secure benefits or disentangle them from red tape.

Senators have a higher profile than representatives and may be more associated with national political issues. Occasionally such associations can hurt them. This was the case in 1978: a strong conservative wind was blowing that year and, partly as a result, a number of well known liberal Democrat senators lost their seats. On the whole, however, the same golden rule applies to Senate elections as to the House: those who serve their constituents well can expect to gain re-election, regardless of party affiliation or ideological disposition (see Box 9.9).

Box 9.9

Local events, national politics

Congressional elections are the Cinderellas of American electoral politics. Even if one lives in the United States – let alone if one observes from outside – much less attention is given to them than to presidential contests. Typically, media coverage is sparse – especially of House contests; most campaigns are sporadic and amateurish, and barely half the voting age population participates (barely one-third when there is no presidential contest).

In keeping with the decentralised character of American government and politics, elections to the House and Senate are in essence local events. The most important task for the candidates is to persuade voters that they will represent the local community effectively. Since most candidates are already incumbents (88 per cent of House members and 64 per cent of senators in 1996) they use the time between elections to cultivate an effective 'home style' which is designed to build trust in them back home. Styles vary considerably and no one style is certain to be successful. The style of Senator Claiborne Pell (D–Rhode Island) was that of a somewhat eccentric patrician uncomfortable with face-to-face politicking and overt publicity seeking. Arkansas Democratic Senator David Pryor's style was more the southern 'good ole boy' who loved to meet and talk with people. Neither senator would have been elected from the other's state. Both styles were effective. Pell was a senator 36 years, Pryor for 18.

According to the American National Election Survey, between 1978 and 1992 voters evaluated House incumbents primarily according to how well they served their constituents' needs, as well as their personal qualities, rather than by their party connections, ideologies or the positions they took on different issues. Not surprisingly, most incumbents during this period were re-elected.

There is nothing fixed, however, about this trend. In certain election years, when challengers find that they can win votes by linking the incumbent to national policy failures and/or unpopular leaders, national factors will come into play more strongly – at least in those races where attractive, well financed challengers effectively exploit these issues in local campaigns. Republicans did this successfully in 1980, Democrats in 1982, and most recently Republicans in 1994 when they won control of the House for the first time in forty years. Not surprisingly, survey results for 1994 show that House voters focused much *less* on constituency service and incumbents' personal qualities and much *more* on the incumbents' party, ideology and policy positions. It was the Democrats who suffered the brunt of this change: losing thirty-four of their incumbents while all House Republicans won re-election. National factors did not play such an important role in 1996.

The relative importance of local factors in congressional election is, however, less important than the *consequences* of these elections. Congressional elections have a major influence on national politics and public policy, not only because they determine which party controls the House and the Senate and the size of the winning party's plurality but also because politicians interpret election results as reflections of voters' preferences. Witness the policy 'revolution' heralded by Newt Gingrich and House Republicans following their victories in 1994. How well congressional elections reflect the concerns of the American public is another matter.

Contributed by John E. Owens, University of Westminster

Incumbency advantage

Sitting members of Congress are well placed to ensure that the benefits of federal largesse reach their constituents. Not only do they draft the legislation concerned, but they benefit from congressional perks which enable them to publicise the good they have done. For example, they exploit the 'franking privilege', which gives them free use of the US Mail to send letters to constituents, including mass mailings detailing members' achievements and local appearances. Although there are rules against using the franking privilege for blatant electioneering, Philip Davies points out that Representative Dennis Hastert (R–Illinois) managed forty-eight references to himself in just four pages, and that Senator Dan Coats (R–Indiana), newly appointed to fill Vice-President Dan Quayle's seat in 1989, spent $1.8 million dollars on franked mail to 'make himself better known to his constituents'. Total spending on Senate and House use of the franking privilege in 1990 reached some $106 million (Davies, 1992, pp. 157–8).

Challengers to incumbents also suffer in other ways. Members of Congress use not only the franking privilege, but also cheap facilities for making video films to circulate back home. Thus, in 1988, the House recording studio charged members $42 for twenty minutes' studio time, when this would have cost challengers over $500 (Pomper *et al.*, 1989, p. 158).

Above all, incumbent members of Congress benefit from their ability to attract far greater campaign donations from interest groups than do their challengers (see Chapter 12).

Until the 1990s, the result of these advantages was high incumbency re-election rates: thus members of the House of Representatives seeking re-election had a success rate of well over 90 per cent in all but the most exceptional years (Bailey, 1989, p. 34).

The three elections from 1992 to 1996 saw a significant increase in the number of House incumbents being defeated. The 1992 election saw twenty-four incumbents defeated, bringing the percentage down to 86 per cent. Then in 1994, the year of the

'Republican Revolution' thirty-five incumbents, all Democrats, were ousted. Yet 1996 saw the figure drop back to twenty-one, all but three of them Republicans.

Before these recent elections, Ross Baker noted that in House elections the term 'incumbency advantage' often seemed an understatement, and that 'incumbency franchise' would be more accurate (Pomper, 1993, p. 158). The 1990s may have brought a greater degree of uncertainty to the iron grip on power of House incumbents, but they nevertheless still enjoy many important advantages over their challengers. For that reason, incumbency re-election rates are unlikely to fall much below 90 per cent on a regular basis.

Incumbency re-election rates for the Senate are historically neither as high, nor as consistent as those for the House. Since the 1960s, the rate has varied from 55 per cent to 96 per cent, with the average around 80 per cent (Bailey, 1989, p. 34; *National Journal*, 7 November 1992, p. 2555). As noted above, senators are more identified with national issues than representatives, and the larger size of their constituencies means they do not have quite the same personal identification with their voters as do House members. Paradoxically, however, the Senate has not mirrored the House experience in the 1990s of an increase in the number of incumbents defeated. Just one incumbent senator was defeated in 1996 and only two in 1994.

It is clear that congressional elections have no necessary connection with presidential elections today. Neither President Clinton in 1992 and 1996, nor President Bush in 1988, had any presidential 'coat-tails' which benefited their parties in Congress. And since the Second World War, only twice has the capture of the White House by the out-party been accompanied by a similar breakthrough in the congressional elections: President Eisenhower in 1952 (House and Senate) and President Reagan in 1980 (Senate only).

Thus, what Ross Baker said of the 1988 elections is substantially true of most others in contemporary American politics: 'In terms of the outcome ... the presidential and congressional contests might have taken place in different countries' (Pomper *et al.*, 1989, p. 153).

Term limits

Notwithstanding the high rate of re-election, members of Congress can take nothing for granted. For in addition to the dangers of an election where the voters are inclined to 'throw the rascals out', the anti-incumbency mood of the 1990s has produced a significant movement to limit the number of terms of office for representatives and senators. This movement is driven by the feeling that if politicians spend too long in Washington, they may become part of a professional, self-serving governing class that are ignorant of and indifferent to the views of the people.

The movement got under way in 1990 when a referendum in Colorado produced a 71 per cent vote in favour of term limits. In the next two years alone, a further fourteen states followed suit. The movement experienced a major setback in 1995, however, when the Supreme Court ruled that the only constitutionally permissible method of imposing term limits on members of Congress was by passing a constitutional amendment (*US Term Limits v. Thornton*). Unsurprisingly, constitutional amendments imposing term limits were duly introduced into Congress (see Box 9.10).

Box 9.10

Constitutional Amendment Imposing Term Limits

H.J. Res. 42
IN THE HOUSE OF REPRESENTATIVES

February 5, 1997

Mr. BLUNT (for himself and Mr. TALENT) introduced the following joint resolution; which was referred to the Committee on the Judiciary

JOINT RESOLUTION

Proposing an amendment to the Constitution of the United States to limit the number of terms a Member of Congress may serve, and to authorize a State to provide longer or shorter term limits for a Member of Congress from that State.

Resolved by the Senate and House of Representatives of the United States of America in Congress assembled (two-thirds of each House concurring therein), That the following article is proposed as an amendment to the Constitution of the United States, which shall be valid to all intents and purposes as part of the Constitution when ratified by the legislatures of three-fourths of the several States:

Article –

Section 1. A Representative shall be limited to three terms in such office, and a Senator shall be limited to two terms in such office ...

Section 2. A Senator or Representative who has served one or more terms in such office as of the date of the ratification of this article, or a part of such term or terms, is deemed to have served one term in such office after the date of ratification for purposes of section 1.

Section 3. A State may, by amendment of the Constitution of that State, provide for term limits with respect to a representative or Senator representing that State that are longer or shorter than the limits provided in section 1.

Section 4. There shall be no time limit within which this article must be ratified by the legislatures of three-fourths of the several States to become valid as part of the Constitution ...

Because constitutional amendment involves a notoriously difficult and protracted political campaign, it remains to be seen whether the anti-incumbency mood will be sustained long enough to bring success. At present it stands as a symbol of the American electorate's belief that centralised political authority needs to be curtailed.

Voting behaviour

The franchise

The right of citizens to vote for their leaders lies at the heart of the democratic political process. Indeed, in assessing the democratic quality of any political system, one of the first questions to be asked is 'who is entitled to vote?'.

As in most western democracies, the franchise in the United States has been greatly expanded since the eighteenth century. Early property and religious requirements imposed by some states had largely disappeared by the 1830s. Yet two great historical struggles for the right to vote remained: the enfranchisement of blacks and women.

An organised women's movement first claimed the right to vote in the manifesto known as the Seneca Falls Declaration, issued in 1848. Yet it was not until the ratification of the Nineteenth Amendment to the Constitution, in 1920, that women were finally permitted to vote throughout the United States. While both proponents and opponents of women's suffrage predicted new, radical departures in voting behaviour as a result, these have largely failed to materialise. As we shall see shortly, however, some significant differences in the way men and women vote have emerged in recent elections.

In terms of possessing the legal right to vote, African Americans were successful much earlier than women. Following the abolition of slavery after the Civil War, the Fifteenth Amendment to the Constitution was ratified in 1870. This declares that, 'The right of citizens of the United States to vote shall not be denied or abridged by the United States or by any State on account of race, color, or previous condition of servitude'.

Despite this categorical assertion, many southern states proceeded to disenfranchise blacks by a variety of devices. For example, a 'literacy test' was often used, whereby would-be voters were required to read and explain a written passage, such as part of the Constitution, before being permitted to vote. With little or no education for African Americans at the time, it was relatively easy for white election officials to deem them unqualified. Payment of a poll tax was also made a condition of voting, something which hit blacks in particular because of their economic subordination. Yet another device was the 'grandfather clause', which gave the vote only to those whose grandfathers had possessed the same right. Since the first post Civil War generation of black voters in the south had grandfathers who had been slaves, they were debarred from voting. Furthermore, this was a self-perpetuating condition inherited by each subsequent generation of blacks.

A less obviously illegal ruse used by southern governments to deprive African Americans of their electoral power was the white primary. The south was a one-party region before the Second World War: Democrats won virtually all elections at every level of government. The real election in southern states, therefore, was the Democratic primary: whoever won that was all but guaranteed victory in the general election. As a *private* organisation, the party believed it could ban blacks from participation in its primaries, without infringing the Fifteenth Amendment's prohibition on *state* discrimination against them. The Supreme Court did not rule otherwise until 1944, in the case of *Smith v. Allwright*.

It was not until the great civil rights movement of the 1950s and 1960s that the legal right of African Americans to vote became a practical reality in the south. With the passage of the Voting Rights Act of 1965, the federal government was empowered to take over the administration of elections in any state where racial discrimination in voting rights was detected. It is now safe to say that, in the United States, with a few exceptions such as the imprisoned and the insane, all citizens over the age of eighteen can vote – if they want to. Box 9.11 sets out the significant dates in the expansion of the franchise.

Non-voting

Despite the constant rhetorical celebration of America's democracy and these heroic struggles to extend the franchise, many Americans do not appear to value the right to vote. Thus, 'With each expansion of suffrage, the percentage of those eligible who do vote has actually declined' (Wayne, 1984, p. 71). This, together with other factors, has resulted in the United States having a lower voter turn-out than almost any comparable democracy. Whereas countries such as Germany and Sweden experience around 90 per cent turn-out, and Britain around 75 per cent, in recent decades barely half of all eligible Americans bother to vote in presidential elections. In mid-term elections for the House and Senate, the situation is even worse: in 1990, for example, the turn-out was just 36 per cent (Davies, 1992, p. 147). Moreover, the trend over recent decades is decidedly downwards, despite an upward turn in 1992 (see Box 9.12).

Such lack of interest in elections by the voters is clearly unhealthy. For many Americans, voting is their primary, if not sole means of participation in the political process. Those who do not vote, therefore, may play no role at all in the democratic process. When the proportion of such non-voters nears 50 per cent, one may

---

Box 9.11

Constitutional milestones in the expansion of the franchise

1787　The Constitution leaves it to the individual states to determine who is qualified to vote

1870　The Fifteenth Amendment is ratified, making it unconstitutional to deprive a person of the right to vote on grounds of race or colour

1913　The Seventeenth Amendment is ratified, requiring the direct election of US senators

1920　The Nineteenth Amendment is ratified, making it unconstitutional to deprive a person of the right to vote on grounds of sex

1964　The Twenty-fourth Amendment is ratified, outlawing the imposition of a poll tax as a qualification for voting in federal elections

1971　The Twenty-sixth Amendment is ratified, lowering the voting age for both federal and state elections from 21 to 18 years

Box 9.12

Voter turn-out in presidential and mid-term elections, 1960–96

Year[a]	Voting age popn	Registered	Turn-out	Percentage turn-out of voting age popn
1996	196,511,000	146,211,960	96,456,345	49.08
1994	193,650,000	130,292,822	75,105,860	38.78
1992	189,529,000	133,821,178	104,405,155	55.09
1990	185,812,000	121,105,630	67,869,189	36.52
1988	182,778,000	126,379,628	91,594,693	50.11
1986	178,566,000	118,399,984	64,991,128	36.40
1984	174,466,000	124,150,614	92,652,680	53.11
1982	169,938,000	110,671,225	67,615,576	39.79
1980	164,597,000	113,043,734	86,515,221	52.56
1978	158,373,000	103,291,265	58,917,938	37.21
1976	152,309,190	105,037,986	81,555,789	53.55
1974	146,336,000	96,199,020	55,943,834	38.23
1972	140,776,000	97,328,541	77,718,554	55.21
1970	124,498,000	82,496,747	58,014,338	46.60
1968	120,328,186	81,658,180	73,211,875	60.84
1966	116,132,000	76,288,283	56,188,046	48.39
1964	114,090,000	73,715,818	70,644,592	61.92
1962[b]	112,423,000	65,393,751	53,141,227	47.27
1960[b]	109,159,000	64,833,096	68,838,204	63.06

[a] Presidential election years are in bold type.

Source: Federal Election Commission

[b] For technical reasons, the registration figures from over a dozen states were not available.

reasonably ask if there is not a malaise affecting popular democracy in the United States.

Another problem created by low voter turn-out concerns the mandate to govern that any president can claim. Consider the position of President Ronald Reagan, the clear winner of the 1984 election, having taken 59 per cent of the popular vote. Once we take into account the fact that the turn-out that year was 53 per cent, we see that President Reagan was supported by less than one-third of those eligible to vote. The Reagan 'landslide' looks far from impressive from this perspective. In 1992, when Bill Clinton took 43 per cent of the vote on a 54 per cent turn-out, he received the active support of just 24 per cent of the electorate.

It is hardly surprising, then, that there have been many studies which have attempted to identify the causes of this worrying phenomenon. Arthur Hadley found evidence to contradict the widespread belief that the typical non-voter was a figure whom he dubbed 'Boobus Americanus' (Hadley, 1978). This stereotype was poor, ill educated, disproportionately southern, female and black. While some non-voters in Hadley's study did correspond to stereotype, many did not. Ruy Teixeira pointed out that a decline in the number of such stereotypical non-voters in the period since 1960 was to be expected: educational levels have risen, southern blacks become freer to vote, and both women and blacks have become more equal citizens to white males in important respects (Teixeira, 1987). There must therefore be other reasons for voter decline in addition to the traditional ones of poverty and lack of education.

Another factor often cited in such studies is the relative difficulty of voter registration in some states. This is exacerbated by the fact that Americans are an unusually and increasingly mobile people, who move state frequently and therefore must re-register frequently under unfamiliar state laws. Unlike in Britain, where government actively solicits citizens to register by sending forms to their homes, many states require individuals to take the initiative, usually by visiting the local registration office. The extra effort thus required undoubtedly deters some eligible voters. Yet as Hadley pointed out, turn-out has been falling even in states where registration is easiest. Moreover, the introduction of the 'motor voter' law in 1993 did not prevent a drop in the 1996 turn-out over 1992 (see Box 9.13).

Box 9.13

The National Voter Registration Act 1993

Popularly known as the 'motor voter' law, the National Voter Registration Act (NVRA) was passed in an attempt to overcome practical barriers to registering to vote. The key elements of the law are:

- Citizens must be allowed to register to vote at the same time as they apply for, renew or change their address on a driving licence. This facility alone can reach 90 per cent of all eligible voters.

- Citizens must be allowed to register at specified government agencies, including those that deal with people considered least likely to possess a driving licence: for example, agencies dealing with the disabled and those receiving public assistance.

- Citizens must be permitted to register by mail, rather than having to visit an office.

- States are obliged to verify the accuracy of voter registration lists on a four-yearly basis.

The NVRA works in terms of increased voter registration. It is estimated that some 20 million voters registered under the Act prior to the 1996 elections. However, the fact that those elections saw a marked decline in actual voting gives support to the argument that practical registration obstacles no longer account for Americans' disinclination to use their most basic democratic right.

Source: League of Women Voters, *The NVRA Factsheet*, 2 January 1997

Underpinning all these contributory factors is what researchers call the issue of *political efficacy*. 'The basic idea of political efficacy is that it taps the extent to which an individual feels that he or she has any power over governmental actions' (Teixeira, 1987, pp. 18–19). In other words, political efficacy concerns the degree to which potential voters believe there is any point in voting. Those who, for one reason or another, believe it makes no difference to them who wins the election will obviously be less likely to vote. On the basis of the turn-out figures quoted above, then, roughly half of eligible voters in the United States believe elections are in essence unimportant to them, if not wholly meaningless. By definition, this constitutes a crisis of American democracy.

Why have Americans come increasingly to take this view since 1960? It is possible that failures and scandals of government, such as Vietnam and Watergate, have caused many Americans to lose faith in the political process. It should also be noted that the 'golden age' of the 1950s, when Americans dominated the world economically and militarily, increasingly gave way to a host of problems which government seemed incapable of solving – racial tensions, the budget deficit, health care, welfare and crime, for example. When a series of presidents fails to solve the nation's major problems, it is perhaps not surprising that the electorate should feel less motivated to vote.

The voters

We now come to one of the most important and interesting questions about voting behaviour in the United States. What factors determine which voters support which candidates? This is a complex question, which must take into account a variety of cultural, ideological and socio-economic factors.

In Europe, for example, we expect social class to be the most powerful, though not the sole, determinant of the way people vote. And while the notion of social class is of some use in analysing voting behaviour in the United States, the greater heterogeneity of American society by comparison with Europe brings many other factors into play. Race, region and religion, for example, are more varied in the United States than in most European societies, and American historical and cultural experience is different from European in significant ways. Box 9.14 shows you the main divisions, or 'cleavages', in the American electorate since 1984.

What does the portrait of the American electorate set out in Box 9.14 tell us about the motivations of voters and the appeal of the parties to different socio-economic groups?

Social class and socio-economic status

We noted above that in European societies, social class is expected to be a major determinant of the way people vote. Yet for historical reasons, class is a difficult concept to employ in the context of the United States. Initially, divisions of class were far less marked in the United States than in, say, Great Britain. To this was added a greater degree of social mobility and an unwillingness on the part of many Americans to define themselves in terms of traditional classes.

Box 9.14

Portrait of the electorate, 1984–96

Percentages

Percentage of 1996 total		1984		1988		1992			1996		
		Reagan (R)	Mondale (D)	Bush (R)	Dukakis (D)	Clinton (D)	Bush (R)	Perot (Ind.)	Clinton (D)	Dole (R)	Perot (Ind.)
	Total vote	59	40	53	45	43	38	19	50	42	8
48	Men	62	37	57	41	41	38	21	44	44	10
52	Women	56	44	50	49	46	37	17	54	38	7
83	Whites	64	35	59	40	39	41	20	43	46	9
10	Blacks	9	90	12	86	82	11	7	84	12	4
5	Hispanics	37	62	30	69	62	25	14	72	21	6
1	Asians	–	–	–	–	29	55	16	43	48	8
66	Married	62	38	57	42	40	40	20	44	46	9
34	Unmarried	52	47	46	53	49	33	18	57	31	9
17	18–29 yr	59	40	52	47	44	34	22	53	34	10
33	30–44 yr	57	42	54	45	42	38	20	48	41	9
26	45–59 yr	60	40	57	42	41	40	19	48	41	9
24	60+	60	40	50	49	50	38	12	48	44	7
23	From the east	53	47	50	49	47	35	18	55	34	9
26	Midwest	58	41	52	47	42	37	21	48	41	10
30	South	64	36	58	41	42	43	16	46	46	7
20	West	61	38	52	46	44	34	22	48	40	8

White Protestant	46	72	27	66	33	33	46	21	36	53	10
Catholic	29	54	45	52	47	44	36	20	53	37	9
Jewish	3	31	67	35	64	78	12	10	78	16	3
White born-again Christian	17	78	22	81	18	23	61	15	26	65	8
Union household	24	46	53	42	57	55	24	21	60	29	9
Republicans	35	92	7	91	8	10	73	17	13	80	6
Independents	26	63	36	55	43	38	32	30	43	35	17
Democrats	39	25	74	17	82	77	10	13	84	10	5
Liberals	20	28	70	18	81	68	14	18	78	11	7
Moderates	47	53	47	49	50	48	31	21	57	32	9
Conservatives	33	82	17	80	19	18	65	17	20	71	8
Not high school graduate	6	50	50	43	56	55	28	17	60	28	11
High school grad.	23	60	39	50	49	43	36	20	52	35	13
Some college	27	61	38	57	42	42	37	21	49	39	10
College graduate or more	26	58	41	56	43	44	39	18	44	46	7
Postgraduate education	17	–	–	50	48	49	36	15	52	39	5
Family income											
under $15k	11	45	55	37	62	59	23	18	60	27	11
$15k-$29,999	23	57	42	49	50	45	35	20	54	36	9
$30k-$49,999	27	59	40	56	44	41	38	21	49	40	10
$50k-$74,999	21	66	33	56	42	40	42	18	47	44	7
$75k and over	18	69	30	62	37	36	48	16	42	50	7

Percentages (Continued)

Percentage of 1996 total	1984 Reagan (R)	1984 Mondale (D)	1988 Bush (R)	1988 Dukakis (D)	1992 Clinton (D)	1992 Bush (R)	1992 Perot (Ind.)	1996 Clinton (D)	1996 Dole (R)	1996 Perot (Ind.)
Family's financial situation is:										
33 Better today	86	14	–	–	24	62	14	67	26	6
44 Same today	50	50	–	–	41	41	18	46	44	8
20 Worse today	15	85	–	–	61	14	25	28	57	8
68 Employed	60	39	56	43	42	38	20	–	–	–
5 Student	52	47	44	54	50	35	15	–	–	–
6 Unemployed	32	67	37	62	56	24	20	–	–	–
8 Homemaker	62	38	58	41	36	45	19	–	–	–
13 Retired	60	40	50	49	51	36	13	–	–	–
Congressional vote										
51 For the Democratic candidate	23	76	27	72	74	11	15	8	7	
47 For the Republican candidate	93	7	82	17	10	71	18	14	77	7

Sources: Adapted from *New York Times*, 5 November 1992, pp. B9–10. Data for 1988 and 1984 based on *New York Times* and CBS News surveys of voters. Data for 1992 based on Voter Research and Surveys exit poll questionnaires. Data for 1996 adapted from Voter News Service exit polls reported in *New York Times*, 10 November 1996, *National Journal*, 9 November 1996, and Pomper *et al.*, 1997

How to read the table

1. Reading from left to right along the top line of numbers:

In 1984, the Republican Ronald Reagan took 59 per cent of the votes cast, while the Democrat Walter Mondale took 40 per cent. In 1988, the Republican George Bush took 53 per cent and the Democrat Michael Dukakis took 45 per cent. In 1992, The Democrat Bill Clinton took 43 per cent, the Republican George Bush 38 per cent and the Independent Ross Perot 19 per cent. In 1996, Bill Clinton took 50 per cent, the Republican Bob Dole 42 per cent and Ross Perot 8 per cent.

2. Reading the numbers for men and women voters:

In 1996, 48 per cent of those who voted were men, and 52 per cent were women (read vertically).

In 1984, men gave their votes 62 per cent to Reagan and 37 per cent to Mondale. Women gave their votes 56 per cent to Reagan and 44 per cent to Mondale (read horizontally). In 1988, men voted 57 per cent for Bush and 41 per cent for Dukakis; women voted 50 per cent for Bush and 49 per cent for Dukakis. In 1992, men voted 41 per cent for Clinton, 38 per cent for Bush and 21 per cent for Perot; women voted 46 per cent for Clinton, 37 per cent for Bush and 17 per cent for Perot. In 1996, men voted 44 per cent for Clinton, 44 per cent for Dole and 8 per cent for Perot.

All subsequent cleavages to be read in the same way.

3. **Identifying a candidate's strengths and weaknesses:**

There are two simple ways to do this:

(a) Compare the vote obtained by a candidate within each cleavage. For example, in 1984, Reagan won 6 per cent more of men's votes than he did of women's votes, (62 per cent to 56 per cent). Similarly, he won 18 per cent more of White Protestant votes than he did of Catholic votes (72 per cent to 54 per cent).

(b) Compare the vote obtained from one group with the overall share of the total electorate's vote. For example, in 1984, Reagan took 59 per cent of the total vote, but 78 per cent of the white born-again Christian vote. We can quickly conclude that something about the candidate made him very popular with this particular group. On the other hand, Reagan's 59 per cent of the total vote fell to just 9 per cent among black voters, thus identifying him as very *unpopular* with that group.

4. **Comparing changes between elections:**

We can also compare party candidates' performances among particular groups between elections. Simple conclusions cannot be drawn from such comparisons, however, because performance is often affected by a change in personnel and a change in historical circumstances. Thus we find that the south gave Reagan (1984) and Bush (1988) huge leads over their Democrat opponents. In 1992 and 1996, however, the south's vote split just about evenly between the two major party candidates. On the basis of this evidence alone, therefore, it is difficult to conclude whether the south is staunchly Republican or not. In this instance, one might want to check how the 1992 and 1996 Republican candidates did in the south compared with their performance nationally (see 3b above).

Yet many of the characteristics associated with social class – income, education, occupation – *do* significantly affect the way Americans vote. Academics refer jointly to these factors as 'socio-economic status' (SES).

As Box 9.14 shows, income is an excellent guide to explaining the way that Americans vote. Quite simply, the higher the family income, the more likely are the adult members to vote Republican. Of course, this does not mean that all wealthy people vote Republican and all poor people vote Democrat. Thus, in 1988, George Bush won 37 per cent of the votes of the poorest group, while Michael Dukakis won exactly the same percentage of the richest group.

Educational attainment is one of the keys to gaining a well paid job. Unsurprisingly, then, the cleavages on education take a similar direction to those on income: at least until we get to those with postgraduate qualifications, the higher the level of education, the greater the inclination to vote Republican. A possible explanation for the relatively high proportion of postgraduates who vote Democrat is that this group includes a large number of teachers, social workers and other similar professionals who tend to hold values which incline them to support the party of the 'have-nots'.

Although Box 9.14 does not include data on occupation, other studies reveal that a higher job status means a tendency to vote Republican. In every election between 1952 and 1988, those whose occupations were classed as professional/business were more Republican than those classed as white collar, and those classed as white-collar workers were more Republican than blue-collar workers (Polsby and Wildavsky, 1995, pp. 303–5; Pomper *et al.*, 1989, p. 133).

Thus, socio-economic status provides a good guide to voting behaviour in the United States. Nevertheless other factors must come into play too.

Ideology

While American political parties are not as clearly defined by ideology as British parties (see Chapter 12), it is reasonable to describe the Democrats as a moderate-liberal party and the Republicans as a conservative party. A voter's ideological leanings may therefore signal his or her voting behaviour. Quite predictably, Box 9.14 shows that those who classify themselves as liberals are strongly Democrat, and those who classify themselves as conservatives are strongly Republican. It is worth emphasising, however, that by far the largest group in this category are those who call themselves moderates, and their vote is less predictable.

Sex and age

It is not difficult to understand why wealthy conservatives vote Republican, given that party's tendency in the twentieth century to favour low taxes, unfettered free enterprise and traditional morality. Similarly, lower-income, blue-collar workers have a natural affinity with a Democratic party that has championed labour union rights, the welfare state and government regulation of employers. Or to take another example, voters from ethnic minority groups logically gravitate towards the Democratic party, which has led the fight for civil rights.

It is not quite so clear, however, why men should be more Republican than women, or why unmarried voters should be more Democratic than married ones. Here we must speculate more than usual. A gender gap of some kind has been present in most elections since 1952. In 1952, 1956 and 1960, women preferred Republicans more than men did. The next three elections all but saw this gender gap disappear, only for it to reassert itself in the election of 1976. Beginning in 1980, however, the gender gap reversed itself: women were now clearly more favourable to Democrats than were men.

Why should there be any gender gap at all, and why should the direction of the gap have changed in the 1980s? The answer to the first question may lie in biological and/or cultural factors. Men are seen as more aggressive than women and this may be reflected in attitudes towards certain policies, such as defence and law and order. The answer to the second might be connected to a change in emphasis in the agenda of issues in the 1980s. In particular, the Republican party under Ronald Reagan and the New Right called for a vast increase in military expenditure, perhaps thereby increasing its attraction for men. The Republicans simultaneously called for a return to 'traditional' or 'family' values, which was seen by some as a threat to gender equality and abortion rights: this may have caused a slippage of women's votes to the Democrats.

Perhaps the issue of family values also explains the tendency of married people, with their more conventional lifestyles, to vote disproportionately for the Republican party.

Is it possible to identify a typical Democratic or Republican voter? Yes, but some caution is required. The various groupings in Box 9.14 cut across each other: for example, better-off voters lean towards the Republicans, while women lean towards the Democrats. It remains a matter of conjecture, then, which way a well-off woman will vote. When we take into account all the other factors which can affect voting behaviour, the permutations make generalisations difficult.

Nevertheless, on the evidence of recent elections, a wealthy, Protestant, married southern white male, with a college degree, is very likely to vote Republican. Conversely, an unmarried, black, female union member of modest financial means, and without a high-school diploma, is very likely to vote Democrat.

We must remember, however, that voting behaviour, like most aspects of politics, is a dynamic phenomenon. Historically, group voting tendencies have changed (as we shall see in more detail in Chapter 11). In each election, parties and candidates must seek to renew their bonds with their traditional supporters and attempt to woo those who are not. Whatever the failings of American voters, politicians may pay a high price for taking them for granted.

 ## Summary

The complex system of elections in the United States has its origins in the Founding Fathers' desire to base the federal government upon popular sovereignty, without instituting a fully fledged democracy or simple majoritarianism. It also reflects their need to mollify the states, particularly the less populous of them, who feared an overweening federal government.

Developments since 1787 have increased the democratic qualities of the American electoral system, both by expanding the franchise and by making more federal politicians directly rather than indirectly elected. Nevertheless, the electorate's faith in the federal government, as measured by the numbers of those actually voting, is in decline. This raises questions about the mandate and representativeness of those who win federal office. Furthermore, the electorate distrusts those who serve in Congress to the point where it overwhelmingly favours the imposition of term limits on them. It is ironic that a system which gives voters several modes of democratic representation at the federal level, should engender such low levels of popular enthusiasm and electoral participation.

Topics for discussion

1. Why did the framers of the Constitution establish different electoral systems for the presidency, the Senate and the House of Representatives?
2. What are the advantages and disadvantages of imposing term limits on federal office-holders?
3. Is it important that so few Americans exercise their right to vote?
4. What are the main determinants of voting behaviour in presidential elections?
5. Are American presidential campaigns too long?

Further reading

Books providing a general introduction to elections and voting behaviour include Philip J. Davies, *Elections USA*; (Manchester: Manchester University Press, 1992); N. Polsby and A. Wildavsky, *Presidential Elections: Strategies and structures of American Politics* (Chatham, NJ: Chatham House, 1995); S. Wayne, *The Road to the White House 1996* (New York: St Martin's Press, 1996); and J. Jackson and W. Crotty, *The Politics of Presidential Selection* (New York: Harper Collins, 1996). The best commentary on individual elections is the series of books edited by G. Pomper *et al.*, the latest of which is *The Elections of 1996: Reports and interpretations* (Chatham, NJ: Chatham House, 1997). For those with access to the Internet the site maintained at the University of Michigan (http://www.lib.umich.edu) is very useful.

References

Bailey, C., 1989, *The US Congress* (Oxford: Basil Blackwell)

Cook, R., 1991, 'New primaries, new rules mark road to nomination', *CQ Weekly Report*, 7 September, pp. 2411–16

Davies, P., 1992, *Elections USA* (Manchester: Manchester University Press)

Hadley, A., 1978, *The Empty Polling Booth* (Englewood Cliffs: Prentice Hall)

Jackson, J. and Crotty, W., 1996, *The Politics of Presidential Selection* (New York: Harper Collins)

Polsby, N. and Wildavsky, A., 1995, *Presidential Elections: Strategies and structures of American politics* (Chatham, NJ: Chatham House)

Pomper, G. *et al.*, 1989, *The Elections of 1988: Reports and interpretations* (Chatham, NJ: Chatham House)

Pomper, G., Arterton, F., Baker, R., Burnham, W., Frankovic, K., Hersey, M., McWilliams, W., 1993, *The Election of 1992* (Chatham, NJ: Chatham House Publishers)

Pomper, G., Burnham, W., Corrado, A., Hershey, M., Just, M., Keefer, S., McWilliams, W., Mayer, W., 1997, *The Elections of 1996: Reports and interpretations* (Chatham, NJ: Chatham House)

Teixeira, R., 1987, *Why Americans Don't Vote* (New York: Greenwood)

Wayne, S., 1996, *The Road to the White House, 1996* (New York: St Martin's Press)

10

The mass media and politics

This chapter analyses the impact of the media, especially television, on elections and politics in general. American politics without television is unthinkable. Not only do voters gain most of their knowledge about politics from television, but candidates gear their campaigns almost entirely to the demands of this particular medium. Moreover, presidents regard the media as a critical element in the art of political persuasion. Unsurprisingly, then, great controversy surrounds the power of the media in politics.

Gerry Rafshoon, a leading media consultant in American politics, tells an amusing story from the 1952 presidential election. Political television was still in its infancy. The Democrats decided for the first time to give their candidate, Adlai Stevenson, a television adviser – a man called Bill Wilson. Stevenson had been introduced to Wilson at the Democratic Convention, yet weeks into the campaign, the candidate had not once called upon his new assistant for advice. Finally, however, in a hotel at a campaign stop, Wilson received a call to come up to Stevenson's suite. Excited at the prospect of getting down to work at last, Wilson hurried to the candidate's room. Stevenson greeted him by pointing to the television in the corner and saying, 'Ah yes, the television man. Can you fix that thing? I can't get a picture' (White and McCarthy, 1985).

A few elections further on, however, no candidate or campaign would be so naive or ignorant about the enormous potential for the use of television in elections. Today, according to one expert, 'Media coverage is the very lifeblood of politics because it shapes the perceptions that form the reality on which political action is based. Media do more than depict the political environment; they *are* the political environment' (Graber, 1989, p. 238). Box 10.1 charts the progress of the partnership between television and politics.

Box 10.1

Key dates in the history of television and politics

1947 First live television broadcast of State of the Union address (President Truman)

1952 First television adverts for a presidential candidate

First use of television consultants in campaigns

First politically significant use of television. Vice-presidential candidate Richard Nixon is threatened with removal from the Republican ticket, after allegations that he had used a secret slush fund for personal gain. Nixon decides to appeal to the public through television. He makes the 'Checkers' speech, confessing that he had received one gift: his children had been given a little dog called Checkers. His children loved the dog and Nixon vowed that they were going to keep him, whatever the critics said. He then asks viewers to contact Republican headquarters if they want him to stay on the ticket. Viewers respond positively and Nixon is saved

1960 First televised presidential debate, between John F. Kennedy and Richard Nixon

1961 President Kennedy gives first live televised presidential press conference

1963 Network TV news programmes extended to 30 minutes

1964 First controversial political advertisement on TV: the 'Daisy Commercial' on behalf of President Johnson. Without mentioning his opponent by name, the advert implies that Barry Goldwater could launch a nuclear war, if elected

1965 US involvement in Vietnam leads to first 'televised war'

1968 Richard Nixon turns to TV advertising specialists to change his negative image: they create the 'new Nixon'

The American press

When we speak of the media we mean television, radio, newspapers and magazines. Although television is undoubtedly the pre-eminent form of the media in the United States, this does not mean that the others are not important. Although the *New York Times* newspaper, for example, is seen by far fewer people than network television, it is both read and taken very seriously by the political elite (see Box 10.2).

As in most democracies, the written press in the United States is privately owned. However, three characteristics distinguish it from the press in, say, Great Britain.

Box 10.2

Leading print media in the United States

	Average circulation, 1991
Newspapers (daily)	
Wall Street Journal	1,795,448
USA Today	1,418,477
Los Angeles Times	1,177,253
New York Times	1,110,562
Washington Post	791,289
Political magazines (weekly)	
Time	4,248,565
Newsweek	3,420,167
US News and World Report	2,351,922

Source: 'Editor and publisher yearbook', in *World Almanac*, 1993, p. 299

Circulation

First, virtually all newspapers are local rather than national publications. Most importantly, the circulation of even the 'quality press' (*New York Times, LA Times* and *Washington Post*, for example) is substantially limited to the city or region of origin. This means that there is a very large number of daily newspapers in total in the United States: 1,586 as of February 1992 (*World Almanac*, 1993, p. 299). On the other hand, precisely because they are restricted in area of circulation, there is far less competition between papers than there is in Britain. Some cities do have more than one newspaper: thus New York has the *Wall Street Journal*, the *New York Times*, the *Daily News* and the *Post*; and Chicago has the *Tribune* and the *Sun-Times*. Most cities, however, have only one of any significance.

Censorship

The second distinguishing aspect is that the American press is much more free from governmental control than the British press. This is owing in large part to the protection provided by the First Amendment to the Constitution, which provides that 'Congress shall make no law ... abridging the freedom of speech, or of the press'. Although originally the amendment restricted only the federal legislature, the Supreme Court has applied it to state legislatures as well since 1931 (*Near v. Minnesota*).

Moreover, the Court has generally interpreted the First Amendment in a fashion that makes it difficult to gag the press. In 1964, in the case of *New York Times Co. v.*

Sullivan, the Court held that a newspaper could not be convicted of libel merely because it published a false story. It was further necessary to prove that the story had been published with actual malice: that is, that the paper knew it was false. This makes it extremely difficult for public officials to intimidate the press with threats of libel suits.

Even where national security is involved, the Court has granted the press wide latitude. Thus, in *New York Times v. United States* (1971), the Court permitted the *Times* to go ahead with publication of the so-called Pentagon Papers, a leaked Defense Department secret history of government policy making on the Vietnam War. The Court held that publication could only be prevented in situations where it would otherwise create immediate and irreparable harm to the nation.

The Supreme Court has also interpreted the First Amendment to give strong protection to political satire. A notable case in this regard occurred in 1988, in *Flynt v. Falwell*. The Reverend Jerry Falwell, the leader of the Moral Majority, a politically conservative Christian group, had been parodied in the most lewd manner by the scurrilous, pornographic magazine *Hustler*. The magazine was owned by Larry Flynt, and Falwell sued him for libel. Despite the fact that the parody contained utterly and maliciously false statements about Falwell's sex life, the Supreme Court ruled unanimously that he could not seek damages from Flynt. They reasoned that since no one could have taken *Hustler*'s portrayal of the reverend's sex life seriously, Falwell could not have been libelled.

These decisions on the First Amendment pay testament to Americans' belief that a free press is indispensable to open and democratic government. They help to ensure that the press, and indeed other media, can speak with a powerful voice in American politics, both by challenging official versions of the truth and by exposing the wrongdoing of government.

Objective journalism

The third distinctive feature of the American press is that, despite the opportunities for irresponsible bias that local exclusivity and First Amendment freedoms create, the major newspapers are far less overtly partisan than those in, say, Great Britain. The journalistic profession in the United States is imbued with a norm of 'factual reporting' and political 'objectivity'. One writer described this norm as follows:

> Objectivity rules contain two primary requirements. *Depersonalisation* demands that reporters refrain from inserting into the news their own ideological or substantive evaluations of officials, ideas, or groups. *Balance* aims for neutrality. It requires that reporters present the views of legitimate spokespersons of the conflicting sides in any significant dispute, and provide both sides with roughly equivalent attention.
>
> (Entman, 1989, p. 30)

Another analyst likened the model of objective journalists to that of medical doctors: 'white-coated specialists describing pathologies as if through microscopes' (Diamond, 1980, p. 235).

Total objectivity is clearly not possible, since the very selection of the items that constitute the news involves judgements which are in part subjective. As we shall see below, many politicians and academics do believe that the American media are politically biased. Nevertheless, it remains true that American newspapers are generally much less inclined to play the role of cheerleader for a politician or political party than are their British counterparts.

Television

Television is by far the most important medium in American politics. Not only do most Americans get the bulk of their information about politics from television, but they trust it more than any other medium. As Box 10.3 indicates, adult Americans spend on average about four hours a day watching television.

Unsurprisingly, very little of this four hours is spent watching news or other programmes about politics. Most Americans watch television as a leisure activity and seek entertainment, not political enlightenment from their television sets. Furthermore, even the main political programmes, such as the prime-time network news, actually convey little information compared with a newspaper. As Robert Spero pointed out, 'The word-count of a half-hour news programme would not fill up much more than one column of one page of the *New York Times*' (Spero, 1980, p. 177).

That said, television is critical to most Americans' knowledge of political affairs, as Box 10.4 indicates.

The reliance of the American public upon television for political information, together with the importance attached to television by politicians themselves, raises several critical questions about the power of television in American politics. Who owns and runs television stations? How does television cover political news? Is television coverage of politics biased? And, perhaps most important of all, how much impact does television have on viewers' political opinions and behaviour? Each of these questions is examined in turn below.

Box 10.3

Hours of television usage per day, 1990

Group	Daily viewing (Hr min.)
Men 18+	3.51
Women 18+	4.28
Teens 12–17	3.15
Children 2–11	3.18

Source: *Television and Video Almanac*, 1992, p. 19a

Use and trustworthiness of media, selected years 1959–88

	1959	1967	1978	1988
Source of most news (%, more than one answer permitted)				
Television	51	64	67	65
Newspapers	57	55	49	42
Radio	34	28	20	14
Magazines	8	7	5	4
Other people	4	4	5	5
Most believable (%, only one answer permitted)				
Television	29	41	47	49
Newspapers	32	24	23	26
Radio	12	7	9	7
Magazines	10	8	9	5
Don't know/no answer	17	20	12	13

Source: Stanley and Niemi, 1990, p. 69

Television ownership and control

Ownership of television in the United States is in private, commercial hands. There is no equivalent of the BBC. There is a small non-commercial television channel (Public Broadcasting Service – PBS) supported financially by a mixture of grants and viewer subscriptions. PBS audiences are very small, however, with a quality political programme such as the MacNeil/Lehrer 'NewsHour' attracting about 1 per cent of the nation's viewers. Similar figures apply to the political programming of cable networks, such as Cable News Network (CNN) and Cable-Satellite Public Affairs Network (C-SPAN) (Entman, 1989, pp. 108–9).

Television broadcasting is thus largely the preserve of private business, and especially of the four main network television companies – the Columbia Broadcasting System (CBS), the American Broadcasting Company (ABC), the National Broadcasting Company (NBC) and the Fox Broadcasting System (FBS). These four corporations sell their programmes to the hundreds of local television stations across the country and are estimated to dominate the programming on about one-third of the nation's television households (Graber, 1989, p. 45). They are also responsible for producing the main national evening news programmes.

American television companies are, in many respects, just like any other business enterprise. They are owned by even larger corporations or by rich tycoons and the main task of the executives who run them is to make profits. Like other businesses, television companies seek to expand their markets: something which may involve buying up other broadcasting companies.

Here, however, there is a degree of governmental regulation. Broadcasting licences are issued by the Federal Communications Commission (FCC), the members of which are appointed by the president, subject to approval by the Senate. In order to ensure that no owner or television company acquires too much media power, the FCC limits the number of media outlets that any one company can own. No company can own more than twelve television stations or own stations that reach more than 25 per cent of the nation's television households (Graber, 1989, p. 44).

Television coverage of politics

The principal way that a television corporation seeks to maximise its profits is to increase the number of viewers who tune into its programmes. The more viewers who watch a programme, the more the television company can charge advertisers who wish to reach that audience. Inevitably, then, virtually all television programmes, including news and current affairs programmes, are designed to pull in the largest audience possible. This has significant consequences for the way in which politics is packaged for television.

Television is a visual medium that most people watch for entertainment. These are two of the principal factors which constrain the coverage of politics on television. Most viewers want visual images which entertain them, whether they are watching an election campaign item or a report of urban rioting. The main ingredients of visual entertainment are movement, drama, emotion and conflict.

Because Americans are relatively uninterested in politics and television therefore devotes relatively little time to it, news items must also be brief and simplified. Finally, because the aim of the company is to maximise its audience, news items should not unnecessarily antagonise any section of the viewing public.

One can immediately see that such constraints raise considerable problems for television coverage of the complex issues which lie at the heart of American politics – the budget deficit, health care, civil rights and foreign affairs, for example. Television takes these important political issues and, in rendering them palatable for viewers, distorts them. Distortion should not be confused with bias: while the latter slants coverage towards a particular political viewpoint, distortion involves misrepresenting events in order to meet journalistic needs.

The result of meeting these needs, say critics, is a diet of trivialised, simplified, emotion-laden items which do little or nothing to develop an informed public. An example of this occurred in the early summer of 1993, when President Clinton went to California as part of his campaign to build political support for his budget proposal. The main story to arise from that tour, however, was not whether the president's plan was a good one, or even whether he had sold the plan well; rather, it was the fact that while aboard Air Force One at Los Angeles Airport, waiting to take off for Washington, he had his hair cut by a fashionable stylist. Since all airport traffic is routinely halted when Air Force One is in the vicinity, the president's hair-cut caused a long delay to other travellers. Moreover, the hair-cut cost $200. The president was pilloried for his alleged indifference to other travellers and his vanity. Moreover, it later emerged that most, if not all of the story, was actually untrue.

The story, however, was entertaining, simple to tell and amenable to visual representation by pictures of the president's hair, Air Force One and the backlog of air traffic at the airport. On the other hand, its political significance is minuscule, except for the irony that it showed Clinton, a master of the political arts, as having been naive about the ability of the media to turn a trivial episode into one that is politically damaging.

On a more serious matter, television coverage of the Vietnam War has frequently been attacked for distorting the nature of the conflict. Television allegedly concentrated on dramatic scenes involving combat, destruction and refugees, even though such scenes were comparatively rare and not typical of the realities of life in South Vietnam. The simple fact is, however, that combat is emotionally and visually exciting, while peasants peacefully tending their rice-paddies is not.

Television bias

As well as being accused of distortion, journalists covering the Vietnam War were also accused of straightforward political bias. Robert Elegant, for example, claimed that many journalists were opposed to the war on political grounds and therefore their reports were negative and damaging to the American cause (Elegant, 1981).

Although the Vietnam War is an outstanding illustration, accusations of political bias in television and press reporting are routine in American politics. Politicians are notoriously thin-skinned and they are quick to attribute media criticism of their actions or policies to political bias. Richard Nixon made such accusations an ongoing feature of his political career. When defeated for the governorship of California in 1962, just two years after he lost the presidential election to John F. Kennedy, Nixon retired from politics, telling journalists at a press conference that, 'You won't have me to kick around any more.'

Even after his successful comeback in the presidential election of 1968, Nixon was convinced that the media were out to get him. Amongst other things, he had his vice-president, Spiro T. Agnew, conduct an aggressive public campaign accusing the media of liberal bias. The names of many journalists also featured on President Nixon's secret Political Enemies List that was discovered during the Watergate scandal.

Beyond Richard Nixon's personal feelings, however, it is almost a staple of conservative politics in the United States to accuse the media of liberal bias. At first glance, this may seem an unconvincing allegation. Most obviously, as already noted, television is a commercial business and one would expect those who run it to share the pro-business values of much of the rest of corporate America. Indeed, it is on precisely these lines that the left usually accuses the media of *conservative* bias.

Nevertheless, the allegation of liberal bias is not altogether without foundation. Most obviously, the four major television networks are based in New York city, the centre of American liberal culture. Moreover, those who work in television are part of an intellectual and cultural liberalism which is strong among the artistic and entertainments community (Dye, 1995; Graber, 1989).

There is also some empirical evidence to support this view. Those who work in television, as opposed to the actual owners of television companies, are far more likely to identify themselves as Democrats or Independents, than as Republicans. One study of executive media personnel in the 1980s found that 33 per cent were Democrats, 58 per cent were Independents and just 9 per cent were Republicans. This led Doris Graber to conclude that 'owners of prominent media hire Democrats and liberal Independents to operate their media properties, although they themselves usually share the Republican leanings of the big business community' (Graber, 1989, p. 62).

It is one thing, however, to identify media personnel as liberal, but quite another to show that their political persuasion results in slanted news coverage. Thomas Dye believes that the liberal bias of the media is most strongly reflected in the actual selection of items that are included in the news:

> Topics selected weeks in advance for coverage reflect, or create … current liberal issues: concern for poor and blacks, women's liberation, opposition to defense spending, and the CIA, ecology, migrant farm labor, tax loopholes and Indian rights and, for nearly two years, Watergate.

> (Dye, 1995, p. 107)

This argument is countered by journalists who claim that television news coverage mirrors society and the public's concerns. This view is buttressed by the point made earlier that, ultimately, television news is an entertainment designed to attract as many viewers as possible, in order to maximise advertising revenue. Content, like other aspects of journalistic coverage, is constrained by the need the please the maximum number of viewers. Any programme which ignored this and instead pursued an agenda of issues that interested only liberals, would soon fall behind in the ratings war.

The liberal bias of the media certainly did not spare President Clinton when he became embroiled in yet another sexual scandal in 1998. Despite the fact that conservative groups had been using such scandal to undermine the Clinton presidency from its inception in 1993, liberal newspapers like the *Washington Post* took the lead in exposing the president's alleged intimate relationship with a White House employee. Moreover, broadcast and print media alike repeated unsubstantiated stories, sometimes from anonymous sources, in their rush to beat their competitors with 'breaking news'.

A further factor which undermines the theory of liberal bias in the American media is the simple fact that reporters are heavily dependent upon government for stories and information. Daniel Hallin disputed the myth of liberal bias in reporting on the Vietnam War by showing that government was not only the major source of information relayed by the media, but also that such information was reported largely unchallenged (Hallin, 1986). What was true of Vietnam coverage is also true of political news in general (Graber, 1989, p. 78). If there is any structural bias in media coverage of politics, it is bias in favour of the government of the day, whatever its political colour.

Impact of television

There is a passionate debate in most countries about the impact of television on people's attitudes and behaviour. It is typically argued that exposure to a heavy diet of explicit television violence or sex leads to antisocial or criminal behaviour in viewers.

Evidence to support this is said to be the number of criminal offenders who cite television programmes as the inspiration to their crime.

On the other hand, it can be plausibly argued that television does not cause violence in people, but rather that people prone to violence are attracted to programmes which portray it graphically. Thus the causal relationship between television and behaviour is in dispute.

The same debate exists in regard to television's coverage of politics. Don Hewitt, the executive producer of the popular politics programme '60 Minutes', tells of a woman who told him that television violence was to blame for John Hinckley's attempt to assassinate President Reagan in 1981. Hewitt responded by asking her how much television John Wilkes Booth had watched before assassinating Abraham Lincoln (White and McCarthy, 1985).

Social scientists have, of course, investigated the impact of television on political behaviour, especially voting behaviour. These studies have failed to produce any evidence that what people see on television affects the way they vote: 'the persistent finding of almost three decades of research has been that the mass media have minimal effects in changing voters' attitudes' (Arterton, 1984, p. 4).

As another analyst pointed out, this conclusion presents us with something of a paradox: 'The public believes that the media have an important impact on the conduct of politics and on public thinking. Politicians act and behave on the basis of the same assumption. But many studies conducted by social scientists fail to show substantial impact' (Graber, 1989, p. 12).

These findings are troubling because common sense tells us that if Americans get most of their political information from television, and if they place a great deal of faith in the reliability of that information, then surely they *must* be influenced by television.

Selective attention

Here as elsewhere, however, common sense may not be right, for media researchers agree that human beings are adept at controlling what information they accept. The most important phenomenon in this respect is selective perception, also known as selective exposure or *selective attention*. Quite simply, viewers will screen out political messages which make them psychologically uncomfortable by contradicting their existing beliefs. Selective attention is thus a defence mechanism against disturbing political information. It can take a variety of forms in practice – the television can be turned off or the channel switched; or the viewer can 'challenge' the unwelcome message by drawing upon different, contradictory evidence or disputing the validity of the source of the message; or the viewer may simply ignore the message.

The importance of selective attention will vary from one individual to the next. Viewers with deeply held political convictions or strong party loyalties are extremely unlikely to be affected by news or propaganda which contradicts their existing opinions. The weaker their knowledge or political beliefs, however, the less they are likely to be discomforted by new political information and the less, therefore, they are likely to invoke the defensive shield of selective attention. Consequently, this section of the population is most vulnerable to the impact of television and any political bias which operates.

It is probable, then, that the main impact of television on the substance of Americans' political beliefs stems from its power to help set the political agenda. By definition, news is what is reported in the media. Selecting newsworthy items from the mass of stories and issues available is a subjective process. However, as noted above, such judgements are likely to be guided at least as much by professional and commercial considerations as by the political bias of the television or newspaper.

It is therefore difficult to avoid the conclusion that the power of the media to influence Americans' political attitudes is frequently exaggerated by those who mistake its pervasiveness for persuasiveness. Nevertheless, as we shall now see, that very pervasiveness is a critical ingredient of the representative process.

The media and elections

Media strategy

In effect, elections take place on television in the United States. Since most Americans get most of their political information from television, candidates for office spend most of their time, effort and money on developing an effective media strategy. To be successful, the first thing they need is exposure: they need to be seen on television as often as possible. The second major condition of a successful media strategy is that this exposure must cast the candidate in a positive light.

Fulfilling both of these demands can be problematic. Take, for example, the relatively unknown politician in a large field of primary candidates. This politician needs to do something that brings favourable publicity onto herself, but the media will prefer to concentrate their attention upon the front-runners in the election. Moreover, those front-runners are likely to be better financed than she is and therefore able to buy more advertising time on television.

The front-runners too, however, may face difficulties in presenting themselves to the public via television. The most obvious problem that may arise is that the media may cover them *too* closely and expose things that they would rather keep hidden. Such was the experience of Senator Gary Hart, the leading candidate for the Democratic party presidential nomination in 1988. When rumours began to circulate about Hart's extramarital affair with model Donna Rice, Hart denied them and challenged the media to produce proof. In hindsight, this was a foolish act of bravado, as evidence soon showed the rumours to be true. The Hart campaign never recovered.

There are ultimately two kinds of media attention with which a candidate has to deal. First there are those situations in which the initiative and control are mainly with the candidate. Most important here are the candidate's public image which he tries to promote and the television advertisements about himself which he pays to have broadcast.

Candidate image

How a candidate looks on television is crucial to his overall strategy of establishing his image in the minds of the electorate. The most basic aspect of this is literally the physical appearance of the candidate. Academics and political consultants agree that it is becoming increasingly difficult for physically unattractive candidates to get elected. They also agree that even great politicians from the past who were not physically blessed, such as Abraham Lincoln, would find it difficult today to pursue a successful political career. Professor Larry Sabato believes that, in effect, candidates are now pre-selected by physical appearance, with their model being the good-looking television presenters: 'We've had a convergence among three types of people. Anchor-persons on television, politicians and game-show hosts all look very much alike today. And that's the effect of television' (Rees, 1992).

The most famous example of the impact of the physical appearance of candidates on television occurred during the 1960 presidential election. In the first televised debate between John Kennedy and Richard Nixon, viewers were presented with a strong contrast between the two candidates. Kennedy was tanned, youthful and dressed in a dark suit which gave him a crisp outline against the pale studio background. Nixon was pale following a recent illness, perspiring and had a dark 'five o'clock shadow'; he also wore a light grey suit which merged his figure with the background. Analysis later showed that those who heard the debate on radio believed that Nixon had won, but those who had watched on television thought Kennedy had won.

Candidate image depends upon more than raw physical appearance, however. Politicians present themselves so as visually to symbolise their character and politics. Jimmy Carter, for example, both as candidate in 1976 and then president, would sometimes dress casually on television in order to try to project an image of being an informal, approachable 'man of the people'.

On the other hand, during the 1980 presidential election, when Carter was under severe public pressure from perceived domestic and foreign policy failures, he sought to emphasise his presidential character by adopting a 'Rose Garden strategy'. This is when an incumbent president invites the cameras in to witness him signing important bills or meeting foreign dignitaries in presidential surroundings, such as the White House Rose Garden. The object is to appeal to the respect that the voters hold for the office, in the hope that this will compensate for any lack of respect for the man or his policies.

Political advertisements

Undoubtedly the main opportunity for a candidate to define himself with the public is the paid television advertisement. Here the candidate, or rather his television consultant, has almost total control over the presentation.

Advertisements may try to establish a candidate's position on certain policy issues, but they are more likely to try to project his image and character. As with commercial advertising, political advertisements seek to entertain and to produce a favourable response to the 'product-candidate', by evoking an emotional rather than a rational response. Thus advertisements have very little to do with conveying information upon which a viewer can base a reasoned voting decision. Rather, advertisements try to make the viewer like the candidate for other, even irrational reasons. Advertisements hope to make viewers prefer a candidate for the same reasons that they prefer a news presenter or game-show host.

Not surprisingly, then, political advertisements have come in for a great deal of criticism for their failure to convey the kind of information that rational voting requires. Critics claim that political advertisements either present false information about candidates or no information at all.

Robert Spero's analysis of political advertisements by presidential candidates adds weight to these criticisms (Spero, 1980). He discovered that these advertisements regularly violated the codes of truthfulness that regulate commercial advertising. They contained both demonstrable lies and seriously misleading statements. Thus, in 1976, the Jimmy Carter campaign ran commercials proclaiming their candidate to be a peanut-farmer and a political outsider, who started out on his quest for the presidency with no organisation, no influential contacts and no money. In fact, Carter was a millionaire owner of a peanut-processing corporation, who had put his campaign organisation into place some three years before the election. He had also served on the Trilateral Commission, where he had established good contacts with leading politicians, academics and businesspeople.

Nevertheless, while such distortion of the truth may be morally reprehensible, it is not clear that it seriously misleads many voters. As Doris Graber says, 'Commercials are perceiver-determined. People see in them pretty much what they want to see – attractive images for their favourite candidates and unattractive ones for their opponents (Graber, 1989, p. 196). As with political news, then, viewers are very good at screening out information which contradicts their existing beliefs, while accepting that which confirms them.

What advertisements can achieve, however, is a crystallisation of a latent feeling that the viewer has about a candidate. This is particularly important in the case of negative advertising, an increasingly common and controversial feature of American election campaigns.

Negative advertising

In terms of political impact, it seems more profitable to attack your opponent than to promote yourself. Typically, campaign consultants will interview a selected panel of voters to find out what they dislike most about the opposing candidate. Advertisements are then produced which attack the opponent on these issues, often in a crude, vicious and misleading manner. At their worst, they attack an opponent's character or distort his or her political record or position.

The first major negative political advertisement was Tony Schwartz's 'Daisy Commercial', screened on behalf of President Johnson during the 1964 presidential campaign. It depicted a little girl counting as she pulls the petals off a flower. Suddenly a male voice is superimposed, counting down from ten to one as if in preparation for a rocket launch. The camera zooms into the eye of the girl, and as the voice reaches zero, a nuclear explosion is heard and the mushroom cloud appears. President Johnson's voice is now heard warning of the dangers of nuclear war.

His opponent, Barry Goldwater, is never mentioned in the commercial. However, the right-wing Goldwater had a well deserved reputation as a hard-line anticommunist, and the daisy commercial played on this to suggest that, if elected, he might be willing to risk a nuclear war. The commercial was scaremongering but its effectiveness depended upon the fact that Goldwater's extremism was already an issue in the public's perception. It was thus a classic example of the power of advertising to sharpen and define an opponent's negative characteristics.

By the late 1980s, negative advertising had become a regular feature of elections at all levels of office and even of primary elections. For example, the 1990 Democratic primary for governor of Texas featured a Jim Mattox advertisement accusing Ann Richards of having used drugs; and a Richards advert mentioning an earlier indictment of Mattox for bribery, even though he had been acquitted (Davies, 1992, p. 95).

The 1988 presidential election was particularly noted for the use of negative advertising by Republicans against the Democratic candidate, Governor Michael Dukakis of Massachusetts. In particular, they played on the fact that a convicted murderer in Massachusetts, Willie Horton, had committed rape while out of prison on a weekend pass. Although many states had such furlough systems, Dukakis was attacked for being 'soft on crime'. Other advertisements attacked him for being unpatriotic, because he had vetoed a state bill requiring schoolchildren to begin the day by reciting the Pledge of Allegiance. The adverts failed to mention that the bill was clearly unconstitutional under well known Supreme Court decisions.

Such advertising may lower the tone of elections and increase the cynicism of the public about politics and politicians in general. Candidates are also aware that the public condemns negative advertising and this may have helped both the Clinton and Dole campaigns in 1996 decide to avoid the worst excesses of character attacks on their opponent. The Clinton campaign concentrated on so-called comparative advertisements, which criticise the opponent's record (Just, *Candidate Strategies and the Media Campaign* 1997, pp. 92–3). This may still be thought of as negative in the sense that it does not concentrate on the candidate's own virtues, but it is also entirely legitimate in a contest between two individuals presenting two different programmes for the public's endorsement.

Ultimately, however, negative advertising can have a significant effect on voter choice. It seems that it is more effective to focus on your opponent's negative features, than merely to emphasise your own positive features. In other words, it is sometimes more effective to play on the electorate's fears rather than its hopes. This is nothing new in electoral politics. It becomes a problem, however, when it is so widespread that voters are presented with a campaign which is almost wholly negative in tone. The danger is that it will simply turn people off politics altogether.

Candidates versus the media

Whereas candidates can control the advertisements that are screened on behalf of their campaign, they are much more vulnerable when it comes to news coverage of elections. Here the supposedly adversarial relationship of politicians and the media comes into play. Candidates want only favourable coverage, while the media wants the truth as they see it, though the truth must be packaged to meet their commercial demands.

Although the media has claimed its victims in the past, as we saw with Gary Hart above, candidates are becoming increasingly adept at manipulating the needs of the media for their own purposes. If television requires pictures, excitement and statements that can be condensed into simple language in a few sentences, then that is what politicians give them.

As a result, American elections are now governed by the 'soundbite' and the 'photo-opportunity'. In fact, campaigning amounts to creating as many opportunities as possible to have the cameras photographing the candidate in attractive settings, and to produce the telling, short phrase that will be broadcast on that evening's news programmes. Thus, in the 1996 campaign, the average length of a candidate quote on the evening news was 8.2 seconds (Just, 1997, p. 98).

Local news coverage is very important in a country the size of and as diverse as the United States, so candidates are given a manic schedule of trips to different parts of the country, spending only enough time in each to provide the media with what they need. As Christopher Arterton argued, 'If a candidate spends one hour in a city, he is likely to receive the same amount of news coverage of that visit as he would during a four-hour or eight-hour stop in the same location. Thus, modern presidential candidates are kept continually on the move by their desire for local news coverage. The scheduler's goal is to set up appearances in three or four major news markets each day' (Arterton, 1984, p. 13).

These appearances are carefully planned, even choreographed, to produce good visuals. Enthusiastic supporters are strategically placed to demonstrate that the candidate is popular. A site may be chosen to produce a positive response from the viewers – for example, Ronald Reagan addressing a crowd against the backdrop of New York harbour and the Statue of Liberty. Or again, the candidate might be filmed eating spaghetti at an Italian American social in order to identify himself with that particular section of the electorate. None of these images tells the voters much about the candidate's policies, but they are appealing and entertaining.

Soundbites fulfil the media's need for simplification and drama at the expense of detailed policy statements. Vice-President Bush's most famous statement about his economic policies was the endlessly repeated 'Read my lips – no new taxes'. Unfortunately, this soundbite returned to haunt him as president when he *did* agree to raise taxes, but at least Bush's slogan purported to say something about policy. In 1992, the Clinton soundbite that took the media's fancy was a sentimental reference to his birthplace that was supposed to rekindle belief in the American dream: 'I still believe in a town called Hope.'

Candidate control of media reporting of elections was taken to extremes by Michael Deaver, Ronald Reagan's media adviser, in the 1984 election. Because Reagan was always liable to make a gaffe when questioned by reporters, Deaver permitted just one press conference with the president during the entire campaign. However, he did supply endless attractive photo-opportunities which the media felt bound to broadcast.

In 1992, the presidential candidates found new ways to bypass the rigours of media interrogation. Instead of reaching the public through interviews with 'heavyweight' political journalists, they appeared instead on popular television programmes, like the 'Larry King Show', 'Phil Donahue' and 'Arsenio Hall' and the rock music station MTV. Here candidates were not in danger of being confronted with difficult questions and they could also provide good photo-opportunities, as when Bill Clinton donned dark glasses and played the saxophone. Ross Perot went even further, simply buying media time to broadcast his own thirty-minute specials.

Even when candidates cannot hide from the political media, they are not without means of trying to ensure that coverage is favourable. All campaigns employ spin doctors whose job it is to move among the media after, say, a televised debate or primary election, trying to persuade them that their candidate was the victor. Bill Clinton's team provided an excellent illustration of this in the 1992 presidential election. In the key New Hampshire primary, Clinton was beaten by Paul Tsongas. Nevertheless, the Clinton team claimed victory by arguing that because the campaign had been hit so badly by sex scandals, his second place was truly remarkable. They even persuaded the media to adopt their description of Clinton as 'The Comeback Kid'.

 ## Summary

Ideally, the media should communicate the kind of political information that the electorate needs in order to make rational voting decisions. Voters should know what policies the candidates propose and what the effect of those policies is likely to be. Voters should also be informed about the past record of politicians and the kind of government they propose to run.

Clearly, however, current media presentation of politics falls far short of these goals. Politicians seem increasingly able to package themselves for television in ways that make them attractive figures, without revealing much about their true selves or their policies. Media personnel may try to penetrate the politicians' veneer, but even when successful they provide mostly a simplistic, trivial and perhaps distorted picture.

It is not clear, however, how much of the blame for this should be laid at the door of the media. For any citizen who wishes to be well informed *can* find newspapers, magazines and television programmes that provide serious and detailed coverage of politics. If the average voter wanted such coverage, then popular print and broadcast media would provide it, for commercial reasons if nothing else. Most Americans, however, appear to value entertainment more than real politics and that, therefore, is what both politicians and the media seek to give them.

 ## Topics for discussion

1. Does media coverage of politics give viewers the information they need?
2. How biased is media coverage of politics?
3. How important is 'image' in elections?
4. Is negative advertising harmful to the political process?

 ## Further reading

An excellent introduction to this subject is Doris Graber, *The Mass Media and American Politics* (Washington DC: CQ Press, 1989). A good discussion of the impact of television on the political process is Robert Entman, *Democracy Without Citizens: Media and the decay of American politics* (Oxford: Oxford

University Press, 1989). A useful chapter on the structure of American media can be found in Thomas Dye, *Who's Running America?* (Englewood Cliffs: Prentice Hall, 1995) For an analysis of the media campaign in the 1996 election, see M. Just (in G. Pomper *et al.*, *The Elections of 1996: Reports and interpretations* (Chatham, NJ: Chatham House, 1997). For a sophisticated analysis of the power of the media in politics, see Daniel Hallin, *The 'Uncensored War': The media and Vietnam* (New York: Oxford University Press, 1986).

 References

Arterton, F., 1984, *Media Politics* (Lexington, Mass: Lexington Books)

Diamond, E., 1980, *Good News, Bad News* (Cambridge, Mass.: MIT Press)

Dye, T., 1995, *Who's Running America?* (6th edn, Englewood Cliffs: Prentice Hall)

Elegant, R., 1981, 'How to lose a war', *Encounter*, August, pp. 73–90

Entman, R., 1989, *Democracy Without Citizens: Media and the decay of American politics* (New York: Oxford University Press)

Graber, D., 1989, *Mass Media and American Politics* (3rd edn, (Washington DC: CQ Press)

Hallin, D., 1986, *The 'Uncensored War': The media and Vietnam* (New York: Oxford University Press)

Rees, L., 1992, 'We Have Ways of Making You Think' (BBC2, broadcast 1992)

Spero, R., 1980, *The Duping of the American Voter: Dishonesty and deception in presidential television advertising* (New York: Lippincott & Crowell)

Stanley, H. and Niemi, R., 1990, *Vital Statistics on American Politics* (2nd edn, Washington DC: CQ Press)

White, T. and McCarthy, L., 1992, 'Television and the Presidency' (BBC 2, broadcast 1985)

11

Political parties

Political parties are a universal and essential feature of western democratic systems. Although often the target of cynical comment, parties are usually recognised as providing a vital link between the governed and the government. At first glance, American parties occupy the same place in the politics of the United States as do their European counterparts in their own countries. Thus, for well over one hundred years, national and local elections have been dominated by the Democratic party and the Republican party. On closer inspection, however, American parties differ significantly from those in Europe. Moreover, America's always relatively weak parties have been in yet further decline over recent decades. As a result, it is appropriate to ask whether parties in the United States any longer play a major role in politics and government.

Origins and history of American political parties

Anti-party feeling and the Constitution

The Founding Fathers took a dim view of political parties. They regarded parties as selfish factions which sought to use governmental power to satisfy their own desires, while neglecting the legitimate interests of other citizens. If such a faction commanded the support of a majority of citizens, a political party might even institute tyranny. In short, parties were viewed as divisive at a time when the country's greatest need was unity.

In *The Federalist* (no. 10) James Madison made clear both his negative view of factions and the ways in which the Constitution was designed to keep them in check. Yet despite his best attempts to create what has been described as a 'Constitution against party' (Hofstadter, 1969, p. 40), it was soon clear that Madison had failed. By the end of George Washington's presidency in 1797, the United States possessed its first party system, pitching the Federalists against the

Jeffersonian Republicans. In his farewell address, Washington warned the country against 'the spirit of faction' that had arisen, but to no avail. In 1800, there occurred the first presidential election fought along clear party lines. What then were the forces which compelled the emergence of political parties?

The first party system

First, and by far the most important, was the simple fact that Americans were divided by self interest and the public policies linked to them. Although free of the extreme class and ideological divisions of Europe, the United States was not without economic, sectional and political rivalries. Thus, economic activity in the south consisted mainly of agriculture, while that of the north east was geared to shipping, banking and commerce. From these differences arose competing views of what constituted good government.

The independent farmers of the south had little need for an active federal government to support their agricultural economy and, therefore, tended to take the view that 'the government governs best that governs least'. Those engaged in commerce, however, required the national government to introduce protective tariffs for American manufacturing and to help establish the creditworthiness of American business. Logically enough, these interests called for an expansive role for the federal government.

Given the fundamental nature of these issues, it comes as no surprise that they quickly emerged as political conflicts. President Washington's Treasury Secretary, Alexander Hamilton, presented Congress with a set of proposals in 1790–91 designed to promote commerce and, along with it, the power of the federal government. Those who supported him were dubbed the Federalists, the name that had first been used to describe the proponents of the Constitution of 1787.

Ironically, the opposition to Hamilton's policies in Congress was led by James Madison, a former Federalist himself and, of course, the opponent of party politics. Along with Thomas Jefferson and others, he saw in Hamilton's policies the threat of a return to autocratic, even monarchic, government as a centralising authority sought to promote the interests of the rich at the expense of 'the common man'. Seeing themselves as the guardians of the American republic, they took the name Republicans. As they increasingly gathered around Jefferson's presidential efforts, they became known as Jeffersonian Republicans.

The split between Federalists and Jeffersonian Republicans was not solely the product of economic self interest and domestic policy. Political philosophy and foreign affairs intervened in respect of American policy towards the Anglo-French war of the 1790s, which followed the French Revolution of 1789. The more aristocratic Federalists supported the British, while the Republicans leaned towards the French.

The second main reason for the rise of political parties in the United States was that which is common to all democracies: the need to organise for competitive elections. While the Jeffersonian Republican party began as a Congressional opposition to a Federalist presidency, the aim of the movement quickly became the capture of the presidency itself. This required not merely organisation in Congress, but also in the country at large.

Republican congressmen therefore began to form Republican clubs at the state and district level. For the election of 1800, Jefferson drew up a party platform designed not merely to ensure his own election to the presidency, but also to produce a Republican majority in Congress.

This brings us to a third reason for the rise and persistence of parties in the United States. The very separation of powers which was designed to inhibit the growth of parties, paradoxically makes them a necessity. Fragmentation of political power invites an organisational network which can bring institutions together for the purpose of advancing particular policies. The best way of producing such institutional coalitions is a party which can offer candidates for each of the institutions in question. Party, then, can supply the glue which holds a fragmented political system together.

This is not to say that the 'Constitution against party' has wholly failed in its goal. For as we shall see, while it did not succeed in containing the spirit of faction, it has helped to ensure that American political parties are weak.

Changes in party systems

The Democratic party

The first party system did not last long, but after the brief Era of Good Feelings, when party politics dissipated, the United States has experienced a series of party systems. Parties have come and gone; and equally importantly, parties which have not changed their name have nevertheless mutated in ways that defy their origins (see Box 11.1).

Both the emergence of new parties and the transformation of established ones have been brought about principally by developments in the fundamental issue agenda of American politics. Such developments have often been accompanied by the rise of new interests and groupings in the American electorate.

Andrew Jackson and the Democratic party

The Democratic party arose in 1828 in conjunction with the presidential candidacy of General Andrew Jackson, the military hero who had defeated the British at the Battle of New Orleans in 1815. The Democratic campaign concentrated heavily on

---

Box 11.1

Party systems in American history

1793–1816	Federalist v. Jeffersonian Republican
1816–1828	No party system: 'Era of Good Feelings'
1828–1856	Democrat v. National Republican/Whig
1856–1932	Democrat v. Republican, *pre New Deal system*
1932–Present day	Democrat v Republican, *New Deal system*

promoting Jackson as a personality. However, it tapped important new sources of electoral support, such as recently enfranchised lower-class voters, particularly in the west, and Irish and German immigrant voters in the cities of the north.

These voters resented what they saw as their opponents' bias towards the interests of the rich, the banks and the corporations, and they enthusiastically bought the image of Jackson as the champion of 'the common man'. The Democrats eventually succeeded in building the first mass, popular party in the United States. However, unlike today, the Democrats at that time believed that the interests of lower-class Americans were best served by opposing the growth of governmental power, especially federal governmental power. They feared that the wealthy were intent on using the federal government not merely to enrich themselves at the expense of other Americans, but also to encroach upon the autonomy of the states' governments.

This fear was famously illustrated when President Jackson fought a running battle with his congressional opponents over their attempt to renew the charter of the National Bank. Jackson saw the bank as the epitome of centralised power in the hands of the rich, and in 1832 he vetoed the recharter bill passed by Congress. In his message accompanying the veto, Jackson proclaimed an egalitarian philosophy. Accepting that some distinctions of wealth were inevitable and natural, he continued: 'but when the laws undertake to add to these natural and just advantages artificial distinctions, to grant titles, gratuities, and exclusive privileges, to make the rich richer and the potent more powerful, the humble members of society – the farmers, mechanics and labourers – who have neither the time nor the means of securing like favours to themselves, have a right to complain of the injustice of their government (Rozwenc, 1963, pp. 88–9).

This philosophy of Jacksonian Democracy embodied themes which have been an ever-present feature of party politics in the United States. In particular, the philosophy is *populist* in its distrust of the combination of federal government power and the economic power of the banks, corporations and the rich. It is *egalitarian* in its belief not in equality, but in equality of opportunity – the right of the 'have-nots' to improve themselves without having to battle against artificial barriers designed to keep them in their place. Its *antielitism* is not radical in the sense that it is anti-capitalist: rather, it celebrates the form of capitalism represented in the American dream, a capitalism which creates individual wealth but does not entrench privilege.

The Democrats' opponents struggled to put together a party which could capture the presidency. Eventually settling on the name of 'the Whigs', they did succeed in electing two presidents: William Harrison and Zachary Taylor. However, these victories followed economic downturns and represented a rejection of the incumbent Democrat, rather than a triumph for Whig principles.

Antislavery and the Republican party

Nevertheless, the Whig belief in promoting national economic development through federal government activity attracted the support of many whose economic self interest was bound up with manufacturing. Most importantly, this included the growing number of white labourers in the country. Unlike farmers, their prosperity was enhanced by tariffs which protected American manufacturing from its overseas competitors. Unlike southerners, they also had good reason to oppose the spread of slavery throughout the country. Since slave labour was inevitably cheaper than free labour, slavery, if allowed to spread, would undercut the opportunities available to white labourers in the north and west. Thus, when the slavery issue came to the fore in the 1850s, it created new electoral possibilities for the Federalist/Whig belief in promoting the national economy.

Slavery was a sectional issue which divided the country along geopolitical lines. As such, the increasing bitterness over the issue split the national parties asunder. The Democrats, whose core was in the agricultural south, gradually became the pro-slavery party; northern Democrats tried desperately to promote a compromise on slavery that would keep the party together. In 1860, however, the Democrat presidential nominating convention broke up on sectional lines, with southerners nominating Breckinridge of Kentucky and northerners nominating Douglas of Illinois.

Antislavery sentiment found its expression in a number of third parties, such as the Liberty party, the Free Soil party, and the American party or 'Know Nothing party'. However, it was the Republican party, founded in 1854, which was able to combine antislavery with other policies and produce a viable electoral alternative to the Democrats.

The Republicans' antislavery policy should not be confused with abolitionism or a belief in racial equality. The Republicans did not propose to end slavery in the United States, but rather to confine it to the states where it already existed. Moreover, most Republicans did not believe in equality of the races. While many accepted that slavery was morally wrong, few advocated racial integration. Indeed, where Republicans acquired sufficient power, as in Kansas, they banned all blacks, free or slave, from entering the state.

The Republicans' antislavery position thus married a moral principle with the self-interest of northern and western white labourers. And the more the Democrats thundered about slaveowners' rights and 'states' rights', the more the Republicans benefited from pro-Union sentiment and resentment of 'southern arrogance' in the north and west.

However, the Republicans were not a single issue party. They campaigned for the protective tariff and free homesteads in the west for white settlers. Moreover, in nominating Abraham Lincoln for the presidency in 1860, the party chose a moderate on the slavery issue and a westerner, rather than a northern radical, such as Senator Seward from New York. The aim was to appeal to the northern and western labourers, without frightening them with radical racial policies. It worked: without capturing a single electoral college vote in the south, or even campaigning there, Lincoln won the presidency with just 39 per cent of the popular vote. As Wilfred Binkley said, 'The successful drive to capture the labor vote was the key to Lincoln's election' (Binkley, 1947, p. 230).

As the Democrats had done earlier, the Republicans had built a successful political party by combining a moral and political vision with the self-interest of a large section of lower-class Americans. Indeed, this progressive aspect appears to be an essential ingredient of successful party politics in the United States. As has been pointed out, 'In its origins, the Republican party, like all the other dominant major parties [Jeffersonians, Jacksonians and New Deal Democrats], was if anything a party of the left, not of the right' (McSweeney and Zvesper, 1991, p. 24).

Two-party politics since the Civil War

Outwardly, the party system has not changed since the Civil War (1861–65). The Democrats and Republicans have remained the only parties with a realistic chance of capturing the Congress or the presidency, although there have been occasional serious third party candidates. As we saw in Chapter 9, third parties are inhibited by the electoral system. Equally important in perpetuating the Democratic/Republican rivalry, however, has been the flexibility of these two parties. Although both have been at times closely identified with particular principles, these have rarely been permitted to stand in the way of policy reorientations deemed necessary for electoral success. In other words, the Democratic and Republican parties have survived because they have been willing to change in response to a changing society. Two features of the parties have greatly facilitated this flexibility: ideological pragmatism and coalition politics.

Ideology and party

The two major American political parties occupy a very narrow ideological space. Both are (and always have been) utterly committed to the preservation of capitalism and constitutional democracy, as indeed have most parties which have appeared on the American scene. Thus, the United States differs strikingly from European democracies in its failure to produce a major political party committed to some form of socialism or of authoritarianism.

There have been a number of socialist parties in the United States, but they have enjoyed little electoral success. At the presidential level, the high point came in 1912 when Eugene Debs, the candidate of the Socialist Party of America (SPA), took 6 per cent of the popular vote. This is puzzling since, in many respects, the factors which promoted socialism in Europe – industrialisation, ruthless exploitation of the working class, demands for socio-economic reforms – were equally present in the United States. Many writers have sought to explain the peculiar weakness of American socialism and have pointed to a combination of causal factors. These range from the underdevelopment of working-class consciousness, owing to ethnic divisions, and the relative affluence of the American working class compared with its European counterparts, to state repression of radical movements, as typified by the Red Scare after the First World War and McCarthyism after the Second World War.

A contributing factor to socialism's electoral failure has been the readiness of Democrats and Republicans to steal the thunder of radicals by adopting at least some of their policies and even co-opting some of the radicals' leaders. For example, in the 1890s, distressed farmers organised the Populist Party. The Populists attacked the banks and corporations for their exploitation of farmers and labourers, especially by their adherence to 'hard money': this was a policy of restricting the amount of money in circulation in line with the available supply of gold. Farmers wanted a 'Greenback policy': the printing of sufficient paper money to reduce the need for credit and high interest rates. While the Republicans stood firm behind hard money, in 1896 the Democrats moved to incorporate the Populists by proposing the expansion of the money supply by allowing the free coinage of silver. The Democrats still lost the election, but the Populists disappeared altogether.

The progressive era

During the Progressive era (1900–17), the clamour for the reform of industrial-urban society became so great that *both* Republicans and Democrats moved to adopt Progressive policies. Each party succeeded in capturing the presidency with a Progressive nominee – Theodore Roosevelt (Republican, 1901–9) and Woodrow Wilson (Democrat, 1913–21).

Progressive Democrats and Republicans were responsible for enacting valuable reforms at the federal and state level. However, their leadership of their respective parties lasted only as long as the public mood demanded reform. In the 1920s, both parties reverted to conservatism, leaving their progressive wings isolated. The two main parties had thus ridden the Progressive wave while it was electorally expedient to do so, but had not become radicalised in the process. Yet during this critical period, they had become sufficiently reformist to persuade the electorate that a genuinely radical third party was unnecessary. This flexibility within an ideologically conservative framework has allowed both Democratic and Republican parties to marginalise radical and third party movements.

The New Deal Democratic party

The greatest success of such flexibility undoubtedly came with the New Deal of the 1930s. An unprecedented seven-year period of economic expansion and prosperity had come to an abrupt, catastrophic end with the Wall Street Crash of October 1929. President Hoover responded to the collapse of the stock market and the ensuing loss of business confidence with orthodox economic measures, including cutting government spending and raising taxes. This only made matters worse and helped to cause the Great Depression. By the time of the next presidential election, in November 1932, the economy and social fabric of the country were in deep crisis. Unemployment nationally had reached 25 per cent , but in many cities it was over 50 per cent or higher.

Worse still, there was little or no welfare provision for the unemployed and their families. Some states did offer support, but even the most generous states could not begin to cope with the scale of social distress. President Hoover refused to countenance any provision of welfare by the federal government. He had once referred to Britain's dole system as 'the English disease', believing that welfare would undermine the American tradition of economic self-reliance.

Furthermore, Hoover was opposed to almost all proposals to stimulate the economy which involved direct action by the federal government, such as government building projects that would create thousands of jobs. Hoover believed that there was no alternative to individualism and free-enterprise capitalism that would not, in the long term, seriously damage the American economic system. Such was his ideological conviction that he led the Republican party into the election promising four more years of the same policies.

The Democratic candidate in 1932, Governor Franklin D. Roosevelt of New York, was also generally orthodox in his economic faith in American capitalism. However, unlike Hoover, he was a pragmatist rather than an ideologue and was prepared to experiment with ways to restore the American economy to health. Moreover, if he was to become only the second Democrat president in the last forty years, he needed to offer the electorate something different from Hoover's rigidity.

Roosevelt therefore turned flexibility and pragmatism into the main planks of his electoral platform. In one speech, for example, he said: 'The country needs, and unless I mistake its temper, demands bold, persistent experimentation. It is sensible to take a method and try it. If it fails, admit it frankly and try another. But above all, try something'.

Roosevelt won the election by a large majority. Having won the election on a promise of flexibility and pragmatism, he proceeded to govern accordingly. Eschewing Hoover's restraint, he threw the energies of the federal government into attempts to solve the major problems of the Great Depression. Moreover, he cared little for whether policy solutions came from the left or the right of the political spectrum. For rather than search for ideological consistency, Roosevelt sought to provide practical help for those who needed it. Roosevelt's 'New Deal' was aimed primarily at helping the underdog – the unemployed, the impoverished farmer, the homeless – but it did so by strengthening banking, manufacturing and landowning interests as well.

So successful was this new philosophy of governmental activism that Roosevelt was re-elected by a landslide in 1936 and went on to win two further elections. Equally important, his party had discovered a new recipe for electoral success. As we noted above, the Democrats had always been the party of limited government and states' rights. With the electoral triumph of the New Deal, however, the Democrats became the party of federal government activism. From now on, the Democrats would argue that the federal government must take responsibility for the economic health of the country and the social well-being of its people. Government regulation of the economy, expansion of the welfare state and continuing social reform became the paramount policies of the 'new' Democratic party.

This transformation of the Democratic party left the Republicans electorally stranded for decades. Since its inception in 1854, the Republican party had identified itself with promotion of the national economy, prosperity and social improvement. However, by allowing the Democrats to seize the initiative during the Great Depression, the Republicans were left with the choice of either opposing the new Democratic creed or adopting a 'me-too' approach. Thus, for years to come, the Republicans found themselves offering the electorate either an unacceptable alternative to New Deal liberalism or no real alternative at all.

Coalition politics

Roosevelt's brand of pragmatic politics was greatly aided by the fact that American political parties have never been ideologically based. That is to say that although parties have advanced particular principles, it is not necessarily those principles which unite the different elements within parties. Thus, in the second half of the nineteenth century, for example, the Democrats' main electoral bases were southerners and the immigrants of the northern cities. These two groups had little in common other than their dislike of the Republican party. Southerners disliked the Republicans because of the Civil War: many immigrants, particularly Catholics, disliked the nativist and pietist tendencies of the Republicans. In that sense, party coalitions were based upon the principle that the enemy of my enemy is my friend. Different groups came together under a party banner in order to share the spoils of victory and to deny those spoils to the common enemy.

In a country as heterogeneous as the United States, attempts to enforce ideological conformity on the party usually end in electoral disaster or worse, as the southern Democrats discovered when they tried to impose a pro-slavery policy on the party before the Civil War. The secret of a successful governing party coalition, then, is to be able to reward one element of the party without causing too much offence to another.

This strategem generally works best when the party concentrates upon sharing out material benefits to coalition members and playing down the importance of ideological, moral or symbolic issues. Roosevelt was the practitioner *par excellence* of this strategem. Thus he won the support of farmers by introducing agricultural subsidies; of the unemployed by creating jobs; of industrial workers by raising wages and supporting trade unions; of the elderly and the infirm by instituting social security; and of black Americans by not excluding them from these benefits. This coalition was new in that it broke previous voting patterns. For example, blacks had until 1936 generally supported the Republican party since it had been responsible for the abolition of slavery.

At the same time, the new Democratic coalition had to keep the lid on issues which could divide the party. The southern wing of the party, for example, had little sympathy with labour unions, liberal social policies and, above all, the civil rights demands of blacks. It is something of a political miracle that for thirty years the Democrats were able to count among their leaders and supporters both those who believed in racial segregation and those who were working for a civil rights revolution. What kept them together for so long were the material benefits in terms of government largesse that such an unholy alliance could bring.

Party realignment

The New Deal enabled the Democrats to initiate what political scientists call 'a partisan realignment'. The notion of partisan realignment views American electoral history in cyclical terms. It argues that one party dominates elections for both the presidency and the Congress – and often state elections, too – for several decades. It dominates the political agenda and normally can rely upon a majority of the electorate to support it. Then, because new issues arise that cut across previous party loyalties, a *critical election* occurs which transfers dominance to the opposition party.

Until the contemporary electoral era cast doubt upon it, realignment theory seemed a useful way of understanding changes in the fortunes of the main political parties. Box 11.2 shows you how certain critical elections were followed by long periods of dominance by one party.

Party dealignment since 1968

In the period since 1968, the cyclical pattern described above appears to have come to an end. First the Republican party seemed to have a lock on the White House but a weak

Box 11.2

Critical elections and partisan realignment

1. Election of Andrew Jackson (D) as president, 1828
Dominance of Democratic party, 1828–60
Years in control of:

Presidency	Senate	House
24	28	24

2. Election of William McKinley (R) as president, 1896
Dominance of Republican party, 1896–1932
Years in control of:

Presidency	Senate	House
28	30	26

3. Election of Franklin D. Roosevelt (D) as president, 1932
Dominance of Democratic party, 1932–68
Years in control of:

Presidency	Senate	House
28	32	32

grip on the Senate and a continuing inability to capture the House of Representatives. When the Republicans finally did capture both houses of Congress at successive elections, in 1994 and 1996, their advance was countered by Bill Clinton's successive victories in the 1992 and 1996 presidential elections (see Box 9.8 in Chapter 9).

While it is always possible that the pattern of partisan realignment will reassert itself in the future, some political scientists have identified factors which may prevent this from happening. Byron Shafer, for example, has expounded the idea of 'electoral order' as an alternative to realignment theory. Shafer suggests that electoral periods involve a more complex and differentiated relationship between issues, parties and government institutions than realignment theory can cope with.

Thus, since the 1960s, there have been three grand issue areas in American politics: social welfare, moral and cultural values, and foreign policy. A majority of the American public are conservative (or traditionalist) on moral issues and foreign policy, but liberal on social welfare. When these majorities come to vote, they respond according to which institution is involved.

The presidency occupies itself more with foreign policy and cultural values, and hence the public majorities on these issues tend to prefer the conservative Republican party for this office. On the other hand, the Congress (and particularly the House) occupies itself predominantly with social welfare policies. Since the public majority is liberal on such issues, it tends to choose the more liberal Democratic party to run this institution (Shafer, 1991).

Shafer's notion of an electoral order worked well in the period from 1968 to 1992, but is challenged by the electoral outcomes of 1994 and 1996. The Republican capture of both the House and Senate in 1994 might have been dismissed as a 'rogue election' had the House, in particular, returned to the Democratic fold in 1996. However, the Republicans retained control of both the House and the Senate in 1996, while simultaneously a Democratic president retained the White House. In short, divided government remained but as a mirror image of its 1968–1992 pattern.

Moreover, President Clinton was re-elected on the basis of a strong economic performance and a promise to protect major welfare programmes, such as Medicare and Social Security – issues which should have given a particular boost to Democratic candidates for the House, according to Shafer's thesis.

An alternative explanation of the 1994 and 1996 elections in particular is that of the 'no majority realignment', proposed by Everett Ladd. He argues that the old realignment theory still works as far as its philosophical/political dimensions are concerned. In other words, a philosophical realignment has indeed taken place since 1968, just as it has done with each major realignment. In this case the philosophical realignment consists of a marked shift to the right, based upon a growing scepticism about the effectiveness of centralised government (Ladd, 1997, p. 5). On most key individual issues, a clear majority of Americans prefer conservative over liberal policy positions (see Box 11.3).

This philosophical realignment, however, has not been matched by a party realignment. When the 1994 elections seemed to threaten one, President Clinton and many other Democrats moved their own positions significantly to the right. Thus President Clinton proclaimed in his 1996 State of the Union address that 'the era of Big Government is over'.

Box 11.3

Public opinion on key issues, 1996

Issue or policy	Percentages for/against
Balanced budget amendment	83/14
Racial preferences in jobs and schools	14/83
Death penalty for murder	79/18
Congressional term limits	74/23
School prayer amendment	73/25
Reducing all government agencies	71/23
Two-year cut-off for welfare payments	71/24
Legalisation of gay marriage	28/67
Reduce defence spending	42/54
Federal flat tax	49/39
Reduce social spending	42/54
Ban abortion except to save mother's life	42/56

Source: Gallup poll, April 1996, in Ladd, 1997, p. 11

However, an alternative, though not incompatible explanation, exists, according to Ladd: 'the chief reason no party has majority status is that large segments of the electorate are abandoning firm partisan ties' (Ladd, 1997, p. 13). Traditional realignment presupposes the existence of parties which are strong enough to exert comprehensive control of the electoral environment. Yet, in recent decades, American parties have actually been in decline in this respect, losing their grip on voters and politicians alike.

Party decline

There is wide agreement that political parties in the United States are no longer the power they once were. In recent decades, social, technological and institutional changes have undermined the importance of parties in their two main spheres of operation: elections and government.

Prior to the 1960s, parties could fairly claim to represent the views and interests of the great mass of Americans. As a result, parties not only dominated the electoral process, but they provided a reasonably effective means of ensuring co-operation between different offices of government. There then followed a sharp decline in many aspects of party influence, leading many analysts to write the obituary for the American party system. Since the 1980s, however, parties have made a determined effort to regain some of their lost influence. While this has not been successful in all respects, parties are no longer in danger of extinction and they play a significant, though not dominant role in both the electoral process and government.

Electoral decline

Partisan identification

Whether partisan identification in the United States is in decline depends in part upon how it is measured. The most common method is to ask voters whether they consider themselves to be Democrats, Republicans or Independents. Some studies also distinguish between 'strong' and 'weak' Democrats and Republicans (McSweeney and Zvesper, 1991, p. 143).

The general picture obtained by such data suggests that after a marked dip in the 1970s, partisan identification has almost recovered to the high levels of the 1950s. Thus, as Box 11.4 shows, although Republicans have made gains at the expense of Democrats, the number of those defining themselves as Independents has only risen by a few percentage points.

These figures tell us only how people think of themselves, rather than how they actually vote. A more reliable guide to party loyalty may be obtained by comparing the figures on self identification with the actual votes cast by these identifiers in elections. By measuring the number of 'deserters' or split-ticket voters, we can see how much hold the party label has on voting behaviour. Studies indicate that split-ticket voting has doubled since the 1950s, encompassing about 25 per cent of the electorate (Reiter,

---

Box 11.4

Partisan identification, selected years 1952–96

Percentages

	Presidential election year				
	1952	1972	1976	1992	1996
Democrats	47	41	40	38	39
Republicans	28	23	23	35	36
Independents	23	35	37	27	26

Sources: Reiter, 1987, p. 38; *New York Times*, 5 November, 1992, p. B9; Pomper *et al.* 1997, p. 179

1987, p. 39). Box 11.5 compares how voters cast their ballots in the elections for president and for the House of Representatives. Although 1996 turned out to be a more consistently partisan year than usual, some 15 per cent of those who voted Democrat in the House election did not vote for Bill Clinton; and 22 per cent of those who voted Republican for the House did not vote for Bob Dole.

In general, then, we can say that about one-quarter of the American electorate do not identify themselves with one of the two main parties. Moreover, even among those who do identify, from one-fifth to one-quarter do not stay loyal to their party. As a result, there is a large body of voters to whom party is meaningless. This group may switch votes from one election to the next, making sustained periods of electoral dominance difficult to achieve.

Box 11.5

Split-ticket voting, 1988–96

House vote	Presidential vote							
	1988		1992			1996		
	D	R	D	R	Ind.	D	R	Ind.
Democrat	72	27	74	11	15	84	8	7
Republican	17	82	10	72	18	14	76	8

Nominating candidates

As noted in Chapter 9, the proliferation of primary elections has all but ended party influence in the selection of candidates for office. Anyone calling himself a Democrat (or a Republican) is entitled to enter a party primary, provided he has fulfilled the technical requirements. And given that candidates these days are largely independent of the party in terms of finance and organisation, they are free to pursue their own electoral strategy regardless of party wishes.

It is even possible for successful primary candidates to be so at odds with the party that the party feels obliged to disown them. Such was the case with David Duke, a former Grand Wizard of the Ku Klux Klan, who won the Republican Senate primary in Louisiana in 1990. President Bush and the National Republican Party urged voters not to support Duke in the primary and publicly denied that Duke was a 'real' Republican.

Financing elections

There were important reforms in the laws governing campaign finance in the 1970s (see Chapter 12). These laws introduced limits on the amounts of money that parties, groups and individuals could contribute to a candidate's election campaign. In the case of presidential elections, public funding of campaigns was also introduced.

One result of these reforms was to eliminate parties as a significant source of direct campaign donations. The national parties today may give only $27,500 to Senate candidates, with state parties being allowed to donate a further $10,000. For the House the figures are $20,000 and $10,000, respectively.

Thus, in the 1980 congressional elections, the percentage of campaign donations by the parties to their candidates was just 4 per cent for the House and 2 per cent for the Senate (Malbin, 1984, p. 39). In the presidential election that year, Reagan and Carter received approximately $29 million of government money, compared with $4 million from the national parties (*ibid.*, 1984, p. 20). Candidates clearly do not rely upon the parties for donations and thus owe them little loyalty or deference.

However, in the wake of further amendments to the campaign finance laws in 1979, parties were given a new lease of life by being permitted to raise and spend so-called soft money. This allowed the parties to raise and spend funds independent of particular candidates: for example, on voter registration and turn-out drives or campaign buttons and bumper stickers. However, in 1992 and 1996 the parties exploited the possibilities of using soft money for generic advertisements at both the federal and state level. In fact, for many, soft money has become seen as a legal method of evading the spirit, if not the letter, of the campaign finance laws of the 1970s. This impression was compounded by the fact that the 'fat cat' contributors to the parties were back on the scene in force and because there were allegations that the Democratic National Committee, in particular, had sought and received soft money contributions from non-Americans (Corrado, 'Financing the 1996 Elections', in Pomper *et al.*, 1997, pp. 152–4). This in turn led to a public demand after the 1996 election for a clean-up of the campaign finance legislation that would eliminate the loopholes being exploited by soft money. However, despite the pledge of President Clinton and others of both

---

Box 11.6

Soft money expenditures, 1980–96

($ million)

	Republican	Democrat
1980	15.1	4.0
1984	15.6	6.0
1988	22.0	23.0
1992	81.4	45.6
1996	149.0	117.3

Sources: Alexander and Bauer, 1991, p. 37; Corrado, 1997, pp. 151–2

---

parties to support such legislation, the principal attempt, the McCain–Feingold bill, was killed by Republicans in the Senate.

Whatever the legalities, there is no denying the phenomenal growth in soft money donations and expenditures in the 1990s (see Box 11.6), and as long as they remain permissible, they ensure a vital new supporting role for the parties in elections.

Campaign services and organisation

As well as a partially revitalised role in funding elections, the parties have also become more energetic in providing their candidates with various services. Thus, 'along with increased funding, the national parties have provided help for their candidates in campaign planning, polling, and the production of campaign advertisements, including experiments in generic national ads for congressional candidates' (Caesar, 1990, p. 121).

Nevertheless, campaigns are resolutely candidate centred and candidate controlled. Candidates have their own strategists, media consultants, pollsters and managers. Moreover, not only has the rise in non-party sources of finance stimulated this independence, but the development of the electronic media has eliminated much of the parties' previous role in communicating with the voters.

Thus the revitalisation of the parties in the electoral process since the 1980s should not be exaggerated. Links between candidates and parties are stronger than they were in the 1970s, but in the key elements of nominations, finance, organisation and communication, parties play, at best, a secondary role.

Party government in decline

We noted above that one reason why parties developed in the United States was the need to co-ordinate the activities of different office-holders. There are two particularly important facets to this function today: co-ordination between different members of Congress and co-ordination between Congress and the president. An examination of both these relationships yields yet further evidence of party decline.

Party unity in Congress

As we shall see in detail in Part V, members of Congress are much more independent of party control than, say, their British counterparts. In the first place, since senators and representatives do not owe their election to the party whose label they wear, they do not feel bound to follow party policy. This is particularly true where the party line is unpopular with the member's constituents.

Secondly, and largely as a result of members' electoral independence, party discipline in Congress is weak. There *are* designated party leaders in Congress, including Whips; Congress is also organised on party lines and party members do meet in caucus to try to develop strategies and policies that will unite the party. Nevertheless, there is little the party can do to force unwilling members to conform to party wishes. Parties do not possess the power of ultimate sanction – deselection of disloyal members. Moreover, members of Congress value their own independence and are therefore content to allow a similar autonomy to their colleagues. Leaders in Congress can offer inducements to members to support the party line, such as help in getting the best committee assignments, but they have less to mete out as punishment. As Senator Tom Daschle (D–South Dakota), the co-chair of the Senate Democratic Policy Committee, put it, a Senate leader trying to influence a colleague's vote has 'a bushel full of carrots and a few twigs' (CQ *Almanac*, 1992, p. 22-B).

Thirdly, as noted above, American political parties are unusually broad coalitions of diverse interests. As a result, one wing of a party may be fiercely opposed on certain policies to another wing. This has produced a situation over the past fifty years, whereby the southern wing of the Democratic party has formed an informal coalition with the Republicans to defeat certain legislation proposed by their northern colleagues. This so-called Conservative Coalition was, for example, responsible for defeating all meaningful attempts at civil rights reform in the 1950s and was invaluable to President Reagan in his efforts to foster a 'conservative revolution' in the early 1980s (Keefe and Ogul, 1993, p. 292).

The number of occasions on which the Conservative Coalition has appeared has declined somewhat since the 1970s, leading to speculation that it may be in terminal decline. The principal reason for this is the partisan realignment of the south. Where once the south overwhelmingly returned Democrats to Washington, it now votes Republican more often than not. This means that, today, there are simply fewer conservative Democrats to line up with the congressional Republicans.

Nevertheless, as Box 11.7 indicates, while the frequency of Conservative Coalition votes has declined, its success rate in those votes is increasing. Moreover, the presence of the moderate Southern Democrat, Bill Clinton, in the White House has not inhibited the Conservative Coalition as much as was initially expected. Thus, when Clinton's very presidency was on the line in August 1993 over his budget proposals, the coalition almost defeated him. Despite a Democratic majority of eighty-two in the

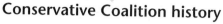

Conservative Coalition history

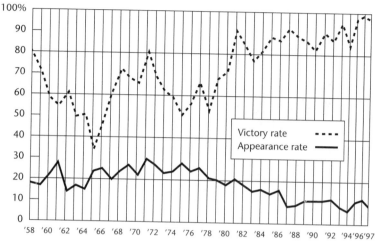

Definition

A voting bloc in the House and Senate consisting of a majority of Republicans and a majority of Southern Democrats, combined against a majority of Northern Democrats.

1997 Data

Senate	23 victories
	2 defeats
	25 appearances in 298 votes
House	55 victories
	0 defeats
	55 appearances in 633 votes

Total Congress appearance rate **8.6%**
Total Congress victory rate **97.5%**

Source: *Congressional Quarterly*, 3 January 1998, p. 21

House, the president's proposals were approved by a margin of just two votes, and a Senate Democratic majority of eight resulted in a tie in the Senate, with the budget being passed only on the casting vote of the speaker, Vice-President Al Gore. In short, conservative members of the Democratic party were not only prepared to defeat Clinton's budget, but also willing to see their votes cripple, even destroy, his presidency.

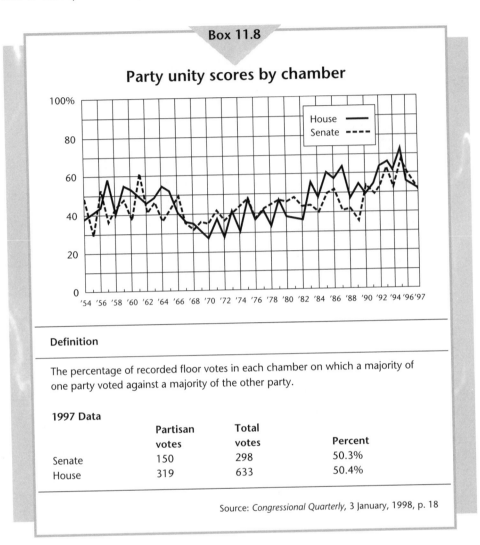

Box 11.8

Party unity scores by chamber

Definition

The percentage of recorded floor votes in each chamber on which a majority of one party voted against a majority of the other party.

1997 Data

	Partisan votes	Total votes	Percent
Senate	150	298	50.3%
House	319	633	50.4%

Source: *Congressional Quarterly*, 3 January, 1998, p. 18

Even aside from the Conservative Coalition, party unity is generally low in the Congress, compared with, say, parliamentary parties in Britain. Box 11.8 shows that the frequency of party votes, defined at the minimum level of those where a bare majority of one party votes in opposition to a bare majority of the other, has been rising in recent years. However, even in the best years, they do not constitute two-thirds of all votes; and in 1997 just 50.4 per cent of House votes and 50.3 per cent of Senate votes were party votes.

Party unity: Congress and president

A second measure of party unity in government can be gained by examining the frequency with which members of Congress vote in support of a president of their own party. Since the 1950s, presidents have on average been able to count on the support of their fellow party members in 72 per cent of House votes and 76 per cent of Senate votes (McSweeney and Zvesper, 1991, p. 168; *Congressional Quarterly*, various years). Thus in the 1997 session of Congress, the average House Democrat backed President Clinton in 71 per cent of the votes on which he took a clear position. This was about the same as in the previous year. By contrast, the average House Republican supported the President in 30 per cent of votes, down from 38 per cent the previous year (*Congressional Quarterly*, 3 January, 1997, p. 17).

These figures suggest that party policy and party discipline are important but not necessarily controlling factors in congressional behaviour. In fact, negotiation and compromise in pursuit of consensus across party lines remains a notable feature of Congress. This is true despite attempts by both parties in the wake of the Republican capture of the House and Senate in 1994, to develop clearer party positions and coherence (see Chapter 16). The markedly increased partisanship of 1994–96 may have pleased more ideologically pure politicians, but it seemed to turn the voters off. The message of the 1996 elections seemed to be that the public expected a Democrat president and a Republican Congress to overcome partisan differences and work together for the good of the country. This, of course, is precisely what the constitutional scheme of separation of powers and checks and balances was intended to promote. As Representative David Skaggs (D–Colorado) commented in 1997, 'We all have to go back to school on a regular basis to remember that this is not a parliamentary system, and the Constitution essentially drives a consensus approach to government in the country (*Congressional Quarterly*, 3 January, 1998, p. 18).

In the next chapter, we will see that politicians in the United States are not simply faced with a choice of pleasing public or party. Moreover, voters themselves do not rely solely or even mainly on parties to represent their interests in government. Political parties, therefore, have a major rival for their claims on voters and politicians alike – interest groups.

Summary

Although the framers of the Constitution thought political parties to be harmful to the political process, the United States quickly developed a two-party system. This was because parties performed useful tasks, such as representing interests, organising elections and co-ordinating government within and between Congress and the presidency. However, because of the great size and diversity of the nation, parties have been based as much on coalitions of interest as they have been on ideology. This has been a factor in weakening party discipline, as has the more recent advent of media coverage of elections and interest-group funding of elections. Elections in America are candidate-centred, rather than party-centred, something which applies as much to voters as it does to candidates themselves. Neither candidates nor voters have very strong ties to party.

Topics for discussion

1. To what extent and why are political parties in decline?

2. What are the advantages and disadvantages of weak party discipline in the federal government?
3. Why has there been party dealignment, but not realignment, since 1968?
4. What are the main differences today between the Democratic party and the Republican party?

 Further reading

One of the most comprehensive introductions to this subject is D. McSweeney and J. Zvesper, *American Political Parties* (London: Routledge, 1991). Good sources on the issue of party decline are M. Wattenburg, *The Decline of American Political Parties, 1952–88* (Cambridge, Mass: Harvard University Press, 1990); and J. Ceaser, 'Political parties – declining, stabilizing, or resurging?', in A. King (ed.), *The New American Political System* (2nd version, Washington, DC: American Enterprise Institute, 1990). On realignment and dealignment, see B. Shafer (ed.), *The End of Realignment? Interpreting American electoral eras* (Madison: University of Wisconsin Press, 1991); and E. Ladd, '1996 elections: The "no majority" realignment continues', *Political Science Quarterly* (Spring 1997, pp. 1–28).

 References

Binkley, W., 1947, *American Political Parties: Their natural history* (New York: Knopf)

Caesar, J., 1990, 'Political parties – declining, stabilizing, or resurging?', in *The New American Political System*, ed. A. King (2nd version, Washington DC: American Enterprise Institute)

Hofstadter, R., 1969, *The Idea of a Party System* (Berkeley: University of California Press)

Keefe, W. and Ogul, M., 1993, *The American Legislative Process* (8th edn, Hemel Hempstead: Prentice Hall)

Ladd, E., 1997, '1996 elections: the "no majority" realignment continues', *Political Science Quarterly* (spring, pp. 1–28)

Malbin, M., ed., 1984, *Money and Politics in the United States: financing elections in the 1980s*, (Chatham, NJ: Chatham House Publishers)

McSweeney, D. and Zvesper, J., 1991, *American Political Parties* (London: Routledge)

Pomper, G. *et al.*, 1997, *The Elections of 1996: Reports and interpretations* (Chatham, NJ: Chatham House)

Reiter, H., 1987, *Parties and Elections in Corporate America* (New York: St Martin's Press)

Shafer, B., ed., 1991, *The End of Realignment? Interpreting American electoral eras* (Madison: University of Wisconsin Press)

12

Interest groups and PACs

Whereas parties have always been weak in American politics, interest groups (or pressure groups) have always been strong. The diversity of American society has encouraged Americans to make full use of their freedom to petition the government, a right guaranteed by the First Amendment to the Constitution. With the huge growth in governmental activity since the New Deal of the 1930s, the importance of representing one's group interests in politics has become paramount. Nevertheless, interest-group activity is the subject of considerable controversy. On the one hand, it is argued that such groups perform a legitimate and valuable representative function. On the other, however, it is alleged that interest groups subvert democracy by making government the pawn of the rich and well organised.

Interest groups

Definitions and origins

An interest or pressure group is an association of individuals or organisations who band together to defend or advance the particular interests they have in common. Those may range from shared business interests and professional status, through common ethnic origins and religion, to shared public policy and ideological convictions. There are literally thousands of interest groups in the United States. Box 12.1 shows you a useful way of categorising them, although some groups clearly overlap the categories.

The United States has always been fertile soil for interest group formation. In 1835, the great French observer of American politics, Alexis de Tocqueville, wrote: 'Americans of all ages, all conditions, and all dispositions constantly form associations. Wherever at the head of some new undertaking you see the government

Box 12.1

Typology of interest groups

Business/Trade	Agriculture	Unions	Professional	Single issue	Ideological	Group rights	Public interest
American Business Conference	American Farm Bureau Federation	American Federation of Labor–Congress of Industrial Organisations (AFL–CIO)	American Medical Association	National Abortion and Reproductive Rights Action League	American Conservative Union	National Association For The Advancement of Colored People (NAACP)	Common Cause
National Association of Manufacturers	National Farmers Union	United Auto Workers	National Education Association	Mothers Against Drunk Driving	People For The American Way	National Organization For Women	Friends Of The Earth
National Automobile Dealers Association	Associated Milk Producers, Inc.	International Association of Machinists and Aerospace Workers	Association of American Universities	National Rifle Association	Christian Voice	American Association of Retired Persons	Children's Defense Fund
					American Civil Liberties Union		

in France, or a man of rank in England, in the United States you will be sure to find an association' (Tocqueville, 1835; 1956, p. 198).

The prevalence of interest groups in American political life is due to four broad factors. First, the sheer diversity of American society has spawned numerous ethnic, social, economic and issue groups. Secondly, as we have already seen, weak parties have failed to fulfil the representative needs of the American people. Thirdly, the fragmented and decentralised structure of American government means that there are numerous points of access to the policy-making process that groups can readily exploit. Fourthly, and particularly true since the 1930s, the rapid expansion of governmental activity means that more and more groups have found their interests affected by public policy.

More recently, the 1960s and 1970s witnessed an 'advocacy explosion' (Berry, 1989, p. 42). Several particular factors contributed to this. Among the most important were the new burst of government programmes associated with President Lyndon B. Johnson's Great Society, the rise of many new divisive political issues (such as race and gender, the Vietnam War and lifestyle issues), and the simple fact that, as some interest groups became prominent, other groups formed in imitation (Cigler and Loomis, 1986).

Furthermore, a little-known variant of the interest group – the political action committee (PAC) – proliferated astonishingly in the 1970s and 1980s, stimulated by new campaign finance laws (see below).

Not surprisingly, the exponential growth of interest groups since the 1960s appeared to eclipse the representative functions of political parties. Moreover, because interest groups conduct much of their activity away from the public view, in the corridors of Congress or the federal bureaucracy, there developed a heightened anxiety over whether representation by interest group was good for American democracy.

Interest group functions

There are, it is said, five principal functions of interest groups: representation, citizen participation, public education, agenda building and programme monitoring (Berry, 1989, pp. 4–5). The last four, however, are really aspects of the central task of self-interest representation.

Interest groups, like parties, are representative institutions, but their aims and methods are not the same. Most importantly, interest groups do not put forward candidates for elected office. Although some interest groups do try to influence electoral outcomes, most concentrate on representing their members' interests in the policy-making process. This means lobbying not only elected politicians but also those who wield power in the bureaucracy and the judiciary.

Interest group methods

Public campaigning

Interest groups operate in a variety of ways. One means of influencing the policy-making process is to stir up public opinion, in the hope that this will put legislators under pressure. One of the oldest forms of interest-group activity in this respect is the public march. This can be very successful, as when a host of civil rights groups got together to organise the 1963 'March on Washington'. The march, coming after almost a decade of public campaigning to end racial segregation, was designed to put pressure on President Kennedy and Congress to take action on the pending civil rights bill. Whatever the precise role of the March in producing the Civil Rights Act of 1964, there can be little doubt that it was a moving spectacle that won converts to the cause.

Public demonstrations can, however, prove counter-productive. Thus, anti-abortion groups organise an annual protest outside the Supreme Court to commemorate the day of the historic 1973 *Roe* decision, which announced a new constitutional right to abortion. When that right seemed threatened in the 1980s, pro-abortion groups began holding counter-demonstrations on the same day.

Another related form of public campaigning is direct action. Here, too, anti-abortion groups have been prominent. For example, Operation Rescue specialises in trying to block access to clinics where abortions are performed. Its members hope that their activities – and their frequent arrest by the police – will stimulate the conscience of judges, legislators and the public and result in a ban on abortions.

Other forms of public campaigning include newspaper and television advertising. In the early 1990s, for example, the National Rifle Association (NRA) produced television advertisements featuring the veteran Hollywood star Charlton Heston as part of its ultimately unsuccessful campaign against the Brady Bill. The legislation aimed only to improve checks on would-be gun purchasers, but the NRA opposes virtually all gun legislation.

Less spectacular, but potentially effective nevertheless, is direct mailing of group members and likely sympathisers. Taking advantage of computerised mailing systems, interest groups can quickly identify and mobilise members on behalf of a particular campaign. During the intense fight over ratification of the Panama Canal Treaties in 1978, conservative groups mailed an estimated 7–9 million letters to members of the public (Berry, 1989, p. 60).

However, although the above strategems for mobilising members and the general public are often employed, the oldest and still most effective activity of interest groups is lobbying.

Lobbying and lobbyists

The most desirable method of influencing policy-makers is through direct contact with them. For that reason, the more affluent and powerful interest groups maintain a permanent office in Washington and employ professional lobbyists to act on their behalf.

These lobbyists may be committed activists in the groups they represent, but these days are increasingly likely to be neutral 'guns for hire' – experts in the legislative process, who sell their skills to those who can afford them. Thus, in 1993, the top lobbying firm of Patton, Boggs and Blow was working to obtain government money to save jobs at Chrysler, supporting a bill to make it easier for the homeless to vote, and fighting a constitutional amendment that would ban flag-burning. In the past, it had also represented Baby Doc Duvalier, the Haitian dictator, and the scandal-ridden Bank of Credit and Commerce International. The firm's most prominent lobbyist, Tommy Boggs, once said: 'We basically pick our customers by taking the first one who comes in the door' (*The Economist*, 27 February 1993, p. 56). The typical working day of a professional lobbyist is described in Box 12.2.

Lobbyists have often acquired their detailed knowledge of the policy-making process from having worked in the federal government – as legislators or legislative assistants, bureaucrats or presidential advisers. Such experience can be invaluable not merely for the expertise acquired but also for the personal contacts and relationships established over the years. Thus, when Senators Russell Long and Paul Laxalt retired in 1986, their services were sought by many Washington law firms which represent clients before government agencies. Both eventually joined Finley, Kumble at salaries of $800,000 a year (Berry, 1989, p. 86).

This so-called revolving door phenomenon has been criticised as unethical, and measures have been taken to try to limit it. In 1978, Congress passed the Ethics in Government Act which forbade certain former executive branch officials from lobbying their previous government agencies within a year of leaving them. In 1989, Congress applied a similar restriction on former legislators and legislative staff. Nevertheless, continuing scandals did little to reassure the public that these measures were sufficient. When President Clinton took office in 1993, therefore, his first executive order extended the one-year limit to five on all top executive branch officials, and banned them from lobbying on behalf of foreign governments and parties for ever.

The revolving door problem is just one of several aspects of lobbying that have given cause for concern in recent years. For example, the first attempt to monitor the activity of lobbyists came with the Regulation of Lobbying Act of 1946. Under this, all

---

Box 12.2

A day in the life of a lobbyist

This is a how the Washington lobbyist for a professional association describes his typical day:

> I am one of those people who gets to work no later than 7.45. The first hour is spent reading the papers – the *Washington Post, Wall Street Journal*, and *New York Times*, trade association publications, and the *Congressional Record* from the prior day. Each of these plays into my need to plan the activities for the current day. The next activity is meeting with the staff for a brief period to check the work plans for any changes. There is then one or more hearings on the Hill in the morning. After lunch, I usually meet with committee staff or use that time to lobby specific members of Congress. I'm usually back by 4.00 to meet with the staff to check on what's happened while I was gone and if we are on top of the work planned for the day. About 5.30 I usually go to some reception or fund-raiser to represent our group. These settings give me an opportunity to swap stories and position with members and other lobbyists who are concerned with the same issues as we are. I usually get home for dinner about 8.00.

Source: Extract from Berry, 1989, pp. 77–8

people hired principally for the task of lobbying Congress were required to register with the House or Senate. Its terms, however, are easily evaded. According to Senator Carl Levin, who introduced more demanding (but unsuccessful) legislation in 1992, around 70 per cent of Washington lobbyists are not registered under the 1946 Act (*CQ Almanac*, 1992, p. 79).

If all that lobbyists did was to act as the eyes and ears of their organisations and try to convert policy-makers to their members' point of view, their activities would be largely uncontroversial. However, what transforms the perspective on interest groups is money – the money they give to legislators in the form of electoral campaign donations. Immediately, then, the suspicion arises that lobbying Congress involves a form of bribery: interest groups enable legislators to get re-elected by financing their campaigns, and legislators in return listen to the pleadings of interest groups and advance their interests through the nation's policy. This suspicion is at the heart of the controversy over interest groups in American politics.

Campaign finance

Interest groups, and particularly business corporations, have always tried to buy favours from legislators by giving them money: hence Will Roger's satirical comment that 'Our Congress is the best that money can buy!' Bribery and corruption were especially rife in the late nineteenth century and the first attempt at reform came with the passage of the Tillman Act in 1907. This banned business corporations from making direct contributions to federal election campaigns.

Nevertheless, the flow of illegal funds continued and it was only when the Watergate scandal broke in 1973, with its revelations of slush funds, huge personal donations and laundered money, that more determined action was taken (Sabato, 1985, p. 4). In 1974, Congress amended the Federal Election Campaign Act (FECA) of 1971 in ways that were to transform, but not necessarily improve, the funding of federal elections.

In an attempt to lower the cost of elections and to reduce the power of rich individuals and organisations, Congress enacted three major reforms. First, it provided public funds for presidential elections. Secondly, it set strict ceilings on the amount of money that any person or group could give to a candidate for the presidency or Congress. Thirdly, it limited the overall amount of money that could be spent on congressional elections.

The limits on spending were quickly challenged in the courts as an unconstitutional restriction on free speech. In *Buckley v. Valeo* (1976), the Supreme Court upheld the restrictions on personal and group donations to candidates, but struck down those which limited expenditures independent of particular candidates and the amount that candidates could spend out of their own pockets, except for presidential candidates who accepted public funds.

Presidential elections

The campaign finance reform legislation of the 1970s largely ended the controversy over rich-individual and interest-group donations to presidential candidates. In the pre-nomination phase, candidates may seek donations from both, though these are strictly limited to a maximum of $1,000 from an individual and $5,000 from a group.

However, the legislation firmly put the emphasis on the public funding of presidential elections. Thus, in the pre-nomination period, the government gives candidates matching funds for each individual donation of $250 or less. Then, full public funding is available for both the nominating conventions and the general election. Although no presidential candidate is obliged to accept public funds and, therefore, the overall limits on campaign expenditure, all major candidates have done so since 1976, with the sole exception of Ross Perot in 1992 and 1996.

Congressional elections

Unlike for presidential elections, the reforms of the 1970s failed to provide public funding for congressional elections. Several reasons lie behind this and subsequent refusals to introduce public funding. Republicans, in particular, tend to believe that using so much taxpayers money is simply wrong.

Nevertheless, the subject keeps forcing itself back onto the agenda for one simple reason: the widespread public belief that interest-group donations to congressional candidates mean that Congress represents interest groups rather than the public. This situation was, if anything, exacerbated by the 1970s reforms. As with presidential elections, individual and group donations to candidates were subjected to limits. Individuals could donate up to $1,000 for each phase of an election, with a maximum to all candidates of $25,000 per year. Groups could give up to $5,000 to one candidate for each phase of an election, with no overall maximum.

With large donations now eliminated, the key to raising campaign funds became soliciting money from as many groups and individuals as possible. It was in this context that political action committees (PACs) came into their own.

Political action committees

Political action committees are a form of interest group which exist for the sole purpose of raising campaign funds. Although they have been in existence since the 1940s, they were rare before the passage of the 1974 FECA amendments. Thus, in 1972, there were just 113 PACs registered with the government. The 1974 amendments, however, stimulated a rapid growth in their number, with the total settling down in the 1990s at around 4,000 (see Box 12.3). Although each PAC was limited in how much it could give to a candidate, there was no limit on how many PACs could make a donation. Logically enough, then, the number of groups proliferated.

Most of these new PACs have been created by business corporations: in 1995 there were 1,670 corporate PACs, compared with 334 labour union PACs and 804 PACs sponsored by trade and professional associations (Hrebener, 1997, p. 198). Moreover, although labour unions are prominent in the list of the biggest donors, business collectively easily outspends labour and other groups in campaign donations. In the 1993/94 election cycle, business outspent labour by some $70 million to $42 million. In the 1995/96 cycle, the gap widened dramatically as business gave $147 million compared with labour's $49 million (Centre for Responsive Politics Web site, http://www.crp.org/, 1998).

Box 12.3

Growth of political action committees, selected years 1972–95

Year	Number
1972	113
1974	608
1980	2,551
1985	3,992
1990	4,172
1995	3,982

Sources: Sabato, 1985, p. 10; Hrebener, 1997, p. 198

Box 12.4

Congressional campaign finance, 1994 and 1996

The senate	1994	1996
Average winner spent	$4, 569, 940	$4, 692, 110
Average loser spent	$3, 426, 509	$2, 773, 756
Most expensive campaign	$29, 969, 695 (Michael Huffington, R–CA, *lost*)	$14, 587, 143 (Jesse Helms, R–NC, *won*)
Average winner's receipts from PACs	$1, 014, 677	$1, 090, 173

The house of representatives	1994	1996
Average winner spent	$516, 126	$673, 739
Average loser spent	$238, 715	$265, 675
Most expensive campaign	$2, 621, 429 (Richard Gephardt, D–MO, *won*)	$5, 577, 715 (Newt Gingrich, R–GA, *won*)
Average winners receipts from PACs	$225, 895	$287, 692

Source: Centre for Responsive Politics Web site, 1998)

A further spur to PAC growth was the rapidly rising cost of running an election campaign for Congress. The increasing use of television was a major factor in this, and the net result was that money raised and spent on congressional elections more than doubled between 1978 and 1986 (CQ *Weekly Report*, 20 March 1993, p. 691). The explosion in the 1990s of 'soft money' donations which evade the campaign finance laws (see Chapter 11) has reduced the percentage of campaign finance raised from PACs, particularly in presidential and Senate elections, yet it is estimated that candidates for the House of Representatives still rely on PACs for 40 per cent of their campaign funds (Centre for Responsive Politics Web site, 1998). Even in the Senate, PAC contributions constitute about 25 per cent of the average winning candidate's campaign expenditure – which is almost exactly the amount that distinguishes the average winning campaign from the average losing campaign (see Box 12.4). In that sense, PAC contributions may be the difference between winning and losing the election. In 1996, then, PACs contributed a vital total of $243 million to campaign funds.

Influence of interest groups and PACs

Closer examination of campaign contributions to congressional candidates sheds considerable light on the motivations behind them.

The first point to note is that not all interest groups have as their primary aim the election of a candidate who shares their political viewpoint. True, ideological groups give overwhelmingly to candidates who champion their preferred policies; and labour unions give funds almost exclusively to Democrats. Thus, in 1996, the largest single union donor, the American Federation of State, County and Municipal Employees, gave a total of just over $4 million to candidates and parties, with 99 per cent going to Democrats. Likewise, the United Auto Workers gave 99 per cent of its $3 million to Democrats, while the Communications Workers of America gave all of its $2,800,000 to Democrats (Centre for Responsive Politics Web site, 1998).

Other groups, however, take a more pragmatic approach. This is especially true of business groups who, until the Republican takeover of Congress in 1994, tended to split their donations equally between the two major parties. While business groups are much more likely to share the economic beliefs of Republicans than of Democrat, they fully appreciated that the Democrats' iron grip on the House and, to a significant extent, on the Senate, meant that it was sensible for them to donate funds to the likely winners. They hoped that this would ensure their access to those who controlled the policy-making process in Congress.

However, once the Republicans wrested control of Congress from the Democrats, the ideological sympathies of business groups were allowed greater play. In a sudden departure from practice, in 1996 business groups gave 70 per cent of their donations to Republicans (see Box 12.5).

As the Centre for Responsive Politics (CPR) commented in its report on this switch, 'If you forget everything else in this report, remember this: money follows power' ('The great PAC flip-flop of 1996, CPR Web site 1998). Thus, the report confirmed that one thing that did not change with the 1996 elections was the tendency of groups to give their funds overwhelmingly to incumbents.

Box 12.5

Business PAC campaign donations to parties, 1988–96

Percentages

	Republicans	Democrats
1988	49.7	50.3
1990	49.4	50.6
1992	46.6	53.4
1994	48.9	51.1
1996	70.0	30.0

Source: Centre for Responsive Politics Web site, 1998

A second notable feature of PAC donations is that they are not necessarily intended to affect the outcome of the elections concerned. In the 1986 House elections, for example, some $23 million in donations went either to candidates who had no major party opponent at all or to those who had won their previous four elections by majorities of at least three-to-one (Stern, 1988, p. 32). Quite simply, many recipients of PAC largesse do not need the money in order to win.

What most PACs – especially corporate PACs – want, therefore, is less to influence elections than to cultivate and influence those who make policy between elections. This is reinforced by the fact that, on average, those with most influence in policy making – committee chairpersons – get 20 per cent more in PAC donations than ordinary House members (Stern, 1988, pp. 5–6). Further support for this view comes from the fact that PACs target their money on incumbents who sit on the committees that deal with legislation most likely to affect their group (see Box 12.6).

Box 12.6

The health care lobby

Health care reform became an increasingly important issue in the United States in the 1990s. As a result, interest groups with a direct interest in health care increased the level of their donations to congressional candidates significantly. For example, their donations for the 1992 election cycle amounted to $19.1 million, an increase of 29 per cent over the 1990 cycle. They targeted members of the four major committees, and their health subcommittees, dealing with medical issues: in the House, the Ways and Means Committee and the Energy and Commerce Committee; in the Senate, the Finance Committee and the Labor and Human Resources Committee.

Top givers, 1989–92

$000

| PAC | House | | Senate | |
	Ways and Means	Energy and Commerce	Finance	Labor and Human Resources
AMPAC (American Medical Association PAC)	346.6	397.8	62.5	54.0
ADPAC (American Dental Association PAC	173.6	242.4	59.0	52.0
AAOPAC (American Academy of Ophthalmology PAC)	136.4	192.7	53.5	n.a.
AHAPAC (American Hospital Association PAC)	106.7	114.2	71.1	61.3
IIAAPAC (Independent Insurance Agents of America PAC)	76.6	99.7	58.0	44.2

Top recipients, 1992 election cycle

House	$000	Senate	$000
Dan Rostenkowski (Chair, Ways and Means)	202.4	Bob Packwood (ranking Republican, Finance)	247.9
Richard Gephardt (Majority Leader)	192.5	Tom Daschle (Finance)	226.4
Pete Stark (Chair, Ways and Means Health Subcommittee)	160.3	Charles Grassley (Finance)	224.1
Henry Waxman (Chair, Energy and Commerce Health Subcommittee	158.0	Daniel Coats (Labor and Human Resources)	223.6
John Dingell (Chair, Energy and Commerce)	111.8	Christopher Dodd (Labor and Human Resources)	218.8

Source: Data from CQ Weekly Report, 31 July 1993, pp. 2048–54

Access or votes?

Lobbyists for interest groups readily concede that they expect something in return for their money, but categorically deny that they are engaged in simple vote-buying. Instead, they hope to obtain access to those who write the nation's legislation. In this way, they are at least assured that policy-makers listen to their side of a policy debate before any action is taken. Lobbyists are aware that legislators are kept extremely busy by the demands of their job and that they have only a limited amount of time to devote to any one issue. If lobbyists get the opportunity to present a legislator with information and a point of view on the issue, there is a good chance that this will influence his thinking. As one lobbyist put it: 'I know what it means to put in a call to a legislator and get a call back and not to get a call back. And if that $500 is going to increase my chances of getting a call back, that is a heck of a lot, because frequently all it takes is the opportunity to talk to a legislator 10 or 15 minutes to make your case. He may not have ten or fifteen minutes to hear the other side' (Sabato, 1985, p. 127).

If a lobbyist can build up a long-term working relationship with a legislator, by providing expert and accurate information, he can acquire the status of a valued and trusted adviser. It may even reach the point where when a relevant issue arises, it is the legislator who contacts the lobbyist to request information (Berry, 1989, p.84).

The essence of this view of pressure-group activity is that influence is only exerted where the legislator receives an informed briefing by a lobbyist and is convinced by it. Donations to campaign funds facilitate the likelihood of that briefing taking place, but they do not buy, or even attempt to buy, legislators' votes.

Although this argument may raise eyebrows given the large sums of money involved, there is evidence to support it. In the first place, even a generous PAC is only one factor in determining a legislator's vote. Party loyalty or personal ideology may be pulling in a contrary direction. Above all, however, a member of Congress will pay the closest attention to what her constituents think on a subject. She is unlikely to risk alienating her voters in order to please a PAC who gave her $5,000.

Moreover, a number of academic studies tend to support the view that legislators do not sell their votes to generous interest groups. By comparing legislators' votes on bills with the campaign donations the studies received from interested groups, they have concluded that while money certainly does buy access, at best it only influences votes at the margins – when legislators have no strong inclinations or contrary pressures being exerted on them (Wright, 1990; Evans, PAC Contributions and Roll – call voting: Conditional Power', in Cigler and Loomis, 1986).

It is also important to remember that a mere correlation of votes with donations does not establish an unambiguous relationship of cause and effect. Quite sensibly, interest groups try to reinforce the position of those whom they know are already sympathetic to their views. In other words, money may follow the voting inclinations and behaviour of legislators, rather than determine them.

Nevertheless, there is other evidence that contradicts this limited view of the influence of campaign finance. In the first place, some members of Congress openly acknowledge that it is difficult to resist the pressure to vote in line with groups who have contributed money. As Representative John Bryant said, 'Anytime someone, whether a person or a PAC, gives you a large sum of money, you can't help but feel the need to give them extra attention, whether it is access to your time or, subconsciously, the obligation to vote with them.' Representative (now Senator) Barbara Mikulski put it less gently: 'I fear we could become a coin-operated Congress. Instead of two bits, you put in $2,500 and pull out a vote' (Sabato, 1985, p. 126).

Box 12.7

Political corruption or constituency service? The case of the Keating Five

The Savings and Loan bankruptcies of the 1980s became the costliest scandal in American political history. The estimated cost to the American taxpayer was between $200 and $300 billion. One conspicuous casualty was Lincoln Savings and Loan, owned by Charles Keating Jr, which crashed in 1989 leaving a bill for the taxpayer of $2 billion. Keating was subsequently imprisoned on fraud and racketeering chargers.

It was obvious that there had been a massive failure in government regulation of these lending institutions in general and of Lincoln Savings and Loan in particular. A Senate committee discovered that, two years before the collapse of Lincoln, no less than five US Senators actively intervened on behalf of Charles Keating to persuade the government regulators to go easy on their investigation of Lincoln. Faced by the concerted action of five senators, the chief regulator said he felt intimidated. When the senators were told that criminal proceedings were likely, three of them withdrew from the matter. Two senators continued to intervene frequently in the regulatory process and one, Senator Cranston, even made an early morning telephone call to the home of one of the regulators.

It emerged that the Keating Five Senators had all received substantial campaign contributions from Charles Keating. Senator Cranston had received almost $1 million during the period that he was intervening on behalf of Keating. While four of the Keating Five were merely rebuked by the Senate, Senator Cranston was formally reprimanded. The Senate committee argued that while Cranston had no corrupt intention, his behaviour gave the appearance of corruption.

The American electoral system requires candidates to solicit campaign contributions from wealthy constituents. If elected, major campaign contributors expect office-holders to give personal and serious attention to their problems. Senator Cranston vigorously rejected the charge of corruption and asserted that he had done nothing worse than most of his Senate colleagues had done.

The consequence of the Keating Five looking after their constituent's interests was that a fraudulently run lending institution stayed in business for two years longer than it should have done, with a significantly increased cost to the taxpayer.

One of the Keating Five, Senator John McCain, is now a leading advocate of campaign finance reform.

Contributed by Robert Williams, University of Durham

While it is members of the House of Representatives who are often seen as most vulnerable to the temptations of PAC money, the Senate is by no means immune. One of the greatest scandals of recent times was the case of the so-called Keating Five (see Box 12.7). In the 1980s, five senators – Cranston, Riegle, Deconcini, Glenn, McCain – had repeatedly intervened with federal regulators on behalf of Charles Keating's Lincoln Savings and Loan Association. The Savings and Loan eventually collapsed in 1989 because of financial irregularities. The ensuing inquiry revealed that the senators who represented Keating during the investigations had received a total of $1.5 million in donations from him. Moreover, the inquiry found that, 'In numerous instances – especially in the cases of Cranston, Riegle and Deconcini – Keating's donations coincided in time with official actions taken by the senators on his behalf' (*CQ Almanac*, 1991, p. 27). Equally worrying, however, Senator Cranston responded to an official reprimand by the Senate Ethics Committee by telling his fellow senators that he had done nothing unusual: 'My behavior did not violate established norms. Here, but for the Grace of God, stand you' (*ibid.*, p. 26).

We noted above that a mere correlation between votes and campaign donations is not enough to establish a clear causal relationship. Nevertheless, some analyses of voting and donations do produce the strong implication that money has determined votes.

Philip Stern's analysis of the lobbying campaign by the National Automobile Dealers Association (NADA) to defeat the 'lemon law' is a case in point. The lemon law was a regulation issued by the Federal Trade Commission requiring secondhand car dealers to inform prospective customers of any flaws in a car of which they were aware. In the early 1980s, NADA campaigned to have Congress veto the regulation. This campaign included making donations to over half the members of Congress and which totalled over $1 million. Box 12.8 shows clearly that the larger the donation, the more likely a member is to vote against the lemon law.

Box 12.8

Campaign donations and the 'lemon law' vote in the House of Representatives, 1982

Amount received from NADA PAC, 1979–82	Percentage of House members voting against the 'lemon law' in 1982
More than $4,000	90.2
$1,000–3,000	88.3
$1–1,000	68
Zero	34.2

Source: Stern, 1988, p. 45

Even such figures as these cannot prove conclusively that NADA bought votes in the House. Nevertheless, episodes such as this and the Savings and Loan Scandal ensure that campaign donations by interest groups will remain a controversial topic.

Interest groups and the public good

Policy

It may be argued that, on balance, interest groups make a valuable contribution to the development of good public policies. As a powerful representative force, their activities help to keep politicians in touch with the needs and demands of different social groups. If one measure of good public policy is its responsiveness and acceptability to the people at large, then interest groups may plausibly be said to be a positive element in the political system.

Yet there are many who claim that interest groups distort the policy-making process and are a prime cause of many of the policy problems which the United States has faced in recent years.

Iron triangles

One such line of criticism is that interest groups have formed a mutually regarding and mutually rewarding relationship with two other political institutions: congressional committees and subcommittees, and the bureaucratic agencies which correspond to the same policy areas. These three-way relationships are known as iron triangles.

The most famous (or infamous) of these iron triangles has been that concerned with national defence. As far back as 1961, President Eisenhower took the opportunity of his Farewell Address to warn the country of the dangers posed by what he termed 'the military–industrial complex'. The three points of the triangle here are arms manufacturers, the government defence establishment, including the armed forces and Defense Department, and members of Congress who represent constituencies whose economies are defence oriented. All three have a vested interest in ever larger defence expenditures. The arms manufacturers reap profits from such outlays; the government defence establishment acquires more power, and members of Congress earn the votes of constituents who gain jobs in the defence plants.

What is missing, as Eisenhower tried to point out, is any concept of the national interest. And the danger is that the iron triangle will cause greater expenditure on arms than the nation needs or can afford. Although the military–industrial complex provides a dramatic example of an iron triangle, similar relationships can be seen to exist right across the range of policy areas (Levine and Thurber, 'Reagan and the Intergovernmental Lobby' in Cigler and Loomis, 1986).

Indeed, in his farewell address in 1989, President Reagan blamed 'special interests' and iron triangles for Americas massive annual budget deficits. They prevented their favourite expenditures from being cut and effectively shut off debate on alternative policies that might be harmful to them, although beneficial to the nation.

Box 12.9

Is pressure group politics biased?

In the past 35 years, the United States has witnessed an explosion of new groups representing interests previously unrepresented in interest group politics, for example people of colour, women, consumers, environmentalists, gays, the physically challenged, and so on. However, while the pressure group system in the United States is undoubtedly open to the formation of new pressure groups when new interests develop in society, interest group politics is also class biased since employers and wealthier individuals are better able to exploit the formal opportunity to form and join interest groups which is enjoyed by all Americans. For example, according to Kay Schlozman, while the pressure group system undoubtedly became much more diverse between 1960 and 1980, business simultaneously increased its over-representation in the pressure group system so that in 1980 more than 70 per cent of pressure groups with a Washington presence represented business interests (Schlozman, 1984). Any scheme for classifying interest groups should acknowledge this basic fact.

Furthermore, despite the presence of pressure groups in Washington DC which speak for the poor and unemployed, there are none which have them as members. To use Abraham Lincoln's description of the United States as a government 'of, by, and for' the people, there are only interest groups 'for' the poor and unemployed but not 'by' them. This inability to form and maintain interest groups with the economically disadvantaged as members contradicts the complacent assumption that the economically disadvantaged can always compensate for their lack of other political resources, especially money, by mobilising large numbers.

Despite the formal equality of opportunity to form and join interest groups, two structural difficulties contribute to a class bias in interest group politics. The first obstacle – the marginal cost of membership – affects those with lower incomes. Wealthy individuals and businesses can almost easily afford membership costs; while membership costs loom large for individuals who are economically marginal. The second obstacle – the collective good free-rider problem – disadvantages groups which seek to organise large numbers of individuals to pursue collective or public goods which are available to non-members. Since individuals can receive the benefits without contributing to their provision, it is rational for them to be free-riders and not to join the organisation even when they support its goals; but if everyone free-rides, then either the pressure group will not be formed or it will collapse. Significantly, the attempt to organise the poor into the mass membership National Welfare Rights Organization in the late 1960s came to grief as a result of both of these problems.

However, since votes also count in a pluralist political system, even if the pressure group system is structurally biased in favour of business and wealthier individuals, undemocratic pressure group politics need not translate into undemocratic public policy.

Contributed by Dr Douglas Jaenicke, University of Manchester. © Douglas W. Jaenicke

Democracy

Finally we come to the most fundamental question of all: are interest groups compatible with democracy? As with most aspects of the interest group debate, opinion remains divided on this (see Box 12.9).

We have already noted that interest groups can be seen as performing a valuable and legitimate representative function. Indeed, at one time, so-called 'pluralist' political theorists argued that interest groups positively advanced democratic values. They believed that since all interests in society could be organised into groups, and because these groups would compete with each other and then compromise, the end-product of interest group activity would mirror the nation's demands as a whole (Truman, 1971).

Pluralist theorists acknowledged the fact that not all interest groups were equal, with corporate groups, for example, having far greater financial resources than others. Nevertheless, it was argued that interest group resources were not cumulative: that is, no one type of group possessed an advantage in all resources. Thus, while corporate groups had an advantage in money, labour or civil rights groups had an advantage in numbers (Dahl, 1961).

The principal critics of the pluralist view have been elite theorists on both the political left and right (Mills, 1956; Dye, 1995). They stress the co-operation that occurs between privileged interest groups, especially those from the corporate sector, and other governmental elites. They deny that this political network is equally open to all-comers, especially groups who lack the financial clout to 'buy themselves a seat at the table'.

Those who defend the role of interest groups today concede some of the arguments made by the critics. Not only is there a real inequality amongst interest groups in terms of resources, but they are not even internally democratic. They tend to be run by a handful of full-time leaders who rarely consult their members on policy issues (Berry, 1989, p. 66).

Nevertheless the sheer number of interest groups tends to support the view that they perform a valuable representative function. They are a vehicle for putting new issues on the public agenda and for encouraging Americans to participate in a small way in their own government. And for all that Americans lambaste the power of special interests in general, they tend to value the role of the groups that represent *them* (Berry, 1989, p. 8).

For both good and ill, therefore, interest groups will remain a powerful force in American politics. They will continue to organise and represent significant sections of the community, and they will continue to provide the financial fuel for congressional elections. This in turn means that they will continue to have a privileged claim on the attention of policy-makers and a privileged opportunity to place private interest at the heart of public policy.

 Summary

The heterogeneous nature of American society has given rise to an impulse to form interest groups. This was encouraged by the constitutional protection of the rights to assembly and to petitition government. As government has grown in its responsibilities, the activities of interest groups have expanded, especially as the fragmented system of government gives numerous points of access to the policy-making process. Interest-group activity is, however, highly controversial, owing mainly to the fact that the groups provide candidates for office with a large percentage of their campaign funds. This has led to the popular belief that Congress is in the grip of rich 'special interests' who put their own needs before those of the nation. While there is contradictory evidence on this issue, there is no doubt that the ability of certain interest groups to gain access to the nation's top policy-makers gives them a very powerful position in the American political process.

Topics for discussion

1. Why are interest groups so numerous in the United States?
2. How did the Federal Election Campaign Acts of the 1970s affect the role of interest groups?
3. How plausible is the argument that interest group money buys access but not votes?
4. Do interest groups impair or enhance American representative democracy?

Further reading

Excellent introductions to this subject include R. Hrebener, *Interest Group Politics in America* (3rd edn, New York: Sharpe, 1997); A. Cigler and B. Loomis, *Interest Group Politics* (3rd edn, Washington DC: CQ Press, 1991), and J. Berry, *The Interest Group Society* (Glenview: Scott, Foresman/Little, Brown, 1989). On PACs in particular, see L. Sabato, *PAC Power: Inside the world of political action committees* (New York: Norton, 1985). On finance laws, see M. Malbin, *Parties, Interest Groups and Campaign Finance Laws* (Washington DC: American Enterprise Institute, 1993). For a useful source of up-to-date information and analysis, visit the Web site of the Centre for Responsive Politics (http://www.crp.org).

References

Berry, J., 1989, *The Interest Group Society* (2nd edn, Glenview: Scott, Foresman/Little, Brown)
Cigler, A. and Loomis, B., 1991,*Interest Group Politics* (3rd edn, Washington DC: CQ Press)
Dahl, R., 1961, *Who Governs?* (New Haven: Yale University Press)
Dye, T., 1995, *Who's Running America? The Clinton years* (6th edn, Englewood Cliffs: Prentice Hall)
Hrebener, R., 1997, *Interest Group Politics in America* (3rd edn, New York: Sharpe)
Mills, C., 1956, *The Power Elite* (Oxford: Oxford University Press)
Sabato, L., 1985, *PAC Power: Inside the world of political action committees* (New York: Norton)
Schlozman, K., 1984, 'What accent the heavenly chorus? Political equality and the American pressure system', *Journal of Politics*, vol. 46, pp. 1006–32
Schlozman, K. and Tierney, J., 1986, *Organized Interests and American Democracy* (New York: Harper & Row)
Stern, P., 1988, *The best Congress money can buy* (New York: Pantheon Books)
Tocqueville, A. de, 1935, *Democracy in America* (Reprinted 1956, New York: Mentor)

Truman, D., 1971, *The Governmental Process* (2nd edn, New York: Knopf)

Walker, J., 1983, 'The origins and maintenance of interest groups in America', *American Political Science Review*, vol. 77, pp. 390–406

Wright, J., 1990, 'Contributions, lobbying and committee voting in the United States House of Representatives', *American Political Science Review*, vol. 84, pp. 417–38

IV

The executive process

The executive branch of American government includes the most visible part of that government – the presidency – and one of its least visible parts – the executive bureaucracy.

The constitutional ambiguity of the extent of the executive power of the presidency, coupled with the fact that the office is held by one person alone, has meant that the presidential role in the political system has depended heavily on the electoral needs and administrative capacities of individual presidents.

However, presidents are by no means alone in exercising their powers. They are surrounded by assistants, and they preside over a large number of federal employees. Although this federal bureaucracy resides within the executive branch, and therefore might appear at first glance to be subordinate to the president, in reality it is better to see the federal bureaucracy as something of a battlefield between presidents and other forces in American politics, both those already examined in Part III (voters, parties, media and pressure groups) and those we shall be looking at in Parts V and VI (Congress and the courts).

Contents

13

Presidential power

It is often said that the president of the United States holds the most powerful political office in the world. This, however, is quite misleading, and confuses the power of the United States as a country with the power of its chief executive. In fact, compared with the leaders of most other democracies, the president of the United States faces a daunting task in imposing his will upon the political system. In this chapter, then, we examine why so much is expected of the American president and yet why so few presidents are able to meet those expectations.

The president of the United States seems to stand at the centre of all American politics, domestic and international. Think of any major action undertaken by the United States in the world, or any important initiative in economic or social policy at home, and automatically one conjures up the image of the president meeting with foreign leaders, making a speech or signing a bill into law at the White House.

In the popular imagination at least, this tendency to identify the nation with the president has led to a fusion of the concepts of political action and presidential action. Aided and abetted by a media obsessed with every aspect of the office, and especially the office-holder, the illusion has been created that all that is necessary for successful political leadership is for the president to have the will to act.

Nothing, however, is further from the truth. While presidents can certainly command attention, they can no more command the political system to do their bidding than King Canute could command the tides. The reference to the delusional monarch is indeed apt. For when the American revolutionaries overthrew the British monarchy in 1776, they signalled their determination to rid themselves of autocratic pretension in all its forms. Thus, when the framers of the Constitution of 1787 designed the presidency, they created a chief executive who was generally more a servant than a master of the national government. At the same time, they created an office with the potential for great political initiative, as some presidents have proved.

The Constitution and the president

Delegates at the Philadelphia convention in 1787 had little difficulty in agreeing on the need for a distinct executive branch – after all, the bedrock of the new Constitution was to be the concept of the separation of powers. With that understood, however, a great deal of consideration was given to what kind of executive office would best serve the nation. In particular, great time was devoted to the question of whether the office should be held by a single person – a unitary executive – or whether several people should be involved – a plural executive.

These deliberations drew upon two distinct and rather contrary experiences. The first was the history of monarchical tyranny that Americans believed they had suffered in the years before the War of Independence. Recognising the dangers of placing too much power in the hands of one person, the delegates contemplated a number of devices that would prevent this: a plural executive of more than one person or an executive council with the power to negate presidential decisions, for example.

The fact, however, that the delegates eventually opted for a single-person, or unitary, office was owing to the influence of a second line of experience. The first American constitution, the Articles of Confederation (1781–89), provided for no national executive power at all, leaving the individual state members of the Continental Congress to enforce collective decisions. The result according to many, was both blatant non-compliance by some states and a general lack of firm administration that bordered on the catastrophic when crises occurred. Perhaps even more important was the political experience of the individual states in this period. As we saw in Chapter 2 (page 30), this experience had led constitutional thinking away from weak executives to strong ones. A major lesson of the decade previous to the Philadelphia convention, therefore, was the need for a vigorous executive branch of government. Although the delegates were determined not to endow the chief executive with unlimited monarchical power, then, they were equally intent upon creating an effective office that could resist unjust or unwise congressional initiatives as well as execute the laws passed by Congress.

The tension between these two aims resulted in a unitary presidency which was given some important, if limited, opportunity to influence the making of national laws and to exercise political leadership, but which was nevertheless looked upon by many Americans with a traditional republican suspicion of executive power. So while some Americans saw great possibilities for leadership in the presidency, more traditionally republican-minded Americans were inclined to see the Constitution as giving to the presidency merely sufficient powers to execute the nation's will once Congress had determined what that was. After all, even in the area of foreign policy, where the president was given greater scope for leadership than in domestic policy, the framers were careful to ensure that the legislature could control the most fundamental policy decisions. In addition, presidents, unlike representatives and senators, were made subject to removal by impeachment for 'the abuse or violation of some public trust' (The Federalist, no. 65). It is in this sense that the earliest popular conception of the president was as a servant rather than a master of the new American government, although the constitutional basis of executive leadership was also created in 1787.

Constitutional powers of the president

A close examination of the president's major powers and duties contained in Article II, Section 2 of the Constitution bears out this portrait of the contradictory intentions that went into the making of the presidency. In the order in which they appear, the president is designated commander-in-chief of the army and navy of the United States; he is given the power to make treaties with other nations; he appoints ambassadors, public ministers, judges of the Supreme Court and all other officers of the United States; 'he shall from time to time give to the Congress information of the state of the Union and recommend to their consideration such measures as he shall judge necessary and expedient' (expedient here means wise); and finally 'he shall take care that the laws be faithfully executed'.

In addition to Article II powers, Article I stipulates that the president has the power to veto legislation passed by Congress. This is an important power: of the approximately 1,500 presidential vetoes to date, fewer than 10 per cent have been overridden by Congress. Moreover, the threat of a veto can be used by presidents to shape legislation. Veto threats often produce important congressional concessions to presidential wishes.

Although these are certainly important powers, they fall far short of – or, in a more profound sense, go beyond – making presidents the popular leaders that they are expected to be today. Modern presidents are 'plebiscitary' presidents; as we shall see, this both strengthens and weakens them. In the original constitutional understanding, presidential power was expected to be used *against* unwise popular demands that might temporarily capture congressional majorities. In this sense, presidents were expected to be stronger than a more plebiscitary executive.

The powers enumerated in Articles I and II are less impressive than may at first appear, simply because each is qualified by associated powers given to Congress. Take for example, presidents' power as commander-in-chief of the armed forces. While this allows them to *conduct* war, it confers no power to *declare* war. That is specifically given to Congress. Furthermore, Congress is specifically endowed with the authority to raise armies, thus creating the potential for Congress to cut off funds for any military activity being pursued by the president. It is clear then that the framers did not intend the president to follow any war policy that did not have the authorisation, or at least acquiescence, of Congress. Rather, the framers believed that military policy, once decided, would be much more effective if placed in the hands of one person who could act quickly and decisively, than if it were left to the slow deliberations and internal conflicts of the legislature.

The nature of executive power

The constitutional powers of the presidency, viewed in conjunction with constraints placed upon them (see Box 13.1), draw our attention to both the positive and negative characteristics that the framers identified with presidential executive power.

The unitary presidency is better suited to action than a plural executive or a numerous legislative house. Presidents can be decisive, since they do not have to bow to the

> ## Box 13.1
>
> ## Presidential powers and congressional checks
>
> | Constitutional grants of power to the president | Constitutional checks by Congress |
> |---|---|
> | ■ Commander-in-chief | ■ Only Congress declares war; only Congress raises and funds armed forces |
> | ■ Power to make treaties | ■ Senate must approve treaties (by two-thirds majority) |
> | ■ Power to appoint ambassadors, Supreme Court justices, other national office-holders | ■ Senate must approve (by simple majority) |
> | ■ Shall recommend 'necessary and expedient' legislation | ■ Only Congress can pass legislation |
> | ■ Must execute laws | ■ Only Congress can fund presidential means and agencies of execution |
> | ■ May veto legislation | ■ May override veto (with two-thirds majority) |

opinion of co-equals. They can therefore act quickly, since they do not have to wait upon the deliberations of others. Moreover, and especially important in foreign affairs, they can maintain secrecy more easily than a body composed of many people. Alexander Hamilton, writing in *The Federalist* and urging the adoption of the new Constitution, compared the virtues of the unitary presidency and the plural legislature as follows:

> Those politicians and statesmen, who have been the most celebrated for the soundness of their principles, and for the justness of their views, have declared in favour of a single executive, and a numerous legislature. They have, with great propriety, considered *energy* as the most necessary qualification of the former, and have regarded this as most applicable to power in a single hand; while they have, with equal propriety, considered the latter as best adapted to deliberation and wisdom, and best calculated to conciliate the confidence of the people, and to secure their privileges and interests.
>
> (*The Federalist*, no. 70, emphasis added)

Congress was clearly expected to have certain strengths to contribute to the legislative process, which Hamilton here states quite flatteringly. However, Hamilton did not expect presidents to exhibit 'servile pliancy ... to a prevailing current, either in the community or in the legislature.' They were rather to use their constitutional position and prestige to make sure that the public good is the object of public policy, even when 'a temporary delusion' induces in the people or in their congressional representatives either neglect of that good or an erroneous perception of it. Presidents were expected not to pursue short-term popularity but to procure 'lasting monuments' of the people's gratitude by risking 'the peril of their displeasure' in the short term. Presidents had to be granted sufficient constitutional power to put them 'in a situation to dare to act [their] own opinion with vigor and decision' (*The Federalist*, no. 71).

Electing the president

That the president was not originally regarded simply as the embodiment of the people's immediate will is indicated by the original system for electing the president. The framers were acutely aware of the numerous examples in history of demagogic leaders who courted popular acclaim in order to acquire dictatorial power. All too often these leaders claimed some kind of mandate from the people and then used it to crush political opposition. The framers addressed this problem partly by placing a barrier between the president and the people. Having at first been inclined to leave the choice of president to Congress, thus making the executive branch distinctly inferior to the legislative branch of government, the framers eventually devised the electoral college as the means of separating the president both from the people and from Congress.

The electoral college is a complex device with some odd features, but as a practical matter, it solved some of the problems confronted by the framers. The framers feared both that a popularly elected chief executive might become too powerful and that a president chosen by the legislature might be too weak to prevent congressional aggrandisement and to execute the laws. In the absence of national political parties, they also doubted that a directly popular election would often result in any candidate receiving a majority of the people's votes; many feared that even with the electoral college system the contest would usually be decided by the fallback method in the House of Representatives.

The electoral college neatly side-stepped the dilemma of a possibly too powerful popularly elected president and a president too dependent on Congress, by placing the choice of president in the hands of the *state* legislatures. Each state was allocated a number of electors in the electoral college equivalent to its congressional delegation, that is, one elector for each of the state's US senators and representatives. These electors were in turn to be chosen in the manner deemed appropriate by each state. Thus, the states were to decide for themselves whether to choose electors by popular vote, special convention or, indeed, by the members of the state legislature. Whichever means was adopted by the states, the fact remained that the common voters could do no more than 'choose the choosers' of the president.

Presidents were not intended to be 'tribunes of the people', but they were intended to have a mandate distinct from that of the Congress. This latter feature was advanced in the spirit of checking the power of Congress and thus also the immediate popular will; it was not intended as an enhancement of popular pressure on government. Popular choice and popular judgement of presidential capacity and achievement were important: presidents were to be republican executives, not independent monarchs. However, it was equally important that this choice and judgement be kept at a distance, otherwise presidents would be insufficiently independent of the people to serve the people's long-term best interests.

The presidency in the eighteenth and nineteenth centuries

The early presidency

The delegates at Philadelphia had many doubts about the office of the presidency: some thought it was so powerless that it might invite movements to change it into a monarchy, while others thought it was far too powerful. The fact that agreement was reached on an independent president with some strong powers was owing, in part, to the fact that everyone assumed that George Washington would be the first president; and since no one doubted Washington's commitment to republicanism or the fact that he would use his powers honourably and without undue personal ambition, they were content to entrust him with significant power. One delegate, Pierce Butler, wrote that the powers of the presidency would not have been so great 'had not many of the members cast their eyes toward General Washington as President; and shaped their ideas of the Powers to be given a President, by their opinions of his Virtue' (Rossiter, 1960, p. 81).

After his death, Washington became the subject of some amusing myth-making that at times hinted at his divinity (see Box 13.2). Nevertheless, as the first president of the United States, Washington did faithfully carry out his duties more or less in line with the framers' expectations. Given his stature with the American people, he inevitably created important precedents that helped to define the office for many years to come.

The most important precedent established by Washington is that he never sought directly to exercise legislative leadership. This is illustrated by the fact that he signed into law congressional bills that he considered unwise. In his view of the presidency, however, he was obliged to accept the legislative leadership of Congress and thus only vetoed two bills during his eight years in office, both minor matters and both on the grounds that he believed them to be unconstitutional. On the other hand, during Washington's administrations, Alexander Hamilton, as secretary of the Treasury, was not unjustifiably accused of leading congressional policy in both domestic and foreign affairs. Hence executive-branch legislative leadership was not entirely a later invention, although the extent to which later presidents invested much personal energy and reputation in this leadership was alien to Washington's style and to his determination to remain above partisan politics.

Congress and Washington tended to respect each other's designated areas of competence with a formality that at times seemed excessive (Cunliffe, 1969, p. 53). There were, however, a few important disputes. In 1793, in pursuit of his powers to conduct relations with other nations, Washington issued a neutrality proclamation with respect to the Franco-British war being waged. Yet such a decision appeared to some to belong more naturally to the body endowed with the power to declare war – Congress. Congress in fact tried to assert its power by passing the Neutrality Act of 1794, but Washington had in effect taken the initiative and determined the policy.

Another difficult episode occurred when Washington tried earnestly to follow the letter of the Constitution in foreign relations. In 1789, in line with his power to make treaties with 'the advice and consent' of the Senate, the president sought to consult the Senate on a treaty he was negotiating with Indians. The Senate responded by asking

Box 13.2

Myth-making and the presidency: George Washington

All nations generate self-serving myths that show the people and the country in a favourable moral light. Quite often, these myths focus upon an individual hero who simultaneously embodies or expresses the national character. As the leader of his country's armed forces during the War of Independence and then the new nation's first president, Washington has attracted more myth-making than any other American.

Undoubtedly the most famous of the Washington myths is the cherry tree story. The young Washington had been playing with his new axe and chopped down his father's cherry tree. When his father asked what had happened to it, Washington cried that he 'couldn't tell a lie', and owned up. His father was not angry, but overjoyed at his son's honesty. A similar tale concerns Washington mastering his mother's wilful sorrel horse, only for the creature to die of a heart attack as a result. As with the cherry tree, Washington does not lie and his mother responds by praising him.

Perhaps the most indicative of Washington's mythic status, however, is the Valley Forge prayer story. During the War of Independence, Washington and his army are at their lowest point and encamped at Valley Forge. One day, Isaac Potts, a member of the pacifist sect of Quakers, is walking through the woods near the encampment. Suddenly Potts hears a voice speaking in earnest. This is how Washington's hagiographer, Parson Weems, tells the story:

> As he approached the spot with a cautious step, whom should he behold, in a dark natural bower of ancient oaks, but the commander-in-chief of the American armies on his knees in prayer. Motionless with surprise, friend Potts continued on the place till the general, having ended his devotions, arose, and with a countenance of angelic serenity, retired to headquarters. Friend Potts then went home, and on entering his parlour called out to his wife, 'Sarah! my dear Sarah! all's well! all's well! George Washington will yet prevail!'
>
> 'What's the matter, Isaac?', replied she, 'thee seems moved.' 'Well, if I seem moved, 'tis no more than what I really am. I have this day seen what I never expected. Thee knows that I always thought that the sword and the gospel were utterly inconsistent; and that no man could be a soldier and a Christian at the same time. But George Washington has this day convinced me of my mistake.' Friend Potts then related what he had seen, and concluded with this prophetical remark: 'If George Washington be not a man of God, I am greatly deceived, and still more shall I be deceived, if God do not, through him, work out a great salvation for America.'
>
> (Boller, 1981, pp. 7–11)

Washington to return in three days when it had had time to deliberate. Deeply offended, Washington went away determined never to request the Senate's 'advice' on a treaty again. Since that episode, presidents seek only the 'consent' of the Senate: that is, they negotiate the treaty first and then present it to the Senate for ratification.

Washington's presidency clarified some of the ambiguities of the constitutional scheme but did not greatly alter it. As well as the episodes discussed above, for example, Washington (with Congress' consent) established the right of presidents unilaterally to dismiss cabinet members and other office-holders, even if these officers had originally been appointed only with the consent of the Senate.

Washington also put a significant gloss on an issue that had caused considerable debate: the length of tenure of the president. Many had argued that any president should be limited to one four-year term of office. While that would have helped to alleviate fears of the presidency being transformed into an hereditary monarchy, it would also have deprived the nation of the services of presidents who had shown themselves to be exceptionally able during their first term, and might discourage some good candidates from seeking the office. The Philadelphia convention eventually decided against putting any limit on the number of terms a president could serve. Yet when Washington chose not to seek a third term, the power of his example prevented any president going beyond two terms, until Franklin D. Roosevelt broke the taboo in 1940.

The presidency in the nineteenth century

The story of the presidency in the nineteenth century is made up of two distinct strands. The first is one of chief executives who more or less willingly deferred to congressional predominance and who can be said to have reigned rather than ruled. Many of these presidents have only an obscure place in American political history, yet they typify the uninspired nature of most presidential politics during this period.

In marked contrast, there are a few outstanding historical figures whose actions demonstrated the *potential* for leadership inherent in the American presidency, at least when the circumstances were right.

Standing head and shoulders above the rest is Abraham Lincoln (1861–65), the first president elected as a Republican and the leader who steered the United States through its greatest domestic crisis, the Civil War. Part of Lincoln's genius was to perceive that, in a major crisis, the limitations imposed on the presidency by the letter of the Constitution must not lead to political paralysis. When the very existence of the Union was seriously threatened, Lincoln exercised 'emergency powers' for which there was no constitutional support; but, as he asked rhetorically in 1864, 'Was it possible to lose the nation and yet preserve the Constitution? … I felt that measures otherwise unconstitutional might become lawful by becoming indispensable to the preservation of the Constitution through the preservation of the nation' (Ragsdale, 1993, p. 51).

Although Lincoln's actions were drastic – suspending the writ of habeas corpus in some places and raising and funding additional armies without congressional approval, for example – they were vindicated by history: and for the most part, they were also later accepted by Congress and the Supreme Court. What Lincoln had successfully demonstrated, therefore, was the existence of inherent emergency powers in the presidency. In other words, there are moments in the nation's life when the president must act because only the president can act.

Of course, the very fact that the Civil War was an extraordinary crisis meant that Lincoln's example did not establish a model for presidential leadership in more normal times. Indeed, after Lincoln's assassination in 1865, Congress reasserted itself very forcefully against his successor, Andrew Johnson, and came within a whisker of impeaching and removing him. For the remainder of the century, presidents were mostly hapless non-entities in the face of congressional power.

Before Lincoln, however, other presidents had demonstrated ways in which their office could be executed energetically. Thomas Jefferson (1801–9) worked closely with his party allies in Congress and channelled legislative proposals through them. Andrew Jackson (1829–37) demonstrated the considerable legislative influence that could be wielded through the president's veto power. Using the veto on purely policy grounds, Jackson proved that the 'negative presidency' could frustrate congressional leadership and require Congress to take account of the president's policy preferences when enacting laws.

Jackson also added a new dimension to the concept of the presidency by being the first president to cast himself as the principal agent of the people. Fuelled by a populistic distrust of the privileged classes, Jackson considered himself a tribune of the people, standing out against the self-serving activities of some of those in Congress.

Lincoln, Jefferson and Jackson were exceptional individuals whose actions fell far short of transforming the institution of the presidency. The main reason for this was not any failure on their part; nor was it owing to a lack of any flexibility in the Constitution permitting change. Rather, it was because there was no real social or ideological demand for change in the institution of the presidency. American government in the nineteenth century was thoroughly imbued with the spirit that there was relatively little that the national government was required to do; and as long as Congress was willing and able to assume leadership in fulfilling those limited responsibilities, the presidency remained pretty much what many of the framers had in mind when they created it: an important office for safeguarding the national interest and administering its laws, but which otherwise accepted the political primacy of Congress.

The modern presidency

The presidency changed when America changed. In the last quarter of the nineteenth century, the United States underwent a rapid socio-economic transformation as industrialisation and urbanisation swept the nation. At the same time, unprecedented millions of immigrants came to the United States, providing much-needed labour. Together these developments helped to create not only great economic advances, but also a far more complex society which required order, reform and continuous management.

By the early twentieth century, those qualities recognised by the framers as belonging to the executive function – especially energy, action and clear purpose – were increasingly demanded of government. As a consequence, not only did presidents emerge who were eager to exercise national leadership, but Congress itself began to recognise its own limitations and to hand over certain of its functions to the executive branch.

The activist presidency

The Progressive presidents, Theodore Roosevelt (1901–9) and Woodrow Wilson (1913–21), are the transitional figures in the switch from the traditional presidency to the modern activist presidency. They recognised the desirability and even the necessity of presidential leadership in both domestic and foreign policy making. Ultimately both presidents met with frustration caused by having a vision of the presidency that went too far for most of their contemporaries. However, they undoubtedly pointed the way towards the modern conception of presidential leadership and power – and to the modern experience of presidential weakness and failure.

Theodore Roosevelt encapsulated a key aspect of both the possibilities and the limitations of the presidency when he spoke of the office as a 'bully pulpit'. Roosevelt appreciated that presidents could exploit their ability to command the attention of the public and of Congress and could call for legislative action with unmatched authority and prestige.

Yet the bully pulpit metaphor also reveals the weakness of the presidency. Just as the churchman can use the pulpit to exhort but not to compel his flock to do the right thing, so too are presidents dependent upon the willingness of Congress and others to follow their leads. The bully, of course, can exert more that just moral pressure: and the president does dispose of both carrots and sticks. Presidents can bestow or withhold the patronage and prestige of their office; they can appeal to the electorate to pressure members of Congress to comply with their wishes, and they can veto legislation that others may cherish.

However, the ability to cajole and even threaten is rarely an adequate substitute for the power to compel. Thus, Roosevelt's own legislative achievements are not impressive by today's standards. An insight into the power and limitations of the presidency can be gained from a look at Roosevelt's policy towards monopoly corporations (or trusts).

Being charged with responsibility for enforcing national laws, Roosevelt was able to order a suit to be taken out against a highly unpopular monopolistic enterprise, the Northern Securities Corporation. When the federal government won its case in 1904, Roosevelt was credited with having struck a great blow for consumers and business competition. Yet Roosevelt achieved no success with his efforts to persuade Congress to pass antitrust legislation, largely because most members of Congress considered such measures to be contrary to their own and the nation's interests. As a result, Roosevelt's policy towards monopolies was a failure.

Woodrow Wilson succeeded in getting more of his legislative agenda acted upon by Congress, but often only at the price of seeing it distorted by congressional amendments or by judicial decisions. Thus when Wilson submitted his own legislative proposals for breaking up the trusts, what emerged was a law that eventually served mainly as a weapon against the formation of labour unions.

The greatest defeat suffered by Wilson was in the realm of foreign policy, where presidents are usually at their most powerful. Wilson was the architect of the plan for the League of Nations, the forerunner of the United Nations that was the product of the bitter experiences of the First World War. Despite his tireless advocacy, however, the Senate refused to give the two-thirds majority necessary to approve the treaty enabling the United States to join the League.

It is well then to remember that even those presidents deemed to be among the most successful in American history were often defeated by political forces they could not control. Nevertheless, what makes Theodore Roosevelt and Woodrow Wilson significant is that they sought to assume the mantle of political and legislative leadership, and to do this not (as the framers had anticipated) by using the constitutional means of recommending legislation uninspired by popular pressure, and of resisting any incompatible congressional policies, but by 'going public', that is by bringing popular pressure to bear upon Congress, in pursuit of what they as president perceived to be the popular will. Both men, quite deliberately and consciously, chose to maximise their power by pushing the 'public presidency' to its limits.

Roosevelt, for example, took a very positive view of presidential power, insisting that the office was blessed with latent, unspecified power. In effect, he believed that any power not specifically withheld from the president by the Constitution or Congress, was his to use on behalf of the people and the nation (see Box 13.3).

Box 13.3

Theodore Roosevelt and the stewardship presidency

In his autobiography, Roosevelt wrote of his theory and practice of the presidency, believing:

> that the executive power was limited only by specific restrictions and prohibitions appearing in the Constitution or imposed by the Congress under its Constitutional powers. My view was that every executive officer, and above all every executive officer in high position, was a steward of the people bound actively and affirmatively to do all he could for the people, and not to content himself with the negative merit of keeping his talents undamaged in a napkin. I declined to adopt the view that what was imperatively necessary for the Nation could not be done by the President unless he could find some specific authorisation to do it. My belief was that it was not only his right but his duty to do anything that the needs of the Nation demanded unless such action was forbidden by the Constitution or by the laws. Under this interpetation of executive power I did and caused to be done many things not previously done by the President and the heads of the departments. I did not usurp power, but I did greatly broaden the use of executive power. In other words I acted for the public welfare, I acted for the common well-being of all our people, whenever and in whatever manner was necessary, unless prevented by direct constitutional or legislative prohibition. I did not care a rap for the mere form and show of power. I cared immensely for the use that could be made of the substance.

Source: Extract from Burns, 1965, pp. 58–9

Seeing himself as the 'steward of the people', he took Andrew Jackson's concept of the president as people's tribune and gave it a positive thrust.

After Wilson, there was a lull in the transformation of the presidency, as those who occupied the White House aspired to follow an earlier model of the chief executive. What is interesting, however, is that Congress itself took concrete steps to enhance the power of the presidency. The outstanding example is the transfer from Congress to the presidency of the prime responsibility for drawing up the national budget. As part of a drive to make government and itself more streamlined and efficient, Congress passed the Budget and Accounting Act of 1921. This put an end to the practice of all parts of the government individually submitting uncoordinated budget requests to Congress. From now on, Congress wanted the newly created Bureau of the Budget to organise a single federal budget proposal. Significantly, Congress located the bureau within the executive branch by placing it under the control of the Treasury Department. Within twenty years, it had moved again, this time under the direct control of the White House. In short, 'in the Budget and Accounting Act of 1921, Congress effectively began the process of ceding control over the budget to the president' (Foley and Owens, 1996, p. 385).

Of course, this does not mean that the Congress accepts the budget submitted by the president. Far from it. However, it does signal congressional recognition that the executive branch is better equipped than the legislative branch to initiate and to co-ordinate the nation's fundamental domestic policy.

Franklin D. Roosevelt and the legislative presidency

Franklin Delano Roosevelt (1933–45) transformed the American presidency. This was in part owing to the unique personality and talents he brought with him to the White House; in part to the changes already introduced by his predecessors; but most of all, the transformation was wrought by crises of truly monumental proportions. Roosevelt became president when the United States was mired in the economic and social catastrophe that was the Great Depression. No sooner had the United States begun to emerge from that trough than it became involved in the even more cataclysmic events of the Second World War.

In short, crisis was the midwife of the presidency we know today. Crisis once again called forth those qualities of the executive branch that are at a premium in such difficult moments – decisiveness, unity of purpose, action and speed. In the case of the Great Depression, a desperate nation demanded fast and effective action, no matter how unprecedented; and, most important of all, perhaps, Congress understood that it could not rival the president's capacity to act even if it had wished to do so. Thus, while individual members of Congress contributed in very significant ways to Roosevelt's New Deal legislative programme, it is rightly remembered as a presidential package of measures.

In 1933, then, all eyes had turned to the president for legislative solutions to serious problems, and they have rarely turned elsewhere since. While there have been times when the American people have not wanted activist government, presidential or otherwise, the fact remains that when action is required, the president is expected to lead.

Expectations of the modern presidency

Modern presidents, then, have to deal with high expectations of their ability to find solutions to major problems. Such expectations constitute a double-edged sword. On the one hand, they are an important resource, because presidents can always insist that their proposals are responses to public demands. The more or less explicit threat is that the public might punish those who thwart the president's attempts to give the people what they want.

On the other hand, the president may become the prisoner of unrealistic public expectations. In the contemporary period, for example, the American public has expected the president to ensure that the economy is healthy and prosperity assured. Presidents, however, have had to contend with economic forces that are simply beyond their control. These may include foreign events such as the huge rises in prices imposed by oil-producing nations in the 1970s. Even closer to home, however, presidents can do relatively little to control the ups and downs of business cycles; and they may have great trouble introducing economic legislation that offends many members of Congress or powerful interest groups.

The institutionalisation of the presidency

Up until this point we have used the terms 'president' and 'presidency' as if they were virtually interchangeable, yet this masks a distinction between the two which is of vital importance in understanding the contemporary executive branch.

As we shall see in the next chapter, the framers of the Constitution clearly understood that the United States would need a bureaucracy to help the president administer the nation. Thus when the new Constitution came into operation in 1789, Congress quickly created the Departments of State, War and the Treasury. Moreover, as more and more demands were made on the national government in the twentieth century, more bureaucratic expertise was required to help draft effective legislation. The natural home of such bureaucracy was, of course, the executive branch of government. In theory, therefore, the demands for greater presidential policy were matched by greater presidential resources.

A less obvious need, however, was for presidents personally to have staff to help them. In 1789 Congress did include a sum for the hiring of a private secretary and a few clerks when it voted the president's expenses, but there was no sense of the need for a White House staff as we know it today. Indeed, well into the twentieth century, the post of secretary to the president could not be considered a major *political* office, even if some of its incumbents took it upon themselves to liaise between the president and important political groups.

A new trend, however, was begun by President Woodrow Wilson. His secretary, Joseph Tumulty, was an experienced politician and had been Wilson's secretary when he served as governor of New Jersey. He liaised with politicians, the press and the Democratic party, and he was involved in all aspects of presidential patronage (Hart, 1995, p. 24).

Along with the politicisation of the role of the president's secretary came a certain increase in the number of the White House staff. Thus from a handful in Washington's day, it had grown to thirty-seven by the time of Franklin D. Roosevelt's first administration (Hart, 1995, p. 28). Nevertheless, this growth had not altered the personal nature of the presidency.

Moreover, such a number was by no means adequate to cope with all the demands made on the president. The basic problem was that the president was required to manage and to co-ordinate an expanding executive branch. When Roosevelt came into office, with a mandate requiring him to assume major new legislative responsibilities, the White House proved woefully understaffed. This inherited problem of an understaffed presidency, combined with a vast new increase in presidential responsibilities, led to the establishment of the Brownlow Committee in 1936 and the consequent institutionalisation of the presidency.

The Brownlow Report

The Brownlow Committee was concerned with the entire organisation and management of the executive branch. When the Brownlow Committee reported in 1937 it stated the general problem in memorably succinct words: 'The President needs help'. Roosevelt himself responded to this by saying:

> The Committee has not spared me; they say, what has been common knowledge for twenty years, that the President cannot adequately handle his responsibilities; that he is overworked; that it is humanly impossible, under the system which we have, for him fully to carry out his constitutional duty as Chief Executive, because he is overwhelmed with minor details and needless contacts arising directly from the bad organization and equipment of the Government. I can testify to this. With my predecessors who have said the same thing over and over again, I plead guilty.
>
> (Rossiter, 1960, p. 128)

The Executive Office of the President

Congress did not enact all of Brownlow's recommendations. As usual, the legislative branch was suspicious that executive branch reorganisation might entail an augmentation of presidential power at the expense of congressional power. Nevertheless, the Reorganization Act of 1939 created what was in effect a presidential bureaucracy quite distinct from the federal bureaucracy.

The first major innovation was the Executive Office of the President (EOP). The purpose of the EOP was to enable the president to direct and to control executive branch activity. Although the president was nominally and constitutionally in charge and accountable, the vast growth of federal bureaucratic activity diluted the president's actual control. The EOP was thus intended to restore presidential power over the executive branch through centralisation and institutionalisation (Foley and Owens, 1996, p. 210).

Within the EOP were located a number of agencies with specific policy tasks. The most important was the Bureau of the Budget (later renamed the Office of

Management and Budget), which was transferred from the Treasury Department to the EOP, precisely to give the president greater control over budgetary policy. In time, other agencies were created within the EOP, such as the Council of Economic Advisers (CEA) in 1946 and the National Security Council (NSC) in 1947 (see Box 13.4).

The White House Office

The 1939 Reorganization Act also saw the creation within the EOP of the White House Office (WHO). In one sense, this was a continuation of the thirty-seven presidential staff who had existed before the 1939 Act. The Brownlow Report only recommended a modest increase in their number – six additional assistants. These were expected to be energetic on the president's behalf but not powerful or high-profile positions.

Roosevelt actually made only three new appointments to his White House staff, but this was because he also continued a policy that had not been officially acknowledged at this point – that of borrowing staff from the departments to give him personal assistance. In this respect, then, 'the importance of the Brownlow report was in legitimating what Roosevelt had been doing all along. It was a ringing manifesto for presidential supremacy, which had not been an accepted fact before the New Deal' (Hess, 1988, p. 34).

The Brownlow recommendations on the White House staff were designed to make the president an efficient manager of a complex and growing executive branch. Yet, as the number of staff has grown over the years, they have created more problems than they have solved. As one academic (and former White House staffer) notes:

If he followed sound management principles, the reasoning went, a president, like any

Box 13.4

The Executive Office of the President (EOP)

Agency	Year established
White House Office	1939
Council of Economic Advisers 1	1946
National Security Council	1947
Office of United States Trade Representative	1963
Council on Environmental Quality	1969
Office of Management and Budget	1970
(formerly Bureau of the Budget)	(1921)
Office of Science and Technology Policy	1976
Office of Administration	1977
Office of Policy Development	1977
National Economic Council	1992
Office for Women's Initiatives and Outreach	1995

other executive, would be measurably assisted through a sensible delegation of his work-load to an enlarged body of intelligent and loyal assistants. ... That something went badly wrong is hardly in dispute.

(Hess, 1988, p. 171).

Hess first came to this conclusion shortly after the Watergate scandal had revealed gross abuses of power by President Nixon's staff. That the problem has continued, however, is evident from the Iran–Contra scandal under President Reagan, when members of the National Security Council defied United States law and the president's own policy, in furnishing arms to Iran and diverting the ill-gotten gains to the Contra rebels in Nicaragua. Meanwhile, more minor tales of the incompetence, arrogance or dishonesty of White House staff are common in all administrations.

Organising the executive branch

As we have seen, the basic intention of Brownlow was to interpose a layer of pres-idential advisers between the president himself and the federal bureaucracy. With hindsight, however, it seems obvious that this would produce as many problems as solutions, for the creation of the EOP involved substantial delegation of presidential power to members of the presidential bureaucracy. Armed with this power, EOP offices and personnel became rivals for control of policy making and policy imple-mentation with each other and with cabinet heads and other leaders of the federal bureaucracy. A strong-minded WHO chief of staff can help presidents manage this rivalry, but cannot end it. In this sense, the creation of the EOP has led to considerable friction within the executive branch.

Moreover, the creation of an expanded White House Office within the EOP has created friction between those who work in the White House and those who work in the presidential and federal bureaucracies. Like other members of the EOP, White House staffers owe their position and, therefore, their loyalty, solely to the president; but they also have the precious asset of proximity to the president. Since proximity easily translates into access to the president, and access into influence, the situation has arisen in which members of the White House staff wield enormous power over public policy, at the expense of the experts in the rest of the EOP and the federal bureaucracy.

Thus, if Watergate and Iran–Contra suggest that the enlargement of the White House staff has made the presidency too powerful, that is only half the story. For it is equally true that the White House staff, while undoubtedly necessary to the efficient running of the executive branch, has failed to make the president the effective manager envisaged by Brownlow.

The presidency today

We have already noted that much is expected of the president today. Yet modern pres-idents encounter failure far more readily than success in meeting those expectations. This 'paradox of presidential power' (Hodgson, 1980, p. 13) is partly explained by the tendency to confuse the power of the United States as a nation with the power of its chief executive. Even in an age of relative American decline, the office is far less powerful an institution than the United States as a nation.

In that sense, public expectations of the presidency are simply too high. This has been compounded by the fact that most presidents since Franklin D. Roosevelt have tried to follow in his footsteps and claimed to be intent upon solving America's major problems through presidential leadership. One should not be too hard upon presidential candidates who promise more than they can possibly hope to achieve – they are only saying what people want to hear and what people will vote for.

Unless and until public expectations of presidents are reduced, presidents must struggle to maximise their potential. They must use to the full the various powers they possess, in a manner which minimises the constraints on their power. This, then, is the yardstick by which the success or failure of modern presidents is generally measured.

Presidential power: the power to persuade

It was Richard Neustadt, first writing in 1960, who coined the phrase 'presidential power is the power to persuade'. He took his cue from President Harry Truman who said of his office: 'I sit here all day trying to persuade people to do the things they ought to have sense enough to do without my persuading them. ... That's all the powers of the President amount to.' Anticipating the election victory of General Eisenhower in 1952, Truman remarked ruefully: 'He'll sit here and he'll say "Do this! Do that!" *And nothing will happen.* Poor Ike – it won't be a bit like the Army. He'll find it very frustrating' (Neustadt, 1964, p. 22).

Truman was certainly entitled to feel frustrated: every year he sent an ambitious legislative programme to Congress and every year Congress refused to act on it. Or in Neustadt's terms, Truman was unable to persuade Congress to act. Yet Truman was by no means a weak or incapable leader. Rather, he simply lacked the brute power to overcome a stubborn, politically unsympathetic Congress that had substantial power of its own.

Let us then examine the power of the presidency today and balance it against the constraining forces that operate against it, and consider the main strategies that presidents can employ.

The power of the president

We saw at the beginning of this chapter that the Constitution gave presidents some very important, albeit circumscribed, powers. They were clearly intended to conduct day-to-day relations with other nations and to nominate people for high office, and they could influence congressional legislation by recommendations and by the threat or the use of the veto power. Although presidents were not intended to exercise popular-based political leadership, we saw how historical developments gradually increased the popular profile of presidential power until it reached the point in the 1930s where such leadership was demanded of the president.

In spite of this development, however, the formal constitutional powers of the president did not increase. On the contrary, the only constitutional change affecting the power of the president was the passage of the Twenty-second Amendment in 1951, which formally restricted presidents to a maximum of two four-year terms in office. This has weakened presidents in their second term.

Since the 1930s, then, presidents have had to deal with rising expectations of their performance while continuing to exercise only those formal constitutional powers that were first given to them in 1789. Some observers complain that, in constitutional terms, the president faces twentieth-century problems armed with eighteenth-century powers. Others note, somewhat to the contrary, that the populistic, extraconstitutional methods that modern presidents have pursued have actually not been as helpful to them and to the nation as more constitutional presidential strategies might have been (Bessette and Tulis, 1981; Milkis, 1993).

The first of these extraconstitutional developments is what we might call acknowledged leadership.

Acknowledged leadership

Rising expectations of the presidency create both possibilities and burdens for the president, for along with rising expectations goes the recognition that presidents must be allowed to exercise leadership, since no other office can so readily provide it. Congress retains the right to refuse presidential leadership in particular instances. For the most part, it has conceded political initiative to the White House, although experience since the 1994 elections shows that this remains a contested development.

Executive orders and agreements

It is important to note that the president can make certain kinds of policy decision without congressional approval. These are not specified in the Constitution, but they have been accepted as inherent in executive power.

Executive orders, which have the force of law, can be made by presidents or by executive agencies. These orders are rules for implementing laws and treaties and for executive-branch procedures. Since the Administrative Procedures Act of 1946, they must be published in the *Federal Register*. Executive orders can be simple housekeeping measures, but they can also constitute important decisions in controversial areas, for example affirmative action regulations and wage and price controls.

Executive agreements are made by presidents directly with heads of foreign governments. Unlike treaties, these agreements bind only the president who makes them, not later administrations (unless they renew them), and they do not require Senate discussion or approval (although Congress can of course refuse any necessary funding, if it comes to light). Therefore executive agreements add greatly to the foreign policy powers of presidents.

Legislative leadership

Because Congress usually acknowledges that the president must lead, it concedes the right of the president to set the political agenda. When a president sets out legislative plans, usually in the annual State of the Union address, Congress is obliged to take them seriously.

None of this means that Congress is obliged to pass the president's legislation, however. Nor is Congress necessarily required to abandon its own members' legislative agenda. In other words, the president, having been allowed to state an agenda, the willingness of Congress to co-operate and to act is contingent upon a set of factors which can vary from one presidency to the next, or even from one year to the next. It is in regard to these contingent factors, then, that presidents must attempt to maximise their formal and informal powers to persuade.

The president as head of state

Although not officially designated as such, the president is the nation's head of state. In some sense, this role combines the political and legislative responsibilities of a prime minister with the ceremonial duties of a monarch. Astute presidents, therefore, will combine these two roles to make themselves more politically irresistible.

When presidents are acting as head of state, they represent, indeed personify, the nation. Because many Americans are highly patriotic, presidents can derive enormous prestige from their ceremonial appearances. Even a president who is not personally held in great esteem can benefit significantly from a good performance as head of state. President Clinton, for example, got a boost to his popularity when he led the nation in mourning over the victims of the bombing of a federal building in Oklahoma City in 1995. Happier occasions also permit the transfer of the nation's pride in itself to rub off on its political leader: a meeting with a foreign dignitary, such as the Pope or Queen Elizabeth; throwing the first ball in the final of baseball's World Series; speaking on air to American astronauts in space. None of these are political events in themselves, but the emotional response they generate in Americans may have the effect of making the people feel good about the leader who stands at their centre.

There are, of course, major political events where the president as head of state, or perhaps, chief diplomat, can shine. A president who holds a summit meeting with important foreign leaders is seen to be a powerful person, acting on behalf of the nation. If the occasion is a glorious one, such as President Nixon's visit to the People's Republic of China in 1972, or President Clinton's White House peace summit with the Palestinian and Israeli leaders in 1994, Americans will feel good about themselves and, probably, their president as well.

In short, as head of state, presidents may well be able to cloak themselves with the same aura of power, prestige and success that the American people identify as their nation's position in the world.

There are circumstances when the tendency of the people to identify the president with the nation can be damaging. This can occur precisely when the nation itself is seen to be unsuccessful and lacking in prestige. The inability to end the war in Vietnam wrecked the presidency of Lyndon B. Johnson; and Jimmy Carter's failure to bring the Iranian hostage crisis to a satisfactory conclusion dealt a major blow to his hopes for re-election in 1980.

Furthermore, it should be noted that foreign policy success alone will not ensure a president's popularity when it matters. Thus George Bush won enormous acclaim from Americans for his handling of the Gulf War in 1991 – and was then turned out of the White House in 1992 for his perceived failure to solve economic problems.

Some presidents are simply lucky or unlucky in the international and national circumstances in which they find themselves. Yet it is also true that some presidents are more adept than others in maximising their influence and power in such circumstances. One important factor in this respect is their use of the media, particularly television.

The president and the media

The media includes a range of print and broadcast outlets, but since the 1950s, it is television that lies at the heart of the relationship between politics and the media. This development has proved an enormous asset – although something of a liability too – for presidents in particular, because the American presidency seems to have been made for television.

As a visual medium, television is better suited to images than to words. This is as true of politics as of any other subject matter. This in turn means that television does not handle complex issues very well, while it excels in telling simple 'stories' which focus on personalities. Thus, of all America's political institutions, the presidency is by far the best equipped to give television what it wants.

While the presidency, like Congress, is composed of thousands of individuals, there is only one president. The presidency has a single public face and it is one which the public knows instantly. Quite simply, the public is more likely to pay attention to a story involving the president than to one involving, say, Congress or the Supreme Court, because the president is a familiar and prestigious person who is instantly recognised as the nation's political leader.

Because the public is likely to take more interest in stories involving the president, television is more likely to turn political stories into presidential stories. It is no accident that political news items, for example, frequently end with a reporter standing in front of the White House commenting on what the president has done or what the president might do.

Moreover, even those members of the public who are not the least interested in politics are often interested in the personal lives of presidents and their families in ways that no other political figure can hope to match. Like the British public and its fascination with royal tittle-tattle, the American public is interested in everything the president does, including the whole first family's taste in food, clothes or music. There is nothing too trivial about the president to be of interest to viewers, and television is only too delighted to give airtime to such entertaining vignettes.

Presidents, therefore, have a vital political ally in television if they can give it what it needs while simultaneously using it to their own advantage. It is widely agreed that Ronald Reagan demonstrated just how powerful an ally television can be to the presidency. In addition to his years of experience as governor of the largest state, President Reagan brought with him to the White House years of experience as a film and television performer. As well as necessary acting skills, however, Reagan had media advisers who ensured that every television appearance was carefully orchestrated, visually attractive and simple in message.

Reagan's media team knew that the media would follow the president wherever he went. By creating pleasing visual images embodying 'feel good' factors about America and the American people, they were virtually guaranteed that these would be transmitted to the public. They did not even mind when the visuals were accompanied by a rather critical commentary, since the public tends to retain the image rather than the words. As one analyst put it:

> The lesson is clear. Maintaining popular support means carefully controlling what is seen rather than what is said. To govern the nation means controlling the videos in the evening news.
>
> (Denton, 1988, p. 71)

The president and the people

Public support is the most important extraconstitutional asset that presidents can have, particularly when they are trying to persuade others to follow their lead. With the aid of television, the president has more completely emerged as 'the people's tribune'.

A new president comes into office with a national mandate. With a popular majority exaggerated by the electoral college system, the president has a better, or at least more obvious claim to speak for the people than any other office-holder.

Moreover, television gives presidents the ability to appeal directly to the people any time they wish. By staging a media event or simply by asking the major networks for time to address the nation, presidents can go right into the living-rooms of Americans and ask for their support and help. If the president can convince the people to contact their members of Congress, this can put enough pressure on the legislators to prove very persuasive indeed.

Of course, the president's reliance upon establishing a close relationship with the people through television is a double-edged sword, especially now that people have become so knowing and cynical about media manipulation. Television can be used by presidents, but it can also turn against them: they can become so dependent on this medium that they become vulnerable to media critiques and to public disenchantment. The experiences of Presidents Johnson and Nixon illustrate this most clearly among recent presidents. Even Ronald Reagan found himself unable to command network coverage of some of his performances. Presidents tend to enter into a Faustian bargain with television, the 'electronic Mephistopheles' (Hodgson, 1980), and eventually they can lose more than they gain.

The president as party leader

Because American political parties are comparatively weak, the fact that the president's party commands a majority in Congress or a majority of the state governorships does not translate into a guarantee of compliance with presidential wishes.

Nevertheless, party loyalty can play an important role in persuading others to follow the president's lead. Presidents have some formal control over their party in the country, in that they appoint the national chairman. Although the national party is far from being hierarchical, it can perform favours and distribute patronage to members and candidates in ways that earn their gratitude and perhaps loyalty.

As far as Congress is concerned, presidents can almost always rely upon their party leaders on Capitol Hill to introduce and to support the presidential legislative agenda. Neither these leaders nor the president can command the support of party members in Congress, however. For while these members would ordinarily prefer to support than to oppose their president, they will be defiant if they believe their own electorate is against the president's policy.

Nevertheless, adroit presidents will do their best to cultivate the loyalty of their party members in Congress by helping them out wherever possible. One of the simplest means of doing this is to invite the members (individually or in small groups) to the White House and have a photographer record the event. The legislators can then proudly display the photograph to their constituents, thereby demonstrating their power and importance as persons 'close' to the president. Or the president can agree to attend a member's fund-raising event, thereby ensuring a far larger turn-out than would otherwise have occurred.

Ultimately, presidents cannot depend on party loyalty alone to secure political victory: even when dealing with members of their own party they must persuade, in the absence of the ability to command. Yet presidents do at least usually begin with fellow party members' goodwill and predisposition to give support. Party loyalty, therefore, is a potential if not guaranteed weapon in the president's armoury.

Modern presidential power and failure

It is generally believed, and it is in some ways clearly true, that the presidency is now a more powerful office than it was in 1789. Historical developments at national and international levels have made the president the undisputed leader of the nation. In recognition of increased presidential responsibilities, Congress has provided the president with a hugely expanded staff, in both the White House Office and the Executive Office of the President more generally. In addition, as we shall see in the next chapter, the federal bureaucracy has grown enormously to further the duties of the executive branch of government.

Equally important, the president can usually command media attention and thus the attention of the ultimate repository of political power, the electorate. With the aid of expert media consultants, presidents can communicate directly with the American people and in this way create support for their political programmes.

In addition, presidents can use the prestige and patronage of their office to cultivate, cajole and even bully other political players into following the presidential lead. This is particularly true of fellow party members, but not exclusively so. Even members of the opposition sometimes need presidential favours and are by no means completely immune to either presidential charms or threats. For whatever the limitations, a call to action by the president of the United States carries a magical quality possessed by no other American politician.

Yet still the presidents fail. Domestic policy difficulties drive them to shore up their ratings with foreign policy successes, which seem easier to accomplish. Even those who survive into a second term seem to leave a disappointing record of achievement. Bill Clinton, for example, came into office promising not merely to introduce a comprehensive health care programme for all Americans, but to send the legislation to Congress within a hundred days of his inauguration. Yet despite two years of intensive discussion and planning, the Clinton administration did not even manage to send a bill to Congress, never mind produce comprehensive health care. For his part, President Reagan succeeded in his goals of reducing income tax and increasing defence expenditure, but only at the price of creating a budget deficit that threatened the long-term economic stability of the nation. Even before the Iran–contra scandal, his public approval ratings and legislative success rate had fallen.

Inadequate formal power or counterproductive informal power?

The first and most frequently offered basic explanation of the failure of modern presidents is that the office possesses insufficient formal power to make it effective. This explanation is cogent up to a point. As we saw at the beginning of this chapter, the president was not intended to act as chief legislator in the manner of a traditional monarch or even a modern prime minister. As a result, the presidency was quite consciously deprived of the formal means of playing those roles.

That remains the position today. No formal structural or constitutional change has taken place that enhances the power of the presidency.

In 1996, Congress – after intermittent discussion for several decades – agreed to grant to the president *line-item veto* authority for certain tax and spending bills ('entitlement' spending was excluded). This statute allowed presidents to veto particular items in bills rather than being obliged to sign or to veto the whole bill. In June 1998, the Supreme Court (in *Clinton v. City of New York*) declared this statutory provision to be unconstitutional, because Article I, Section 7 of the Constitution gives presidents the right to veto whole bills, not parts of them. Even if presidents were armed with a line-item veto, it is not clear that this would enhance their legislative role. They might instead simply become more deeply mired in the Washington insider bureaucratic struggles that make politics so alienating to many American citizens.

In certain respects, the president is worse off than ever in the contemporary period. Since the 1970s, allegations about criminal actions of presidents have been subject to searching investigations by independent counsels and special prosecutors appointed under provisions of laws enacted by Congresses jealous of energetic executives. This constraint on executive action has sometimes been vigorously pursued. Expansive and expensive investigations of the Iran-Contra scandal under Reagan in the 1980s and early 1990s, and of financial and sexual-legal scandals under Clinton during the later 1990s, helped to persuade many observers – left, right and centre – of the unwisdom of the independent counsel laws.

However, even if Congress were to loosen or to abolish such institutional constraints on presidents, there remain significant political constraints. For since the 1960s, the electorate has developed a taste for handing control of the White House to one party and control of one or both chambers of Congress to the other. This tendency to 'divided government' has further weakened presidents' already shaky hold on party loyalty as a means of achieving their goals.

Perhaps more important still, however, is the breakdown of the political consensus that at least made executive–legislative co-operation achievable in earlier periods. Presidents now often have to overcome not merely the institutional rivalry that the framers built into the constitutional scheme, but partisan hostility as well.

This tendency towards divided government is in part a result, and in turn one of the causes, of the tendency for modern presidents to depend on the informal sources of power. They are led to this 'public presidency' strategy by its promise to make them less dependent on deliberative co-operation and compromise with Congress, by the prospect of using public pressure to compel Congress to go along with them.

This leads to the second explanation of presidential failure. While informal or extra-constitutional developments have increased the potency of the presidency, they have been accompanied by other changes that counterbalance the advantage gained, and they often entail diminishing presidential stature. They have therefore produced a presidency of which much more is expected, yet to which little more has been given with which to achieve.

This second explanation of the failures of modern presidents does not emphasise the weaknesses of their formal constitutional position – indeed, it suggests that recent presidents, intent on developing their extraconstitutional roles, may have overlooked ways to use their constitutional powers as effectively as (for example) Jefferson, Jackson and Lincoln used them. This explanation emphasises instead the ultimately counterproductive character of their informal, more populist attempts to base their power on public opinion. Modern presidents have deployed this strategy much more frequently and casually than the protomodern presidents (Theodore Roosevelt and Woodrow Wilson) who invented it. They have found that using this less constitutional, more plebiscitary strategy tends to make even relatively successful presidents captives of popularity ratings, opinion polls, focus groups and television politics. Thus, while Ronald Reagan enjoyed success in his budget negotiations with Congress during his first year as president, he found it difficult to repeat this success in subsequent years because his strategy of 'going public' depended on the difficult task of constantly replenishing his supply of popular support (Kernell, 1986, chapter 5).

Moreover, even if 'public presidents' succeed in retaining their public connection and sympathy, they risk becoming more isolated from Congress, which resents being pressured by a public led by the president. In this situation, public posturing by both president and Congress can replace reasonable negotiations and co-operation between them.

Therefore, in many ways in the 'public presidency' universe, short-term successes are compatible with longer-term failures.

Strengths and weaknesses of the public presidency

It is certainly true that the new direct relationship that has developed between the president, the media and the people can be manipulated to promote presidential popularity. However, while this is of enormous benefit to the president in politics, it does not necessarily bring equivalent benefits for presidential governance or for longer-term perception of political success.

The distinction between politics and governance is an important one. Politics here refers to the contest for authority and power, with public opinion being the principal arbiter and measure of victory. Governance, however, is about how authority and power are used in actually running the country. While the two are closely related in some respects, they are also different in others.

A concrete example may help to illustrate the point. In 1995, the Democrat president Bill Clinton was engaged in a budget stand-off with the Republican-controlled Congress. At its worst, the federal government was obliged literally to shut down many of its operations through lack of funding. Eventually, President Clinton won the political battle, because a clear majority of the public came to blame Congress for the crisis. In particular, Clinton was able to portray the position of Congress as being inspired by an unreasonable desire to undermine precious entitlements, such as Medicare and social security. In doing so, the president cleverly drew on both his standing as the people's steward guarding their fundamental interests, and on his considerable communication skills. His main rival, the Republican Speaker of the House, Newt Gingrich, proved no match and emerged from the fight with his public standing greatly damaged.

However, while the president won a significant political victory and thereby secured a second term in office, he did little to enhance his power to govern. Although the Republican Congress was forced to give way on some details of the budget, it did nothing to dissipate its hostility towards the Clinton administration. Thus, in 1996, it was Congress that won the battle over welfare reform and in November that year, it was the Republican party that won a majority of seats in the House and Senate elections. Clinton had thus won a political battle, but not the right to govern on his own terms.

Except in conditions of major crisis, it may be doubted whether any president will be able to govern on anything like his or her own terms – by which, of course, is meant the terms on which they were elected to office. Modern presidents may certainly aspire to at least short-term popularity, but effective governance is likely to remain beyond their reach unless there is an unusually favourable configuration of contingent factors, or unless they can learn to exploit their constitutional powers more effectively and thereby gain more durable popularity as well as policy-making success.

 Summary

The Constitution created a presidency with great potential power, but Americans' republican principles and low expectations of federal government activity have often kept presidents' exercise of power limited in practice. One of the principal innovations of modern presidents, both liberal and conservative, is their great reliance on the public rhetorical possibilities of the office as a way of bringing public pressure to bear on congressional deliberations. It is not clear that this 'public presidency' strategy delivers as much as it promises to presidents who use it, but it seems difficult for them to use a more patient approach when so much is expected of them.

Topics for discussion

1. What are the most significant constitututional powers of the president?

2. What most decisively brought about the 'modern presidency'?

3. Is 'going public' a necessary strategy for contemporary presidents? Is it compatible with fidelity to the constitutional design of the presidency?

4. How has the end of the cold war changed the presidency?

Further reading

The presidency is discussed in *The Federalist*, nos 67–77; see especially nos 70 and 71. Godfrey Hodgson colourfully describes some of the dilemmas of the modern presidency in *All Things to All Men: The false promise of the modern American presidency* (New York: Touchstone, 1980). Samuel Kernell, *Going Public: New strategies of presidential leadership* (Washington DC: CQ Press, 1986) considers the difficulties of the 'public presidency' that has arisen since the Second World War. Both political and constitutional aspects of the presidency are studied in the essays in Joseph M. Bessette and Jeffrey Tulis (eds), *The Presidency in the Constitutional Order* (Baton Rouge: Louisiana State University Press, 1981) and in Sidney M. Milkis, *The President and the Parties: The transformation of the American party system since the New Deal* (New York: Oxford University Press, 1993). Terry Eastland makes a case for a rhetorically robust but more constitutionally based presidency in *Energy in the Executive: The case for the strong presidency* (New York: Free Press, 1992).

References

Bessette, J. M. and Tulis, J., eds, 1981, *The Presidency in the Constitutional Order* (Baton Rouge: Louisiana State University Press)

Boller, P. F., 1981, *Presidential Anecdotes* (New York: Oxford University Press)

Burns, J. M., 1965, *Presidential Government* (Boston: Houghton Mifflin)

Cunliffe, M., 1969, *American Presidents and the Presidency* (London: Erye & Spottiswoode)

Denton, R. E., 1988, *The Primetime Presidency of Ronald Reagan* (New York: Praeger)

Foley, M. and Owens, J. E., 1996, *Congress and the Presidency* (Manchester: Manchester University Press)

Hart, J., 1995, *The Presidential Branch* (2nd edn, Chatham, NJ: Chatham House)

Hess, S., 1988, *Organizing the Presidency* (2nd edn, Washington DC: The Brookings Institute)

Hodgson, G., 1980, *All Things To All Men: The false promise of the modern American presidency* (New York: Touchstone)

Kernell, S., 1986, *Going Public: New strategies of presidential leadership* (Washington DC: CQ Press)

Milkis, S. M., 1993, *The President and the Parties: The transformation of the American party system since the New Deal* (New York: Oxford University Press)

Neustadt, R. E., 1964, *Presidential Power* (New York: Mentor)

Ragsdale, L., 1993, *Presidential Politics* (Boston: Houghton Mifflin)

Rossiter, C., 1960, *The American Presidency* (2nd edn, London: Harcourt Brace & World)

14

The federal bureaucracy

The executive branch of the federal government includes a vast array of experts organised into departments and agencies. Their purpose is to serve the government, and especially the president, by providing specialist knowledge to policy-makers and by administering national laws and policies. However, some argue that the civil service has an uneasy and sometimes hostile relationship with the president and that it constitutes an unelected and independent source of governmental power. In this chapter, we examine how the federal bureaucracy came to occupy such a controversial position in American government and whether its critics are right.

The executive branch of the United States government employs almost 3 million men and women, that is, virtually one in forty of all Americans in work. While a large civil service is common to most modern societies, this is a remarkable number of government employees for a nation which prides itself on its individualism and its belief in limited government. Nevertheless, the phenomenal growth in the size and range of the federal bureaucracy since 1789 is no aberration. Rather, it has been a logical response to the increasing complexity of American society and the unrelenting growth in federal government responsibilities.

Main elements of the federal bureaucracy

The cabinet

Even in 1789, when George Washington became the first president of the United States, there was a clear recognition of the need for specialist departments within the executive branch. Washington's cabinet consisted of three department heads – state, treasury and war – and an attorney-general. Along with the postal service, these constituted the executive branch establishment.

Box 14.1

Government departments under President Clinton, 1995

Department	Number of civilian employees
State	24,869
Treasury	155,951
Defense	830,738
Justice	103,262
Interior	76,439
Agriculture	113,321
Commerce	36,803
Labor	16,204
Health and Human Services	59,788
Housing and Urban Development	11,822
Transportation	63,552
Energy	19,589
Education	4,988
Veterans Affairs	263,904

Source: US Bureau of the Census, 1996

Today there are fourteen departments (see Box 14.1), and their heads, or secretaries, form the core of the president's cabinet. As the number of employees in the departments indicates, cabinet secretaries are responsible for a wide number and variety of policy programmes. Indeed, along with the independent agencies and commissions (see below), the department secretaries administer some 1,400 federal programmes.

Beneath the department secretary, is an under-secretary and several assistant-secretaries. These top officials and other senior appointees, about 3,300 in total, are nominated by the president but require Senate confirmation (DiClerico, 1995, p. 165). While the president can usually rely upon getting his nominees confirmed, the Senate has developed a marked tendency in recent years to seize opportunities to reject nominees. Thus President Bush fought a losing battle to have former Senator John Tower confirmed as secretary of defense. The Senate was ostensibly concerned about Tower's alleged history of heavy drinking and womanising, but some observers believed that the Senate was simply engaged in a power play to undermine the president. In his first term, President Clinton had to withdraw his first two nominations for attorney-general because the nominees ran into serious trouble in the Senate over their failure to make social security payments for their domestic employees.

Presidential selection of cabinet secretaries

Presidents are free to nominate whomsoever they wish to cabinet posts. Most cabinet appointees either have strong political ties to the president's party or are respected for skills and expertise displayed outside the political arena. A president may well also take into account the likely reaction to an appointment from the main groups that deal with a particular department. Thus the president may appoint to the Treasury Department someone who is trusted and respected by bankers and the business community and to the Labor Department someone who is similarly appealing to unions. This would certainly explain President Clinton's first term appointments of the economically conservative Lloyd Bentsen at Treasury and the economically liberal Robert Reich at Labor. In these appointments, Clinton was trying to reassure the respective 'clients' of Treasury and Labor that the administration would be sympathetic to their interests and views.

President Clinton had yet another criterion in making his cabinet appointments. In an effort to consolidate his support among diverse sections of the community, he wanted a cabinet that 'looked like America'. This translated into a policy that became known as EGG – Ethnicity, Gender and Geography. Clinton kept his promise by appointing more women and members of ethnic minorities to his cabinet than any president before him. In his second administration, four cabinet posts went to women: Madeleine Albright as secretary of state; Janet Reno as attorney-general (Justice Department); Alexis Herman as secretary of labor; and Donna Shalala as secretary of health and human resources. Clinton also appointed the first Puerto Rican-born American to a position of cabinet rank when Aida Alvarez became head of the Small Business Administration.

When making cabinet appointments, then, the president combines political and practical criteria. Ideally, his appointees will obtain Senate confirmation with ease, earn the respect of those who deal with particular departments and also satisfy the president's supporters and the public at large. Of course, the president also wants his cabinet secretaries to further his goals and policies, in as far as he has any. As we shall see below, this can prove quite difficult.

The cabinet in operation

The American cabinet is a weak body in that it meets solely at the president's discretion and discusses only those topics that the president chooses to put before it. Furthermore it has no collective responsibility for the administration's policy. Thus, as Louis Koenig writes: 'The cabinet ... has rarely been a source of advice upon which the president continuously relies. It exists by custom and functions by presidential initiative and is therefore largely what the chief executive chooses to make of it' (Koenig, 1996, p. 188).

President Kennedy actually only held six cabinet meetings in three years, while President Nixon was of the view that 'No [president] in his right mind submits anything to his cabinet' (Pious, 1996, p. 277). Consequently the cabinet exists collectively only to serve goals of secondary importance, such as acting as a sounding board for new and possibly controversial ideas or for trying to co-ordinate public pronouncements on administration policy.

Individually, however, department secretaries can wield considerable influence over policy in their own area of competence and perhaps outside of it as well. This is likely to be the case when the secretary heads one of the more prestigious departments, such as State, Defense or the Treasury, or when he is a particularly valued adviser to the president.

Finally, some presidents have used subgroups of the cabinet as important policy-makers on particular clusters of issues. Thus the Reagan administration created 'cabinet councils', each with six to eleven cabinet members, to advise in areas such as economic affairs, natural resources and environment and food and agriculture (Whicker, 1990, p. 57). Some of these worked well, while others met infrequently and produced little of any value. Much of their effectiveness depends upon the ability of different cabinet members to co-operate without allowing 'turf fights' and egos to get in the way.

Ultimately, however, the cabinet amounts to far less than the sum of its individual parts. Department secretaries are highly important members of the executive branch, not because they collectively devise administration policy, but because individually they are responsible for carrying out administration policy on vital matters. In that sense, they are the real heads of the federal bureaucracy.

Independent agencies and commissions

While there are only fourteen departments, there are dozens of agencies and commissions within the federal bureaucracy. Some of these play an enormously important role in implementing government policy and regulating key areas of public business. Thus the Equal Employment Opportunity Commission (EEOC) has developed many of the policy guidelines which attack race and sex discrimination in employment; the Federal Reserve Board (the Fed) is a major influence in economic policy through its power to set interest rates; and the Federal Communications Commission (FCC) oversees broadcasting policy and sets national standards. Others are far more obscure, such as the American Battle Monuments Commission and the Physician Payment Review Commission.

Like department secretaries, the chairpersons of these agencies are appointed by the president. However, while secretaries can be sacked at will by the president, agency heads are usually appointed for a set term of office, something which gives them greater autonomy from the White House. As we shall see below, agency heads can thwart or even defy the president on policy by exploiting their independence and status.

Career civil service

The great mass of the federal bureaucracy consists of career civil servants. Their numbers grew steadily in the nineteenth century: while there were some 20,000 federal employees in the 1830s, this had more than doubled by the end of the Civil War to 53,000 and then reached 131,000 by 1884 (Garraty, 1968, p. 253). Moreover, serious problems had emerged regarding the professionalism of these employees.

Patronage and professionalism in the civil service

It had always been understood that the main role of the federal bureaucracy was to serve the president. For that reason, the president was given the power to appoint civil servants, even though the most senior of them, such as cabinet secretaries, were subject to Senate approval. However, under the presidency of Andrew Jackson (1829–37), the right to appoint civil servants became a crude power of patronage, with appointees receiving their public posts as rewards for political service rather than for their administrative skills or expert knowledge. This in turn led to a civil service that was often both inefficient and corrupt.

This deterioration in the quality of the federal bureaucracy reached its lowest point in the late nineteenth century. By this time, appointments were so thoroughly in the hands of corrupt party bosses that President Benjamin Harrison (1889–93) found himself unable even to select his own department secretaries. All the cabinet posts had literally be sold by the party bosses to pay the election expenses.

At a lower level of the federal bureaucracy, steps had already been taken to end corruption and cronyism. In 1881, President James Garfield had been assassinated by a disappointed office-seeker, creating an irresistible demand for civil service reform as a consequence. In 1883, the Pendleton Act (or Civil Service Reform Act) was passed. This 'classified' certain positions within the federal bureaucracy, subjecting applicants to competitive examination. The Act also created the Civil Service Commission to oversee recruitment, thus further undermining corrupt political control. Finally, the president was empowered to place further posts within the classified category, with the result that by the end of the century, roughly half of all federal employees were in classified positions (Garraty, 1968, pp. 257–8). The Pendleton Act may therefore be seen as the foundation stone of the modern American civil service, bringing genuine specialist knowledge and administrative skill to prominence within the federal bureaucracy.

The qualities of bureaucracy

As in most countries, there are unflattering stereotypes of civil servants in the United States. Sometimes they are viewed as slow and obstructive, sometimes as interfering and unappreciative of the needs of the 'real world'. Yet bureaucracy and civil servants bring valuable, even vital, qualities to American government. As theorists of bureaucracy from Hegel onwards have pointed out, these negative and positive attributes of bureaucrats are actually two sides of the same coin, so it is difficult to have the advantages of modern bureaucracy without the disadvantages.

The 'permanent government'

Unlike politicians who come and go, the federal bureaucracy brings a sense of permanence and continuity to American government. Many policy programmes transcend the terms of office of presidents and members of Congress and it is clearly important for those affected by the programme to know that its operation is not dependent upon the whim, inexperience or ignorance of incoming politicians.

Moreover, career civil servants constitute a governmental store of knowledge about issues, problems and programmes. No new presidential administration, however radical in intent, would wish or be able to redesign all the federal government's major policies. And even the most ambitious of administrations would still depend to a considerable degree upon the advice and assistance of the bureaucracy in formulating and, above all, implementing new policy.

Bureaucratic creativity and administrative law

The federal bureaucracy is no mere passive repository of expertise and experience. Frequently it plays a major part in legislating by filling in the details of congressional legislation. It is very common for Congress to write legislation in broad terms, leaving detailed 'guidelines' for the implementation of the bill to departments and agencies. This has created a mass of so-called administrative law (as opposed to the statutory law of Congress).

Administrative law can be highly creative. For example, when Congress passed the Civil Rights Act of 1964, it failed to define what it meant by 'discrimination' on grounds of race or sex. It was therefore left to the federal bureaucracy to determine exactly what constituted discrimination and what kinds of evidence would demonstrate its existence in any particular context. In the field of race discrimination in employment, it was the Department of Labor, through its Office of Federal Contract Compliance (OFCC), that initiated a policy of affirmative action to fulfil the aims of the 1964 Act. In 1968 and 1971, the OFCC issued guidelines which established numerical goals and timetables for the greater employment of minority group members in certain jobs; and then decided that a disproportionately low employment rate of such members in any occupation was proof of discrimination. Whether this was a good policy or not, it was undoubtedly a radical development from what Congress had in mind when it passed the basic legislation in 1964.

Bureaucratic rationalism and neutrality

As well as bringing collective knowledge and experience to bear on problems, the federal bureaucracy is also presumed to be rational in proposing solutions. More precisely, civil servants are supposed to discount political and partisan considerations and to give advice which is politically objective. Elected politicians rarely have the luxury of being able to avoid the demands of interest groups or public opinion, but, sheltered as they are from such political pressures, civil servants are expected to give their political masters neutral advice.

This expectation stems, of course, from the basic assumption that the federal bureaucracy is willing and able to serve political masters of differing political complexion. Even when the change from one administration to the next is unusually sharp, as when President Reagan replaced President Carter in 1981, the federal bureaucracy is supposed to serve the new as faithfully as it served the old. We shall see below, however, that this bureaucratic ideal of political neutrality is viewed with considerable scepticism by politicians, who see political motivations in the resistance to administration policy that they frequently encounter. For the moment, it is sufficient to note that there is solid evidence to suggest that Democrats greatly outnumber Republicans in the career civil service. Moreover, even those bureaucrats who define themselves as

Independents have political attitudes that are far closer to Democrat than to Republican philosophy (DiClerico, 1995, p. 166).

These statistics are not especially surprising, given the fact that the Democratic party has traditionally favoured governmental activism, while the Republican party has often attacked it. It is only logical that those who harbour a belief in governmental activism should be more likely to seek government employment than those who do not.

Controlling the federal bureaucracy

Having described the basic contours of the federal bureaucracy, it is now necessary to analyse the power that it wields: for if the ideal of the bureaucracy is of a body of disinterested experts, advising the president on policy matters and faithfully carrying out his wishes, the reality is significantly different.

Presidential control of the bureaucracy

Most presidents have found dealing with the bureaucracy to be one of the most frustrating aspects of their job. President Truman (1945–53) once commented that 'I thought I was the president, but when it comes to these bureaucracies, I can't make them do a damn thing'. Years later, President Carter indicated that things had not changed much: 'Before I became president, I realized and was warned that dealing with the federal bureaucracy would be one of the worst problems I would have to face. It has been even worse than I had anticipated' (DiClerico, 1995, pp. 163–4).

Bearing in mind that these were Democratic presidents experiencing difficulty in controlling the bureaucracy (see also Box 14.2), it is safe to assume that Republican presidents must expend even more effort if they wish to tame the bureaucracy.

Indeed, President Reagan entered office determined to do something to bring the bureaucracy under his control. He started at the top, making sure that his cabinet secretaries were ideologically sympathetic to his conservative goals. Then, instead of leaving the secretaries to select their own sub-cabinet top officials, the Reagan White House took control. They insisted that all secondary and tertiary positions in the departments were given only to those who had voted for Reagan, who were known Republicans and who were known conservatives (DiClerico, 1995, pp. 189–90). Moreover, President Reagan insisted that both cabinet and sub-cabinet appointees be briefed not by the permanent civil servants, but rather by White House staff indisputably loyal to the president.

Reagan had other plans for the career bureaucrats. The president had campaigned for office proclaiming that, 'Government isn't the solution: government is the problem.' Strongly opposed to 'big government' and what he considered to be intrusive bureaucracy, President Reagan quickly set about reducing both the number of civil servants in domestic policy agencies and departments and the number of federal regulations. He also made extensive use of the powers given to the president under the Civil Service Reform Act of 1978. This allowed him to reassign senior career bureaucrats who were classified as part of the senior executive service. Needless to say, some of

Box 14.2

President Clinton and the Federal Reserve Board

Early in his presidency, Bill Clinton learned the power of the bureaucracy of which he was the titular head. His Republican predecessor, George Bush, re-appointed his fellow Republican, Alan Greenspan, to a second term as chairman of the Federal Reserve Board in March, 1992. Because the chairman of the Fed served for four years and could not be sacked for political reasons, President Clinton was obliged to work with Greenspan for at least most of his first admin-istration. Clinton wanted to see a lowering of long-term interest rates, since this would help to fulfil his much-publicised promise to reinvigorate the economy and create new jobs. However, it is the Chairman of the Fed, not the president of the United States, who determines interest-rate policy. Clinton's advisers told him that Greenspan would only lower interest rates if the President introduced budget cuts, because only if the budget deficit were reduced would the stock exchange dealers in government bonds feel safe in lowering their rates. On hearing this,

> Clinton's face turned red with anger and disbelief. 'You mean to tell me that the success of the programme and my re-election hinges on the Federal Reserve and a bunch of (expletive) bond dealers?'

Source: Extract from Woodward, 1994, p. 84

these reassignments were made to undermine the power and influence of those deemed insufficiently supportive of the president's agenda.

President Reagan certainly gained increased control of the bureaucracy through making ideological sympathy and personal loyalty determining factors in appoint-ments. In other respects though, the degree of change he wanted was limited by the fact that his appointees necessarily were often lacking in experience and competence in administration (DiClerico, 1995, p. 192).

'Presidentialising' the bureaucracy

President Reagan was merely raising to a new level the process of 'presidentialising' the bureaucracy: that is, using his appointment power to try to bring the bureaucracy under closer political control (Rourke, 1991). Why should presidents have to work so hard to ensure the loyalty of the members of their cabinet and of the sub-cabinet and permanent civil servants?

Going native

As far as political appointees are concerned, there is always the fear in the White House that they will 'go native'. This means that, instead of imposing the president's agenda on the permanent bureaucracy, they come to share the bureaucracy's outlook and start to resist the White House. This can happen where the cabinet secretary or deputy secretary disagrees with presidential policy or simply believes that the civil service has a better policy. Or going native can occur simply as a result of the fact that political appointees to the bureaucracy spend far more time in the company of civil servants than they do with senior White House personnel. Little by little, the appointee becomes socialised by the culture of the department or agency.

The president may use the appointments process to try to minimise this, but he may also try to increase the involvement of White House staff in the departments and agencies. This can cause serious friction between presidential aides and civil servants, who resent interference from those they consider to lack the requisite knowledge and experience to make sound decisions.

Politicising the bureaucracy

There is a very fine line between strengthening presidential control of the bureaucracy and politicising the bureaucracy. It is possible to see President Reagan's actions as either an attempt to force the bureaucracy to follow his legitimate requests as its chief, or as an attempt to persuade the bureaucracy to become part of an ideological or partisan crusade. There is no bright line that separates policy making from policy implementation. Equally, it is difficult to identify the line between loyally serving an administration and abandoning the virtues of bureaucratic neutrality and professionalism. As is so often the case in US politics, there is a trade-off to be made between following the democratic imperative and searching for rational and effective policy.

Political versus bureaucratic values

Disputes between presidents and bureaucrats have their roots in one basic factor: the two have real differences in outlook. Presidents and their White House assistants see themselves as bearers of a democratic mandate. The president, as candidate, has presented his policies to the people and received their approval. He is therefore fully entitled to implement the policies he chooses. Even where there was no clear policy commitment during the election, the president has a mandate to use the power the people have given him to do as thinks best for the nation.

As democracy's champion, the president embodies what some see as the core values of democracy: responsiveness, direction and revitalisation. The values of the modern administrative state, however, are different; here the emphasis is upon continuity, professionalism, expertise and effectiveness. All of these values may be desirable but they are not always compatible. Thus a president will, quite reasonably, wish to demonstrate to his supporters that the government can respond to their needs and can be made to perform more economically. Bureaucrats, however, may not see the drive to satisfy a particular section of the electorate as a factor in producing a rational policy response to a problem; or a reduction in their capacity as a means to more effective administration.

Moreover, if presidents and other politicians are most likely to believe that their loyalty lies with the electorate, bureaucrats will tend to identify with their department or even with a particular programme operated by their department. It is not uncommon for senior civil servants to spend twenty-five or thirty years working within the same policy area. During that time they may acquire not merely a knowledge of the subject that greatly surpasses that of politicians, but also a belief that their programmes must continue for the good of the people. In that sense, politicians and bureaucrats can have quite different visions of what constitutes 'good' public policy.

Bureaucratic political resources

The differences of values that produce tensions between the president and the bureaucracy can, as we have seen, lead to a struggle between them for control of policy. The president can use his appointment powers and his White House staff as instruments of control. The bureaucracy, however, is by no means without its own resources in these power struggles.

The first and most obvious weapon of the recalcitrant bureaucrat is delay. This is particularly the case in the United States, where the president may serve only four or, at most, eight years in office. Simply by refusing to follow the spirit of the president's orders or by throwing up seemingly endless objections to proposed changes, civil servants may succeed in a waiting game with the White House.

Iron triangles

Beyond that, however, lies the fact that bureaucrats can and do build alliances with other political actors. Most notably, they form mutually beneficial relationships with committees in Congress and with interest groups. These 'iron triangles' are based upon the fact that all three elements have a common interest in a particular policy area or programme.

Congress and the bureaucracy

Throughout this chapter we have looked at the bureaucracy as if it were simply under the aegis of the president. Yet it is important to understand that Congress, as well as the president, has a significant measure of control over the bureaucracy. This means that the bureaucracy must seek to satisfy its congressional master, as well as the White House.

The principal instruments of congressional control of the bureaucracy are its general legislative power and its appropriations power – the 'power of the purse'. Congress uses its legislative power to create, abolish or merge departments, to inaugurate new programmes and agencies, and to fix terms of appointment and other structural details. It is true that Congress has ceded the initiative to undertake such reorganisations to the president in recent decades, but it retains the power to veto presidential reorganisation plans and to institute its own.

It uses its appropriations power to fund departments, agencies, programmes and, not least, civil servants. Since money is the oil that makes the machinery of government turn, the federal bureaucracy cannot afford to alienate its source in Congress.

Congress therefore establishes the structural and financial parameters of the federal bureaucracy, and presidential control must be exercised within those constraints. From the perspective of those who work for the federal bureaucracy, this makes the presidency their day-to-day manager, but it makes the Congress the manager upon whom they are ultimately dependent for their sheer existence.

Congress also has another major instrument of control over the federal bureaucracy: oversight. This is the right to investigate the operation of any part of the executive branch, and will normally include holding hearings and calling executive branch personnel to testify before a congressional committee. Depending on the outcome of the investigation, Congress may reward certain departments or programmes with better finance or more staff, or it may shut them down altogether.

There is, however, a two-way relationship between Congress and the bureaucracy. Bureaucrats seek funding, enlargement, programmes and discretion from the congressional committees with which they deal most closely. For the bureaucracy, discretion comes in the form of statutory language that it is simply broad or unclear. Either way, it gives bureau chiefs discretionary power to make important decisions.

Members of congressional committees also stand to gain from their relationship with the bureaucracy. Most importantly, they wish to ensure that programmes administered by bureaux bring benefits to their constituents back home. Most members of Congress seek membership of committees that deal with matters closest to the heart of their electorate. Thus those members who represent agricultural constituencies will want, first, membership of the Agriculture Committee and, second, membership of its sub-committees that deal with the particular branches of agriculture most important to the constituency's economy. Thus, if a bureau is responsible for distributing subsidies to dairy farmers, then members of Congress with a lot of dairy farmers in their electorate will want to ensure first, that the subsidies are large enough, and second, that 'their' dairy farmers get them.

We can see here the basis for a mutually supportive and beneficial relationship between members of Congress and the bureaucracy. In this example, both have an interest in maintaining and enhancing dairy subsidisation programmes, even if the president, in the interests, say, of budget deficit reduction, would like to reduce or eliminate them.

The third element in the 'iron triangles' is the interest groups and their paid lobbyists. With regard to the bureaucracy, lobbyists seek access to and influence over decisions made within the civil service. This can involve participation in the writing of administrative law or even in the appointment of particular individuals to key posts. In return, lobbyists will work to enhance the power and prestige of the bureau by testifying before Congress that it is doing a fine and important job, and by lobbying the president to the same effect.

As we saw in Chapter 12, interest groups and Congress have a strong relationship based on the need of lobbyists to gain access to those who legislate in their areas of concern and the need of members of Congress to obtain election campaign funds from interest groups and their political action committees. Thus, bureaux, congressional committees and interest groups have tight bonds of mutual self interest that can unite them against a president who wishes to make unwelcome changes. To put it another way, any president who tries to exercise total control over 'his' bureaucracy may soon discover a wall of resistance which is at times impossible to break down.

Issue networks

Iron triangles are accompanied by what Hugh Heclo has called issue networks (Heclo, 1978). These characterise the way that policies are debated in certain areas of economic regulation, especially in cases where federal agencies (for example, the Environmental Protection Agency) have economy-wide purview rather than being restricted to a certain segment of the economy (for example, farming). Issue networks are in one sense more democratic than iron triangles: they are more open and can involve many more participants. One becomes part of an issue network simply by becoming recognised as an expert in the field, somebody who needs to be consulted. Compared with iron triangles, issue networks are more amorphous, more complex, less predictable and less amenable to control. They are less reliable as building blocks of durable coalitions. They can be better at prolonging debate than at reaching decisions. So their appearance on the scene has complicated an already complex policy-making system.

Bureaucratic agencies involved in issue networks are subject to many pressures, and for that reason are, if anything, even less likely to be decisively influenced by either presidents or Congress. This newer pattern of policy making thus underlines many of the doubts that had already been raised about the role of bureaucracy in the American political system.

This is not to say that policy making always goes badly wrong, and that considerations of the long-term public interest are always left out of the equation. Indeed, the phenomenon of issue networks can be seen as a sign that ideas do matter in public policy (Reich, 1988), but the tendency towards short-term electoral bias in members of Congress, coupled with the equally self-interested behaviour and the limited outlook of bureaucrats, does make any upbeat portraits of the policy-making process somewhat optimistic.

Bureaucracy and effective government

We saw in the previous chapter that the president of the United States has many demands made upon him, but inadequate means of ensuring that he satisfies them. As chief executive, one might think that he could at least count upon the federal bureaucracy to carry out his wishes, but this is simply not the case. Just as the president must struggle to exert influence over Congress, so too he must treat the bureaucracy as a potential rival rather than a willing partner.

At first glance, this may seem a wholly regrettable state of affairs. How can the United States have good government if its chief political officer is thwarted even by those whose supposed reason for existence is to assist him? Nevertheless, there is another side to this situation. Koenig writes that:

> It is good for democracy but bad for an effective presidency – though by no means always for either – that the chief executive possesses a highly imperfect capacity to induce the vast officialdom of the executive branch to abide by his purposes and follow his directives.
>
> (Koenig, 1996, p. 181).

What Koenig has in mind here is that total presidential control of the bureaucracy could and sometimes does lead to presidential abuse of that power. President Nixon, for example, put pressure upon the Internal Revenue Service (IRS) and the Federal Bureau of Investigation (FBI) to aid him in his attempts to destroy those he considered his political enemies. A civil service that believed it had no means of resisting such unconstitutional demands could easily be turned into a weapon that undermined or even destroyed democracy.

As in other aspects of American politics, then, we must look at the bureaucracy through the perspective of the separation of powers and checks and balances. Effective government and democratic responsibility require that the president should be able to direct the bureaucracy and have it co-operate with his legitimate policy initiatives. On the other hand, effective government and democratic values also require that the bureaucracy not be left wholly vulnerable to a president animated by crass and even unconstitutional motivations.

In short, the fact that the federal bureaucracy in the United States possesses a measure of autonomous power is neither surprising nor unwarranted. However, the fact that its self-interest sometimes defeats the national interest as embodied in presidential policy is a genuine cause for concern.

Summary

We have seen that, despite its ideological opposition to 'big government', the United States has developed a vast federal bureaucracy. This bureaucracy brings considerable virtues to American government, especially expertise, experience, professionalism, political neutrality and continuity. However, the very size and authority of the federal bureaucracy make it difficult for the president, the supposed head of the executive branch, to control it. This is exacerbated by the ability of the bureaucracy to form alliances against the president with other political actors. The tensions that exist between the president and the bureaucracy give rise to conflicting and seemingly insoluble concerns about an ineffective presidency and an overpoliticised bureaucracy.

Topics for discussion

1. When is the bureaucracy justified in resisting presidential leadership?
2. Is bureaucratic professionalism compatible with democratic principles?
3. Are iron triangles a positive feature of American politics?
4. Is the federal bureaucracy too powerful?

Further reading

There are few books devoted solely to the bureaucracy which are appropriate at this level, but the best is Francis E. Rourke, *Bureaucracy, Politics and Public Policy* (Boston: Little, Brown, 1984). A useful collection of short essays about presidential/bureaucratic issues is James Pfiffner (ed.), *The Managerial Presidency* (Pacific Grove: Brooks/Cole, 1991). Three books which deal more generally with the presidency have excellent sections on the bureaucracy: Louis Koenig, *The Chief Executive* (6th edn, Fort Worth: Harcourt Brace, 1996); Richard Pious, *The Presidency* (Boston: Allyn & Bacon, 1996); and Richard DiClerico, *The American President* (4th edn, Englewood Cliffs: Prentice Hall, 1995). On the cabinet, see Anthony Bennett, *The American President's Cabinet: From Kennedy to Bush*, (Basingstoke: Macmillan, 1996).

References

DiClerico, R., 1995, *The American President* (4th edn, Englewood Cliffs: Prentice Hall)

Garraty, J., 1978, *The New Commonwealth* (New York: Harper & Row)

Heclo, H., 1978, 'Issue networks and the executive establishment', in *The New American Political System*, ed. A. King (Washington DC: American Enterprise Institute)

Koenig, L., 1996, *The Chief Executive* (6th edn, Fort Worth: Harcourt Brace)

Pious, R., 1996, *The Presidency* (Boston: Allyn & Bacon)

Reich, R., ed, 1990, *The Power of Public Ideas* (Cambridge, Mass. Harvard University Press)

Rourke, F., 1991, 'Presidentializing the bureaucracy: from Kennedy to Reagan', pp. 123–4 in *The Managerial Presidency* J. Pfiffner (Pacific Grove: Brooks/Cole)

US Bureau of the Census, *Statistical Abstract of the United States* (Washington DC, 1996)

Whicker, M., 1990, 'Managing and organising the Reagan White House', in *The Reagan Presidency*, eds D. Hill, R. Moore and P. Williams (Basingstoke: Macmillan)

Woodward, B., 1994, *The Agenda: Inside the Clinton White House* (New York: Simon & Schuster)

The legislative process

As we saw in Part IV, the office of the presidency looms large in the legislative process. Yet for all the importance of the presidency in proposing and drafting legislation, it is a basic fact of political life in the United States that only Congress can pass national laws. This means that the legislative efforts of the president, interest groups and, indeed, all political actors at the national level, must ultimately focus on the Congress.

In Part V, therefore, we examine the legislative power and role of Congress, especially in relation to the presidency (Chapter 15). We also examine the way Congress is organised and the impact that its internal structural and processes have on its legislative and other governmental functions (Chapter 16).

Contents

15

Congress and the president

Congress and the president are rivals for political power generally, and legislative power in particular. To a considerable extent, this rivalry is a 'zero-sum' game: any increase in the power of one player inevitably means a corresponding loss of power for the other. Nevertheless, as a responsible national legislature, Congress cannot simply devote itself to institutional self-preservation. It must pass laws to advance the national interest and, to do this, it needs to co-operate with the president. In this chapter, we trace the origins and development of this ambiguous relationship with the presidency and assess the contemporary balance of power between the two. We also ask whether Congress is any longer either willing or able to provide legislative leadership for the country.

Legislative power: the constitutional design

Legislative power is the power to pass laws. It lies, therefore, at the heart of the policy-making process and, indeed, is a central attribute of what we more generally call political power. Although the framers of the Constitution were concerned that no single institution should accrue too much political power, it is clear that they entrusted legislative power mainly to the Congress. True, the president was also given a role in the legislative process, but it was not until the twentieth century that he began to expand this role at the expense of Congress and to assume legislative leadership.

Legislative powers of Congress

Article I of the Constitution begins by stating that 'All legislative powers herein granted shall be vested in a Congress of the United States, which shall consist of a

Senate and House of Representatives'. Section 8 of Article I goes on to specify the particular powers which the framers wished to transfer from state legislatures to the federal legislature. Among the most important of these *enumerated powers* are the power to levy taxes; the power to regulate both international and interstate commerce; and the power to declare war. The general functions of Congress are set out in Box 15.1.

The framers did not intend that the new Constitution signify a general transfer of legislative power from the states to the Congress, hence, the detailed specification of the matters on which Congress was entitled to pass laws. The Tenth Amendment to the Constitution (1791) reinforced the fact that the legislative ambit of Congress was strictly limited by stating that 'The powers not delegated to the United States by the Constitution ... are reserved to the States respectively, or to the people'.

Nevertheless, legislative range of Congress *did* expand, thanks in particular to the doctrine of *implied powers*. The seeds of this were sown in the last paragraph of Article I,

---

Box 15.1

Functions of Congress

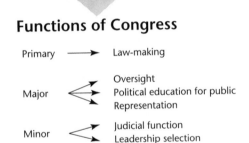

These are seven functions of Congress, categorised by their importance (Keefe and Ogul, 1993, p. 16). The primary and major functions are discussed in this chapter. The minor functions can be briefly summarised: the judicial function consists mainly of the role of Congress in the process of impeachment. This procedure allows for the removal of presidents and federal judges from office for 'high crimes and misdemeanours'. Rarely used, the most famous instance of impeachment came in 1974 when President Nixon resigned after the House Judiciary Committee investigating the Watergate scandal voted to indict him on three counts. Had Nixon not resigned at that point, the Senate would have acted as the 'jury' in his impeachment trial. In 1998, President Clinton faced the possibility as a result of a four-year inquiry into alleged financial and sexual misconduct.

The leadership function is an unwritten but important contribution to political life: it allows politicians to develop their skills and reputations, with the Senate in particular often providing a launch-pad for the presidency. In recent years, however, the Senate has produced vice-presidents rather than presidents. Thus, none of the last four presidents (Clinton, Bush, Reagan and Carter) served in the Senate, though three of their vice-presidents had done so (Gore, Quayle and Mondale). President Bush had also served in the House.

Section 8 of the Constitution. This entitled Congress 'to make all laws which shall be necessary and proper for carrying into execution the foregoing powers'. This was intended merely to enable Congress to use its enumerated powers, rather than to provide it with an additional, general grant of power. However, expansive interpretation of the 'necessary and proper clause' by the Supreme Court has allowed Congress to legislate on virtually any matter it wishes.

The key Supreme Court decision came early, in *McCulloch v. Maryland* (1819). Here the Court decided that 'necessary and proper' meant convenient, rather than indispensable, to the exercise of an enumerated power. Subsequent Court decisions, such as those legitimating the New Deal legislation of the 1930s, recognised the political reality that national problems required national solutions, even if this meant allowing Congress to encroach upon state legislative power as conceived by the framers in 1787. Consequently, 'Nowadays, so long as Congress's actions do not violate specific constitutional rights of individuals or interfere with Constitutional powers delegated by the Constitution to the president or federal courts, there is little that Congress wants to do that it lacks constitutional authority to do' (Peltason, 1988, p. 36).

Legislative powers of the president

As we have seen, Article I of the Constitution stated that Congress was endowed with *all* legislative power. This, however, is not quite true. Congress is indeed legislatively supreme to the extent that it alone can pass a law, yet the president was given a certain degree of both influence and actual power in the legislative process.

The power given to the president was negative power, in the form of the veto, for Article I, Section 7 of the Constitution requires that all bills passed by Congress must be signed by the president before they can become law. Moreover, it explicitly states that the president need not sign a bill if he has objections to it: instead, he can simply return the bill unsigned to Congress, stating the reasons for his veto. Congress can only override that veto by a two-thirds majority of both the Senate and the House. Mustering such a majority of both chambers is no easy matter and thus the presidential veto is a formidable weapon with which to counter the legislative power of Congress.

As well as this negative power, the president was invited by the Constitution to influence the legislative agenda of Congress. Article II, Section 3 instructs him as follows: 'He shall from time to time give to the Congress information of the state of the Union, and recommend to their consideration such measures as he shall judge necessary and expedient ...'. As the wording of the clause suggests, it was not intended that the president recommend legislation to Congress on a routine basis. Nevertheless, it does indicate an awareness on the part of the framers that Congress might not always be capable of providing the legislative leadership that the country needs.

These avenues of presidential intrusion into the legislature's domain are, of course, applications of the principle of checks and balances. Yet while the framers intended the president to be able to check congressional legislative power, they did not intend that he should be able to usurp it, for that would have violated that other cardinal principle of the Constitution, the separation of powers. Thus, the balance struck by the Constitution was one weighted heavily in favour of congressional dominance in the legislative field: 'It is clear that the original design was intended to give Congress the legislative authority that was, in fact, the power to determine national policy' (Wayne, 1978, p. 7).

Today, however, that balance of power has been largely reversed. To be sure, the constitutional framework has barely been altered with respect to legislative power. However, historical forces, interacting with institutional capacities, have engendered a transfer of substantial legislative power from Capitol Hill to the White House.

The changing balance of legislative power

In the eighteenth and nineteenth centuries, Congress dominated the legislative process. From time to time, a strong president such as Jefferson, Jackson or Lincoln might challenge that supremacy, but most presidents readily conceded that legislation was in essence a matter for the Congress. Furthermore, demand for national legislation was limited during this period and Congress had little need to seek help from the presidency in accomplishing its constitutional duties. In the post Civil War era, the presidency came close to being eclipsed altogether by a powerful and confident Congress.

Ironically, it was precisely at this zenith of congressional power that the socio-economic changes that were to undermine it were sweeping the nation. The Industrial Revolution eventually brought forth an unprecedented demand for national legislation. The federal government was asked to legislate on such matters as the regulation of the new giant corporations; on the conditions of work in factories; the problems of small farmers; public health and safety; child labour; trade union rights and a host of other pressing issues.

By the end of the Progressive era (1900–17), not only had a new legislative activism been generated, but the presidency had moved to centre-stage of the legislative process. President Theodore Roosevelt declared his office a 'bully pulpit' from which he could spur Congress into action. The other major Progressive president, Woodrow Wilson, became the first since John Adams to deliver his State of the Union address personally before the Congress. Moreover, he personally lobbied for bills on Capitol Hill and sometimes provided his supporters there with draft legislation (Wayne, 1978, p. 15).

What the Progressive period had demonstrated was that an activist federal government required a new level of presidential energy and initiative. Not only could the president personally dramatise legislative issues in a way that a collective body like Congress could not match; but, more important still, much of the new legislation required technical expertise that members of Congress simply did not possess. This was to be found rather in the federal bureaucracy, located within the executive branch.

These indications of an emerging new balance of legislative power between Congress and president became unmistakable – and irreversible – during the Great Depression of the 1930s. With the exception of the Civil War, the Depression was the greatest domestic crisis in American history. Industry and agriculture had all but collapsed, unemployment reached 50 per cent in some areas, and welfare provision was wholly inadequate. After enduring this misery for some three years under President Herbert Hoover, the country turned to Franklin D. Roosevelt for remedial action.

Roosevelt's first one hundred days in office are rightly famous for the flood of major legislation which he sent to Congress. What is particularly striking, however, is not merely the energy and ingenuity of the president and his advisers, but the reception given by Congress to this legislative bombardment. A body which had hitherto had the reputation of moving at a snail's pace, approved radical new proposals by huge majorities in a matter of days or, sometimes, hours. On some occasions, members had not even received copies of the legislation before voting for it. Moreover, when such legislation proved inadequate to the country's needs, members demanded still further legislative initiatives from the executive branch.

Roosevelt's New Deal saw more than mere legislative initiative pass from Congress to president. Many new bureaucratic agencies were created by the legislation, bodies such as the Securities and Exchange Commission, the National Labor Relations Board and the Social Security Administration. Having been set up with broad grants of power, these agencies proceeded to make detailed policy decisions on a routine basis. Such decisions amounted to the substantive exercise of legislative power, yet the agencies were located within the executive, not legislative, branch of government. The great expansion in bureaucratic structures and responsibilities under Roosevelt thus entailed a significant diminution in the legislative power of Congress relative to that of the presidency.

The New Deal years witnessed a transformation in the expectations of the presidency. Henceforth, the nation, including Congress, would look to the president and his advisers for the solution to the problems it faced. After Roosevelt, presidents would be measured by their ability to generate legislative proposals and support for them in Congress. For its part, the legislative role of Congress now was in essence to approve, amend or disapprove the president's proposals. It is almost as if the constitutional roles have been reversed: the role of Congress is to check and balance the president's legislative power by 'vetoing' legislation it thinks unwise or undesirable. While such negative legislative power is important, it provides no basis for Congress to supplant the presidency in legislative leadership.

Events since the 1930s have generally had the effect of enhancing the legislative dominance of the presidency. Most importantly, the emergence of the United States as a world superpower has maximised the foreign policy powers inherent in the presidency. However, in the field of domestic affairs too, the sheer volume of legislation, combined with an ever greater need for technical expertise, has also made presidential leadership the central feature of the legislative process.

This presidential aggrandisement begs the question of how Congress has responded to the erosion of its power and what role it is left to play in the legislative process today. Above all, we need to examine the reasons for its decline and the likelihood of Congress ever recapturing its former pre-eminence.

Congress today: mandate and the legislative agenda

In the early autumn of 1993, the *Congressional Quarterly* looked forward to the legislative battles ahead. It noted that President Clinton was in an inherently weak position, having been elected the previous November by a plurality rather than a majority of the voters. Yet, it reported,

> this fall's legislative calendar is a reminder of Clinton's power to determine what Congress fights over – even if he lacks the clout to control the outcome. Congress's agenda for the rest of the year is jammed with White House proposals on trade, health care and other domestic policies.
>
> (*CQ Weekly Report*, 4 September 1993, p. 2295)

Even a relatively weak president, then, sets the legislative agenda of Congress. Put another way, Congress has lost the capacity and the will to determine the legislative priorities of the nation. This has come about for a number of reasons. First, there are causes which arise from the electoral characteristics of Congress.

Electoral factors in congressional decline

While Congress contains members from all parts of the nation, it is not, in important respects, a truly national body. Each member of Congress is elected by a discrete, local electorate. Even the two senators elected from the same state are usually chosen in different years, when issues and political moods may well be quite distinct. Moreover, those seeking election to Congress are not normally bound by a common set of policies or manifesto, or, indeed, by strong party or ideological loyalties. An attempt to overcome this weakness occured in 1994, when most Republican candidates for the House of Representatives signed up to the Contract with America. It was ultimately unsuccessful, however, either in attracting the attention of the public, as opposed to the media, or in legislative achievement (see below, p. 333).

All this means that congressional elections are in essence local elections, fought on local issues, with candidates offering themselves as representatives and guardians of local interests. As a result, when those elected on such a basis gather in Washington, they can scarcely claim to represent a national constituency or be in possession of a national mandate. In this sense, Congress as a whole is not much greater than the sum of its parts.

This is not to suggest that members of Congress have no concern with national issues or no idea of the national interest; nor indeed does it mean that Congress cannot influence the legislative agenda or take important legislative initiatives. Yet, in the end, members of Congress owe their election – and re-election – to their ability to represent their local constituents' interests, rather than those of the nation, and local and state interests are not only different from the national interest, they may actually conflict with it. For example, members from tobacco-growing areas may well feel bound to oppose proposed limitations on cigarette advertising, even while they concede that a reduction in smoking would be in the national interest. Another example of such a conflict of interest was visible in 1993 when President Clinton's budget deficit reduction proposals included a tax increase on petrol. It surprised no one that some of the most vehement opposition to the measure came from members of his own party who represented states with major oil interests. Even with his presidency on the line,

Clinton could not win the support, for example, of Senators Bennett Johnson of Louisiana and Dave Boren of Oklahoma.

In short, Congress stands accused of *parochialism*, a narrowness of vision and a self interest which gives priority to local concerns over those of the nation. This parochialism may lead Congress to behave in a frankly irresponsible manner. In 1985, for example, it passed the Gramm–Rudman–Hollings Act, which proposed to eliminate the national budget deficit by 1991. Such a rapid elimination of the deficit necessitated some very tough choices on spending cuts. Knowing its own limitations, Congress provided that where cuts could not be agreed among its members, the comptroller general should make across-the-board cuts. When this procedure was later declared unconstitutional by the Supreme Court, Congress amended the Act to give the responsibility for making the cuts to the Office of Management and Budget. Why was Congress so willing to yield its power to others? 'No mystery surrounded the rationale for this provision. By opting for automatic, across-the-board cuts, thus relinquishing its budgetary authority, Congress sought to protect its members from having to go on the record by voting for painful spending cuts that were sure to be felt in the constituencies' (Keefe and Ogul, 1993, p. 10).

This parochialism contrasts with the national outlook, standing and responsibility of the president. He is chosen by a national constituency, all voting on the same day and on the same set of contemporary issues. Although, as we saw above with President Clinton, his claim to represent the nation may be undercut by the size of his majority, he may nevertheless genuinely claim to be the main embodiment of the nation's concerns and policy preferences. Quite simply, he has a mandate from the nation which Congress cannot rival. Along with this mandate comes a responsibility which cannot easily be shirked. He is therefore entitled to establish the legislative agenda and take the initiative in drafting legislation.

Institutional factors in congressional decline

In relation to the presidency, Congress has serious institutional weaknesses which inhibit its ability to provide legislative leadership. These weaknesses stem from disadvantages in both organisation and capacity.

Bicameralism

The internal organisation of Congress leads to a fragmentation of power that makes legislative coherence extremely difficult. In one basic respect, this fragmentation has its roots in the Constitution. The framers decided that Congress should be a bicameral body, composed of two chambers with more or less equal legislative power. By stipulating that all bills must be approved by both chambers in identical form, they established the possibility that one house could negate the legislative initiatives of the other. This potential for inter-chamber conflict was made all the greater by designing different electoral bases for the House of Representatives and the Senate. Even after the passage of the Seventeenth Amendment in 1913, when the Senate joined the House in being directly elected, the different electoral cycles and types of constituency represented by the two ensured that they would often have distinctive or opposed priorities.

This constitutionally ordered fragmentation of the Congress contrasts with the unitary design of the presidency. Furthermore, Congress established internal structures which only exacerbate the problem.

Committee power

One of the conditions for providing leadership *outside* of Congress is effective leadership *within*, yet the committee structure of Congress makes coherent, unified policy leadership difficult to achieve. As we shall see in detail in the next chapter, Congress carries out its legislative tasks by delegating substantial authority to specialist committees. Although each chamber as a whole must approve any bill, that approval is often a formality, a largely unproblematic ratification of the decisions taken by the committee. Moreover, power is fragmented still further by the fact that committees in turn delegate considerable power to their subcommittees. The practical result is that, on most occasions, the subcommittee recommendation is accepted by the full committee and the full committee recommendation is accepted by the chamber as a whole.

Unsurprisingly, then, congressional committees and subcommittees are frequently spoken of as 'little legislatures'. As long ago as the late nineteenth century, Woodrow Wilson observed that 'Congress in session is Congress on public exhibition, whilst Congress in its committee rooms is Congress at work' (Bailey, 1989, p. 103).

From the very beginning, members of Congress were aware that the use of committees threatened to disperse and undermine the power of Congress as a whole. They sought, therefore, to limit the lifetime and autonomy of committees. However, as the nineteenth century wore on, an increasing legislative workload, combined with an increasing membership of both chambers, made division of labour a necessity (Smith and Deering, 1990, p. 28). Thus, for mainly practical reasons, the structure of legislative power became more fragmented than had originally been deemed desirable.

Leadership and party weakness

At one time, this fragmentation of power towards committees was compensated by strong party leadership, particularly in the House of Representatives. The key figure here was the Speaker. At first little more than a formal presiding officer, the Speaker, chosen by the majority party, gradually accumulated important powers. The most significant of these was control over appointments to committees, including the committee chairs. Moreover, the Speaker personally chaired the House Rules Committee, which in effect determined which bills would progress and which would not. The Speaker was thus in a position to make or break a legislator's career, by determining both his committee service and the fate of his (and his constituents') legislative preferences. 'By the turn of the twentieth century, the Speakers' powers were almost complete, their hegemony virtually unchallenged' (Keefe and Ogul, 1993, p. 275). In short, there was a centralised authority in the House.

Eventually, however, members rebelled against this control of their interests and careers. A series of decisions in 1910–11 stripped the Speaker of some of his most important powers, including his right to make committee assignments and his position on the Rules Committee. This inevitably resulted in a fragmentation of authority, which persists to this day.

As for the Senate, it has never experienced the kind of centralised power that the House once knew. It has been noted that 'senators tend to regard themselves as unregimented ambassadors from their states' (Bailey, 1989, p. 154). They are, therefore, most reluctant to subordinate themselves to others and expect to be treated as a co-equal by those at the head of the party.

Although there has been some strengthening of party discipline in recent years, party leaders have little control over members who wish to go their own way. Both the House and the Senate have a hierarchy of party leaders and whips (see Chapter 16), but as former senator Alan Cranston put it: 'A lot of leadership is just housekeeping now. Occasionally you have the opportunity to provide leadership, but not that often. The weapons to keep people in line just aren't there' (Keefe and Ogul, 1993, p. 272).

Without an effective and coherent internal leadership, Congress is simply incapable of either putting together a legislative agenda or ensuring that an agenda is acted upon. Such leadership as Congress recognises, therefore, must come from outside and that means first and foremost, the presidency (see Box 15.2).

A further disadvantage of the Congress is its relative lack of specialised knowledge compared with the presidency. As we saw in the previous chapter, the president is the head of a vast federal bureaucracy, employing thousands of specialists on every aspect of likely legislation. Whenever a problem arises, then, the president is well placed to ascertain its origins and scope and to draw up legislative proposals accordingly.

Members of Congress are in essence amateurs in policy matters, although they may

---

Box 15.2

Legislative power

Presidential advantages	Congressional advantages
■ Can recommend laws	■ Exclusive right to pass laws
■ Veto	■ Veto override
■ National constituency	
■ National mandate	**Congressional disadvantages**
■ National perspective	■ Local constituencies
■ Unitary structure	■ Local mandates
■ Unitary authority	■ Parochialism
■ Bureaucratic expertise	■ Bicameral division
	■ Weak internal authority
Presidential disadvantages	■ Fragmented committee power
■ No power to pass laws	

have a measure of expertise in one or two areas, thanks to previous careers and service on specialist committees. Nevertheless, they can rarely match the bureaucratic experts.

Since the 1970s, Congress has taken steps to establish its own bank of policy specialists in an attempt to reduce its dependence upon executive branch expertise. It established new specialist support agencies, such as the Office of Technology Assessment (1972) and the Congressional Budget Office (1974), and doubled the staff of existing agencies like the Congressional Research Service and the Government Accounting Office. Furthermore, between 1970 and 1986, the number of committee staff increased by 250 per cent and the personal staff of members by 60 per cent (Mezey, 1989, p. 133).

While these changes have undoubtedly provided Congress with an independent source of expertise and information, it is by no means clear that they have enabled Congress to perform its legislative tasks any better. Critics have argued, for example, that increased support personnel means that legislators spend more time on managing their staff than deliberating on public policy. Moreover, it is the staff who in effect perform many of the legislative tasks previously done by members. Thus, 'A recurrent complaint is that staffs have encroached on the members' role in policymaking' (Keefe and Ogul, 1993, p. 201).

Other critics argue that the Congress has proved incapable of making good use of the information now available to it. Most notably, Congress tends to ignore information which suggests policies that might conflict with political considerations, such as constituency interests (Mezey, 1989, p. 134).

It would be a mistake to think that the president is wholly free of these electoral and institutional weaknesses that bedevil congressional leadership. Nevertheless, whatever its own failings, the presidency is more unified, better resourced and more nationally focused than the Congress. The cumulative impact of these advantages, at a time when more – and more complex – national legislation is deemed desirable, is that the president must lead. Consequently, Congress is left only with what Arthur Maas has called leadership reserve. Congress may still exercise leadership, but only when the president chooses not to lead himself. Such leadership reserve can only be exercised episodically, says Maas, because Congress lacks the will and capacity to do so on a regular basis. 'Furthermore, the president is free at any time to include any subject in his programme and thereby to be the leader. The Executive always has the resources for this. As a general rule, whenever the president is disposed toward leadership, it is his to be had' (Maas, 1983, p. 14).

However, the fact that the president may choose to lead at any time does not mean that the Congress is bound to follow.

Congressional co-operation and resistance

It is worth emphasising that this fundamental shift in legislative power from the Congress to the presidency was accomplished without any significant formal change in the constitutional structure. The president is now expected to do far more than in 1787, but there has been no constitutional recognition of the fact. Congress, then, retains 'all legislative power'.

Many have recognised what Godfrey Hodgson called this 'paradox of presidential power'. In terms of practical politics, it means that the president is powerless to command Congress to act. All he can do is urge, bully, cajole, woo and induce legislators to pass his proposals. In the famous phrase of Richard Neustadt, presidential power is 'the power to persuade' (Neustadt, 1960). If so, then the legislative power of Congress can be described as 'the power to refuse'. For in the final analysis, Congress, or even just one of its chambers, retains the autonomy to refuse the president outright or to amend his proposals out of all recognition.

For any legislation to pass, therefore, Congress and the president must co-operate. Yet co-operation is not easily achieved. As we have already noted, the president and members of Congress operate on different electoral cycles and are answerable to different constituencies. In other words, over and above any policy differences, they do not necessarily share the same legislative interests in terms of political survival.

Congressional–presidential liaison

Congressional liaison is one of the most important aspects of the modern presidency. To a significant extent, a president's legislative success or failure turns upon the skill of his liaison staff in operating the politics of persuasion. As John Hart put it:

> The congressional relations staff act as the president's eyes and ears on Capitol Hill, as lobbyists, as providers of vital services to members of Congress, and sometimes as policy advisers inside the White House.
>
> (Hart, 1987, p. 111)

This last point can be crucial, since Congress will usually take more notice of White House liaison staff who are able to speak for the president.

Nevertheless, both liaison staff and members of Congress have no illusions about the extent to which their real differences of interest can be ignored. Larry O'Brien, chief of congressional liaison under Presidents Kennedy and Johnson, and one of the most skilful practitioners of his art, put it this way: 'I never expected any member to commit political suicide in order to help the President, no matter how noble our cause. I expected politicians to be concerned with their own interests; I only hoped to convince them our interests were often the same' (Wayne, 1978, p. 155).

Party ties

In many political systems, party is the mechanism which links the executive to the legislature, but, as we saw in Chapter 11, parties in the United States are relatively weak. Presidents cannot simply assume that members of their own party in Congress will support them, as President Carter discovered. Although there was a clear Democratic majority in both houses of Congress, the Carter administration proved inept at mobilising party support there. As a result, some of his most important legislation, such as his energy bill, was badly delayed, significantly amended or quite simply dumped.

Weak parties do present some advantages to the president. Most obviously, a president whose party is in the minority in one or both chambers of the Congress can make an ideological or pragmatic appeal to members of the other party. President Reagan was able to do this in 1981 in persuading the House of Representatives to pass his tax and budget proposals. Although the Republicans were in the minority, enough conservative Democrats supported the president to ensure his success.

Nevertheless, party *is* one of the levers a president has in trying to persuade Congress to act, and so he will, if wise, make a considerable effort to liaise with his party's congressional leadership. For their part, party leaders in Congress do generally see one of their most important duties as maximising support for (or opposition to) the president's legislation. The Speaker of the House of Representatives and the majority and minority leaders and whips in both chambers are right in the middle of executive–legislative relations. If of the same party as the president, they will represent his wishes to fellow party members. In turn, however, the members also expect their leaders to represent their views to the president. Party leaders are thus engaged in a fine balancing act. They must avoid being seen as someone who fails to defend the interests of the institution and membership to which they themselves belong (Keefe and Ogul, 1993, pp. 270–1).

Even if they wished to do so, party leaders have little power to compel members to follow the party line. Party leaders can be helpful to a member in her daily work, providing information or useful contacts, even assisting her to get a desired committee assignment or legislative favour. In principle, therefore, they could withdraw such assistance. In practice, however, they are not likely to push her too hard if she has good grounds for opposing the party line. As former majority leader (and later, Speaker) Jim Wright put it: 'The majority leader is a conciliator, a mediator, a peacemaker. Even when patching together a tenuous majority, he must respect the right of honest dissent, conscious of the limits of his claims upon others' (Keefe and Ogul, 1993, p. 269). As always with members of Congress, those with the strongest claim are the constituents whose votes sent her to Washington.

In fact, on some occasions, these claims are so strong that even the party leaders do not follow the party line. President Clinton experienced this in 1993, when he was trying to secure passage of the North American Free Trade Agreement (NAFTA). This eliminated trade restrictions between the United States, Canada and Mexico. Its opponents believed that whatever economic benefits it might bring, it would certainly entail the loss of manufacturing jobs in the United States, since companies would move to Mexico in pursuit of cheap labour.

Among those leading the fight against NAFTA were House Majority Leader Richard Gephardt (Missouri) and House Majority Whip David Bonior (Michigan). Thus the two House Democrats who ranked behind only the Speaker in the party's congressional hierarchy, found the pull of constituency interests to be greater than loyalty to their party's president.

It is not altogether surprising, then, that presidents are by no means guaranteed passage of their legislative proposals, even when they have given a clear lead and their party controls both houses of Congress. As Box 15.3 indicates, however, presidents whose party do not control Congress are at a disadvantage, as are those in their second term of office and therefore in the process of becoming 'lame ducks'.

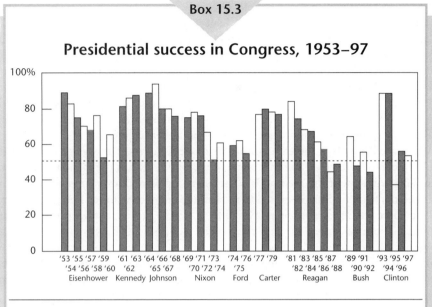

Box 15.3

Presidential success in Congress, 1953–97

Definition

How often the president won his way on roll call votes on which he took a clear position.

1997 Data

Senate
45 victories
18 defeats

House
29 victories
46 defeats

Total Clinton success rate **53.6%**

The graph shows how often Congress supported the president on roll call votes on which he took a clear position. Some caution must be shown in comparing presidents, since a higher support rate could indicate simply that a president did not take clear positions on controversial issues.

Source: Adapted from *CQ Weekly Report*, 3 January 1998, p. 14

Congressional support for presidents

Many factors help to explain why Congress supports some presidents more than others. Most obviously, a majority of members will support a president when they believe that his proposals are likely to solve a particular problem in an appropriate and successful manner. In these instances, Congress and president are of the same mind and there is relatively little need for either to draw upon its 'heavy guns'.

What about those instances where there is no easy agreement to be reached? This is often the case when controversial or difficult legislation has been proposed. What are the factors that come into play when members of Congress are reluctant to support the president, but he is determined to secure passage of his legislation? What induces members to vote for legislation when appeals to ideology, party and the public interest have failed?

As with most aspects of the congressional process, the electoral connection is vital here. The president has a number of carrots and sticks with which he can win over recalcitrant members by supporting or threatening their chances of re-election.

Where a bill involves the expenditure of money, the most powerful inducement a president can offer is to ensure that some of it will be spent in the member's district or state. This will benefit the member's constituents by providing them with jobs or services and make them more disposed to re-elect the member who secured these benefits.

If no direct material benefit is available, a president can confer prestige upon a member. Thus, in order to win the crucial support of Representative Marjorie Margolies-Mezvinsky (D–Pennsylvania) for his 1993 deficit-reduction bill, President Clinton promised to hold an important conference in her district in order to help overcome any constituent backlash against her support for the president. In this case, it did not work, and Margolies-Mezvinsky lost her seat in 1994.

Presidents can also grant access to the White House to a member and, perhaps, some of her constituents. The visit can be publicised back home, as can a photograph of the event signed by the president. All of this can be used to convey the impression that the member is an important and influential player in national politics.

As well as being able to confer material benefits and prestige, a president can also offer his services during the member's re-election campaign. A member facing a strong challenge at the next election is grateful to a president who can use his influence to ensure a successful campaign. It appears that the vote of Senator Dennis DeConcini (D-Arizona) on the 1993 budget bill was won by an offer to swing the Democratic National Committee (DNC) behind the senator in his 1994 primary battle. DeConcini believed that the support among Democrats that the president and the DNC could mobilise outweighed any damage that might be caused by reversing his previous pledge to oppose tax increases.

A president can also refuse to provide such services as those discussed above, thereby turning carrots into sticks. In addition, however, he can directly bring pressure to bear by appealing over the heads of members to their constituents. President Reagan used this tactic to considerable effect. The basic method was to appear on television, present his proposals and then ask all the viewers who wanted to see them passed to call or write to their members of Congress to urge them to support the president. Members who were subsequently inundated with tens of thousands of letters and calls would thus feel the electoral heat and perhaps think twice about defying a popular president. In other words, a president on occasion will challenge members for the loyalty and support of their constituents.

The legislative power of Congress, then, is severely constrained by institutional weaknesses and outside political pressures. Initiative and leadership have passed to the executive branch. As we saw in Chapter 12, pressure groups and PACs contribute vital funds to members at election time and make legislative demands on the back of them.

The president expects support for the policies for which he believes he has an electoral mandate. Party leaders expect solidarity. Above all, constituents expect members to serve their interests. A member of Congress has to steer her way through all these often conflicting pressures, try to produce effective legislation and secure her own re-election.

The balance of evidence suggests that it is the constituency service/electoral needs axis which generally determines congressional behaviour. What suffers as a result is the performance and reputation of Congress as a deliberative body, legislating for the national good. Thus, it is frequently observed that there is a marked difference between the attitudes of voters to, on the one hand, Congress as a whole and, on the other hand, to their particular representatives and senators. In recent decades, opinion polls reveal that, on average, less than one-third of the public approves of the way Congress is doing its job. In 1990, the number of those approving dropped to just 23 per cent (Keefe and Ogul, p. 14), although a steady improvement beginning in 1996 saw approval ratings in one poll reach the dizzy heights of 47 per cent in January 1998 (Washington Post/ABC News poll, January 1998).

These figures contrast noticeably with much higher approval ratings for individual members of Congress. Thus the same Washington Post/ABC News poll of January 1998 had 74 per cent of respondents approving of the job being done by their own member of the House of Representatives and 68 per cent believing that their Representative deserved to be re-elected.

It seems, therefore, that the American public tends to believe that the main purpose of Congress is to represent in a narrow sense the interests of members' constituents, leaving it primarily to the president to represent and lead the nation. This supposition was, however, challenged by the so-called Republican Revolution of 1994.

The Republican 'Revolution' of 1994

In 1994, the Republican party captured the House of Representatives for the first time since 1952. It also captured a majority in the Senate. Even more impressively, the Republicans held onto the House (and the Senate) in 1996, thus winning consecutive House majorities for the first time since 1928.

Under the aggressive leadership of Newt Gingrich (R–Georgia), the House Republicans fought the 1994 elections in a manner that sought to remedy some of the longstanding weaknesses in congressional power described above. Thus they attempted to overcome the parochialism of both congressional elections and congressional legislative activity by 'nationalizing' their approach.

The Contract with America

Gingrich was determined that the House Republicans should fight the 1994 elections on the basis of a common manifesto which, if successful, would provide a mandate for party unity and legislation in the 104th Congress (1995/96). A media event was staged on the steps of the Capitol in which some three hundred Republican candidates for the House signed a pledge to act on a series of key legislative items within a year.

In some respects, the Contract with America was a gimmick. Thus while House

Republicans may genuinely have intended to act in united and determined fashion on an agreed agenda of measures, this could by no means guarantee that those measures would become law. First, the Republicans in the Senate made no commitment either to support the House legislative agenda or to heighten party unity. Secondly, even if the two chambers of Congress could produce an agreed bill, there was every possibility that the Democrat in the White House would veto it. In short, the Contract with America stood little chance of performing the functions of a manifesto and legislative agenda in any real sense.

Furthermore, it appears not to have made much of an impact upon the American electorate. A survey undertaken at the time of the 1994 election revealed that 71 per cent of voters had never heard of it. Moreover, while 7 per cent said the Contract was more likely to make them vote Republican, 5 per cent said it was less likely to do so (Jacobson, 1996, p. 209). On the other hand, although voters may not have been able to recall the contract itself, it is possible that it helped Republicans to establish their campaign themes more clearly in the public's mind (Hershey, 1997, p. 208).

Moreover, the contract did have an effect on House Republicans, making them more willing to act in unified fashion and more amenable to strong party leadership from the new Speaker, Newt Gingrich. However, to a significant degree, this proved unsustainable. While stronger partisanship and greater ideological coherence enabled House Republicans to fulfil the contract pledge in so far as they brought their main legislative proposals to a vote in the House, none, with the exception of major welfare reforms, had been enacted into law as the 1996 elections approached. In part, this was because traditional factors inhibiting the effectiveness of Congress reasserted themselves to a greater or lesser extent.

First, the conservative ideological drive of the majority of House Republicans tended to alienate the small but potentially important moderate wing of the party, especially on items that were not in the contract. For example, in 1995 the Republican leadership attempted to undermine existing environmental protection laws, but thereby caused a sufficient number of moderate Republicans to vote with the Democrats to defeat their party's proposals (Hershey, 1997, p. 212).

Predictably enough, the Senate Republicans declined to follow the lead of their House colleagues. As we shall see in the next chapter, senators are far less willing to submit to party discipline or centralised leadership than members of the House. Therefore while House Republicans rejected traditional bargaining and compromise with those who disagreed with them, Senate Republicans were more realistic.

The real war was, of course, with Democrat President Clinton and the climactic battle came with the struggle over the 1995 budget. The House rejected Clinton's budget, pushing instead for cuts in expenditure that would produce a balanced budget. In turn, the president refused to sign the congressional budget bill, because it threatened important programmes such as Medicare and education. The new fiscal year came into force on 1 October 1995, with the impasse still in place. In the past, Congress had dealt with this by authorising temporary funds to keep the wheels of government in motion. With Gingrich to the fore, however, the Republicans refused to do this, which in turn led to the shut-down of many governmental offices and government-run tourist attractions.

This tactic rebounded badly on Gingrich and the Republicans. Cleverly exploiting his role of the nation's leader, President Clinton was able to portray his opponents as irresponsible extremists. When public opinion polls decisively pinned the blame for the crisis on the Republicans, they were forced to back down. Indeed, only when, in the summer of 1996, House Republicans decided to revert to the time-honoured strategy of compromise with the president and Senate on a number of important issues, did they succeed in putting onto the statute books any elements of the Contract with America (Hershey, 1997, p. 216).

As noted above, the Republicans retained control of the House (and Senate) in 1996, but with a reduced majority and, therefore, with even less chance to force through a partisan agenda. While conservative Republicans pushed their cherished items again in 1997, they 'failed to muster enough votes to overcome either bipartisan opposition or the prospect of a presidential veto' (*Congressional Quarterly*, 20 December 1997, p. 3103). Moreover, Speaker Gingrich faced two serious attempts to unseat him, and committee chairs reasserted their power against the party leadership (see next chapter). Finally, leadership of the congressional Republican party slipped from the House to the Senate in the form of the more pragmatic Senate majority leader, Trent Lott of Mississippi.

The Republican Revolution of 1994 was a failure. A bold attempt at party government foundered on the rocks of the Constitution's structures and the political and legislative constraints they impose. Even though supported by a public mood favourable to Republican ideology and a majority in both chambers of Congress, it proved impossible to govern from Capitol Hill.

Of course, President Clinton found it difficult to govern from the White House, even when Democrats controlled Congress, but when bargaining and compromise failed, it was the president who emerged the victor from the struggle with Congress. Indeed, it should be remembered that even if the House Republicans had succeeded in exercising political leadership in the 104th Congress, they would probably have ceded it to a Republican president, had one been elected in 1996. In that sense, the Republican Revolution was perhaps never much more than a 'second-best' option, born, in part, of the failure to capture the natural home of political leadership in the United States – the presidency.

The inability of Congress to perform successfully the legislative leadership role as originally conceived by the framers, has led some commentators to emphasise the value of other aspects of the legislature's duties. Louis Fisher, for example, believes that one of the most important tasks of Congress is 'the daily grind of overseeing administration policies' (Fisher, 1985, p. 334). This brings us, then, to a consideration of the function known as 'congressional oversight'.

Congressional oversight

You will search the Constitution in vain for an explicit reference to the oversight function of Congress, yet the very notion of 'checks and balances' invites Congress to ensure that the executive branch does not abuse its power.

Moreover, there are clauses of the Constitution which do explicitly give Congress the right to constrain executive power. For example, the president is required to obtain the support of two-thirds of the Senate before any treaty he has negotiated can become law (Article II, Section 2(ii)). The same clause requires a simple majority of the Senate to approve presidential nominations for the Supreme Court, ambassadorships, cabinet secretaries and, indeed, all federal officials save those exempted by Congress itself. Congress may also exploit the 'power of the purse' given to it by the Constitution: for the exercise of executive power depends to a considerable extent on the willingness of the legislature to vote the necessary funds.

To these Constitutional controls, Congress itself added the right to hold public investigations into the activities of the executive branch. This has been described as an 'inherited power' of Congress, because it follows from the British Parliament's practice of conducting investigations for the purpose of gathering information with a view to legislation (Peltason, 1988, p. 74). It has not been restricted to the generation of new legislation, but also includes the right to investigate whether the executive branch is properly administering existing legislation.

Congressional oversight, then, involves both substantive powers and investigative authority over the executive branch. Yet there is still no common succinct definition of what it is. Indeed, Congress itself has employed different terms at different times. Thus, the Legislative Reorganization Act of 1946 referred to 'continuous watchfulness', whereas the Legislative Reorganisation Act of 1970 mentioned 'legislative review' (Hart, 1987, p. 140). Part of the difficulty arises from the fact that Congress tries to accomplish more than one objective through oversight.

In the first place, as the term 'oversight' suggests, Congress tries to ensure that the executive branch faithfully administers programmes and legislation as Congress intended. This is in essence a retrospective form of oversight. It may involve, for example, examining policy guidelines drawn up by a bureaucratic agency or monitoring expenditures to see that they are in line with congressional intentions. At the level of personnel, oversight may seek to establish whether individual bureaucrats are performing their duties satisfactorily.

Secondly, oversight more generally can be seen as part of the legislative–executive struggle over policy. In this aspect, oversight capacity may be used prospectively to establish future policy. For example, when the Senate rejected President Reagan's nomination of Robert Bork to the Supreme Court in 1987, it purported to have doubts about his temperament and judicial qualifications for the job. In fact, the underlying reason for rejecting Bork was simply that he was too right wing and would indubitably strengthen the radical conservative bloc on the Court. This was not the use of the oversight power to monitor the executive branch, but rather to undermine its will.

Thirdly, there are more narrowly self-interested motivations and purposes behind some exercises in oversight. Thus, 'the ostensible goal of legislative oversight is to promote rationality, efficiency and responsibility in the bureaucracy. Although some legislators have high regard for this goal, they are also concerned with promoting their own careers and causes (Keefe and Ogul, 1993, p. 407). This may take the form of interceding with the bureaucracy on behalf of a constituent or interest group, or, more spectacularly, using the power of investigation for self-promotion, as Senator Joe McCarthy did so notoriously in the 1950s.

Congressional oversight, therefore, is best seen as a series of practices by which Congress can project its power into the executive branch (see Box 15.4). The purpose

Box 15.4

Instruments of congressional oversight

- Hearings/investigations
- Legislative veto
- Appointments
- 'Power of the purse'

- Required reports
- Sunset legislation
- Informal contact

of oversight *may* be to ensure bureaucratic efficiency and responsibility, but it may also be exercised in pursuit of institutional and individual aggrandisement.

Effectiveness of oversight

There is a broad consensus among scholars that Congress does not perform its oversight functions very well. Peter Woll concluded, for example, that 'effective oversight performance is at best sporadic' (Woll, 1985, p. 145). Thus, from time to time, there are spectacular congressional hearings which have a major impact: the Watergate hearings which led to the resignation of President Nixon in 1974 is the most obvious example. Other hearings, however, produce meagre results, even when considerable time and effort are expended on them by Congress. For all the publicity and drama of the Iran–Contra hearings of 1987, little effective action was taken against members of the Reagan administration who had breached both law and government policy in selling arms to Iran and channelling the proceeds to the counter-revolutionary forces in Nicaragua.

Similarly, if we consider the appointment power of the Senate, rejection of the president's nominee is the exception, with routine approval the rule. In 1990, for example, President Bush sent some 2,443 nominations to federal posts to the Senate. Of these, 2,145 (87.8 per cent) were approved, 11 were withdrawn and 287 (11.7 per cent) were not confirmed (Keefe and Ogul, 1993, p. 400). The rejection of presidential nominees to the most important posts is an embarrassing blow to any president, as when President Bush's first nominee as defense secretary, John Tower, was rejected in 1989, or when President Clinton had to withdraw his first two nominees as attorney-general, Zoe Baird and Kimba Wood, in 1993. Generally such failures are due to perceived personal weaknesses on the part of the individual nominee concerned – in these cases, Tower's alleged excessive drinking and womanising, and Baird's and Wood's failure to pay social security taxes for domestic staff. When the president selects nominees without such personal vulnerabilities, the Senate rarely denies him his choice.

These are legitimate exercises of oversight power by the Senate, particularly if one considers the peccadillos of nominees to be relevant to their ability to perform the duties in question. On the other hand, the Senate frequently approves the appointment of federal office-holders who are not obviously qualified for the post and whose main asset appears to be a record of political support for the president. Likewise, some of those rejected, including the three mentioned above, *are* eminently qualified in terms of experience and knowledge. Thus, it is difficult to make the case that Senate confirmation powers constitute an effective exercise of oversight.

Nevertheless, while public, formal oversight by Congress may produce little tangible evidence of effectiveness, it may be that informal oversight is more productive. By definition, the effect of informal oversight is impossible to measure. Yet, it seems logical, at least, to assume that the daily, routine contacts which members of Congress have with federal bureaucrats attune the executive branch to the preferences, interests and objections of the legislative branch. Bureaucrats, therefore, will try to anticipate the views of legislators and, if possible, accommodate those views when devising and implementing policy (Keefe and Ogul, 1993, pp. 411–12).

Political education for the public

The legislative and investigative functions of Congress involve informed, public debate on the major political issues confronting the nation. As a result, Congress may be said to have an important role to play in educating the public. It may further be argued that an increasing tendency in recent years to allow hearings, floor debates and even committee sessions to be televised has enhanced the importance of this function of Congress.

While political elites, including the media, may take advantage of congressional activity to inform themselves on political issues, it is rare that the public takes much notice of what Congress does. As we have already seen (Chapter 11), the public gets most of its political information from television and television coverage of politics is generally brief and superficial. Certainly it excludes detailed coverage of congressional debates or hearings, unless something quite sensational is involved. Thus, while detailed coverage of Congress is available on the C-Span cable channel, this is not part of the viewing habits of the vast majority of the American public.

The significance of the educative function of Congress, therefore, is not that the public actually pays attention to what Congress is saying, but that congressional activities provide a major source of political information for those who wish to know what government is doing. In this respect, Congress plays an important part in ensuring an open system of government.

Congress is, in many respects, an institution under attack. In terms of its major functions, it seems to have lost the will or capacity to perform them to the public's satisfaction. As we saw above, public opinion polls indicate that it is held in low esteem. As a consequence, many states have introduced term limits in an attempt to improve congressional performance.

Yet Congress should not be shouldered with all the blame for its failings. Most democracies have experienced a drift of power from the legislative to the executive in the twentieth century. Moreover, for historical and cultural reasons, Congress does not have strong political parties to help it perform effectively. On the other hand, there is little doubt that the internal structures and processes of Congress also play their part in hampering legislative performance. The next chapter examines those in detail.

Summary

Although Congress retains its exclusive power to enact laws, much of the initiative in legislation has passed to the presidency. This is due largely to the institutional advantages enjoyed by a unitary executive compared with a fragmented legislative branch. Another major cause, however, is the tendency of members of Congress towards parochialism and the desire to serve their constituents in order to enhance their prospects of re-election. This does not mean, however, either that Congress has yielded all rights to initiate legislation or that it passively accepts what the president puts before it. While the Republican Revolution of 1994 may not have succeeded in restoring congressional pre-eminence in the field of legislation, it was a powerful reminder of the fact that the president and the Congress remain rivals for legislative power and that co-operation between the two is essential if laws are to be enacted.

 ## Topics for discussion

1. What explains the shift in legislative initiative from the Congress to the presidency in the twentieth century?
2. What are the principal purposes of 'legislative oversight' and how effective is Congress in pursuing them?
3. How accurate is the view that Congress is a fundamentally parochial institution?
4. Under what conditions might Congress regain its old pre-eminence in the field of legislation?

 ## Further reading

The best single text on Congress is perhaps W. Keefe and M. Ogul's *The American Legislative Process* (8th edn, Englewood Cliffs: Prentice Hall, 1993). A little more dated, but still a useful introduction to the basics of Congress is C. Bailey, *The US Congress* (Oxford: Basil Blackwell, 1989). Two books which address the crucial relationship of the presidency and Congress are M. Foley and J. Owens, *Congress and the Presidency: Institutional politics in a separated system* (Manchester: Manchester University Press, 1996) and C. Jones, *Separate But Equal Branches: Congress and the presidency* (Chatham, NJ: Chatham House, 1995). A book which deals mainly with the presidency, but also has a good section on relations with Congress is J. Hart, *The Presidential Branch* (2nd edn, Chatham, NJ: Chatham House, 1995). For analysis of congressional elections, see M. Hershey, 'The congressional elections' in G. Pomper *et al.* (eds), *The Elections of 1996: Reports and interpretations*, (Chatham, NJ: Chatham House, 1997). If you are fortunate to have access to it, *Congressional Quarterly* is a marvellous source of up-to-date information and analysis. There are also a number of sites on the Internet which provide useful information, the most comprehensive of which is Thomas at http://thomas.loc.gov.

 ## References

Bailey, C., 1989, *The US Congress* (Oxford: Basil Blackwell)
Fisher, L., 1985, *Constitutional Conflicts between Congress and the President* (Princeton: Princeton University Press)

Hart, J., 1987, *The Presidential Branch* (Chatham, NJ: Chatham House)

Hershey, M., 1997, 'The congressional elections', in *The Elections of 1996: Reports and interpretations*, eds G. Pomper *et al.* (Chatham, NJ: Chatham House)

Jacobson, G., 1996, 'The 1994 House elections in perspective', *Political Science Quarterly*, vol. 111, no. 2, pp. 203–23

Keefe, W. and Ogul, M., 1993, *The American Legislative Process: Congress and the States*, (8th edn, Englewood Cliffs: Prentice Hall)

Maas, A., 1983, *Congress and the Common Good* (New York: Basic Books)

Mezey, M., 1989, *Congress, the President and Public Policy* (Boulder: Westview)

Neustadt, R., 1960, *Presidential Power* (New York: Wiley)

Peltason, J., 1988, *Corwin and Peltason's Understanding the Constitution* (11th edn, New York: Holt, Rinehart & Winston)

Smith, S. and Deering, C., 1990, *Committees in Congress* (2nd edn, Washington, DC: Congressional Quarterly Press)

Wayne, S., 1978, *The Legislative Presidency* (New York: Harper & Row)

Woll, P., 1985, *Congress* (Boston: Little, Brown)

16

Congressional structures and processes

Like most legislatures, Congress has its own distinctive set of structures, processes and institutional norms. We saw in the previous chapter how some of these can help or hinder Congress in the performance of its major tasks. In this chapter, we take a closer look at congressional practices in order to understand how the legislative process works. We also examine the members of Congress themselves – what kinds of people they are, what their methods of work and their career aspirations are.

A bill becomes law

There are many bills introduced into Congress every session, but very few become law (see Box 16.1). Many bills are introduced without any serious expectation that they will be passed. However, even the most earnestly and widely supported bills have to struggle to overcome the many obstacles and opportunities for sabotage and derailment that await them. As we saw in the previous chapter, the parochialism and fragmentation of power within Congress, combined with the absence of strong party loyalties and disciplines, makes the path of legislation unusually incoherent and uncertain.

In formal terms, all bills follow more or less the same route (see Box 16.2). The complexity of the legislative process stems from the fact that problems may arise at any step along the path. For example, the requirements of bicameralism mean that separate bills must be introduced into both House and Senate. However, not only may the two chambers pass different amendments, but the two bills may be different from the outset, depending on the distinctive goals and strategies of the bills' sponsors. The wording of a bill is vital if its sponsor has a strong preference for a particular committee to take jurisdiction of it. Thus seeking a 'friendly' home in each of the two chambers may require differences in the initial House and Senate bills.

Box 16.1

A statistical portrait of Congress, selected years 1989–97

		1997	1995	1993	1991	1989
Days in session	Senate	153	211	153	158	136
	House	132	168	142	154	147
Average daily hours	Senate	7.1	8.7	8.3	7.6	7.4
	House	7.6	9.1	6.9	6.1	5.1
Bills introduced	Senate	1,839	1,801	2,178	2,701	2,548
	House	3,662	3,430	4,543	5,057	4,842
Recorded votes	Senate	298	613	395	280	312
	House	640	885	615	444	379
Laws enacted		140[a]	88	210	243	240
Vetoes		2[a]	9	0	3	10

[a] Up to 5 December, with 13 bills awaiting presidential action

Source: Adapted from *Congressional Quarterly*, 6 December 1997, p. 3025

Committees and legislation

The main legislative work begins when the standing committee which takes jurisdiction of a bill when it is introduced assigns it to one of its subcommittees, for it is at the subcommittee stage that there are hearings, proposed amendments and the first major vote.

Committee hearings

Hearings involve the calling of witnesses to appear in public before the subcommittee. Such witnesses are typically from the executive branch or from interest groups, although independent experts and constituents may also appear. Witnesses are expected to supply information about a problem in which they have an interest or of which they have experience. The formal purpose of hearings, then, is to inform Congress so that it may take appropriate legislative action.

In theory, those who testify before congressional subcommittees may be supportive, hostile or neutral to the bill concerned. In practice, it is often the case that the chairs of the subcommittees and their staff carefully select witnesses who will support their own position. Indeed, the very purpose of hearings may be less to acquire information otherwise unavailable, than to allow committee members to perform in the limelight (Woll, 1985, p. 114–15).

Nevertheless, whether intended for information gathering, personal advancement or

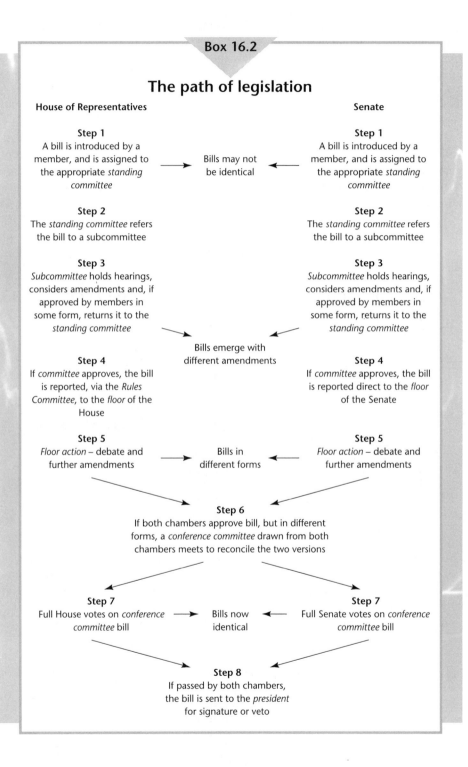

Box 16.2

The path of legislation

House of Representatives   **Senate**

Step 1
A bill is introduced by a
member, and is assigned to
the appropriate *standing
committee*

Bills may not
be identical

Step 1
A bill is introduced by a
member, and is assigned to
the appropriate *standing
committee*

Step 2
The *standing committee* refers
the bill to a subcommittee

Step 2
The *standing committee* refers
the bill to a subcommittee

Step 3
Subcommittee holds hearings,
considers amendments and, if
approved by members in
some form, returns it to the
standing committee

Step 3
Subcommittee holds hearings,
considers amendments and, if
approved by members in
some form, returns it to the
standing committee

Bills emerge with
different amendments

Step 4
If *committee* approves, the bill
is reported, via the *Rules
Committee*, to the *floor* of the
House

Step 4
If *committee* approves, the bill
is reported direct to the *floor*
of the Senate

Step 5
Floor action – debate and
further amendments

Bills in
different forms

Step 5
Floor action – debate and
further amendments

Step 6
If both chambers approve bill, but in different
forms, a *conference committee* drawn from both
chambers meets to reconcile the two versions

Step 7
Full House votes on *conference
committee* bill

Bills now
identical

Step 7
Full Senate votes on *conference
committee* bill

Step 8
If passed by both chambers,
the bill is sent to the *president*
for signature or veto

for symbolic reassurance to the public that Congress is open and democratic, the fact is that hearings rarely make any direct difference to the content of legislation. Quite simply, witnesses are unlikely to provide significant information of which Congress is not already aware. On the other hand, hearings may help to generate or solidify a coalition behind the bill (Smith and Deering, 1990, p. 142). Committee hearings can focus the attention of Congress and the country on an issue and, by parading the evidence of witnesses, mobilise support for legislation that has already been drawn up.

There are several different types of committee in Congress (see Box 16.3). The basic type is the *standing committee* and their *subcommittees*. These are permanent committees. This means that they automatically continue in existence from one Congress to the next, unless Congress decides to abolish or amalgamate them. Perhaps the most important feature of standing committees and subcommittees is that they have

---

Box 16.3

Committees in the 105th Congress (1997/98)

Senate
- Agriculture, Nutrition and Forestry
- Appropriations
- Armed Services
- Banking, Housing and Urban Affairs
- Budget
- Commerce, Science and Transportation
- Energy and Natural Resources
- Environment and Public Works
- Select Committee on Ethics
- Finance
- Foreign Relations
- Governmental Affairs
- Committee on Indian Affairs
- Judiciary
- Labor and Human Resources
- Rules and Administration
- Special Committee on Aging
- Small Business
- Select Committee on Intelligence
- Veterans Affairs

House
- Agriculture
- Appropriations
- Banking and Financial Services
- Budget
- Commerce
- Education and the Workforce
- Government Reform and Oversight
- House Oversight
- International Relations
- Judiciary
- National Security
- Resources
- Rules
- Science
- Small Business
- Standards of Official Conduct
- Transportation and Infrastructure
- Veterans Affairs
- Ways and Means
- Permanent Select Committee on Intelligence

Joint committees
- Joint Economic Committee
- Joint Committee on the Library
- Joint Committee on Printing
- Joint Committee on Taxation

legislative jurisdiction over one or more policy areas. Thus, in the Senate, the Armed Services Committee deals with defence-related issues only. On the other hand, the Banking, Housing and Urban Affairs Committee deals with different policy areas that are not directly related to each other. Senate and House Committees do not necessarily have precisely parallel jurisdictions. Thus the issues dealt with by the Senate Labor and Human Services Committee are handled in the House by the Appropriations Committee. The fact that the House has 435 members, compared with just 100 senators, means that the House has greater scope for both more and larger committees and subcommittees.

The second type of committee is the *select* or *special committee*. These are not formally permanent, nor do they have legislative authority. Their main task is to investigate or highlight particular issues or problems. The most famous of such committees are those which investigate scandals, such as the Watergate Committee or the Iran–Contra Committee.

Select committees can, however, become standing committees or, at least, acquire the same permanence and legislative status as they possess. The infamous House Committee on Un-American Activities, which investigated alleged communist subversives in the 1940s and 1950s, was made permanent in 1945, though it had existed as a select committee since 1938. More recently, the Intelligence Committees of both houses have become permanent, even though they are not listed as standing committees in the rules of the two chambers. Normally, select and special committees are established with specified time limits on their existence, but in the case of the Intelligence Committees, these limits have been dropped (Smith and Deering, 1990, pp. 5–6).

The third major type of committee is the *conference committee*, made up of members of both the Senate and the House. These have the vital task of harmonising, or *reconciling*, the House and Senate versions of the same bill. In order to accomplish their task, members of a conference committee must necessarily devise amendments to the bills as passed by the two chambers. They can, therefore, wield substantial legislative power. Of course, the conference committee bill must be approved by both House and Senate, but faced with a choice of that bill or no legislation at all, the conference committee version is usually adopted.

The fourth type is the *joint committee*. Currently there are five of these. Composed of members of both House and Senate, they are non-legislative committees, but some do make significant contributions to policy making. For example, the Joint Committee on Taxation has a large staff of experts and its work services the two legislative taxation committees, the House Ways and Means Committee and the Senate Finance Committee.

Mark-up sessions

When any hearing on a bill has been completed, the subcommittee will 'mark up' the legislation: that is, it takes the initial bill and amends it through additions and deletions. This mark-up process usually involves an attempt by the chairperson of the subcommittee to produce a broad consensus among the members. Thus mark-up sessions may involve intense political bargaining between individual members of the committee

> **Box 16.4**
>
> # A typical committee/subcommittee structure
>
> **Subcommittees of the House Resources Committee**
> - National Parks and Public Lands
> - Fisheries Conservation, Wildlife and Oceans
> - Energy and Mineral Resources
> - Water and Power
> - Forests and Forest Health

and between members of the majority and minority parties. Bargaining and compromise are desirable because a bill with broad support stands a much better chance of surviving the later stages of the legislative process than one which is divisive and likely to attract hostile actions (Woll, 1985, p. 117).

The subcommittee stage of a bill's progress is usually the most important. Although not the final stage, it is at this point that the real specialist members of Congress, together with their even more specialised staff, have the opportunity to define the basic shape of the bill. Other members not on the subcommittee tend to defer to the expertise of those who are, unless they have a particular reason for opposing them. This is especially true of the House, whose large membership encourages legislative specialisation. Senators, owing to their much smaller numbers, are obliged to sit on more subcommittees and committees and are therefore somewhat less specialised and less deferential.

'Subcommittee Bill of Rights'

In the 1970s, several important reforms enhanced the power and prestige of subcommittees. The reforms had two main goals: first, to free subcommittees from the control of full committee chairpersons, and secondly, to disperse power more widely among members. House Democrats set the ball rolling in 1971 when they limited each member to the chair of no more than one legislative subcommittee. Until this reform, the chairs of full committees dominated subcommittees by heading several subcommittees themselves. The new limitation automatically gave more members the opportunity to chair subcommittees, thus dispersing and democratising power. In its first year of operation, the rule change brought in sixteen new subcommittee chairpersons, most of whom were younger and less conservative than their predecessors (Vogler, 1983, p. 151).

In 1973 came the 'Subcommittee Bill of Rights'. This transferred significant power over subcommittees from full committee chairpersons to the Democratic group, or *caucus*, on each committee. Henceforth, the caucus would decide who would chair the subcommittees and also ensure that all members be given a major subcommittee assignment. Other reforms ended full committee chairpersons' control over the referral of legislation to subcommittees: they had previously used their position to either block referral completely, thus preventing any progress on the bill, or to refer it to a sub-committee under their personal control. Now referral would be automatic and subcommittee jurisdictions strictly delineated.

The reforms continued in 1974 when the number of subcommittees was increased by a new rule requiring all full committees with more than twenty members to establish at least four subcommittees. This was aimed squarely at Wilbur Mills, the chairman of the key Ways and Means Committee, which deals with taxation. Mills had kept control of policy for over fifteen years by refusing to establish any subcommittees at all (Vogler, 1983, p. 152).

Still more changes followed, all with the same aim of increasing the power and autonomy of subcommittees. As David Vogler wrote: 'The greatest effect of these reforms was to shift the site of most congressional lawmaking from the full committee to the subcommittee level. ... It is clear that subcommittees in the House have come into their own as new centres of power' (Vogler, 1983, p. 154).

Power in the Senate had always been more decentralised than in the House, but in 1977 it too reorganised its committee and subcommittee structures. The number of committees was reduced by one-fifth and subcommittees by one-third. Each senator would also now be limited to service on no more than three committees and eight subcommittees. Furthermore, no senator could chair more than three committees and subcommittees.

Whatever benefits the subcommittee reforms produced, they also exacerbated the problem of fragmentation within Congress (see Box 16.4). Congress has itself recognised this and there were attempts to modify some of the measures of the 1970s. These attempts failed, however, largely because, for most members, the admitted loss in institutional coherence was outweighed by the gain in the power and autonomy of sub-committee members. Subcommittees give members their best chance to make their mark in the legislature and, consequently, with the voters back home. Too many of them are therefore simply unwilling to forgo the opportunities the strengthened sub-committees offer them.

The 1994 Republican Revolution

As noted in the previous chapter, however, the remarkable Republican victory in the 1994 elections led to an attempt to instil stronger party government into the House of Representatives. The new Speaker of the House, Newt Gingrich, fully appreciated that such a change must inevitably involve a reduction in the decentralising force of committee and subcommittee autonomy and set about reforming committee structures accordingly. The House Republican Conference authorised Gingrich to select committee chairs and to ignore claims of seniority where deemed appropriate. In addition, the tenure of committee and subcommittee chairpersons was limited to a maximum of six years. The Speaker was also given greater influence over committee assignments and the choice of committee to which bills are referred. Moreover, three committees and thirty-one subcommittees were abolished altogether (Foley and Owens, 1996, p. 36).

Yet by the beginning of the 105th Congress (1997–98), much of the revolution had been undone. As with other aspects of the Republican Revolution of 1994, the roots of this return to traditional arrangements lie in the failure of the House Republicans to secure passage of their key legislative priorities by pure partisanship. Forced in 1996 to compromise in order to get action on welfare reform and other items, the House Republicans found that committees were the best forum for bargaining and making deals across party lines (*Congressional Quarterly*, 22 March 1997, p. 9).

For similar reasons, committee chairs have regained much of their power to initiate and control legislative initiatives; where bipartisanship is essential to enacting legislation, committee leaders are better placed than party leaders to assess and manage the potential for acceptable compromise.

Reporting bills

Many bills fail to progress beyond the subcommittee stage. If, however, the subcommittee can agree and approve a version of the bill, then it is sent back to the full committee for consideration. The full committee may choose to hold further hearings and mark-up sessions, though on the whole it will accept the recommendations of the subcommittee. At this point, if the committee approves the bill, it is reported to the floor for consideration by the full chamber. The vast majority of bills are never reported: one count in the mid-1980s revealed that only 12 per cent of House bills and 24 per cent of Senate bills survived the committee stages of the legislative process (Bailey, 1989, p. 98).

House rules

At this point, the House and Senate processes diverge. In the House, the reported bill must go to the *Rules Committee* where it will be given a 'rule' determining the conditions of debate and the extent to which amendments may be offered. If the majority party is united on the bill and wishes to protect it, the committee can give it a rule which forbids amendments altogether. In the Senate, however, this is possible only where there is a unanimous vote to limit debate or amendment. Given that just one senator alone can prevent such limitation, Senate bills are more vulnerable to hostile amendment on the floor than House bills.

Floor action

Floor action refers to the activities of the whole chamber when a bill is reported to it. In essence this means debate, amendments (unless a 'rule' determines otherwise) and the final vote.

As noted above, the extent of such activities may be restricted in the House, but the Senate has a rule of unlimited debate. Because senators may talk for as long as they like, they can exploit it to try to exact further concessions from the bill's supporters or even to kill the legislation altogether. When organised with real determination, this is known as a filibuster. The filibuster is at its most effective when several senators combine to keep debate going. One such effort in 1893, designed to prevent repeal of the Silver Purchase Act, lasted for forty-six days (Woll, 1985, p. 55).

However, precisely because the filibuster is a method by which a minority can block the wishes of even a clear majority of senators, considerations of both democracy and efficiency have led to attempts to restrict its force. In 1917, the Senate approved a cloture rule, otherwise known as Rule 22. This allowed debate to be ended if two-thirds of the Senate voted to do so. Cloture was significantly strengthened as a weapon against the filibuster in 1975, when the number of votes required to end debate was reduced to sixty members. This more than doubled the number of successful cloture votes to over 50 per cent of those attempted (Woll, 1985, p. 57). Nevertheless, it is a fact of life in the Senate that if the minority party has forty-one seats or more and can hang together, it can prevent a bill from being to put to a vote. In other words, the majority party in the Senate has little choice but to take a bipartisan approach to legislating.

Conference

If both the Senate and the House pass a bill, it goes to a *conference committee*. A conference committee is composed of a delegation of members from both the House and the Senate. Their task is to take the two versions of the bill passed by the Senate and the House and reconcile them: that is, produce a common version of the bill. This may involve both removing clauses from the original versions and adding completely new clauses. An agreed version, known as the Committee Report, is accepted once it has been signed by a majority of each chamber's delegation. It is then sent back to the House and Senate for a final vote.

The conference stage of a bill can be of enormous importance. In the first place, it is rare for a conference report to be defeated in the Senate or House. Equally important, no amendments to a conference report are permitted. Senators and representatives are therefore confronted with what is called a straight 'up or down' vote – a simple choice between approving or disapproving the report as it stands. Whatever is agreed in the conference committee, therefore, will almost certainly be what becomes law.

The membership of conference committee delegations are usually dominated by those who serve on the standing committees and subcommittees. They tend to use the conference stage to remove floor amendments of which they disapprove and, as a result, the conference committee tends to be yet one more instrument by which the specialised committees of Congress dominate the legislative process.

Bargaining and compromise in the legislative process

The legislative process as outlined above offers a series of points at which a bill may be fundamentally altered or defeated altogether. Each stage provides individual members of Congress, interest groups and representatives of the executive branch with a point of access to the legislative process (see Box 16.5). Combined with a set of detailed and complex rules governing legislative procedure, this makes negative legislative action far easier than positive legislative action. In simple terms, it is easier to prevent than to secure the passage of a bill.

Given the difficulty of operating on partisan lines, the best method for securing the passage of a bill is to ensure that it serves the interests and needs of as many individual members as possible. This means that for each new bill, its sponsors must try to build

Box 16.5

New forms of legislating

On 17 July 1995, Representative Skaggs, a Democrat from Colorado, rose to his feet in the House of Representatives to lambast the legislative tactics of Speaker Gingrich. He asserted that the new Republican majority was 'distorting the normal legislative process around here, acting against House rules by *using the appropriations process to rewrite law and reshape policy*, so that they can achieve, by stealth, objectives that lack real public support'. He claimed that:

> We saw the start of this pattern with the first recission bill, with its pages of legislative language waiving environmental and forest management laws, language that under the normal rules of the House should not have been in any bill of that kind. We are seeing it again now in the Interior appropriations bill, which we will take up later today with its provisions to dissolve the National Biological Service, transfer its functions to the US Geological Service, again *legislating on an appropriations bill*. ... Later this week we will see it in even more outrageous ways when the full Committee on Appropriations takes up the bill to fund the Environmental Protection Agency. That bill has more riders than the Long Island Railroad. Most of them are intended to prevent the government from doing its job in protecting our water, our air, our wetlands, our health.
>
> *(Congressional Record,* 17 July 1995, p. H7016)

Representative Skaggs' complaint was directed at the Republicans' use of the appropriations process to change policy through the 'back door'. The legislative process in Congress traditionally has two parts: the authorisation process and the appropriations process. First, a law needs to be enacted which authorises government action to deal with a particular problem. The authorisation will also specify an amount of money that the government may spend on programmes established by the law. Then, provision needs to be made in an appropriations bill to provide the money that has been authorised. The appropriation may be any amount up to the figure specified in the authorisation.

Splitting the legislative process into two parts means that debate about the merits of government action should take place during consideration of the authorising legislation. The authorising committee will hold hearings on a bill at which interest groups can air their views. Amendments to the bill may then be adopted to take account of perceived deficiencies. The role of the Appropriations Committees in the House and Senate, theoretically, is to determine levels of funding for programmes based on the budgetary position of the United States. A problem with this traditional pattern of law-making, however, is that reconciling differences between competing interests is often difficult during the authorisation process. Individual representatives and senators have considerable power to obstruct legislation. To overcome this problem, the Republican leadership in the 104th Congress (1995/96) decided to use the appropriation rather than the authorisation process to change the law. Riders or clauses were added to appropriation bills which changed government policy. Because appropriation bills are protected under congressional rules, individual legislators had far less opportunity to obstruct than would have been the case with authorisations. The technical language of appropriation bills had the further advantage of allowing unpopular changes to be disguised.

These new forms of law-making allowed the Republican leadership to drive policy change through Congress in a way that would otherwise have been impossible – but at a price. Representative Vento, a Democrat from Minnesota, articulated these concerns in a speech on the floor of the House in February 1996. He argued that:

> If you want to change the policy, let us have a vote on this floor and vote it up or down. But to undercut it by not funding these particular policies and hiding behind that particular artifice I think is wrong, I think it is irresponsible, and I think it is inconsistent with the sound policy making that should characterize this body. We ought to be looking at what the impact is on the economy, we ought to be looking at what the scientific evidence is, we ought to be looking at what is morally right or wrong with regard to these issues, and we ought to be looking at what the people we represent think, what their views are.

(*Congressional Record*, 27 February 1996, p. H1292)

Contributed by Dr Christopher J. Bailey, Keele University

a coalition which will support it through the difficult process which lies ahead. However, since the specific interests and needs of individual members may vary considerably, this inevitably entails bargaining and compromise on the details of the legislation. If a bill involves a distributive policy, that is, one which involves the allocation of funds or other benefits, then the simplest method of building a successful coalition is to make sure that enough members' constituencies benefit from the expenditure. If little or no money is involved, as with a civil rights bill, then bargaining and compromising will revolve around the terms and language of the legislation: some members may seek to strengthen the bill, while others try to dilute it.

In either case, the effect on the original bill can be very significant. Ensuring the passage of a distributive bill may simply necessitate spending more money than the nation's financial position makes desirable. This could contribute to a budget deficit or to other programmes being starved of vital finance. Diluting the terms and language of legislation may render it less effective or even completely worthless. An interesting example of this is the Civil Rights Act of 1960. Congress responded to the mounting pressure of the civil rights movement by trying to ensure greater compliance with existing laws. In order to gain the necessary support from southern members, however, the enforcement provisions of the 1960 Act were so watered down that the legislation could not possibly achieve its original goals. As the leading civil rights activist (and later Supreme Court justice) Thurgood Marshall observed, 'The 1960 Civil Rights Act isn't worth the paper it's written on.' The *New York Times* apparently agreed, since it did not bother to report the passage of the Act on its front page. Congress had thus wasted considerable time and energy on a bill rendered worthless by the need for bargaining and compromise; and it was very quickly obliged to take up consideration of a new civil rights bill.

In short, the need to bargain, compromise and make deals may well undermine the achievement of good public policy. Nevertheless, it continues to be a central feature of the congressional process because there is no other, more effective method of aggregating the interests of individual members in a fragmented legislative body.

Members of Congress

Although Congress is a representative institution, its members are not at all typical of the population at large. They are disproportionately old, male, white and wealthy compared with those who elect them. There is also a very large number of lawyers in Congress. Although less prevalent today than a generation ago, lawyers still make up about three-fifths of senators and two-fifths of representatives. The next largest pro-fessional category is those with a background in banking and business: around one-quarter of senators and one-third of representatives (Bailey, 1989, p. 55).

Some of these imbalances are less worrying than others. For example, the predomin-ance of lawyers is hardly surprising, given that politics is all about the making of laws. The gender and ethnic imbalances, on the other hand, indicate that there remain considerable barriers preventing members of historically disadvantaged groups from entering the corridors of power. As a result of the 1996 elections, there were, for example, just 51 women in the 435-member House and 9 in the 100-member Senate. Given that women constitute over 50 per cent of the population, it is evident that the national legislature remains overwhelmingly a male preserve.

Nevertheless, there are more women members of Congress today than there have ever been. There has also been progress in the number of members who come from ethnic minorities (see Box 16.6).

For minority candidates, it is clearly easier to get elected to the House than to the Senate. This reflects two main factors. First, because House districts are smaller than those for the Senate, they may contain concentrations of minority voters who consti-tute a relatively high percentage of the district's electorate. This factor was given added impetus in the early 1990s, when the Justice Department put pressure upon states to create 'majority-minority districts'. However, a series of Supreme Court decisions, beginning with *Shaw v. Reno* (1993) has ruled many of these districts unconstitutional as racial gerrymanders.

The second, and closely related, factor which makes it difficult for minority can-didates to get elected to the Senate is that many white voters seem very reluctant to support them. Since whites constitute a large majority in all states, the state-wide elect-oral constituency of senators militates against the success of minority candidates. As a result, unless there is a marked change of attitude on the part of white voters, minor-ity membership of the House may already be close to its maximum possible level. It is likewise difficult to imagine much further progress being made in the Senate.

Congressional careers

Once elected to Congress, however, members from all backgrounds face a similar career structure. Apart from their own talents and ambitions, the main determinant of

Box 16.6

Women, African Americans and Hispanic Americans in Congress, selected years 1973–97

	Women		African Ams		Hispanic Ams	
	%	No.	%	No.	%	No.
1973						
Total population	51.3		11.1		4.6	
House members	3.7	16	3.4	15	1.1	5
Senate members	0.0	0	1.0	1	1.0	1
1983						
Total population	51.4		11.7		6.4	
House members	5.1	22	4.6	20	2.2	9
Senate members	2.0	2	0.0	0	0.0	0
1993						
Total population	51.2		12.3		9.0	
House members	10.8	47	8.7	38	3.9	17
Senate members	6.0	6	1.0	1	0.0	0
1997						
Total population	51.2		12.7		10.6	
House members	11.7	51	8.5	37	4.4	19
Senate members	9.0	9	1.0	1	0.0	0

Source: Adapted from Hershey, 1997, p. 231

their success is committee work. As we have seen, it is in committee that the main legislative work of Congress is done, and so it is also here that members have a chance to make their name. They want to demonstrate to their party leaders, colleagues and the media that they are able and intelligent; but most of all they want to demonstrate to the voters back home that they have the skills and power to secure major benefits for their district or state. This is because the first goal of all members of Congress is to win re-election: that is the precondition of any other goals, such as making public policy or gaining influence and prestige within Congress (Mayhew, 1974, p. 16). The first aim of a new member of Congress, then, is to secure a seat on the most electorally advantageous committee.

Committee assignment

All committees and subcommittees are organised along party lines. That is to say, that the party which has an overall majority in the chamber as a whole is entitled to have a majority of the seats on every committee and subcommittee. Logically enough, then, it is the two parties who allocate their members to committees. Each party in each chamber has a committee on committees, although their official names vary somewhat. In the Senate, there are the Democratic Steering Committee and the Republican Committee on Committees. In the House, there are the Democratic Steering and Policy Committee and the Republican Steering Committee (Foley and Owens, 1996, pp. 116–18).

Although the precise manner of choosing members of the committees on committees is different in each case, all involve some balance of party leaders and members elected by the caucus. This reflects the need for harmony between party leaders and rank-and-file members if the two groups are going to work together effectively in the forthcoming sessions. Party leaders will want to ensure that committees are filled with those who will work well towards party goals, while rank-and-file members require assignment to their preferred committee. On the whole, it is the committee preferences of rank-and-file members which dominate the assignment process, subject to availability.

Members' committee preferences differ according to their personal interests and how they choose to attempt to advance their careers. From this perspective, committees can be divided into four groups: prestige committees, policy committees, constituency committees and unrequested committees (Smith and Deering, 1990). A member bent on building up his power within the House might well aim for the House Rules Committee since this has considerable sway over the progress of most legislation. On the other hand, a member from a mainly rural area might request a place on the Agriculture Committee in order to ensure that she can protect the interests of the farming communities in her constituency. Then again, a senator with presidential aspirations might seek a place on the Foreign Affairs Committee in order to acquire and demonstrate expertise in matters that preoccupy most residents of the White House (see Box 16.7.)

The seniority principle

Once on a committee and subcommittees, members will almost invariably rise through the ranks largely on the basis of seniority. Seniority is acquired by years of continuous service on a committee. Thus a member who has served twelve years continuously on the same committee outranks one who has served only ten years.

The seniority system has certain advantages for members of Congress. First, those with most legislative experience of the issues dealt with by a committee will also be its highest ranking and most influential members. Secondly, it guarantees all members 'promotion' on a neutral basis: a member knows she need only wait her turn to rise to the top, probably to become chairperson of a subcommittee or even full committee. This also helps to avoid recriminations and feuds between members over promotions.

There are disadvantages to the seniority system, however. For example, it promotes the longest-serving committee members regardless of their talent, diligence or loyalty to party and colleagues. Seniority thus also frustrates more able but junior members of Congress. It was for reasons such as these that Congress gradually abandoned the absolute application of the seniority rule in 1970s. A series of changes gave the party caucuses the ultimate power to overturn the assignment of committee chairs based on seniority.

This was used in 1975 to unseat three incumbent committee chairpersons who owed their position to seniority. The next major departure from seniority did not occur until

Box 16.7

Committee preferences

Although some of the categories below overlap to a considerable extent, they do indicate the main motivations expressed by members when seeking particular committee assignments.

Prestige committees
Attract members primarily because of the status they confer.

Examples
House Appropriations Committee
House Ways and Means Committee
House Rules Committee
Senate Appropriations Committee
Senate Armed Services Committee
Senate Foreign Relations Committee

Policy committees
Attract members primarily because of the opportunity to influence policies of personal interest and national importance.

Examples
House Banking and Financial Services Committee
House Education and the Workforce Committee
House Judiciary Committee
Senate Armed Services Committee
Senate Finance Committee
Senate Small Business Committee

Constituency committees
Attract members primarily because of the opportunity to service the needs of a particularly important section of voters.

Examples
House Agriculture Committee
House Resources Committee
House Science Committee
Senate Agriculture, Nutrition and Forestry Committee
Senate Energy and Natural Resources Committee
Senate Environment and Public Works Committee

Unrequested committees
Fail to attract members because they offer few career or electoral benefits.

Examples
House Standards of Official Conduct Committee
Senate Rules and Administration Committee

Source: Adapted from Smith and Deering, 1990, pp. 87, 101

1985. In that year, the seventh-ranking member of the House Armed Services Committee, Les Aspin, campaigned successfully for the chair against the incumbent chairman and senior member, David Price. Price was considered by Democrats to be too supportive of President Reagan's policies and also suffered from ill health. Aspin promised more effective opposition to administration policies and duly won in a vote of House Democrats. More recently, in 1995, House Speaker Newt Gingrich, backed by the Republican caucus, ignored seniority in regard to the chairs of three committees.

Despite these exceptions, however, seniority remains the dominant principle in determining who shall rise to become chairpersons of congressional committees. To a considerable extent, this is because it avoids the problem of finding a better method of appointment: 'Reliance on seniority, unless there is an overwhelming reason to oppose the most senior member, resolves the question of choosing between the alternatives and minimises internal party strife' (Smith and Deering, 1990, p. 134).

Party leadership

Apart from the power that comes through committee service, members of Congress may also seek to become party leaders. As we saw in the previous chapter, party leaders do not have the disciplinary powers that would enable them to control party members. This is particularly true when party policy conflicts with members' constituency interests. Nevertheless, party leaders in Congress are in position to command the respect, if not the absolute loyalty of fellow party members. Although there are no formal rules governing who may occupy these top-level party positions, it is usually those who have served in Congress for some considerable time who are chosen. A second key factor is their personality and style. As befits an institution in which party is a significant though not dominant feature of members' behaviour, prospective party leaders must be seen as people who can energetically pursue party goals whilst simultaneously respecting individual legislator's autonomy. Tact, persuasion and goodwill towards colleagues are usually among the required qualities of party leaders. Box 16.8 lists the party leaders in the 105th Congress.

Speaker of the House

Speaker of the House is the most important party position in either chamber of Congress. This is in part owing to the fact that it is the only leadership position created by the Constitution. Originally intended as a non-partisan presiding officer, the Speaker is today the leader of the majority party in the House. All members take part in the election of the Speaker at the beginning of each new Congress. However, the vote is normally strictly partisan.

The Speaker possesses important powers which help him lead his party and the House. He is influential in determining the committee assignments of members of his party, who are therefore mindful of his opinion of them. He can influence the outcome of legislation through his power to choose the committee to which a bill is assigned, and he largely controls appointments to the Rules Committee, which determines how a bill will be handled on the floor of the House.

Box 16.8

Party leadership in Congress
Main office-holders in the 105th Congress (1997/98)

Republicans	Democrats
House	**House**
Speaker	–
Newt Gingrich (Georgia)	–
Majority Leader	*Minority Leader*
Dick Armey (Texas)	Richard Gephardt (Missouri)
Majority Whip	*Minority Whip*
Tom Delay (Texas)	David Bonior (Michigan)
Senate	**Senate**
Majority Leader	*Minority Leader*
Trent Lott (Mississippi)	Thomas Daschle (South Dakota)
Majority Whip	*Minority Whip*
Don Nickles (Oklahoma)	Wendell Ford (Kentucky)

When the president is of a different party, the Speaker can also take on the role of unofficial 'leader of the opposition'. Speaker Tip O'Neill tried to do just this during the first six years of the Reagan administration. Even so, O'Neill was not able to hold his party together in opposition to President Reagan's tax and budget proposals, thus underlining once again the limits of party authority in Congress. Speaker Newt Gingrich sought to go beyond oppositional status in the 1990s and tried to wrest national political leadership from President Bill Clinton. However, this failed and Gingrich succeeded only in lowering his standing in public opinion polls, as respondents saw him as aggressive and extreme.

In 1997, Gingrich's bid for power was further reined in when there were two attempts by some House Republicans to unseat him as Speaker. Although both failed, the fact that they were in part caused by resentment of Gingrich's increasing power served as a salutary reminder to the Speaker that his tenure in office cannot be taken for granted. As a result, Gingrich's power was significantly reduced. Finally, as a result of the poor showing by Republican House candidates in the 1998 mid-term elections, Gingrich was obliged to step down as speaker. Ultimately, therefore, the Speaker's power is dependent upon the will of the party caucus in the House. If it wants a strong leader, it will have one; but if it prefers to devolve power to committee chairs, there is little he can do about it.

House majority and minority leaders and whips

House majority and minority leaders and whips are chosen in intra-party elections. The majority leader's principal task is to support the work of the Speaker. He also has a distinct advantage on the floor of the House, because he is always first to be recognised by the Speaker. The minority leader, by definition, has no supportive relationship with the Speaker. He does, however, carry out similar functions to those of the majority leader – liaising between party members, gathering intelligence and trying to persuade them to follow party policy. If the president is of the same party, then the minority leader will have an additional important task of liaising with the White House.

The main function of the majority and minority whips is to advise party members about important votes that are coming up and finding out their members' voting intentions. In this they are assisted by an elaborate network of junior whips. However, despite the large number of whips in the House, their influence over members' voting behaviour is limited. Despite the significantly increased activities of party leaders in the 1990s (Foley and Owens, 1996, p. 153), the fact remains that representatives are not dependent upon their party for either nomination or election to Congress. This means that party leaders lack the decisive weapon enjoyed by their homologues in many other political systems: the power to deprive a member of his or her seat.

House caucus and conference chairpersons

The Democratic caucus and the Republican conference consist of all the members of the respective parties. If members wished it, the chairpersons of these two groups could wield considerable power, even more than that of the Speaker and majority and minority leaders. Since the caucus or conference chooses all other party leaders, it has the potential to define the hierarchy of party leadership.

In practice, members who do not accept binding party discipline see little need for powerful caucus or conference leaders. Nevertheless, chairing the caucus can be a useful step on the political ladder for an ambitious member of Congress.

Senate party leaders

There is no equivalent position to that of the Speaker in the Senate. The presiding officer stipulated in the Constitution is an outsider, namely the vice-president of the United States.

This means that the majority and minority leaders take on the mantle of party leaders. The majority leader, for example, has some of the same responsibilities as the Speaker, including scheduling legislation, organising the chamber and acting as a focal point for party unity. The minority leader, when the president is of the other party, may also try to emulate the speaker by assuming the role of 'leader of the opposition'.

However, owing to the differences in culture between the two chambers, these positions are of less importance in the Senate than they are in the House. Senators are more individualistic and less deferential than members of the House. This means that leadership in the Senate must be even more collegial in nature. Gone are the days of the 1950s when Lyndon B. Johnson, with the aid of a few senior senators, could cajole or even bully members into compliance. The Senate is much more a body of equals than it was then, and party leaders are expected to work in a co-operative rather than hierarchical manner. Combined with the fact that they have no formal, constitutional basis for their power, they have little choice but to do so.

Congressional staffs

Senators and representatives are clearly the most prominent members of the Congress, but they are not the only important group in the legislature. Increasingly, the staff who support congressional committees and the individual members themselves are being seen as vital participants in the legislative process. Indeed, these congressional staff have been characterised as 'the invisible force in American lawmaking' (Fox and Hammond, 1977).

There has been a rapid increase in the number of these personal and committee aides in the past fifty years, as well as in the number of those working for congressional support agencies. Between 1967 and 1977, the number of staff working in the offices of members of Congress in Washington almost doubled, from 5,804 to 10,486. In the case of senators, in 1967 they had an average of 17.5 staff per member, including those working back at the offices in the state; by 1991, the average was 57 per member. Committee staff also grew rapidly in number, from a total of 1,337 in 1970 to 3,231 in 1991. When those working for support agencies, such as the Congressional Research Service were included, it made for a total of some 24,000 staff working for Congress in the early 1990s (Hart, 1995, p. 188). Although the levels stabilised at the end of the 1970s, owing mainly to financial constraints, and were then cut by the Republicans when they captured Congress in 1994, the thousands of congressional staff who remain must clearly fulfil important functions.

Committee staff

The rapid growth of committee staff began with the Legislative Reorganization Act of 1946. This permitted each standing committee to employ up to four professional staff and six clerical aides. The number was increased in 1970, and then in 1974 the House raised its number to eighteen professional assistants and twelve clerical aides (Smith and Deering, 1990, p. 149). A variety of factors accounts for the increase. In the first place, Congress simply has to cope with more legislative work than before – this reflects the general growth in governmental activity in the United States since the Second World War.

Secondly, the marked upsurge in the 1970s was stimulated by the attempt to reassert congressional power *vis-à-vis* the presidency. Congressional laxity was seen as partly responsible for the Vietnam and Watergate episodes, and increased staff was considered one means of strengthening both the legislative and oversight functions of Congress.

Thirdly, the subcommittee revolution of the 1970s also played a part, particularly in the House of Representatives. Between 1970 and 1990, the share of staff in the House attached to subcommittees, as opposed to full committees, rose from 23.2 per cent to 45.2 per cent (Smith and Deering, 1990, p. 152).

Committee staff, and many personal staff, are thus closely involved in all the main functions of Congress. They organise hearings, draft legislation, meet interest groups and negotiate between members on details of policy and votes. Critics argue that they have become more influential than the elected legislators themselves, or that, rather than help deal with the congressional workload, they actually increase it unnecessarily in order to justify their existence.

Certainly, even major bills, such as the Budget and Impoundment Control Act of 1974, are marked up, given initial consideration and redrafted by staff (Fox and Hammond, 1977, p. 143). While the ultimate approval of such legislation remains with members themselves, there can be little doubt that the duties of congressional staff afford them considerable opportunities for influencing the content of national legislation.

Personal staff

As already noted, some of the staff attached personally to members of Congress carry out legislative and oversight functions. There is evidence to suggest, however, that most of the work done by personal staff is connected to the representative roles of members (Vogler, 1983, p. 130). Employed either in Washington DC or in offices back in the state or district, they deal with constituents' complaints and problems, schedule meetings and personal appearances for the member and try to ensure a flow of good publicity. They also conduct frequent polls in order to try to keep their member in tune with political developments and moods among their constituents.

As usual with members of Congress, the electoral connection here is all too apparent. The ultimate task of personal staff engaged in representative work is to provide the high level of constituency service and political intelligence that will ensure their member's re-election. Given today's incumbency re-election success rates of better than 90 per cent, the creation of large personal staffs seems to have paid off.

 Summary

The central feature of legislative activity in Congress is the committee. Although the precise amount of power wielded by committees and their chairpersons varies over time, committees remain central because it is in committee that the details of legislation are hammered out. Committees are also important because they are the principal instrument of career progression for members. This is both because they offer the best opportunity for members to service their constituents' interests, thus enhancing their electoral prospects; and because service on a committee over time usually brings a steady increase in power and prestige with colleagues.

Party is also a significant factor in the organisation of Congress, because it brings coherence and discipline to legislative activity. Ultimately, however, members of Congress remain individualists who will come together with party colleagues when it appears to be in their interest, but will not hesitate to exploit the fragmented structures and processes to serve the needs of their constituents and their own careers. Legislating in Congress is therefore a complex and difficult process. It requires considerable bargaining and compromise in order to accommodate the diverse interests of members; for without such accommodation, it is relatively easy for a minority of members to block the legislative process.

Topics for discussion

1. Why is the committee system central to the legislative process in Congress?

2. Why is it so difficult to centralise authority within Congress?

3. What are the most important differences between the Senate and the House of Representatives?

4. What are the advantages and disadvantages of a national legislature that finds it difficult to legislate?

Further reading

See suggestions at the end of Chapter 15 (page 339).

References

Bailey, C., 1989, *The US Congress* (Oxford: Basil Blackwell)

Foley, M. and Owens, J., 1996, *Congress and the Presidency: Institutional politics in a separated system* (Manchester: Manchester University Press)

Fox, H. and Hammond, S., 1977 *Congressional Staffs: The invisible force in American lawmaking* (New York: Free Press)

Hart, J., 1995, *The Presidential Branch* (2nd edn, Chatham, NJ: Chatham House)

Mayhew, D., 1974, *Congress: The electoral connection* (New Haven: Yale University Press)

Hershey, M., 1997, 'The congressional elections', pp. 205–40 in *The Elections of 1996: Reports and interpretations*, eds G. Pomper *et al.* (Chatham, NJ: Chatham House)

Smith, S. and Deering, C., 1990, *Committees in Congress* (2nd edn, Washington DC: Congressional Quarterly Press)

Vogler, D., 1983, *The Politics of Congress* (4th edn, Boston: Allyn & Bacon)

Woll, P., 1985, *Congress* (Boston: Little, Brown)

part

VI

The judicial process

'We are under a Constitution, but the Constitution is what the judges say it is.' So said Charles Evan Hughes, politician and jurist, and later to become Chief Justice of the United States Supreme Court. His perceptive remark succinctly identifies the vital connection between the American political system and the American judiciary. As we saw in Part I, American politics is conducted within the framework of a written Constitution which establishes the powers of different branches of government, as well as many of the fundamental rights and liberties of American citizens.

The Constitution, however, is a brief document, written mostly in broad, even vague language. Its precise meaning in any particular situation is rarely self-evident. Consequently, the application of constitutional law requires constitutional interpretation, and that has become the primary function of the federal judiciary, especially the United States Supreme Court.

In Part VI, we examine first the origins of the Supreme Court's role as the authoritative interpreter of the Constitution, and the procedures and processes through which it plays that role (Chapter 17). We then go on to analyse how and why the Supreme Court transcends its judicial role and is, in many ways, a political body. We assess, too, its overall importance and its impact upon American politics and society (Chapter 18).

Contents

17

The Supreme Court and judicial review

The key to understanding the Supreme Court is to appreciate that it is both a judicial and a political body. This means that its formal structures and procedures are in essence those of a court of law, while its agenda, its interpretation of the Constitution and its impact are inescapably political. In this chapter we focus primarily upon the legal and judicial aspects of the Court; although as befits the dual nature of the institution, even here it is impossible to avoid a political dimension.

Article III of the Constitution deals with the judicial power of the American system of government and it makes the United States Supreme Court the nation's highest judicial body. Most importantly, it is the final court of appeal from the lower federal courts and the court systems of the fifty States in all cases involving the Constitution or federal laws.

In line with the principle of separation of powers, the framers of the Constitution wanted to ensure that the judges, or *justices*, of the Supreme Court would be truly independent of both the executive and legislative branches. They also wanted the Court to be beyond the control of the electorate. For these reasons, justices of the Supreme Court are appointed, not elected; and they are appointed for life, so that their tenure of office does not depend on pleasing either the people or their political representatives. There is no doubt, therefore, that the framers wanted a genuinely independent Supreme Court that would settle legal disputes without fear or favour.

Article III, however, says nothing about a political role for the Court. In particular, it does not say that the Supreme Court has the power to declare legislation or executive branch policies unconstitutional. Yet it is precisely this power over federal and state legislation that has changed the Court from being a mere judicial body into a major political force in the American system of government. Let us examine how and why this came about.

Judicial review

The foundation of the Supreme Court's legal and political power is the American version of the doctrine of *judicial review*. This empowers the Court to declare any law or action of a governmental institution to be unconstitutional. This entails a majority of the nine justices deciding that a challenged law or administrative action violates one or more clauses of the Constitution. When a law is declared unconstitutional by the Court, it is null and void. The power of judicial review extends beyond *constitutional interpretation*, however. The Supreme Court also adjudicates alleged violations of federal laws by state laws or by the actions of private organisations. This is known as *statutory interpretation*.

There is, however, a crucial difference between constitutional interpretation and statutory interpretation. If the Supreme Court interprets a federal statute in a way that offends Congress, then the legislators can simply amend the law to nullify the Court's decision. If, on the other hand, a Court decision is based upon constitutional interpretation, then Congress has no power to overturn it. True, it can initiate the process of constitutional amendment, but this is extremely difficult to bring to a successful conclusion. In virtually all cases, then, a decision of the Supreme Court based upon constitutional interpretation is final, unless the Court can be persuaded to change its mind.

The power of judicial review, therefore, has serious implications for the operation of American democracy. Since, in principle, all governmental policies can be challenged in the federal courts as unconstitutional, it can be argued that the Supreme Court, as the final court of appeal, is superior to both the Congress and the president in matters of legislation and public policy. Indeed, critics of the Court have sometimes alleged that the United States has 'government by judiciary'.

In fact, such charges are a gross exaggeration. As we shall see, there are many practical restrictions on the power of judicial review. Nevertheless, because the Supreme Court is recognised as the authoritative interpreter of the Constitution, it has a stature and role in American government that makes it a political force to be reckoned with. Remarkably, however, it is not at all clear that the framers of the Constitution intended the Court to play such an important role.

Inventing the Supreme Court

As noted above, Article III of the Constitution clearly created a *court* when it opened with the words 'The judicial power of the United States shall be vested in one Supreme Court, and in such inferior courts as the Congress may from time to time ordain and establish'.

As many scholars have pointed out, however, Article III makes no mention of judicial review or of the power of the Supreme Court to declare legislation unconstitutional. Nor does the Judiciary Act of 1789, by which Congress created the first federal court system. In other words, both the Constitution and the first Congressional legislation on the matter are silent on the very power that today makes the Supreme Court a major actor in American politics.

The explanation for this silence lies in the fact that, even in 1787, the idea that unelected judges should be able to nullify the Acts of elected legislators was controversial. Those who opposed judicial review believed it was simply undemocratic and would be employed on behalf of conservative policies. Those who favoured it argued that fears of judicial autocracy were fanciful, though they did hope that judicial review would act as a brake on the 'democratic excesses' of the electorate. No agreement was reached at Philadelphia and accordingly, the wording of Article III was left vague.

The proponents of judicial review, however, continued their campaign. In the course of the public debates over ratification of the new Constitution, Alexander Hamilton established their basic case in a three-step argument in *The Federalist* (no. 78). First, he pointed out that since the Constitution was the supreme law of the United States, legislative Acts which conflicted with it must be illegitimate. Secondly, in the event that such a conflict was alleged to exist, some body or another must be empowered to interpret the Constitution in order to arbitrate the dispute. Thirdly, Hamilton argued that the Supreme Court was the logical institution to play this role: after all, courts had traditionally performed the task of interpreting other forms of law. Moreover, to allow legislative bodies to exercise review, as some suggested, would create the unsatisfactory situation in which legislators would sit in judgement on the constitutionality of their own actions. To say the least, this would raise doubts about their impartiality in the matter.

Hamilton made one further argument of great importance: he denied that giving the Court the power to strike down Acts of Congress and state legislatures would make the federal judiciary the most powerful branch of government. On the contrary, he famously predicted that a Supreme Court endowed with judicial review would prove 'the least dangerous branch' of the government, because it possessed 'neither Force nor Will, but only judgement'.

By this, he meant that the Court was inherently weaker than either the Congress or the presidency. Those two branches controlled both expenditure and law enforcement and without these, the Court was in no position to implement its decisions. It would have to rely on the co-operation of Congress and the president. Furthermore, Congress and the president were driven by the will and desires of the population, something which could lead to rash actions. The justices of the Supreme Court, on the other hand, would not be ideological partisans: they would be impartial legal technicians – judges – who merely established the facts of whether a given law conflicted with a given clause of the Constitution.

Plausible as it was, Hamilton's argument did not yet convince the country. As a result, the early years of the Supreme Court were exceedingly dull and uneventful. Without the power of judicial review, the Court lacked stature compared with the Congress, the presidency or even the higher offices of state government. As a consequence, it proved difficult to persuade people of high standing to serve on the Court and it appeared destined to play only a minor part in the nation's government.

Marbury v. Madison: a political coup

The transformation in the role and power of the Supreme Court came in 1803, as a direct result of the bitterly fought presidential election of 1800. The more conservative

Federalist party, having lost that election to the Jeffersonians, sought to use their remaining months in office to make the unelected judiciary a bastion of Federalist power. Most significantly, the outgoing Federalist secretary of state, John Marshall, was appointed chief justice of the Supreme Court.

In the case of *Marbury v. Madison* (1803), Marshall and his colleagues staged a political coup by claiming the power to declare an Act of Congress unconstitutional (see Box 17.1). With consummate skill, Marshall avoided a political war with the Jeffersonians – a war the Court was bound to lose – yet simultaneously won implicit acceptance of the power of judicial review. To Chief Justice John Marshall, then, goes the ultimate credit for making judicial review of legislation a significant reality of American political life.

We will examine in the next chapter how the Marshall Court and its successors used the power it had awarded itself. First, though, it is important to understand how the process of judicial review works. For this reminds us that, no matter how embroiled it becomes in politics, the Supreme Court operates in a manner quite different from other

---

Box 17.1

Marbury v. Madison (1803) and the creation of judicial review

Chief Justice Marshall headed a thoroughly Federalist Supreme Court when the *Marbury* case came before it. Yet the politics of the issues involved were most delicate. Towards the end of the outgoing Federalist administration of President John Adams (1797–1801), several new justices of the peace were appointed, all staunch Federalists, but their commissions were not delivered before the new administration of President Thomas Jefferson (1801–9) took over. Given the bitter rivalry between Federalists and Jeffersonians, the new secretary of state, James Madison, refused to complete delivery of the commissions, one of which was destined for William Marbury. Marbury went to court, claiming that Section 13 of the Judiciary Act of 1789 empowered the Supreme Court to order Madison to complete delivery of his commission.

The Court sympathised with Marbury, but knew that a decision in his favour would invoke the wrath – and disobedience – of the Jefferson administration. Since this would damage the Court's prestige and, therefore, its potential use as an instrument of Federalist power, the Marshall Court ruled in favour of Madison. However, it did so in a manner that made the Court a vital player in the future of American politics. Marshall argued that he could not order Madison to complete Marbury's commission because Section 13 of the Judiciary Act violated the Constitution by enlarging the Court's power of *Original Jurisdiction*; and that such an enlargement could only be achieved by constitutional amendment, and not by federal statute. Many scholars doubt the validity of Marshall's argument. However, it was politically adroit. Mollified by their immediate victory, the Jeffersonians did nothing substantial to negate the Court's claim to the power of judicial review and the power to declare an act of Congress unconstitutional.

political institutions. Quite simply, it is a *court*, and therefore its procedures are those of a court.

Stages of judicial review

Initiating a case

There are several formal steps through which any Supreme Court case proceeds. The first is that an individual, organisation or governmental body must decide to *litigate*, that is, to bring a law suit in a lower federal court or a state court. These litigants must do more than merely allege that someone has violated the Constitution: they must show that they have personally suffered some concrete harm as a result of the violation.

In theory, this first stage means that litigation cannot be used simply as a forum for political debate or controversy. For example, the requirement that the litigants must have a real stake in the case aims to prevent people from challenging laws simply because they oppose them on political grounds.

It is also important to note that the judiciary cannot take the initiative on an issue, unlike the president or the Congress. Rather, it must wait until the issue is placed before the courts in the form of a law suit. Moreover, it is not usually possible to take a case straight to the Supreme Court: litigants must work their way up through the hierarchy of lower courts (see Box 17.2), and so a case may take several years before the Justices settle the question definitively.

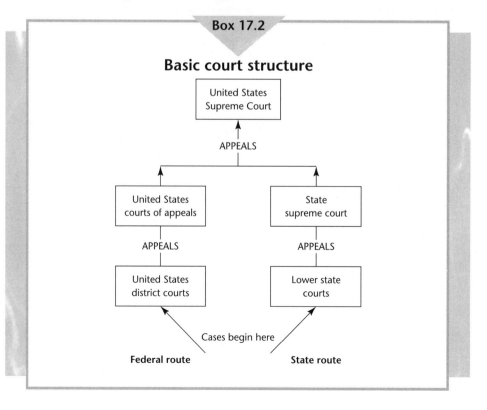

Box 17.2

Basic court structure

These constraints on the Court's freedom of manoeuvre are in line with the language of Article III of the Constitution, which says that the Court's power extends to all 'cases and controversies' arising under the Constitution. Cases must be real legal disputes, not merely hypothetical or political arguments.

Interest group intervention

In practice, litigation today is frequently initiated by specialist interest groups whose strategies are legal but whose mission is entirely political. These groups seek out individuals who have real cases and effectively take them over. They provide individual litigants with the legal and financial resources to take their case through the expensive minefield of preparing and arguing cases in the judicial system, if necessary going through one or more appeals to get to the Supreme Court. These organisations hope that by winning a concrete case for the individual, they will simultaneously win a constitutional ruling that will benefit others. In short, these interest groups sponsor or manufacture test cases which they hope will have wide social and political significance.

Perhaps the most famous example of the successful use of the courts to bring about political reforms is that by the National Association for the Advancement of Colored People (NAACP). This group sponsored some of the main cases in the racial segregation controversies of the 1950s and 1960s and became a role model for other litigation groups.

The American Civil Liberties Union (ACLU) is another group which frequently sponsors litigation on behalf of liberal political causes. In the 1970s, for example, it created a specialist branch, the Women's Rights Project, which proved successful in persuading the Supreme Court that the Constitution should be interpreted to ban most of the legal distinctions between men and women.

Class-action suits

An important legal device which greatly aids the political use of the courts by interest groups is the so-called class-action suit. This means that an individual who brings a case may do so not merely on her own behalf, but also for all those similarly situated. An example would be that of an African American parent whose children are denied entry to a school because of their race. As well as suing to have her own children admitted, a class action enables her to sue on behalf of all African-American parents throughout the entire country whose children are similar victims of racial discrimination. Class-actions, then, combined with the activities of litigation interest groups, ensure that major political issues are frequently brought to the courts, albeit in the guise of lawsuits.

Appeals

As noted above, the first round of a constitutional case takes place in a federal district court or a state court. (The only exceptions being the one or two cases each year which come direct to the Court under its *Original Jurisdiction*). When the decision is announced in the lower court, the loser may appeal to either a federal appeals court or a state's highest court. These courts may affirm or reverse the lower court's decision, but either way, the loser may then try an appeal to the Supreme Court.

At this point, however, we come to a most important feature of the Supreme Court. It is not obliged to hear any appeal. Originally, there were a considerable number of appeals that the Court was obliged to hear. Owing to the Court's increasingly heavy workload, however, Congress has removed virtually all mandatory appeals and has left the Court with full discretion over its docket. Thus, as Box 17.3 indicates, the justices receive thousands of petitions for appeal each year, mostly in the form of petitions for review called *writs of certiorari*. From these, however, the Court frequently accepts less than one hundred for full consideration: that is, cases accepted and decided with written opinions.

Moreover, the Court is not obliged to give any reason for its refusal to hear the thousands of appeals it rejects each year. This means that the justices can avoid involvement in an issue if they wish. A prime example of this occurred during the Vietnam War, when antiwar activists wanted the Court to pronounce the war unconstitutional because President Johnson had never asked Congress for a formal declaration of war. Although there was a clear constitutional issue here, the Court did not think it wise to take upon itself such a momentous decision as war and peace. As a result, it either refused to hear appeals at all or settled them in a way that avoided the issue of the constitutionality of the war.

The Supreme Court's agenda

The Supreme Court, then, has a large measure of control over its own agenda and this flexibility can at times be most useful. On the other hand, the Court does have an obligation to settle constitutional conflicts and it would be of little value as an institution if it avoided every controversial issue. As Justice William O. Douglas (1939–75)

Box 17.3

The Supreme Court's discretionary control

Term	Cases decided with full opinions	Review denied
1992/93	119	6,110
1993/94	96	6,513
1994/95	95	6,971
1995/96	92	6,384
1996/97	101	6,517

Source: Adapted from the annual statistical review of the Supreme Court, *Harvard Law Review*, various years

once observed, 'Courts sit to determine questions on stormy as well as calm days.' Moreover, as we shall in the next chapter, the cases that are brought before the Court are often precisely those which are politically controversial. So as the nineteenth-century commentator Alexis de Tocqueville famously said (admittedly with a measure of exaggeration), 'Scarcely any political question arises in the United States that is not resolved, sooner or later, into a judicial question.'

Judicial decision making: the formal procedures

The basic procedures that the justices of the Supreme Court follow in deciding a case are relatively straightforward. First comes the decision whether or not to take an appeal at all: five votes are formally needed to grant judicial review of a case, but the custom is that the 'rule of four' applies. Thus if four justices favour review, a fifth justice will supply the additional vote.

Next, the Court schedules a date for *oral argument*. This is when lawyers for each party to the case will appear before the justices and in public to present the arguments for their clients. Normally, each side is allowed thirty minutes to speak, but the lawyers may be frequently interrupted by questions from the justices. The record suggests that the justices are rarely swayed by the oral arguments, and the questions they put to the lawyers are intended mainly to draw attention to a point which they have already decided is dispositive, one way or the other.

This is in part because before oral argument, the lawyers will have submitted detailed, written *briefs* stating their arguments in full. Furthermore, interest groups also frequently submit briefs at this stage. Although not always a party to the case, an interest group is allowed to participate as an *amicus curiae* (literally, friend of the court). In its amicus brief, the interest group will hope to place before the justices evidence or arguments that they may find persuasive. Some briefs rely on the special expertise of the group concerned. For example, in cases concerning abortion rights, the American Medical Association submitted briefs which addressed the specifically medical aspects of the abortion issue. Other groups may offer innovative legal arguments or, like the National Organization for Women, hope to impress the justices with the fact that their large membership deems abortion rights to be fundamental to their lives.

Another significant participant at this point may be the federal government, in the form of the solicitor-general. Coming below the attorney-general, the solicitor-general is the second-ranking member of the Department of Justice. The solicitor-general frequently appears before the Court, either because the United States is itself a party to the case, or because it has a particular view to articulate as an *amicus curiae*.

For much of the period since 1870, when the office was created, the solicitor-general was regarded by the justices as a valued source of neutral, legal expertise. Because of this, the solicitor-general was often referred to as 'the tenth justice'. However, like virtually every other aspect of the Court's environment, the office has recently become much more politicised. Under President Reagan, for example, the solicitor-general was sent to the Court as the standard-bearer of the administration's crusade against abortion rights and affirmative action. As a consequence, the office lost some of the respect previously shown to it by the justices.

Case conference

After reading the briefs and hearing the oral arguments, the justices meet in a *case conference* to discuss and to take preliminary votes. Many cases are decided unanimously. However, of those cases deemed sufficiently important to warrant written opinions, over half involve at least one dissenting justice, as Box 17.4 indicates.

In theory, a five-to-four decision is as authoritative as a unanimous decision. In practice, however, the former is far more vulnerable to attack than the latter. First, a five-to-four split indicates that there may be good constitutional reasons for believing the case to have been decided wrongly. Secondly, a five-to-four decision can easily be reversed when one of the majority justices leaves the Court and a new one is appointed. A unanimous decision, on the other hand, is well nigh unassailable. In the major cases where it is possible, therefore, the justices work hard to produce unanimity, including making compromises over the wording and scope of the opinion. This will help to sustain a decision which is likely to meet with resistance in some quarters. Unanimity was an important feature, for example, of the Court's desegregation decision, *Brown v. Board of Education* (1954), and also of its decision ordering President Nixon to release the 'Watergate tapes' (*US v. Nixon*, 1974).

After the vote, the chief justice, provided he is with the majority, assigns himself or another member of the majority the task of producing a formal, written *opinion* explaining the Court's decision. If, however, the chief justice is in the minority, then the most senior associate justice in the majority assigns the opinion. Those justices in the minority may well decide to write a *dissenting opinion*, explaining why they

---

Box 17.4

Unanimity rates on the Court: decisions with full opinions

Term	Unanimous decisions	With concurring opinions	With dissenting opinions
1992/93	35 (30.7%)	16 (14.0%)	63 (55.3%)
1993/94	25 (28.7%)	12 (13.8%)	50 (57.5%)
1994/95	28 (32.6%)	8 (9.3%)	50 (58.1%)
1995/96	29 (38.7%)	3 (4.0%)	43 (57.3%)
1996/97	32 (37.2%)	7 (8.1%)	47 (54.7%)

Source: Adapted from the annual statistical review of the Supreme Court, *Harvard Law Review*, various years. The number of cases in this table are calculated slightly differently from those in Box 17.3, above, so the totals do not necessarily agree

disagree with the majority. Yet a third type of opinion is the *concurrence*, in which a justice usually explains that he agrees with the majority's decision but for different reasons than those given in the Court's opinion.

Before the Court's decision is formally announced, draft versions of these opinions are circulated among the justices for their comment and may well be amended as a result. Votes may even be switched at this stage. Eventually, the Court announces its decision and the opinion(s) are published (see Box 17.5).

Although few people outside of politics, the law schools and the media actually read Supreme Court opinions, they are nevertheless very important. The opinion of the Court is both an explanation and a justification of the Court's decision. An opinion which fails to convince those who read it will give ammunition to those who disapprove of the result. For example, the opinion of the Court in *Roe v. Wade* (1973), which announced a new right to abortion, was deemed seriously flawed even by some who support abortion rights. This has strengthened the hand of pro-life activists who wish to see *Roe* overturned.

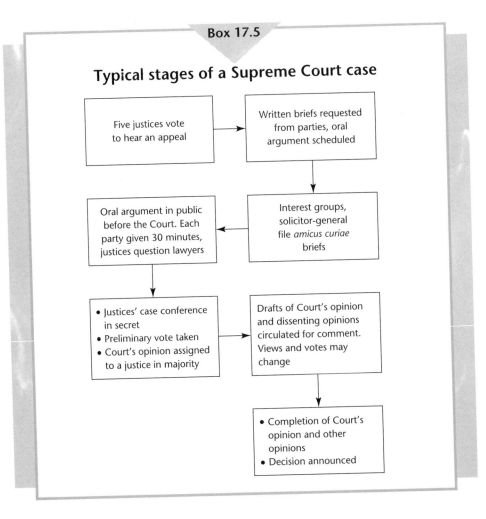

Box 17.5

Typical stages of a Supreme Court case

Five justices vote to hear an appeal

→ Written briefs requested from parties, oral argument scheduled

Oral argument in public before the Court. Each party given 30 minutes, justices question lawyers

← Interest groups, solicitor-general file *amicus curiae* briefs

- Justices' case conference in secret
- Preliminary vote taken
- Court's opinion assigned to a justice in majority

→ Drafts of Court's opinion and dissenting opinions circulated for comment. Views and votes may change

- Completion of Court's opinion and other opinions
- Decision announced

Judicial reasoning and politics

The procedures outlined above are those of a court, not those of what we traditionally think of as a political institution. Moreover, as we saw from Alexander Hamilton's defence of judicial review, Supreme Court justices were expected to eschew politics and to carry out their duties in a politically neutral manner. Yet today there are many judicial scholars who argue that it is neither possible nor even desirable for the justices to escape from their own political, philosophical or moral values. Others, however, believe that the Court can usually make decisions that are politically neutral and that it should at least always attempt to do so. Let us examine each of these arguments in turn.

Judicial traditionalism

Until the twentieth century, the notion of politically neutral, or value-free, Supreme Court justices was largely accepted. At the heart of this concept was the belief that when a justice struck down a law as unconstitutional, he was not enforcing his own values but rather the values enshrined in the Constitution by the framers. The justice merely used his legal knowledge and skills to discover what the will, or intention, of the framers actually was and how it should be applied in the particular case before the Court.

Justice Owen Roberts expressed this view of judicial neutrality in 1936 in the case of *US v. Butler*. The decision in *Butler* was one of a series in which the Court struck down some key elements of President Franklin D. Roosevelt's New Deal. Many people thought the justices were simply motivated by their ideological conservatism. Roberts, however, rejected this accusation:

> It is sometimes said that the Court assumes the power to overrule or control the action of the people's representatives. This is a misconception. The Constitution is the supreme law of the land ordained and established by the people. All legislation must conform to the principles it lays down. When an Act of Congress is appropriately challenged in the courts as not conforming to the constitutional mandate, the judicial branch of government has only one duty – to lay the article of the Constitution which is invoked beside the statute which is challenged and to decide whether the latter squares with the former. All the Court does or can do is to announce its considered judgement upon the question. The only power it has, if such it may be called, is the power of judgement. This Court neither approves nor condemns any legislative policy.

Roberts sought to make a vital distinction between the *political result* of a Supreme Court decision and *the process* by which that decision was made. Thus, although the decision in *Butler* had great political significance because it scuppered President Roosevelt's policy for agricultural recovery, that did not mean that the Court's decision was motivated by a desire to defeat that policy. All Roberts and his colleagues had done, he maintained, was judge that the policy was at odds with the design of the Constitution. That was a quite separate question from whether the policy was good for the country.

Today, judicial traditionalists emphasise that the justices of the Supreme Court must follow the original intentions of those who framed the Constitution. They argue that the doctrine of *original intent* prevents justices from inflicting their personal policy preferences on the country. In turn, this secures the legitimacy of judicial review in a democracy. For if, on the contrary, the justices abandon original intent and substitute their own or some other set of values for those intended by the framers, then unelected judges are in effect selecting the values and policies that govern the country. Such a situation, they claim, is more akin to judicial autocracy than representative democracy.

As we shall see shortly, many doubt whether judicial neutrality is really possible. However, there are plenty of instances in which justices of the Supreme Court have clearly voted in line with what they see as the command of the Constitution, even though this meant going against their own personal values. For example, in the 1972 case of *Furman v. Georgia*, Justice Harry Blackmun declared himself to be personally opposed to capital punishment, yet he voted to uphold the constitutionality of various state death penalty laws. And in 1989, in the highly emotive decision in *Texas v. Johnson*, Justice Anthony Kennedy voted to uphold the right to burn the American flag as a political protest, even though he expressed his distaste for that activity. He ruefully noted that, 'The hard fact is that sometimes we must make decisions we do not like. We make them because they are right, right in the sense that the law and the Constitution, as we see them, compel the result.'

Judicial modernists

Other justices and scholars see many problems in the doctrine of original intent. In the first place, it is by no means always easy to establish exactly what the framers did intend. We have already seen that they left Article III unclear on the role and powers of the Supreme Court and the same lack of precision characterises many other clauses of the Constitution. What is an 'unreasonable search and seizure' (Fourth Amendment) or a 'cruel and unusual punishment' (Eighth Amendment)? Traditionalists argue that where the text of the Constitution is unclear, the historical record surrounding it will help. Not so, say the modernists: evidence such as debates in Congress may simply reveal that politicians who supported a particular Constitutional clause did so for different reasons and with different understandings of what was intended.

However, modernists believe that even if the original meaning of a clause is clear, it does not follow that the justices should be bound by it. After all, they argue, much of the Constitution was written in 1787 and those who drafted it could not possibly foresee the needs and values of American society in future centuries. Chief Justice Marshall, the architect of judicial review, identified this dilemma early on. In 1819, in *McCulloch v. Maryland*, he wrote that the Constitution was 'intended to endure for ages to come, and, consequently, to be adapted to the various crises of human affairs.' Marshall thus created the concept of the *living Constitution*. In this view, the Constitution is an organism which must grow and adapt as society develops. It is the duty of the Court to interpret it flexibly, so that the country is not oppressed by the dead hand of the past.

In effect, this power to reinterpret the Constitution in the light of changing societal needs can amount to the power to amend the Constitution. For this reason, Woodrow Wilson, once famously wrote that 'The Supreme Court is a constitutional convention in continuous session.' Of course, the original Constitution did provide for a process of amendment in Article V, but this is too cumbersome to be invoked on every occasion that a significant innovation is required. Many scholars and, indeed, judges believe that while the Supreme Court must be faithful to the spirit of the original Constitution, it must define that spirit by reference to contemporary values. As Justice William Brennan said in 1985 in response to traditionalist criticisms: 'We current justices read the Constitution in the only way that we can: as twentieth-century Americans.'

Virtually all justices today accept that their task of interpreting the Constitution involves some measure of 'updating'. A clear example is the current interpretation of the Eighth Amendment's ban on 'cruel and unusual punishments': even those who most admire intentionalism agree that ear-clipping, branding and other punishments familiar to the framers in 1787 are no longer permissible.

What divides the justices, then, is the degree of creativity they allow themselves in applying the Constitution. At one end of the spectrum is the 'intentionalist' or 'strict interpretivist' whose ideal it is to follow closely the will of the framers (see Box 17.6). At the opposite end are the 'non-interpretivists' who not only pay little or no heed to the original meaning of the Constitution, but are also willing to create new rights on subjects that the framers had never even contemplated. Between these two extremes are those justices, probably a majority, who take a pragmatic approach, trying to harmonise fidelity to original meaning with the demands of contemporary realities.

Judicial role

We can see from the foregoing discussion that the concept of 'judicial role' is an important one in understanding how the Court works. Unlike others involved in making decisions that determine public policy, most Supreme Court justices do not believe that

---

Box 17.6

Approaches to constitutional interpretation

Traditionalist	Pragmatist	Modernist
Strict Interpretivism or *Strict Construction*, follows the original intent of the framers	Balances traditionalist concerns against those of modernists	*Non-interpretivism* or *Broad Construction*', disregards original intent, creative in applying contemporary values to interpret the Constitution

they can simply vote for their own political preferences. Even the most non-interpretivist of justices will at least argue in his written opinion that his vote is explained by his understanding of what the Constitution requires, rather than his personal notions of good public policy. As the traditionalist scholar and failed Supreme Court nominee, Robert Bork, once commented with acid humour, 'The way an institution advertises tells you what it thinks its customers demand.' For the fact is that the public *does* expect the justices of the Supreme Court to behave like judges, and not like politicians. Moreover, much of the authority and prestige which the Court possesses depends upon being perceived as, if not totally above politics, then at least different from 'politics as usual'.

The Supreme Court therefore has a delicate role to perform in American politics. On the one hand, it is expected to be a judicial body which is politically impartial, and which must attempt to transcend passing political passions and uphold the eternal values of the Constitution. On the other hand, it is expected to resolve the sometimes highly charged political controversies which come before it in the form of lawsuits, with the inevitable result that its decisions will have a profound political impact and be attacked vehemently by whichever party has lost the case. Moreover, these judicial decisions are often made under considerable political pressure, since the presidency, the Congress, interest groups, legal scholars, the media and the public may all seek to influence the Court in its decision.

In the next chapter, we examine how well the Court has performed this delicate balancing act. We will see that the Court has become increasingly politicised in all its aspects, including the process by which new Supreme Court justices are appointed. Finally, we shall assess whether, for all the controversies that surround the Court, its power to make public policies has been exaggerated.

 ## Summary

The Supreme Court was established as a judicial body and thus its formal structures and processes are those of a court of law. However, the acquisition of the power of judicial review transformed the Court. Authorised now to declare legislation and executive decisions unconstitutional, the Court necessarily became involved in the policy-making process. Moreover, because constitutional interpretation often requires the justices to define vague and highly political concepts, such as equality and liberty, it is an inherently political process. The Supreme Court therefore has a dual nature, part judicial and part political. Its decisions can have a major impact on public policy and its judicial decision-making processes require an infusion of political, moral and philosophical reasoning.

 ## Topics for discussion

1. What grounds are there for doubting that the framers of the Constitution intended the Supreme Court to exercise the power of judicial review?

2. To what extent is constitutional interpretation an inherently political exercise?

3. How, if at all, do the Supreme Court's legal structures and processes restrict its political power?

4. What is the significance of interest group participation in the Supreme Court's decision-making process?

5. Is it acceptable from the point of view of democratic principles that the Supreme Court can 'update' the Constitution?

 Further reading

Two very useful reference works on the Supreme Court are: *The Oxford Companion to the Supreme Court of the United States* edited by Kermit L. Hall (Oxford: Oxford University Press, 1992) and *The Supreme Court Compendium: Data, decisions and developments* edited by Lee Epstein *et al.* (Washington DC: CQ Press, 1994). Recent introductory level books on the Supreme Court include Robert J. McKeever's *The United States Supreme Court: A political and legal analysis* (Manchester: Manchester University Press, 1997) and David G. Barnum's *The Supreme Court and American Democracy* (New York: St Martin's Press, 1993). More sophisticated discussions of the interaction between politics and law and the policy-making role of the Court include: David M. O'Brien's *Storm Centre: The Supreme Court in American Politics* (4th edn, New York: Norton, 1997) and Robert J. McKeever's Raw *Judicial Power: The Supreme Court and American society* (2nd edn, Manchester: Manchester University Press, 1995). On the appointment process, useful introductions are provided by Laurence Tribe's *God Save This Honorable Court: How the choice of Supreme Court justices shapes our history* (New York: Mentor, 1985) and Henry Abraham's *Justices and Presidents* (3rd edn, New York: Oxford University Press, 1992). There are two very useful websites relating to the Court freely available via the Internet. The first, at Cornell University contains all the decisions and opinions of the Supreme Court since 1990 as well as most of its important decisions prior to that. It also explains other aspects of the Court's work and environment and is at http://www.supct.law.cornell.edu. The second allows you to hear tapes of oral arguments and is operated by Professor Jerry Goldman at Northwestern University. The address is http://court.it-services.nwu.edu/oyez.

The Supreme Court and American politics

We saw in the previous chapter that the Supreme Court's power of judicial review makes it a potentially powerful player in American politics. In this chapter, we examine how the Court has used this power in different historical periods. We also analyse the constraints upon the political role and power of the Court and assess its overall significance in the political system. Finally, we examine the men and women who wield the power of judicial review – the justices of the Supreme Court – and the nature of the process by which they are appointed.

The Supreme Court's role as the authoritative interpreter of the Constitution has been applied to two broad areas of government and politics. First, the Supreme Court defines the powers of other governmental offices established by the Constitution. Thus it settles disputes over the relative powers of Congress and the presidency, and over the relative powers of the federal government and the governments of the fifty states. In other words, the Court interprets the Constitution to determine exactly what is required by the separation of powers and by the principle of federalism. Thus, in *Clinton v. New York* (1998), the Court declared unconstitutional the congressional grant of a line-item veto to the president. The Court reasoned that the Constitution empowered the president to veto only an entire bill, rather than a part of one, and therefore that the only way he could acquire a line-item veto was through the process of constitutional amendment.

Secondly, the Supreme Court settles disputes over the constitutional legitimacy of particular legislative Acts or other policy decisions. Of course, sometimes both these kinds of dispute are involved in the same case. However, it is useful to bear this distinction in mind when considering the controversies that have arisen over the Court's decisions, for, generally speaking, decisions on the precise parameters of the powers of the president or Congress do not generate much public excitement. When a case involves the legitimacy of particular policies, however, that is when the Court is likely to occupy the public limelight, simply because such policies tend directly to affect the daily lives of individuals, interest groups and various sections of the community. This does not mean that decisions regarding federalism and separation of powers are not important: they unquestionably are since they can have significant implications for the operation of government throughout the United States. However, as we now go on to examine the uses of judicial review in American history, we will find that on the whole, the power of the Court becomes controversial when it decides cases that involve controversial policy decisions.

Judicial activism and judicial self-restraint, 1789–1954

The prominence and power of the Court has varied over the years. In some eras, the Court has practised *judicial activism*: this means that the Court has asserted its power, even when faced with hostile challenges from the Congress, the president or the public. Such periods of activism are indicated by the unusually large number of federal or state laws which the Court has struck down as unconstitutional. They may also be characterised by innovations in constitutional interpretation and the suspicion that the justices are motivated by their own political viewpoints. As a result, judicial activism has usually been controversial.

In contrast to judicial activism stands *judicial self-restraint*. When the Court practises restraint, it is cautious, passive and, above all, shows great deference to the elected branches of government. The Court seeks to avoid making controversial decisions and rarely declares an Act unconstitutional. It also tends to avoid innovations in constitutional interpretation and instead follows precedent, that is, the principles announced in past decisions.

We have already noted that, after a quiet start, the Supreme Court became a dynamic institution under the leadership of Chief Justice John Marshall. After the Marshall Court (1801–35) had established the legitimacy of judicial review in *Marbury v. Madison*, it proceeded to make bold decisions which had a major impact upon the political and economic future of the United States. In particular, the Marshall Court strengthened the federal government at the expense of the power of the individual States and also ensured that national commerce and capitalism were given free rein. For example, in *McCulloch v. Maryland* (1819), Marshall announced the doctrine of 'implied powers' which gave Congress broader control over commerce policy than had been indicated on the face of the Constitution. Furthermore, in cases such as *Dartmouth College v. Woodward* (1819), *Gibbons v. Ogden* (1824) and *Brown v. Maryland* (1827), the Marshall Court curtailed the power of the states to interfere with commercial contracts and trade.

Under the leadership of Chief Justice Roger B. Taney (1836–64), the Court generally practised self-restraint. Taney, like President Andrew Jackson who had appointed him, was associated with the political opposition to a strong federal government and was therefore disinclined to follow Marshall's line. Typical of the Taney Court's restraint was the decision in *Luther v. Borden* (1849). The case involved the state of Rhode Island, where two rival governments each proclaimed their legitimacy. The Court refused to resolve the dispute by inventing the doctrine of 'political questions'. A 'political question' was said to be one whose resolution had been consigned by the

Constitution to the elected branches of government. In fact, then as now, the doctrine of political questions is little more than a device by which the Court can avoid politically delicate decisions.

Unfortunately for the Taney Court, it is remembered less for its characteristic restraint than it is for its lone, disastrous foray into judicial activism. In *Dred Scott v. Sanford* (1857) the Court helped precipitate the Civil War (1861–65). Giving a much broader ruling than was required by the facts of the case, the southern-dominated Court declared that the Missouri Compromise on slavery, worked out by Congress, was unconstitutional. This meant not only that the westward expansion of slavery could continue, but also that Congress could not fashion a compromise between pro-slavery and antislavery forces.

It should be noted, however, that under both Marshall and Taney, it was rare for a law to be declared unconstitutional. Between 1800 and 1860, just two federal laws and thirty-five State laws suffered this fate. To a great extent, these figures reflect the fact that levels of legislative activity were still low at this stage in the nation's history.

This situation began to change drastically with the onset of industrialisation in the last quarter of the nineteenth century (see Box 18.1). As government tried to regulate the explosion in economic activity and cure the social ills which accompanied it, the Supreme Court established itself as the last bastion of laissez-faire economics. While it did permit some economic regulation and some social reform, the Court increasingly interpreted the Constitution's guarantees of liberty to protect the economic rights of individuals and corporations against interference from both federal and state government. For example, in *Adair v. United States* (1905) the Court struck down a Congressional Act outlawing 'yellow-dog contracts'. These obliged workers to agree not to join a union as a condition of employment. The justices reasoned that the Act violated the constitutionally guaranteed freedom of contract of both employer and employee to make any agreement they wished.

In the same year, the Court decided in *Lochner v. New York* (1905) that freedom of contract also prevented the state from restricting the maximum hours of work of bakery workers to sixty a week; and in yet another infamous case, *Hammer v. Dagenhart* (1918), the Court ruled that Congress had no power to prohibit factories from using child labour.

Although these decisions were by no means without constitutional basis, they were activist and controversial. The Constitution makes no mention of freedom of contract, for example. Rather the justices interpreted the general guarantee of liberty in the Fifth and Fourteenth Amendments to include freedom of contract, and then exalted that right above the general power of government to provide for the public welfare. In simple political terms, however, the Court was imposing a set of values and policies upon the country which the electorate and their chosen representatives no longer supported.

The Court in political crisis

This ongoing crisis came to a head during the Great Depression of the 1930s. In the presidential elections of 1932 and 1936, the nation gave impressive victories to the Democratic party candidate, Franklin D. Roosevelt. He had promised the voters a

Box 18.1

Federal and state laws declared unconstitutional by the Supreme Court 1790–1989

Decade	Federal laws	State laws
1790–1799	0	0
1800–1809	1	1
1810–1819	0	7
1820–1829	0	8
1830–1839	0	3
1840–1849	0	9
1850–1859	1	7
1860–1869	4	24
1870–1879	7	36
1880–1889	5	46
1890–1899	5	36
1900–1909	9	41
1910–1919	6	112
1920–1929	18	131
1930–1939	14	84
1940–1949	2	58
1950–1959	5	59
1960–1969	19	123
1970–1979	20	181
1980–1989	16	161

Source: adapted from Epstein, L., *et al.* pp. 96–128

'new deal'. Together with a large Democratic majority in Congress, Roosevelt experimented with various forms of governmental intervention in an attempt to alleviate the economic and social catastrophe that had befallen the country. The Supreme Court, however, declared some of his most important policies unconstitutional. The National Industrial Recovery Act of 1933 was struck down in *Schechter v. United States* (1935) and the Agriculture Adjustment Act of 1933 in *US v. Butler* (1936).

Roosevelt's response was to do battle with the Court. In 1937, he proposed a bill that purported to aim at helping the ageing justices to cope with their workload. For each justice over the age of seventy, the President would be empowered to appoint an additional member of the Court. As it so happened, six of the nine current justices were over seventy, so at one fell swoop, Roosevelt would be able to make six new appointments to the Court. Assuming he would appoint only those known to support the New Deal, this would bring an end to the Court's resistance. It was clear to all that this was a crude attempt to bring the Court to heel and the proposal became known as the Court-packing plan.

There was considerable opposition to the Court-packing plan, even among Roosevelt's regular supporters in Congress. They feared that, if passed, it would violate the principle of the separation of powers and create a dangerously dominant presidency. Before Congress had to vote, however, the Court itself rendered the bill politically unnecessary. In *West Coast Hotel v. Parrish* (1937), the Court surprised everyone by upholding the constitutionality of a minimum-wage law of a type that it had previously struck down. Moreover, language in the Court's opinion suggested that henceforth, economic liberties would take second place to government's view of what was required by the public welfare. And so it proved. Since 1937, the Supreme Court has virtually abandoned the field of economic regulation to the Congress, the president and the states.

Political lessons of the Court-packing plan: the Supreme Court and the political majority

Although there continues to be a debate over the precise reasons for the Court's change of direction in 1937, there is no doubt that it was a severe political setback for the Court. It had engendered considerable public hostility over the previous decades and had lost much of its prestige. The justices were viewed by many as political reactionaries rather than impartial interpreters of the Constitution.

The Court's strategic error in the 1930s was in overestimating the degree to which the Supreme Court can resist an insistent political tide. Ultimately, the power of the Court rests upon the respect it can command. It can rely upon a degree of automatic respect because of its constitutional position. Beyond that, however, it must continuously nurture and renew its status as the guardian of the nation's fundamental values, as expressed in the Constitution. In order to do that, it must convince the nation that its decisions as a whole are in the country's long-term interests. In this sense, the justices do have a 'constituency' like other political actors. In the 1950s, a leading political scientist, Robert Dahl, advanced the argument that the Court never remains out of step with the national political majority for very long (Dahl, 1957).

This in turn highlights a very important aspect of the Court's role in American government: it acts as a legitimator of political change. The New Deal involved a marked break with American traditions of politics and governmental responsibility, yet by eventually conferring its constitutional blessing upon this shift, the Court signalled that it was an acceptable addition to the fundamental political values and practices of the nation.

More recently, a study of the Court's decisions in relation to public opinion tended to support this view that the Supreme Court is in essence a majoritarian institution (Marshall, 1989). The fact is that, if the Court becomes isolated from all major exterior sources of support – Congress, the presidency and the public – it has insufficient independent resources to withstand a concerted attack. In short, if the Court is to embark upon controversial, activist decisions, it must have strong allies among the elected branches of government.

The Supreme Court crisis of the 1930s was, however, an extreme example of judicial extravagance. It paid dearly for its intransigence by losing virtually all of its power over socio-economic legislation. Nevertheless, because the precise role of the Court is not fixed in the Constitution, or anywhere else, it has the potential to construct a new agenda for itself. Before the Civil War, it worked to strengthen the national government and national commerce. From the onset of industrialisation until 1937, its self-assigned task was to nurture laissez-faire economics. In the 1950s, after a period of passivity and self-restraint, it emerged in yet another new guise: defender of civil liberties and the interests of subordinate social groups.

The Supreme Court since 1954

In hindsight, the year 1954 can be recognised as a watershed in the history of the Supreme Court. For it was then that the Court took on not just a new agenda of issues, but a significantly different method of constitutional interpretation.

Brown v. Board of Education (1954)

The catalyst for these changes was a decision ordering an end to racial segregation in the nation's school systems. It had long been the practice, particularly but not exclusively in the southern and border states, to require black and white children to attend separate schools. The Supreme Court had validated this and other forms of racial segregation in *Plessy v. Ferguson* (1896). There the Court ruled that, providing facilities were 'separate but equal', racial segregation did not violate the Fourteenth Amendment's guarantee of equal protection of the laws.

In *Brown v. Board of Education* (1954), the Court unanimously voted to reverse its *Plessy* decision. Under the leadership of its new chief justice, Earl Warren (1953–69), it argued that separate facilities were inherently unequal: the mere desire to segregate by race implied the inferiority of one of the races compared with the other. Therefore, racial segregation did indeed violate the Fourteenth Amendment's command that the states must give all persons the 'equal protection of the laws'.

Although unarguably the right moral decision, *Brown* was rather unconvincing in terms of constitutional interpretation, as even sympathetic scholars acknowledged. The decision could not be justified by original intent, as the historical record made clear. In fact, the members of Congress who approved the Fourteenth Amendment in 1866 lived and worked in a Washington, DC, which itself operated a racially segregated school system. There was not the slightest indication that they intended to put an end to that system.

In *Brown*, therefore, the Court ignored history and judicial precedent, and relied instead upon some rather flimsy social science evidence purporting to show that black children suffered psychological damage as a result of segregated schooling. The Court's reasoning, however, was regarded as secondary to the overwhelming moral rightness of the decision. Legal scholars, in spite of their misgivings, applauded the decision. This encouraged the Warren Court along a new path of using constitutional interpretation as a means of promoting what many Americans considered to be benign social reforms. The *Brown* decision thus illustrates the fact that the Court can sometimes get away with decisions whose constitutional underpinnings are shaky, provided they are viewed as just and desirable by other politicians and the public.

The Warren Court became increasingly bold, activist and eventually, bitterly controversial. After *Brown*, a series of decisions swept away every law which required racial segregation. However, the Court also turned its activist guns onto other targets. In *Baker v. Carr* (1962), the Court reversed a relatively recent precedent, *Colegrove v. Green* (1946), and ordered the state of Tennessee to reapportion its legislative districts. The population in some counties was much greater than in others, with the result that counties containing two-thirds of the state population chose only one-third of the members of the state legislature.

Once again, the political case for the Court's decision was overwhelming, but the constitutional basis was less convincing. Most importantly, the *Colegrove* decision had held that the Court had no power to adjudicate reapportionment cases: these fell into the category of 'political questions' whose resolution had been consigned by the Constitution to other branches of government. Now the Warren Court rejected that restraint and narrowed the range of 'political questions'.

More controversy followed over reapportionment as a result of *Gray v. Sanders* (1963), *Wesberry v. Sanders* (1964) and *Reynolds v. Sims* (1964). Here the Warren Court not only ordered legislative reapportionment, but actually prescribed the apportionment formula to be applied throughout the country: 'one man, one vote'. (In later cases, this was rephrased as 'one person, one vote'). At first glance, this may appear reasonable and fair. However, it is simply not a formula required by the Constitution. Most obviously, the United States Senate itself is not based upon one person, one vote, but rather two senators per state, regardless of population. If the Constitution permits the Senate to be grossly malapportioned because there are deemed to be other benefits resulting from the scheme, upon what basis can the Court declare that the Constitution finds such malapportionment intolerable elsewhere?

Once again, however, the fact that the Court reached a manifestly just result in other respects overcame objections that it was not so much interpreting the Constitution, as reading into it the justices' own notions of what was good for the country. This type of judicial decision making came to be known as results-oriented jurisprudence: this means that Supreme Court decisions are determined (and evaluated) by the social and moral good that they achieve, rather than by what the Constitution mandates. Moreover, the reapportionment cases illustrated another important change in the nature of judicial review. For much of its history, the Court's activism had been predominantly negative, telling government what it could *not* do. The Warren Court's activism now developed a positive aspect, telling government what it *must* do and also *how* to do it.

In cases such as *Brown* and *Baker*, where there is a wide consensus on what actually *is* the social and moral good, the Court's decisions prove politically acceptable when they are in accord with that consensus. However, in cases involving such issues as abortion, homosexuality, pornography, and government-sponsored religion, no such consensus exists. It is over just these types of cases that the contemporary Supreme Court has claimed authority and caused a backlash against its power and role in the political system.

In 1969, President Nixon appointed Warren Burger as chief justice. By 1975, Nixon and his Republican successor, Gerald Ford, had appointed a further four new justices. They had been appointed to practise judicial self-restraint, and many expected the Burger Court (1969–86) to launch a counter-revolution against the Warren Court's liberal activism. However, with a few exceptions, this failed to materialise. Indeed, in many respects, the Burger Court was even more activist than the Warren Court. Many scholars took this as a sign that the Court's role in the political system had undergone a fundamental change. No longer would there be cycles of activism and restraint: the Court would now be more or less permanently activist. Judicial review, it seemed, had become the means through which policy on socio-moral issues would be made in the United States.

The Burger Court's decisions certainly gave ammunition to this theory. It announced innovations in constitutional interpretation by holding that the Fourteenth Amendment banned traditional gender classifications (*Reed v. Reed*, 1971); that the Eighth Amendment banned all existing State death penalty laws (*Furman v. Georgia*, 1972); that women had a constitutional right to terminate pregnancies by abortion (*Roe v. Wade*, 1973); and that the Constitution's requirement of race equality in the law did not disbar affirmative action policies that avoided 'quotas' but which were intended to gave racial minorities certain advantages in college applications (*Regents of the University of California v. Bakke*, 1978).

Decisions such as these provoked considerable anger among conservatives and, at both the state and federal levels of government, there were determined and partially successful attempts both to reverse them and to force the Court to abandon its activism. This backlash revealed once again that, when it provokes significant opposition, the Court's decisions can suddenly take on the appearance of great vulnerability.

Supreme Court decisions: implementation and resistance

There are several formal means at the disposal of other branches of government if they wish to reverse a constitutional decision by the Court. Most obviously, they can attempt to pass a constitutional amendment. However, this is a difficult, time-consuming and uncertain device. As a result, it has been employed successfully on only four occasions in American history. The Eleventh Amendment overturned *Chisholm v. Georgia* (1793); the first part of the Fourteenth Amendment overturned *Dred Scott v. Sanford* (1857); the Sixteenth Amendment reversed *Pollock v. Farmers' Loan and Trust Co.* (1895); and the Twenty-Sixth Amendment reversed *Oregon v. Mitchell* (1970).

Nevertheless, despite the slim prospects of success, members of Congress often introduce constitutional amendments as a symbolic gesture to express their hostility to the Court. Thus, for example, within eighteen months of the Court's decision banning school prayer (*Engel v. Vitale*, (1962)), no less than 146 constitutional amendments to reverse it were introduced into Congress.

An even worse success rate characterises a second device to overturn a Court decision: *withdrawal of appellate jurisdiction*. The Constitution allows Congress to vary the kinds of case which may be taken on appeal to the Supreme Court. If Congress dislikes the Court's decisions on, say, abortion, it can simply remove the Court's right to

hear appeals in cases involving abortion. In fact, such withdrawal of appellate jurisdiction has happened on only one occasion: just after the Civil War, Congress removed
the Court's right to hear appeals involving convictions for sedition by a military commission. In 1958 the Jenner–Butler bill, designed to withdraw the Court's jurisdiction
over certain national security issues, failed to pass the Senate by just one vote. On the
whole, however, proposals for the withdrawal of appellate jurisdiction, like constitutional amendment, are in essence symbolic. They are not an effective means of actually
reversing the Court, but they do fire a warning shot across the Court's bows.

The failure of so many proposals to reverse the Court by withdrawing appellate
jurisdiction or amending the Constitution reveals something important about the
Court's power. No matter how much the justices may anger Congress by particular
decisions, a majority of its members are deeply reluctant to inflict permanent, structural damage upon the Court. Frequent surgery upon the Court with such blunt instruments would soon leave it incapable of truly independent decision making – and it
is that independence which makes the Court so valuable in settling constitutional
conflicts.

In the previous chapter, however, we noted Alexander Hamilton's observation that
the Court was inherently weak because it had to rely on others to implement its decisions. The history of the Court bears this out. An early illustration came in *Worcester
v. Georgia* (1832), when the Marshall Court offended anti-Indian sentiment by telling
the state it could not make laws for the local Cherokee nation. Not only did Georgia
refuse to obey the order, but President Andrew Jackson is reputed to have said: 'John
Marshall has made his decision. Now let *him* enforce it.' Three years after the Court's
decision, most of the Cherokees were forcibly removed from the state.

In modern times, non-compliance with Court decisions is fairly common. The most
famous example concerns the 'massive resistance' to the *Brown* school desegregation
decision, organised by southerners. Ten years after the Court made its order, hardly any
black children in the deep south were attending integrated schools. Southern governors
such as George Wallace (Alabama) and Orval Faubus (Arkansas) openly led the resistance. As a result of the latter's activities, President Eisenhower was obliged to use
federal troops in order to allow black children to enter Little Rock High School in 1957.

Even then, however, Arkansas, like the rest of the south, did not implement
desegregation. As one analyst wrote:

> The statistics from the Southern states are truly amazing. For ten years, 1954–64, virtu-
> ally *nothing* happened. Ten years after *Brown* only 1.2 percent of black schoolchildren in
> the South attended school with whites. ... Despite the unanimity and forcefulness of the
> *Brown* decision, the Supreme Court's reiteration of its position and its steadfast refusal to
> yield, its decree was flagrantly disobeyed.'
>
> (Rosenberg, 1991, p. 52)

Box 18.2 shows the pace of desegregation, or rather the lack of it, in certain southern
states.

It is obvious that the mere fact that the Court ordered states to desegregate their
schools was wholly insufficient to bring about any significant change. Compliance
with *Brown* only came in the late 1960s, after Congress and President Johnson combined to produce legislation which allowed stricter enforcement and which provided

Box 18.2

Black children in desegregated southern elementary and secondary schools

	1954/5		1959/60		1964/5	
	%	No.	%	No.	%	No.
Alabama	0	0	0	0	0.03	101
Arkansas	0	0	0.09	98	0.81	930
Georgia	0	0	0	0	0.40	1,337
Louisiana	0	0	0	0	1.1	3,581
Mississippi	0	0	0	0	0.02	57
South Carolina	0	0	0	0	0.10	265

Source: Adapted from Rosenberg, 1991, pp. 345–6

Box 18.3

Impact of the increase in federal funds on the pace of desegregation in southern schools

	Federal funds as percentage of state education budget		Percentage of Black children in integrated schools	
	1963/64	1971/72	1964/65	1972/73
Alabama	7.6	21.5	0.03	83.5
Arkansas	11.1	21.2	0.81	98.1
Georgia	7.1	15.7	0.40	86.8
Louisiana	4.8	14.6	1.1	82.9
Mississippi	8.1	27.8	0.02	91.5
South Carolina	7.5	18.7	0.10	93.9

Source: Adapted from Rosenberg, 1991, p. 99

financial 'carrots and sticks' for state school systems. Particularly important were the Civil Rights Act of 1964 and the Elementary and Secondary Education Act of 1965. Box 18.3 indicates the impact of the increase in federal funds for Southern state school systems on the pace of desegregation.

Non-compliance with *Brown* was simply illegal. On the issue of the Court's death penalty decisions, however, many states used a more legitimate means of resistance. In *Furman v. Georgia* (1972) the Court had not ruled that capital punishment was in itself unconstitutional. Rather it said that current laws were so infrequently, randomly and capriciously applied that they amounted to 'cruel and unusual punishment' in violation of the Eighth Amendment. Nevertheless, most observers agreed that the Court had accomplished the effective abolition of capital punishment. A majority of states, however, simply refused to accept that result. Some thirty-five of them passed new death penalty laws, including fifteen who dealt with the issue of arbitrariness by making the death sentence mandatory for certain offences. Faced with this evidence of continuing support for capital punishment, the Court backed away from its near-abolitionist position. In *Gregg v. Georgia* (1976), Justice Stewart conceded that, 'It is now evident that a large proportion of American society continues to regard the death penalty as an appropriate and necessary criminal sanction.'

The Court's 1973 abortion decision produced several forms of resistance. States which favoured illiberal abortion statutes placed many obstacles in the path of women seeking terminations. Many refused to allow abortions to be performed in public hospitals, leaving women reliant upon private clinics which might be located hundreds of miles away. Others introduced cumbersome administrative procedures which required women to attend the abortion facility more than once. A favourite strategy, emulated by Congress in 1976 with the passage of the Hyde Amendment, was to withdraw public funds for poor women seeking abortions, even though funds were available for childbirth expenses and, indeed, all other types of medical treatment. In the first full year of the operation of the Hyde Amendment, the number of Medicaid (publicly funded) abortions fell from 200,000 to less than 2,000. The Reagan administration also joined the attack by banning any federally-funded pregnancy counselling service from providing advice or information on abortion. On several occasions, President Reagan's solicitor-general also intervened as *amicus curiae*, urging the Court to reverse its decision in *Roe*.

The Court had thus ruled that states could not ban abortions; but the response of many states and the other branches of the federal government was to do their utmost to undermine that policy. The result was that although women retained a theoretical right to abortion, many experienced some difficulty in turning that right into a practical reality. The constraints upon the Court, then, are less the formal ones of reversal by constitutional amendment or withdrawal of appellate jurisdiction; rather, they are the pressures and indirect restrictions which arise from the unwillingness of the elected branches to implement the Court's decisions. In short, the main constraint upon the Court is the political hostility that its decisions engender.

There is, however, yet one other major way in which Supreme Court decisions may be changed by the actions of elected politicians. That is through the appointment process.

Supreme Court appointments

The power to appoint Supreme Court Justices is shared by the president and the Senate. Article II, Section 2(ii) of the Constitution stipulates that the president shall nominate new justices 'with the advice and consent of the Senate'. In other words, the Senate has the power to confirm or reject the president's nominees. Here again the constitutional system of checks and balances provides the executive and legislative branches with an 'invitation to struggle'. Yet the president usually has the upper hand in such struggles, simply because the Constitution gives him the initiative in the appointment process. The Senate can reject the president's nominee, but it knows it cannot replace that nominee with its own preferred candidate. It must always calculate, therefore, whether the rejection of one nominee will lead to the appointment of a better one. Nevertheless, in recent decades, the Senate has become a lot more assertive in the appointment process than in the first two-thirds of the twentieth century.

Presidential nominations to the Court

Presidents have no power over how many nominations they can make to the Court. With justices being appointed for life, presidents must wait until a member of the Court either resigns or dies. As Box 18.4 shows, some presidents are luckier in this respect than others. Most obviously, President Carter had no opportunity at all to nominate a justice during his single term, while President Bush made two nominations; and while Presidents Johnson and Nixon served for similar lengths of time, the latter filled twice as many vacancies as the former.

Presidents rightly cherish their opportunities to make nominations to the Court. In the short term, it allows them to place political allies and sympathisers in another branch of the federal government. In the long term, those justices and their political viewpoints will still be influencing government long after the presidents themselves have left office.

Box 18.4

Number of Supreme Court vacancies per president since 1945

President	Years in office	Number of vacancies
Truman	1945–53	4
Eisenhower	1953–61	5
Kennedy	1961–63	2
Johnson	1963–69	2
Nixon	1969–74	4
Ford	1974–77	1
Carter	1977–81	0
Reagan	1981–89	3
Bush	1989–93	2
Clinton	1993–(97)	2

Take the case of Justice William O. Douglas, nominated by Franklin D. Roosevelt in 1939. Roosevelt died in office in 1945, but Douglas did not retire from the Court until 1975, some thirty years after Roosevelt died. In fact, while no president may serve more than eight years (up to ten years exceptionally), the average length of service of justices appointed since 1937 is fifteen years (excluding those still serving). Moreover, of those twenty-two justices, three served more than thirty years, a further three more than twenty years, and a further eight more than fifteen years. The longest-serving of the current Court is Chief Justice William Rehnquist. Appointed as an associate justice in 1971, Rehnquist has been on the Court for twenty-seven years – that is, some twenty-two years more than the length of time his appointing president, Richard Nixon, occupied the White House.

Criteria for nomination

There are no formal requirements for those who serve on the Court. While it is convention that nominees should possess a law degree, they are not required to have practised law, never mind have experience as a judge. Many of the justices considered to be outstanding had no judicial experience prior to their nomination: thus, Chief Justice Warren had been governor of California and an unsuccessful Republican vice-presidential candidate. Justice Hugo Black (1937–71) had been a senator and Justice Felix Frankfurter (1939–62) a law professor and adviser to President Franklin D. Roosevelt.

There would appear to be no connection between prior judicial experience and greatness on the Court, perhaps because the functions of the Court require political and philosophical skills, as much as they require purely legal skills. However, recent Republican presidents, all striving to appoint strict constructionists, have nominated only those with at least some judicial experience. The thinking is that those with personal experience of judging, as opposed to politics, will behave more 'judicially' and less 'politically' once they are on the Court.

Since the 1950s, it has been the custom of presidents to submit the names of potential nominees to the Committee on the Federal Judiciary of the American Bar Association. The committee ranks potential nominees to the Court according to their perceived competence, integrity and judicial temperament. Although the committee has no formal powers with respect to nominations, its ratings may influence the Senate's decision whether or not to confirm a nominee. For example, in 1987, Robert Bork was given the highest ranking of 'well qualified'; but the fact that the vote was not unanimous added fuel to the political fire which eventually engulfed the nominee.

The overwhelming criterion for nomination is political compatibility with the president. This can be identified in a number of ways. Most obviously, presidents usually nominate those affiliated with their own party. Of the 109 justices who have served on the Court up to 1997, only 13 have not been members of the nominating president's party. Even then, such cross-party nominees have usually been known to share the president's ideology.

Another way the president may try to ensure that the nominee is compatible with his own views is to nominate a friend or political ally. President Lyndon B. Johnson went to great lengths in 1965 to put his long-time friend and adviser Abe Fortas on the

Court. First he manufactured a vacancy by persuading justice Arthur Goldberg to accept the bait of becoming ambassador to the United Nations. Then he successfully nominated Fortas to the Court. Three years later, when Earl Warren expressed his wish to retire, Johnson tried to elevate Fortas to the chief justiceship. This failed, in part precisely because Fortas was known to be so close to the president and so the nomination smacked of cronyism.

It was President Reagan, however, who established the most elaborate method of screening nominees for political compatibility. During his administration, all potential candidates for nomination to the Supreme Court, or lower federal courts, were vetted by a President's Committee on Federal Judicial Selection. This committee analysed all the published writings and statements of those being considered for nomination. Candidates would be interviewed and asked their views on issues about which the administration felt strongly. Indeed, under presidents Reagan and Bush, it was widely perceived that the 'litmus test' for any nominee to the Court was opposition to the *Roe v. Wade* (1973) abortion decision, although both administrations denied this.

Beyond political compatibility, the president may have a variety of secondary, and in essence symbolic, criteria for nomination. Until the early twentieth century, presidents considered the nominee's home state to be important, because it was thought desirable that the Court should reflect the country's regional diversity. In the twentieth century, a desire for ethnic diversity has been a factor. In 1916, Louis Brandeis became the first Jew to be appointed to the Court and the tradition of a 'Jewish seat' continued until the retirement of Abe Fortas in 1969. In 1967, Thurgood Marshall became the first black Supreme Court justice. When he retired, President Bush nominated another black, Clarence Thomas, to fill his seat.

Such nominations are not free of political calculation. The president will hope to reap electoral rewards for his actions by showing his symbolic support for the group concerned. This was certainly a factor for President Bush in nominating Justice Thomas. Bush was widely perceived as unsympathetic to the cause of racial equality and the nomination gave him the opportunity to curry favour with African American voters. Similar considerations lay behind President Reagan's 1981 nomination of the first woman Supreme Court justice, Sandra Day O'Connor. Reagan was not noted for his enthusiasm for gender equality and, in the 1980 election, he had received a lower percentage of the votes of women than of men. The nomination of Justice O'Connor was a means of countering this 'gender gap'.

However, these secondary criteria should not obscure the overriding importance of political considerations. Thus, for example, President Reagan made sure he appointed a *conservative* woman and President Bush made sure he appointed a *conservative* African American. Quite simply, the political stakes are too high in Supreme Court nominations to make it otherwise.

Senate confirmation and rejection

The president has sole prerogative over who is *nominated* to the Court, but the Senate has equally sole prerogative over who is *confirmed*. Historically, about one in five presidential nominees to the Court fail to be confirmed by the Senate. Sometimes they are rejected outright by Senate vote; sometimes their nominations are withdrawn before a vote because of the certainty of defeat.

The historical frequency of Senate rejections of presidential nominees to the Court is not, however, even, and a marked change in that respect took place at the end of the 1960s. Box 18.5 shows the comparative fate of nominations in the periods 1937–67 and 1967–97.

Two facts in Box 18.5 stand out. First, in the earlier period, all twenty-two nominees were confirmed, while in the later period five out of eighteen failed to make the Court.

Secondly, in only eight of the twenty-two earlier nominations did the Senate bother to record a vote: even then, not one of the recorded votes indicated substantial opposition to the nominee. In the second period, however, all nominations were subject to a recorded vote, save those which were withdrawn. Moreover, those votes show that, as well as the three rejections, there was a serious attempt to deny confirmation on three further occasions, most notably in the case of Clarence Thomas.

In short, between 1937 and 1967, there were twenty-two almost wholly problem-free Senate confirmations of presidential nominees to the Court. Since 1967, however, eight out of eighteen presidential nominations have met substantial opposition in the Senate. Clearly then, the appointment of Supreme Court Justices has become a major political battleground, with far less certainty of presidential success than before. Why has this happened?

The fundamental reasons have to do with the increasing realisation since the 1960s of the political nature and importance of the Court in the policy-making process. As we noted above, the Warren Court engaged in results-oriented decision making and thereby initiated some strikingly liberal policies. By 1968 a conservative backlash against the Court was under way, and Republican presidents such as Nixon, Reagan and Bush were determined to place new justices on the Court who would halt or even reverse the liberal advances. Thus, because the Court behaved in an explicitly political manner, presidential nominations took on a more explicitly political aspect.

A second source of increased friction between the Senate and the president was the emergence of divided government, in which one party controls the Congress and the other the White House. This deprives the president of the crutch of a partisan majority in the Senate. It is no coincidence that four of the five failed nominations were inflicted by a Senate with a Democratic majority upon a Republican president. Nevertheless, divided government is by no means the whole story. President Eisenhower, for example, had four of his five successful nominees confirmed by a Senate with a Democratic majority, and Justices Souter and Kennedy of the present Court won easy confirmation by Democratic Senates, despite having been nominated by Republican presidents.

What has changed, then, along with the politicisation of both the Court's role and the criteria for presidential choice of nominees, is the way the Senate views its role in the appointment process. According to Laurence Tribe, there has until recently been a tendency for Americans to believe in 'the myth of the Spineless Senate' (Tribe, 1985). This myth argues that Supreme Court appointments are the prerogative of the president; and that the Senate should confine itself (and it usually has) to the rejection of nominees who are not qualified for the job. Above all, the Senate should not reject

Box 18.5

Senate confirmation/rejection of Supreme Court nominees, 1937–97

1937–67			1967–97		
Nominee (year of Senate action)	Result	Vote	Nominee	Result	Vote
Hugo Black (1937)	Con.	63–16	Abe Fortas[a] (1968)	With.	—
Stanley Reed (1938)	Con.	—	Warren Burger (1969)	Con.	74–3
Felix Frankfurter (1939)	Con.	—	Clement Haynsworth (1969)	Rej.	45–55
William Douglas (1939)	Con.	62–4	G. Harrold Carswell (1970)	Rej.	45–51
Frank Murphy (1940)	Con.	—	Harry Blackmun (1970)	Con.	94–0
Harlan Stone[a] (1941)	Con.	—	Lewis Powell (1971)	Con.	89–1
James Byrnes (1941)	Con.	—	William Rehnquist (1971)	Con.	68–26
Robert Jackson (1941)	Con.	—	John Paul Stevens (1975)	Con.	98–0
Wiley Rutledge (1943)	Con.	—	Sandra Day O'Connor(1981)	Con.	99–0
Harold Burton (1945)	Con.	—	William Rehnquist[a] (1986)	Con.	65–33
Fred Vinson (1946)	Con.	—	Antonin Scalia (1986)	Con.	98–0
Tom Clark (1949)	Con.	73–8	Robert Bork (1987)	Rej.	42–58
Sherman Minton (1949)	Con.	48–16	Douglas Ginsberg (1987)	With.	—
Earl Warren (1954)	Con.	—	Anthony Kennedy (1988)	Con.	97–0
John Harlan (1955)	Con.	71–11	David Souter (1990)	Con.	90–9
William Brennan (1957)	Con.	—	Clarence Thomas (1991)	Con.	52–48
Charles Whittaker (1957)	Con.	—	Ruth Bader Ginsberg (1993)	Con.	96–3
Potter Stewart (1959)	Con.	70–17	Stephen G. Breyer (1994)	Con.	87–9
Byron White (1962)	Con.	—			
Arthur Goldberg (1962)	Con.	—			
Abe Fortas (1965)	Con.	—			
Thurgood Marshall (1967)	Con.	69–11			

Con. = Confirmed Rej. = Rejected With. = Withdrawn

[a] Sitting associate justice nominated to the chief justiceship

nominees because of their political ideology or judicial philosophy. By and large, says the myth, the President is entitled to place on the Court whomsoever he wishes.

The rejection of one in five nominees would seem to support Tribe's view that such an understanding of the appointments process is indeed mythical. Yet upon closer inspection, the myth would appear to merit greater credence. One study suggests that only a handful of the pre-1968 rejected nominees were voted down for their political views and only one for what might be termed his judicial philosophy. (Vieira and Gross, 1990). In the former category, we find for example the first rejected nominee, John Rutledge, nominated as chief justice by President Washington in 1795. His political crime was to have denounced the Jay Treaty with England; the treaty's Senate supporters decided to punish him by rejecting his nomination.

Prior to the modern period, the sole candidate rejected because of his judicial philosophy was John Parker, nominated in 1930 by President Hoover. Parker was certainly well qualified and was supported by the legal community. He was rejected, however, largely because of his anti-union record. Parker was the last nominee to be rejected until Abe Fortas in 1968. For almost forty years and through twenty-four nominations, then, the myth seems to have applied. However, whether a new phenomenon or a new phase in an old phenomenon, the contemporary struggles over Supreme Court appointments are an important feature of American politics.

Senate confirmation battles

When the president and the Senate do battle over a Supreme Court nominee, they are fighting for a major political prize: influence over the future direction of a co-equal branch of the federal government. The more political the Court's decisions, the more both president and Senate want that influence.

Take, for example, the historically unprecedented rejection of two successive nominees under President Nixon. During the 1968 presidential election campaign, Nixon had attacked the Warren Court for a number of its liberal-activist decisions. He promised to appoint new justices who would practise strict construction. The president also had a second political goal: to appoint a Southerner to the Court. Nixon believed, rightly, that the traditionally Democratic, but conservative south was potentially a Republican stronghold. The appointment of a southerner, Clement Haynsworth of South Carolina, was therefore part of Nixon's plan to woo the region away from the Democrats.

Haynsworth was undoubtedly qualified for the office, but Democrats seized upon an alleged minor breach of judicial ethics as an excuse for rejecting him. Nixon's response was to nominate G. Harrold Carswell of Florida, a federal judge with a background of racial bigotry and incompetence. Nixon wanted to punish the Senate for the rejection of Haynsworth by obliging them to accept someone far worse. Nixon falsely assumed that the Senate would not dare reject two successive nominees. However, he made it easy on the Democrats by nominating a man who was clearly unsuitable. Senator Roman Hruska unintentionally damned Carswell with faint praise when he famously remarked of the nominee: 'Even if he is mediocre, there are a lot of mediocre judges and people and lawyers. They are entitled to a little representation, aren't they?'

The politics of appointment reached new heights of intensity with the nominations of Robert Bork and Clarence Thomas. On each occasion, the nomination was believed to be more than usually important because the other justices were more or less evenly divided on many of the big issues. The appointment of one new justice could swing the Court one way or the other on abortion rights, for example. As a result, both president and Senate went all out for victory against the backdrop of a massive lobbying campaign by interest groups on both sides. Senate hearings were televised live and the whole nation became absorbed in the fate of a Supreme Court nominee.

Robert Bork was a noted judicial scholar and a judge of some considerable experience. What led to his defeat was the fact that he had been the nation's foremost critic of the modern Court's failure to follow the doctrine of original intent. As such, he was portrayed by his opponents as being 'outside the judicial mainstream' and therefore lacking in 'judicial temperament'. This was untrue, but Bork *was* a controversial figure and President Reagan nominated him precisely because he was a high-profile scourge of liberal judicial activism. Certainly Bork's own fidelity to original intent would undoubtedly lead him to conservative decisions in most cases. In nominating Bork, therefore, the president deliberately issued a challenge to the Senate Democrats, apparently in the belief that they could not prevent him from shifting the Court decisively to the right.

Many liberal interest groups joined in the battle, raising huge sums of money to persuade Senators and the public that Bork was an extremist. According to one estimate, groups such as the National Abortion Rights Action League (NARAL), the National Organization for Women (NOW) and People for the American Way spent around $15 million on their anti-Bork campaign (Hodder-Williams, 1988, p. 628). Conservative groups such as the National Right to Life Committee (NRLC) and the National Conservative Political Action Committee (NCPAC) mounted a counter-campaign, though not quite on the same scale. Robert Bork himself appeared before the Senate Judiciary Committee to answer questions on his judicial views for over thirty hours.

The final vote against Bork was almost, but not quite, strictly partisan. Only two Democrats voted for Bork, while six Republicans voted against him. Ultimately, the rejection of Robert Bork was political and partisan. It was significant, however, that senators professed that they rejected Bork because he did not possess 'judicial temperament', rather than admitting that they simply did not like the way he would vote once seated on the Court.

A similar legitimating device was used to cloak the essentially political reasons that almost led to the rejection of Clarence Thomas in 1991. President Bush had wrong-footed Senate Democrats by nominating a conservative who was also black. It was difficult for liberals to oppose the appointment of only the second African American justice in the Court's history. Nevertheless, liberals wanted to defeat the nomination because Thomas' record indicated he would tip the balance of the Court further, perhaps decisively, to the right. However, Thomas was not the kind of antagonistic figure who could unite the liberal opposition.

The anti-Thomas campaign was therefore foundering until one of his former colleagues, Professor Anita Hill, alleged that Thomas had sexually harassed her some ten years before. Thomas denied the allegations and there was an absence of corroborative evidence to determine which of the two was the more credible. Despite this, liberals now had a 'legitimate' and 'non-political' reason for doubting Thomas' fitness for a seat on the Court. As a result, the anti-Thomas campaign gathered sudden momentum and only fell short of securing his rejection by three votes.

Thomas survived because although there was again a strong partisan aspect to the Senate vote, this was qualified by other political considerations for some senators. Only two Republicans voted against Thomas, but eleven Democrats voted for him. Of these, eight were from the south and were particularly dependent for election upon the support of black voters. When polls told them that, in spite of Professor Hill's allegations, these voters believed Thomas should be confirmed, they cast their votes in line with constituency opinion. Thus, even though the Thomas vote was not simply partisan, it was wholly political.

The history of recent Supreme Court appointments suggests that the conditions for presidential success have changed. The Senate is still reluctant to be *seen* as opposing a nominee on purely political grounds. Thus, Antonin Scalia and Anthony Kennedy were unanimously confirmed, even though their judicial views (and votes) were close to those of Bork and Thomas. In this sense, the president still has the upper hand in the appointment process. However, if the president makes a mistake in selecting his nominee, either by going out of his way to provoke the Senate (Carswell, Bork), or by picking someone with a possible skeleton in the cupboard (Douglas Ginsburg's admitted marijuana smoking, Thomas' alleged sexual harassment), he thereby gives politically motivated opponents the 'judicial' legitimation and momentum they need to reject the nominee.

On the evidence of his nominations of Ruth Bader Ginsburg (1993) and Stephen G. Breyer (1994), President Clinton appeared to absorb these lessons of recent bitter nomination battles. While both the nominees were chosen because they shared broadly the president's political philosophy, he was also careful to select candidates who were well respected by the Republican opposition in the Senate. Thus both Ginsburg and Breyer had an easy ride to confirmation.

Post-appointment performance: do presidents get what they wanted?

Nothing guarantees that a president's successful nominee will vote as anticipated once on the Court. Justices of the Supreme Court are answerable to no one for their decisions, and it may be that their behaviour on the Court departs significantly from what their pre-Court record suggested. President Eisenhower expected Chief Justice Warren to be a moderate conservative, just like himself. Instead, Warren led the Court in a liberal-activist direction, causing Eisenhower to comment later that nominating Warren was 'the biggest damned-fool mistake I ever made'. President Nixon nominated Justice Blackmun as a strict constructionist, but on abortion and many other issues Blackmun voted with the liberal non-interpretivists. Likewise, current justice David Souter, nominated by President Bush, has turned out to be much more liberal than many Republicans expected.

These, however, are the exceptions that prove the rule. By and large, justices *do* turn out the way their nominating president had hoped. Thus, if the president gets the chance to fill sufficient vacancies, he can change the Court's direction altogether. Thus, although President Franklin D. Roosevelt's Court-packing plan was never passed by Congress, his eventual nominees to the Court ensured that New Deal-type legislation was deemed acceptable under the Constitution. The more recent Reagan–Bush campaign to shift the Court in a more conservative direction also paid off in many ways, though not as decisively as conservative Republicans had hoped: abortion rights have been significantly undermined, affirmative action policies much more difficult to pursue and convicted murderers more likely to be executed.

At the same time, on particular issues or in particular cases, justices do not necessarily do what their nominating presidents desire. Thus, although justices O'Connor, Kennedy and Souter have undermined the Court's 1973 abortion decision, they have not squarely reversed it, as both presidents Reagan and Bush urged. In part, at least, this is owing to the fact that most justices of the Supreme Court are not simply politicians in disguise. They cannot escape their political environment entirely, but there are also judicial imperatives that may constrain them. Law, even constitutional law, requires a good measure of stability and consistency of principle. If the Court simply tacks with every change in the prevailing political winds, it risks losing the very character that makes it distinctive and authoritative in American politics. As the three Justices wrote when refusing to reverse *Roe v. Wade*:

> The Court must take care to speak and act in ways that allow people to accept its decisions on the terms the Court claims for them, as grounded truly in principle, not as compromises with social and political pressures having no bearing on the principled choices that the Court is obliged to make. Thus, the Court's legitimacy depends on making legally principled decisions under circumstances in which their principled character is sufficiently plausible to be accepted by the Nation.
> (Joint opinion of Justices O'Connor, Kennedy and Souter, *Planned Parenthood of Southeastern Pennsylvania v. Casey*, 1992)

It is no accident that the word 'principle' appears four times in just two sentences, for it goes to the very heart of the notion of having a written constitution, whose principles are superior and more enduring than the views of the latest legislative majority. The Supreme Court is the guardian of the Constitution and is therefore duty-bound to resist political pressures that conflict with the principles it contains. In the long run, the appointment process will ensure that the Supreme Court falls into line with the political majority on most issues. In the meantime, the Court provides a valuable, if imperfect, insurance against legislative and executive abuse.

Summary

Throughout American history, the Supreme Court has oscillated between judicial activism and judicial self-restraint. When the Court has been activist, opponents have charged that the supremacy of the Constitution has been perverted to create the supremacy of the Supreme Court in the American political system. In fact, there are enough formal and informal constraints upon the Supreme Court's power to ensure that this does not happen, and in the long term, the Court usually does comply with the wishes of the majority. Nevertheless, precisely because the Supreme Court is a judicial body endowed with significant political power, presidents go to considerable lengths in the appointment process to shape the direction and decisions that the Court will take.

Topics for discussion

1. What are the distinguishing features of the concepts of *judicial activism* and *judicial restraint*?

2. How powerful is the Supreme Court?

3. Should we regard the Supreme Court as in essence a legal or a political body?

4. What does a president look for in a Supreme Court nominee?

5. Why are some Supreme Court nominations so controversial?

Further reading

See suggestions at the end of Chapter 17 (page 379)

References

Dahl, R., 1957, 'Decision-making in a democracy: the Supreme Court as a national policy-maker', *Journal of Public Law*, vol. VI, pp. 279–95

Hodder-Williams, R., 1988, 'The strange story of Judge Robert Bork and a vacancy on the United States Supreme Court', *Political Studies*, vol. XXXVI, pp. 613–37

Marshall, T., 1989, *Public Opinion and the Supreme Court* (Boston: Unwin Hyman)

Rosenberg, G., 1991, *The Hollow Hope: Can courts bring about social change?* (Chicago: University of Chicago Press)

Tribe, L., 1985, *God Save This Honorable Court* (New York: Mentor)

Vieira, N. and Gross, L., 1990, 'The appointments clause: Judge Bork and the role of ideology in judicial confirmations', *Journal of Legal History*, vol. XI, pp. 311–52

part VII

The policy process

In this final part of the book we examine the policy-making process in the context of four major issues on the agenda of contemporary American politics. While there are some significant differences between policy making on domestic issues and the making of foreign policy, there are also striking similarities. Policy making on all issues in the United States is conducted within a constitutional framework that encourages the participation of multiple players in multiple fora – a fragmentation which can create serious problems in the generation of coherent and effective policy. Each of the chapters also pays considerable attention to the historical and ideological contexts of the issues concerned, since these are crucial factors which make some policy outcomes much more likely than others.

Contents

19

Welfare

Even more consistently than in foreign policy, issues in domestic policy illustrate the characteristic features of policy making in the United States. Despite a broad consensus on the purpose and scope of the welfare state, conflicts on these questions have formed an important part of the political agenda in the twentieth century. These continuing conflicts illustrate the open and adversarial character of the policy-making process, to which many centres of political and economic power contribute, and which rarely results in simple and unchallengeable policy directions. Welfare politics also shows the frequent relevance of racial antagonisms, and of the intertwining of economic with cultural and moral issues.

In the 1992 presidential election campaign, the successful Democratic candidate, Bill Clinton, promised to 'end welfare as we know it', that is, to introduce drastic changes in the governmental system of assistance to poor families. The new Republican majority elected to Congress in 1994 was also committed to radical reforms of the welfare system, and this Congress presented President Clinton with three bills incorporating such reforms, the first two of which the President vetoed, and the third of which he signed in August 1996. The Personal Responsibility and Work Opportunity Act, with effect from 1 July 1997, established a new framework for the welfare system, replacing the long established but controversial main federal welfare programme of Aid to Families with Dependent Children (AFDC) with a more decentralised programme, Temporary Assistance to Needy Families (TANF). The TANF system, like welfare-to-work schemes currently being pursued in some other western democracies, sets up strict work requirements and time limits for recipients (Box 19.1).

Many advocates and opponents of the 1996 Act agreed that it constituted a drastic change in welfare policy. However, this tough new welfare regime had been gestating for a number of years. The terms of the welfare debate in the 1980s and 1990s that produced the 1996 reforms echoed the discussions of many previous

Box 19.1

The TANF system

Under the programme of Temporary Assistance to Needy Families (TANF), which came into effect in 1997 to pay for welfare, the federal government now gives each state a fixed sum of money each year (a TANF block grant). The amount for each state is based on that state's previous level of AFDC spending (this varies widely from state to state), but it is fixed for six years, rather than being (as under AFDC) an open-ended categorical grant matching all state expenditures. (On the distinction between categorical and block grants, see Chapter 4, page 92.)

Under TANF, states remain free to spend as much of their own funds on welfare as they choose, although they must spend at least 75 per cent of what they spent in recent past years in order to receive the full federal grant.

Further conditions apply to TANF block grants: states must impose strict *work requirements* and *time limits* on welfare beneficiaries, and they must maintain effective enforcement of *child support* orders (for example by revoking driving, professional and recreational licences of delinquent parents).

Able-bodied adults in welfare families are expected to work (whether in regular paid employment or in community service jobs) within two years of first receiving assistance. The TANF block grant will be reduced (by penalties rising two percentage points yearly from 5 per cent to 21 per cent) for states that do not get specified percentages of their welfare adults into work by specified deadlines (rising yearly to 50 per cent of all families and 90 per cent of two-parent families by 2002).

Moreover, starting in 2001, no family (except the 20 per cent of cases that each state is allowed to classify as hardship cases) is to receive federally funded welfare cash (as distinguished from in-kind and service) benefits if an adult in that family has already received benefits for a total of five years. States are permitted to impose shorter lifetime limits.

States are also permitted (but not required) to deny benefits to unmarried teenage mothers and to limit the number of children for whom a welfare family will be paid additional support.

decades. In order to understand the treatment of this issue today, we need to study its emergence in earlier American political experience. We begin by examining the character of the American welfare state, to see the role played within it by welfare in the narrower sense commonly used in American political speech.

The logic of the American welfare state

Those who study and those who experience the welfare state in the United States often assert that it defies logic: the welfare 'system', they say, is incoherent and illogical, with no guiding principle. This is a defensible conclusion that commands assent up to a point: one of the undeniable characteristics of the American welfare state is its incremental development and patchwork coverage, and we shall be looking at some of the reasons for this. However, there is a logic or at least a dominant ethos in the American welfare state. It is illuminating to explore the way that Americans have in general thought about how the welfare state fits into their liberal democratic polity. Understanding the ethos of the American welfare state can help in understanding its intricacies and apparent contradictions.

Both extreme laissez-faire and complete socialism (total government control of the economy) have their advocates in the United States, but something between these two extremes has developed and prevailed. Laissez-faire is seen as incompatible with democracy (popular demands for government action in certain circumstances); complete socialism is seen as incompatible with liberty. American 'liberals' and 'conservatives' (as these labels have been used since the 1930s) argue about which economic policies the various levels of American governments should pursue. Liberals tend to favour a more active role for government in economic matters, especially for the federal government; conservatives tend to be more sceptical. However, they agree that governments at all levels have limited but substantial economic powers and responsibilities.

One of the issues in political economy that American liberals and conservatives both agree and disagree upon is the proper role of government in the provision of social welfare. The collapse of the postwar consensus in the 1960s and 1970s (analysed in Chapter 5) involved growing disagreements about welfare policy. These disagreements continue today to engage the passions and the reflections of American citizens, even though Americans also continue to agree on many of the fundamentals of welfare policy:

1. The necessity of promoting welfare by means of government but also of limiting the scope of the welfare state in order to preserve limited government.

2. The right of citizens to a degree of protection against economic insecurity.

3. The necessity of paying attention to the moral as well as the economic effects of welfare policies.

4. The ensuing distinction between social insurance and social welfare.

5. The importance of the non-governmental contribution to welfare.

These five fundamentals are examined below.

The welfare state and limited government

Modern liberal democracy is a fundamentally secular regime: it seeks to promote the happiness of people primarily not by saving their souls but by securing their rights to material comforts. Yet even this limited end of modern politics can demand unlimited resources: when can one have enough of the basic goods of life? Therefore the duty to provide 'welfare' can seem like an open-ended commitment of government, authorising it to go beyond any constitutional limits in order to serve its purpose. The welfare state is in this way logically somewhat at odds with the idea of limited government. In

American politics, this problem of fitting welfare policies into a limited government has been addressed by understanding the welfare state as strictly limited in scope and as constrained by certain moral considerations.

Socialist commentators see welfare states as tools of capitalism, which are therefore likely to be stingy and directive, serving the interests of the rich by supervising and appeasing the poor. Laissez-faire conservatives see welfare states as destructive of political and economic freedom. Less doctrinaire American conservatives have been able to agree with many American liberals on a middle view that sees the welfare state as a counterforce to the excesses and hazards of industrial capitalism and markets, but a counterforce that can be arranged in such a way that it neither significantly undermines the productivity of the market system nor leads to unlimited government. The New Deal exemplified this way of thinking. It was intended by its architects to reform economic practices and financial institutions in order to promote a productive market economy, and to relieve severe economic distress which the market economy caused or at least did not cure. It recognised a collective social responsibility to protect the right of individuals to earn an adequate living, and to help them provide against certain economic hazards connected with old age, unemployment, illness and disability. Thus in 1936, President Franklin D. Roosevelt, in one of his 'fireside chats' broadcast to the nation by radio, spoke of the government's duty to protect individuals 'in the opportunity to use their labor at a return adequate to support them at a decent and constantly rising standard of living, and to accumulate a margin of security against the inevitable vicissitudes of life' (Rosenman, 1938–50, vol. 5, pp. 338–9).

Protection against economic insecurity

Modern welfare states are generally said to be animated by three purposes: encouraging social solidarity, reducing inequality, and protecting against economic insecurity. In the United States, the last purpose has been most prominent: protecting citizens against 'the inevitable vicissitudes of life' in an economic world in which industrialisation and urbanisation have increased not only wealth but also the risks of unemployment and work-related accidents.

The other two purposes, social cohesion and equality, have also been present, confusing many issues. For example, the federal provision of retirement pensions, primarily a protection against economic insecurity, also serves as a means of redistributing income since beneficiaries receive from the pension fund more than they have contributed to it by way of payroll taxes. Moreover, it is worth noting that traditional republican concerns (going back as far as Plato's *Laws*) that economic inequalities among citizens should not become too great have been voiced in the United States not just by socialists but also by mainstream liberals from the earliest times (for example by James Madison). However, welfare policies are generally most successfully justified in the United States not in terms of reducing economic inequality but in terms of helping those temporarily or permanently unable to earn enough to provide their own economic security. Social cohesion or solidarity is to be served by making a work ethic widely shared. Reducing inequality and ending poverty – if those are goals – are goals to be served primarily by economic growth and such means as publicly funded education and legally protected unions rather than directly by income redistribution.

The morality of welfare

One of the reasons that welfare policies sometimes become very controversial in the United States is that welfare is understood as not just an economic issue but also a moral issue. It is not just conservatives since the 1970s who have been concerned with the adverse moral impact of government-provided welfare. In the early years of the New Deal, Roosevelt insisted on moving government away from providing material relief to millions (although that was temporarily necessary), towards setting up contributory insurance schemes for pensions and for support for the unemployed: while these schemes of insurance were a 'sound means' of making people more secure, 'continued dependence upon relief induces a spiritual and moral disintegration. ... To dole out relief in this way is to administer a narcotic, a subtle destroyer of the human spirit' (Rosenman, 1938–50, vol. 5, pp. 19–21; Berkowitz, 1991, p. 14; Katz, 1986, p. 226) In this view, held by many liberals as well as by conservatives, the overriding purpose of welfare policy must be to maintain the dignity of individuals, and most individuals in liberal democracies earn dignity by (among other ways) earning their living. The spirit of welfare assistance is the same as that of the nineteenth-century homestead laws that made public land cheaply available to families to enable them to earn their living by cultivating the land. Dignity requires an equality of opportunity to earn unequal rewards, and governmental action might be necessary to maintain or to restore that equal opportunity, but long-term governmental support of able-bodied adults (the 'undeserving poor') is a very dubious policy from this point of view. This raises a troubling problem in cases where these adults are in charge of children; American welfare policy has embodied the contradictory desires to help the children and to avoid encouraging the irresponsibility of the adults. Many disputes about welfare between conservatives and liberals have centred upon the question of whether government policies should encourage families headed by married couples, or should instead be indifferent or even enthusiasic about the increase in households headed by single parents.

Insurance versus welfare

It is such moral considerations as these that have helped make the American welfare state a two-tiered system, divided between the social insurance side and the welfare side. More than twice as much government spending is devoted to the insurance side. The insurance side, with little or no means (income and assets) testing, and with the vast majority of workers paying into it (by dedicated payroll taxes) and eventually being able to collect from it, enjoys relatively strong public support. The welfare side, financed through general revenues and benefiting only those unfortunate enough to meet tests for low income, carries more stigma, and arouses controversies often far out of proportion to the amount of spending involved. It also tends to be concerned as much with rehabilitating its clients by providing services, as with handing over cash or vouchers for food and housing. It is this moral aspect of the American welfare state, as well as the different arrays of majorities and minorities that appear on the insurance side and on the welfare side, that renders policy making so different on the two sides.

The advantages of private sector welfare

In addition to its potentially demoralising effects on beneficiaries, another reason that government provision of welfare is often thought to be suspect is that providing welfare by means of government bureaux and compulsory taxation is considered both more demeaning and less socialising than doing it by voluntary associations. (The opposite view was taken by twentieth-century communist regimes, which outlawed such associations and considered voluntary charity as a sign of the failure of state provision.) Not just governments but many social institutions too provide welfare: families, friends, religious charity organisations, charitable clubs, non-profit human service agencies such as the Red Cross, the Volunteers of America, the Family Service Association of America, and so on. There are tens of thousands of small organisations in this voluntary welfare sector, supported by money and time donated in any given year by more than half of the American population aged 14 and over (Karger and Stoesz, 1990, p. 116). Many worthy causes not (or at least not at first) served by governmental programmes have been helped by these organisations. Many beneficiaries prefer voluntary to government help. Many citizens are happy to contribute through voluntary organisations to people for whom they would not support government programmes. Several commentators on American politics from the Antifederalists onwards have worried about the decline of America's network of 'intermediary institutions' between governments and individual citizens, but the involvement of millions of citizens in these voluntary social organisations continues to contribute to American civil society and American welfare efforts.

However, in addition to its base in private philanthropy, which amounts to 2 per cent of GNP (Ginsburg, 1992, p. 102), it must also be noted that this voluntary part of private sector welfare benefits from government encouragement such as tax exemptions, and increasingly depends heavily upon more direct government subsidies in many cases, in the form of grants and contracts. For example, Catholic Charities USA, a large national network of social service agencies, receives two-thirds of its revenue from federal, state and local governments (Arenson, 1995). Many of the organisations in the poorest parts of the country are those most highly dependent on government grants. Therefore the hope of financially hard-pressed governments that the voluntary sector might take significant amounts of welfare responsibility off their hands needs to be tempered.

The private welfare sector also includes a significant amount (about 14 per cent of GNP) of 'welfare capitalism': the provision by private employers of such welfare services as health care plans or insurance and pensions (US Bureau of the Census, 1996, p. 370). As President Clinton found during his first term in his abortive attempt to extend federal government responsibility for health care, the presence of this large private welfare sector can impede the expansion of the welfare state, when the private welfare interests feel threatened by greater government involvement.

The welfare state before the New Deal

British colonial America had a welfare regime based on the English poor laws. These laws made the relief of the destitution of local residents the responsibility of local governments and churches, while also empowering those bodies to turn away the poor who were not settled in the community, and those whose parents, grandparents, children or grandchildren could support them. They also empowered local authorities to apprentice the children of paupers to farmers or artisans, and to require work from able-bodied recipients of assistance. In several cities in late eighteenth- and early nineteenth-century Britain and America, reformers interested in rehabilitating the poor to make them more independent citizens succeeded in introducing the institution of the poorhouse, which served as a refuge for the helpless and a deterrent to the able-bodied poor. However, this proved to be a relatively expensive (and not necessarily more humane) alternative to earlier methods of poor relief, which therefore persisted (Katz, 1986, chapters 1–2).

The responsibility of local (town or county) governments for regulating and relieving local residents who were extremely poor remained a major part of the welfare state until it was overwhelmed by the depression of the 1930s, when the federal government stepped in to help. (Most states and some localities maintain such General Assistance programmes today, often restricted to disabled or elderly persons who do not qualify for federally funded relief.) However, there were a few developments between the Civil War and the Depression that served as precedents and bases for New Deal and later welfare policy, or as durable parts of the complex and incrementally-grown American welfare state.

Pensions

The first of these developments was the programme of pensions for Civil War veterans and widows. This programme, set up in 1862, financed by general revenues, eventually paid benefits to a majority of elderly, native-born white males in the northern states. This was a large item in the federal budget, and before the First World War the US government spent much more on old-age assistance than Britain did (Katz, 1986, p. 200; Skocpol, 1992). On the eve of the Great Depression of the 1930s, the federal government, mainly because of the veterans' pensions, was paying 58 per cent of public welfare expenses (Katz, 1986, p. 208). Independent retirement – a luxury that was not experienced by any but wealthy Americans in the nineteenth and early twentieth centuries, when children more generally took care of their elderly parents – was receiving greater attention in social thinking in this period. A few states adopted modest old-age public pension plans. However, the more general adoption of public old-age pensions was resisted until the depression. Pensions developed by 'welfare capitalism' – the provision of welfare services by business corporations for their employees – while never very comprehensive, nevertheless provided a plausible reason for resisting movements for more tax-funded pensions, until the depression bankrupted many corporate pension schemes.

In the 1910s and 1920s, public pension programmes were started for some state and local government employees – police, firefighters, teachers – and for federal civil servants, the latter financed (as Social Security pensions were to be) by employee contributions rather than by general revenues. Also in these two decades, all but two states established non-contributory systems of mothers' pensions (which usually went to widows), designed to provide public support for poor children without separating children from their families by apprenticing or institutionalising them. These pension systems were part of a set of Progressive reforms based on an intensified focus on childhood as a precious time. These reforms also included child labour legislation, compulsory school attendance laws, the institution of juvenile courts, and public health projects directed especially at women and children (Katz, 1986, chapter 5). The state systems of mothers' pensions were a precedent for the federal assistance to dependent children that began in 1935 and continued to 1997 in the largest (and most controversial) part of the welfare (non-insurance) side of the federal welfare state, Aid to Families with Dependent Children (Temporary Assistance for Needy Families from 1997).

Workers' compensation

Most states passed workers' compensation legislation in the 1910s, to address the problem of high industrial accident rates and uncertain legal liabilities. These programmes, still operative today, generally require or at least encourage employers to buy liability insurance, either from the state or from a private insurer. They were designed with employers' and insurance companies' as well as employees' interests in mind, and therefore do not invariably ensure prompt and adequate compensation, but they did establish the principle that such compensation is a matter of right.

Unemployment insurance

Loss of employment is a constant hazard in a market economy. During the first decades of the twentieth century, a few business corporations attempted to reduce unemployment in their firms by evening out production schedules; and some provided benefits for workers who were nevertheless laid off. However, organised labour did not favour legislation for compulsory unemployment insurance until the depression of the 1930s began raising the level of unemployment to unprecedented heights (from 3 per cent in 1929 to 25 per cent in 1933). The first state to pass such legislation (Wisconsin) did so in 1932, and three other states followed suit before 1935, when New Deal legislation required all states to adopt unemployment insurance.

New Deal innovations

State and local initiatives in welfare policy in the decades before the 1930s made it possible to argue that states and localities (along with business corporations) were doing the job, so the federal government need not intervene. However, that argument became much less convincing during the deep and prolonged depression of the 1930s, which greatly increased the incentives of state and local governments to seek help from the federal government. Co-operative federalism (discussed in Chapter 4, page 86) thus came into being in service to the welfare state.

With unemployment running up to 25 per cent nationally (much higher – up to 80 per cent – in some cities), state and local governments and private corporations were simply unable to cope with the increased demands on welfare services. Without federal government action, the possibility of mass starvation and civil disorder loomed large. After the elections of 1932, the federal government did take action, first on the welfare or relief side and then on the social insurance side of welfare policy.

The most immediately effective federal action was to help the state and local relief efforts. They were supplemented by two kinds of federal action: (1) federal subsidy (by matching grants) of the disbursements – and of the expansion and reorganisation – of state and local relief agencies, and (2) federal public works programmes. The first of these – the pure relief programmes – were ended after a few years; Roosevelt's administration took the view that this – and certainly the relief of 'unemployables' – should revert to being a state and local responsibility, with the federal government continuing to bear responsibility for employable victims of the national economic emergency, but only by enrolling them in works projects. These public works programmes, which required work for payment rather than being a mere dole, lasted longer – until the Second World War – and employed as many as 3 million workers at a time (a large number, but still less than one-third of the total unemployed). However, they too were thought of as temporary measures, to be ended (as they were) when the economy recovered, as it did finally only with the War.

For the longer term, the social insurance side of the welfare state was at the centre of the focus of New Deal policy-makers. Roosevelt's Cabinet Committee on Economic Security initiated the more durable parts of New Deal welfare policies by drafting the Social Security Act passed by Congress in 1935. This Act established the framework that still exists for federal old-age insurance, unemployment compensation, and federal assistance for state provisions for blind and disabled persons and for dependent children:

1. **Old-age and survivors' insurance (Title II of the Social Security Act).** This programme of federal pensions and death benefits to workers (and their surviving dependants) who retire at age 65 (or die before then) was not immediately politically popular, since its contributory taxes started in 1937 but it did not pay benefits to anyone until 1942. (Title I of the Social Security Act thus appropriated money to support existing state old-age assistance plans.) However, that was the key fact about this programme that eventually made it the most politically unchallengeable part of the American welfare state: it was understood not as a 'relief' programme but as an insurance programme, with benefits related not to a means test but to the contributions of the eventual beneficiaries (and their employers). Its attraction, and its political defensibility, lay in its approach to universality: a large majority were beneficiaries – although in its original form, it was also made more immediately politically defensible by excluding from its provisions certain

employments, such as agricultural labour and domestic service in a private home, occupations that included many non-whites and women.

2. **Unemployment compensation**. Legislation regarding unemployment and its attendant needs is more difficult to formulate than that regarding old age, since every case of unemployment is different from all others, whereas age is an easy criterion to use in all cases. Reaching political agreement on old-age insurance (benefiting almost all people over 65, deemed too old to be expected to work), was therefore easier than reaching agreement on unemployment compensation laws (benefiting a minority of able-bodied workers), even when unemployment was as widespread as it was in the 1930s. In fact, there was general agreement that this programme, like old-age pensions, would not benefit anyone immediately: the new laws would apply only to workers laid off in the future, with a work record established after the new laws took effect. There was also agreement that benefits would be limited to a number of months: they were not to become a dole. There was disagreement on whether unemployment compensation should be dealt with directly by the federal government, or whether the federal government should simply require the states to tackle this problem (four of them had already done so). There was also disagreement on whether the polity at large should be responsible for compensating unemployed workers, or whether (as in Wisconsin, the American pioneer in this field of legislation) individual employers should be primarily responsible, thus giving them an incentive for hesitating to lay off workers (by financing the scheme only through employers' contributions, and varying these in accordance with the employers' record of avoiding lay-offs). Both President Roosevelt and Congress came down on the side of allowing states great freedom to establish whatever kind of system they chose, and simply required that all states did establish a system (by imposing a punitive payroll tax in states that neglected to do so). This decentralised unemployment system, which is still in place, leaves each state to determine eligibility rules and the amount and duration of benefits payments (although the federal government can and sometimes does step in to top up states' unemployment programmes). It does not establish incentives for state employment offices to publicise job opportunities in other states, nor for states to tax employers heavily enough to provide very generous levels of compensation.

3. **Aid to the blind and disabled.** In 1935, the federal government began making grants to states to support approved state plans for financial assistance 'to needy individuals who are blind' (Social Security Act, Title X), and for diagnosis and care of 'children who are crippled or who are suffering from conditions which lead to crippling' (Social Security Act, Title V). In 1956, the Social Security Act was amended to extend assistance to those over 50 with permanent disabilities; in 1958, this was extended to cover their dependants, and it was further extended in 1960 to cover disabled workers of any age whose disability prevented their working for at least a year.

4. **Aid to Dependent Children (ADC).** This provided federal grants to assist state plans giving financial support to children under 16 years of age who had been 'deprived

of parental support or care by reason of the death, continued absence from the home, or physical or mental incapacity of a parent' (Social Security Act, Title IV), and who were living in the home of a relative (usually a mother). Like aid to the blind, ADC is a means-tested form of assistance, but was – in 1935 – a similarly uncontroversial part of the Social Security Act. The expectation was that widows with children would eventually be covered by old age and survivors' insurance (Title II). ADC was considered to be a pro-family policy, supporting mothers' pension programmes that were already operating in most states. Poor widows and orphans – like the old, the blind and the disabled – were regarded as among the deserving poor, blameless for their plight. Like the blind and disabled (and the old, at least temporarily), they were given relief ('welfare') rather than social insurance, but relief that was relatively unstigmatised because these groups were judged to be morally deserving as well as economically needy.

Like unemployment compensation, administration of ADC by individual states (including setting of benefit levels, which therefore varied widely – and still do) reassured those who were worried about federal interference with the discriminatory treatment of racial minorities. This decentralisation also meant that a variety of 'morals tests' could be applied. For example, some states required that a 'suitable home' (such as one with no illegitimate children) was being provided for the dependent child.

The Housing Act of 1937 began federal involvement with another aspect of the welfare state: the government subsidy of housing projects intended to provide 'decent, safe and sanitary dwellings for families of low income'. Under this Act and its later versions, the federal government has developed programmes of subsidy both for housing construction and for rent and mortgage payments. Because housing is an issue in which many conflicting interests and strongly held views are involved, these programmes have had problems and failures, but they have helped greatly to reduce the proportion of overcrowded and substandard housing units.

New Deal innovations in welfare policy constituted a very significant increase in government – especially federal government – responsibility for welfare. They increased states' commitments to welfare policies, and improved the administrative capacity of the welfare systems in many states. Spending on welfare programmes vastly increased at both federal and state level, although the increase was more dramatic at the federal level, rising from 2 per cent of the total in 1932 to 62 per cent by 1939 (Katz, 1986, p. 246).

The New Deal also increased the complexity of the American welfare state, with its many different and somewhat overlapping programmes, gaps in coverage, many different overseers, and variety of levels of benefits and eligibility rules in different states. New Deal welfare policies were a product of and a spur to American federalism. State governments were built into almost all of the federal programmes as administrators, and they retained much financial responsibility, especially in cash relief programmes.

Individual states had both liberal and conservative reasons for insisting on this federal basis of welfare policy. Certain states felt themselves to be the senior partners to the federal government in terms of experience and liberal commitment. For example, Wisconsin social insurance experts worried that the federal government with its underdeveloped administrative capacity would undermine that state's progressive legislation. Southern states, mindful of their peculiar racial laws and aware of their strength as essential parts of the New Deal Democratic party coalition, would not have approved of any great bypassing of states' prerogatives. On the other hand, it should be noted that many poor blacks were helped by the New Deal, especially by work relief programmes that were administered by the federal government with an eye to equal rights (Katz, 1986, pp. 244–5).

Welfare policy was only one way – and it was not intended to be the most important way – in which the New Deal helped people in economic trouble in the depression years. The most effective help was looked for from economic recovery – which came durably only with the Second World War. Coupled with this was an insistence that the 'footsoldiers of industry' – ordinary workers, as opposed to the captains of industry – should gain from economic recovery: New Deal legislation protecting the rights of labour unions to organise and to bargain collectively was at least as important as welfare policy in advancing the interests and the dignity of many Americans.

Expansion and reform of the welfare state in the 1960s and 1970s ▬

In the fifteen years following the Second World War, while western European governments were expanding their welfare states, the United States remained conservatively attached to its successful economy as the source of economic security. Democratic presidential administrations still sought expansions of federal welfare initiatives in such areas as health care (and they advised and approved large welfare states in Japan and western Europe), but conservative Congresses did not usually support these initiatives. In the 1940s and 1950s, the private health insurance industry expanded, often in employment-related plans, and states set up disability schemes that involved private insurance companies. Development of these non-governmental and state government provisions for certain welfare services made it much more difficult to find political support for the expansion of these services by the federal government, although (as noted above) Congress (and a Republican president) did add disability provisions to the Social Security law in 1956, 1958 and 1960.

However, as in other OECD (Organization for Economic Co-operation and Development) countries, welfare state spending greatly increased from the 1960s up to the mid-1970s (although faster than some, and from a lower base). Whereas from 1940 to 1960, public expenditures for social welfare had increased from 9 to 10 per cent of GNP, from 1960 to 1976 (a peak), they increased to over 20 per cent of GNP. The governmental proportion of total social welfare spending (government plus voluntary) rose from 65 to 73 per cent (Gilbert, 1983, pp. 7, 139–40, 142). The ratio of federal to state and local government spending on social welfare rapidly increased in these years, from slightly less than 1 to its current level of about 1.5. From 1971 onwards, social welfare expenditures replaced military spending as the largest item in the federal budget (US Bureau of the Census, 1996, p. 332).

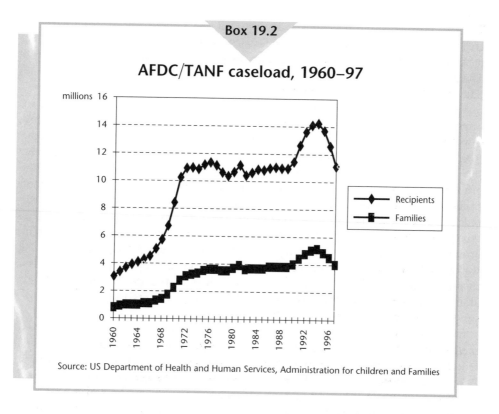

Box 19.2

AFDC/TANF caseload, 1960–97

Source: US Department of Health and Human Services, Administration for children and Families

Much of this growth in the welfare state was on the insurance side; as the number of people entitled to social security benefits grew, relief programmes shrank. The major exception was the numbers receiving Aid to Dependent Children, which had increased steadily from the beginning of the programme, and which grew dramatically from 3.1 million in 1960 to 10.8 million in 1974 (Patterson, 1981, p. 171). In 1962, the ADC programme (Title IV of the Social Security Act) was changed to include grants for care-givers (thus the title was changed to Aid to Families with Dependent Children, AFDC), and states were given the option (made mandatory in 1988) to extend AFDC as-sistance (at least for a temporary period) to families with both parents present but unemployed (AFDC–Unemployed Parents) – see Box 19.2.

Poverty, welfare and welfare rights

American thinking about poverty changed in the early 1960s. Poverty came to be seen as less tolerable and more curable in the affluent society of postwar America. Pursuing some earlier initiatives and studies, President Lyndon B. Johnson declared a 'war on poverty' in January 1964. Although poverty was not restricted to minority groups, the

War on Poverty was closely connected to the civil rights movement of these years. The civil rights march on Washington in August 1963 helped create the atmosphere for the passage of the Economic Opportunity Act (as well as the Civil Rights Act) of 1964. The preamble to this Act stated the policy that the law was intended further: 'to eliminate the paradox of poverty in the midst of plenty in this Nation by opening to everyone the opportunity for education and training, the opportunity to work, and the opportunity to live in decency and dignity.' The assumption was that the main causes of poverty were cultural deprivation and blocked opportunities, rather than the structure of the economy. Therefore, the preferred strategy was to provide not money but services and rehabilitation: education (including preschool and adult literacy programmes, and part-time jobs for needy students), training (including work-training programmes and residential vocational training centres for unemployed 16–21 year-olds), legal services, and housing, community health and nutrition programmes. Thus this strategy to end poverty depended on employment being provided by economic growth, rather than relief (even work relief) being provided by government. The welfare state could help produce employable workers; the economy would have to produce jobs for them. In fact, economic growth in the 1960s and early 1970s, along with increased government cash and in-kind payments to poor people, did substantially reduce poverty, especially among the old.

In spite of this optimistic strategy aimed at rehabilitating welfare clients to move them towards self dependence, more and more poor Americans came to rely on the federally funded relief programme, AFDC, which by the 1950s had replaced General Assistance (relief by state and local governments) as 'America's major welfare program' (Berkowitz, 1991, p. 93), and which grew rapidly in the 1960s and early 1970s. The postwar baby boom and the migration of poor citizens from the south (where agriculture was being mechanised) to more liberal northern and western states (with more generous AFDC benefits) accounted for much of this growth; liberalised federal grant rules also accounted for some of it. Some of the growth was also caused by the greater assertiveness of potential beneficiaries, who were learning to think in terms of 'welfare rights', and to assert that publicly funded welfare was superior to voluntary charity, the need for which they took to be a sign of the inadequacy of the welfare state. Although the Supreme Court refused to recognise a constitutional right to welfare, for federally funded programmes successful legal challenges were mounted against waiting requirements that some states imposed on new residents (the Court spoke of the right to move in search of 'opportunities for self-preservation and advancement' *Shapiro v. Thompson*, (1969) and against some of the 'morals' tests that had been used to make some claimants (particularly non-whites) ineligible. Welfare rights activists, along with the availability of Medicaid to AFDC recipients after 1965, successfully encouraged a much larger percentage of eligible people to apply for aid, and a larger percentage of applications were successful.

However, these successes of the welfare rights movement were also signs of underlying political weakness. The assertion of welfare rights was less a case of majoritarian politics, with the majority of people demanding and agreeing upon rights, than it was a case of a few experts demanding rights for certain groups of poor people. The focus was on the minorities – on 'pockets of poverty'. More majoritarian approaches to poverty (for example family allowances) were not pursued. As AFDC grew in size, and as its champions grew in assertiveness, its legitimacy in general public opinion actually decreased, primarily not because of its growing financial costs (benefit levels did not keep pace with inflation), but because of the growing public perception of its beneficiaries as set apart from the majority, and as less morally deserving than the original beneficiaries of this programme. From a support for (typically white) widows with dependent children, AFDC was gradually changing to a programme supporting many divorced or never-married single parents, still mainly women, but increasingly blacks (although black families have always been and remain today a minority of assisted cases, albeit now a substantial minority – 39 per cent in 1993 [US Bureau of the Census, 1996, p. 383]). It is difficult to separate the moral from the ethnic or racial elements of this changing perception, but in the light of the stigma traditionally attached to relief of able-bodied adults of whatever colour (except widows with young children), and the general view that children are better off being raised by fathers and mothers, it seems reasonable to speculate that even if no racial consideration had affected the public judgement, there would still have been strong objections raised against the shift from supporting widows and orphans, who had general sympathy, to supporting young unmarried mothers and illegitimate children unsupported by their fathers. Perhaps the greatest single cause of the growing public unpopularity of AFDC was the fact that in these decades, women in general, including many mothers of young children, were working – and were expected to work – in paid employment outside the home. By 1975, a majority of mothers with school-age children held jobs outside the home. The argument became: why should non-AFDC mothers (including single parents), or anyone else for that matter, work and pay taxes to support AFDC mothers staying at home? In the judgement of one historian, this failure of welfare programmes to respond to modern conditions doomed these programmes to unpopularity (Berkowitz, 1991, pp. xiv, 10).

Welfare reforms

The real and the merely alleged shortcomings of AFDC placed welfare reform firmly on the political agenda, where it remains today. During the first years of the Republican presidential administrations of Richard Nixon (1969–74), attempts were made to reform welfare in a comprehensive way that would make a clean break from the 'welfare mess' that Democratic administrations were accused of foisting upon the nation. Nixon favoured the proposal to abolish AFDC and to substitute for it a federally guaranteed minimum income (or 'negative income tax') for all American families, whether that income currently came from welfare or from employment. The idea of this proposed Family Assistance Plan (never enacted) was to switch from the antipoverty strategy that emphasised rehabilitation of culturally deprived clients of the social services, hoping to transform them into 'employables', to an income strategy that proposed simply to top up the incomes of all poor families, including the working

poor. Among other effects, this was intended to address the problem of work disin-
centives in the AFDC programme, which reduced its payments in proportion to clients'
income from work; and the problem of AFDC's built-in incentives for mothers to live
separately from their children's father (and from their own parents) in order to be eligible for relief, and for fathers to avoid supporting their children. However, the Family
Assistance Plan met the fatal objections, from conservatives, that it seemed to be
admitting that welfare was a right rather than a need based on physical or cultural disability, or (alternatively) that it threatened to stigmatise the working poor by including
them in the welfare system, and that its own system of work incentives (allowing some
income from employment to be disregarded) might well fail (in part because of workers' loss of the health care grants available to welfare recipients); and, from liberals,
that the proposed minimum income was too low, and that it was wrong even to try to
set up work incentives that would drive welfare mothers out of the house to low-paid
jobs.

In 1975, Congress would agree to establish a kind of negative income tax in the
form of the Earned Income Tax Credit (EITC) to top up the incomes of the poor
working families with children, but it did not agree to the Family Assistance Plan's
proposal to give a uniform guaranteed income to those who depend solely on AFDC
relief. In 1977, President Carter's version of that proposal, in his Program for Better
Jobs and Income, was also rejected by Congress.

Thus, for all their differences about which poor people deserve to be helped by
welfare, the coalition of conservatives and liberals that defeated Nixon's Family
Assistance proposal seemed to agree on the need for American politics to maintain the
traditional sharp distinction between the world of welfare (public help for the deserving poor) and the world of employment. This helps to make sense of the fact that the
same Congress that rejected the Family Assistance Plan nevertheless enacted (in 1972)
Supplementary Security Income (SSI), a programme that consolidated and federalised
assistance to the needy old, blind and totally and permanently disabled (that is, the
unemployable deserving poor) and that pays them a uniform national guaranteed
minimum income; while (in 1971) it required able-bodied adult AFDC recipients not
caring for children under six years of age (the employable undeserving poor) to join the
Work Incentive programme, a federal welfare-to-work training scheme that had been
set up in 1967.

The only major federal programme that was changed in a way that bridged the
worlds of welfare and work was the Food Stamp programme, a system of vouchers
(originally designed to supplement farm income, therefore administered by the
Department of Agriculture) sold at a discount to those eligible for welfare. In 1970,
Congress extended the eligibility for this programme to the non-welfare poor, and
made the vouchers available without cost to poor families with children. In 1977, purchase requirements were removed for all recipients. More recently, the expansion of
this programme has been slowed: in the early 1980s, food stamp eligibility was tight-
ened, and the number of recipients slightly dropped, although spending continued to
rise, and by 1991 numbers climbed back to 1980 levels; the welfare reform law of
1996 added a work requirement for able-bodied recipients with no dependent
children.

Social security, Medicare and Medicaid

While 'welfare' (AFDC) was thus becoming more controversial, 'social security' (old-age and disability pensions) – the main item on the insurance side of the welfare state – was moving in the opposite direction, becoming more expensive but also more popular and politically difficult to attack. The postwar economic boom, and the baby boom that helped make AFDC larger, helped to ensure the viability of social security old-age pensions, at least up to the economically less promising years that started in 1973. In spite of its kinship with European welfare state insurance systems, social security came to be portrayed as a pragmatic, quintessentially American system, helping older citizens to live in dignity and independence. It benefits not only old people (and most people become old), but also their children and grandchildren, who in earlier periods would have been expected to support them. Therefore, once it became established and the immediate welfare demands of the depression were no longer pressing, it became politically irresistible for Congress to agree on enlarging the benefits. From its earliest years, benefits were steadily increased and extended to more people. (The tax basis supporting these benefits has also increased, although less steadily, since Congress has often been able to delay tax increases.) In 1972, the decision was taken to index benefits to inflation – which soon proved to be a more expensive enhancement than had been expected.

The most significant addition to social security was Medicare, a federal health insurance programme for the elderly that started in 1965. This was (and is) really a kind of hybrid of insurance and welfare, since it was clear from the outset that it would have to be financed by general revenues (the welfare mode) as well as by contributions from future beneficiaries' social security taxes (the insurance mode). In fact, Medicare came out of Congress in a package that also included Medicaid, a programme that provides federal grants (administered differently in different states) to supplement state payments of medical expenses of welfare recipients (that is those in receipt of AFDC, SSI and other federally funded relief). Many social policy advocates had wanted to include health insurance in the Social Security Act of 1935, but it was decided that such a proposal might make opposition to the Act overpowering; besides, there was a problem in providing widespread insurance for medical services which were not then widely available. The development of the health care industry in the intervening years, and the restriction of the federal government's intervention to the elderly and the poor, made Medicare and Medicaid politically acceptable.

There have been increasing financial pressures on social security since the adoption of Medicare, because of rises in life expectancy and health care costs attributable to expensive new drugs and technology, as well as to the tendency of Medicare and Medicaid clients to seek health care that they might have been unwilling or unable to seek had they been paying for it themselves. However, like social security pensions, Medicare has enjoyed strong public and interest group support, even from many health care providers who had initially opposed it but later learned to appreciate government funding.

Boxes 19.3–19.5 summarise the financing and the significance for household income of the various elements of the American welfare state.

Box 19.3

Major federal government outlays (highlighting social welfare spending), fiscal year 1994

	$bn	Percentage of total
GDP	6,931	
Total federal government outlays	**1,461**	**100**
Military	282	19
Net interest on federal government debt	203	14
Old-age and disability programmes:	533	36
Social Security	320	
Medicare	145	
Federal employee retirement and disability	68	
Benefit programmes for persons with low incomes:	246	17
Medicaid	82	
Other medical care services	11	
Pensions for needy veterans	3[a]	
SSI	24	
AFDC	14	
Foster care	3	
Social services and child care grants	7[b]	
Training and employment programmes	5[c]	
EITC	17	
Food benefits and nutrition programmes	37	
Housing benefits and energy assistance	28	
Education aid	15[d]	
Other federal outlays related to social welfare	106	7
Unemployment compensation	29	
Education (excluding d above)	19	
Health research	11	
Social services (excluding b)	7	
Training and employment services (excluding c)	3	
Consumer and occupational health and safety	2	
Veterans benefits and services (excluding a)	35	

AFDC Aid to Families with Dependent Children   EITC Earned Income Tax Credit

SSI Supplementary Security Income

Source: US Bureau of the Census, 1996, pp. 334–5, 371, 445

Box 19.4

Benefit programmes for persons with low incomes, fiscal year 1994

	Average monthly recipients millions	Expenditures Federal $bn	State and local $bn
Medicaid	34.0	82	61
Other medical care services	13.5[a]	11	6
Pensions for needy veterans	0.8	3	–
SSI	6.4	24	4
AFDC	14.2	14	12
Foster care	0.2	3	2
Social services and child care grants	na[b]	7	5
Training and employment programmes	na[c]	5	0.7
EITC	54.2	17	0
Food stamps and nutrition programmes		37	2[d]
Food stamps	28.9		
School lunch programme	14.0		
Women, infants and children (WIC)	6.5		
School breakfast programme	5.2		
Child and adult care food programme	1.1		
Nutrition programme for elderly	na		
Housing benefits and energy assistance		28	0.4[e]
Low-income housing assistance	2.9		
Low-rent public housing	1.4		
Interest reduction payments	0.5		
Other housing programmes	1.1		
Low-income energy assistance	6.1		
Education aid	na	15	1
General Assistance	1.1	–	3

na Not available

[a] Excludes state and local recipients (not available)

[b] Only available relevant figure is for child care for AFDC recipients: 0.5 million

[c] Some relevant figures available:

Training for disadvantaged	0.8 million
AFDC JOBS programme	0.6 million
Job Corps	0.1 million
Summer youth employment	0.6 million

[d] Excludes state and local expenditures on school lunch programmes (not available)

[e] Excludes state and local expenditures on low-rent public housing (not available)

Source: US Bureau of the Census, 1996, p. 371

Box 19.5

Number of families receiving various kinds of income, 1994

	Number of families millions	Percentage of total
Total number of families	69.3	100
Type of income:		
Earnings	58.6	85
Pensions:		
Social security (and railroad retirement)	16.2	23
Military pensions	1.0	1
Federal employment pensions	1.2	2
State or local employment pensions	1.8	3
Private pensions	6.5	9
Supplementary Security Income (SSI)	2.4	3
Public assistance (AFDC, General Assistance)	3.9	6
Unemployment compensation	5.5	8
Workers' compensation	1.9	3
Education assistance	4.8	7
Veterans' payments	1.8	3
Child support	4.2	6
Alimony	0.2	0.3

Since families can receive more than one type of income, the numbers and percentages add up to more than the total number of families

Source: US Bureau of the Census, 1996, p. 370

Welfare debates and reforms since the 1970s

The slowdown in economic growth in the mid-1970s began to make the continued expansion of the welfare state questionable, although growing economic inequality also strengthened the case for the welfare state for those Americans who regarded reduction in that inequality as one of its purposes. In welfare policy, as in other areas, the politics of incremental growth has given way to 'decrementalist' politics, with politicians competing to deliver tax cuts and to find the least unpopular spending cuts.

This change of economic and political climate has affected even the social security, insurance side of the American welfare state. The indexing of pension benefits to price inflation (cost-of-living allowances), agreed in 1972, began to look less sustainable in the new stagflationary economic conditions, with prices rising faster than wages (and social security taxes based on wages). In 1977, social security taxes were raised with, for the first time, no corresponding increase (in fact, with a slight reduction) in benefits. Continued financial pressure on social security compelled an agreement in 1983 to delay cost-of-living increases and to phase in raising the standard retirement age to 67. In the 1990s a similar financial crisis built up in the Medicare system, forcing Congress in 1997 to agree to cuts in projected spending. These are unlikely to be the last of such difficult adjustments in financing social security.

The insurance side of the American welfare state faces fewer problems of moral legitimacy than the welfare side (although questions are raised about the justice of paying state pensions to the wealthy), but more problems of cost (since they cost so much more). In the United States as in other western democracies, expectations from publicly funded retirement and health care programmes are being lowered. The American government, like governments elsewhere, increasingly uses tax incentives to encourage private saving for and spending on these services, as supplements or substitutes for public saving and spending. This trend seems set to continue, in spite of the prospect of federal government budget surpluses at the end of the 1990s. One reason this trend is popular is that private pension investments in equities appear more profitable than the social security system's investments in risk-free government bonds.

On the welfare side, reforms continue to be inspired not so much by financial considerations (although those always play a role) as by cultural or moral considerations. Debates over welfare policy have been part of the 'culture wars' in American politics that erupted in the 1960s and that have affected other, often related issues such as religion, abortion, pornography, illegitimacy, drugs, multiculturalism and affirmative action. Neo-conservatives and neo-liberals both expressed scepticism about the ability of government (especially the federal government) to achieve its social policy goals, and voiced concerns not only about the need for fiscal prudence but also about the decline of the work ethic, of family and individual responsibility, and of voluntary associations. Some argued that welfare was an area in which government policy had been effective but counterproductive, demoralising (if not actually otherwise impoverishing) the people it was intended to benefit, and sustaining a pathological culture of dependency, irresponsibility, illegitimacy, drugs and crime. Even if this argument was incorrect, growing perceptions of its plausibility set the world of welfare farther apart from mainstream America. Conservative critics of welfare gained in confidence while liberal defenders were losing theirs.

Given this growing critical pressure building up since the 1960s, one might think that radical reform of welfare along the lines of the 1996 Personal Responsibility and Work Opportunity Act was a long time coming, especially since the number of people receiving AFDC never dropped dramatically, and began rising sharply again in the 1990s. However, there were earlier welfare-to-work efforts in many states, and some softer versions of the 1996 reforms in earlier federal legislation.

Experience with work requirements for federal welfare recipients had not been unambiguously successful. In 1971, California (at Governor Ronald Reagan's suggestion) began requiring able-bodied AFDC adults in that state to pay for their welfare grants with community service jobs. However, since they were paid for these 'workfare' jobs at the minimum wage (high compared with welfare grants), not many hours of work per week were actually required to pay off the grant, and it was not clear that workfare served either as a deterrent to welfare applicants or as good experience in preparing them for other employment. In the same year, Congress began requiring all able-bodied adult AFDC recipients not caring for children under six years of age to enrol in a work incentive (WIN) programme and (when selected) attend work-training sessions and consult state employment offices. The WIN programme was low in participation (few were selected) and unimpressive in results, because of low funding, complicated administrative arrangements, and lack of incentives for administrators to make the programme work – welfare administrators are more geared up to getting benefits to their clients than to encouraging them to find jobs; and employment officers find non-welfare clients more promising users of their services (Bane and Ellwood, 1994, p. 21).

During Ronald Reagan's presidency (1981–89), Congress rejected his 1981 proposal to require all states to establish workfare plans, although it made it easier for states to do so. In 1988, a coalition of conservatives and liberals in Congress agreed to the Family Support Act. This Act seemed to strengthen requirements that able-bodied adult welfare recipients accept job training and placement services, threatening loss of their (but not their children's) benefits if they failed to show good faith efforts in this direction, and promising them help in the form of child support enforcement, and payments for child care and extension of Medicaid coverage when they left the welfare rolls for paid employment. However, it set low participation targets, and allowed states to count as participants those completing high school or postsecondary education and those holding community work (workfare) jobs. The Family Support Act anticipated the 1996 reforms by leaving it up to individual states to find ways of transforming welfare adults into long-term job-holders, but (in contrast to the 1996 law) did not strictly require that the states succeed. In this respect, the Act was 'a sheep in wolves' clothing' (Marmor *et al.*, 1990, p. 233). Even if the states had been given greater incentives to succeed, they might have failed to produce many success stories because of the economic recession of 1989–92, which ended hopes that welfare rolls might soon start declining.

Further anticipations of the 1996 law appeared in state experimentation. The administrations of George Bush (1989–93) and Bill Clinton (1993–) continued the practice of the Reagan administration in granting temporary waivers from AFDC rules in order to allow states to try various new welfare policies. Thus Wisconsin reduced AFDC benefits of parents with truant teenage children, Ohio required all teenage AFDC beneficiaries to attend school, several states set higher allowances for earnings before reductions in benefits, and some imposed time limits on benefits. By 1996, 43 states had received waivers, so AFDC was already at least temporarily interrupted if not for ever ended as a relatively uniform federal welfare system, and the initiative in welfare policy had passed to the states. (See Box 19.6.)

The main provisions of the 1996 reforms (which are set out at the beginning of this chapter) horrified some liberal critics with their unprecedentedly strict work requirements and time limits. The reforms were greatly influenced by the Republican takeover of Congress after the 1994 elections; Republicans in Congress then paid less attention to reaching a compromise with the Democratic president. President Clinton signed the bill with some reluctance, promising to work to reverse some of its terms. Yet the major theme of these reforms (if not its accompanying but somewhat contradictory

Box 19.6

Welfare reform: the Wisconsin model

The state of Wisconsin, under Republican governor Tommy Thompson, introduced a major welfare-to-work programme in 1987, which inspired welfare reforms both at the federal level in the United States and by the Labour government in Britain. Wisconsin was allowed to experiment under a waiver from national regulations granted by the federal government, and it has revised the programme several times.

The goals of the programme are:

■ to encourage the work ethic
■ to develop a sense of individual responsibility
■ to end welfare dependency
■ to demonstrate that the states require less federal regulation
■ to reduce the costs for taxpayers
■ to stimulate the state economy through lower taxes

The programme operates on the assumption that everyone can work. Instead of receiving welfare benefits, efforts are made to move the unemployed directly into jobs. Those not 'job-ready' have to attend compulsory training courses, and work at trial jobs subsidised by the state government, or participate in 30-hour-per-week community service jobs. Mothers are expected to work after their child is 12 weeks old, and welfare income is not related to the number of children. Benefits are reduced for the parents of teenage truants from school. Child care is subsidised and medical services provided free.

Supporters argue that:

■ the number of families on welfare has dropped from 100,000 in 1986 to 30,000 in 1997 owing to workfare
■ welfare should be based on reciprocal responsibilities to society
■ welfare encourages teenage, single-parent families which are more prone to social misbehaviour such as crime
■ work experience provides the necessary skills and attitudes to obtain a long-term job
■ workfare destroys the expectation that welfare is a possible alternative to work
■ welfare creates an underclass of permanent welfare dependents
■ the increase in the number in work and off welfare reduces the costs to taxpayers

Opponents argue that:

■ the reduction in welfare recipients is largely a result of a growing economy and demand for workers
■ citizens should be entitled to benefits as a right

■ single parents should stay at home to look after their children

■ training and work experience fail to lead to long-term jobs

■ government should not coerce people into work

■ women and racial minorities are the main targets

■ workfare is more expensive than welfare because of the provision of training, child care and job subsidies

Contributed by Dr Nigel Ashford, University of Staffordshire

attempts to cut federal welfare spending) is a venerable strain in American welfare policy, which Clinton and many other Democrats had also endorsed: the emphasis on work rather than welfare as the means of obtaining human dignity. Clinton's own welfare reform plan (presented to Congress in June 1994) had included time limits (which had become a popular idea) and strong work requirements for welfare recipients. He agreed with more conservative politicians that 'work is the best social program this country has ever devised' (Clinton, 1994, p. 174).

It remains to be seen whether states will actually bring themselves to enforce the five-year lifetime limits on welfare cash benefits (no one will be subject to it until 2001), and whether in the mean time they will manage to get the adults in half of their welfare families (including 90 per cent of two-parent welfare families) working at least thirty hours per week, as they are required to do in order to maintain their full federal TANF grant. Welfare-to-work programmes, as state experience in the early 1990s again showed, are more expensive (at least in the short term) than welfare as simple income support: they require more attention to individual cases. It is difficult to evaluate their long-term effects.

During the first year of the new welfare regime, there were some reasons for optimism. The end of the economic recession in 1992 was helpful, in that it started reducing the number of welfare recipients. News of the new regime seems to have deterred some potential applicants. The new regime itself can also claim some of the credit for the reduction in numbers. From 1994 to 1998, the number of AFDC TANF recipients fell by 30 per cent, from a record annual high of 14.2 million to less than 10 million. The downward trend in caseloads allows states reductions in their work participation targets. Moreover, since the amount of each state's TANF block grant is based on that state's welfare spending in its most expensive recent years, states have a useful windfall to spend on some of the things that might help welfare recipients find and keep jobs, such as child care and reliable transportation. (The 1996 law also provides a new child care block grant, which allows states to spend the money on those at risk of becoming welfare applicants, as well on those currently on welfare.)

However, it was also recognised that an economic recession could severely strain the states' capacity to meet the targets now set for work participation. Even without a recession, it may be asking too much of the economy to produce suitable and sufficiently well paid jobs for more than 50 per cent of welfare adults, many of whom lack the education, experience, and hard and soft skills required for employment. The Democratic mayor of Milwaukee, Wisconsin – a state in the forefront of welfare-to-work reforms – has remarked that, 'Most people have underestimated the abilities of welfare recipients to work and care for their families' (DeParle, 1997, p. 7). However, many welfare recipients do experience problems that make employment more difficult, such as bad health, housing instability, drug addiction and domestic violence. Although half of welfare beneficiaries stop claiming benefits within a year of starting, they often return to welfare dependence. The proportion of welfare cases that currently exceed the new five-year lifetime limit is closer to one-third than one-fifth, which is the proportion of hardship exceptions to the five-year limit allowed in each state under the new law, and in some areas that national average is greatly exceeded (Conte, 1996, p. 1068). There is also some concern about the fact that a greater proportion of whites and non-Hispanics than of blacks and Hispanics have been leaving the welfare rolls under the new regime.

If the 1996 reforms do prove to be more-or-less successful, the likely implications of that success are subject to conflicting speculations. Some conservatives are counting on the reforms to curtail the level of government activity and spending. Some liberals hope that a large movement of employable people out of the welfare system might make it politically easier to make welfare benefits more generous for those who remain in the system, and that the creation of a more confident and self-reliant class of working poor might move American politics to the left.

 ## Summary

The logic of the American welfare state emphasises protection against economic insecurity, and the moral as well as the economic effects of welfare policies. Family and other private providers remain important sources of welfare goods and services. However, the welfare state has grown both incrementally and, in some periods (for example the 1930s and 1960s–1970s) quite rapidly. It now includes programmes of general assistance, pensions, medical care for the old, workers' compensation, unemployment insurance, aid to the disabled, aid (including topping up earned income) to families with dependent children, food stamps and medical care for the poor, and housing. Most of these programmes are based on co-operation between different levels of government, and the level of assistance varies from place to place. The financial costs of pensions and the moral costs of aid to families have made welfare state reforms a current political preoccupation.

Whatever the fate of the welfare reforms that were enacted in 1996, it seems likely that the American welfare state will continue to exhibit its two-tiered character, institutionally and mentally divided into welfare and social security (or insurance). It also seems likely that it will continue to consist of significant efforts by both federal and state governments, with the federal government more exclusively involved in the social security side of things, and states and localities more involved with welfare than with social security. Social security (insurance), which benefits from majority participation, will surely continue to be less politically vulnerable than welfare, but will also be subjected to reform considerations as its financial costs increase and as private sector pensions and medical savings plans grow. The reform of welfare is likely to remain a controversial issue as long as it continues to serve as a proxy for wider political and cultural issues that unsettle American politics in its third century.

 Topics for discussion

1. What is distinctive about the welfare state in the United States?

2. Why is it often said that the welfare state in the United States defies logical analysis? Does it?

3. What has driven reforms of (a) the Social Security programme, and (b) AFDC?

4. How are state and local governments involved in welfare policy?

 Further reading

Edward D. Berkowitz surveys and analyses the growth and character of the welfare system in *America's Welfare State: From Roosevelt to Reagan* (Baltimore: The Johns Hopkins University Press, 1991). Michael B. Katz, *In the Shadow of the Poorhouse: A social history of welfare in America* (New York: Basic Books, 1986), reviews a longer period of welfare state history. Theodore R. Marmor, Jerry L. Mashaw and Philip L. Harvey explore the logic of the American system in *America's Misunderstood Welfare State: Persistent myths, enduring realities* (New York: Basic Books, 1990). Mary Jo Bane and David T. Ellwood, *Welfare Realities: From rhetoric to reform* (Cambridge, Mass.: Harvard University Press, 1994), reveals some of the thinking that has gone into current reforms of welfare policies. Federal government statistics and policy statements on welfare can be accessed via the Internet site of the Children and Families Administration of the Department of Health and Human Services: http://www.acf.dhhs.gov.

 References

Arenson, Karen W., 1995, 'Charities rebut Gingrich: their services heavily dependent on US aid', *International Herald Tribune*, 5 June, p. 3

Bane, Mary Jo, and Ellwood, David T., 1994, *Welfare Realities: From rhetoric to reform* (Cambridge, Mass.: Harvard University Press)

Berkowitz, Edward D., 1991, *America's Welfare State: From Roosevelt to Reagan* (Baltimore: The Johns Hopkins University Press)

Clinton, Bill, 1994, 'Remarks by the President on welfare reform to officials and participants of the Future Now Program,' *Social Justice*, vol. 21

Conte, Christopher, 1996, 'Welfare, work and the states,' *CQ Researcher*, vol. 6, no. 45, pp. 1057–79

DeParle, Jason, 1997, 'US city pioneers a shift off welfare to workfare', *International Herald Tribune*, 8 May, pp. 1, 7

Gilbert, Neil, 1983, *Capitalism and the Welfare State: Dilemmas of social benevolence* (New Haven: Yale University Press)

Ginsburg, Norman, 1992, *Divisions of Welfare: A critical introduction to comparative social policy* (London: Sage)

Karger, Howard J. and David Stoesz, 1990, *American Social Welfare Policy* (New York: Longman)

Katz, Michael B., 1986, *In the Shadow of the Poorhouse: A social history of welfare in America* (New York: Basic Books)

Marmor, Theodore R., Mashaw, Jerry L. and Harvey, Philip L., 1990, *America's Misunderstood Welfare State: Persistent myths, enduring realities* (New York: Basic Books)

Patterson, James T., 1981, *America's Struggle Against Poverty* (Cambridge, Mass.: Harvard University Press)

Rosenman, Samuel I., ed., 1938–50, *The Public Papers and Addresses of Franklin D. Roosevelt* (13 vols, New York: Russell & Russell)

Skocpol, Theda, 1992, *Protecting Soldiers and Mothers: The political origins of social policy in the United States* (Cambridge, Mass.: Harvard University Press)

US Bureau of the Census, 1996, *Statistical Abstract of the United States* (116th edn, Washington DC)

20

The politics of race and affirmative action

Race relations undoubtedly constitutes the most intractable social problem in the United States. This is especially true of the matter of race equality between black and white Americans. While the context of racial tension has changed over the centuries, from slavery, through segregation to the modern civil rights era, the difficulty of overcoming discrimination and assuring equality of the races still presents an enormous challenge to the American political system. In this chapter, we examine the political controversy surrounding one attempt to meet that challenge – the policy of affirmative action.

As an immigrant nation of diverse racial and ethnic origin, it is not surprising that the United States has experienced related social and political tensions from time to time. For the most part these have arisen from discrimination by Americans of white, Anglo-Saxon, Protestant ancestry (WASPs) against groups who are culturally different and are deemed to pose some kind of threat to the cultural and political status quo. Jewish, Chinese and Irish Americans, for example, have all been the victims of discrimination and prejudice in American history. With the passage of time, however, these groups have been able to move into the mainstream of American economic, social and political life. As a consequence, they have achieved equality of status and condition, even if elements of prejudice remain.

In the case of African Americans, however, this general pattern of eventual inclusion and equality still does not apply. As we will see, by almost every major criterion of achievement, be it education, employment or income, blacks lag behind whites to a significant degree. And while many white Americans deny that discrimination remains a major problem today, most blacks are convinced that racism continues as a powerful force. Thus, as Andrew Hacker writes:

> Black Americans are Americans, yet they still subsist as aliens in the only land they know. Other groups may remain outside the mainstream – some religious sects, for

example – but they do so voluntarily. In contrast, blacks must endure a segregation that is far from freely chosen. So America may be seen as two separate nations. Of course, there are places where the races mingle. Yet in most significant respects, the separation is pervasive and penetrating. As a social and human division, it surpasses all others – even gender – in intensity and subordination.

(Hacker, 1995, pp. 3–4)

Both objectively and subjectively, then, racial tension between black and white America continues to bedevil American politics. Indeed, at the end of the twentieth century, there is no consensus on the causes of racial inequality, never mind on the solutions for it.

Historical context

Prior to the Civil War (1861–65) the vast majority of blacks in the United States were slaves (see Box 20.1). This meant that they had few legal rights and were regarded as little more than property. Despite Thomas Jefferson's inspirational proclamation in the Declaration of Independence (1776) that 'all men are created equal', the United States came into existence as a slave society. Thus, while the Constitution of 1787 did not mention slavery by name, certain of its clauses recognised and protected the institution. Article I, Section 2, for example, allowed slaves to be counted as three-fifths of

Box 20.1

Racial composition of the United States, 1790–1990

Percentages

Year	Whites	Enslaved blacks	Free blacks
1790	80.7	17.8	1.5
1830	81.9	15.6	2.5
1860	85.7	12.6	1.7

Year	Whites	Blacks	Others
1870	87.1	12.7	0.2
1900	87.7	11.6	0.7
1930	89.6	9.7	0.7
1960	88.6	10.5	0.9
1970	87.5	11.1	1.4
1980	83.2	11.7	5.1
1990	75.3	11.9	12.8

Source: Hacker, 1995, p. 253, US Census data

Box 20.2

Civil War Amendments to the Constitution

Thirteenth Amendment (ratified 1865)
Neither slavery nor involuntary servitude, except as a punishment for crime whereof the party shall have been duly convicted, shall exist within the United States, or any place subject to their jurisdiction ...

Fourteenth Amendment (ratified 1868)
All persons born or naturalized in the United States, and subject to the jurisdiction thereof, are citizens of the United States and of the State wherein they reside. No State shall make or enforce any law which shall abridge the privileges or immunities of citizens of the United States; nor shall any State deprive any person of life, liberty, or property without due process of law; nor deny to any person within its jurisdiction the equal protection of the laws ...

Fifteenth Amendment (ratified 1870)
The right of citizens of the United States to vote shall not be denied or abridged by the United States or by any State on account of race, color, or previous condition of servitude ...

a person when it came to apportioning seats in the House of Representatives, although slaves were not allowed to vote. And Article I, Section 9 excluded abolition of the slave trade before 1808 or the imposition of a tax on imported slaves greater than ten dollars per head.

Slavery was eventually abolished by the Thirteenth Amendment to the Constitution, ratified in 1865(see Box 20.2). By that time, however, over two hundred years of slavery in the American colonies and then the United States, had established the deep roots of today's race problems. African Americans were not voluntary immigrants to America, but either transported slaves or the descendants of such. Moreover, not merely were black Americans deprived of their freedom and civil rights, but an elaborate culture of white supremacy stamped all slaves as *racially* inferior and unworthy of equal status with whites, be it social, legal or political.

Even when the Civil War Amendments were passed, therefore, most white Americans continued to believe that such inferiority justified a lower status for African Americans. This was most obvious in the former slave states of the south, where racial discrimination and segregation quickly became entrenched in most aspects of public and private life. Even outside of the south, though, African Americans endured the inferior education, employment and housing that most white Americans believed was merited by perceived biological and cultural differences between the races. Gross inequality and subordination of African Americans were thus the hallmarks of race relations in the United States for a century after the abolition of slavery.

The civil rights era (1954–80)

The first half of the twentieth century saw the beginnings of political agitation by and on behalf of black Americans for full equality. Organisations such as the National Association for the Advancement of Colored People (NAACP), founded in 1910, and the Congress of Racial Equality (CORE), founded in 1942, pressed the federal government for action on equality of opportunity in employment and education and on the full implementation of the civil rights promises of the Fourteenth and Fifteenth Amendments. While they won the occasional victory, however, the government was not prepared to make a strong commitment to race equality. Indeed, the federal government often practised discrimination within its own jurisdictions. Prejudice aside, most elected politicians were not prepared to jeopardise the support of the white majority in the cause of a minority population which did not vote in great numbers.

The major breakthrough came in 1954 when the Supreme Court, the unelected branch of the federal government, declared unconstitutional the many state laws which required public schools to be racially segregated. More fundamentally, this decision in *Brown v. Board of Education* signalled the end of the doctrine of 'separate but equal' in American life. This had permitted states to pass laws which, in effect, created an apartheid system throughout the south and border states. Blacks and whites were separated in parks, restaurants, public transport, and indeed in virtually all respects. However, separate facilities were never remotely equal, so that segregation was a graphic, daily reminder that whites considered blacks to be an inferior race. By putting an end to such *de jure* racial separation, the *Brown* decision marked the beginning of a phase in American politics when African Americans would achieve full equality in law.

As well as the abolition of all forms of statutory racial segregation by the Supreme Court, the civil rights era saw Congress pass historic bills, such as the Civil Rights Act of 1964 and the Voting Rights Act of 1965. The former banned, for example, racial discrimination in employment and in public accommodations such as restaurants and hotels. The Voting Rights Act obliged states to end various practices that were designed to prevent African Americans from exercising their Fifteenth Amendment right to vote.

These Acts constitute a landmark in the history of the American political system: for the first time since the Civil War era, the elected branches of the federal government decided to try to bring about race equality through legislative action. As we shall see, this was to have far-reaching consequences not merely for race policy, but also for political and electoral conflict.

The civil rights consensus

After centuries of legalised discrimination, the civil rights legislation of the 1960s constituted a major breakthrough for African Americans, since formal rights are a precondition of racial equality. Success came in part because civil rights organisations were able to create a broad consensus within the nation and the political system that the time for equality and inclusion was long overdue. This they did by appealing to both the values and the self interest of white America.

To take the latter first, the massive demonstrations organised by the civil rights movement threatened social order. Although the protests were guided by the principle of non-violent civil disobedience, they were often met with severe police and white citizen brutality. Such dramatic public violence needed to be quelled not only to prevent further escalation but also to save the United States embarrassment in the international community. It was also important that business corporations feared that the violence and instability associated with the resistance to desegregation would harm commerce and profits. Thus, 'many corporate leaders, always looking at the social costs of doing business in the South, had concluded that desegregation was inevitable; that the federal government's appropriate role was to ensure the civil order which was essential to business expansion' (Marable, 1991, p. 80).

The civil rights movement also succeeded, however, because it appeared to share the cultural and political values of white Americans. Indeed, for many civil rights activists as well as liberal politicians and white citizens, African Americans were simply seeking inclusion and assimilation within the dominant, that is, white, value system of the country. The undoubted leader of the movement, the Reverend Martin Luther King, appealed to a vision of society in which discrimination and prejudice were vanquished, government treated all citizens as equals and in which race was irrelevant. King's appeal for the construction of a 'colour-blind' society coincided happily with the rhetoric, if not the reality, of mainstream American politics.

White politicians, outside of the south, were therefore willing to embrace the cause of race equality, especially those who hoped to garner the votes of the increasingly significant black population in many urban areas. There was, then, a strong element of bipartisanship in civil rights legislation, with the main political divide being between the south and the rest of the country, rather than between Democrat and Republican. The Voting Rights Act of 1965, for example, was passed by majorities of 328 to 74 in the House of Representatives and by 79 to 18 in the Senate (Marable, 1991, p. 90).

Limits of formal equality

The biracial, bipartisan consensus behind the civil rights movement began to unravel, however, almost as soon as it had formed. The main reason for this was that the emphasis of the agenda switched from formal and legal equality to equality of condition or 'substantive equality'. As noted above, the civil rights legislation passed under President Johnson (1963–69) swept away all official barriers to equality of opportunity in employment, education, housing and so on. What it could not do was to turn those opportunities into substance. While African Americans now had the right to attend the best schools or obtain the best-paid jobs, few among them had the qualifications to make those rights a reality.

This gap between formal equality and substantive equality was well recognised at the time. President Johnson and many others saw the Civil Rights Act of 1964 and the Voting Rights Act of 1965 as the beginning, rather than the end, of the campaign for race equality (see Box 20.3).

> **Box 20.3**
>
> ## President Lyndon B. Johnson and racial equality
>
> The following extract is from President Johnson's speech at Howard University, Washington DC, 4 June 1965:
>
> > Freedom is the right to share fully and equally in American society – to vote, to hold a job, to enter a public place, to go to school. It is the right to be treated in every part of our national life as a person equal in dignity and promise to all others.
> >
> > But freedom is not enough. You do not wipe away the scars of centuries by saying: Now you are free to go where you want, do as you desire, and choose the leaders you please. You do not take a person who, for years, has been hobbled by chains and liberate him, bring him up to the starting line of a race and say, 'You are free to compete with all the others', and still justly believe that you have been completely fair.
> >
> > Thus, it is not enough to just open the gates of opportunity. All our citizens must have the ability to walk through those gates. This is the next and more profound stage of the battle for civil rights. We seek not just freedom but opportunity – not just legal equality but human ability – not just equality as a right and a theory, but equality as a fact and as a result.
>
> Source: Extract in Curry, 1996, pp. 18–19

Affirmative action

The recognition that much more needed to be done to achieve genuine racial equality led to the gradual adoption of a series of governmental policies that collectively became known as affirmative action. The term has never been defined with precision. When first used in the early 1960s it indicated 'outreach' programmes, in which government or private employers took steps, for example, to encourage African Americans to apply for jobs from which they had previously been excluded.

By the late 1960s, however, a much stronger set of affirmative action policies began to emerge. Congress, the presidency and the Supreme Court all pushed employers to adopt statistical goals in the hiring and promotion of African Americans and certain other minorities. Similarly, many universities began to set aside a specific number of places for minority students. The clear purpose of these statistical affirmative action plans was to oblige public and private institutions to do more than pay lip service to racial equality. Good intentions were no longer sufficient and concrete results in terms of jobs and university places were deemed necessary to prove that real progress towards racial equality was being made.

Typical of these policies was the Philadelphia Plan, drawn up by the administration of President Nixon (1969–74). Promulgated in 1969, it required all companies bidding for federal contracts to set numerical targets for the hiring of racial minorities, as well as timetables for their achievement. The Philadelphia Plan inspired many local units of government to adopt similar policies, and statistical affirmative action quickly became a familiar feature of hiring and promotion decisions in employment and in admissions to higher education.

The politics of affirmative action

By the early 1970s, the government had a fairly clear approach to ensuring race equality. First, the basic principle of law and policy was that of non-discrimination. No American should be disadvantaged on grounds of race, colour or ethnic origin.

Secondly, where the effects of past discrimination were visible in employment, education or housing, for example, remedial policies should be employed which achieve concrete progress. The most obvious way to identify the lingering effects of past discrimination was deemed to be through a statistical analysis revealing a disparity between, say, the number of African Americans in the local workforce and the number employed by a company within that locality. The most direct means of remedying that disparity was aggressively to seek to recruit more African American employees, if necessary by reserving jobs for them until the disparity disappeared.

All federal and state government departments and agencies were obliged to operate affirmative action policies. Moreover, many private businesses and educational institutions adopted similar policies, often because they feared expensive law suits would be brought against them if they did not. The key government body here was the Equal Employment Opportunity Commission (EEOC), created by the Civil Rights Act of 1964. Although it started rather slowly, the EEOC became a central player in elaborating and enforcing race equality policy. In particular, it initiated or supported lawsuits against companies which operated discriminatory practices.

The government's twin-track approach to race equality quickly generated political difficulties, however. In the first place, many white and some black Americans think the two basic principles of non-discrimination and compensatory race preferences are at odds with each other. While they agree that the principle of non-discrimination is sound, they think it is violated when African Americans are given preference over whites in employment or educational opportunities. This is compounded when African Americans are preferred to white Americans with higher qualifications. These opponents of affirmative action regard it as 'reverse discrimination', involving the unconstitutional and otherwise undesirable distribution of benefits according to racial classification. Their ideal is a 'colour-blind' meritocracy in which race is no longer relevant and individuals advance on the basis of their talent. Since affirmative action policies are anything but colour-blind, they argue that the means of achieving race equality are fundamentally at odds with the goal.

These philosophical criticisms are usually voiced by those who are generally conservative in political matters. While they declare themselves committed to race equality and non-discrimination, they also believe that, over thirty years after the civil rights 'revolution', black Americans should not expect favours from government. Rather they should do as other minorities have done in American history: rely upon their own industry and talents to improve their condition.

This individualistic approach to race equality fits well with the broader conservative antipathy toward activist government. However, opposition to affirmative action runs deeply throughout the white community in the United States, especially, perhaps, among working- and middle-class whites who are by no means adverse to governmental activism when it benefits them. Thus, for some whites, self-interest leads them to oppose affirmative action, because jobs, promotions, contracts or university places reserved exclusively for non-whites necessarily deprive whites of opportunities.

Liberals and affirmative action

Liberals take a more collectivist approach to race equality than the conservatives just described. They believe that American society in general owes a great deal to African Americans and that means that even individual whites today, who have never knowingly discriminated against blacks, must accept some of the responsibility and bear some of the burden of achieving equality.

Liberals, moreover, believe that government can do much to promote race equality: 'Although less confident now than in the past, most liberals still put their faith in public policies. Hence the view that a variety of programmes, many of them quite expensive, will be needed if black Americans are to be brought to parity with whites. ... Much more will have to be spent in areas such as education, health services, housing, and job training' (Hacker, 1995, p. 62).

Unsurprisingly in the light of such views, liberals continue to defend government-enforced affirmative action. They see affirmative action as an effective means of ensuring greater race equality and one that is justified by the need to remedy centuries of discrimination. As well as these moral and pragmatic considerations, liberals argue that affirmative action is not unconstitutional. Although they share with conservatives the goal of a colour-blind society, they believe that it is unrealistic to ignore the past in getting there. Moreover, they distinguish between racial classifications designed to stigmatise a particular race and those which are intended bring a disadvantaged group to parity. Thus affirmative action, unlike the segregation of the past, does not stamp the other race as inferior, but merely makes blacks and whites more equal.

Liberals also do not share the outrage often expressed by opponents of affirmative action at the perceived violation of individualistic and meritocratic principles involved. They point out that many whites benefit from advantages of birth and social connections which may be unrelated to individual talent. They also remind Americans that preferences are sometimes sanctioned by law where exceptional compensation is deemed appropriate: for example, the employment and educational preferences accorded to military veterans.

Proponents and opponents of affirmative action clearly disagree on the remedy it involves. Moreover, they disagree over the major causes of racial inequality in contemporary America.

The basic problem

Before discussing political conflict over the solutions to racial inequality, then, it is important to understand differing perceptions of what the problem actually is.

There is no dispute about the fact of racial inequality. As Boxes 20.4 to 20.8 indicate, blacks lag behind whites in income, educational achievement, longevity and a host of other areas.

Even where African Americans are doing better than before in absolute terms, they are not necessarily closing the gap on whites. Indeed, as the figures for child mortality and for imprisonment demonstrate, in relative terms some things are getting worse. Moreover, where blacks are catching up with whites, as on family income, the pace is painfully slow.

Box 20.4

Race and infant mortality rates, 1940–91

Deaths per 1,000 births

	White	Black	Black multiple
1940	43.2	72.9	1.69
1950	26.8	43.9	1.64
1960	22.9	43.9	1.92
1970	17.8	32.6	1.83
1980	11.0	21.4	1.95
1991	7.7	17.0	2.21

Source: Hacker, 1995, p. 257, US Census data

Box 20.5

Race and incomes, 1992

	White[a] $	Black[a] $	Black as a percentage of white
Families	38,909	21,161	54.4
All men	21,645	12,754	58.9
All women	11,036	8,857	80.3
Employed men	31,012	22,369	72.1
Employed women	21,659	19,819	91.5

[a] Income figures are medians

Source: Hacker, 1995, p. 100, US Census data

Box 20.6

Education and earnings of blacks, 1992

Income

Education	Percentages of whites	
	Men	Women
High school not finished	78.6	86.0
1–3 years of college	83.9	91.8
Bachelor's degree	76.4	96.6
Master's degree	87.0	93.9

Source: Hacker, 1995, p. 101, US Census data

Box 20.7

Black share of family income, 1959–92

Percentage of total family income

1959	1969	1979	1989	1992
5.4%	6.1%	6.8%	7.2%	7.3%

Source: Hacker, 1995, p. 259, US Census data

Box 20.8

Race and prisoners, 1930–93

Percentage of total prison population

	White	Black	Other
1930	76.7	22.4	0.9
1950	69.1	29.7	1.2
1970	60.5	35.8	3.7
1993	43.2	44.9	11.9

Source: Hacker, 1995, p. 204, US Census data

Causes of racial inequality

There is among many African Americans in particular the suspicion that racial prejudice still motivates many, if not most whites. This prejudice may manifest itself in personal or institutional behaviour and may be blatant or subtle. It may also be committed by individuals and institutions who genuinely do not consider themselves to be prejudiced.

A notorious example of apparent racism, both institutional and individual, occurred in the Rodney King case. In March 1991, King, an African American, was stopped in his car by the Los Angeles police on suspicion of drink-driving. The officers claimed that King refused to obey their orders and that they were obliged to use 'managed force' upon him. By chance, however, a local resident filmed the police actions on videotape. What that showed was the repeated beating and kicking of the inebriated Mr King while he lay on the ground or tried to get up. Four police officers, all white, were duly charged with assault.

For the black community, the beating of Rodney King was deplorable but not unusual. The Los Angeles Police Department had a particularly bad reputation for racism. What really caused bitterness was the trial of the four officers. First, the defence succeeded in having the trial moved out of Los Angeles to the overwhelmingly white Simi Valley area. This meant that the number of blacks on the jury would be minimal and, in the end, there were actually none. The jury was composed of ten whites, one Asian American and one Hispanic. Then, despite what seemed to many people the incontrovertible evidence of the unjustified use of force on the amateur video, that jury found the officers not guilty on all charges.

As soon as the verdict was announced in April 1992, blacks took to the streets and rioted in Los Angeles and other cities around the nation. The result of this explosion of violence was over forty people killed, two thousand injured and over five thousand arrested (*The Observer*, 3 May 1992). Once again, a single episode of suspected racism had released all the underlying racial tensions in American society. For most blacks, the police, the court system and the individual jurors had clearly acted from racist motivations. They also immediately linked the individual treatment of Rodney King to the generally discriminatory nature of American society.

This in turn brings out what remains the fundamental divide between blacks and whites in the United States today. According to a Washington Post–ABC News poll, differing but still clear majorities of both blacks (90 per cent) and whites (60 per cent) believed that the four police officers should have been found guilty and that the federal authorities should bring further charges against them. However, when asked whether the King case 'shows that blacks cannot get justice in this country', only 25 per cent of whites agreed, compared with 75 per cent of blacks. Faced with the same evidence, therefore, blacks and whites still draw opposed conclusions about the significance of race in American life (*The Observer*, 3 May 1992).

A second, more subtle example serves to illustrate how the racial divide affects political perceptions in the United States. Congress has enacted legislation imposing mandatory prison sentences for drug dealing. Dealers in crack cocaine, however, are punished much more severely than those who supply cocaine powder. Thus, someone

Box 20.9

Race of drug defendants, October 1994–September 1995

	Crack cocaine	Powder cocaine
White	5%	18%
Black	88%	41%
Hispanic	7%	41%

Source: US Sentencing Commission, *Washington Post*, 15 April 1997

convicted of dealing more than fifty grams of crack must be sentenced to at least ten years imprisonment: a dealer in powder, however, must be found with over five thousand grams before the same mandatory minimum sentence is imposed. The principal justification offered for the distinction is that crack dealing typically involves greater and more serious violence than the trade in powder.

Ostensibly, there is no race angle on this issue. The US Sentencing Commission, however, reported to Congress in 1995 that the law disadvantages African Americans. It produced figures which gave some support to the popular view that powder is a drug used by 'yuppie' whites, while crack is almost exclusively the drug of black ghetto youths (see Box 23.9).

While there is undoubtedly a disparate racial *impact* here, it is far less clear that there is any discriminatory *intent*. For the same sentencing standards apply to people of all races convicted of dealing in crack. Yet it may be asked, would Congress, an overwhelmingly white body, have passed such a law if its effect was to treat whites much more severely than blacks? In other words, was Congress in part motivated by considerations of race, conscious or unconscious? In 1997, in *Edwards v. United States*, the Supreme Court unanimously agreed to let the law stand. However, lawyers for the African American crack dealer involved in the case argued that, 'There is a perception among African Americans that there is no more unequal treatment by the criminal justice system than in the crack v. powder cocaine racially-biased federal sentencing provisions' (*Washington Post*, 15 April 1997).

Race, class and culture

For many blacks and white liberals, then, discrimination and prejudice remain central to current conditions of racial inequality, even if they are by no means the whole story. Conservatives, however, including some African Americans, do not agree. Although they acknowledge that racial prejudice still exists, they believe that the end of legal and overt discrimination has left blacks with the same opportunities for self-advancement as other minority groups have had in American society. Thus, whatever prejudices

Box 20.10

President Clinton's urban policy

The 1992 Los Angeles riots dramatically forced urban policy to a high position on the domestic political agenda. The riots underscored the degree to which African Americans and other inner city minorities still suffered from social exclusion, communal conflict and limited economic opportunities. President Clinton's first term therefore brought an urgent reassessment of federal programmes for the inner cities with emphasis upon community betterment through local economic development and neighbourhood enterprise.

In spite of the president's support for community capitalism, Republican criticism of urban policy intensified. Republicans focused upon the inefficiencies of the Department of Housing and Urban Development (HUD) as an oversized, high-spending federal bureaucracy. During Clinton's second term, HUD responded by radically rethinking its role by shifting its policy focus away from top-down bureaucratic solutions and towards the efficient and effective implementation of community-level policies. Vice-President Al Gore's Community 2020 seminar series endorsed this approach as well as relating economic policy initiatives to the president's Initiative on Race and his vision of 'One America in the 21st Century'.

African Americans, Latinos and other minorities therefore could be empowered to take greater responsibilities for neighbourhood improvement by working with corporate sponsors and non-profit organisations. Empowerment Zones (EZs) enabled public/private partnerships to regenerate poor neighbourhoods, deal with drugs and tackle crime in what HUD termed, 'comeback communities'.

In 1996, HUD published *America's New Economy and the Challenge of the Cities*. The message was that deprived inner city neighbourhoods could use local talents and information technology to promote local enterprise and assist business development. The inner cities would connect with expanding metropolitan regions by ensuring that the unemployed benefited from new job opportunities in expanding sectors of the economy. The 1997 HUD report, *The State of the Cities*, envisaged a central role for urban communities in the nation's economic future.

Clinton and Gore have thus enthusiastically revived urban policy by making it relevant to the nation's quest for economic competitiveness. Poor urban communities must have a part to play in wealth generation if they are not to remain marginalised and prone to social conflict.

Contributed by Dr Brian Jacobs, University of Staffordshire

white Americans may have towards blacks, they cannot prevent blacks from 'making it' these days.

In dismissing the centrality of present-day discrimination, conservatives, and even some liberals, emphasise other causes of racial inequality (see Box 20.3). Most important, they stress the fact that most blacks are held back not so much by their race as by their poverty. For example, in a famous work, William Julius Wilson argued that:

'class has become more important than race in determining black life-chances in the modern industrial period' (Wilson, 1980, p. 150).

In that sense, it is argued, policies attacking discrimination miss the point. Wilson, not a conservative, believed that affirmative action programmes did little to help the great majority of blacks who were poor, even if it did open doors for some well educated African Americans. What most blacks need, then, are policies that address the issue of economic inequality, rather than racial inequality *per se*.

Thomas Sowell highlights other possible causes of racial inequality than racial discrimination:

> there are many reasons, besides genes and discrimination, why groups differ in their economic performances and rewards. Groups differ by large amounts demographically, culturally, and geographically – and all of these differences have profound effects on incomes and occupations.
>
> (Sowell, 1984, p. 42)

Glenn Loury argues that the rising number of young blacks living in single-parent families has a highly damaging effect on their education and career prospects and that affirmative action policies do not tackle this problem. In fact, affirmative action, he believes, has done – and can do – little to ameliorate racial inequalities:

> [Affirmative action] policy advances under the cover of providing assistance to disadvantaged persons when in fact, by its very nature, its ability to assist poor blacks is severely limited. In reality affirmative action is a symbolic policy, signifying the nation's commitment to right historical wrongs endured by blacks. ... But it has become divorced from the social and economic context of racial inequality as it actually exists in our society.
>
> (Curry, 1996, p. 51)

Critics of affirmative action, then, not only believe that it is undesirable and unconstitutional to distribute benefits according to race, they also believe it is largely ineffective in helping those who most need assistance. Moreover, they argue that it has drawbacks even for those it does help. Loury, for example, argues that blacks who reach top positions in mainstream institutions operating affirmative action policies must always ask themselves whether they would have succeeded without race preferences:

> Racial preferences undermine the ability of black people to be confident that they are as good as their achievements would suggest. In turn, this limits the extent to which the personal success of any one black can be a source of inspiration guiding the behaviour of other blacks. ... The universality of affirmative action as a vehicle for advancing black achievement puts even the 'best and brightest' African Americans in the position of being supplicants of benevolent whites. Ultimately, this way of thinking is destructive of black self-esteem.
>
> (Loury, in Curry, 1996, p. 54)

The politics of affirmative action

We have seen that the philosophical debate on race has undergone a transformation since the 1960s. Whereas there was once a broad agreement on the existence and causes of race inequality – and therefore on the solutions, as well – there is now quite bitter controversy. The agenda of affirmative action divides America and it divides black and white Americans. Unsurprisingly, the debate has moved out of academic circles and into the mainstream political arena. Moreover, it has become a sharply partisan issue.

The Democrats and affirmative action

The Democratic party is the political home of most liberals and most African Americans. In the 1996 presidential election, for example, 84 per cent of black Americans voted for Bill Clinton and just 12 per cent for the Republican candidate, Bob Dole. This stands in stark contrast to the white vote, which split 46 per cent for Dole and 43 per cent for Clinton (Pomper *et al.* 1997, p. 180). In fact, blacks have been staunch Democrats since the New Deal of the 1930s and their support has been a major factor in making the Democratic party the main vehicle of the civil rights lobby and affirmative action policies.

As a result, when Democrats have controlled the White House or the Congress, those institutions have defended affirmative action policies. Since 1968 the Democrats have had greater control of at least one chamber of Congress than of the presidency. This means that, for most of that period, Congress has maintained its support for affirmative action, while the White House has fought against it.

During the same period, the Supreme Court has swung from being generally, though by no means unconditionally, supportive of affirmative action to being generally, though not absolutely, hostile to it. This change has been brought about largely by Republican success in capturing the White House since 1968. For this in turn has given Republican presidents the right to nominate new justices to the Supreme Court; and of the five nominated by presidents Reagan and Bush, four have consistently judged that most affirmative action policies violate constitutional principles.

The Republicans and affirmative action

Just as white voters prefer Republican candidates in presidential elections, so, unsurprisingly, do conservatives. Whereas just 2 per cent of the electorate in 1996 described themselves as liberal Republicans and 13 per cent as liberal Democrats, conservative Republicans constituted 21 per cent and conservative Democrats 6 per cent (Pomper *et al.* 1997, p. 179).

With very little support among blacks and liberals, but the backing of a majority of whites and conservatives, it is logical that the Republican party has led the crusade against affirmative action. It first took a clear line in opposition to affirmative action in 1980, when Ronald Reagan easily won the party's nomination for the presidency. Once in power, the Reagan administration not merely condemned affirmative action, but used the powers of the executive branch to attack it. When Reagan's vice-president, George Bush, became president in 1989, he modified the anti-affirmative action rhetoric but was still determined in his opposition to 'racial quotas'.

Affirmative action policy since 1970

Affirmative action policy is thus the result not merely of philosophical debate but also of partisan and institutional conflict. As a consequence, affirmative action policy has often been confused. The Congress, the presidency and the Supreme Court have vied with each other to determine the fate of affirmative action policy. While no institution or party has yet been able to claim total victory, it became clear in the 1990s that those who oppose affirmative action have had the better of the struggle.

Statistical affirmative action was initially, however, the product of consensus between all three branches of the federal government. Thus, pursuant to President Johnson's Executive Order 11246 (1965), requiring would-be federal contractors to operate affirmative action, the Department of Labor's Office of Federal Contract Compliance (OFCC) drew up guidelines in 1968 and 1971 which in effect obliged firms to use statistical goals and timetables for the greater 'utilisation' of minorities. Subsequently, in 1969 the Republican Nixon administration put its seal of approval on statistical affirmative action with the promulgation of the Philadelphia Plan.

The Supreme Court added its weight to this new direction in race policy in 1971 in the case of *Griggs v. Duke Power Co.* A unanimous Court ruled that company practices which had the effect, though not the intent, of discriminating against minorities contravened the Civil Rights Act of 1964. Although the legislative history of the 1964 Act appeared to rule out numerical quotas, the Court approved their use in establishing and remedying the 'disparate impact' of hiring policies on racial minorities.

For its part, Congress went along with statistical affirmation action. First, it failed to take any legislative steps to correct the Court's interpretation of its 1964 statute. Secondly, it enacted the Equal Employment Opportunity Act of 1972, which extended the coverage of the 1964 Act and strengthened the powers of the EEOC to sue companies which engaged in discrimination.

Towards the end of the 1970s, however, the political mood in the country shifted sharply to the right. As well as the rising popularity of conservative economic views, there was a resurgence of traditional social values which emphasised individual and family responsibility. Conversely, there was an attack on 'social engineering' by 'big government'. On the specific issue of affirmative action, there was a growing feeling among whites that blacks should not expect 'favours' from government, especially when these were granted at the direct expense of whites. This resentment became reinforced as the country moved into a difficult economic period, when resources and opportunities were more constrained than at any point since the Great Depression of the 1930s.

Matters came to a head when the question of quotas was brought under the political spotlight. Enormous publicity and heated debate surrounded the Supreme Court case of *Regents of the University of California v. Bakke* in 1978. The university's Davis Medical School had set aside sixteen of its one hundred places each year for disadvantaged or minority students. In practice, only minority students entered the school through this route, leaving the clear impression that this was indeed a 'racial quota'. Moreover, minority students entering through this route did not need such high grades as those who entered through the mainstream route. Thus the case arose when a white student, Allan Bakke, was rejected by Davis even though he had higher grades than almost all the minority students admitted. He alleged that he had been discriminated on account of his race, in violation of the Equal Protection clause of the Fourteenth Amendment.

The Supreme Court was sharply divided on the question. Four justices believed the Davis scheme did not constitute discrimination, because such racial preferences, intended to remedy past wrongs, did not stigmatise whites as inferior. Four other justices, however, were convinced that the Davis scheme was impermissible and that Allan Bakke must be given a place there.

That left Justice Lewis Powell with the deciding vote. He took a position between the two groups. He held that Davis was operating a racial quota and that this violated the Equal Protection clause. However, he also said that universities could operate plans such as that used by Harvard, which allowed minority group status to be counted as a plus for an applicant. He ordered Davis to admit Allan Bakke.

The *Bakke* case crystallised the issue of reverse discrimination, with Allan Bakke emerging as a symbol of the 'new inequality'. Yet the Supreme Court soon showed that it was willing to tolerate racial preferences under some conditions. In 1979, in *United Steelworkers v. Weber*, it upheld a company scheme that awarded every other promotion to minority employees, even where white employees with more seniority were available. The Court accepted that the scheme was justified by remedial goals. In 1980, in *Fullilove v. Klutznick*, the Court upheld the federal Public Works Employment Act of 1977. Through this legislation, Congress required 10 per cent of federal grants to state and local government for public works to go to minority firms.

Thus, as the Reagan administration took office, it seemed that the Supreme Court and the Congress were in reasonable harmony over affirmative action. Racial preferences and at least some forms of quota system did not constitute race discrimination under either the Civil Rights Act of 1964 or the Equal Protection clause of the Fourteenth Amendment. Intended not as a stigmatisation of whites, but as a remedy for centuries of discrimination against blacks, they offered an apparently reasonable and practical method of achieving real racial equality.

The Reagan administration set about capitalising on white popular resentment and upsetting this elite consensus. Strongly opposed in principle to affirmative action, it placed people unsympathetic to race preferences into key agencies, including Clarence Thomas as head of the EEOC and Edwin Meese at the Justice Department. When the Supreme Court considered affirmative action issues, the solicitor-general was sent to make the case against the constitutionality of race preferences and quotas.

Most important of all in the long term, President Reagan nominated new justices to the Court who seemed likely to regard affirmative action with far less tolerance than their predecessors. Between them, Republican presidents Reagan (1981–89) and Bush (1989–93) placed five new justices on the Court: Sandra Day O'Connor (1981), Antonin Scalia (1986), Anthony Kennedy (1987), David Souter (1991) and Clarence Thomas (1992). With the exception of Souter, these appointees have viewed affirmative action with great constitutional disfavour. Eventually, in alliance with Chief Justice Rehnquist, they formed a majority of five which struck major blows against affirmative action.

Since the 1980s, affirmative action policy has largely, though not exclusively, been determined by the Supreme Court. For once affirmative action had been challenged by white 'victims' as reverse discrimination, the Court was called upon to decide whether the broad principle, as well as particular applications of it, were permissible under the Constitution and certain statutes such as the Civil Rights Act of 1964. The president and Congress could thus try to influence the Court's decisions and, in cases decided on statutory grounds, overturn them, but there is no denying that the Court has been the dominant player in setting affirmative action policy since the 1980s.

At first, the Reaganite assault on affirmative action achieved success only on the details of particular affirmative action policies, rather than on its fundamental principles. For example, in *Firefighters v. Stotts* (1983) and *Wygant v. Board of Education* (1986), the administration helped persuade the Court that where affirmative action policies caused whites to be made redundant from their jobs, but blacks with less seniority were retained, the burden on whites of remedying past discrimination against blacks was simply too great. The Court explicitly stated that firing someone on grounds of race was much more serious than hiring based on race. In this respect the Reagan administration could be pleased that limits had been placed on the reach of remedial race preferences.

On the other hand, the administration lost a more important battle over the issue of 'victim specificity'. This holds that remedial race preferences are only constitutionally permissible when designed to compensate a particular individual who has proved that he or she personally has been a victim of racial discrimination. This stands in contrast to the liberal view that a history of societal discrimination against minorities in general is sufficient justification for remedial race preferences. In *Wygant* and then *Sheet Metal Workers v. EEOC* (1986), a majority of the justices rejected victim specificity. While they also rejected general societal discrimination as sufficient justification for race preferences, they held that where a general pattern of discrimination against minorities in a particular profession or institution is proved, individual blacks need not also prove they personally have been victimised.

This was a crucial victory for supporters of affirmative action. For if victim specificity is required, then affirmative action is rendered useless as an instrument of social reform. For while individual blacks may win their cases, their efforts will not only be time consuming and very expensive, but they will only benefit a small percentage of the black workforce.

As is often the case, however, a president's Supreme Court appointees fulfil his hopes and expectations after he has left office. This is certainly true of the Reagan administration's campaign against affirmative action. In 1989, for example, a series of cases amounted to a major victory for the conservative cause. In *Richmond v. Croson*, the Court ruled unconstitutional a set-aside scheme run by the city of Richmond, Virginia. The city had ordered 30 per cent of the value of all municipal building contracts to go to minority-owned businesses. Although justified as a remedial measure, the Court ruled that the city had produced no convincing evidence of discrimination in the Richmond construction industry on a scale that justified a 30 per cent set-aside. Even more important, however, was that *Croson* was the first case in which a majority of the justices held that all race preference policies, whether designed to help blacks or whites, must be subject to strict scrutiny by the Court. Strict scrutiny is the most exacting standard of judicial review and it is rare that legislation survives it. *Croson*, therefore, seemed to be a clear signal that the days of most affirmative action plans were numbered.

Other Supreme Court decisions of 1989 did, however, provoke a Democrat-dominated Congress to hit back at the Court. One of these cases was *Wards Cove v. Atonio*. This decision significantly undermined the 1971 *Griggs* ruling on disparate impact. Whereas under that ruling *employers* were required to justify a statistical imbalance of the races in their workforce, the Court now shifted the burden of proof to *employees* to demonstrate that it was caused by discrimination. It also set arduous standards for that proof.

Democrats responded by passing the 1990 Civil Rights Act, in effect reversing *Wards Cove* and seven other cases which affected affirmative action in various technical ways. President Bush vetoed the Act, however, condemning it as a quotas bill. Eleven Republican senators joined fifty-five Democrats in voting to override the veto, but they fell just one vote short of the two-thirds majority required. The bill was introduced in the following session, this time, however with a new clause declaring that 'nothing in the amendments made by this Act shall be required to construe or encourage an employer to adopt hiring or promotion quotas on the basis of race, color, religion, sex or national origin'. This was a significant concession by liberals to conservatives and President Bush signed the 1991 Civil Rights Act into law.

The anti-affirmative action majority on the Court continued to make headway into the 1990s. In 1995, for example, in *Adarand v. Pena*, the Court extended the *Croson* requirement of strict judicial scrutiny to federal as well as local and state affirmative action policies. Until this point, the Court had always held that Congress had a particular responsibility to ensure compliance with the Fourteenth Amendment and this gave it greater latitude in devising race equality policy.

By this time, of course, the Democrat president Bill Clinton was in office. He defended the principle of affirmative action and stated his belief that many federal affirmative action programmes could meet the Court's new standards. He therefore ordered a thorough review of all these policies and declared his philosophy of affirmative action to be 'Mend it, don't end it'.

Opponents of affirmative action have continued their campaign, however. In 1996, voters in California approved by referendum the California Civil Rights Initiative (CCRI), which banned the use of every form of race preference by state and local government institutions. The full impact of the referendum has still to be gauged, but it seems clear that African Americans will lose out in significant ways. Thus, minority admissions to the most prestigious universities in the state system for the year 1998–99 seemed set to fall drastically in the wake of the CCRI. In the spring of 1998, administrators at Berkeley had offered minority applicants 61 per cent fewer places than in the previous year and the comparable figure at the Los Angeles campus was 36 per cent, ('All Politics' Web site, 2 April 1998).

Meanwhile, the Republican-controlled Congress is considering the Dole–Canady bill, designed to negate Clinton's 'Mend it, don't end it' approach, by abolishing all race preferences and quotas operated by the federal government.

If all or most forms of affirmative action are eventually eliminated, however, the problem of racial inequality is unlikely to go away. Unless its opponents devise alternative means of reducing the many substantive gaps between white Americans and African Americans, racial tensions and resentments will persist (Box 20.10). The evidence of recent history suggests that where the political system fails, those tensions will find release in protest and violence on the streets. Thus if the end of the battle over affirmative action is indeed in sight, the larger problem of racial inequality seems destined to endure.

Summary

Affirmative action policies were introduced in a pragmatic attempt to make the promise of racial equality become a reality. They were intended as remedies for centuries of discrimination and disadvantage. However, when affirmative action took the form of preferences for ethnic minorities over white Americans and of statistical goals and quotas, opposition developed quickly. Opponents believe that affirmative action is simply reverse discrimination, but discrimination nonetheless. It therefore violates American values of individualism, formal equality and meritocracy. In basic terms, it is not 'fair'. Supporters believe that affirmative action policies are simply the most effective means of overcoming continuing individual and institutional racism, both conscious and unconscious, and the burden on the majority population is both moderate and dispersed throughout society. Given that affirmative action came to be perceived, rightly or wrongly, as harmful to the majority of the population, it is unsurprising that the force of the majority was eventually brought to bear against it.

Topics for discussion

1. Does adherence to the principle of non-discrimination preclude all affirmative action policies?

2. What alternatives to affirmative action are likely to advance the cause of racial equality?

3. Is racism the main cause of racial inequality in the United States today?

4. Why have opponents of affirmative action gained the upper hand in contemporary US politics?

Further reading

Much of the literature on affirmative action is polemical and unbalanced. For an accessible introduction to the topic, which also gives space to various opinions for and against, see George C. Curry, *The Affirmative Action Debate* (Harlow: Addison-Wesley, 1996). A much more sophisticated, but still objective, analysis of the controversy over affirmative action is John David Skrentny, *The Ironies of Affirmative Action: Politics, culture, and justice in America* (Chicago: University of Chicago Press, 1996). An extended but accessible presentation of the arguments for and against affirmative action is Albert Mosley and Nicholas Capaldi, *Affirmative Action: Social justice or unfair preference?* (Lanham, MD: Rowman and Littlefield, 1996). An excellent overview of racial inequality in the United States today is Andrew Hacker, *Two Nations: Black and white, separate, hostile, unequal* (New York: Ballantine, 1995).

References

Curry, G., ed., 1996, *The Affirmative Action Debate* (Harlow: Addison-Wesley)
Hacker, A., 1995, *Two Nations: Black and white, separate, hostile, unequal* (New York: Ballantine)

Marable, M., 1991, *Race, Reform and Rebellion: The second reconstruction in black America, 1945–90* (Jackson: University of Mississippi Press)

Pomper, G., Burnham, W., Corrado, A., Heeshey, M., Just, M., Keetee, S., McWilliams, W., Mayee, W. eds, 1977, *The Elections of 1996: Reports and interpretations*, (Chatham, NJ: Chatham House)

Sowell, T., 1984, *Civil Rights: Rhetoric or reality?* (New York: Quill)

Wilson, W., 1980, *The Declining Significance of Race: Blacks and changing American institutions*, (Chicago: University of Chicago Press)

21

Abortion

This chapter examines what has undoubtedly been the most controversial social issue in the United States over the past three decades. As well as being interesting and important in its own right, abortion politics provides an illuminating case study of the policy-making process. It brings into dramatic light the operation of the core constitutional principles of federalism, the separation of powers, and checks and balances. It also reveals the conflict that can arise over policy-making between different government institutions and between different interest groups.

In August 1994, Dr John Britton was shot and killed as he was leaving his clinic in Pensacola, Florida. It came as no surprise to learn that the man arrested for his murder, Paul Hill, was a militant anti-abortion activist. A similar murder had taken place the previous year and groups such as the Army of God had been bombing clinics for some time. What made Dr Britton a target was the fact that his clinic performed abortions. While this was perfectly legal, it was also dangerous given the rise in anti-abortion violence. Indeed, Dr Britton had adopted the practice of wearing a bullet-proof vest to work, but even this could not save him.

The murder of John Britton came after some twenty-five years of acrimonious political conflict, during which the political system of the United States struggled to establish a policy on abortion that could satisfy, or at least placate, different points of view and demands. The fact that it has failed to do so is partly owing to the highly emotive character of the abortion issue. It also reflects, however, the unusual degree to which different institutions of American government can pursue and enforce different and contradictory policies on the same issue.

The rise of the abortion issue: state legislation

As recently as the early 1960s, abortion policy was not an issue at all in American politics. In the first place, abortion was one of many policy areas that the constitutional principle of federalism had assigned to the individual states. Thus, abortion was not an issue on which the national government was expected to have a policy. Secondly, most states had determined their abortion policies in the second half of the nineteenth century and there had been little reconsideration of them since. Those nineteenth-century abortion laws were generally very restrictive, usually only permitting abortion when the mother's life would otherwise be endangered.

Nothing much changed until the 1960s when two distinct, but mutually reinforcing developments occurred. The first concerned abortion as a *medical issue*. In 1962, the pregnancy of Sherri Finkbine, a resident of California, became national news. Finkbine had been taking tablets containing the drug Thalidomide, which soon became infamous for causing severe fetal deformities. Finkbine's doctors initially recommended that she have her pregnancy terminated, but the hospital stalled because it was not clear whether the abortion would be legal under California law. Finkbine then flew to Sweden for the abortion. The fetus was, indeed, badly deformed and would not have lived, according to the Swedish doctors.

Shortly after, there was an epidemic of rubella (German measles) in California. It was well known that the fetuses of pregnant women who contracted rubella were often seriously deformed. Yet doctors who wished to perform abortions on such women were again uncertain whether the state's nineteenth-century law made these abortions illegal.

As a result of the Finkbine case, the rubella epidemic and a longstanding concern over the evils of illegal 'back-street' abortions, the medical profession in the United States began to campaign for liberalised abortion laws. What they sought were laws which allowed abortions where doctors considered there was danger not merely to the mother's life, but also to her physical and psychological well-being. These medical factors, then, lay at the heart of the drive for abortion reform in the 1960s.

Towards the end of that decade, the second development occurred. This was the movement for women's liberation or gender equality, (see Chapter 7). Along with other radical movements that arose in the 1960s, the women's movement was determined to challenge the established political, social and economic order. However, the movement quickly came to the conclusion that, unless women had control over their reproductive capacities, all other reforms would be undermined. How, for example, could women compete with men on an equal basis in the workplace if they could suddenly be incapacitated by an unwanted pregnancy? While easy access to contraception had gone a long way in mitigating such problems, the women's movement believed that women would never have true reproductive freedom, and therefore equality with men, unless they had the right to abortion. In the words of one feminist writer, abortion was 'a condition of women's liberation' and 'a paradigmatic feminist demand' (Petchesky, 1981, p. 210).

In 1967, the National Organization for Women (NOW) made reproductive freedom, including abortion, part of its Women's Bill of Rights. This was clear evidence that the movement for liberalised abortion had now transcended its purely medical parameters. While groups such as NOW were certainly concerned with women's health, they were equally convinced that women's freedom involved the right to choose abortion regardless of whether there were medical problems or not. They wanted 'abortion on demand' as a fundamental political right. In time, this would significantly alter the public perception of the abortion issue. Instead of being seen primarily as a serious health matter, on which deference was due to the medical profession, it became perceived by many as a controversial political issue, associated with a radical, feminist agenda for widespread social change.

Until the early 1970s, the medical image of the abortion issue predominated, and health care professionals led successful movements for liberalised abortion in a number of states. For example, the legislatures of California, Colorado and North Carolina all passed reform bills in 1967. These new laws, although widening access to abortion, placed the emphasis upon health (or *therapeutic*) grounds for abortion. As a result, doctors rather than pregnant women themselves took the ultimate decision over whether an abortion would take place. This failed to satisfy the women's movement, which wanted women to be empowered to make the decision. They also wanted abortion legalised even for *non-therapeutic* reasons.

The first such radical success came in New York in 1970. Following a campaign which for the first time included significant activities by women's groups, the state legislature passed a new law which in effect permitted abortion on demand during the first three months of pregnancy (Tribe, 1990, p. 141). Unlike the earlier reform campaigns in California, North Carolina and Colorado, the debate over the New York law was highly charged and acrimonious. Indeed, no sooner had it been passed than anti-abortion groups began to campaign for its repeal. In 1972, the state legislature voted to do just that, only for Governor Nelson Rockefeller to thwart them by using his veto.

By 1972, a majority of states had considered reforming their nineteenth-century abortion laws. Some had actually passed new laws; others had rejected them. Although the issue was beginning to take on the character of a fundamental ideological conflict between pro-choice and pro-life pressure groups, its explosiveness was diluted by the fact that a different battle was being fought in each of the fifty states. Moreover, this federalism aspect allowed different outcomes in different states, so that each side to the conflict could count some victories, as well as defeats. However, that was about to change with the intervention of the Supreme Court.

The Supreme Court and *Roe v. Wade*

As we saw in Part VI, the Supreme Court has a policy-making role in American politics. Through its power of judicial review, the Court can order any branch of American government, federal or state, to change its policies if those policies are deemed to violate the Constitution. Of course, there are relatively few policy areas addressed by the Constitution and accordingly, the Court intervenes only infrequently in the policy-making process. On the other hand, since the 1950s, the Court has shown a marked appetite for asserting the civil liberties of individuals against government regulation: and in 1973, the Court decided to extend its liberal judicial activism to the issue of abortion.

The campaign for the reform of abortion laws had not confined itself to the arena of state legislatures. Some pro-abortion activists were hopeful that they could convince the judiciary that abortion rights were so fundamental to women's freedom that they should be recognised as constitutionally protected. They were encouraged in this by a

Supreme Court decision of 1965, *Griswold v. Connecticut*. In that case, the justices had upheld the right of married couples to use contraceptives in the face of a state ban. They concluded that the Constitution protected certain privacy rights of citizens, including the right to choose whether to beget children. In 1972, the same right was extended to non-married couples (*Eisenstadt v. Baird*).

There were, however, significant obstacles to a Court decision upholding abortion rights against restrictive state laws. First, the 'right to privacy' announced in *Griswold*

Box 21.1

The *Roe v. Wade* case

In this landmark case, the Supreme Court voted 7 to 2 to hold that the Constitution, through its unenumerated right to privacy, protected a woman's right to choose to terminate a pregnancy by abortion. The justices also recognised that states had certain legitimate interests in abortion decisions – preserving maternal health and protecting potential life. The Court therefore sought to balance the competing interests of the mother's right to abortion against the states interests within the following chronological framework:

First trimester (first three months of pregnancy)
In consultation with her physician, a woman is free to choose to have an abortion. The state may not interfere with this decision. As abortion is medically safer than continuing pregnancy during this period, the state has no reason to prevent the abortion to protect maternal health. As the embryo/fetus is not capable of life outside the womb at this stage, the state has no reason to prevent the abortion in order to preserve potential life.

Second trimester (second three months of pregnancy)
A woman is still free to choose an abortion, in consultation with her doctor, but because abortion now poses a greater medical risk to her than continuing the pregnancy, the state's interest in preserving maternal health becomes operative. It can therefore regulate the conditions under which terminations take place, such as the kinds of hospital and clinic which may perform them. However, since the fetus is still not capable of life outside the womb, the state has no right to prevent the abortion pursuant to its interest in protecting potential life.

Third trimester (final three months of pregnancy)
At about the end of the second trimester, the fetus becomes 'viable', that is, it is capable of living outside the mother's womb, with or without artificial means of support. The state's interest in protecting potential life is thus relevant to this stage of the pregnancy. In addition to regulating the conditions under which abortion may take place, therefore, it can now ban them altogether, but with one major exception: if her doctors agree that continuing the pregnancy poses a threat to her life or health, the mother may still choose an abortion.

was rather tenuous: no such right is mentioned in the Constitution and many legal scholars were unconvinced by the rationale for declaring its existence as an 'unenumerated right'. Secondly, even if the right to privacy was sound, it was not obvious that it could be applied to abortion: a termination of pregnancy not only took place in a public facility, it also involved the elimination of a 'living' entity – the embryo or fetus. Thirdly, abortion policy had always been considered the province of the states and not the federal government, including the Supreme Court.

Nevertheless, to the surprise of even pro-abortion activists, the Court not only found that the right to abortion was constitutionally protected, but also devised a very liberal framework within which that right could be exercised. In essence, a woman in the first six months of pregnancy, and having consulted a physician, could not be prevented by government from having an abortion; and even in the last three months of pregnancy, she had the right to an abortion if there was otherwise a threat to her life or health (see Box 21.1).

The *Roe* decision did not give pro-choice activists everything they wanted. It did not, for example, allow abortion on demand at all stages of pregnancy and the medical profession still had considerable influence over a woman's decision. Nevertheless, it was so liberal that every state law except New York's was rendered unconstitutional. In effect, the Supreme Court had constitutionalised and nationalised abortion rights, leaving the states with little control over this area of social policy.

While *Roe* was welcomed as a great victory by pro-choice activists, it simultaneously caused deep offence to two distinct elements in the country. First, it antagonised state legislatures who had been deprived of their policy-making powers. Secondly, it disturbed, if not outraged, many who considered that abortion would now be undertaken 'lightly', that is, without any medical justification (Box 21.2 sets out the actual figures before and after *Roe*, and Box 21.3 the numbers of abortions, by selected characteristics). In his dissenting opinion in *Roe*, Justice Byron White alleged that the Court had approved abortion 'on the whim or caprice' of pregnant women. Those

---

Box 21.2

Number of abortions performed, selected years 1972–92

	No. of abortions
1972	586,800
1975	1,034,200
1978	1,409,600
1982	1,573,900
1985	1,588,600
1988	1,590,800
1992	1,520,000

Sources: US Bureau of the Census, 1993, p. 83; 1992 figure from *The Economist*, 16 July 1994

> ### Box 21.3
>
> ## Abortions, by selected characteristics, 1988
>
> | | Percentage of all abortions |
> |---|---|
> | **Age** | |
> | Under 15 years | 1 |
> | 15–19 years | 25 |
> | 20–24 years | 33 |
> | 25–29 years | 22 |
> | 30–34 years | 12 |
> | 35–39 years | 6 |
> | Over 40 years | 2 |
> | | |
> | **Race** | |
> | White | 65 |
> | Non-white | 35 |
> | | |
> | **Marital status** | |
> | Married | 17 |
> | Unmarried | 83 |
> | | |
> | **Weeks of gestation** | |
> | Less than 9 weeks | 50 |
> | 9–10 weeks | 27 |
> | 11–12 weeks | 12 |
> | 13 or more weeks | 11 |
>
> Source: US Bureau of the Census, 1993, p. 83

who disagreed with the Court, therefore, set out to reassert the states' powers and to reverse the abortion policy of *Roe v. Wade*.

Pressure groups and abortion policy

In the late 1960s, groups campaigning for women's equality, like NOW, began to address the issue of abortion as part of their concept of reproductive freedom. They were supported to a greater or lesser extent by a wide variety of other interest groups. Some were dedicated to the abortion issue and related reproductive matters. These included NARAL, the National Association for the Repeal of Abortion Laws, founded in 1969. (While keeping the same acronym, NARAL has changed its name twice. After *Roe*, it became the National Abortion Rights Action League, and in 1994, it changed again to the National Abortion and Reproductive Rights Action League.) Another major campaigner for abortion rights was the Planned Parenthood Federation of America (PPFA). In addition to these policy groups, many professional organisations backed at least therapeutic abortions: these included the American Medical Association (AMA), the American Psychiatric Association (APA) and the American Public Health Association (APHA). There were also ethnic and religious groups which supported abortion rights, including the American Jewish Congress (AJC). In short, the abortion rights campaign was quite well advanced in that most crucial feature of contemporary American politics, interest group activity.

Until the *Roe* decision, anti-abortion activism was confined largely to the Catholic Church, although the defeat of an abortion reform referendum in Michigan in 1972 was brought about partly by the founder of the National Right to Life Committee (NLRC), John C. Willke (McKeever, 1993, p. 82).

Such was the shock of *Roe*, however, that it galvanised the anti-abortion movement. The Catholic Church was still central, particularly its Pastoral Plan for Pro-Life Activities, launched in 1975, but opposition to *Roe* went beyond traditional Catholic dogma. Many social conservatives, particularly in the middle and lower-middle classes, felt not merely that abortion involved the taking of innocent life, but that it was part of a broader threat to traditional family values (Conover and Gray, 1983). They swelled the ranks of groups such as the NLRC, the League for Infants, Fetuses and the Elderly (LIFE) and the Christian Coalition. In the 1980s, more militant anti-abortion groups emerged, such as Operation Rescue.

A fierce conflict soon developed between pro-choice and pro-life groups, as they preferred to call themselves. Pro-choice groups adopted a defensive posture, seeking to preserve the gains made in *Roe*. Pro-life groups went on the attack. They prompted sympathetic politicians to introduce pro-life measures into Congress and state and local legislatures; they supported these measures in the courts through *amicus curiae* briefs; and they launched public campaigns, including an annual March For Life outside the Supreme Court in Washington, on the anniversary of the *Roe* decision (22 January). All this activity quickly paid dividends.

Congress and abortion policy

Abortion is the kind of divisive policy issue of which many legislators prefer to steer clear, for whatever they may gain in votes and campaign donations from supporting one side, they are likely to lose as much, if not more, by alienating the other. Before *Roe*, members of Congress could avoid taking a stand on abortion by arguing that it fell within the exclusive jurisdiction of state legislatures. Once *Roe* had nationalised abortion rights, however, they were put under pressure to take a public position by pro-life legislative proposals. These included constitutional amendments to outlaw virtually all abortions; statutory measures declaring the fetus to be a legal person and therefore having all the same rights to life and liberty as American citizens; and bills that would remove the right of the Supreme Court to hear cases involving abortion. All of these failed. In part, this was because of opposition by pro-choice legislators, but it was also because they were such drastic measures and in effect embodied a frontal assault on the Supreme Court and its authority in interpreting the Constitution.

The Hyde Amendment

Many members of Congress were ready, however, to do something to placate the rising anger of the pro-life movement. In 1976, they passed the Hyde Amendment. The pro-life Representative Henry Hyde (R–Illinois.) introduced a rider to the Health, Education and Welfare Appropriations bill, that cut off Medicaid funds for virtually all abortions. Medicaid, is the federally funded health care programme for America's poor. The Hyde Amendment continued to permit Medicaid funds to be used for all health care associated with pregnancy. However, not even therapeutic abortions (medically necessary) would henceforth be covered unless the mother's life was otherwise endangered. In subsequent years, other exceptions to the amendment's ban were included: thus the measure passed in 1993 allowed Medicaid funds for abortion where pregnancy had resulted from rape or incest.

Nevertheless, the Hyde Amendment achieved its main goal of eliminating virtually all Medicaid abortions. In 1978, its first full year of operation, the number of such abortions fell from 295,000 the previous year to just 2,000 (Petersen, 1984, p. 170). While it did not affect the abortion rights of the great majority of women who were not eligible for Medicaid health care, it certainly made it very difficult for poor women to exercise their constitutional rights as declared in *Roe*.

Congress had thus shied away from a direct attack on *Roe*, but had undoubtedly undermined the new abortion right by the indirect method of refusing public funds to facilitate its exercise. The same tactic lay behind the Adolescent Family Life Act of 1981. This Act gave grants to organisations to promote chastity among teenagers, but no organisation giving contraception or abortion counselling was eligible for funds (McKeever, 1993, p. 259). In effect, then, Congress used its control of the public purse to adopt a compromise position in the pro-choice/pro-life conflict.

Presidential abortion policy

Views on abortion transcend party lines in the United States. For the most part, however, the pro-choice movement has made its home in the Democratic party, and the pro-life movement in the Republican party. Given the ascendancy of Republicans in the White House since the *Roe* decision, it comes as no surprise to learn that the executive branch has opposed the judicial branch over abortion. This was particularly true of presidents Reagan and Bush.

Despite the fact that both presidents regularly called for a constitutional amendment, they lacked the means directly to overturn the Supreme Court's decision in *Roe*. They did, however, possess a number of powers that could, like Congress, attack it indirectly. They employed three such powers in particular. First, they used executive orders and administrative guidelines to cut any kind of support for abortion counselling. Most notably, President Reagan issued a 'gag rule' in 1988, forbidding anyone employed on a federally funded health programme from even discussing the subject of abortion with a patient.

Secondly, the Reagan and Bush administrations instructed the solicitor-general to intervene in abortion cases before the Supreme Court and to urge the justices to reverse their decision in *Roe*.

Thirdly, and most controversial of all, President Reagan employed presidential powers of appointment to pack the federal judiciary with judges antagonistic to *Roe*. Through the newly created President's Committee on Federal Judicial Selection, the Reagan administration sought to appoint only those judges with a conservative judicial philosophy. Such a philosophy usually entails opposition to the *Roe* decision and the administration was widely perceived by its opponents as operating a 'litmus test' for judicial nominees: did they oppose the constitutional right to abortion?

At the Supreme Court level, President Reagan's plan worked well enough until he attempted to appoint Robert Bork in 1987. Bork was a knowledgeable but controversial constitutional theorist and judge. He was deeply hostile to the Court's reasoning in *Roe* and, indeed, in many other modern cases. His nomination also came at a time when the Court was thought to be evenly balanced on the merits of *Roe* and hence Bork was regarded as a certain fifth and decisive vote to overturn it (Hodder-Williams, 1988). A massive movement was mounted to persuade the Senate to reject Bork's nomination. At the heart of it were the leading pro-choice interest groups, as well as others concerned with the preservation of the civil rights gains of the past twenty-five years (Bronner, 1989). Together, they assured Bork's defeat.

Nevertheless, President Reagan appointed three new members of the Court: Sandra Day O'Connor, Antonin Scalia and Anthony Kennedy. President Bush appointed two further Justices: David Souter and Clarence Thomas. Gradually, these changes were to place the survival of *Roe* in great jeopardy. Together with congressional actions, abortion policy at the federal level of government was in turmoil: the Supreme Court had in effect established a policy which said that women were free to have an abortion for any reason up to six months of pregnancy and thereafter for serious health reasons; Congress made clear its distaste for that policy by banning the use of federal money to fund it, thereby effectively discriminating against America's poorest women; and Presidents Reagan and Bush were doing all they could to get the Supreme Court to reverse itself on abortion, while also making it as difficult as possible for women to receive advice and information on their constitutional rights.

State responses to *Roe*

Some states welcomed the new liberal abortion policy announced by the Supreme Court. Others, however, either refused to comply with it or sought to undermine it by adopting regulations which were clearly intended to make it difficult in practice for women to obtain abortions. Rhode Island, for example, responded by passing a law stating that life begins at conception, that a fetus was a legal person and that physicians performing abortions not necessary to save the mother's life would be liable to criminal prosecution. Pennsylvania and Missouri enacted laws requiring a woman wishing to have an abortion to obtain her husband's consent. Other states simply surrounded the abortion decision with a maze of regulatory and administrative procedures designed to deprive women of a real choice (Ford, 1983). Still others banned abortions from being performed in public hospitals, leaving women reliant upon private clinics. While this posed no great problem in the country's major metropolitan centres, women in rural areas and smaller towns often had to travel hundreds of miles to obtain abortion services, sometimes having to go to another state. In short, many states observed what they took to be the letter of *Roe v. Wade*, while doing everything possible to violate its spirit.

Public opinion on abortion

While interest groups, the Supreme Court, president, Congress and states all vied with one another for control of abortion policy in America, each naturally sought to influence public opinion. Yet despite the raging political battle in the corridors of government and, indeed, in the streets of America, public opinion has remained stable. In particular, the rival sets of interest groups have both been unable to shift majority public opinion away from its middle-of-the-road position. As Box 21.4 indicates, there has never been majority backing either for the unfettered right to abortion championed by pro-choice groups or for the virtual ban on abortions advocated by pro-life organisations. That said, the 'pure' pro-choice position receives significantly greater support than the 'pure' pro-life position.

In essence, a majority of Americans favour liberal access to abortion services for health reasons, but disapprove of non-therapeutic abortions. Moreover, the majority does not believe that public funds should be available for abortions for any reason.

Box 21.4

Public opinion on abortion, 1972–91

Percentage supporting legal abortion for specified reasons

	Therapeutic			Non-therapeutic			
Year	Risk of fetal defect	Risk to mother's health	Rape	Wants no more children	Not married	Can not afford	Any reason
1972	74.3	83	74.1	37.6	40.5	45.6	–
1973	82.2	90.6	80.6	46.1	47.3	51.7	–
1974	82.6	90.4	82.7	44.6	47.9	52.3	–
1976	81.6	88.7	80.4	44.6	48.2	50.8	–
1978	80.1	88.3	80.4	39.0	39.6	45.4	32.2
1980	80.3	87.7	80.2	45.2	46.3	49.6	39.4
1982	78.4	87.5	79.8	43.4	43.2	46.7	36.5
1984	77.4	87.0	76.7	41.1	42.2	44.4	37.2
1987	74.8	84.4	75.6	39.3	38.5	42.8	37.3
1989	78.3	87.5	79.9	42.7	43.3	45.8	38.6
1991	79.4	88.0	82.3	42.7	42.9	46.1	40.8

Source: Adapted from Epstein *et al.*, 1994, p. 599

Box 21.5

Support for *Roe v. Wade*, 1974–91

Percentage supporting Roe

	Harris poll	Gallup poll
February 1974	52	–
November 1974	–	47
March 1976	54	–
February 1979	60	–
May 1981	56	45
June 1983	–	50
September 1985	50	–
December 1988	–	57
July 1989	61	58
July 1991	–	56

Source: Epstein *et al.*, 1994, p. 600. Note: As Epstein *et al.* themselves note, both Harris and Gallup surveys ask misleading questions about *Roe*, since they indicate that the Court only made abortion legal during the first trimester.

In other words, both the Supreme Court's *Roe* decision and the policy preferences of pro-choice groups would appear to be well to the left of public opinion; and presidential policy under Reagan and Bush and the position of pro-life groups appear to be sharply to the right of public opinion. As always, however, one must treat public opinion surveys with some caution. For example, while a majority of the public disapproves of non-therapeutic abortions, some polls show a majority simultaneously claiming to support the Court's decision in *Roe* (see Box 21.5).

Whether these incompatible majorities reflect the different wording of the questions asked, or the ignorance or indecisiveness of many Americans, is not clear. What is more certain, however, is that public opinion is more supportive of a compromise on abortion policy than are the activists on both sides of the conflict.

The Supreme Court Revisits *Roe v. Wade*

The *Roe* decision was by no means the Supreme Court's last word on abortion policy. In the first place, the decision established a policy framework for the competing claims of women and government, rather than a detailed policy covering all aspects of abortion. Secondly, as we have see, many simply did not accept the decision and sought to thwart its implementation. Inevitably, many of these state and federal responses to *Roe* were challenged as unconstitutional and found their way to the Supreme Court. In a series of cases continuing to the present day, therefore, the justices had the opportunity to flesh out the policy framework of *Roe* in greater detail; and, if they wished, to incorporate some of the objections to their original decision. Naturally, the arrival of newly appointed justices at the Court would play a large part in any such reconsiderations.

As noted above, *Roe* was approved by a majority of 7 to 2 of the justices. Gradually, however, that majority was whittled away. In 1976, in *Planned Parenthood v. Danforth*, a 6-to-3 majority struck down Missouri's spousal consent law. In 1977, the Court actually upheld Connecticut's law cutting off public funds for non-therapeutic abortions (*Maher v. Roe*), and three years later, the Court upheld the Hyde Amendment, cutting off funds for both non-therapeutic and therapeutic abortions (*Harris v. McRae*). These cases did not involve a challenge to the basic right to choose an abortion, but many commentators suspected they indicated waning enthusiasm on the Court for defending *Roe v. Wade* (Box 21.6).

Those suspicions were further raised by the Court's decisions in *Akron v. Akron Centre for Reproductive Health* (1983) and *Thornburgh v. American College of Obstetricians* (1986). In both these cases, legislatures adopted 'regulations' which were, in fact, a transparent attempt to put pressure on women not to have abortions at all. For example, the Akron ordinance, written by a lawyer for the Ohio Right To Life Society, contained an 'informed consent' provision, requiring that certain information be given to a woman before she could have an abortion. The information in question was blatant pro-life propaganda designed to make the woman believe that the embryo/fetus was a person and that abortion was a major medical procedure. Writing for the Court, Justice Lewis Powell described this information as a 'parade of horribles' intended 'not to inform the woman's consent but rather to persuade her to withhold it altogether'.

The law at issue in *Thornburgh* contained similar provisions, and Justice Harry Blackmun's majority opinion sharply rebuked Pennsylvania, commenting that 'the States are not free, under the guise of protecting maternal health ... to intimidate women into continuing pregnancies'. It was worrying for pro-choice activists, however, that the 6-to-3 majority of *Akron* was now reduced to 5-to-4 in *Thornburgh*. In other words, one more switch in the vote in a future case, and not only would anti-abortion regulations like those enacted by Akron and Pennsylvania become constitutional, but the basic right to have an abortion might also disappear.

It was after the *Thornburgh* decision that President Reagan made his ill-advised and unsuccessful attempt to put Robert Bork on the Supreme Court. The campaign to defeat the Bork nomination had the effect of reinvigorating the pro-choice movement. Having become somewhat complacent after *Roe*, and relying too much on the Court to fight off the assault of pro-life groups and the Reagan administration, the battle over the Bork nomination made the pro-choice movement realise how close it was to losing the constitutional right to an abortion. If the Court ever allowed *Roe* to be reversed, either wholesale or in part, then the conflict over abortion rights would be returned to the states and, possibly, Congress. In short, abortion policy would be determined once again by legislatures.

It was precisely that outcome that many predicted for the Court's next major con-

---

Box 21.6

Leading abortion cases in the Supreme Court since *Roe*

Planned Parenthood v. Danforth, 1976
A 6-to-3 majority declares unconstitutional a Missouri law requiring a woman to obtain her husband's consent for an abortion

Maher v. Roe, 1977
A 6-to-3 majority *upholds* the constitutionality of a Connecticut law cutting off Medicaid funds for non-therapeutic abortions

Harris v. McRae, 1980
A 5-to-4 majority *upholds* the Hyde Amendment passed by Congress, which cut off Medicaid funds for non-therapeutic *and* therapeutic abortions, except where necessary to save the mother's life

Akron v. Akron Centre for Reproductive Health, 1983
A 6-to-3 majority declares unconstitutional an Akron (Ohio) ordinance placing various conditions upon a woman's right to choose an abortion. These included an 'informed consent' provision, a twenty-four hour delay between signing the consent form and having the operation, and a requirement that the fetal remains be disposed of 'in a humane and sanitary manner'

Thornburgh v. American College of Obstetricians, 1986
A 5-to-4 majority strike down several provisions of a Pennsylvania statue, similar to those in *Akron*

Webster v. Reproductive Health Services, 1989
A 5-to-4 majority *upholds* provisions of a Missouri abortion law, even though at least one appears to violate the trimester system established in *Row v. Wade*. Of the majority justices, only Justice O'Connor seems unwilling squarely to reverse *Roe*. Chief Justice Rehnquist declares *Roe* to be 'modified'

Planned Parenthood v. Casey, 1992
A 5-to-4 majority *upholds* several provisions of a Pennsylvania statue similar to those declared unconstitution in *Akron* and *Thornburgh*. The trimester system of *Roe* is abolished. However, to the surprise of many, five justices nevertheless vote to sustain the basic constitutional right to choose an abortion

---

sideration of the abortion issue in 1989, in *Webster v. Reproductive Health Services*. Again, a number of unmistakably anti-abortion 'regulations' were at issue in the statute from Missouri. These included a preamble declaring that life begins at conception and a fetal viability examination in the second trimester – even though *Roe*'s framework had said that States could not act on their interest in protecting potential life until the third trimester. More openly, both the state and the Bush administration urged the Court to overrule *Roe*.

The pro-choice movement was as pessimistic as the pro-life movement was optimistic. After all, the Court now contained not only the two original dissenting justices in *Roe*, (Rehnquist and White), but three Justices appointed by President Reagan (O'Connor, Scalia and Kennedy). There was, then, a likely majority for abandoning *Roe v. Wade*. Fearing the worst, the pro-choice movement put on a show of political strength by organising a demonstration of some 300,000 people outside the Court on the day the case was argued.

There was, however, no clear-cut decision in *Webster*. This was owing principally to the tight-rope walked by Justice O'Connor. On the one hand, she agreed with Rehnquist, White, Scalia and Kennedy, that all the provisions of the Missouri statute were permissible, but on the other hand, she alone insisted that this was not incompatible with *Roe*. As a result, it was not possible to muster a majority to overturn *Roe* and Chief Justice Rehnquist was obliged to say that it was modified and narrowed, but its basis left undisturbed.

If *Webster* resolved little in the abortion conflict, its tolerance of the Missouri regulations was an invitation to states to pass similar laws and even to test further the limits of the Court's increasing willingness to allow them to regulate the constitutional right to abortion. As Justice Blackmun wrote in dissent, the Court's opinion was 'filled with winks, nods, and knowing glances to those who would do away with *Roe* explicitly'.

The fundamental issue left hanging in *Webster* was whether the Supreme Court still held to the view that there was a right contained in the Constitution that allowed a woman to have an abortion, even when her state legislature was vehemently opposed. By the time the next major case came along in 1992, it seemed certain that that issue would be resolved, for in the years since *Webster*, President Bush was able to replace two of *Roe*'s staunchest champions on the Court – Justices William Brennan and Thurgood Marshall – with two nominees of his own – David Souter and Clarence Thomas. In fact, of the original majority of seven justices in *Roe*, only Harry Blackmun remained. The constitutional right to abortion seemed doomed.

In *Planned Parenthood v. Casey*, however, the Court reaffirmed *Roe* in a manner which secured the basic constitutional right, while allowing still further state regulation. The Pennsylvania law under review contained, amongst others, a twenty-four hour waiting period and informed consent provision reminiscent of those declared unconstitutional in *Akron* and *Thornburgh*; it also contained a provision requiring a woman intending to have an abortion to notify her husband of the fact. In yet another complicated voting line-up, a bloc of seven justices upheld the waiting period and informed consent provisions, thereby in effect overruling *Akron* and *Thornburgh*. Moreover, the trimester system was explicitly abandoned and states could henceforth adopt regulations that applied at any stage of pregnancy, provided they did not put an 'undue burden' on the woman's right to choose.

A different bloc of five justices, however, declared the spousal notification provision unconstitutional. Much more important still, the same bloc reaffirmed the basic constitutional right to abortion. The key group of justices in *Casey* consisted of Sandra Day O'Connor, Anthony Kennedy and David Souter. In their joint opinion upholding the fundamental element of *Roe*, the three justices emphasised the importance of stability in the law. First, they said, some stability in abortion law was due to women who needed it and had grown used to it:

For two decades of economic and social developments, people have organized intimate relationships and made choices that define their view of themselves and their places in society, in reliance on the availability of abortion in the event that contraception should fail. The ability of women to participate equally in the economic and social life of the Nation has been facilitated by their ability to control their reproductive lives.

Secondly, the three justices emphasised the importance of stability for the concept of a society governed by laws and for the Supreme Court as the interpreter of the Constitution. While they implied that they did not necessarily agree with the *Roe* decision as originally made, they argued that to overrule it now would create the impression that they had retreated in the face of the political pressure applied by the pro-life movement. Such an impression would seriously diminish respect for the both the law and the Court itself. Without absolutely compelling evidence that *Roe* had been wrongly decided, therefore, they would not overturn it while 'under fire' or 'surrender to political pressure'.

Abortion policy today

Political developments since *Casey* have consolidated the abortion policy established there. Most important was the election of Bill Clinton, the first pro-choice president since 1976. Clinton reversed the administrative orders put in place by presidents Reagan and Bush, including the 'gag order'.

Moreover, in his first eighteen months in the White House he had the opportunity to appoint two new Supreme Court justices. In 1993, Justice Byron White, one of the original dissenters in *Roe*, announced his retirement and was replaced by Judge Ruth Bader Ginsburg. As a lawyer, Ginsburg had worked on many of the key gender equality cases of the 1970s and although somewhat critical of the legal reasoning in *Roe*, she is known to support the constitutional right to abortion. In 1994, the author of the Court's opinion in *Roe*, Harry Blackmun, also retired, to be replaced by Judge Stephen Breyer. Although his record on the issue is limited, he too is thought to support the essence of *Roe v. Wade*. As far as the Supreme Court is concerned, therefore, the basic constitutional right to an abortion looks set to remain in the foreseeable future. At the end of its 1997 term, the Court had only three justices – Rehnquist, Scalia and Thomas – who would reverse it altogether. This explains the fact that the Supreme Court has not decided any major case on the fundamental right to abortion since *Casey*.

Of course, abortion policy is more complicated than the basic constitutional issue. Beyond the right to have an abortion is the problem of obtaining an abortion in practice. We saw above how the Hyde Amendment cut off federal funds for abortion for poor women, and this shows no sign of changing – all attempts to overturn the ban have been easily defeated in both the House and Senate.

States are free to use their own funds to pay for abortions for indigent women, but only a few do this. For most American women, therefore, the right to an abortion depends partly on their ability to pay. Poverty is compounded by the fact that, following the decisions in *Webster* and *Casey*, some states have clamped down on abortions being performed in public hospitals. Many women therefore have to travel long distances to private abortion clinics; and the costs involved are further increased by the waiting period provisions of many state laws, which may necessitate an overnight stay in a hotel.

It is not merely public hospitals which are performing fewer abortions: fewer doctors and clinics are offering abortion services. According to one count, in 1992, 18 per cent fewer clinics provided abortion services compared with ten years earlier (*The Economist*, 16 July 1994). This may be due to the intimidatory tactics of extreme anti-abortion groups like the Army of God and Operation Rescue. As well as murderous bombings and attacks on clinics and doctors, some groups have become effective at physically blocking access to clinics that provide abortions. Here, however, there is now some sign of policy cohesion at the federal level. In 1994, Congress passed the Freedom of Access to Clinic Entrances Act (FACE), making it a federal criminal offence to blockade abortion clinics or threaten those who wish to enter them. Also in 1994, the Supreme Court decided unanimously that the Racketeer Influenced and Corrupt Organizations Act (RICO) could be used to prosecute those conspiring to organize such clinic blockades, (*National Organization for Women v. Scheidler*). Further cases will be needed, however, to clarify just how far government can go in stopping clinic protests, without violating the First Amendment free speech rights of anti-abortion protesters.

If FACE was a congressional success for the pro-choice movement, it also suffered a major setback in 1993 when Congress abandoned consideration of the Freedom of Choice Act. This was an attempt to codify the abortion rights of *Roe v. Wade* into federal law, thus contradicting many of the state law provisions permitted by the Court in *Webster* and *Casey*. Originally introduced during the Bush presidency, it was hoped that the arrival of the pro-choice Bill Clinton in the White House would ensure its passage. However, when it proved impossible to obtain a consensus on what restrictions the Act should contain, legislators decided not to proceed (*National Journal*, 5 March, 1994).

The conflict over abortion continues, then, but has reached a stalemate for the foreseeable future. The Supreme Court looks set to defend the basic right to abortion, a right of which some 1.5 million women avail themselves every year. Since this represents over a quarter of all pregnancies, it is clear that the pro-choice movement is driven as much by social need as by ideology (*The Economist*, 16 July 1994).

Meanwhile the pro-life movement continues to campaign for the abolition of that right. It searches for new tactics and issues by which to maintain the pressure on abortion rights. Thus it seized on the rarely practised procedure known as 'partial-birth abortion' to advance its case that abortion involves the killing of an innocent life. Such was the success of this campaign that the Republican-controlled Congress outlawed it. As is typical of the abortion issue, however, this was immediately countered by the actions of a different political institution – President Clinton vetoed the ban in 1997.

 ## Summary

Since the Supreme Court's intervention in *Roe v. Wade* in 1973, abortion has been the most intractable of all policy issues in the United States. The policy-making process has struggled to contain it. In part, this is because the opposing factions do not merely disagree over policy, but also have fundamentally different sets of values about individual freedom and social values. The conflict is also fuelled, however, by the fact that the fragmented nature of the American policy-making process, characterised by numerous access points and fora, always seems to offer determined protagonists another chance of turning defeat into victory. It is hardly surprising, therefore, that political activists who are dealing with matters of life and death take full advantage of what the system has to offer.

Further reading

Much of the literature on abortion is highly partisan, but the following three books can be recommended as informative and reasonably dispassionate: Elizabeth Adell Cook, Ted G. Jelen and Clyde Wilcox, *Between Two Absolutes: Public opinion and the politics of abortion* (Boulder: Westview, 1992), Barbara Hinkson Craig and David M. O'Brien, *Abortion and American Politics* (Chatham, NJ: Chatham House, 1993), and Malcom L. Goggin (ed.), *Understanding the New Politics of Abortion* (London: Sage, 1993). A useful study of pro-abortion interest groups is Susan Staggenborg, *The Pro-Choice Movement: Organization and activism in the abortion conflict* (Oxford: Oxford University Press, 1991). On the roots of anti-abortion ideology, see Kirsten Luker, *Abortion and the Politics of Motherhood* (Berkeley: University of California Press, 1984), and Pamela Conover and Virginia Gray, *Feminism and the New Right: Conflict over the American family* (New York: Praeger, 1983).

References

Bronner, E., 1989, *Battle for Justice* (New York: Doubleday)

Conover, P and Gray, V., 1983, *Feminism and the New Right: Conflict over the American family* (New York: Praeger)

Epstein, L. Seqal, J., Spaeth, H., Walker, T., 1994, *The Supreme Court Compendium* (Washington DC: Congressional Quarterly, Inc.)

Ford, N., 1983, 'The evolution of a constitutional right to an abortion', *Journal of Legal Medicine*, IV, pp. 271–322

Hodder-Williams, R., 1988, 'The strange story of Judge Robert Bork and a vacancy on the United States Supreme Court', *Political Studies*, vol. XXXVI, pp. 613–37

McKeever, R., 1993, *Raw Judicial Power? The Supreme Court and American society* (Manchester: Manchester University Press)

Petchesky, R., 1981, 'Antiabortion, antifeminism, and the rise of the new right', *Feminist Studies*, vol. VII, pp. 206–46

Petersen, K., 1984, 'The public funding of abortion services', *International and Comparative Law Quarterly*, vol. XXXIII, pp. 158–80

Tribe, L., 1990, *Abortion: The clash of absolutes* (New York: Norton)

US Bureau of The Census, 1993, Statistical Abstract of the United States (113th edn, Washington DC)

22

Foreign policy

At the close of the twentieth century, the foreign policy of the United States stands at a crossroads. Following the collapse of its cold war nemesis, the Soviet Union, the United States is the only nation which can plausibly claim to be a superpower. On the other hand, it has also had to deal with problems of relative economic decline, as Japan and the European Union among others, emulate and even surpass America's economic performance. How should the United States respond to both the opportunities and the limitations of the new global environment? In this chapter, we examine the roots and traditions of American foreign policy and the processes and institutions which have grown up to serve it. This analysis helps us to understand not merely how and why it came to be the world's greatest power, but also how the United States sees its place in the world – past, present and future.

Nature of foreign policy

Foreign policy is a broad term, covering many different spheres of policy and action. Its concerns include defence and national security, overseas trade and commerce, global stability and conflict, and the values and rules which govern relations between states. The instruments for carrying out foreign policy are equally varied: economics, diplomacy and military action each offers a wide range of means of pursuing foreign policy goals.

The goals themselves are innumerable in a complex and interdependent world, but may broadly be subsumed under three headings: defence, economic prosperity and ideology. In its pursuit of economic prosperity and national security, the foreign policy of the United States resembles that of other nations: these are, after all, the basic necessities that all countries seek in their dealings with other nations. As such, they loom large in the *realist* school of foreign policy which holds, for example, that the United States should only intervene militarily in international conflicts when there is a clear and substantial American economic or security interest at stake (Kegley and Wittkopf, 1987, p. 77).

The ideological content of American foreign policy is, however, more distinctive. It has its roots in the earliest years of the American colonies, when settlers from Europe set out to build a new and better society than those they left behind. Inspired by religious idealism, they eschewed the corruption and strife of Europe. They saw themselves as pilgrims in a land that God had reserved for a special destiny: the creation of a society morally, socially and politically superior to any that had gone before. Unsurprisingly, therefore, they also believed that their new society would serve as a model for the future progress of the human race. As John Winthrop, the leader of those who established the Massachusetts Bay colony in 1630, told his group: 'We must consider that we shall be as a city upon a hill, the eyes of all people are upon us' (LaFeber, 1989, p. 9).

This sense of *mission* inevitably found its way into American foreign policy. After all, a belief in one's distinctiveness and superiority as a nation is bound to colour one's relations with other nations not so blessed. Yet this 'myth of superiority', as Henry Steele Commager called it, did not demand an inflexible policy in dealing with the outside world. On the contrary, it justified both remaining aloof from international politics and leading crusades for a better world (Commager, 1974). Thus, whether discussing nineteenth-century isolationism or twentieth-century globalism, we quickly encounter the moralistic underpinnings of American foreign policy.

Some believe that such American idealism is little more than rhetoric, designed to cloak the presence of the baser motivations of national self-interest. Indeed, it would be foolish to argue that politicians do not attempt to dignify their policies, foreign or domestic, with the language of higher moral purpose. On the other hand, as Michael Hunt has pointed out, such rhetoric only works and continues to be employed because it taps deep-seated beliefs in American culture:

> In the United States, foreign-policy rhetoric has been peppered with widely understood codewords. References in speeches, school texts, newspaper editorials, and songs to liberty, providential blessings, destiny, and service to mankind have been fraught with meaning shared by author and audience. Precisely because of their explanatory power and popular appeal, such simple but resonant notions become essential to the formulation and practical conduct of international policy.
>
> (Hunt, 1987, p. 16).

This does not mean that we must accept that American foreign policy actually is more moral than that of other nations. Rather, it means that we must seriously consider the possibility that American foreign policy makers – and the American public at large – do conceive of their foreign policy as something more than the mere pursuit of national self-interest.

This tradition of *idealism* in American foreign policy is often said to be at odds with the tradition of realism, noted above. As we shall see, 'They compete with each other as conceptions of how the United States ought to define its foreign policy objectives, even while they coexist with one another. While one tradition may predominate over the other at any single point in time ... neither has managed to obliterate the influence of the other' (Kegley and Wittkopf, 1987, p. 78).

US foreign policy, 1789–1941

The early republic

It is sometimes thought that, before the Second World War, American foreign policy was generally isolationist. This, however, is misleading. The fact that the United States showed reluctance to join the great European powers in vying for international supremacy, does not mean that it shunned contact with them. Indeed, both geopolitical factors and economic self-interest demanded that the United States devote great care and attention to its relations with the likes of Great Britain, France, Spain and Russia (Box 22.1).

At the very moment when the United States secured its independence from Britain, it was surrounded by European colonial powers. Not only were these powers potential or actual rivals to the United States' commercial and territorial interests, but their incessant bellicosity towards each other threatened to engulf the new nation. American

---

Box 22.1

American neutrality in foreign affairs

Presidents George Washington and Thomas Jefferson made a strong stand in favour of neutrality in international politics, fearing in particular that joining permanent alliances with other nations would inevitably drag the United States into wars that were not in its interests. Furthermore, they believed that adherence to such neutrality placed the United States upon superior moral ground.

Extract from George Washington's farewell address, 1796

Observe good faith and justice toward all nations. Cultivate peace and harmony with all. … It will be worthy of a free, enlightened and at no distant period a great nation to give to mankind the magnanimous and too novel example of a people always guided by an exalted justice and benevolence …

The great rule of conduct for us in regard to foreign nations is, in extending our commercial interests, to have with them as little political connection as possible …

Europe has a set of primary interests which to us have none or a very remote relation. Hence she must be engaged in frequent controversies, the causes of which are essentially foreign to our concerns. Hence, therefore, it must be unwise in us to implicate ourselves by artificial ties in the ordinary vicissitudes of her politics or the ordinary combinations and collisions of her friendships or enmities.

Extract from Thomas Jefferson's first inaugural address, 1801

About to enter, fellow citizens, on the exercise of duties which comprehend everything dear and valuable to you, it is proper you should understand what I deem to be the essential principles of our Government. … Equal and exact justice to all men, of whatever state or persuasion, religious or political; peace, commerce, and honest friendship with all nations, entangling alliances with none …

diplomacy was thus confronted with the difficult task of maintaining good relations with all of these bitter enemies.

Geopolitical considerations were made more complex by the fact that the health of the early American economy was dependent upon international commerce. American exports increased greatly in value in the years following independence. Even more important was the income generated by US shipping, which carried goods across both the Atlantic and Pacific oceans (LaFeber, 1989, pp. 41–2).

These issues of national self-interest also, however, intersected with ideological positions. These revolved around the political conflicts generated by the French Revolution of 1789 and which fuelled the Napoleonic wars until 1815. Many Americans, most notably Thomas Jefferson, sympathised with the republican radicalism of the French, with whom they identified as fellow revolutionaries. More conservative Americans, including George Washington and his Federalist supporters, were shocked by the excesses of the French Revolution. Moreover, as substantially products of English culture and tradition themselves, they were drawn towards the side of the mother country.

Thus, while the idealism embodied in the myth of American superiority might otherwise have persuaded the United States to adopt a truly isolationist position from the start, less noble but more immediate considerations demanded an active foreign policy.

The foreign policy of the Washington administration was thus more akin to 'active neutrality' than isolationism. Seeking to avoid becoming embroiled in war, the President issued the Neutrality Proclamation in 1793. Two years later, and in spite of British attacks on American shipping, he signed the Jay Treaty with Britain. Although many Americans denounced the treaty as a surrender to British naval muscle, Washington was motivated by the need to avoid a costly, perhaps suicidal, war with Britain (LaFeber, 1989, p. 46).

Also in 1795, Washington signed the Pinckney Treaty with Spain which allowed Americans tax-free use of New Orleans. This Spanish port lay at the mouth of the Mississippi River and was thus vital to American traders in the West.

Having secured friendly relations with Britain and Spain, it was not surprising that relations with France deteriorated. French attacks on American shipping increased dramatically in the last years of the eighteenth century, and the possibility of war arose. Once again, however, the United States avoided military conflict: the Convention of 1800 made financial concessions to France in return for recognition of America's trading rights as a neutral country.

The United States had thus established the central principles of its foreign policy very quickly. These were, first, to pursue honest and open relations with all countries: this was not only morally right, but would allow Americans to trade freely. Secondly, the United States must avoid becoming involved in conflicts having their origin in the corrupt Old World of Europe. Once again, this stance blended moral principle with economic and defence needs: the United States would indulge neither in intrigue nor war and simultaneously ensure that no nation felt compelled to invade American territory or attack American commerce.

However, these principles could not totally be preserved in the face of the recurring pressures emanating from the Napoleonic wars. In 1807, the Jefferson administration faced increasing restrictions on American shipping from both Britain and France. Sticking to its principle of non-involvement, the United States government passed the Embargo Act which closed American ports and banned exports. The problem was that this idealistic stand did great harm to the country's own economy. Before he left office in 1809, Jefferson bowed to domestic economic pressures and reopened the country's ports. The ban on British and French ships remained, but this brought no change in their hostile behaviour.

The War of 1812

American resentment at foreign restrictions on their shipping came to focus principally on Britain, who had also been in league with native Americans who were resisting the attempts of the US government to take over yet more of their land. Eventually, President James Madison decided that war against Britain was the only solution and, in 1812, obtained a declaration of war from Congress.

This was no mere war of self-defence, however. Madison hoped to seize Canada, just as the previous year he had seized western Florida from Spain. American forces also took the opportunity to push native Americans still further to the west. In short, the United States sought to expand its territory through war, making its foreign policy uncomfortably similar to those of the corrupt Old World.

The 'War of 1812' came perilously close to being a humiliating disaster for the United States. The British navy was far too powerful and soon controlled the Atlantic coast. British troops landed in Washington in 1814 and set fire to the city, forcing the US government to flee. On Christmas Eve, 1814, the United States signed the Treaty of Ghent with Britain, which simply restored prewar boundaries and gave the United States nothing on the crucial issue of neutrals' shipping rights. It could have been far worse had the British not wished to concentrate their resources on bringing the Napoleonic wars to an end in Europe, rather than on the difficult task of conquering the United States.

However, what saved the war for the United States was the fact that news of the Treaty of Ghent was slow in crossing the Atlantic. Thus, in January 1815, General Andrew Jackson defeated a British invasion at New Orleans, establishing not only his own reputation as a great American hero, but also transforming the war from an American catastrophe into a phenomenal victory over the world's greatest military power.

It is clear then that the period from 1789 to 1815 was far from being one of American isolationism in foreign policy. Moreover, while successive administrations espoused idealistic sentiments, the period demonstrated that the United States was willing to employ both the means and the ends of foreign policy that it condemned in other nations. This was confirmed over the next one hundred years. For although a century of peace in Europe released the United States from entanglement in Old World conflicts, Americans turned their energies to acquiring vast swathes of new territory in the New World.

Territorial expansion and conquest in the nineteenth century

In the period before the American Civil War (1861–65), the United States grew from an eastern seaboard nation to a vast continental power. This was achieved by a combination of war and shrewd diplomacy. After the Civil War, considerable effort was spent in 'taming' the great western territories, a process that included the near-genocide of those native Americans who resisted the loss of the land that had been promised to them in perpetuity by the US government. Once the continental United States was consolidated, there began the first major attempt to extend American power overseas. Once again, therefore, it is something of a misnomer to characterise this era as one of isolationism. Rather, it was a period when the United States' foreign policy paid scant attention to European politics and concentrated upon relations with other nations in the New World (Box 22.2).

Manifest destiny

Whether it concerned war, diplomacy or land purchase, American foreign policy was impelled by the notion of what became known as 'manifest destiny'. Coined in the 1840s, the term denoted the belief that the whole of the New World was destined by God to be owned and run by the people of the United States. Although territorial expansion was eventually limited, there were many who believed that Canada, Mexico, Central America, the Caribbean and perhaps South America would all one day become part of the United States – and by military conquest, if necessary (LaFeber, 1989, p. 134). Indeed, as early as 1823, the government had announced officially that it viewed the New World as a place where the political and social values of the United States were destined to hold sway.

The Monroe Doctrine of 1823

The original intention behind President James Monroe's address to Congress in 1823 (see Box 22.3) was to warn the European powers that they should cease to regard New World territories as targets for inclusion in their empires. Although he made no threats against existing European colonies, Monroe decreed that the political and social future of nations in the Americas would be constructed along the democratic and republican lines of the United States itself.

In its original form, therefore, the Monroe Doctrine was not so much an attempt to lay claim to the territories of the Americas, as a warning to the Old World not to impede the 'natural' development of societies in the New. Such development, of course, coincided with the economic and security interests of the United States in the Americas.

As the nineteenth century progressed, however, American expansionism saw the Monroe Doctrine transformed into a rationalisation of the New World as a United States' sphere of influence. Moreover, the United States went to war to acquire what were, in effect, colonial possessions.

Box 22.2

Key dates in American territorial expansion

1803   **The Louisiana purchase**
President Thomas Jefferson buys the Louisiana territory from France for $15 million. The new territory, stretching from the Mississippi River to the Rocky Mountains, doubles the size of the United States and eventually is made into thirteen new states

1819   **The Transcontinental Treaty**
Spain cedes Florida to the United States after an American threat to take it by force. In return, the United States recognises Spain's claim to Texas (but see the Treaty of Guadelupe–Hidalgo below)

1830–35   **Expulsion of native Americans**
The Choctaw, Chickasaw, Creek and Cherokee nations are forcibly removed from the south to the Oklahoma Indian Territory across the Mississippi River. Likewise, the Fox and Sauk are removed from the north to Oklahoma

1846   **Buchanan–Pakenham Treaty**
Having threatened war, President James K. Polk agrees to divide the disputed Oregon Territory with Great Britain. This pushes the north-west American boundary to the 49th Parallel

1848   **Treaty of Guadelupe–Hidalgo**
Following the annexation of Texas from Mexico in 1845, the United States goes to war with Mexico. It gains the California Territory, running from Texas to California, thereby increasing the US land-mass by some 50 per cent

1853   **The Gadsden purchase**
The United States purchases a small but significant piece of land from Mexico, extending the southern borders of what were to become the states of Arizona and New Mexico. Its great value is that it permits the completion of a southern transcontinental railroad

1867   **The Alaska purchase**
For the sum of $7.2 million, Russia sells the United States Alaska – a territory over twice the size of Texas

1862–90   **Indian wars in the west**
A series of wars against native American nations, resulting in their mass annihilation and the removal of those left alive from their territories to reservations

The Spanish–American War of 1898

The war of 1898 arose from rebellions by the remnants of the Spanish Empire in the Caribbean and the Pacific to achieve independence. On the pretext of a Spanish attack upon the USS *Maine*, the United States entered the conflict on the side of the rebels in

---

Box 22.3

The Monroe Doctrine, 1823

In his seventh annual message to Congress, President James Monroe alluded to recent discussions with Russia and Great Britain about rival claims in the northwest of the American continent; and to continuing warfare in Europe. He then asserted the principle:

> that the American continents, by the free and independent condition which they have assumed and maintain, are henceforth not to be considered as subjects for future colonization by any European powers ...
>
> In the wars of the European powers in matters relating to themselves we have never taken any part, nor does it comport with our policy to do so. It is only when our rights are invaded or seriously menaced that we resent injuries or make preparation for our defence. With the movements in this hemisphere we are of necessity more politically connected, and by causes which must be obvious to all enlightened and impartial observers. ... We owe it therefore, to candour and to the amicable relations existing between the United States and those powers to declare that we should consider any attempt on their part to extend their system to any portion of this hemisphere as dangerous to our peace and safety ...
>
> Our policy in regard to Europe ... is not to interfere in the internal concerns of any of its powers; to consider the government *de facto* as the legitimate government for us; to cultivate friendly relations with it, and to preserve those relations by a frank, firm, and manly policy, meeting in all instances the just claims of every power, submitting to injuries from none.

Cuba. Victory over Spain was achieved quickly, but Cuban independence was not the outcome. Rather, Cuba became a US 'protectorate'. The 1903 treaty settlement allowed the Cubans to determine their own internal laws, but Senator Orville Platt's amendment to the original version gave the United States ultimate control. In particular, the Platt Amendment gave the United States the right to intervene militarily in Cuba 'to protect its independence'; and granted the United States a 99-year lease on a naval base at Guantanamo Bay.

The war also saw the United States annex the Philippines, Puerto Rico and Hawaii. The Filipinos, who had originally welcomed the Americans as allies against Spain, fought a bloody but unsuccessful guerilla war against the American occupying forces for three years. It eventually required some 120,000 US troops to subdue the Filipinos, whose deaths from the fighting, starvation and the American concentration camps may have reached 200,000 (LaFeber, 1989, p. 202).

In the wake of the war, it was clear that the United States was now behaving as an imperial power, much like the nations of Europe. Moreover, the American empire was founded not merely on economic and territorial ambition, but on the notion of a racial hierarchy (Hunt, 1987, p. 78). Just as Europeans justified colonialism in terms of 'the white man's burden', most Americans deemed latins, orientals and blacks to be so far inferior to Anglo-Saxons that they could not be entrusted with self-rule.

An oft-repeated, though apocryphal story, reveals how Americans rationalised their imperialism at the end of the nineteenth century. The story has President McKinley telling an audience of churchmen how he had prayed late into the night for divine guidance on what to do with the Philippines after the Spanish had been defeated:

> And one night it came to me in this way – We could not give the Philippines back to Spain: that would be cowardly and dishonourable. We could not turn them over to France and Germany, our commercial rivals in the Orient: that would be bad business. There was nothing left to do but take them all, and educate the Filipinos, and uplift and civilise them, and by God's grace do the very best by them as our fellow men for whom Christ also died. And then I went to bed, and went to sleep and slept soundly.
>
> (LaFeber, 1989, p. 200).

The hard realities of the new American imperialism were, however, easy enough to discern. In 1903, when Colombia refused the United States permission to construct a canal from the Atlantic to the Pacific on its territory, the administration of President Theodore Roosevelt sponsored a local revolution which led to the creation of the state of Panama. The Panama Canal was duly constructed and placed under American control.

The following year, the president placed the official seal on the new American hegemony in the western hemisphere. In the Roosevelt Corollary to the Monroe Doctrine (see Box 22.4), he announced that the United States was assuming responsibility for maintaining stability and order in the Americas. Henceforth, when nations in the region behaved irresponsibly, the United States would intervene, with armed force if necessary, to correct the situation.

In the years around the turn of the century, then, the United States appeared ready to assume the global role to which its economic wealth, large population and dynamic expansionism were so suited. That, however, did not happen for another fifty years. The principal reason is that a countertendency in American ideology reasserted itself: isolationism, or more precisely, the desire to avoid entanglement in European conflicts.

Box 22.4

The Roosevelt Corollary, 1904

'It is not true that the United States feels any land hunger or entertains any projects as regards the other nations of the Western Hemisphere save such as are for their welfare. All that this country desires is to see the neighbouring countries stable, orderly, and prosperous. Chronic wrongdoing, or impotence which results in a general loosening of the ties of civilised society, may ... ultimately require intervention by some civilised nation, and in the Western Hemisphere the adherence of the United States to the Monroe Doctrine may force the United States, however reluctantly, in flagrant cases of such wrongdoing or impotence, to the exercise of the international police power.'

The First World War and the interwar years

President Theodore Roosevelt's successors did not share his enthusiasm for military action, but they were convinced that the United States must pursue an activist international policy. They were fully aware that the American economy depended more than ever on overseas markets, a fact which led the United States to adopt an 'open door' policy with regard to international trade. This would allow American business to have access to markets and raw materials on the same terms as other nations. The administration of President Taft (1909–13) thought this could best be achieved through 'dollar diplomacy', whereby American capital investment in other nations would guarantee the United States both economic access and political influence.

Along with economic self-interest, went a desire to export 'American values': republicanism, democracy, free enterprise and individualism. Under President Woodrow Wilson (1913–21), idealism in foreign policy reached new heights, culminating in Wilson's attempt to create a new framework for the conduct of politics between nations.

On the outbreak of the First World War in Europe in 1914, the familiar combination of economic self interest and American values persuaded Wilson to remain neutral. This permitted American business to make huge profits from selling to both sides of the conflict, while simultaneously refusing to descend to the levels of European power politics.

Gradually, however, the war encroached unbearably on American freedom to trade, particularly German U-boat attacks upon American merchant ships. By 1917, Wilson realised that the United States must become a belligerent if it wished to protect its economic interests. Moreover, Wilson understood that if the United States was to influence the postwar settlement and international order, it would have to negotiate as a victor.

In April 1917, Wilson sought and obtained a declaration of war from Congress. Declaring that neutrality was no longer feasible or desirable, Wilson proclaimed a crusade to make the 'world safe for democracy'. The president continued in idealistic vein in his 'Fourteen Points' speech to Congress, in January 1918. Although it played to the economic interests of the United States, with its advocacy of absolute freedom of navigation and the open door in trade, the speech also envisaged self-determination for all nations and international peace based upon collective security. This latter idea would relieve nations of the need to engage in balance-of-power politics and arms races to protect themselves. Instead, the pooled force of what shortly became the League of Nations would deter and punish aggressor nations.

Whatever initial enthusiasm Americans may have had for Wilson's idealistic proposals, the experience of war and its aftermath left them severely disillusioned. It became evident during the negotiations over the peace settlement that America's European allies did not share Wilson's vision of a new world order. Rather, they seemed intent upon conducting business as usual as they sought only to serve their own national interests.

When Wilson proved unable to change European habits, Americans turned inwards. Ironically, the president, by raising exaggerated hopes and then failing, 'laid the foundation for a pervading postwar isolationism' (Graebner, 1984, p. 2). In effect,

American participation in the First World War served only to confirm the view that the United States could and should avoid entanglement in Europe. The most important immediate consequence of this disillusionment was the Senate's rejection of United States membership in the League of Nations. In the longer term, it led the United States to retreat ever deeper into isolationist behaviour, even in the face of blatant aggression by Nazi Germany in the 1930s.

The Second World War

Wilsonian internationalism still had its supporters in the United States in the interwar years, particularly among the makers of foreign policy. However, isolationism was strong in the Congress. Many Progressive politicians from the mid-west and western states were principled opponents of what they saw as the threat to American virtue stemming from involvements in Europe. Senators such as William Borah of Idaho and Gerald Nye of North Dakota argued fiercely against any repetition of First World War engagements. In the 1930s they were joined by demagogic populists, such as Senator Huey Long of Louisiana and the publisher William Randolph Hearst. Between them, they managed to defeat President Franklin D. Roosevelt's 1935 proposal for the United States to join the World Court of the League of Nations. They followed this by passing three separate Neutrality Acts in the period from 1935 to 1937.

Thus, even after Roosevelt had begun helping the British and, indeed, the Soviet Union, to fight against Germany, he admitted to the British prime minister, Winston Churchill, that isolationist opposition in Congress prevented him from declaring war (LaFeber, 1989, p. 382).

Roosevelt's dilemma was solved by the decision of Hitler's ally, Japan, to attack the American Pacific Fleet at Pearl Harbor, Hawaii, on 7 December 1941. In the light of such aggression, Roosevelt had no difficulty persuading Congress to declare war on Japan. Germany responded by declaring war on the United States. Thus the Americans, who had spent the past twenty years desperately trying to avoid military entanglements, now found themselves at war across both the Atlantic and the Pacific.

The United States emerged from those conflicts as the world's dominant economic and military power. During the war years, the American economy had recovered fully from the Great Depression. While the American economy boomed, the major European powers, whether in victory or defeat, had suffered economic devastation. Consequently, the end of the Second World War saw the United States uniquely positioned to lead the world out of the economic chaos of the previous two decades.

Moreover, economic dominance translated ineluctably now into political and military dominance. The United States needed a thriving capitalist world economy if its own businesses were to prosper. However, the world capitalist economy could only recover if stable and supportive political conditions existed: and the sole country with the power to assure such conditions was the United States. American policy-makers recognised this and moved their country towards a position in international politics that in effect reversed some 150 years of foreign policy tradition. Unsurprisingly, that change in policy also necessitated a transformation in the structures and processes of American foreign policy making.

The cold war

Historians disagree about the origins of the cold war – that permanent state of crisis and tension between, principally, the United States and the Soviet Union, which lasted from the late 1940s to the late 1980s. The liberal school of western scholars blame the aggressive, expansionist actions and rhetoric of the Soviets, particularly in eastern Europe, for provoking the conflict, for between 1945 and 1948, the Soviet Union gradually installed puppet regimes in East Germany, Poland, Hungary, Czechoslovakia and Bulgaria. Moreover, with the spread of communism to other countries, including Rumania, Yugoslavia and, in 1949, China, many in the west perceived a Moscow-directed plan to conquer the world for communism.

Revisionist historians, however, point to American political and economic aggression, backed by the threat of military force. Certainly the United States was determined to create a postwar economic order that would serve its own interests. In 1944, the United States called an international meeting at Bretton Woods, New Hampshire. The outcome of that meeting was that while the United States would promote economic growth through the loan and investment of billions of American dollars, the world, including the British Empire, would have to open itself to US trade.

The Bretton Woods agreement created two new powerful instruments for American economic domination: the International Bank for Reconstruction and Development – or the World Bank, as it is often called – and the International Monetary Fund (IMF). Primed with American finance and dominated by American administrators, these two institutions would help to ensure that the world would provide the United States with necessary export markets and outlets for capital investment.

Although many countries stood to gain from increased American investment, they were aware that the price to be paid was economic subordination to the United States. Thus, the British prime minister, Winston Churchill, resisted American terms at Bretton Woods: 'US officials, however, simply steamrolled over London's objections' (LaFeber, 1989, p. 411).

If a close ally such as Great Britain was fearful of the consequences of the new American economic domination, it is not surprising that the Soviet Union was deeply suspicious. Although the Soviet Union and United States had been allies during the Second World War, this had been a marriage of convenience. Even as the United States entered the war, Senator (later, President) Harry Truman said the Soviets were as 'untrustworthy as Hitler and Al Capone' (Hunt, 1987, p. 156). Soviet communism and American capitalism lay at opposite ideological poles and each viewed the progress of the other as a threat to its own existence. Thus, while President Franklin D. Roosevelt had hoped that the wartime collaboration with the Soviet leader, Josef Stalin, might continue after the war, the old mutual suspicions quickly re-emerged.

To the Soviet Union, the United States represented not merely an economic threat, but a military danger as well. This danger was most dramatically embodied by America's exclusive possession of the atomic bomb. When the United States had used the bomb to end the war with Japan, it had done so, in part, to save the lives of thousands of American troops who would surely have been killed in the course of a traditional invasion. Yet the atomic devastation of Hiroshima and Nagasaki was also intended 'to make clear to the world that the United States was ruthless enough to drop the bomb on live targets' (McCormick, 1989, p. 45).

Thus, American foreign policy makers hoped that they could exploit their atomic monopoly and practise 'atomic diplomacy' upon the Soviets. Unfortunately, the Soviets reacted to these pressures in ways that only heightened tensions: 'atomic diplomacy reinforced Russia's security fears, strengthened its disposition to control its Eastern European buffer zone more tightly, undermined soft-liners on German policy, and led Soviet leaders to create a crash atomic bomb project of their own' (McCormick, 1989, p. 45)

Containment

Wherever the responsibility for the cold war should lie, the fact is that in the years following the Second World War, relations between the United States and the Soviet Union deteriorated rapidly. Rightly or wrongly, from the American viewpoint, the Soviet Union was an aggressive, expansionist state, armed with a messianic ideology that saw war with international capitalism as inevitable. This was the prism through which American policy makers viewed not merely Soviet conquests in eastern Europe, but the activities of all communists throughout the world.

The decisive episode for US foreign policy came in 1947 and arose from the civil war taking place in Greece between local communists and royalists. Up to this point, Britain had been backing the royalists in an attempt to prevent the emergence of the first communist government in western Europe. Britain, however, was bankrupt and informed the United States that it could no longer sustain its effort. It also had to withdraw support from Turkey, which was coming under pressure from its Soviet neighbour.

President Truman, and his secretary of state, Dean Acheson, decided that the time had come to confront the Soviet threat. They had been primed for a new policy by the ideas of an American diplomat in Moscow, George Kennan. In February 1946, Kennan had sent a long, secret telegram to Washington, giving his analysis of the nature of Soviet aggression. The following year, Kennan, using the pseudonym 'X', published his views in an article entitled 'The sources of Soviet Conduct'. Kennan believed that the Soviet Union was inherently aggressive for a number of reasons, including its ideology and its sense of national insecurity. Although he did not believe that the Soviets had any immediate plans to go to war with the West, they would, he argued, try to exert pressure whenever and wherever the opportunity presented itself. They must, therefore, 'be contained by the adroit and vigilant application of counter-force at a series of constantly shifting geographical and political points.' Thus, the policy of containment was born. Truman decided in 1947 that Greece and Turkey were the places to begin application of the doctrine.

The Truman administration was ready to transform the United States into the 'world's policeman', yet such a change, involving global responsibilities and entanglements, went against the grain of a century-and-a-half of American foreign policy tradition. The president therefore faced the task of convincing the American people and a Congress controlled by the opposition Republican party, that such a new departure was necessary and in the best interests of the United States. At a meeting with congressional leaders in February 1947, Truman and Acheson argued that it was imperative to stop communism in Greece and Turkey, before the 'infection' spread through the entire Middle East and Europe. The leading Republican foreign-policy spokesman,

Senator Arthur Vanderberg, agreed, but reportedly told Truman that if he wanted to get aid for Greece and Turkey from Congress, he would have to 'scare hell out of the American people'.

In his speech before Congress, on 12 March 1947, President Truman tried to do just that. Describing the sources of world tensions and conflict in simplistic but stirring terms, Truman declared: 'I believe that it must be the policy of the United States to support free peoples who are resisting attempted subjugation by armed minorities or by outside pressures.' While Truman was only asking for $400 million to help Greece and Turkey, his speech placed no geographical limits on his pledge to resist communism. Containment in Greece and Turkey, then, was merely the first step toward a policy of global containment.

As we saw in Part II, a broad consensus quickly developed behind the policy of containment or 'the Truman doctrine', as it was sometimes called. Despite disagreements over specific aspects of policy, the politicians, media and people of the United States shared the belief first, that Soviet communism and its allies posed a mortal threat to the non-communist world, including the United States; and secondly, that this justified American intervention in all corners of the globe, no matter how distant from the United States or how costly in American resources. Even after the reassessment that followed the defeat in Vietnam, it was only a few years before many in America believed that a new or second cold war was necessary to preserve American values, security and influence.

Unsurprisingly, then, the four decades of commitment to global anticommunism had a considerable impact upon the way in which American foreign policy was formulated. We now turn, therefore, to an examination of how foreign policy has been made in the United States, particularly since the end of the Second World War.

The foreign policy-making process

The transformation in US foreign policy wrought by the onset of the Cold War called into being the modern foreign policy-making process. The Constitution of 1787 had indicated the broad powers of the president and Congress in this field. It was, however, only when foreign policy assumed the scale and importance that it did in the cold war, that a massive and elaborate set of arrangements was needed to serve the nation's new global crusade.

The constitutional framework

In keeping with its overall strategy, the Constitution of 1787 divided the power to make foreign policy between the president and the Congress (see Box 22.5). Thus, while the president was made responsible for the negotiation of treaties with foreign nations, they must be approved by a two-thirds majority of the Senate, (Article II, Section 2(ii)). And while the president is commander-in-chief of the armed forces, only Congress has the power to declare war (Article II, Section 2(i) and Article I, Section

Box 22.5

The separation of powers in foreign policy

Constitutional powers of the president

- Commander-in-chief of the armed forces
- To make treaties
- To nominate ambassadors and top foreign policy makers, e.g. the secretary of state
- To 'receive' representatives of foreign governments

Constitutional powers of the Congress

- To declare war
- To ratify or reject treaties
- To confirm or reject ambassadorial and government nominees
- To 'raise and support' armies

8(i), respectively). Thus the great constitutional scholar Edward Corwin described this sharing of power as 'an invitation to struggle for the privilege of directing American foreign policy' (1957, p. 171).

Growth of presidential power in foreign policy

It is clear beyond doubt that, today, the president has predominant power in the foreign policy making process. This does not mean that the president's power is absolute or that its pre-eminence is bound to continue. Indeed, as we shall see, the end of the cold war and other global developments have undoubtedly diminished the power of the presidency in foreign affairs.

Nevertheless, the presidency has distinct advantages over other policy makers, especially Congress, and some of these are traceable to the original constitutional design. For example, the president (and vice-president), as the only office-holder chosen by a national electorate, can lay claim to be the main political embodiment of the nation. Moreover, arising from his explicit powers to conduct day-to-day relations with other nations, and his more general status as chief executive, the president was clearly intended to perform the role that we now call 'head of state'.

It is also the case that the different structures of the presidency and Congress make the White House, rather than Capitol Hill, the more natural home for foreign policy making. Foreign policy decisions often require a measure of secrecy, specialised knowledge, cohesion and the ability to act decisively. All these characteristics play to the strengths of the executive branch rather than a Congress composed of 535 autonomous and often parochial individuals, whose deliberations are conducted largely in public. If, as is often asserted, foreign policy making is inherently authoritarian, then the presidency is the American governmental institution that comes closest to fitting the bill. However, as we shall see, it would be unwise to overstate the abilities of the presidency in this respect. The point here is that the presidency is *relatively* superior to the Congress in its ability to conduct foreign policy.

Nevertheless, the modern predominance of the presidency in foreign policy owes more to historical developments than it does to constitutional logic. In particular, the onset of the cold war transformed both the quantitative and qualitative dimensions of American foreign policy making.

Quantitatively, the cold war, with its commitment to global containment, simply required a vast increase in the foreign policy and war making capacity of the US government. As well as generating an enormous growth in the foreign policy making establishment, it also called into existence a permanent standing army of unprecedented proportions peaking in 1968 at the height of the Vietnam War (see Box 22.6).

Given the president's roles as chief executive and commander-in-chief, both these developments occurred within the executive branch of government, with a concomitant increase in presidential power. In other words, the cold war enhanced the constitutional powers of the president by bringing to the fore his responsibilities as commander-in-chief and head of the foreign policy making bureaucracy.

The cold war as crisis

The cold war was a permanent crisis in American foreign policy because it constituted a continuing threat to national security. It was, moreover, a crisis that could lead to nuclear war at any given moment. In such a climate of fear and danger, American foreign policy underwent a *qualitative*, as well as quantitative, change. Now it became unwise, perhaps even foolhardy and unpatriotic, to challenge presidential predomin-

---

Box 22.6

US armed forces, selected years 1950–93

Thousand personnel

Year	Army	Navy	Marines	Air Force	Total
1950	593	381	74	411	1,459
1955	1,109	661	205	960	2,935
1960	873	617	171	815	2,475
1968	1,570	764	307	905	3,546
1975	784	535	196	613	2,128
1980	777	527	188	558	2,051
1985	781	571	198	602	2,151
1990	732	579	197	535	2,044
1993	572	510	178	444	1,705

Source: Bureau of the Census, 1996, p. 357

ance in foreign policy. This did not mean that presidential conduct of foreign policy was beyond criticism, but at no point until the failure in Vietnam did Congress attempt to wrest a significant measure of foreign policy making power from the president.

This was true even when explicit powers of Congress were involved. For example, although Congress alone possesses the power to declare war, it was content to allow the president to initiate wars, as well as less significant military actions, without its approval. Thus, neither President Truman (Korea) nor President Johnson (Vietnam) sought or obtained a declaration of war from Congress.

By the early 1970s, some believed that such developments in foreign policy making powers had helped to create an 'imperial presidency' (Schlesinger, 1973). According to this view, presidential power was now more akin to that wielded by an emperor than an elected chief executive in a democracy. If so, however, it must be said that Congress had willingly acceded to the surrender of much of the substance of its constitutional powers. In the climate of the cold war and the foreign policy consensus it produced, Congress was content to trust to the superior resources and judgement of the president in matters of foreign policy.

As we saw in Part II, the Vietnam War did mark something of a turning point in presidential–congressional relations in foreign policy making. Nevertheless, it remains the case today that there is simply no alternative to presidential leadership in conducting foreign affairs. Congress may take a closer interest in foreign policy and frustrate the president more than before; interest groups and public opinion may also be more influential with the increase in 'intermestic issues' (see below). The president, however, is uniquely able to give direction and vigour to US foreign policy. To a considerable extent, this is owing to the fact that he sits at the apex of a vast network of foreign policy making bureaucracies.

The foreign policy-making establishment

Until the cold war, the United States government had made do with relatively few foreign policy making institutions and personnel. The State Department, whose main responsibility is diplomacy, was created in the early days of the new Constitution in 1789, as was the Department of War. In 1798, a Department of the Navy was added, but there was no further growth in specifically foreign policy-making institutions until the cold war.

In 1947, Congress passed the National Security Act. This created a Department of Defense, combining the previous War and Navy departments and adding a new military service, the Air Force, the National Security Council and the Central Intelligence Agency (CIA). Together with the State Department and the President himself, these three institutional products of the cold war have dominated American foreign policy making over the past half-century.

Let us look briefly at each of these five main players.

The president

The character and interests of the individual president can go a long way in explaining the substance and management of American foreign policy in any given period. Some presidents are far more interested in foreign policy than domestic policy. In recent times, Presidents Nixon and Bush stand out as 'foreign policy presidents', while Presidents Johnson and Clinton at least attempted to devote their main energies to domestic rather than foreign policy. One of the results of Nixon's deep interest in international politics was that he took personal charge of foreign policy, deliberately appointing 'weak' secretaries of State and defense and relying instead for advice on his national security adviser, Henry Kissinger.

Other factors than the president's predilections may determine the extent to which he concentrates upon foreign policy. Up to a point, for example, it is true that Republican presidents may have a greater propensity to concentrate upon foreign policy than Democrats, because they do not share the latter's commitment to the creative use of governmental power to improve society at home. This was particularly true of President George Bush, for example.

On the other hand, Democrat presidents have often been forced by circumstances beyond their control to devote considerable time to foreign policy, as was the case with President Truman and the cold war, and President Johnson and Vietnam. Even President Clinton, elected in part because of a backlash against his predecessor's perceived neglect of domestic policy, quickly found himself under attack for devoting insufficient time to America's world role.

It has also been argued that presidents have been drawn into greater involvement in foreign policy because, in comparison with domestic policy, they are less constrained by Congress. This gives presidents more scope for initiative and action and, hence, a better chance of attaining their policy objectives (Wildavsky, 1975). To some extent, however, this explanation has been undermined by a more assertive Congress in the wake of the disastrous 'presidential war' in Vietnam.

Furthermore, in an increasingly interdependent world, the dividing line between domestic and foreign policy has become blurred. For example, when President Carter imposed a ban on grain sales to the Soviet Union, as punishment for the latter's 1979 invasion of Afghanistan, he did not foresee the impact this would have on America's grain farmers. So badly hit were they by the loss of income from these sales, that they prevailed upon the arch anticommunist Ronald Reagan to drop the ban when he replaced Carter in the White House.

Thus, it has become common today to talk of 'intermestic' issues and policies – issues with significant implications for both international and domestic politics. As we saw in Chapter 15, Congress will always try to assert its power against the president when the domestic – and therefore intermestic – policy at issue is concerned with the immediate self-interest of the American electorate.

Such is the importance of foreign policy to the United States today, that no president can afford to neglect or delegate responsibility for it to others without running great risks, for not only are American economic and security interests closely bound up with events in the wider world, but also American prestige is easily tarnished by foreign policy mishaps. In varying degrees, the presidencies of Lyndon B. Johnson (Vietnam), Jimmy Carter (the Iran hostage crisis), Ronald Reagan (the Iran–Contra scandal) and Bill Clinton (the failed intervention in Somalia) were all damaged by foreign policy failures.

Box 22.●●

The Helms–Burton Act: Congress makes foreign policy

Following the downing of two American planes by Cuban forces, large majorities in the House and Senate passed the Helms–Burton or Cuban Liberty and Solidarity Act in March 1996. The Act strengthened existing economic sanctions against Cuba, and contained several measures designed to dissuade foreign companies from investing in the island. The United States has been an active opponent of the communist regime in Cuba since Fidel Castro came to power in 1959, and the end of the cold war has not led to any substantial change in its position. Sponsors of the Helms–Burton bill argued that it would put additional pressure on Castro by further isolating the country economically, but its opponents claimed that the legislation would be both difficult to implement and detrimental to American goals. Eight dissenters in the House International Relations Committee described it as an 'extreme bill that damages US national interest'.

Congressional initiatives of this type often meet with such criticisms, and Congress is generally considered to be ill-equipped to deal with foreign affairs. All of the factors which have restricted the ability of Congress to perform its legislative functions have been regarded as even more of a handicap with respect to foreign policy. It is argued that its parochial outlook restricts the interest of its members in foreign policy issues, whilst its fragmented structures and defective legislative tools limit its ability to have a substantial impact on policy. Even on the occasions when Congress has acted decisively, its efforts have frequently been criticised for either overly restricting executive leeway, or ignoring the wider implications of policy. In short, Congress has been seen to lack both the incentives and means to make coherent foreign policy, and in recognition of this fact, many members have traditionally deferred to the policy preferences of the presidency.

The end of the cold war, the onset of divided government, the increasing overlap between foreign and domestic policy, and the impact of the budget deficit, however, have led many observers to suggest that Congress is now more likely to become involved in the foreign policy process, which means that attempts to legislate foreign policy may become more frequent. The Helms–Burton Act therefore provides a useful opportunity to examine when Congress is likely to involve itself in foreign affairs, and to assess the results of its efforts.

Helms–Burton confirms that Congress does possess the incentives and means to make foreign policy under certain circumstances. The political strength of Cuban Americans provided electoral incentives for the new Republican majority to take action, as did the opportunity to put a Democrat president under pressure in an election year. Policy goals also motivated a number of law makers, many of whom have an intense personal interest in Cuba. Importantly, Congress also had the necessary tools to make policy in this area, because of its constitutional authority to regulate trade.

Despite confirming that Congress will make foreign policy under certain conditions, the Act also highlights congressional limitations. Critics argued that Congress was perhaps overly responsive to domestic pressure, and therefore ignored the wider implications of the policy. The most controversial element of the Act (Title III) allows US citizens who owned property nationalised by the Castro regime, to sue foreign companies who either buy or 'traffic' in it. Opponents have claimed that this provision violates international law, will clog up US courts, and may assist Castro by turning the US into a scapegoat for Cuba's economic problems. The provision has also antagonised a number of America's trading partners, including Canada, Mexico and the European Union.

Another section of the law (Title II) sets out the conditions under which the president can assist a post-Castro government. Opponents argued that by laying out in rigid terms when and how the president can intervene, Title II may prevent US intervention during a crucial period of political transition in Cuba. This demonstrates the problems of using legislation to lay down future policy, as it may prove inflexible and restrictive.

The Helms–Burton Act, therefore, raises many questions about the results of congressional activism in foreign policy. On the one hand, it has led to a drawn-out dispute with some of America's trading partners, suggesting that criticisms of legislative short-sightedness were valid, and it is unclear what effect the Act will have on the Cuban economy. On the other, the legislation has proved more flexible than some predicted. Its supporters accepted that the president should be able to suspend the rights of claimants to litigate under Title III, if he deemed it to be in the national interest. By using this authority, Clinton has avoided many of the logistical problems associated with implementing this provision. He also used the suspension to gain an agreement with the European Union to link further investment in Cuba to its record on human rights. Despite its many flaws, the law has therefore had some effect by indirect means, prompting the president to act on the issue of foreign investment in Cuba, and providing him with a bargaining chip to use in negotiations with America's allies.

Helms–Burton therefore demonstrates the potential for legislation to be effective, if only in an indirect manner, but its many limitations also highlight the problems associated with such attempts. Irrespective of the advantages and disadvantages, it is also a clear indication of the fact that Congress will, under certain circumstances, attempt to make foreign policy.

Contributed by Peter J. Ingram, Keele University

The State Department

Of all the agencies and federal bureaucracies engaged in foreign policy making, the State Department is, in principle at least, the first among equals (Kegley and Wittkopf, 1987, p. 372). It was created in 1789 for the purpose of conducting US foreign relations. This means, among other things, representing the United States through its embassies and consulates throughout the world; negotiating treaties with other nations; acting as a repository of specialised knowledge about other nations and developments in international politics; and drawing up policy recommendations for the president and then, perhaps, implementing them. It also houses bodies with specialised functions, such as the Agency for International Development (AID), the Arms Control and Disarmament Agency (ACDA) and the United States Information Agency (USIA).

Apart from the relatively small number of top political appointees to the State Department, its thousands of employees are true bureaucrats: that is, career specialists who tend to spend their whole working life in the department. As such, the State Department can reasonably claim to be the most authoritative and wide-ranging source of information and perspective upon the world outside the United States.

For all that, the State Department is not only a much-criticised body, but some presidents have regarded it as untrustworthy and consequently have preferred to rely on others as their principal source of policy advice. There are various reasons for this distrust, although in many ways they all relate to the same point: that the president and his personal advisers believe that State Department personnel are out of tune with domestic political perspectives and demands. For example, the State Department is variously accused of being elitist, arrogant and indecisive, with a marked tendency to 'go native' when stationed abroad.

There is undoubtedly something in all of these criticisms. For example, there is a 'subculture' within the State Department that leads Foreign Service officers to believe that outsiders cannot understand the subtleties of their craft and should, therefore, bow to their superiors (Kegley and Wittkopf, 1987, p. 376).

It is also true that the State Department can appear indecisive and prone to fudging issues. Within Washington, it has few natural allies to help buttress a strong position on any given issue: it lacks the Defense Department's enthusiastic backing by the arms industry, the CIA's patriotic appeal or the president's electoral support. Outside the United States, the State Department has to maintain good relations with a couple of hundred nations and international bodies. Compromise may often be the best way forward, given that a decisive stand may win friends only at the cost of making enemies (Hilsman, 1990, p. 194).

Nevertheless, these accusations are usually brought to bear when the White House fears that the State Department will not be sufficiently supportive of the administration's position, or when other policy-makers wish to undermine the department in order to advance their own policy agenda. Thus Republicans, in or out of office, tend to distrust Foggy Bottom (the area of Washington where the State Department is located), because they see it as dominated by the East Coast Liberal Establishment. In the 1950s, the populist demagogue senator Joe McCarthy made accusations of State Department sympathy with communism central to his more general witch-hunt for subversives; and as noted above, President Nixon quite deliberately subordinated the State Department to his national security adviser, Henry Kissinger, because he assumed from the start that the department was likely to view his administration with something less than enthusiasm. Yet even liberal Democrats have been critical ·and unwilling to rely upon the State Department: President Kennedy once described it as 'a bowl of jelly' because of its inability to be decisive and dynamic (Hilsman, 1990, p. 194). Even John Kenneth Galbraith, a quintessential member of the East Coast Liberal Establishment, complained to Kennedy that the ethos at the State

Department was 'that God had ordained some individuals to make foreign policy without undue interference from presidents and politicians,' (Kegley and Wittkopf, 1987, p. 381).

Ultimately, the bureaucrats of Foggy Bottom are too independent in their judgements and too distant from the White House inner circle to dominate, or even lead, foreign policy making.

The Department of Defense

Often referred to as the Pentagon, because of the shape of the building in which it is housed, the Department of Defense is a powerful player in the foreign policy making process. It has the vital task of ensuring that the United States is militarily capable of defending the nation and its interests, both at home and abroad. This responsibility immediately confers great power and influence upon the Pentagon, particularly during a prolonged period of international crisis, such as the cold war.

However, there is more to the power of the Defense Department than its formal role, important though that is. The key to Pentagon power in Washington is the enormous defence budget (see Box 22.7).

The massive expenditures by the Defense Department attracts two major sources of support: arms manufacturers and the Congress. The arms industry is eager to support Pentagon requests for ever larger and more sophisticated military hardware, since it stands to gain massive profits from supplying these weapons. Arms industry interest groups therefore have a strong incentive to lobby both Congress and the president for the increased militarisation of US foreign policy. Worse still, it is sometimes alleged,

---

Box 22.7

Federal expenditures on national defence, selected years 1960–96

Year	Total expenditure $bn	Percentage of federal outlays	Percentage of GDP
1960	53.5	52.2	9.5
1965	56.3	42.8	7.5
1970	90.4	41.8	8.3
1975	103.1	26.0	5.7
1980	155.2	22.7	5.1
1985	279.0	26.7	6.4
1990	328.4	23.9	5.5
1996 (est.)	303.3	16.9	3.6

Source: Bureau of the Census, 1996, p. 351

the Defense Department and the arms industry deliberately exaggerate the threat posed to the United States by foreign countries in order to justify ever higher expenditure on armaments.

The second group which has a strong interest in sustaining high defence expenditures is Congress, or more specifically, those members of Congress whose districts and states benefit from arms industry employment and the presence of military bases and installations. By voting for military programmes and distributing the benefits amongst their constituents, members of key congressional appropriations and armed services committees can obtain a substantial boost to their chances of re-election.

By the late 1950s, there was increasing concern about this relationship between the Defense Department and the arms industry and its implications for both foreign policy and the nation's budget. In his farewell address of 1961, President Eisenhower felt moved to warn the country about the military–industrial complex (see Box 22.8).

Eisenhower's address inspired a debate, which continues to this day, over the validity of the 'military–industrial complex thesis'. While the more extravagant notions of a conspiracy by the military–industrial complex to control foreign policy lack convincing proof, there is considerable evidence to support the essence of the thesis. Kegley and Wittkopf, for example, writing from the perspective of the mid-1980s, listed seven basic reasons for lending it 'substantial credibility':

1. Employment in America is significantly dependent upon military expenditures: one in ten jobs is directly or indirectly linked to such expenditures.

2. Congress has at times gone beyond presidential requests in voting defence appropriations. It is argued, for example, that Congress was responsible for increasing expenditures on the MX missile from roughly $150 million to $600 million per missile in the 1980s.

Box 22.8

The military–industrial complex

Extract from President Eisenhower's farewell address, 1961

'This conjunction of an immense Military Establishment and a large arms industry is new in the American experience. The total influence – economic, political, even spiritual – is felt in every city, every statehouse, every office of the Federal Government. We recognize the imperative need for this development. Yet we must not fail to comprehend its grave implications. Our toil, resources, and livelihood are all involved. So is the very structure of our society.

In the councils of government we must guard against the acquisition of unwarranted influence, whether sought or unsought, by the military–industrial complex. The potential for the disastrous rise of misplaced power exists and will persist.

We must never let the weight of this combination endanger our liberties or democratic processes ...'

3. Profits in the defence industries are higher than those in most other manufacturing sectors. This is owing in no small measure to the generous manner in which the Pentagon treats defence contractors: for example, handing out millions of dollars in grants and interest-free loans, repaying the costs of even unsuccessful bids, and allowing tax deferments on profits.

4. Sheer extravagance, waste and fraud: for example, the Lockheed corporation being paid $640 for an airplane toilet seat.

5. Universities, which should keep a critical eye on the military–industrial complex, have in fact been seduced by it: they accept millions of dollars' worth of research contracts connected to defence expenditures.

6. Defence industry consulting firms and think-tanks have mushroomed over the years. Most employ former members of the Defense Department and the Armed Forces, and their advice to their former employers usually supports the wishes of the military–industrial complex.

7. Defence expenditures have remained a priority, even during times of massive budget deficits (see again Box 22.7) (Kegley and Wittkopf, 1987, pp. 271–4).

In some respects, this evidence is not at all surprising. American politics generally gives considerable scope to coalitions of interest – bureaucracies, legislators, pressure groups – to work for public policies that reward themselves in various ways. In other words, we should expect the military–industrial complex to be self-promoting in the same way that farmers, the Department of Agriculture and members of Congress from farm states, are self-promoting over agriculture policy. However, given the huge sums of money involved and the absolutely critical nature of defence policy, such comparisons are of limited validity.

It should be noted that the evidence above does not suggest that the military–industrial complex routinely advocates war as a solution to foreign policy problems. While the rhetoric of some may be hawkish or worse, neither the civilians who head the Defense Department nor the military commanders they manage are always the strongest proponents of war. For example, it was General Matthew Ridgeway who did most to persuade President Eisenhower not to intervene in Vietnam in 1954. Thus,

> In general the military–industrial complex favours a high degree of preparedness and 'tough' foreign policies, but they shy away from entering wars, especially limited ones. Once committed to fighting, however, the military will usually oppose any settlement short of victory.
>
> (Hilsman, 1990, pp. 310–11)

The power of the Defense Department (and its allies) to assert itself in the foreign policy making process is then considerable, though by no means absolute. And as with all the players in this particular game, it must compete with others for influence over policy.

The National Security Council

The National Security Council (NSC) was created by Congress in 1947 to 'advise the President with respect to the integration of domestic, foreign, and military policies relating to national security' (Kegley and Wittkopf, 1987, p. 345). In other words, the creation of the NSC was recognition of the fact that, with the advent of the cold war, the United States needed better co-ordination of foreign policy. In line with these objectives, Congress required that the president, vice-president, secretaries of state and defense, the chairman of the joint chiefs of staff and the director of the CIA must all be members of the NSC. It also created a new post of 'special assistant to the president for national security affairs', often referred to more briefly as the national security adviser (NSA). From time to time, different presidents have added others to the membership of the NSC, for example, the Treasury secretary and the attorney-general.

In its early years, the NSC made some important contributions to American foreign policy, none more so than National Security Council Memorandum 68 (NSC-68) of 1950. This review of US global strategy in the light of the Soviet acquisition of the atomic bomb and the Chinese Communist revolution in 1949, established the broad thrust of American cold war policy for the next twenty years. Most importantly, NSC-68 instigated a massive militarisation of US global strategy, involving an increase in the military budget from $14 billion in 1950 to $53 billion in 1952 (McCormick, 1989, p. 94).

Yet it took some time before the NSC and, in particular, the national security adviser, achieved top status in the foreign policy making establishment. As part of the Executive Office of the President, the precise role and influence of the NSC and NSA is left to the discretion of the president. Truman, for example, originally did not attend NSC meetings and during both his and Eisenhower's administrations, the national security adviser was little more than 'a glorified clerk-secretary to the NSC, overseeing its agenda and following up the president's decisions' (Hilsman, 1990, p. 134).

Moreover, under Eisenhower, the NSC was heavily criticised for failing to produce rational policy choices for the president, owing to its tendency to promote incoherent compromises between the preferences of the Council's members (Kegley and Wittkopf, 1987, p. 347). While Kennedy put the NSC and NSA to better use by requiring clear policy alternatives to be submitted to him, it was not until the Nixon administration that they achieved great prominence. This was owing mostly to Nixon's determination to reduce the power of the foreign policy making bureaucracy, particularly the State Department, and to his appointment of Henry Kissinger as national security adviser.

Kissinger increased the number of professional staff on the NSC to about 150, compared with a dozen or so under Kennedy (Hilsman, 1990, p. 137). This allowed him to produce policy recommendations that rivalled those of State and Defense. Combined with the fact that President Nixon simply placed greater trust in Kissinger than in any other adviser, this ensured that the NSC and Kissinger became the principal source of foreign policy advice to the president.

President Carter's NSA, Zbigniew Brzezinksi, was also a principal presidential adviser. Even if he never achieved the prominence of Henry Kissinger, Brzezinski was a rival for influence with Secretary of State Cyrus Vance. Indeed, when the NSA and the secretary of state clashed once again in 1980 over the plan to use commandos to release the American hostages held in Iran, it was Vance, not Brzezinski, who resigned his office.

Since the Carter years, the roles of the NSC and NSA have changed again. President Reagan had no less than six different national security advisers during his eight years in office. Reagan also adopted a 'hands-off' approach to the operation of the NSC, something which helped to allow the Iran–Contra scandal to develop.

Using the NSC as their base, Reagan's third and fourth NSAs, Robert McFarlane and John Poindexter, together with a marine officer attached to the NSC, Colonel Oliver North, employed illegal methods in an attempt to solve two of the president's major foreign policy problems. The first was to secure the release of American hostages being held by Iranian-backed groups in the Lebanon. The second was to provide money for the American-backed counter-revolutionaries in Nicaragua, the *Contras*. Congress had cut off all funds for the *Contras* in 1984, but the Reagan administration was determined to find ways of keeping them supplied.

North secured approval from his NSC superiors to sell arms to Iran in the hope that they, in turn, would use their influence to secure the release of the hostages in the Lebanon. This was done, in spite of the administration's oft-stated policy of not selling arms to Iran. The profits from the sales were then illegally diverted to the *Contras*, in defiance of the Congressional ban.

Such activity was far from what Congress had in mind when it created the NSC in 1947. Thus, the Iran–Contra scandal demonstrates that the NSC can play whatever role the president wishes or allows it to. Equally, the role of the national security adviser may vary from glorified clerk, to chief architect of foreign policy, to overseer of covert policy operations.

The Central Intelligence Agency

The mere mention of covert activities immediately calls to mind the CIA. Yet although the CIA has rightly become synonymous with American espionage and secret operations in foreign countries, it was not created with these in mind. Rather, as its name suggests, it was founded in 1947 to provide better intelligence about the world that the United States was now seeking to lead. In particular, there was a perceived need to co-ordinate the intelligence gathered by the different intelligence agencies of various government departments. It was made responsible to the NSC and thereby to the president.

Almost immediately after its creation, however, the CIA acquired responsibility for covert operations. This was prompted by the communist coup in Czechoslovakia in 1948, after which President Truman authorised the CIA to undertake sabotage and subversion in such a way that, if these operations were discovered, the United States government could plausibly deny responsibility for them (LaFeber, 1989, p. 459).

Since then, the CIA has become the most notorious and controversial institution in American government. It has claimed, or been charged with, responsibility for such acts as interfering in Italian elections since 1948 in order to ensure victory for the Christian Democrats against their Communist opponents; installing the Shah on the Iranian throne in 1953; planning and executing the bungled Bay of Pigs invasion of Cuba in 1961; devising Operation Mongoose, a series of assassination attempts on President Fidel Castro of Cuba in the 1960s; running a secret army and war in Laos during President Johnson's administration; helping to organise the murder and overthrow of the elected Marxist president of Chile, Salvador Allende, in 1973; blowing up oil terminals and other targets in Nicaragua during the Reagan administration; and, of course, carrying on a continuous campaign of espionage and clandestine operations against the Soviet Union and its eastern European allies.

However, the notoriety of the CIA and the extensiveness of its activities, should not be confused with the question of its power in the foreign policy making process. True, the CIA has some of the characteristics of a 'state within a state' (Hilsman, 1990, p. 201). Its need for secrecy, both in intelligence gathering and covert operations, has meant that it is left largely free of normal outside scrutiny and accountability. The 1970s witnessed several attempts to make the CIA more accountable: for example, the Hughes–Ryan Amendment of 1974 required covert operations to be reported to certain congressional committees, and new Senate and House Intelligence Committees were established to exercise more systematic oversight.

On the whole, however, these reforms have made little significant difference to the secrecy which shrouds the CIA. The simple fact is that, once the need for an organisation such as the CIA is accepted, it is somewhat counterproductive to expose its activities to a Congress where secrets are difficult to keep, still less to the public, media and other nations. Indeed, even Congress recognised this overriding need for secrecy, by partially reversing its earlier reforms in the 1980s (Dumbrell, 1990, pp. 150–1).

On the other hand, it must be remembered that the CIA is responsible to and under the control of the president. For all the mythology of the CIA as a 'cowboy operation', engaging in reckless and unauthorised secret operations, it is more accurate to see it as a highly professional bureaucratic agency acting at the behest of the president or the NSC. Indeed, this was the conclusion reached by the Pike Committee of the House of Representatives, after it had examined CIA covert operations between 1965 and 1975: 'the CIA, far from being out of control, has been utterly responsible to the instructions of the President and the Special Assistant to the President for National Security Affairs' (Dumbrell, 1990, p. 153). Or again, the 1987 Tower Commission investigation into the Iran–Contra scandal concluded that, 'The Central Intelligence Agency acted as a willing accomplice, but the NSC called the shots' (Ragsdale, 1993, p. 17). Thus, while the accountability of the CIA is a legitimate source of concern in a democracy, condemnation of its 'objectionable' activities is more properly addressed to the White House.

Other administration influences

The State Department, the Pentagon, the National Security Council and the CIA – these are the major bodies within the administration which are specifically dedicated to helping the president to decide American foreign policy. There are, however, others who wield influence in this sphere, particularly where the economic interests of the United States loom large on the horizon.

The Department of the Treasury is an influential force in foreign policy making, particularly in relation to factors which affect the value of the US dollar. Specific responsibilities include exchange rates, tariffs and the balance of trade. The Treasury secretary also acts as the US governor of the International Monetary Fund (IMF), the World Bank and other regional international financial agencies.

Situated within the White House, the Office of the United States Trade Representative has a growing influence, in line with the increasing economic interdependence of the United States and the outside world. The major responsibility of the US trade representative is to negotiate trading agreements with other nations, most famously the General Agreement on Tariffs and Trade (GATT).

Other bodies which can influence foreign policy include the Department of Commerce, whose main responsibilities lie in implementing trade policy, and the Departments of Agriculture and Labor, whose domestic 'clients' find themselves increasingly affected by the impact of international events and agreements.

Bureaucratic politics

It can be seen then that the president is not short of advice on foreign policy from within his administration. Yet such an array of potential influences can be a problem, as well as a source of strength. Ideally, the American foreign policy making bureaucracies should produce rational and effective decisions. Together, they should be able to gather and interpret information stemming from the outside world; analyse and discuss different policy alternatives in response to it; decide upon and implement the policy that maximises the chances of fulfilling the broad goals of US foreign policy. In this 'rational actor' model of policy making, specialised bureaucracies are dedicated to providing the president with all he needs to make the correct decision, as defined by American national interests.

No policy-making machinery works perfectly and we should not expect all American foreign policies to be wholly rational, either in conception or implementation. Nevertheless, many scholars view rationality-centred models as fundamentally flawed. Instead, they posit theories of foreign policy making that emphasise self-serving competition between the different bureaucratic organisations that have some say in the formulation and execution of foreign policy (Dumbrell, 1990, chapter 2; Kegley and Wittkopf, 1987, chapter 13; Hilsman, 1990, part 1). For the sake of simplicity, these theories will be subsumed here under the heading 'bureaucratic politics'.

Bureaucratic politics sees the president less as someone who commands the agencies created to serve him, and more as someone who struggles to manage and contain their separate wills. Each organisation is parochial in outlook and reluctant to entertain novel or rival ideas; it also seeks to expand its own influence and range of responsibilities. The negative results of these characteristics are several: organisations compete rather than co-operate with each other. This in turn leads to dogmatic and exaggerated viewpoints being expressed, in the hope that this will maximise the organisation's power when the inevitable bargaining begins between different agencies. As a result, foreign policy decisions are often incremental and insufficiently responsive to new circumstances, as well as being a 'fudge'.

Perhaps worse still, agencies which have substantially lost out when the president finally makes a decision, will quite deliberately seek to thwart its implementation. Perhaps the most famous example of this emerged during the Cuban Missile Crisis of 1962. The previous year, President Kennedy had ordered the State Department to remove American Jupiter missiles from Turkey. The missiles were not only obsolete, but placed so close to the border with the Soviet Union, that they were unnecessarily provocative. The Turkish government, however, wanted the missiles to remain and the State Department, therefore, thought it best to ignore Kennedy's order and leave the missiles in place. Thus, at the height of the missile crisis the following year, Kennedy was surprised and angry to find the Soviets able to make the reasonable point that Soviet missiles in Cuba were no more threatening than American missiles in Turkey.

Presidents, then, cannot simply assume that 'their' bureaucracy will be co-operative. They must act forcefully, decisively and even punitively when dealing with the bureaucracy, if they wish to see their foreign policy goals achieved.

Non-governmental influences

Public opinion

It is generally agreed that public opinion is much less influential in the making of foreign policy that it is in domestic policy. From the perspective of most members of the public, foreign policy is figuratively and literally distant from their everyday lives. Unlike the core domestic issues of employment, the cost of living and education, for example, most foreign policy issues make little impact upon the consciousness of the average American.

This general indifference to foreign policy issues leads to low levels of knowledge about them. Time and again, studies have shown the American public to be woefully ignorant of contemporary and recent foreign affairs, even those which have received considerable coverage in the media. Thus in 1985, only 63 per cent of those surveyed knew that the United States had supported *South* Vietnam during the Vietnam War; 44 per cent did not know that the United States and the Soviet Union were allies during the Second World War, with 28 per cent believing the two had been at war with each other; and in 1983, 47 per cent did not know whether the Reagan administration supported or opposed the Sandinista government of Nicaragua (Kegley and Wittkopf, 1987, p. 288).

This public lack of concern has some significant consequences for the foreign policy making process. Most importantly, it helps to make that process one dominated by elites, thereby reinforcing its intrinsically authoritarian nature. In this respect, foreign affairs provides a major exception to the democratic openness of the general American policy-making process.

The combination of public ignorance and elite control and secrecy makes public opinion on foreign policy malleable, if not downright manipulable, and the main beneficiary of this is unquestionably the president. As the personification of the national identity and pride, the president is generally trusted by the public to act in the nation's best interest. This frequently means that the public accepts whatever policy decisions the president makes and supports them enthusiastically. In times of crisis, this is termed the 'rally round the flag' phenomenon. In short, most of the time, presidents lead, rather than follow, public opinion on foreign policy.

However, none of the above should be read as meaning that public opinion is irrelevant to foreign policy. In the first place, presidents do pay considerable attention to public opinion poll data on foreign affairs. Any politically astute president will wish to know 'the outer limits of consent' of the American public, if only in order to gauge the possible repercussions of any decision he takes.

Secondly, under certain circumstances, the public *does* take a strong interest in foreign policy and may have clear policy preferences. This is particularly true where US military action is being contemplated and has become more critical in the wake of the defeat in Vietnam (see Part II). Although the precise role of American public opinion in the Vietnam War is still hotly debated, there is no doubt that the slowly dwindling public support for the war did limit the options of both Presidents Johnson and Nixon. The dominant issue for the public was less the morality of US intervention in Vietnam, than its human costs in terms of US casualties (Mueller, 1971).

Thus, since Vietnam, presidents have been wary of adopting policies that might lead to intensive and prolonged military engagement. Moreover, presidents are now less willing to intervene militarily unless they have overwhelming evidence that success is probable. The American public is still very tolerant of presidential policies it deems successful, as the invasions of Grenada (1983) and Panama (1991) demonstrate. On the other hand, so concerned are presidents now about hostile public reaction to US war casualties, that they tend to disengage quickly when losses are incurred. This was the prime reason for the withdrawal of US troops from the Lebanon under President Reagan in 1984 and from Somalia under President Clinton in 1994.

Public opinion can also be aroused by other issues which connect close to home, such as trade agreements or immigration policy. In addition, media portrayal of human suffering caused by war can also put pressure on government to act.

Nevertheless, it remains the case that, exceptions aside, the American public knows or cares little about foreign policy; rarely determines its votes in elections by reference to foreign affairs; and rarely makes irresistible demands on either the Congress or the president over foreign policy issues.

Pressure groups

Unlike the general public, certain pressure groups know and care about foreign policy. For example, both business and labour groups take a close interest in trade policy because it directly affects the profits and jobs of their members. Thus, business groups lobbied strongly in favour of President Clinton's decisions in 1994 to lift the trade embargo on Vietnam and to renew China's 'most favoured nation' trading status. In both cases, American business saw great opportunities for investments and profits in these former enemy nations, and hence countered pressures from those who wished to punish China for its human rights abuses and Vietnam for its alleged foot-dragging over the fate of US prisoners of war.

As well as groups motivated primarily by economic interests, there are those which can be termed 'ethnic lobbies' (Dumbrell, 1990, p. 176). Among the most prominent of these are the American Israeli Public Affairs Committee (AIPAC) and the Irish Northern Aid Committee (NORAID).

AIPAC is often credited with a major role in maintaining strong American commitment to Israel and, indeed, there is some evidence to support that (Dumbrell, 1990, p. 176). On the other hand, it is easy to overestimate AIPAC's influence. First, it is often the case that AIPAC is pushing at an open door: the United States has had important ideological and strategic interests in sustaining a strong Israel and its policy might well have been the same without the lobbying by AIPAC. Moreover, the US government has ignored AIPAC when its interests have so dictated: for example, in 1983, President Reagan pushed ahead with his policy of selling advanced warning aircraft (AWACs) to Saudi Arabia, despite a considerable lobbying effort against it by AIPAC.

Other ethnic lobbies have far less influence than AIPAC. Although presidents may pay lip-service to such groups, and offer them symbolic victories in the hope of cultivating their electoral support, they would not allow ethnic pressure groups to determine the nation's policy. Thus, while NORAID and the wider Irish lobby may have been instrumental in persuading President Clinton to allow Gerry Adams of Sinn Fein into the country in 1994, the Clinton administration continues to support the broad approach of the British government on the status of Ulster.

As with public opinion, then, the influence of pressure groups over foreign policy is more limited than in the domestic sphere. Thus, 'Interest groups may be effective on certain special issues. More often, however, it would appear that the foreign policy process is relatively immune from direct pressure by interest groups' (Kegley and Wittkopf, 1987, p. 280).

Foreign policy in the 1990s

We have seen that in the era of the cold war, the United States developed a new international grand strategy – containment – and a new foreign policy establishment – the National Security state. But what of these two pillars of American foreign policy now that the cold war which engendered them has disappeared?

It is difficult to exaggerate the fundamental changes in international politics represented by the end of the cold war. Gone is the rigid, bipolar confrontation that sucked in virtually every nation on earth and threatened them with nuclear annihilation. Gone is the conflict that obliged the United States to maintain a massive standing army and a network of alliances all around the globe. Gone is the need to engage in proxy wars in places like Korea, Vietnam, Afghanistan, the Horn of Africa and Central America. Above all, gone is the great superpower rival, the Soviet Union, with its ideology and economy in ruins. Truly, the end of the cold war is an occasion for rejoicing in the United States. As the sole remaining superpower, the United States has regained the unequalled military status that it enjoyed briefly at the end of the Second World War.

For all its peerless military power, however, the United States has struggled somewhat to define its role and ambitions in the post cold war era. Partly this is an inevitable consequence of the uncertainties that followed from the collapse of the cold war system. For all its terrible aspects, the cold war provided a relatively stable and predictable framework in which to formulate American foreign policy; and not least, the cold war produced an unusually long period of peace between the two major powers, when compared with earlier eras in international relations (Kegley, 1991). The United States now has to deal with a world in which it has no major enemy and no simple yardstick for evaluating and responding to the challenges and conflicts in the outside world. To a considerable extent, therefore, the United States finds itself in uncharted waters and it is understandable that it needs time to set its compass.

However, there is more to America's international dilemmas than the novelty of the situation it finds itself in. Calculations of what international strategy the United States *should* adopt cannot be made without a simultaneous consideration of what role it is *capable* of adopting: and here we come to the question of the *relative decline* of the United States.

It has been apparent since the 1970s that the United States has been in relative economic decline: that is, while still the world's greatest economy, the United States has been losing ground to other countries in matters such as its economic productivity and its share of world trade. Nothing symbolises this more than the fact that, since the 1980s, the United States has had an annual trade deficit with Japan averaging around $50 billion a year. Moreover, during the same period, the United States passed from being the world's greatest *creditor* nation to the world's greatest *debtor* nation. Although the years of the Clinton presidency witnessed a sustained recovery in the economy, the fact remains that the United States has to fight harder than ever before to maintain its economic status.

This relative decline of American economic power inevitably has repercussions for its global political and military strategies. Indeed, it has even been considered possible that the United States might go the way of previous hegemonic nations by falling prey to 'imperial overstretch': this occurs when a nation's global interests and obligations are too great for its economy to sustain (Kennedy, 1988, p. 515). Just as Great Britain and others before it failed to reconcile the gap between overseas demands and domestic capacity, so too the United States may lose its hegemonic status. As we saw in Part II, there were already signs of such imperial overstretch during the Vietnam War.

Furthermore, in the years since Vietnam, other domestic issues have increasingly come to demand attention. While the longstanding problem of an annual federal budget deficit averaging well over $200 billion is now solved, it has helped to generate a continuing preoccupation with low taxation and lean government expenditures. In addition, with the disappearance of the international communist threat, the public tends to believe that domestic programmes should be given priority over at least some kinds of foreign policy expenditures. In short, there are far fewer funds available today for defence and foreign affairs than there were during the cold war. Indeed, the 1997 congressional appropriation for international affairs was less than half it was in 1984, in part because 'the cold war used to provide a fiscal fig-leaf for what would now be immediately denounced as profligacy' (Naim, 1997/8, p. 38).

In short, as the world's sole superpower, the United States has greater opportunities, choices and responsibilities as a result of the end of the cold war. Simultaneously, however, the resources available to be devoted to this international agenda are diminishing as a result of relative economic decline and the rival claim to resources of domestic crises. Thus it is ironic that 'as the external environment has widened the range of choices for the United States, its domestic situation has narrowed them' (Art and Brown, 1993, p. 2).

The phenomenon of globalisation has brought additional problems for American foreign policy makers. The opening up of international trade and competition has created greater freedom for non-governmental organisations (NGOs). These include multinational corporations with agendas that may differ from that of the United States government. Moreover, such corporations may have direct access to foreign governments eager for inward investment and thus the US government may simply be bypassed (Naim, 1997/8, p. 39).

In the light of these new challenges and constraints, it is hardly surprising that the first post cold war administrations of Presidents Bush and Clinton have struggled to articulate a new vision of America's role in the world.

The new world order

For a brief period in the early 1990s, it seemed that the United States had found the solution to its foreign policy dilemmas. President Bush, flushed with the success of the American-led multinational force in expelling Iraq from Kuwait, announced the arrival of a new world order (see Box 22.9). He and other foreign policy makers set out

---

Box 22.9

The new world order

'You see, as the cold war drew to an end we saw the possibilities of a new order in which nations worked together to promote peace and prosperity. I'm not talking here of a blueprint that will govern the conduct of nations or some supernational structure or institution. The new world order does not mean surrendering our national sovereignty or forfeiting our interests. It really describes a responsibility imposed by our successes. It refers to new ways of working with other nations to deter aggression and to achieve stability, to achieve prosperity and, above all, to achieve peace.

It springs from hopes for a world based on a shared commitment among nations large and small, to a set of principles that undergird our relations. Peaceful settlements of disputes, solidarity against aggression, reduced and controlled arsenals, and just treatment of all peoples.

This order, this ability to work together got its first real test in the Gulf war. For the first time, a regional conflict – the aggression against Kuwait – did not serve as a proxy for superpower confrontation. For the first time, the UN Security Council, free from the clash of cold war ideologies, functioned as its designers intended – a force for conflict resolution and collective security ...

The new world order really is a tool for addressing a new world of possibilities. The order gains its mission and shape not just from shared interests, but from shared ideals. And the ideals that [have] spawned new freedoms throughout the world have received their boldest and clearest expression in our great country, the United States. Never before has the world looked more to the American example. Never before have so many millions drawn hope from the American idea. And the reason is simple: Unlike any other nation in the world, as Americans, we enjoy profound and mysterious bonds of affection and idealism. We feel our deep connections to community, to family, to our faiths.

But what defines this nation? What makes us Americans is not our ties to a piece of territory, or bonds of blood. What makes us Americans is our allegiance to an idea that all people everywhere must be free. This idea is as old and endur- ing as this nation itself – as deeply rooted, and what we are as a promise implicit to all the world in the words of our own Declaration of Independence.'

(President George Bush, Remarks at Maxwell Air Force Base War College, Alabama, 13 April 1991)

'Twice before in this century after world wars, US presidents have led efforts to create an international mechanism for collective resistance to aggression – first, President Wilson and the League of Nations and then President Roosevelt and the United Nations. Yet, now, with the end of the cold war, in the Persian Gulf for the first time an international body – the UN – has played the role dreamed of by its founders – orchestrating and sanctioning collective resistance to an aggressor. The potential for the UN to continue to play this role, and the new willingness of many nations to contribute money and military units, are the foun- dation stones of a new era of international security – a new world order charac- terized by a growing consensus that force cannot be used to settle disputes and that when the consensus is broken, the burdens and responsibilities are shared by many nations.

The new world order is neither a *Pax Americana* nor a euphemism for the US as a world policeman. It is simply an attempt to deter aggression – and to resist if necessary – through the collective and voluntary action of the international community.'

(Robert Gates, Deputy National Security Adviser, Address to the American Newspaper Publishers' Association, Vancouver, 7 May 1991)

a vision of a global order in which the United States continued to offer leadership, but other nations assumed a greater responsibility for the human and economic costs of keeping the peace and maintaining stability.

For President Bush, the new world order was founded upon 'universal' values of capitalism, liberal democracy, free trade and the renunciation of aggression as an instrument of foreign policy. Nations which transgressed the new order by using force should expect to be met by the collective force of the international community, especially the United Nations. The United States would offer military leadership to the international community, but would not attempt to turn this into a *Pax Americana*.

The Bush concept of a new world order struck some familiar themes in American foreign policy. Thus, American values were, in fact, universal values and the United States a political and social model to which other nations aspire. The idealist tradition in American foreign policy also appears in the advocacy of collective security and the implicit assertion (made explicit in Gates' address: see Box 22.9), that US policy is geared to the good of the international community as a whole, rather than the entrenchment of American power.

However, 'Even the most favourable reading of the diplomacy and rhetoric of the "new world order" project could not fail to ignore its central affirmation of the primacy of American global power' (McGrew, 1994, p. 220). Yet if the new world order suggested an America still hankering to play the role of world policeman, US foreign policy under President Clinton had a significantly different emphasis.

The Clinton administration came in for sustained criticism for its alleged failure to define a coherent agenda and strategy for US foreign policy (Haas, 1997; Naim, 1997/98). While such critics acknowledge that President Clinton had to contend with new constraints, they underestimate the extent to which he did in fact possess both a vision and a foreign policy for the changed world of the 1990s. As Michael Cox has argued:

> Clinton (like Ronald Reagan) assumed office with a fairly clear view of the world and the sort of policies he would have to pursue in order to enhance American power. Of course, unlike his neo-conservative predecessor, his main interest was not in the evil empire but in the world economy; and the principal means he hoped to use to mobilize Americans behind his policies was not anti-communism but raw economic self-interest.
>
> (Cox, 1995, pp. 22–3)

Logically enough, therefore, Clinton's emphasis was upon strengthening American power through restoring its economic competiveness. This in turn involved both domestic policy, such as bringing the budget deficit under control, and foreign policy, such as the formation of a free-trade zone in the western hemisphere in the form of the North American Free Trade Agreement Treaty (NAFTA) of 1993.

It is important to stress, however, that this new emphasis on geopolitics does not entail a wholesale retreat from American military leadership. As events in the former Yugoslavia demonstrated in the 1990s, even an economically powerful European Union possessed neither the will nor the means to promote and sustain a resolution to civil war. The Dayton Agreement on Bosnia could never have worked without American leadership. Furthermore, the renewed crisis with Iraq in 1998 over its alleged store of weapons of mass destruction produced a convincing demonstration of America's readiness to use its military might to impose its will, even when most of its allies in the Gulf War refused to support its stand.

It is true that the United States has not developed a comprehensive global strategy to replace containment, but then there is no clear agreement that one is necessary. The precise direction of American foreign policy in the post cold war context is thus still a matter of debate. Three basic schools of thought can be discerned: American primacy, neo-isolationism and new internationalism (McGrew, 1994, pp. 226–34).

Those who advocate American primacy are motivated by a mixture of realism and idealism. They believe that the United States must maintain and enhance its preponderance of power in the world in order to shape it in ways that favour American economic interests and political values. To do otherwise risks allowing a hostile world environment to develop, perhaps forcing the United States once again to rely upon military might to secure its prosperity, and even its democracy, at home. Along with these powerful elements of realism goes the belief that it is America's historic mission to universalise its political and economic values.

Neo-isolationists also blend realism with idealism in their desire to return to the foreign policy principles and practices of the early republic. They advocate 'selective engagement' with the outside world, guided in this by economic self-interest. They see the end of the cold war as an opportunity to focus attention once again on domestic matters, rebuilding a strong, prosperous and stable society at home.

New internationalism views neither neo-isolationism nor primacy as a realistic option. On the one hand, nations are too interdependent to permit successful partial withdrawal from the world, and power is too fragmented to allow the United States to reassert its primacy for very long. Instead, the United States must pursue multilateralism, offering leadership to, but not attempting to dominate, institutions such as the United Nations. Within the global framework of peace and stability delivered by such multilateralism, the United States can concentrate on renewing its economic strength. With military force no longer a viable means of achieving international ends, and economic power widely dispersed, the new internationalism in effect calls for an end to any American pretence to be a superpower. Instead, the new internationalism envisions the United States as one of many nations enjoying peace, security and free trade and offering international leadership based economic strength and moral standing.

There are clearly areas of overlap between these three schools of thought. Most importantly, perhaps, they all stress the need to strengthen America's economic position. However, it is still not clear which blend of realism and idealism the United States will take forward as its foreign policy for the twenty-first century. There has always been a measure of ambivalence in America's engagement with the outside world and that appears unlikely to change. Nevertheless, it is hard to imagine the United States adjusting easily to the status of 'just another nation' in an increasingly interdependent world. For in the oft-quoted words of the American Revolutionary, Thomas Paine, the United States still considers itself to be 'the last best hope of mankind', and reluctantly or otherwise, many nations still look to the United States for leadership in a world where order is a fragile commodity.

 ## Summary

American foreign policy has always been a blend of realism and idealism and of internationalist and isolationist tendencies. Nevertheless, there has been an almost inexorable rise of the United States to the status of world power and then lone superpower. Parallel with this has occurred a gradual rise in the importance of the presidency within the foreign policy making process. While the current context of international relations and domestic politics suggests something of a diminution in the power of both, it is unlikely that either the United States or the presidency will lose its centrality in global and American politics.

Topics for discussion

1. What do we understand by the terms *idealism* and *realism* in the context of American foreign policy?

2. Why did the United States rise to become a Superpower?

3. What are the major constraints upon presidential power in foreign policy making?

4. What are the main foreign policy dilemmas facing the United States today?

5. Is isolationism a myth in the history of American foreign policy?

Further reading

There are many useful introductory texts on the making of American foreign policy, but among the best are J. Dumbrell, *The Making of US Foreign Policy* (Manchester: Manchester University Press, 1990), and C. Kegley and E. Wittkopf, *American Foreign Policy: Pattern and process* (5th edn, Basingstoke: Macmillan, 1996). A more sophisticated treatment can be found in R. Hilsman, *The Politics of Policy Making in Defence and Foreign Affairs* (2nd edn, Hemel Hempstead: Prentice Hall, 1990). A very readable history of US foreign policy is W. LaFeber, *The American Age: US foreign policy at home and abroad since 1750* (London: Norton, 1989). For an assessment of post cold war foreign policy, see M. Cox, *US Foreign Policy after the Cold War: Superpower without a mission?* (London: Pinter, 1995).

References

Art, R. and Brown, S., 1993, *US Foreign Policy: The search for a new role* (Basingstoke: Macmillan)

Commager, H., 1974, 'Myths and realities in American foreign policy', in *Defeat of America: Presidential power and the national character*, ed. H. Commager (New York: Touchstone)

Corwin, E. (1957) *The President: office and powers* (New York: New York University Press)

Cox, M., 1995, *US Foreign Policy after the Cold War: Superpower without a mission?* (London: Pinter)

Dumbrell, J., 1990, *The Making of US Foreign Policy* (Manchester: Manchester University Press)

Graebner, N., 1984, *America as a world power: A realist appraisal from Wilson to Reagan* (Wilmington: Scholarly Resources)

Haas, R., 1997, 'Fatal distraction: Bill Clinton's foreign policy', *Foreign Policy*, vol. 108, Fall, pp. 112–123

Hilsman, R., 1990, *Politics of Policy Making in Defence and Foreign Affairs* (2nd edn, Hemel Hempstead: Prentice Hall)

Hunt, M., 1987, *Ideology and US Foreign Policy*, (New Haven: Yale University)

Kegley, C., ed., 1991, *The Long Postwar Peace* (London: Harper Collins)

Kegley, C. and Wittkopf, E., 1987, *American Foreign Policy: Pattern and process* (5th edn, Basingstoke: Macmillan)

Kennedy, P., 1988, *The Rise and Fall of the Great Powers* (London: Unwin Hyman)

LaFeber, W., 1989, *The American Age: United States foreign policy at home and abroad since 1750* (London: Norton)

McCormick, T., 1989, *America's Half-century: United States foreign policy in the cold war*, (Baltimore: The Johns Hopkins University Press)

McGrew, A., 1994, 'The end of the American century?', in *The United States in the Twentieth Century: Empire*, ed. A. McGrew (London: Hodder & Stoughton)

Mueller, J., 1971, 'Trends in popular support for the wars in Korea and Vietnam', *American Political Science Review*, vol. 65, pp. 358–75

Naim, M., 1997/98, 'Clinton's foreign policy: a victim of globalization?', *Foreign Policy*, vol. 109, Winter, pp.34–45

Ragsdale, L., 1993, *Presidential Politics* (Boston: Houghton Mifflin)

Schlesinger, A., 1973, *The Imperial Presidency* (Boston: Houghton Mifflin)

US Bureau of the Census, 1996, *Statistical Abstract of the United States* (116th edn, Washington DC)

Wildavsky, A., 1975, 'The two presidencies', in *Perspectives on the Presidency*, ed. A. Wildavsky (Boston: Little, Brown)

Action of Second Continental Congress, July 4, 1776

The unanimous Declaration of the thirteen United States of America

WHEN in the Course of human Events, it becomes necessary for one People to dissolve the Political Bands which have connected them with another, and to assume among the Powers of the Earth, the separate and equal Station to which the Laws of Nature and of Nature's God entitle them, a decent Respect to the Opinions of Mankind requires that they should declare the causes which impel them to the Separation.

WE hold these Truths to be self-evident, that all Men are created equal, that they are endowed by their Creator with certain unalienable Rights, that among these are Life, Liberty and the Pursuit of Happiness – That to secure these Rights, Governments are instituted among Men, deriving their just Powers from the Consent of the Governed, that whenever any Form of Government becomes destructive of these Ends, it is the Right of the People to alter or to abolish it, and to institute new Government, laying its Foundation on such Principles, and organizing its Powers in such Form, as to them shall seem most likely to effect their Safety and Happiness. Prudence, indeed, will dictate that Governments long established should not be changed for light and transient Causes; and accordingly all Experience hath shewn, that Mankind are more disposed to suffer, while Evils are sufferable, than to right themselves by abolishing the Forms to which they are accustomed. But when a long Train of Abuses and Usurpations, pursuing invariably the same Object, evinces a Design to reduce them under absolute Despotism, it is their Right, it is their Duty, to throw off such Government, and to provide new Guards for their future Security. Such has been the patient Sufferance of these Colonies; and such is now the Necessity which constrains them to alter their former Systems of Government. The History of the present King of Great-Britain is a History of repeated Injuries and Usurpations, all having in direct Object the Establishment of an absolute Tyranny over these States. To prove this, let Facts be submitted to a candid World.

HE has refused his Assent to Laws, the most wholesome and necessary for the public Good.

HE has forbidden his Governors to pass Laws of immediate and pressing Importance, unless suspended in their Operation till his Assent should be obtained; and when so suspended, he has utterly neglected to attend to them.

HE has refused to pass other Laws for the Accommodation of large Districts of People, unless those People would relinquish the Right of Representation in the Legislature, a Right inestimable to them, and formidable to Tyrants only.

HE has called together Legislative Bodies at Places unusual, uncomfortable, and distant from the Depository of their public Records, for the sole Purpose of fatiguing them into Compliance with his Measures.

HE has dissolved Representative Houses repeatedly, for opposing with manly Firmness his Invasions on the Rights of the People.

HE has refused for a long Time, after such Dissolutions, to cause others to be elected; whereby the Legislative Powers, incapable of the Annihilation, have returned to the People at large for their exercise; the State remaining in the mean time exposed to all the Dangers of Invasion from without, and the Convulsions within.

HE has endeavoured to prevent the Population of these States; for that Purpose obstructing the Laws for Naturalization of Foreigners; refusing to pass others to encourage their Migrations hither, and raising the Conditions of new Appropriations of Lands.

HE has obstructed the Administration of Justice, by refusing his Assent to Laws for establishing Judiciary Powers.

HE has made Judges dependent on his Will alone, for the Tenure of their Offices, and the Amount and Payment of their Salaries.

HE has erected a Multitude of new Offices, and sent hither Swarms of Officers to harrass our People, and eat out their Substance.

HE has kept among us, in Times of Peace, Standing Armies, without the consent of our Legislatures.

HE has affected to render the Military independent of and superior to the Civil Power.

HE has combined with others to subject us to a Jurisdiction foreign to our Constitution, and unacknowledged by our Laws; giving his Assent to their Acts of pretended Legislation:

FOR quartering large Bodies of Armed Troops among us;

FOR protecting them, by a mock Trial, from Punishment for any Murders which they should commit on the Inhabitants of these States;

FOR cutting off our Trade with all Parts of the World;

FOR imposing Taxes on us without our Consent;

FOR depriving us, in many Cases, of the Benefits of Trial by Jury;

FOR transporting us beyond Seas to be tried for pretended Offences;

FOR abolishing the free System of English Laws in a neighbouring Province, establishing therein an arbitrary Government, and enlarging its Boundaries, so as to render it at once an Example and fit Instrument for introducing the same absolute Rules into these Colonies;

FOR taking away our Charters, abolishing our most valuable Laws, and altering fundamentally the Forms of our Governments;

FOR suspending our own Legislatures, and declaring themselves invested with Power to legislate for us in all Cases whatsoever.

HE has abdicated Government here, by declaring us out of his Protection and waging War against us.

HE has plundered our Seas, ravaged our Coasts, burnt our Towns, and destroyed the Lives of our People.

HE is, at this Time, transporting large Armies of foreign Mercenaries to compleat the Works of Death, Desolation, and Tyranny, already begun with circumstances of Cruelty and Perfidy, scarcely paralleled in the most barbarous Ages, and totally unworthy the Head of a civilized Nation.

HE has constrained our fellow Citizens taken Captive on the high Seas to bear Arms against their Country, to become the Executioners of their Friends and Brethren, or to fall themselves by their Hands.

HE has excited domestic Insurrections amongst us, and has endeavoured to bring on the Inhabitants of our Frontiers, the merciless Indian Savages, whose known Rule of Warfare, is an undistinguished Destruction, of all Ages, Sexes and Conditions.

IN every stage of these Oppressions we have Petitioned for Redress in the most humble Terms: Our repeated Petitions have been answered only by repeated Injury. A Prince, whose Character is thus marked by every act which may define a Tyrant, is unfit to be the Ruler of a free People.

NOR have we been wanting in Attentions to our British Brethren. We have warned them from Time to Time of Attempts by their Legislature to extend an unwarrantable Jurisdiction over us. We have reminded them of the Circumstances of our Emigration and Settlement here. We have appealed to their native Justice and Magnanimity, and we have conjured them by the Ties of our common Kindred to disavow these Usurpations, which, would inevitably interrupt our Connections and Correspondence. They too have been deaf to the Voice of Justice and of Consanguinity. We must, therefore, acquiesce in the Necessity, which denounces our Separation, and hold them, as we hold the rest of Mankind, Enemies in War, in Peace, Friends.

WE, therefore, the Representatives of the UNITED STATES OF AMERICA, in GENERAL CONGRESS, Assembled, appealing to the Supreme Judge of the World for the Rectitude of our Intentions, do, in the Name, and by Authority of the good People of these Colonies, solemnly Publish and Declare, That these United Colonies are, and of Right ought to be, FREE AND INDEPENDENT STATES; that they are absolved from all Allegiance to the British Crown, and that all political Connection between them and the State of Great-Britain, is and ought to be totally dissolved; and that as FREE AND INDEPENDENT STATES, they have full Power to levy War, conclude Peace, contract Alliances, establish Commerce, and to do all other Acts and Things which INDEPENDENT STATES may of right do. And for the support of this Declaration, with a firm Reliance on the Protection of divine Providence, we mutually pledge to each other our Lives, our Fortunes, and our sacred Honor.

John Hancock.

GEORGIA, Button Gwinnett, Lyman Hall, Geo. Walton.
NORTH-CAROLINA, Wm. Hooper, Joseph Hewes, John Penn.
SOUTH-CAROLINA, Edward Rutledge, Thos Heyward, junr., Thomas Lynch, junr., Arthur Middleton.

MARYLAND, Samuel Chase, Wm. Paca, Thos. Stone, Charles Carroll, of Carrollton.

VIRGINIA, George Wythe, Richard Henry Lee, Ths. Jefferson, Benja. Harrison, Thos. Nelson, jr., Francis Lightfoot Lee, Carter Braxton.

PENNSYLVANIA, Robt. Morris, Benjamin Rush, Benja. Franklin, John Morton, Geo. Clymer, Jas. Smith, Geo. Taylor, James Wilson, Geo. Ross.

DELAWARE, Caesar Rodney, Geo. Read.

NEW-YORK, Wm. Floyd, Phil. Livingston, Frank Lewis, Lewis Morris.

NEW-JERSEY, Richd. Stockton, Jno. Witherspoon, Fras. Hopkinson, John Hart, Abra. Clark.

NEW-HAMPSHIRE, Josiah Bartlett, Wm. Whipple, Matthew Thornton.

MASSACHUSETTS-BAY, Saml. Adams, John Adams, Robt. Treat Paine, Elbridge Gerry.

RHODE-ISLAND AND PROVIDENCE, C. Step. Hopkins, William Ellery.

CONNECTICUT, Roger Sherman, Saml. Huntington, Wm. Williams, Oliver Wolcott.

The Constitution of the United States

We the people of the United States, in order to form a more perfect union, establish justice, insure domestic tranquility, provide for the common defense, promote the general welfare, and secure the blessings of liberty to ourselves and our posterity, do ordain and establish this Constitution for the United States of America.

Article I

Section 1. All legislative powers herein granted shall be vested in a Congress of the United States, which shall consist of a Senate and House of Representatives.

Section 2. The House of Representatives shall be composed of members chosen every second year by the people of the several states, and the electors in each state shall have the qualifications requisite for electors of the most numerous branch of the state legislature.

No person shall be a Representative who shall not have attained to the age of twenty five years, and been seven years a citizen of the United States, and who shall not, when elected, be an inhabitant of that state in which he shall be chosen.

Representatives and direct taxes shall be apportioned among the several states which may be included within this union, according to their respective numbers, which shall be determined by adding to the whole number of free persons, including those bound to service for a term of years, and excluding Indians not taxed, three fifths of all other Persons. The actual Enumeration shall be made within three years after the first meeting of the Congress of the United States, and within every subsequent term of ten years, in such manner as they shall by law direct. The number of Representatives shall not exceed one for every thirty thousand, but each state shall have at least one Representative; and until such enumeration shall be made, the state of New Hampshire shall be entitled to chuse three, Massachusetts eight, Rhode Island and Providence Plantations one, Connecticut five, New York six, New Jersey four, Pennsylvania eight, Delaware one, Maryland six, Virginia ten,

North Carolina five, South Carolina five, and Georgia three.

When vacancies happen in the Representation from any state, the executive authority thereof shall issue writs of election to fill such vacancies.

The House of Representatives shall choose their speaker and other officers; and shall have the sole power of impeachment.

Section 3. The Senate of the United States shall be composed of two Senators from each state, chosen by the legislature thereof, for six years; and each Senator shall have one vote.

Immediately after they shall be assembled in consequence of the first election, they shall be divided as equally as may be into three classes. The seats of the Senators of the first class shall be vacated at the expiration of the second year, of the second class at the expiration of the fourth year, and the third class at the expiration of the sixth year, so that one third may be chosen every second year; and if vacancies happen by resignation, or otherwise, during the recess of the legislature of any state, the executive thereof may make temporary appointments until the next meeting of the legislature, which shall then fill such vacancies.

No person shall be a Senator who shall not have attained to the age of thirty years, and been nine years a citizen of the United States and who shall not, when elected, be an inhabitant of that state for which he shall be chosen.

The Vice President of the United States shall be President of the Senate, but shall have no vote, unless they be equally divided.

The Senate shall choose their other officers, and also a President pro tempore, in the absence of the Vice President, or when he shall exercise the office of President of the United States.

The Senate shall have the sole power to try all impeachments. When sitting for that purpose, they shall be on oath or affirmation. When the President of the United States is tried, the Chief Justice shall preside: And no person shall be convicted without the concurrence of two thirds of the members present.

Judgment in cases of impeachment shall not extend further than to removal from office, and disqualification to hold and enjoy any office of honor, trust or profit under the United States: but the party convicted shall nevertheless be liable and subject to indictment, trial, judgment and punishment, according to law.

Section 4. The times, places and manner of holding elections for Senators and Representatives, shall be prescribed in each state by the legislature thereof; but the Congress may at any time by law make or alter such regulations, except as to the places of choosing Senators.

The Congress shall assemble at least once in every year, and such meeting shall be on the first Monday in December, unless they shall by law appoint a different day.

Section 5. Each House shall be the judge of the elections, returns and qualifications of its own members, and a majority of each shall constitute a quorum to do business; but a smaller number may adjourn from day to day, and may be authorized to compel the attendance of absent members, in such manner, and under such penalties as each House may provide.

Each House may determine the rules of its proceedings, punish its members for disorderly behavior, and, with the concurrence of two thirds, expel a member.

Each House shall keep a journal of its proceedings, and from time to time publish the same, excepting such parts as may in their judgment require secrecy; and the yeas and nays of the members of either House on any question shall, at the desire of one fifth of those present, be entered on the journal.

Neither House, during the session of Congress, shall, without the consent of the other, adjourn for more than three days, nor to any other place than that in which the two Houses shall be sitting.

Section 6. The Senators and Representatives shall receive a compensation for their services, to be ascertained by law, and paid out of the treasury of the United States. They shall in all cases, except treason, felony and breach of the peace, be privileged from arrest during their attendance at the session of their respective Houses, and in going to and returning from the same; and for any speech or debate in either House, they shall not be questioned in any other place.

No Senator or Representative shall, during the time for which he was elected, be appointed to any civil office under the authority of the United States, which shall have been created, or the emoluments whereof shall have been increased during such time: and no person holding any office under the United States, shall be a member of either House during his continuance in office.

Section 7. All bills for raising revenue shall originate in the House of Representatives; but the Senate may propose or concur with amendments as on other Bills.

Every bill which shall have passed the House of Representatives and the Senate, shall, before it become a law, be presented to the President of the United States; if he approve he shall sign it, but if not he shall return it, with his objections to that House in which it shall have originated, who shall enter the objections at large on their journal, and proceed to reconsider it. If after such reconsideration two thirds of that House shall agree to pass the bill, it shall be sent, together with the objections, to the other House, by which it shall likewise be reconsidered, and if approved by two thirds of that House, it shall become a law. But in all such cases the votes of both Houses shall be determined by yeas and nays, and the names of the persons voting for and against the bill shall be entered on the journal of each House respectively. If any bill shall not be returned by the President within ten days (Sundays excepted) after it shall have been presented to him, the same shall be a law, in like manner as if he had signed it, unless the Congress by their adjournment prevent its return, in which case it shall not be a law.

Every order, resolution, or vote to which the concurrence of the Senate and House of Representatives may be necessary (except on a question of adjournment) shall be presented to the President of the United States; and before the same shall take effect, shall be approved by him, or being disapproved by him, shall be repassed by two thirds of the Senate and House of Representatives, according to the rules and limitations prescribed in the case of a bill.

Section 8. The Congress shall have power to lay and collect taxes, duties, imposts and excises, to pay the debts and provide for the common defense and general welfare of the United States; but all duties, imposts and excises shall be uniform throughout the United States;

To borrow money on the credit of the United States;

To regulate commerce with foreign nations, and among the several states, and with the Indian tribes;

To establish a uniform rule of naturalization, and uniform laws on the subject of bankruptcies throughout the United States;

To coin money, regulate the value thereof, and of foreign coin, and fix the standard of weights and measures;

To provide for the punishment of counterfeiting the securities and current coin of the United States;

To establish post offices and post roads;

To promote the progress of science and useful arts, by securing for limited times to authors and inventors the exclusive right to their respective writings and discoveries;

To constitute tribunals inferior to the Supreme Court;

To define and punish piracies and felonies committed on the high seas, and offenses against the law of nations;

To declare war, grant letters of marque and reprisal, and make rules concerning captures on land and water;

To raise and support armies, but no appropriation of money to that use shall be for a longer term than two years;

To provide and maintain a navy;

To make rules for the government and regulation of the land and naval forces;

To provide for calling forth the militia to execute the laws of the union, suppress insurrections and repel invasions;

To provide for organizing, arming, and disciplining, the militia, and for governing such part of them as may be employed in the service of the United States, reserving to the states respectively, the appointment of the officers, and the authority of training the militia according to the discipline prescribed by Congress;

To exercise exclusive legislation in all cases whatsoever, over such District (not exceeding ten miles square) as may, by cession of particular states, and the acceptance of Congress, become the seat of the government of the United States, and to exercise like authority over all places purchased by the consent of the legislature of the state in which the same shall be, for the erection of forts, magazines, arsenals, dockyards, and other needful buildings; – And

To make all laws which shall be necessary and proper for carrying into execution the foregoing powers, and all other powers vested by this Constitution in the government of the United States, or in any department or officer thereof.

Section 9. The migration or importation of such persons as any of the states now existing shall think proper to admit, shall not be prohibited by the Congress prior to the year one thousand eight hundred and eight, but a tax or duty may be imposed on such importation, not exceeding ten dollars for each person.

The privilege of the writ of habeas corpus shall not be suspended, unless when in cases of rebellion or invasion the public safety may require it.

No bill of attainder or ex post facto Law shall be passed.

No capitation, or other direct, tax shall be laid, unless in proportion to the census or enumeration herein before directed to be taken.

No tax or duty shall be laid on articles exported from any state.

No preference shall be given by any regulation of commerce or revenue to the ports of one state over those of another: nor shall vessels bound to, or from, one state, be obliged to enter, clear or pay duties in another.

No money shall be drawn from the treasury, but in consequence of appropriations made by law; and a regular statement and account of receipts and expenditures of all public money shall be published from time to time.

No title of nobility shall be granted by the United States: and no person holding any office of profit or trust under them, shall, without the consent of the Congress, accept of any present, emolument, office, or title, of any kind whatever, from any king, prince, or foreign state.

Section 10. No state shall enter into any treaty, alliance, or confederation; grant letters of marque and reprisal; coin money; emit bills of credit; make anything but gold and silver coin a tender in payment of debts; pass any bill of attainder, ex post facto law, or law impairing the obligation of contracts, or grant any title of nobility.

No state shall, without the consent of the Congress, lay any imposts or duties on imports or exports, except what may be absolutely necessary for executing it's inspection laws: and the net produce of all duties and imposts, laid by any state on imports or exports, shall be for the use of the treasury of the United States; and all such laws shall be subject to the revision and control of the Congress.

No state shall, without the consent of Congress, lay any duty of tonnage, keep troops, or ships of war in time of peace, enter into any agreement or compact with another state, or with a foreign power, or engage in war, unless actually invaded, or in such imminent danger as will not admit of delay.

Article II

Section 1. The executive power shall be vested in a President of the United States of America. He shall hold his office during the term of four years, and, together with the Vice President, chosen for the same term, be elected, as follows:

Each state shall appoint, in such manner as the Legislature thereof may direct, a number of electors, equal to the whole number of Senators and Representatives to which the State may be entitled in the Congress: but no Senator or Representative, or person holding an office of trust or profit under the United States, shall be appointed an elector. The electors shall meet in their respective states, and vote by ballot for two persons, of whom one at least shall not be an inhabitant of the same state with themselves. And they shall make a list of all the persons voted for, and of the number of votes for each; which list they shall sign and certify, and transmit sealed to the seat of the government of the United States, directed to the President of the Senate. The President of the Senate shall, in the presence of the Senate and House of Representatives, open all the certificates, and the votes shall then be counted. The person having the greatest number of votes shall be the President, if such number be a majority of the whole number of electors appointed; and if there be more than one who have such majority, and have an equal number of votes, then the House of Representatives shall immediately choose by ballot one of them for President; and if no person have a majority, then from the five highest on the list the said House shall in like manner choose the President. But in choosing the President, the votes shall be taken by States, the representation from each state having one vote; A quorum for this purpose shall consist of a member or members from two thirds of the states, and a majority of all the states shall be necessary to a choice. In every case, after the choice of the President, the person having the greatest number of votes of the electors shall be the Vice President. But if there should remain two or more who have equal votes, the Senate shall choose from them by ballot the Vice President.

The Congress may determine the time of choosing the electors, and the day on which they shall give their votes; which day shall be the same throughout the United States.

No person except a natural born citizen, or a citizen of the United States, at the time of the adoption of this Constitution, shall be eligible to the office of President; neither shall any person be eligible to that office who shall not have attained to the age of thirty five years, and been fourteen Years a resident within the United States.

In case of the removal of the President from office, or of his death, resignation, or inability to discharge the powers and duties of the said office, the same shall devolve on the Vice President, and the Congress may by law provide for the case of removal, death, resignation or inability, both of the President and Vice President, declaring what officer shall then act as President, and such officer shall act accordingly, until the disability be removed, or a President shall be elected.

The President shall, at stated times, receive for his services, a compensation, which shall neither be increased nor diminished during the period for which he shall have been elected, and he shall not receive within that period any other emolument from the United States, or any of them.

Before he enter on the execution of his office, he shall take the following oath or affirmation: – 'I do solemnly swear (or affirm) that I will faithfully execute the office of President of the United States, and will to the best of my ability, preserve, protect and defend the Constitution of the United States.'

Section 2. The President shall be commander in chief of the Army and Navy of the United States, and of the militia of the several states, when called into the actual service of the United States; he may require the opinion, in writing, of the principal officer in each of the executive departments, upon any subject relating to the duties of their respective offices, and he shall have power to grant reprieves and pardons for offenses against the United States, except in cases of impeachment.

He shall have power, by and with the advice and consent of the Senate, to make treaties, provided two thirds of the Senators present concur; and he shall nominate, and by and with the advice and consent of the Senate, shall appoint ambassadors, other public ministers and consuls, judges of the Supreme Court, and all other officers of the United States, whose appointments are not herein otherwise provided for, and which shall be established by law: but the Congress may by law vest the appointment of such inferior officers, as they think proper, in the President alone, in the courts of law, or in the heads of departments.

The President shall have power to fill up all vacancies that may happen during the recess of the Senate, by granting commissions which shall expire at the end of their next session.

Section 3. He shall from time to time give to the Congress information of the state of the union, and recommend to their consideration such measures as he shall judge necessary and expedient; he may, on extraordinary occasions, convene both Houses, or either of them, and in case of disagreement between them, with respect to the time of adjournment, he may adjourn them to such time as he shall think proper; he shall receive ambassadors and other public ministers; he shall take care that the laws be faithfully executed, and shall commission all the officers of the United States.

Section 4. The President, Vice President and all civil officers of the United States, shall be removed from office on impeachment for, and conviction of, treason, bribery, or other high crimes and misdemeanors.

Article III

Section 1. The judicial power of the United States, shall be vested in one Supreme Court, and in such inferior courts as the Congress may from time to time ordain and establish. The judges, both of the supreme and inferior courts, shall hold their offices during good behaviour, and shall, at stated times, receive for their services, a compensation, which shall not be diminished during their continuance in office.

Section 2. The judicial power shall extend to all cases, in law and equity, arising under this Constitution, the laws of the United States, and treaties made, or which shall be made, under their authority; – to all cases affecting ambassadors, other public ministers and consuls; – to all cases of admiralty and maritime jurisdiction; – to controversies to which the United States shall be a party; – to controversies between two or more states; – between a state and citizens of another state; – between citizens of different states; – between citizens of the same state claiming lands under grants of different states, and between a state, or the citizens thereof, and foreign states, citizens or subjects.

In all cases affecting ambassadors, other public ministers and consuls, and those in which a state shall be party, the Supreme Court shall have original jurisdiction. In all the other cases before mentioned, the Supreme Court shall have appellate jurisdiction, both as to law and fact, with such exceptions, and under such regulations as the Congress shall make.

The trial of all crimes, except in cases of impeachment, shall be by jury; and such trial shall be held in the state where the said crimes shall have been committed; but when not committed within any state, the trial shall be at such place or places as the Congress may by law have directed.

Section 3. Treason against the United States, shall consist only in levying war against them, or in adhering to their enemies, giving them aid and comfort. No person shall be convicted of treason unless on the testimony of two witnesses to the same overt act, or on confession in open court.

The Congress shall have power to declare the punishment of treason, but no attainder of treason shall work corruption of blood, or forfeiture except during the life of the person attainted.

Article IV

Section 1. Full faith and credit shall be given in each state to the public acts, records, and judicial proceedings of every other state. And the Congress may by general laws prescribe the manner in which such acts, records, and proceedings shall be proved, and the effect thereof.

Section 2. The citizens of each state shall be entitled to all privileges and immunities of citizens in the several states.

A person charged in any state with treason, felony, or other crime, who shall flee from justice, and be found in another state, shall on demand of the executive authority of the state from which he fled, be delivered up, to be removed to the state having jurisdiction of the crime.

No person held to service or labor in one state, under the laws thereof, escaping into another, shall, in consequence of any law or regulation therein, be discharged from such service or labor, but shall be delivered up on claim of the party to whom such service or labor may be due.

Section 3. New states may be admitted by the Congress into this union; but no new states shall be formed or erected within the jurisdiction of any other state; nor any state be formed by the junction of two or more states, or parts of states, without the consent of the legislatures of the states concerned as well as of the Congress.

The Congress shall have power to dispose of and make all needful rules and regulations respecting the territory or other property belonging to the United States; and nothing in this Constitution shall be so construed as to prejudice any claims of the United States, or of any particular state.

Section 4. The United States shall guarantee to every state in this union a republican form of government, and shall protect each of them against invasion; and on application of the legislature, or of the executive (when the legislature cannot be convened) against domestic violence.

Article V

The Congress, whenever two thirds of both houses shall deem it necessary, shall propose amendments to this Constitution, or, on the application of the legislatures of two thirds of the several states, shall call a convention for proposing amendments, which, in either case, shall be valid to all intents and purposes, as part of this Constitution, when ratified by the legislatures of three fourths of the several states, or by conventions in three fourths thereof, as the one or the other mode of ratification may be proposed by the Congress; provided that no amendment which may be made prior to the year one thousand eight hundred and eight shall in any manner affect the first and fourth clauses in the ninth section of the first article; and that no state, without its consent, shall be deprived of its equal suffrage in the Senate.

Article VI

All debts contracted and engagements entered into, before the adoption of this Constitution, shall be as valid against the United States under this Constitution, as under the Confederation.

This Constitution, and the laws of the United States which shall be made in pursuance thereof; and all treaties made, or which shall be made, under the authority of the United States, shall be the supreme law of the land; and the judges in every state shall be bound thereby, anything in the Constitution or laws of any State to the contrary notwithstanding.

The Senators and Representatives before mentioned, and the members of the several state legislatures, and all executive and judicial officers, both of the United States and of the several states, shall be bound by oath or affirmation, to support this Constitution; but no religious test shall ever be required as a qualification to any office or public trust under the United States.

Article VII

The ratification of the conventions of nine states, shall be sufficient for the establishment of this Constitution between the states so ratifying the same.

Done in convention by the unanimous consent of the states present the seventeenth day of September in the year of our Lord one thousand seven hundred and eighty seven and of the independence of the United States of America the twelfth. In witness whereof We have hereunto subscribed our Names,

G. Washington-Presidt. and deputy from Virginia
New Hampshire: John Langdon, Nicholas Gilman
Massachusetts: Nathaniel Gorham, Rufus King
Connecticut: Wm: Saml. Johnson, Roger Sherman
New York: Alexander Hamilton
New Jersey: Wil: Livingston, David Brearly, Wm. Paterson, Jona: Dayton
Pennsylvania: B. Franklin, Thomas Mifflin, Robt. Morris, Geo. Clymer, Thos. FitzSimons, Jared Ingersoll, James Wilson, Gouv Morris
Delaware: Geo: Read, Gunning Bedford jun, John Dickinson, Richard Bassett, Jaco: Broom
Maryland: James McHenry, Dan of St Thos. Jenifer, Danl Carroll
Virginia: John Blair–, James Madison Jr.
North Carolina: Wm. Blount, Richd. Dobbs Spaight, Hu Williamson
South Carolina: J. Rutledge, Charles Cotesworth Pinckney, Charles Pinckney, Pierce Butler
Georgia: William Few, Abr Baldwin

Amendment I

Congress shall make no law respecting an establishment of religion, or prohibiting the free exercise thereof; or abridging the freedom of speech, or of the press; or the right of the people peaceably to assemble, and to petition the government for a redress of grievances.

Amendment II

A well regulated militia, being necessary to the security of a free state, the right of the people to keep and bear arms, shall not be infringed.

Amendment III

No soldier shall, in time of peace be quartered in any house, without the consent of the owner, nor in time of war, but in a manner to be prescribed by law.

Amendment IV

The right of the people to be secure in their persons, houses, papers, and effects, against unreasonable searches and seizures, shall not be violated, and no warrants shall issue, but upon probable cause, supported by oath or affirmation, and particularly describing the place to be searched, and the persons or things to be seized.

Amendment V

No person shall be held to answer for a capital, or otherwise infamous crime, unless on a presentment or indictment of a grand jury, except in cases arising in the land or naval forces, or in the militia, when in actual service in time of war or public danger; nor shall any person be subject for the same offense to be twice put in jeopardy of life or limb; nor shall be compelled in any criminal case to be a witness against himself, nor be deprived of life, liberty, or property, without due process of law; nor shall private property be taken for public use, without just compensation.

Amendment VI

In all criminal prosecutions, the accused shall enjoy the right to a speedy and public trial, by an impartial jury of the state and district wherein the crime shall have been committed, which district shall have been previously ascertained by law, and to be informed of the nature and cause of the accusation; to be confronted with the witnesses against him; to have compulsory process for obtaining witnesses in his favor, and to have the assistance of counsel for his defense.

Amendment VII

In suits at common law, where the value in controversy shall exceed twenty dollars, the right of trial by jury shall be preserved, and no fact tried by a jury, shall be otherwise reexamined in any court of the United States, than according to the rules of the common law.

Amendment VIII

Excessive bail shall not be required, nor excessive fines imposed, nor cruel and unusual punishments inflicted.

Amendment IX

The enumeration in the Constitution, of certain rights, shall not be construed to deny or disparage others retained by the people.

Amendment X

The powers not delegated to the United States by the Constitution, nor prohibited by it to the states, are reserved to the states respectively, or to the people.

Amendment XI

The judicial power of the United States shall not be construed to extend to any suit in law or equity, commenced or prosecuted against one of the United States by citizens of another state, or by citizens or subjects of any foreign state.

Amendment XII

The electors shall meet in their respective states and vote by ballot for President and Vice-President, one of whom, at least, shall not be an inhabitant of the same state with themselves; they shall name in their ballots the person voted for as President, and in distinct ballots the person voted for as Vice-President, and they shall make distinct lists of all persons voted for as President, and of all persons voted for as Vice-President, and of the number of votes for each, which lists they shall sign and certify, and transmit sealed to the seat of the government of the United States, directed to the President of the Senate; – The President of the Senate shall, in the presence of the Senate and House of Representatives, open all the certificates and the votes shall then be counted; – the person having the greatest number of votes for President, shall be the President, if such number be a majority of the whole number of electors appointed; and if no person have such majority, then from the persons having the highest numbers not exceeding three on the list of those voted for as President, the House of Representatives shall choose immediately, by ballot, the President. But in choosing the President, the votes shall be taken by states, the representation from each state having one vote; a quorum for this purpose shall consist of a member or members from two-thirds of the states, and a majority of all the states shall be necessary to a choice. And if the House of Representatives shall not choose a President whenever the right of choice shall devolve upon them, before the fourth day of March next following, then the Vice-President shall act as President, as in the case of the death or other constitutional disability of the President. The person having the greatest number of votes as Vice-President, shall be the Vice-President, if such number be a majority of the whole number of electors appointed, and if no person have a majority, then from the two highest numbers on the list, the Senate shall choose the Vice-President; a quorum for the purpose shall consist of two-thirds of the whole number of Senators, and a majority of the whole number shall be necessary to a choice. But no person constitutionally ineligible to the office of President shall be eligible to that of Vice-President of the United States.

Amendment XIII

Section 1. Neither slavery nor involuntary servitude, except as a punishment for crime whereof the party shall have been duly convicted, shall exist within the United States, or any place subject to their jurisdiction.

Section 2. Congress shall have power to enforce this article by appropriate legislation.

Amendment XIV

Section 1. All persons born or naturalized in the United States, and subject to the jurisdiction thereof, are citizens of the United States and of the state wherein they reside. No state shall make or enforce any law which shall abridge the privileges or immunities of citizens of the United States; nor shall any state deprive any person of life, liberty, or property, without due process of law; nor deny to any person within its jurisdiction the equal protection of the laws.

Section 2. Representatives shall be apportioned among the several states according to their respective numbers, counting the whole number of persons in each state, excluding Indians not taxed. But when the right to vote at any election for the choice of electors for President and Vice President of the United States, Representatives in Congress, the executive and judicial officers of a state, or the members of the legislature thereof, is denied to any of the male inhabitants of such state, being twenty-one years of age, and citizens of the United States, or in any way abridged, except for participation in rebellion, or other crime, the basis of representation therein shall be reduced in the proportion which the number of such male citizens shall bear to the whole number of male citizens twenty-one years of age in such state.

Section 3. No person shall be a Senator or Representative in Congress, or elector of President and Vice President, or hold any office, civil or military, under the United States, or under any state, who, having previously taken an oath, as a member of Congress, or as an officer of the United States, or as a member of any state legislature, or as an executive or judicial officer of any state, to support the Constitution of the United States, shall have engaged in insurrection or rebellion against the same, or given aid or comfort to the enemies thereof. But Congress may by a vote of two-thirds of each House, remove such disability.

Section 4. The validity of the public debt of the United States, authorized by law, including debts incurred for payment of pensions and bounties for services in suppressing insurrection or rebellion, shall not be questioned. But neither the United States nor any state shall assume or pay any debt or obligation incurred in aid of insurrection or rebellion against the United States, or any claim for the loss or emancipation of any slave; but all such debts, obligations and claims shall be held illegal and void.

Section 5. The Congress shall have power to enforce, by appropriate legislation, the provisions of this article.

Amendment XV

Section 1. The right of citizens of the United States to vote shall not be denied or abridged by the United States or by any state on account of race, color, or previous condition of servitude.

Section 2. The Congress shall have power to enforce this article by appropriate legislation.

Amendment XVI

The Congress shall have power to lay and collect taxes on incomes, from whatever source derived, without apportionment among the several states, and without regard to any census of enumeration.

Amendment XVII

The Senate of the United States shall be composed of two Senators from each state, elected by the people thereof, for six years; and each Senator shall have one vote. The electors in each state shall have the qualifications requisite for electors of the most numerous branch of the state legislatures.

When vacancies happen in the representation of any state in the Senate, the executive authority of such state shall issue writs of election to fill such vacancies: Provided, that the legislature of any state may empower the executive thereof to make temporary appointments until the people fill the vacancies by election as the legislature may direct. This amendment shall not be so construed as to affect the election or term of any Senator chosen before it becomes valid as part of the Constitution.

Amendment XVIII

Section 1. After one year from the ratification of this article the manufacture, sale, or transportation of intoxicating liquors within, the importation thereof into, or the exportation thereof from the United States and all territory subject to the jurisdiction thereof for beverage purposes is hereby prohibited.

Section 2. The Congress and the several states shall have concurrent power to enforce this article by appropriate legislation.

Section 3. This article shall be inoperative unless it shall have been ratified as an amendment to the Constitution by the legislatures of the several states, as provided in the Constitution, within seven years from the date of the submission hereof to the states by the Congress.

Amendment XIX

The right of citizens of the United States to vote shall not be denied or abridged by the United States or by any state on account of sex.

Congress shall have power to enforce this article by appropriate legislation.

Amendment XX

Section 1. The terms of the President and Vice President shall end at noon on the 20th day of January, and the terms of Senators and Representatives at noon on the 3rd day of January, of the years in which such terms would have ended if this article had not been ratified; and the terms of their successors shall then begin.

Section 2. The Congress shall assemble at least once in every year, and such meeting shall begin at noon on the 3rd day of January, unless they shall by law appoint a different day.

Section 3. If, at the time fixed for the beginning of the term of the President, the President elect shall have died, the Vice President elect shall become President. If a President shall not have been chosen before the time fixed for the beginning of his term, or if the President elect shall have failed to qualify, then the Vice President elect shall act as President until a President shall have qualified; and the Congress may by law provide for the case wherein neither a President elect nor a Vice President elect shall have qualified, declaring who shall then act as President, or the manner in which one who is to act shall be selected, and such person shall act accordingly until a President or Vice President shall have qualified.

Section 4. The Congress may by law provide for the case of the death of any of the persons from whom the House of Representatives may choose a President whenever the right of choice shall have devolved upon them, and for the case of the death of any of the persons from whom the Senate may choose a Vice President whenever the right of choice shall have devolved upon them.

Section 5. Sections 1 and 2 shall take effect on the 15th day of October following the ratification of this article.

Section 6. This article shall be inoperative unless it shall have been ratified as an amendment to the Constitution by the legislatures of three-fourths of the several states within seven years from the date of its submission.

Amendment XXI

Section 1. The eighteenth article of amendment to the Constitution of the United States is hereby repealed.

Section 2. The transportation or importation into any state, territory, or possession of the United States for delivery or use therein of intoxicating liquors, in violation of the laws thereof, is hereby prohibited.

Section 3. This article shall be inoperative unless it shall have been ratified as an amendment to the Constitution by conventions in the several states, as provided in the Constitution, within seven years from the date of the submission hereof to the states by the Congress.

Amendment XXII

Section 1. No person shall be elected to the office of the President more than twice, and no person who has held the office of President, or acted as President, for more than two years of a term to which some other person was elected President shall be elected to the office of the President more than once. But this article shall not apply to any person holding the office of President when this article was proposed by the Congress, and shall not prevent any person who may be holding the office of President, or acting as President, during the term within which this article becomes operative from holding the office of President or acting as President during the remainder of such term.

Section 2. This article shall be inoperative unless it shall have been ratified as an amendment to the Constitution by the legislatures of three-fourths of the several states within seven years from the date of its submission to the states by the Congress.

Amendment XXIII

Section 1. The District constituting the seat of government of the United States shall appoint in such manner as the Congress may direct:

A number of electors of President and Vice President equal to the whole number of Senators and Representatives in Congress to which the District would be entitled if it were a state, but in no event more than the least populous state; they shall be in addition to those appointed by the states, but they shall be considered, for the purposes of the election of President and Vice President, to be electors appointed by a state; and they shall meet in the District and perform such duties as provided by the twelfth article of amendment.

Section 2. The Congress shall have power to enforce this article by appropriate legislation.

Amendment XXIV

Section 1. The right of citizens of the United States to vote in any primary or other election for President or Vice President, for electors for President or Vice President, or for Senator or Representative in Congress, shall not be denied or abridged by the United States or any state by reason of failure to pay any poll tax or other tax.

Section 2. The Congress shall have power to enforce this article by appropriate legislation.

Amendment XXV

Section 1. In case of the removal of the President from office or of his death or resignation, the Vice President shall become President.

Section 2. Whenever there is a vacancy in the office of the Vice President, the President shall nominate a Vice President who shall take office upon confirmation by a majority vote of both Houses of Congress.

Section 3. Whenever the President transmits to the President pro tempore of the Senate and the Speaker of the House of Representatives his written declaration that he is unable to discharge the powers and duties of his office, and until he transmits to them a written declaration to the contrary, such powers and duties shall be discharged by the Vice President as Acting President.

Section 4. Whenever the Vice President and a majority of either the principal officers of the executive departments or of such other body as Congress may by law provide, transmit to the President pro tempore of the Senate and the Speaker of the House of Representatives their written declaration that the President is unable to discharge the powers and duties of his office, the Vice President shall immediately assume the powers and duties of the office as Acting President.

Thereafter, when the President transmits to the President pro tempore of the Senate and the Speaker of the House of Representatives his written declaration that no inability exists, he shall resume the powers and duties of his office unless the Vice President and a majority of either the principal officers of the executive department or of such other body as Congress may by law provide, transmit within four days to the President pro tempore of the Senate and the Speaker of the House of Representatives their written declaration that the President is unable to discharge the powers and duties of his office. Thereupon Congress shall decide the issue, assembling within forty-eight hours for that purpose if not in session. If the Congress, within twenty-one days after receipt of the latter written declaration, or, if Congress is not in session, within twenty-one days after Congress is required to assemble, determines by two-thirds vote of both Houses that the President is unable to discharge the powers and duties of his office, the Vice President shall continue to discharge the same as Acting President; otherwise, the President shall resume the powers and duties of his office.

Amendment XXVI

Section 1. The right of citizens of the United States, who are 18 years of age or older, to vote, shall not be denied or abridged by the United States or any state on account of age.

Section 2. The Congress shall have the power to enforce this article by appropriate legislation.

Amendment XXVII

No law varying the compensation for the services of the Senators and Representatives shall take effect until an election of Representatives shall have intervened.

Index